The
Pan-African
Movement

The
Pan-African
Movement

A History of Pan-Africanism in America, Europe and Africa

Imanuel Geiss
translated by Ann Keep

Africana Publishing Co.
A Division of Holmes & Meier
Publishers, Inc.
New York

To my friends in Harlem
who have helped me to understand
so many things

First published as Panafrikanismus *by Europäische Verlagsanstalt*
© 1968 Europäische Verlagsanstalt
English translation published in the United States of America, 1974
by Africana Publishing Company
a division of Holmes & Meier Publishers, Inc.
101 Fifth Avenue
New York, N.Y. 10003
© 1974 Methuen & Co Ltd
Printed in Great Britain

Library of Congress Cataloging in Publication Data

Geiss, Imanuel.
  The pan-African movement; a history of pan-Africanism
in America, Europe, and Africa.

  Translation of Panafrikanismus.
  Bibliography: p.
  1. Pan-Africanism—History. I. Title.
DT31.G5513   320.5′4′096   74-6107
ISBN 0-8419-0161-9

Contents

Preface

The present volume was researched in 1964–6, written in 1967, first published in German in 1968, translated into English 1970–73 and published in English in 1974. The author has, as far as possible, tried to keep up with the current literature on the subject which accumulated between 1967 and 1973. Without the help of a specialized institute it proved impossible to be comprehensive. What could technically be incorporated into the English translation by 1973 was made use of. Some works can only be mentioned summarily: Adekunle Ajala's *Pan-Africanism. Evolution, Progress and Prospects* (London, 1973) deals mainly with the period after 1958, although the introductory pages are rather conventional in treating the historical background. The recollections of Ras Makonnen, *Pan-Africanism from within* (Nairobi, London, 1973) could be made use of for some points only in the page-proof stage of the book. Too late for the book the author learned of an earlier article by J. Ayo Langley, 'Pan-Africanism in Paris, 1924–46', *Journal of Modern African Studies*, VII, 1 (1969), pp. 69–94. A biography on Sylvester Williams by Owen C. Mathurin, Trinidad, has been announced but apparently not yet published. Finally, it may be added that apart from the dissertation prepared by Werner Ustorf on Kimbanguism at

Hamburg University, mentioned in Chapter 8, n. 65, two more dissertations at Hamburg, which deal with particular aspects of the development of Pan-Africanism in greater detail, will be completed by 1975:
Erhard Kamphausen on the Ethiopian Movement in South Africa,
1883–1910, and Gunter Rusch on the reaction of the Basle Mission and
the Presbyterian Church of Ghana on the rise of African nationalism,
1896–1966.

Translator's note

The orthography of quotations accords with the original where such
quotations have been verified on re-translation from the German; in
other cases the rendering is that of the author.

Introduction

The historical roots of Pan-Africanism

Pan-Africanism is probably one of the most complex phenomena in modern history, but also one of the hardest to pin down. Since it is one of the political forces active on the current world scene, and since scholarly research into it has scarcely begun, the literature on the subject is still unsatisfactory. Nevertheless the origins of the Pan-African movement do lend themselves to scholarly treatment.

Until recently the only works about Pan-Africanism available were sketchy surveys, mostly written by non-historians. These early efforts were certainly useful at the time, but on the whole they gave a superficial view. The first of these sketches came from the pen of W. E. B. Du Bois, the leading Afro-American historian, sociologist and journalist. His *œuvre*, which has a strong autobiographical element, contains numerous references to the history of Pan-Africanism.[1] He influenced George Padmore, author of what became for many years the standard work on the subject.[2] Subsequent historical accounts borrowed quite heavily from Padmore, and sometimes even reproduced his actual phrasing.

The first survey written from a broader viewpoint was by Philippe Decraene, an editor of *Le Monde* specializing in African affairs.[3] In

1961 his colleague on the London *Observer*, Colin Legum, produced a similar sketch, which likewise devoted little space – a mere fourteen pages – to the most important period between 1900 and 1958.[4] Nevertheless Legum was the first to take account of the stimulating research carried out by George Shepperson, professor of African history at the University of Edinburgh.

One year earlier Shepperson had written a pioneering article exploring the contacts forged between Africans and Afro-Americans in the USA and the West Indies, which he showed had begun at a surprisingly early date and had been relatively intensive.[5] The wealth of material cited, and the fact that he was able to consult the Schomburg Collection in Harlem, New York, the best specialized library in the field, make this article a mine of information for other students of the question. The present work is also deeply indebted to this pioneering effort. As well as other important essays on Pan-Africanism[6] Shepperson published, together with a colleague from Glasgow, a detailed study of the origins of nationalism in Nyasaland (today Malawi) which is especially important for our theme on account of the material it contains about contacts between Africans and Afro-Americans.[7]

In 1960 the American Society of African Culture (AMSAC) devoted its third annual meeting in Philadelphia to a discussion of the problem of movements for African unity. The papers, published in 1962, include a historical retrospect by Rayford Logan,[8] professor at Howard University, Washington, DC – the leading Afro-American university. Logan had worked with Du Bois in the 1920s. Except for a few personal reminiscences, his paper did not venture beyond the limits set by Du Bois and Padmore.

The first detailed account of Pan-Africanism to appear in German was published by Hanspeter F. Strauch in 1964.[9] Its historical section is forty-five pages long and more comprehensive than all previous surveys since Padmore. Strauch refers to a few more sources than is usual in such works, but some passages read like a German paraphrase of Padmore.[10] Finally the history of Pan-Africanism is treated in numerous articles of varying length and in chapters of general works, paying some attention to its historical development – mostly relying on Padmore, Decraene and Legum.[11] A Portuguese study has an instructive chapter on the 'Liga Africana' in the 1920s.[12]

Du Bois and Padmore were responsible for all the current clichés about the history of Pan-Africanism. This is all the more unsatisfactory in that both men were among its most articulate spokesmen. Since Padmore quotes amply from Du Bois, our picture of the development of the Pan-African movement in the last resort indirectly reflects the subjective views of Du Bois. As the 'father of Pan-Africanism' in any case had a tendency to self-adulation,[13] the result is doubly inadequate.

Our problem is thus to replace the personally biased view of Pan-Africanism given by Du Bois and Padmore with a more objective one. Any further attempt to base generalizations on, let alone draw conclusions from, fragmentary and limited knowledge could only add to the prevailing confusion and make people reluctant to deal with Pan-Africanism at all.

The present volume is an attempt to provide the first detailed and comprehensive account of the development of Pan-Africanism during the decisive years between 1900 and 1945. Its aim is to bring together the information that exists in a large variety of sources and to place it in a meaningful historical context. In order to understand twentieth-century Pan-Africanism it will also be necessary to explore its historical antecedents in the nineteenth and late eighteenth centuries more systematically than was done by Padmore – who correctly appreciated their significance, but dealt with them briefly and in an amateurish way.[14] Furthermore an effort will be made to include in Part I all the elements that make up the total picture, which we shall often have cause to refer back to in Part II.

Since this is the first attempt to provide an account of Pan-Africanism that rests on a foundation of concrete historical fact, it will be necessary to make frequent reference to persons and organizations of which we know little more than the name. Thus a great deal will still remain vague and colourless. Regrettable as this is, it seemed more important to bring together the maximum possible amount of information, leaving it to later investigators to follow up certain points of detail. The working hypothesis presented here is subject to revision or modification by the authors of monographic works, some of which are already in progress or appeared while this study was in the press.[15] Since it would take a long time for all of these monographs to be published – indeed, the end is not in sight – it seemed advisable to proceed with the present volume rather than to delay it any further.

The chief sources used are nineteenth- and twentieth-century books and pamphlets, supplemented by a number of periodical publications. Some of these have been as good as forgotten, while others are to be found, if at all, only in one or another of the great public libraries. Some hitherto untapped sources have been utilized which are important for anyone wishing to re-examine critically the prevalent picture of the history of Pan-Africanism. Of these the most important is that part of the Du Bois papers deposited in Accra,[16] to which Mrs Shirley Graham-Du Bois kindly allowed me access. There is also some interesting material in the papers of Lapido Solanke, founder and for many years general secretary of the West African Students' Union (WASU) in London. I am most indebted to Mrs Du Bois and Mrs Solanke for permission to consult these two archives. On one hitherto unknown aspect of the Pan-African movement's nineteenth-century antecedents new material is available in the papers of Dr Thomas Hodgkin in Oxford. At this point I should like to thank the latter's great-grand-nephew, Mr Thomas Hodgkin, who shares his political sympathies, for allowing me to make use of these papers, for providing me with valuable contacts in Accra and for many other useful tips. I am especially indebted to the Deutsche Forschungsgemeinschaft for generously supporting me in my research; the library staff of the Schomburg Collection in Harlem, New York, and of Howard University, Washington, DC; the libraries of the Universities of Ibadan and Accra; the Rhodes House Library; the Bodleian Library, Oxford; the Colonial Office Library, the British Museum Library (especially the Newspaper Department in Colindale), for bearing so patiently with my requests; and to Professor Clemens Heller and M. Robert Cornevin, both of Paris, for their kindness in supporting my research in Paris. I should also like to thank most warmly Professor George Shepperson, Edinburgh, for his frequent encouragement, and Mr Christopher Fyfe, Edinburgh, for kindly making critical suggestions to improve the completed manuscript.

Bremen, January 1974

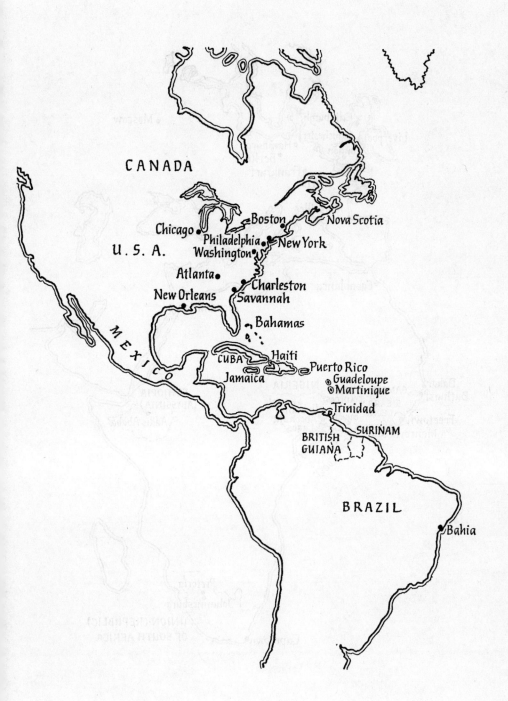

CANADA

Chicago

U. S. A.

Boston
Philadelphia
Washington
Atlanta
New Orleans

New York
Nova Scotia

Charleston
Savannah

MEXICO

Bahamas

CUBA
Jamaica

Haiti
Puerto Rico
Guadeloupe
Martinique

Trinidad

BRITISH
GUIANA

SURINAM

BRAZIL

Bahia

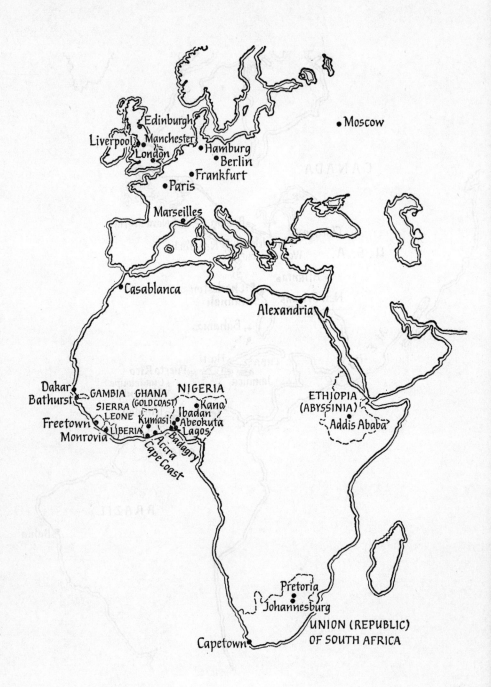

Edinburgh

Moscow

Liverpool• •Manchester
London•

•Hamburg
•Berlin
•Frankfurt

•Paris

Marseilles•

•Casablanca

Alexandria•

Dakar•
Bathurst• GAMBIA GHANA NIGERIA
SIERRA (GOLDCOAST)
LEONE Kumasi• •Kano
Freetown• LIBERIA •Ibadan
Monrovia• •Abeokuta
Badagry•Lagos
Accra
Cape Coast

ETHIOPIA
(ABYSSINIA)
Addis Ababa•

Pretoria•
•Johannesburg

Capetown•

UNION (REPUBLIC)
OF SOUTH AFRICA

Part I   The social and intellectual background

1 What is Pan-Africanism? An attempt at a definition

It is still difficult, perhaps even impossible, to provide a clear and precise definition of Pan-Africanism. It is a complex problem which can best be approached historically. By looking at its various manifestations we can arrive at simple and comprehensive formulae, compare them with objective reality and modify them continually in the light of modern knowledge.

By Pan-Africanism we understand:

1 Intellectual and political movements among Africans and Afro-Americans[1] who regard or have regarded Africans and people of African descent as homogeneous. This outlook leads to a feeling of racial solidarity and a new self-awareness and causes Afro-Americans to look upon Africa as their real 'homeland', without necessarily thinking of a physical return to Africa.

2 All ideas which have stressed or sought the cultural unity and political independence of Africa, including the desire to modernize Africa on a basis of equality of rights. The key concepts here have been respectively the 'redemption of Africa' and 'Africa for the Africans'.

3 Ideas or political movements which have advocated, or advocate,

the political unity of Africa or at least close political collaboration in one form or another.

Even this provisional definition is unsatisfactory and will not please everyone. But it will serve as a working tool for historical analysis, if used with due caution.

In addition to the difficulties encountered in defining the concept, two other factors make the history of the Pan-African movement complex and difficult to comprehend. Firstly, developments occurred simultaneously on three continents – in North America (USA and the West Indies), in Africa (especially West Africa) and Europe (especially England) – sometimes influencing one another but sometimes in isolation. Secondly, these developments must be seen within the framework of the general history of Africa, America and Europe, so that one always has to bear in mind a fair amount of world history, even though one cannot draw the line as precisely as one might wish.

Furthermore, Pan-Africanism developed on different planes of varying significance. If we take the political aspect in each period as the criterion, we may distinguish six such planes.

1 Pan-Africanism frequently took the form of a movement of all coloured and colonial peoples, which has been called since Bandung the 'Afro-Asian solidarity movement', or the 'Pan-Colonial' or, earlier, 'Pan-Coloured' movement.

2 In most cases Pan-Africanism was understood as 'Pan-Negroism', i.e. was defined primarily in racial terms. This view ignored Arabic North Africa and concentrated on the solidarity between Black Africans and Afro-Americans.

3 Only after the unity of the whole African continent had become the goal, and Afro-Americans of the New World had been excluded, did Pan-Africanism attain the form from which it derives its name and the meaning generally associated with it today.

Two sub-categories may be further distinguished: the drive for the unity of Black Africa south of the Sahara and that for the unity of the entire continent including the Arabic north.

4 A regional union has frequently been regarded as a preliminary stage on the road to continental unity, especially in British West Africa during the earlier years. Only in very recent times have such ideas been taken up in other regions as well, notably in East Africa.

5 The fifth plane to be considered is the national one. Until a short time ago it was at this level that concrete action as a rule took place, whereas theoretical discussions, propaganda and agitation were oriented mainly to the supra-national plane.

6 Nationalism frequently first developed on a tribal level (e.g. in the case of the Fanti).

Pan-Africanism has hardly ever been a clearly defined, precise or rational concept. On the contrary, it has been (and still is) a matter of hazy, vague emotions – a vision or a dream, as Du Bois put it.[2] Nevertheless it is possible to isolate a rational kernel from the chaos of declarations and proclamations, even though this rational element is all too often subordinated to a feeling of resentment and despair at the injustice prevalent in the world and at White domination. Here one has to be particularly careful about the way in which one launches upon a critical analysis, and the definitions outlined above will be found helpful. For what may at first sight appear to the unsympathetic European (if he takes any notice of these ideas at all) as products of the fevered imagination of frustrated and half-educated negroes – a hotchpotch of confused and ill-digested notions – emerge when viewed historically as an unconscious, inarticulate demand by Pan-Africans[3] for equal rights for Africans and people of African descent. Its opposition to the idea and practice of racial discrimination and hierarchical relationships among men, makes Pan-Africanism *par excellence* the ideology of decolonization in Africa.[4] It stands for the economic, technological, social and political modernization of a whole continent.

Pan-Africanism is thus predominantly a modern movement. It is the reaction of the most advanced, most intensively Europeanized Africans and Afro-Americans to contact with the modern world. Its representatives have been Africans or Afro-Americans who in many cases had an academic education in Europe, America or West Africa, or who were exposed for a long time to modern influences in their own country. They embraced the European and North American principles of equality and democracy and on this basis elaborated their own ideology of emancipation from White supremacy. Africans who completed their studies in Europe or in the USA, or who stayed there voluntarily for a considerable length of time and then returned to their African homelands, acted as a ferment of modernization upon traditional society; like the Afro-Americans, they protested against racial discrimination and European colonialism, turning against their White masters the very political and intellectual principles they had learned from them.

A process of this kind is not uncommon in history. One finds it wherever an advanced culture comes into contact with a stagnant and backward society, wherever the conflict between the old and the new produces a fresh awareness in a society that has been stirred into movement. It usually leads to a division between those who unreservedly want rapid and consistent modernization and those who want to preserve what is traditional, or at least to progress slowly. Between the element favouring radical modernization and that favouring conservation one finds an intermediate group which in one way or another would like to combine the old and the new. For them, as for the conservatives, a largely idealized past serves as a useful means of formulating their new self-awareness.

Parallels to this aspect of Pan-Africanism can be discovered in the recent history of almost all modern societies. In Germany the Romantics invoked the medieval empire as a response to the challenge of the French Revolution.[5] The Slavs looked back to their history in medieval times, in shaking off foreign economic, social and political domination, and on this basis developed a modern national consciousness. This led to the revival of so-called 'unhistorical' nations, to demands for national self-determination, and ultimately to the emergence of individua nation states. In Russia there was a sharp cleavage between 'Westerners' and 'Slavophils', between exponents of rational, modern Western ideas and those Romantics who sought to revive the country's own traditions.[6]

These parallels may help us to understand the African cultural renaissance and the political movement of Pan-Africanism. These are ambivalent reactions to modernizing influences and to the White supremacy associated with them. In this case, too, we may observe the dialectic of cultural contact, the tension between the (few) advocates of consistent modernization and those who favour some kind of combination of the new and the old. It is worth bearing in mind that Pan-Africanism is but one instance of a universal phenomenon, which takes different forms according to time, place and historical setting.[7] Just as Pan-Slavism and Slav nationalism were closely linked, so Pan-Africanism and African nationalism are interconnected. Pan-Africanism may be seen as African nationalism extended to embrace either the entire African continent or Black Africa alone.

The reaction of the most modernized Africans and Afro-Americans to contact with the modern world reflects three simultaneous processes: the transition from a gradual modernization of society to new levels of 'social aggregation'; the clash between modern and traditional elements; and an attempt to integrate them. For a century African society has been evolving from traditional agrarian forms to more modern ones. This results at first in an inevitable confusion and a bewildering eclecticism; this is probably best represented by Nkrumah and his philosophy of 'Consciencism',[8] a deliberate attempt to combine ideas of a traditional African character with ideas from the Arabic–Islamic world and from Western Europe (with Marxism–Leninism being treated as a Western influence).

It is inevitable that the relatively sudden and massive confrontation of a traditional and largely isolated society with the modern world should lead to a long period of transition and confusion. For the modern world is itself no compact, uniform, rational structure; it has developed in a complex process of chaotic and violent conflict. For this reason Pan-Africanism reflects the tensions and contradictions of the modern world, especially as they have been transplanted to African soil, as well as the confusion that springs from the blending of modern and traditional African elements. This explains the frequent vacillations between traditionalism and modernism which one can observe time and time again among exponents of Pan-Africanism.

These considerations enable us to define Pan-Africanism in both a narrower and a broader sense. The narrower definition is limited to the political movement for the unification of the African continent, perhaps to the Pan-Negro movement (planes 3 and 2). The broader definition includes cultural and intellectual movements, even those that aim at a wider solidarity, i.e. anti-colonialism or Afro-Asianism. A distinction of this kind roughly corresponds with that drawn by George Shepperson between 'Pan-Africanism' (in the narrower sense) and 'pan-Africanism' (in the broader sense).[9]

With some justification the beginning of Pan-Africanism in the narrower sense may be dated as recently as 1958, when two Pan-African conferences were held on African soil (both in Accra), and the 'diaspora' first began to return to the 'promised land' of Africa. If this is so, the period before 1958 is only the prehistory of Pan-Africanism, and one can distinguish between a 'narrower' and a 'broader' prehistory corresponding to the narrower and broader definitions of the term. Its prehistory in the narrower sense begins with the first Pan-African conference in London in 1900;[10] that in the broader sense goes back to the late eighteenth century.[11]

Prior to 1900 there was no Pan-Africanism in the narrower sense, either in name or form. If Pan-Africanism proper was a reaction to classical European imperialism and colonialism, approximately from the 'scramble for Africa' (in the late nineteenth century) onwards, the first quasi-Pan-African impulses may be considered as a reaction to what might be called European 'proto-imperialism' in the eighteenth and nineteenth centuries, characterized by the slave trade across the Atlantic and by slavery and racial discrimination in the New World. By analogy one may speak of a 'proto-Pan-Africanism' before 1900.

An attempt to study Pan-African prehistory in the broader sense requires an investigation into the historical conditions for its appearance in about 1900. One would have to describe and analyse the soil from which Pan-Africanism could spring, including the social changes in Africa (especially British West Africa), the West Indies and among Afro-Americans in the USA from the late eighteenth century.[12] Moreover, from the late eighteenth century onwards individual Africans and Afro-Americans formulated ideas which may be categorized as 'Pan-African' in the broader sense or as 'proto-Pan-African'. One thus faces the problem of exploring the tradition of Pan-Africanism before it appeared in articulate guise in 1900, i.e. its historical continuity.[13]

The slave trade and Pan-Africanism:
a triangular relationship

One of the wittiest definitions of Pan-Africanism is that it is 'a delayed boomerang from the time of slavery'.[14] This is more than a *bon mot*: if one examines the facts more closely, one will appreciate the geographical pattern underlying the historical development of Pan-Africanism. This is identical with the well-known 'triangle' of the transatlantic slave trade: Western Europe (especially England) – Africa (especially West Africa) – the New World (the West Indies and USA). Along the same routes taken by the 'goods' which made the slave trade profitable – in particular the slaves themselves, who were treated as chattels – there travelled ideas which from the late eighteenth century onwards were to make Pan-Africanism a political force – at first unconsciously, but later knowingly.

The boomerang metaphor has several variations. All three points of the slavers' triangle became centres for the development of Pan-Africanism. In Africa it was primarily West Africa which provided the first, and most, slaves for the New World. In West Africa it was the Gold Coast (Ghana) that was the focal point of the traffic in slaves, owing to the large number of forts and trading stations there. It is accordingly no coicidence that at an early stage the Gold Coast was the stronghold of African proto-nationalism and the proto-Pan-Africanism associated with it. The first African critic of the trans-atlantic slave trade, and a precursor of proto-Pan-Africanism, was Ottobah Cugoano, a Fanti from the Gold Coast.[15] One of the key figures of twentieth-century Pan-Africanism, M. Garvey,[16] in fact came from Jamaica, but is traditionally regarded as a negro of Koromantee stock.[17] His ancestors had been sent to the New World from Fort Koromanti on the Gold Coast, and thus almost certainly came from what today is Ghana. In America the Koromantee were regarded as 'difficult' slaves because of their independent and rebellious spirit, and Garvey the Pan-African agitator was indeed a real firebrand.

After Ghana the most important Pan-African centre in West Africa was the southern part of modern Nigeria; it provided the largest contribution to the slave trade in the nineteenth century. A contemporary of Cugoano was an Ibo, the ex-slave Equiano who was known as Gustavus Vassa. His criticism of the slave trade and racial discrimination was less harsh than that of Cugoano,[18] and one recalls that Ibo slaves at that time had a reputation for being relatively easily managed. Modern nationalism came late to the Ibos, but they took to it all the more vehemently, particularly under the leadership of Nnamdi Azikiwe.[19] The Yoruba in Western Nigeria provided the last major contingent of slaves in the first half of the nineteenth century. This was a result of their lengthy civil war in the years after 1817. They were the first to return to their homeland as free men after a relatively brief period of slavery, often during the first generation; some of them came from Brazil and Cuba, others from Sierra Leone. The so-called 'Sierra Leoneans' in particular produced the first generation of African intellectuals and proto-nationalists in Nigeria during the later period.[20]

Scarcely less important was the historical function of the smaller West Indian islands. They were, so to speak, the hub around which the entire system of slave trading and slavery in the New World revolved.[21] It was in the West Indies, not long after their discovery by Columbus, that slavery developed with the Spaniards as the masters. Slavery spread to North America in 1619 and for two centuries thereafter the West Indies served as the first port of call for millions of African negro slaves on their way to North and South America. Here generally they were first sold into slavery, or else remained for several months to become acclimatized. West Indian slavery was particularly brutal and oppressive, and became the model for slavery throughout the African continent.

As early as the sixteenth century the Caribbean islands were the scene of slave revolts against the Spaniards. Such risings took place time and time again until the best-known revolt, the only one to have immediate political consequences, broke out in Haiti in 1791. This not only led to Haiti's emergence in 1804 as the first independent negro republic, a lonely status which it was to enjoy for a long time to come,[22] but had direct repercussions in the southern states of the USA.[23]

It was no accident that in Haiti slavery was first enshrined in a legal code. The initial step was taken in 1685 when Louis XIV issued the 'Code Noir' for the French possessions, chiefly San Domingo (Haiti). However, it was inspired primarily by paternalistic motives and was intended in the first place to regulate, and frequently also to improve, the generally intolerable working and living conditions of the negro slaves.[24] Just three years later, in 1688, the British colony of Barbados took over the 'Code Noir' and developed it as the first 'Slave Code'.

The West Indies were in the forefront of attention among those Frenchmen who during the revolutions of 1789 and 1848 sought to abolish the slave trade and later slavery itself; the same was true of the British. The abolition of slavery by the revolutionary Convention of 1794, its reintroduction by Napoleon I, and his attempt in 1803 to reconquer Haiti which had become to all intents and purposes autonomous – all these factors accelerated the emancipation of Haiti in 1804.[25] The abolition of slavery in the British Empire between 1834 and 1838 led to the emergence in the British West Indies, as in South Africa, of a free African population, the most advanced elements of which were in surprisingly close contact with West Africa, with liberal humanitarian groups in England and with Afro-Americans in the USA.[26]

After the emancipation of 1834–8 Afro-Americans from the West Indies took an active part in Christian missionary work in Africa. The West Indian regiments which were stationed in rotation there and on the coast of West Africa likewise contributed to the formation and strengthening of contacts between Africa and the New World.[27] Some soldiers stayed on in Africa after completing their military service, or else returned there either temporarily or permanently.[28] Together with the early missionaries came artisans, traders, catechists and later administrative officials, as well as the occasional journalist, from the West Indies. West Indians brought with them to West Africa not only modern manual skills and techniques but also a consciousness of solidarity among all persons of African descent.[29] But their function was rather that of a catalyst in the process of modernization than that of an element in the new élite which was forming, since their exceptional status as outsiders in the service of the White man produced tensions in their attitude towards their African environment. On the other hand an officially encouraged immigration took place after 1838 of recently emancipated slaves, who had been brought to Sierra Leone to fill vacancies on the plantations left by the liberation and the falling off in the supply of slaves to the West Indies after 1807.[30]

It was the West Indies, too, that produced men of great significance in the development of Pan-Africanism such as Edward W. Blyden, Sylvester Williams, Marcus Garvey, George Padmore and Claude McKay, to mention only the most important among those who spoke English; Du Bois's father and grandfather came from Haiti. A role of similar importance was played by West Indians from the French possessions in the development of nationalism in francophone Africa and the 'Négritude' movement after World War I: René Maran, Gaston Monnerville, Aimé Césaire and Frantz Fanon all came from Guadeloupe and Martinique; Jean Price-Mars came from Haiti. Most of Du Bois's followers in his Pan-African Congress movement in France after 1919 were politicians and intellectuals from the French Antilles.[31] West Indians played a leading part in dissolving the colonial system. They acted as a ferment of modernization in African society and promoted radical ideas among Afro-Americans in the USA – and to some extent also among Africans in England and France after World War I.[32]

As a movement worthy of the name, Pan-Africanism first appeared among Afro-Americans in the New World in about 1900. But in the earlier struggle against the slave trade and slavery traditions developed which led to Pan-Africanism, and this abolitionist movement also forms part of the background to Pan-Africanism.[33]

These preliminary remarks lead one to ask why Pan-Africanism was to remain principally a matter for people living in English-speaking areas. Pan-Africanism developed an astonishing mobility across the oceans along the triangular route of the slave trade. Horizontal mobility and the consequent broadening of intellectual and political horizons were possible on a large scale in the British Empire from the late nineteenth century onwards, the more so since links with the English-speaking USA were never completely broken. Only the British Empire granted its colonial territories a considerable, if not absolute, freedom of the press, the rudiments of a parliamentary system (through the institution of Legislative Councils) and a minimum of personal liberty and political opportunity. Even when colonial imperialism reached its climax about 1900 the British Empire offered Africans and Afro-West Indians more opportunities to develop a consciousness of their own political identity than they had under any other colonial power. In the process of decolonization the British Empire proved to be 'democratizable', a fact which gives it a unique position in world history. By generally peaceful means the colonies of White settlement gained their independence first, then the 'Brown' (Asian) ones and later still the 'Black' (African and West Indian) ones. African and West Indian nationalists were at all times aware of the advantages they enjoyed under British rule.[34]

The French-speaking peoples, on the other hand, did not participate in the Pan-African movement until after 1919.[35] The 'Négritude' movement was predominantly non-political, cultural, literary and philosophical. The relatively few politically active elements in the French West Indies and in French Africa as a rule sought political and social equality within the framework of the French system – in accordance with the French doctrine of assimilation and 'la République Française une et indivisible'. Even after 1919 nationalists from the francophone area at first remained for a long time a small forgotten minority without any direct political influence.[36] Contacts with anglophone Pan-Africanism remained sporadic and episodic. It was not until 1958 that a certain change came about when Guinea under Sekou Touré voted for immediate independence and sought to associate itself with the Pan-African movement, represented at that time primarily by Ghana. Mali followed in 1960 after her breach with Senegal.

Africans from other European colonies participated scarcely at all in the Pan-African movement, apart from an episode involving the *assimilados* of the Portuguese colonies in 1921 and 1923.[37] Until Nasser's Egypt became interested in Pan-Africanism the Arab element was represented only by Mohamed Ali Duse, who came from the Anglo-Egyptian Sudan.[38] The contribution to Pan-Africanism of Portuguese- or Spanish-speaking Afro-Americans is practically non-existent. But even in English-speaking colonies West Africa was the real focal point. In East Africa, apart from the isolated figure of Jomo Kenyatta, little was heard of Pan-Africanism before 1958. Although Jomo Kenyatta was one of the organizers of the Manchester Pan-African Congress in 1945, and its resolution calling for the complete independence of Kenya, Uganda, Tanganyika, Nyasaland and Somaliland was reported in the East African press, he focused the attention of his colleagues primarily on Kenyan problems after he returned home in 1946.[39] Chilembwe's rising in Nyasaland in 1915[40] remained a local phenomenon, and in South Africa early attempts were consistently frustrated by apartheid, even before its practice became formally institutionalized in 1948.[41]

In the USA, in accordance with the historical boomerang effect of slavery, the strong Afro-American element naturally played a leading part. Its active role in the abolitionist movement and its struggle for emancipation after the Civil War produced an intellectual and political tradition from which Pan-African impulses were later able to develop.[42]

Finally we may mention the philanthropic and humanitarian element in England, which from the late eighteenth century onwards time and time again stood up for the rights of Africans and Afro-Americans. At the beginning the struggle was to prohibit the slave trade, and later slavery, in the British colonies and then in the independent African territories.[43] Indirectly these circles thereby became the pacemakers of European colonial-imperialism. However, in the beginning of the twentieth century elements of the British left who followed the radical abolitionist tradition, as well as Quakers and other groups, provided practical and political assistance to the nascent Pan-African and African nationalist movements *inter alia* by their impact on Parliament and on public opinion.[44]

For the reasons mentioned it is legitimate to concentrate upon the movements in the English-speaking areas of West Africa, the West Indies, the USA and England. History is made between the three or four extremities of this historical triangle (in fact a quadrangle). Numerous activists weave a complex pattern across the Atlantic, as though with the shuttle of a loom. Since the four principal geographical areas continually influenced one another directly or indirectly one cannot use a purely chronological approach even for specific regions. Nor must one be tempted to break up the history of Pan-Africanism into a series of biographies of its exponents; however, since the careers of many of these men reflect a 'Pan-African' quality, the biographical dimension must not be neglected. Finally we do not intend to undertake a systematic arrangement according to subject matter, for this would result in a political science treatise that would presume prior knowledge of the course of historical development. Moreover, the sense of historical dynamism would be lost by a static and categorized approach.

In this work an attempt will be made to study the development of Pan-Africanism in its historical context, with the aid of all the components mentioned above. We shall use chronological data, biographical and systematic data and information that is regionally and geographically limited. The reader must expect to be taken rapidly to and fro across the Atlantic and through time. It will help to prevent him from losing the thread if he bears in mind the triangular geographical pattern of the slave-trading era, and a few historical landmarks:

1787   *Beginning of proto-Pan-Africanism in the broadest sense.*[45]
1807   *Slave trade prohibited for British citizens.*
1834–8 *Emancipation of slaves in the British Empire.*
1861–5 *American Civil War and the emancipation of slaves.*
1900   *First Pan-African Conference in London.*[46]
1919   *First Pan-African Congress in Paris.*[47]
1945   *Fifth Pan-African Congress in Manchester.*[48]
1958   *First Pan-African Conferences on African soil.*[49]

This study will reveal fascinating chains of circumstances, interrelationships extending across space and time often made still more complex by the continual appearance, in one form or another, of the elementary factors of the slave trade and abolitionism. To give a rough idea of the complexity of such 'intellectual genealogies', as one might call them, we may look at the antecedents of Nkrumah. During the Ashanti War of 1863 John B. Small, a company clerk in one of the West Indian regiments, arrived on the Gold Coast. Here he witnessed the beginnings of the Methodist mission, which had been active on the Cape Coast since 1835. After returning home to the West Indies, Small emigrated to the USA where he joined an Afro-American Methodist church, the 'African Methodist Episcopal Zion' (AMEZ), intending to carry out missionary work under its auspices in Africa. In 1896 he was elected bishop in AMEZ and visited the Gold Coast, where he laid the foundations of the AMEZ mission. At that time he invited two talented young Methodists to study theology in the USA at the AMEZ divinity college. One of these men was Aggrey, the leading African pedagogue during the first quarter of the twentieth century. He was later Nkrumah's teacher at Achimota College near Accra and encouraged Nkrumah to study in the USA. There Nkrumah pursued his studies at Afro-American universities. He felt himself drawn to the tradition set by his teacher Aggrey, but also came under the strong influence of Garvey who originated from Jamaica. In 1945, on his way back to Africa, he stopped in England where he was influenced by Padmore whose position within the Pan-African movement was quite unique.[50]

Theoretically there are an infinite number of rational ways whereby one could coordinate all the relevant dates, facts, persons, ideas, organizations, locations and events. For this reason there are also numerous grounds on which objection could be taken to the method adopted here. Other writers doubtless might find different, perhaps better, arrangements of the material. We have settled for the one which seemed the most fittting in order to clarify as far as possible the complex evolution of Pan-Africanism and its prehistory. The hazards involved in such a pioneer attempt may perhaps lead critics to look with indulgence upon the deficiencies inevitable when one is investigating something so many-sided, so complex and as yet so inadequately researched.

2 The significance of the transatlantic slave trade and American slavery

Pan-Africanism, as a protest movement of the African and Afro-American peoples against White domination, cannot be understood without looking at the historical background; in particular, the slave trade and slavery and the abolitionist movement to which they gave rise; the history of Afro-Americans in the USA and the West Indies; and the Christian missions with the schools which they founded. From the mid-nineteenth century onwards the impact of the missionaries and traders led to the gradual development of a small but influential class of modernized Africans, especially in West Africa (Gold Coast, Sierra Leone, Nigeria) and South Africa. These men came into contact with England and the USA, as well as with West Indians who had come to Africa, which helped to broaden their intellectual horizon and led to an intensification of their political consciousness.[1] The first contacts between Europe and West Africa go back to the late fifteenth century when the Portuguese were feeling their way along the African coast in search of 'Wangara', the legendary land of gold,[2] and the sea-route to India – an endeavour which from the beginning of the fifteenth century was powerfully stimulated by Henry the Navigator. What began as barter trade gradually became, after the discovery of America, a commerce in slaves, who were needed to satisfy the ever-growing demand for cheap labour in the mines and plantations of the Caribbean and later also to assist in the colonization of South, Central and North America.[3] Gradually merchants and slave-dealers from almost all the European maritime countries succeeded in breaking the monopoly originally enjoyed by the Portuguese and joined in the profitable slave trade. The age of the chartered companies in the seventeenth and eighteenth centuries was a time of greatness for the British, French and Dutch on the Guinea Coast, and even for the Danes, Swedes and at times the Prussians as well.[4]

The slave trade was most profitable when African slaves could be settled in a colony in the New World belonging to a state which also possessed forts or factories on the West African coast. For this reason the maritime powers which participated in the slave trade tried to gain a footing in the West Indies. The Spaniards, who were the first to arrive, were from the mid-seventeenth century onwards displaced by the British French, Dutch and Danes. The British conquered Jamaica under Cromwell in 1655 (it was not until 1808 that they took over Trinidad from the Spaniards) and later in British Guiana on the north-eastern coast of South America; the French took Martinique, Guadeloupe and the western half of San Domingo. The Dutch won large areas of Brazil from the Portuguese around the mid-seventeenth century, but eventually all that remained of their imperial dream was Surinam (Dutch Guiana) and the island of Curaçao. The Danes secured for themselves St Thomas Island. During the seventeenth century pirates became the first plantation-owners, quietly acquiring considerable wealth with the aid of cheap labour from Africa. The basis of the economy was the cultivation of cane-sugar. Besides this there were coffee, cotton, indigo, rice, cocoa, tobacco and other 'colonial goods', for which there was a growing demand in Europe. At the end of the eighteenth century the richest and most flourishing of these West Indian colonies was the French colony of San Domingo, which later became Haiti.[5]

The beginnings of a modernized middle class on the Gold Coast

Across the Atlantic in West Africa European settlements were less numerous. To maintain the slave trade it was enough to establish a few forts, fortified or non-fortified trading-stations and warehouses. Several forts were erected by the French in what is now Senegal and by most of the other European powers on the Gold Coast (where there was the greatest concentration of trading posts) with the co-operation of the local inhabitants, who also had an interest in keeping the slave trade going smoothly.

The settlements of the various powers were at first intermingled, which excluded the formation of spheres of interest of any size. The influence of the Europeans was restricted to the immediate vicinity of the forts, as far as their cannon could reach and no further. This led to the development of a tutelary relationship between the Europeans and the Africans in the area of the forts, whereby the latter withdrew when threatened to the safety offered by the guns of 'their' Europeans. A more extensive though indirect influence could be obtained only by carrying on normal commercial relations.

Two major centres of European power came into being on the Gold Coast, one in the west around Cape Coast (British) and Elmina (Portuguese) and the other around Accra in the east.

In the shelter of the European forts there arose quasi-urban settlements of coastal tribes which took the same name as their fort. The population of these new towns on the coast profited from the slave trade either directly as middlemen, or indirectly by providing supplies for the forts and the troops stationed there. In the capacity of middlemen the coastal people, most of whom were Fanti or Ga, procured from the relatively large states which arose in the interior the slaves needed for the slave trade. Their chiefs associated with the Europeans as equals and were treated as such by the merchants whose interest it was to keep up an uninterrupted supply of slaves.

A smaller number of Africans on the coast entered directly into the service of Europeans as soldiers, clerks, cooks, gardeners etc.; they were frequently mulattoes who lived directly beneath the walls of the forts or even inside them. The first schools which were founded by individual missionaries or chaplains of these forts, such as Cape Coast Castle and Christiansborg, were designed for the children of these mulattoes. They also served as the first bases from where the missionaries who became active on the Gold Coast in about 1830 could carry on their work.

From what at first appeared to be an insignificant mulatto element there gradually developed large Europeanized families, especially on the Gold Coast. Their European names and light skin were external evidence of descent on the paternal side from Europeans, usually merchants – the Brews, for example, who were related to a large number of other families of similar origin,[6] the Hayfords, Bannermanns and Hutton-Mills, to mention only a few of the best-known such families. From about 1850 onwards they could also be distinguished by their European style of life, modern education and professional skills: they gained their living as merchants and lawyers, and also in the infant colonial administration. This new group, termed by the British 'educated natives' or 'middle class', formed a kind of aristocracy vis-à-vis the rest of the African population during the latter half of the nineteenth century, if only by the fact that its members had a monopoly of European education and modes of life; at the same time they attached importance to the maintenance of good relations with the leading elements in traditional society. Thus they were not nearly so detribalized as superficial observers then and later tended to assume. On the contrary, from the mid-nineteenth century onwards there developed a kind of symbiosis between the two groups: the modernized element became the spokesmen for African interests vis-à-vis the Europeans, whereas the chiefs prevented the great families from becoming totally alienated from their fellow-tribesmen. Gradually members of the 'educated class' came to assume the position of 'traditional rulers', as when the Fanti elected leaders from several 'royal' families. The best-known example is that of J. R. Ghartey, who rose from being a mere merchant in Anomabu to become King Ghartey IV of Winneba; even today he occupies an honourable place in the history of Ghanaian nationalism.[7] This modernized middle class, although small in numbers, was of great importance in its social and later political function as the representative of an African proto-nationalism which provided the foundation upon which Pan-Africanism could develop. For this to happen Africans had to leave their homelands to study abroad, whence they returned imbued with the political ideas that were prevalent in the countries of their White masters. There they also became conscious of the existence of people of African descent who lived outside Africa, and established contact with them.

The process whereby the Pan-African movement took shape was exceedingly slow when one looks at it in a long-term perspective. Moreover, it is doubtful whether the social changes which took place on the Gold Coast would have sufficed to provide the igniting impulse in the twentieth century. For European influence at first seeped only slowly and hesitatingly into West African society. The number of Whites who could play a part in breeding the mulatto element was restricted; so, generally, was the length of time they spent on the Coast. It is true that during the eighteenth century a few Africans came to Europe, and at least three of them obtained a comprehensive modern academic education: Capitein, Amo and Quaque.[8] But on their return they were unable to exercise a decisive influence upon society. Even so, Quaque was in charge of an elementary school on the Cape Coast for nearly fifty years, until his death in 1816, where the young men who prompted the Methodists to organize their mission were educated.[9] Also the financial profit obtained by Africans from the slave trade was dissipated without producing any modernizing effect upon African society. The money was invested in easily retailed consumer goods from Europe, such as clothing, furniture, gin or umbrellas (the outward symbols of a ruler's power and prestige). West Africa lacked the independent economic basis, the modern social and intellectual infrastructure, which might have allowed the modest profit gained from the slave trade to spark off a primary accumulation of capital on the European model, and thus have promoted industrialization and further modernization.[10]

Slavery in the New World

By an irony of history, the African slaves who comprised the objects of the transatlantic slave trade, or rather their descendants, were unable to accelerate the process of modernization in Africa itself. The negroes exported to the West Indies and America received there the first elements of modern education and culture and were introduced into a rapidly modernizing society, especially in the USA. Although they were condemned to remain at the lowest level of this society, the fact that they played a part in the process of modernization represented a certain progress for Afro-Americans by comparison with their fellow-countrymen left behind in Africa. Even under slavery, so unpropitious for any kind of education, some elements of modern ways of thinking gradually seeped down to the slaves. Modernization made a certain amount of progress after the emancipation of individual slaves or whole groups, but could not make real headway until after the abolition of slavery. In the British West Indies slaves were freed in two stages, in 1834 and 1838; in the French Antilles (after the intermezzo of 1794–1803),[11] except for Haiti, not until 1848 and in the USA only in 1863–5.

In the New World mulattoes played a greater role, at least quantitatively, than in West Africa, acting so to speak as a transmission belt in the process of modernization. Here the social order was relatively stable and their numbers were larger than in Africa, both in absolute terms and relatively. African girls were held in high esteem as concubines and wet-nurses by those who could afford to pay for them. Mulattoes generally accounted for a higher proportion of house-slaves, whose lot was by and large more bearable than that of the field-hands. Not all of them were actually the children of the White master concerned or otherwise related to him; slave children were sold by their parents or other kinsmen as house-slaves to other proprietors since this meant that they would be more adequately provided for than if they were employed working in their own master's fields. A more humane way of dealing with slaves which was practised more and more frequently during the eighteenth century was manumission, or emancipation as individuals. Those freed in this way were often also given the means to acquire an education or even sums of capital. Most of those emancipated in the USA and the West Indies before the abolition of slavery were mulattoes and it was they who later led the first Afro-American organizations.[12]

Simultaneously there evolved in the West Indies a society of classes graded hierarchically according to the lightness of their skin, with the Whites at the top of the social pyramid, the mulattoes in the middle, and the Blacks at the bottom. The mulattoes took on the function of a 'middle class' and looked down in turn upon the 'negroes' as 'the masses'.

The most elaborate example of a society differentiated according to criteria of race and class and based on slavery was to be found in Haiti on the eve of the French Revolution.[13] In Haiti the large plantation-owners, many of whom had been born in the country (Creoles) and known as the *grands blancs*, had secured for themselves a position at the top of the pyramid. Far below them were the mass of European petty proprietors and others who had no land, such as artisans, clerks, employees etc., the *petits blancs*. Then came the mulattoes, some of whom were already better off than the *petits blancs* but were inferior to them as regards political rights; they were distinguished among themselves according to the darkness of their skin.[14] Prior to the French Revolution they had control of one-fifth of the land and resisted any diminution of their social privileges. Even lower down the scale were the first free Blacks, while the mass of slaves (mostly Black) had absolutely no rights whatever. They, too, were graded broadly into house-slaves and field-hands.

It is perhaps no coincidence that the complex system of slavery which existed in Haiti was the first to collapse during the French Revolution. But even here the old class and racial system of the colonial period survived, in a concealed and shamefaced way: scarcely mentioned by name but very widely practised, often by those who paid lip service to the ideals of equality and civil rights.[15]

Among Afro-Americans in the USA the hierarchical structure of society was camouflaged in the same way, according to the lightness or darkness of skin colour, but it was equally effective. The light-skinned elements were clearly in control, although naturally enough they denied that there was any connection between the colour of one's skin and one's position within Afro-American sub-society. At any rate most leading Afro-Americans in the ecclesiastical and political fields, to mention only the two historically most important fields of activity, were light-skinned. Their dominant position was of course not due to any mysterious supposed hereditary superiority of the White race but to the fact that they often had an easier start in life than Black Afro-Americans. In the USA, as in the West Indies, the differences between mulattoes and Blacks was also a frequent cause of latent tension even in the age of slavery. In the 1920s these tensions came to the fore in the conflict between Garvey, the full-blooded negro from Jamaica who appealed above all to the racial pride of the Black 'masses', and the light-skinned Afro-American intellectuals and political leaders. In a more subtle form the difference between the two groups was manifested in their attitude to Africa, and thus also to Pan-Africanism.[16]

For Africans deportation into slavery was a psychological catastrophe of the first order. The sudden decline in status from that of a free person to that of a slave was in itself a sufficient cause of deep shock; added to this was their forceful removal from conditions which if not exactly idyllic were at least relatively orderly, and then the suffering endured on the march to the coast, the long period of waiting at the trading-stations or forts before they were transported and finally their sale and shipment to an uncertain future across the Atlantic. It was widely believed that in the White men's country Africans were eaten.[17] Then came the hardships of an unaccustomed sea voyage, which in those days at any rate was no source of pleasure even in comfortable circumstances. Even White sailors on warships, trading vessels or slave-ships lived in miserable conditions, and the incidence of sickness was probably hardly any lower among White emigrants from Europe than it was among African slaves. But the unbearable conditions in the overcrowded little ships, on which the hatches were usually battened down for fear of riots and were at any rate always heavily guarded, was made still more agonizing by the preceding shock and the fear of an uncertain future.

In principle there were two possible kinds of reaction: apathy and protest. Apathy offered the greater chance of survival; resistance led almost inevitably to death, which many Africans preferred to seek in order to escape their desperate plight. So far as protest was concerned, again there were in principle two kinds: active and passive. Forms of passive resistance included a refusal to eat, a hunger strike until death supervened, as was frequent, or a plunge into the sea, which was invariably fatal on the high seas, and usually in coastal waters as well on account of the sharks. The active form of resistance was the slave revolt, which occurred mostly near the African or American coast.

After the dangerous and onerous voyage came a new shock for the slaves, most of whom were enfeebled or sea-sick: the sale. In the USA a popular procedure was the 'scramble': eager purchasers rushed on to the ships and sought out their 'goods' for themselves in a wild rush, each wanting to get the best slaves first. The 'scramble' was a real pandemonium for the slaves, already sufficiently frightened and un-nerved.[18]

The system of slavery was constructed in such a way as to nip in the bud the ever-present menace of a slave revolt.[19] This meant that the slaves had to be deprived of the chance to organize in secret. The most important means of communicating any human sentiment, including the idea of conspiratorial action, is the possession of a common language which in itself creates a community of interest among those who speak it. To prevent such a common language from developing the masters had two possible ways of keeping their slaves isolated, neither of which was one hundred per cent foolproof. Either the slaves could be kept together in tribal groups, so as to make it more difficult for them to learn as a *lingua franca* the prevailing European language, or else one could try to level and stamp out all tribal differences. In the first case one got numerous small groups of slaves separated from one another by linguistic differences, who could only conspire in small numbers and within a restricted locality. In the second case the members of a tribe were to all intents and purposes isolated from one another, their memories of Africa as far as possible blotted out and their cultural identity denied. The Spaniards and Portuguese adopted the strategy of deliberately preserving tribal differences; the British and Americans preferred the strategy of levelling and assimilation.

Neither strategy wholly attained its objective. In Latin America it was impossible to prevent the slaves from learning Spanish or Portuguese as well as their African vernacular, if only because the Portuguese and Spaniards attempted to Christianize the slaves, often even on the slave-ships. Moreover, some 'national' groups such as the Hausa and Yoruba became so strong during the nineteenth century that compact minorities developed, and African religious and political movements could be carried on across the Atlantic. The Yoruba, who arrived in large numbers from 1817 onwards, like their fellow-tribesmen who were liberated on the high seas by the British navy and were settled in Sierra Leone,[20] tended to keep together in groups, to help one another to buy their freedom from slavery and then to return, in large or small groups, to Yorubaland, or at least to the West African coast. There the 'Brazilians' and 'Cubans' joined the 'Sierra Leoneans' as in Nigeria, or else the immigrants formed the nucleus of a new class, as happened in Togo where the Olympios have been one of the leading families on the coast for over a century. The Spaniards and Portuguese built a safety-valve into their system of slavery by making it relatively easy to secure individual manumission. In the nineteenth century slaves were encouraged to obtain their freedom by hard work or to purchase it, and then to return to Africa. Despite this one must guard against the error of judging Latin American slavery merely by the legal provisions and so idealizing it. Until the nineteenth century the system was probably just as harsh as it was in North America.[21]

In the British possessions, and later in the USA, the strategy of dividing the slaves by extinguishing all traces of tribal individuality likewise collapsed. The slaves had to learn English and thus had an almost universal means of communication; on the other hand they could not engage in conspiratorial activities without their masters knowing. Manumission was made more difficult and was not practised on any notable scale until after the mid-eighteenth century (and then only with considerable hesitation), thanks to the preaching and example of certain radical Quakers; after a century of crises and convulsions slavery was abolished as late as 1863–5.[22] Apart from temporary fluctuations around 1800 and some particular exceptions, the Anglo-American slave system was opposed to giving the slaves any intellectual, religious or practical instruction which went beyond enabling them to fulfil their immediate utilitarian purpose. As far as possible they were to be kept on the level of dumb beasts. They had to perform hard physical labour on the plantations, open up new territory, build roads and work treadmills as substitutes for machines in the primitive establishments where cane-sugar was produced. To give slaves religious instruction would have implied a recognition that they had human souls; for this reason it was taboo and in some areas of the south even expressly prohibited.[23] It was only in the north and in southern towns that milder forms of slavery developed.[24] On the other hand, in contrast to the Spanish and Portuguese colonies, the basically democratic structure of American society gave the Afro-Americans, once they had become emancipated in larger numbers after the close of the eighteenth century, a better chance to organize and to voice their grievances in an articulate manner. The fact that their treatment as individuals was harsher than in Latin America also gave them an additional impulse to become politically active. In Latin America the situation was the reverse: the slave system was in legal terms less harsh but it was practically impossible to form a political organization in an authoritarian and feudal colonial environment. This explains why no notable contribution towards Pan-Africanism could be expected from Latin America.

In the West Indies and in North America racial discrimination was more marked than in Latin America. In the English-speaking world negro slaves were despised not only on account of their status but also on account of their race, even when the Afro-Americans had won the status of free men and had attained a measure of prosperity. Contrary to the intentions behind the policy of cultural assimilation, modern racism drew Afro-Americans back towards their native continent to a much greater extent than was the case in Latin America. The colour of their skin and the texture of their hair identified them for ever as members of an 'inferior race'; from this stigma they were unable to escape. One of the arguments against them was the assertion that Africa had no culture and no history, which was to provoke defiant protests from many Afro-Americans[25] as well as later from Africans.

Thus all Afro-Americans, regardless of whence they or their ancestors came from in Africa or what social position they had held in African society or now held in the USA, were lumped together as racially 'inferior'. It was therefore quite natural that those who lived in the diaspora of the New World, in permanent exile as it were, should have been more inclined to see Africa and the Africans as a unit than the Africans who remained in their traditional tribal societies, largely isolated from one another.[26] The Afro-Americans adopted the image of Africa held by their White masters, who as outsiders recognized a unity in Africa and Africans which was all but hidden from those who actually lived on that continent. This is not unusual; for instance both Teutons and Slavs obtained their collective names from their neighbours, Romans in the first case and Germans in the second.

The relationship to Africa

Thus among Afro-Americans and former slaves the concept of Africa came to be formed sooner than among the Africans themselves. Apart from the considerations advanced above, we only have the evidence of the earliest writings by Afro-Americans, ex-slaves in England and Africans. It is hard to be more precise since we know practically nothing about what Africans or slaves in the New World really thought until they themselves had the chance to articulate their ideas in a form accessible to the modern historian. Publications in the form of books or pamphlets by former negro slaves in England began as late as the close of the eighteenth century, and then only sparsely. Afro-Americans followed at the beginning of the nineteenth century and Africans in Africa in the mid-nineteenth century.[27] Even then it is usually difficult to say just what was a reflection of the opinions circulating in European society, or to distinguish between main and secondary currents of thought, between an expression of the literary or ideological conventions of the day and an original contribution by a Black author. At least as a theoretical consideration one cannot exclude the possibility that the first publications of this kind were entirely or partly inspired, or even partly written, by British philanthropists towards the close of the eighteenth century. At present, however, there is no evidence for this assumption, and until some is forthcoming the first literary products attributed to ex-slaves in England should be treated as their own authentic work, no more in debt to previous or contemporary ideas than any other literature.[28]

At this point we may also deal with the possible objection that one cannot draw generally valid deductions from the sparse literary evidence left by the few fortunate ones who came to England in the late eighteenth century, learned how to read and write, developed a facility for expressing their ideas and had the chance to publish them. Such an objection must not be taken lightly and cannot be refuted conclusively. But there is nevertheless a great likelihood that the first authors were indeed representative of the views held by thousands of their anonymous fellow-countrymen before and during the time of writing. Without access to the modern techniques of psephology it is a tricky business to make deductions about the ideas of whole groups from those of individuals, and even the psephologists rely upon representative sampling. Therefore the keenest sceptic must allow that the early literary testimony has some value, at least as illustrative of the opinions held by its authors.

It must also be borne in mind that ex-slaves in England had an image of Africa which was based, in part at any rate, on their own youthful experiences, however blurred their childhood memories may have been. The first Afro-American authors in the USA as a rule did not have such personal experiences. Their attitudes towards Africa reflected those of the dominant White elements in society, either adopting a negative picture or else reversing the values in protest by accepting unconditionally a positive and partly romanticized image of Africa.[29] In either case the notion of 'Africa' and 'Africans' is the elementary precondition for the development of Pan-African concepts. These intellectuals employed relatively rational arguments, even if they were inspired by an emotional sense of indignation at the slave trade and slavery. They were personally the furthest removed from Africa; their relationship to Africa was thus extremely abstract, reflecting book knowledge and their own cerebrations rather than concrete experiences. Forced to generalize by their inadequate knowledge, they often tended to adopt romantic and idealized notions which could powerfully affect their basically rational approach – best exemplified perhaps by the case of W. E. B. Du Bois.[30]

Matters are somewhat different as regards the non-intellectual element of Afro-Americans, the field-slaves, mostly Blacks, after the Civil War. Since they often came directly from Africa and since the plantations were virtually isolated from the outside world these field-slaves were better able to preserve the memory of their old homeland and to keep up its traditional customs. On the question of the so-called 'survivals' of Africa there has arisen a certain controversy among American historians, which we cannot go into in detail here.[31] For the present it is enough to state that the Afro-Americans in general were not so radically cut off from their African past as has usually been assumed. Moreover, the extent of such survivals varied from place to place. The strength of the African cultural element and modernization varied greatly from such places as former Dutch Surinam, where at an early date thousands of slaves achieved a kind of independence and withdrew into the jungle where they lived under quasi-African conditions, to the Yoruba groups in Brazil such as the Bahia, in the West Indies, parts of the southern USA and to the large American cities.[32] Some elements of African culture survived in the New World under conditions of slavery, such as the dominant position of the woman within the family, a continuation in modified form of the matriarchal order found among many West African peoples. Religious concepts, too, lived on, sometimes in a superficially Christianized form, particularly marked in the negro Baptist churches and even more so in the typical syncretic Voodoo cult, especially on Haiti.[33]

Some indirect evidence about the attitude of the slaves towards Africa may be gleaned from the slave songs, forerunners of the negro spirituals.[34] These often couched their protest against slavery in the figurative language of the Old Testament. The slaves compared themselves to the people of Israel in Egyptian bondage; 'Heav'n', 'Jerusalem' or 'Zion' stood for an Africa which had receded into a mythical past. The widespread concept that the slaves would return to Africa after their death was expressed in the idea of going to 'Heav'n' or 'Jerusalem' after crossing the Atlantic, called the 'River Jordan'. The idea that men's souls went to Africa after death in America was noted by a French author at the beginning of the nineteenth century[35] and re-appeared, surprisingly enough, in a somewhat spectacular form in the middle of World War II.[36] The greater the distance that separated an Afro-American from the original milieu of slavery, the greater the likelihood that his memory of Africa would have faded. According to Du Bois, his family knew only one African melody handed down from generation to generation, whose words nobody could any longer understand; this was their sole memory of Africa.[37]

Upon this substratum of a sentimental and superstitious link back to Africa there developed among many uneducated Afro-Americans a desire to return to Africa physically, and among intellectuals a spiritual and political interest in Africa. However, and this point needs to be emphasized, such attitudes to Africa were by no means uniform among the negro élite. It may be assumed that most Afro-Americans adopted the White stereotype of a barbaric, savage Africa devoid of history, so that many of them felt ashamed of their African origin and developed a deeply rooted inferiority complex of which traces remain to this day.[38] Hence spokesmen for the free coloured people opposed all projects for deporting them forcibly to Africa, arguing that that continent was backward and barbaric.[39] The more successful and wealthier an Afro-American became, despite all the handicaps facing him in American society, the greater his inclination to avoid being identified with Africa. Those with an interest in Africa were only a minority among the educated classes, yet from this minority sprang the decisive impulses that led to the development of Pan-Africanism.

The poor, mainly dark-skinned 'masses' were more willing to consider returning physically to Africa, as is shown by the fact that projects for a voluntary (as opposed to more or less forcible) return time and again met with a favourable response.[40] This latent sentiment was later directed into quasi-political channels by Garvey with his 'Back-to-Africa' movement.[41] Thus it is understandable that among the strongest advocates of a return to Africa were such men as W. E. Blyden, Martin R. Delany and Garvey – full-blooded negroes who, in contrast to many mulattoes, were still proud of their black skin.

3 The beginnings of proto-Pan-Africanism: 1787

Any attempt to establish the beginning of a phenomenon so complex as Pan-Africanism must always remain a difficult enterprise. The normal approach would be to opt for a period of several years, or at the most decades, broad enough to allow for the imprecision inseparable from all historical transitions. In trying to explain the appearance of Pan-Africanism in the narrower sense of the word in 1900 we found it necessary to go ever further back into time until suddenly, towards the close of the eighteenth century, we came to a point where all our sources had their origin. It turned out that in one particular year a number of events took place which all sooner or later, directly or indirectly, led to the emergence of Pan-Africanism in the narrower sense. These little rivulets were destined one day to flow into the mainstream of the Pan-African movement. So far as proto-Pan-Africanism is concerned, the epoch-making year was 1787 – two years prior to the outbreak of the French Revolution.

All these events took place at the corners of the geographical triangle within which the slave trade was carried on – and within which Pan-Africanism developed. Later, in the twentieth century, the focal point in the development of this movement was to shift from the USA via

England to West Africa; it is thus no accident that in 1787 most of the events of interest to us occurred in North America, three in England, and only one in West Africa; even this was initiated by Europeans.

Such a striking accumulation of historical events relevant to our theme cannot be observed in any other year, although one might put in a claim for 1688. This saw the 'Glorious Revolution' in England which gave rise to the liberal and parliamentary system with which in later years Pan-Africans were to identify. The 'Glorious Revolution' created the political conditions in the British colonies at a later date which permitted the growth of African nationalism and Pan-Africanism. In 1690 John Locke's *Two Treatises on Government* was published, providing the ideological foundation of British liberalism. John Locke later became an important 'witness for the defence' invoked by the American revolutionists, and later by Pan-Africans, in their fight for equality and freedom.

In sharp contrast to the liberal victory in England was the adoption of the first Slave Code on the British West Indian island of Barbados in 1688. This later served as the model for the legalization of slavery in the British colonies on the North American mainland: first in 1712 in South Carolina where the basic Slave Code, revised in 1739, remained in force until slavery was abolished at the end of the American Civil War. In 1770 Georgia adopted the Slave Code from South Carolina and at a later date Florida adopted that of Georgia.[1] It is also no coincidence that shortly after 1688 the Quakers were banished from Barbados 'because they sought to Christianize and educate their slaves'.[2]

Of a more specific kind were two other events which likewise belong to the prehistory of Pan-Africanism in the widest sense. In 1688 Mrs Aphra Behn, an Englishwoman, published a novel called *Oroonoko*. The eponymous hero was a Koromantee slave in the New World, whose fate is described in a sentimental tone and with complete sympathy. The author made use of her personal experiences during a slave riot in Dutch Surinam and for the first time represented a leader of rebellious slaves as a positive literary figure. The novel enjoyed great success, was adapted for the stage by Thomas Southerne and was performed in London theatres for almost a hundred years from 1696. Along with Montaigne's essay on cannibalism it helped to stimulate the eighteenth-century enthusiasm for the 'noble savage' which by way of Defoe and Rousseau led to the philanthropists' commitment to the suppression of the slave trade and their favourable attitude towards the Africans. The word 'noble' has a double use in *Oroonoko*: the 'noble savage' was not only morally superior to his White master but was also aristocratic, an African prince of aristocratic character and mentality, whereas the author showed no interest whatsoever in the plebeian mass of slaves, except as a foil for Oroonoko.[3]

Finally, in 1688 there appeared the first written protest against the slave system – in Germantown, Philadelphia. The work of some Quakers of German origin who came from the Krefeld area, it was published at a time when most Quakers, in so far as they could afford them, themselves owned slaves in the West Indies and the North American colonies, as did William Penn, the founder of Philadelphia. The protest from Germantown, *Remonstrance against Slavery and the Slave Trade*, therefore aroused no initial response.[4] In spite of this it marked the beginning of abolitionism which belongs to the historical background to Pan-Africanism. It was to take almost exactly another century before in 1787 there appeared a significant minority of Quakers who rejected slavery[5] and before abolitionism could take shape on American soil as a continuous organized movement.

The beginnings of abolitionism and Afro-American organizations in America

Before abolitionism assumed an organized form there were long and bitter quarrels among the members of the 'Society of Friends', as the Quakers were properly called, during the course of which most advocates of what was to become the abolitionist movement were excluded from the Quaker community. The written protest from Germantown was followed in 1693 by the first printed attack upon slavery which, however, was confined to the keeping of slaves by Quakers.[6] The most energetic abolitionist agitator during the eighteenth century was Anthony Benezet, who belonged to a Huguenot family which had been expelled from France by the revocation of the Edict of Nantes (1685). Benezet was born in St Quentin in 1713. Two years later he came to London by way of Holland. In 1731 he was in Philadelphia, where he joined the Quakers and became the most ardent advocate of the suppression of the slave trade. As early as 1750 he established a school for negroes in Philadelphia. Two of his publications exerted a considerable influence upon the abolitionist movement then in the process of formation,[7] and later indirectly also upon the Afro-Americans and the African nationalists.[8] By the time Benezet died in Philadelphia in 1784 there was in that city an organization devoted to the fight against slavery, founded in 1775 by the Quakers. After some years of passivity, the abolitionists reorganized themselves in 1787, also in Philadelphia, and adopted a new statute which enabled non-Quakers to be enrolled as members. The chairman was none other than the famous Benjamin Franklin. American abolitionism may therefore be said to have begun in 1787.

The date and location were not fortuitous, for it was in that year that there assembled in Philadelphia, then the largest city in the thirteen newly independent states, the Constitutional Assembly, at which the United States of America were formally established and the Constitution passed. Among the questions that forced themselves upon the delegates' attention was that of slavery. The newly organized abolitionists submitted their first petition to Congress requesting it to abolish slavery throughout the USA. Most members favoured the abolition of slavery but the delegates from South Carolina and Georgia, two of the slave-owning states, threatened that they would not join the union if they had to abandon slavery, the basis of their wealth. The fathers of the Constitution agreed upon a complicated compromise. Matters affecting the internal order of a state within the federation (i.e. a decision about slavery) remained a question for its (White) citizens; the federal government could not interfere. For this reason the Constitution made no mention of slavery (except for an oblique reference to 'other persons' in the famous 3/5 clause). It was assumed that it would disappear of its own accord as education and enlightenment progressed. But to forestall a possible expansion of slavery, the Northwestern Ordinance of 1787 stipulated that the new territories in what was then called the Northwest – for practical purposes the entire Middle West of the USA – should be exempt from slavery. It was also decided that after twenty years no more slaves should be imported into the USA.[9] The crucial problem remained unsolved and its settlement was merely postponed. This led to the gradual development of ever greater tension between North and South, which finally exploded in the American Civil War.

The establishment of the USA, and indeed also the foundation of the abolitionist movement among the American Quakers, are part of general world history. The same year saw the first efforts at independent organization among free Afro-Americans in three important fields of activity: the churches, freemasonry and education. On 12 May 1787 a group of free Afro-Americans, under the leadership of Richard Allen and Absolom Jones, founded the Free African Society in a Methodist church in Philadelphia in protest against the spread of racial discrimination. This was a preliminary step to the foundation of the Bethel church in Philadelphia in 1794, which in 1816 united with other local churches to form the African Methodist Episcopal church (AME), the first independent Afro-American denomination. This likewise took place in Philadelphia, and the first bishop to hold office was Richard Allen. Between 1796 and 1820 a similar situation arose in New York, leading to the founding of the African Methodist Episcopal Zion church (AMEZ). It differed from Allen's church mainly in the addition of the single word 'Zion' and a strong emphasis upon its independence, so that the two rival bodies, despite many attempts, have never merged.[10] The independent negro churches made a great contribution to the growth of political consciousness among Afro-Americans, above all by their protest against a compulsory return to Liberia. This agitation, still under Allen, in 1817 and 1830 unleashed the militant phase of abolitionism. The preachers and bishops of these churches were the first Afro-American intellectuals; it was they who wrote the first polemical treatises against the teaching of racial inequality.[11] Towards the close of the nineteenth century the two churches started missionary work in Africa. The schools, colleges and universities which they founded and supported produced an intellectual élite which, through its interest in Africa, enabled Pan-Africanism to develop. Finally, two bishops of the AMEZ church were among the initiators of the Pan-African movement in 1900.[12]

1787 also saw the formal establishment in Boston under Prince Hall of the first freemasonic lodge in the USA, the Free African Lodge, which received its charter as an independent lodge from the Grand Lodge in London. It had come into being informally in 1775 or 1776 as an offshoot of a lodge founded by an Irish regiment stationed in Boston during the Revolutionary War. With their ideology of equality and fraternity, in theory applicable to all men and all races, the freemasons played their part in the struggle of Afro-Americans for legal equality.[13]

Prince Hall, a very light-skinned mulatto from Barbados, may be regarded as the first Afro-American advocate of equal rights in the important field of education. He was the spirit behind a petition addressed on 17 October 1787 by the free negroes to the Parliament of Massachusetts in which they asked for their children to be given educational facilities, arguing that in the final instance they had loyally paid their taxes. The petition was rejected, but this gave the impulse to the founding of a school for negro children in Prince Hall's house in 1798.[14] The significance of schools in the progress of the Afro-Americans cannot be exaggerated. Their struggle to obtain emancipation and legal equality may almost be regarded as a struggle to acquire the right to modern education. The founding of this school and of the Free African Society were two indirect sources of Pan-Africanism.

British abolitionism and the foundation of Sierra Leone

The way events were moving in 1787 can be seen by examining the similar trends in Great Britain, where in the same year the abolitionist movement also took shape with the formation of a committee for the suppression of the slave trade led by William Wilberforce, Thomas Clarkson and Granville Sharp.[15] Like the American Quakers in Philadelphia, with whom they were in correspondence, they acted as a kind of lobby for the abolition of the slave trade, at first discreetly supported by William Pitt. As parliamentary spokesman for the so-called 'Clapham Sect' (after Clapham, the London suburb in which most of the leading abolitionists lived), Wilberforce became the most famous representative of British abolitionism. But his impact would have been impossible without the work of Clarkson and Sharp, whose extensive research provided the material for a successful propaganda campaign on a scale that had hitherto never been seen. The struggle to abolish first the slave trade and then slavery itself had far-reaching historical consequences, as we shall see.

In 1787, in the same year that the Constitutional Assembly met in Philadelphia to give the thirteen British ex-colonies a new federal constitution, the first settlers landed in Sierra Leone, forming the first colonial settlement in tropical Africa. This seemingly insignificant event was also to have far-reaching consequences, for from this time onwards Sierra Leone became, after the Gold Coast, the second most important centre in the modernization of African society along the west coast.[16] The early history of Freetown and the colony of Sierra Leone leads us right into the problems of proto-Pan-Africanism, and therefore at least an outline of the main events must be given.

Before abolitionism became an organized movement in England certain individuals engaged in the struggle against the slave trade and slavery. The most important was Granville Sharp, who in 1772 won his first success when the judge Lord Mansfield made his famous ruling in the case of James Somerset. According to this every slave who set foot upon British soil became a free man automatically, since the institution of slavery was unknown to the law of England. Since their former masters often no longer bothered about them, they formed a kind of sub-proletariat in English society. In time their numbers appear to have grown considerably, although one may dismiss as a scare-mongering exaggeration the description of a contemporary according to whom they were to be found throughout the country and were well organized.[17]

The 'Black Poor' apparently became a problem after the American War of Independence, when a number of ex-slaves arrived from America who had either fought on the side of the British as Loyalists or at the end of the war had left the future USA with the Loyalists, mostly for Canada. The 'Black Poor', many of them destitute and vagrant, were now regarded as a burden.[18] Their cause was first taken up by a Committee for Relieving the Black Poor led by the philanthropist Jonas Hanway, founded at the beginning of 1786; its *spiritus rector* was Granville Sharp, who even drafted a charter on their behalf. In 1786 a certain Dr Henry Smeatham, who had spent several years on the West African coast and then in the West Indies, published a plan for settling coloured persons in Sierra Leone.[19] His project was not a very serious one and was mainly designed to further his own financial interests; it was supported by two London merchants who valued the opportunity it presented to invest in cotton plantations. Sharp, who apparently was at first unaware of the background to the plan, took the matter up.

Even before this it had been suggested that the growing number of ex-slaves supported by the committee should be deported overseas, for instance to Nova Scotia in Canada. Now attention centred upon the West African coast. Approached by the committee, the British government promised financial and material support. After a certain amount of effort Hanway succeeded in winning over the ex-slaves themselves to the idea, though they had at first been rather suspicious of it, for among other reasons they feared that they might be sent back to slavery.

In this situation the scarcely philanthropic motives of Dr Smeatham and his two backers became known; Smeatham died, and Sharp wanted to call off the entire project. But the ex-slaves who were willing to be settled, and who had elected fifteen of their number to speak for them, insisted on being sent back to Africa; they said that they had heard from an inhabitant of Sierra Leone that they would be well received there. Sharp changed his mind and the government kept its promise. The founding of Sierra Leone and Freetown was thus in the last resort due to former slaves, some of whom had come to Britain from Africa via America. With their settlement on the West African coast the triangle was, so to speak, complete.

In 1792 the first colonists were reinforced by settlers from Nova Scotia. They were also ex-slaves who had joined the British and the Loyalists in the American War of Independence and had subsequently settled in Nova Scotia. They came directly from Halifax without passing through England. Some of them actually originated from Sierra Leone; one of them found his mother again, and another the man who had sold him into slavery and to whom he gave a gift for having unwittingly been the instrument of his conversion to Christianity.[20]

The third group of settlers came to Sierra Leone in 1799, likewise from Nova Scotia. For them, too, this had only been a port of call: they were so-called 'maroons' from Jamaica. They were the descendants of former slaves who, after the British had taken possession of the island in 1655, had attained a kind of tolerated autonomy in the mountains of the island. In 1795, influenced by the revolution in nearby Haiti, some of them launched a new guerilla war against the White planters; the maroons capitulated after Cuban bloodhounds were about to be used against them. Contrary to the terms whereby they surrendered, they were deported and settled in Nova Scotia, whence some of them came to Freetown in 1799.

When a new group of colonists arrived in Sierra Leone in the years after 1808, freed by the British fleet, they found that the first waves of settlers had already grown together to form a social group opposed to newcomers. The latter originated directly from Africa, and had not yet familiarized themselves with the ways of life in a modernizing society; they were therefore at first regarded as backward.

Cugoano's criticism of the slave trade and slavery

The plan to colonize Sierra Leone was welcomed by Ottobah Cugoano in a book which appeared in the same year 1787.[21] Cugoano heard about the preparations from Equiano, who was originally to have accompanied the first settlers to Sierra Leone but owing to differences of opinion withdrew from the expedition and stayed behind in England.[22] It is thus understandable that, while basically favourable to the undertaking, Cugoano should have criticized sharply the way in which it was carried out.[23]

Cugoano was a Fanti who had been kidnapped as a child while visiting relatives and had first been taken to the West Indian island of Grenada. Here he was brought up by Lord Hoth who brought him to England, where as a manservant he learned to read and write. In 1787 he published his book, which as quickly as the following year appeared in a French translation with a foreword by Abbé Grégoire, the leading figure in the Société des Amis des Noirs, founded in Paris in 1786 or 1788. According to Piatoli, an Italian who apparently suggested the translation or arranged for it to be made, Cugoano's book 'caused the greatest sensation'.[24] In 1788 Cugoano was in the employment of Cosway, the painter. Piatoli took him to be between thirty-six and forty years of age; he described him as religious and added: 'The Bible is his principal object of study. . . . He is married to an English-woman and is on very good terms with her.'

Apart from his comments on the Sierra Leone project, which illustrate the deeper connection between the events of 1787 in Britain and West Africa, Cugoano's book is of importance for three other reasons. In the first place Cugoano was the first African to demand the total abolition of the slave trade and emancipation of slaves. The latter demand is all the more noteworthy in view of the fact that most White abolitionists only came round to this standpoint much later. Secondly, Cugoano made two concrete proposals, one of them negative and the other positive and both of which were implemented later. After the slave trade had been generally prohibited, the British fleet was to enforce the ban. In lieu of the slave trade and slavery 'there might be a very considerable and profitable trade carried on with the Africans', which could be expanded into peaceful collaboration between the Africans and the British.[25] Cugoano also discussed the wages that free workers should receive.

Of even greater interest to historians is the striking prophecy which Cugoano dared to make about a reversal of the conditions that then prevailed – two years before the French Revolution and almost two centuries before decolonization. Here we already find the dialectical shift, the boomerang effect of slavery, formulated in an impressive form, partly in mystical and eschatological language:

History affords us many examples of severe retaliations, revolutions and dreadful overthrows; and of many crying under the heavy load of subjection and oppression, seeking for deliverance. And methinks I hear now, many of my countrymen, in complexion, crying and groaning under the heavy yoke of slavery and bondage, and praying to be delivered. . . . Yet O Africa! Yet, poor slave! The day of thy watchmen cometh, and thy visitation droweth nigh, that shall be their perplexity. Therefore I will look into the Lord; I will wait for the God of my salvation; my God will hear me. Rejoice not against me, O mine enemy; though I be fallen, I shall yet arise; though I sit in darkness, the Lord shall yet be a light unto me . . . and I shall behold his righteousness. Then mine enemies shall see it, and shame shall cover them which said unto me, Where is the Lord thy God, that regardeth thee: Mine eyes shall behold them trodden down as the mire of the streets. In that day thy walls of deliverance are to be built, in that day shall the decree of slavery be far removed. What revolution the end of that predominant evil of slavery and oppression may produce, whether the rise and considerate will surrender and give it up, and make restitution for the injuries that they have already done, so far as they can; or whether the force of their wickedness, and the iniquity of their power, will lead them on until some universal calamity burst forth against the abandoned carriers of it on, and against the criminal nations in confederacy with them, is not for me to determine? But this must appear evident, that for any man to carry on a traffic in the merchandize of slaves, and to keep them in slavery; or for any nation to oppress, extirpate and destroy others; that these are crimes of the greatest magnitude, and a most daring violation of the laws and commandments of the Most High, and which, at least, will be evidenced in the destruction and overthrow of all transgressors. And nothing else can be expected for such violations of taking away the natural rights and liberties of men, but that those who are the doers of it will meet with some awful visitation and righteous judgement of God, and in such a manner as it cannot be thought that his just vengeance for their iniquity will be the less tremendous because his judgements are long delayed.[26]

Thus at the beginning of the prehistory of Pan-Africanism we find an almost prophetic and solemn condemnation of all those who either were responsible for the slave trade and slavery or who profited thereby. The curse – fortunately for those concerned – has not yet come wholly to fulfilment, and its mystical religious content may be disregarded here. But Cugoano's insight into the nature of European–North American hegemony and its dialectical consequences is nevertheless an impressive illustration of what a modern writer has called 'the delayed boomerang from the time of slavery'.[27] The boomerang effect of the slave trade and slavery, and later that of colonialism and imperialism, will be discussed more fully below. Not only was it evident in the events of 1787 we have mentioned – at any rate to the historian – but at least one object of the slave trade, Cugoano, described it in the language of ecstatic prophecy.

4 Sierra Leone and Nigeria: abolitionism and the Christian missions

For some time after the dramatic prelude of 1787 proto-Pan-Africanism did not make itself felt very powerfully. Meanwhile the economic, social and political processes were at work which were to enable Pan-Africanism proper to emerge, and the interconnections between them were becoming apparent. This development lasted throughout the nineteenth century. It led first to a reinforcement of slavery in the USA but also, in the British Empire, to the abolition of the slave trade in 1807 and of slavery in 1834–8. In the USA slavery was abolished as late as 1863–5, as a by-product of the Civil War; nevertheless by the end of the century Afro-Americans, although now free in a formal sense, felt themselves scarcely less oppressed than they had been before as slaves – at least in the southern states. On the other hand, with the Monroe Doctrine the USA coined the popular slogan 'America for the Americans' which, appropriately modified, became almost a touchstone of Pan-Africanism: 'Africa for the Africans'.

Around 1800 British abolitionism and Christian missionary fervour led to the first permanent commitments in Africa which went beyond commercial relations and the maintenance of coastal forts. This provided the basis for imperialism which, in the last third of the nineteenth century, constructed the European colonial system which reached its apogee in 1900. The defence of African interests against European colonial imperialism and racism in Africa, and of Afro-American interests against racial discrimination in the USA, gradually led to a new racial consciousness among the most modernized groups, both in West Africa and in the New World. Modern means of communication facilitated contact between the two élites which were in any case mobile. Finally, after decades of preparation, an extraneous event brought these various currents together: the World Fair in Paris in 1900, exemplifying a mobile worldwide society undergoing rapid modernization.[1]

The two great movements which created the historical conditions of Pan-Africanism – abolitionism and the Christian missions – are closely interlinked and can hardly be distinguished clearly from one another, either as regards their motives or their historical effect. Both are derived from the same roots: the humanitarian spirit of the Enlightenment and the new missionary zeal nurtured by the Evangelical movement in late eighteenth-century England. The leading abolitionists were keen promoters of the Christian mission and the early missionaries were inspired by the philanthropy of the abolitionists. Both movements originated in Britain. By 'the Christian missions' we understand those of the Protestant Anglo-Saxon churches; the missionary work carried out by the negro Methodists deserves special attention.[2] The Anglo-Saxon missionary movement of the late eighteenth and early nineteenth centuries was part of a larger phenomenon, the spread of Christianity whose historical roots go back further[3] than those of abolitionism, which is a relatively modern movement. On the other hand, the phase of missionary activity relevant to the development of Pan-Africanism only began after abolitionism had appeared, so that the thread which had been abandoned in 1787 was taken up again by this latter movement.

The Sierra Leone Company and suppression of the slave trade

There can hardly be any doubt about the primarily humanitarian character of the motives that led Thomas Clarkson, Granville Sharp and William Wilberforce to join forces in May 1787 with the object of abolishing the slave trade.[4] But they too lived in the real world, and needed allies and money for the campaign they had undertaken. These they could only attain by combining the prospect of practical advantages with their humanitarian intentions. Like Cugoano before them,[5] they pointed to the possibilities of engaging in a lucrative trade with Africa and of cultivating cotton there. In support of their ideas they could invoke, as well as John Locke, Adam Smith who used economic arguments to justify his rejection of slavery.[6] The abolitionists were respectable members of English society who appealed in an ingenious way to widespread feelings of sympathy for the 'noble savage'; they thus evoked an astonishingly powerful echo among the aristocracy and prosperous members of the middle class.

Wilberforce, a young member of Parliament for Hull who had hitherto attained little prominence, secured the attention of his friend Pitt[7] for whom the abolitionist movement was a kind of instrument with which to wreak revenge upon France. French support had proved decisive in the War of American Independence. Having concluded peace with the victorious colonists, Pitt hoped to strike a blow against a sensitive point in the French economy. The abolition of the slave trade would obstruct the importation of cheap slave labour into San Domingo (Haiti). The abolitionists submitted a large number of petitions, which with Pitt's help led to the appointment of a committee to hear evidence about the slave trade. The evidence given in this committee, particularly once it was available in printed form, gave the abolitionist cause a decisive psychological breakthrough so far as the general public was concerned. As early as May 1788 the parliamentary campaign began in earnest when the abolition of the slave trade was raised in the House of Commons for the first time.

Granville Sharp, who had actually initiated the settlement in Sierra Leone, did not regard the expedition of 1787 as a unique act, as a transient act of philanthropy. He was not concerned just with deporting the 'Black Poor' or opening up a lucrative field of activity for some resourceful entrepreneurs. On the contrary, he was first and foremost concerned with the well-being of his Black protégés. In February 1790, in order to ensure that the new settlement in Sierra Leone should be maintained, he proposed to found a company. Its purpose, however, was not to make profits for the shareholders. The founding members of the Sierra Leone Company included Wilberforce and Henry Thornton, a rich banker and a member of Parliament. The appearance of the new company put an end to the autonomy enjoyed by Sharp's 'Province of freedom' which was now ruled from London by a board of thirteen directors including Sharp, Wilberforce, Clarkson and Thornton.

After Parliament had given its approval in 1791, shares were issued at the price of £50 each with a subscription limit of £150,000,[8] at that time a considerable sum. In June 1792 approximately 1800 shareholders had bought 4518 shares at the price of £225,900.[9] The largest amount was held by Thornton, who had 58 shares. Although there was no prospect of any profit, there was greater readiness than had been expected to sink money *à fond perdu*. As is clear from the list of original subscribers, the shareholders came from the same social milieu as those who shortly before had made possible by subscription the publication of the letters of Ignatius Sancho, a former slave living in England. The number of subscribers, approximately 1800, happens to be the same.[10]

The society used its funds to rebuild Granville Town, the first settlement in Sierra Leone, which had been burned down during a conflict with a neighbouring tribe; it was now given the name of Freetown. New settlers arrived from Nova Scotia in 1792 and 1799.[11] After initial difficulties the colony consolidated itself, despite the many changes of governors sent out by the Sierra Leone Company and despite the tensions between the settlers and those governors like Zachary Macaulay, father of the well-known Thomas B. Macaulay, whose pious zeal led them to take a strong line towards the settlers.[12] But then came the inevitable setbacks and material losses: defensive measures had to be taken against the French (whose fleet burned down Freetown in September 1794 during the Revolutionary War)[13] and the neighbouring coastal tribes; the work of opening up the country and supporting the settlers absorbed so much money that even a subsidy from the British government could not cover the expenses. British trade had suffered as a result of the war and the Continental Blockade, and philanthropic zeal had also slackened. In 1807 the Sierra Leone Company succeeded in transferring its burden to the British government. On 1 January 1808 Sierra Leone became a British Crown Colony, the first one upon African soil. The abolitionists secured for themselves a continued influence upon Sierra Leone by founding an 'African Institution'.[14]

By 1807 abolitionism had scored its decisive initial success, the prohibition against British subjects participating in the slave trade. They could only win this victory once the West Indian planters' lobby at Westminster had been broken as a result of the erosion of their economic power.[15] As a parliamentary committee of inquiry found, after hearing statements by all the interested parties, the price of West Indian sugar had fallen for several years after 1799, whereas in most plantations the costs of production had risen above the takings, with the result that they had sunk into a hopeless misery. The main reason for this was an overproduction of sugar-cane, and this in turn was caused *inter alia* by the fact that for several years there had been none of the usual devastating hurricanes and that as a consequence of the Napoleonic wars and the Continental Blockade foreign markets had been closed, whereas the 'hostile colonies', i.e. the French, Spanish and Dutch sugar islands, had gained easy access to the European market in ships flying the American flag.[16] Spokesmen for the West Indian lobby argued that the wealth of the West Indies, and thus of the British Empire, depended on an uninterrupted supply of cheap labour; but this became untenable once the economic ruin of the sugar industry was inevitable for the reasons shown.

In 1807 the British government made a humanitarian virtue out of economic necessity: as from 1 May, trade in slaves was prohibited. The historical impact of this step was considerable: logically the ban had to be expanded into a general one. As a result of the decision of 1787, further import of slaves into the USA was likewise officially banned from 1 January 1808; since there were, however, no legal penalties against offenders the American slave trade continued to flourish even without any legal basis. Attempts by the British government to reach agreement with the USA on joint enforcement of the prohibition led to considerable tension between the two countries in the middle of the nineteenth century; the Americans would only adhere formally and temporarily to the agreements they had in fact made, such as that on joint control of West African waters. They failed to implement their laws against the slave trade and always protested strongly against American ships being searched by the British navy even when the slave traders' ships flew the American flag improperly.[17] The southern states, which were over-represented in the government, Congress and the army, were not interested in an effective suppression of the slave trade. Some extremists even pressed for the slave trade to be legally restored; the North resisted this suggestion, which helped to inflame the passions that led to the outbreak of the Civil War.

The British were more successful in their attempts to persuade other European countries to follow their lead. A recommendation in this sense was made by the Congress of Vienna to the signatories of the treaties, which led to a system of bilateral agreements on the suppression of the slave trade and, later, of slavery itself. One of the most important consequences was that most European countries conceded to the British fleet the right to search vessels on the high seas in tropical waters in order to detect camouflaged slave-ships. Nevertheless the transatlantic slave trade continued until the American Civil War.

The beginnings of missionary activity and modern education in Sierra Leone

The prohibition of the slave trade raised the question of control. The British government authorized the Royal Navy to patrol the West African coast in order to stop offences against the prohibition. As a base for the West African squadron, Freetown with its fine harbour was well suited; it also became the seat of a court at which slave-traders apprehended on the high seas were brought to trial. The question arose as to what was to be done with the liberated slaves. They could not simply be sent home, since they would then be quickly enslaved again. In this case, too, Sierra Leone provided an ideal solution. Here the emancipated slaves could live on African soil in a relatively free community of Africans and Afro-Americans, protected by the British Crown against being enslaved afresh. Between 1808 and 1863, when the final shipload of slaves originally destined for the USA was disembarked in Freetown, approximately 50,000 Africans came to Sierra Leone in this way. They were settled in Freetown and in nearby villages which sprang up at the beginning of the nineteenth century.[18]

The emancipated slaves, called 'liberated Africans' or 'recaptives', were well suited to be objects of the missionary fervour reawakened by the Evangelical movement. From 1808 onwards the Church of England set up schools and churches in Sierra Leone and achieved considerable success; later the same vigorous activity was displayed in Nigeria.

The Christian missions in tropical Africa can look back upon a long and chequered history, which in modern times begins with the Bull of Pope Nicholas V in 1454. This gave the Portuguese the right to take possession of all newly discovered land inhabited by pagans south of Cape Bojador, to attack, subject and force into permanent slavery 'Saracens, heathen and other enemies of Christ' on condition that these infidels were converted to Christianity.[19] This obligation explains the

Portuguese practice of getting their ship's chaplains, or those of their forts, to baptize whole shiploads of slaves before they were transported, so that the papal command might be carried out at least in a formal sense. Missionary attempts of a more serious kind were restricted to the royal courts of Benin and Angola as well as Mozambique, but they were deprived of any real hope of lasting success since they were far too obviously linked to Portuguese expansion, including the slave trade. The Catholic missions only gained a firm footing in Black Africa at the close of the nineteenth century.

The revival movement towards the close of the eighteenth century was itself a continuation of the impulse that had led John Wesley of Oxford to found the Methodist Church. In 1795 it led to the creation of the London Missionary Society. This organization sent six missionaries to Sierra Leone in 1797 to convert the heathen Susu tribes, but the enterprise ended in failure.[20] As a result the London Missionary Society refused to send any further missionaries to Sierra Leone. Thereupon the leaders of the Evangelical revival movement, including Wilberforce, Thornton and Clarkson, founded a Church of England missionary society which in 1813 adopted the title of Church Missionary Society (CMS), still in use today.[21] After the discouraging experience of the London Missionary Society it was impossible to find any missionaries in England willing to go to Sierra Leone. For this reason the CMS gladly made use of an old connection with a Lutheran missionary seminary in Berlin (later the Berliner Missionsgesellschaft), which trained missionaries but had no mission field of its own. In 1804 the first two German missionaries arrived in Freetown with the object of converting the Susu. Until 1816 twenty-four more German missionaries followed, of whom sixteen soon died, mostly from malaria. In 1816 the CMS suspended the Susu mission in order to take up work among the 'recaptives'. In contrast to the first settlers, who as a rule came from America already as Christians (mostly Methodists and Baptists), the emancipated slaves were still heathen, presenting an ideal field of activity to the CMS mission. By introducing the ex-slaves into the modern world through school and church it could take credit for an important historical achievement in this part of Africa.

The Sierra Leone Company, according to its charter, was obliged to set up schools for African children. In 1799, on his return to London, Zachary Macaulay brought with him to Clapham from Sierra Leone twenty-three boys and four girls for whom he opened a school, the

'African Academy'. It was supervised by a board which included Wilberforce, Sharp, Macaulay, the Rev. J. Venn and others – all of those named except Venn being men we have referred to above.[22]

From the day the first slave-ship was brought to Freetown by the British navy, 10 November 1808, until 1816 approximately 16,000 freed slaves arrived in Sierra Leone. They were settled in Freetown and eleven nearby colony villages which came into existence between 1809 and 1819;[23] most of these had their own village school. In 1816, in one of the oldest colony villages, Leicester, the CMS set up an additional school, the Christian Institution, in which 350 boys and girls received a practical training. In addition to reading, writing and arithmetic (the 'three Rs') the boys learned a trade as joiners, brick-layers etc., while the girls learned sewing, gardening, laundering etc. After the Christian Institution had virtually ceased to exist, the governor suggested founding a college for boys only. In 1827 Fourah Bay College[24] was founded as a kind of theological secondary school. It has had an eventful history and after all kinds of ups and downs became the precursor and nucleus of what is now the university of Sierra Leone, still called Fourah Bay College.[25] Its first pupil was Samuel Crowther, who in 1822 as a boy aged fifteen was freed from a slave-ship and came to Freetown. He rose to become one of the most famous 'Sierra Leoneans', as they were called, and has his place in the prehistory of African nationalism in West Africa.[26]

In March 1845 fourteen pupils were taken from Fourah Bay College to form the nucleus of an independent secondary school, the CMS Grammar School in Freetown.[27] Just one month later higher education for girls began in Sierra Leone with the setting up of the Female Institution in Freetown. Like Fourah Bay College, the CMS Grammar School was run by Anglican clergy, at first Europeans but from 1854 occasionally also Africans. Simultaneously experiments were made with training in practical subjects, then known as the 'industrial system'. For this reason in 1854 the grammar school was amalgamated with a 'normal school' at Kissy.[28] But the 'normal school' did not flourish, as little as did similar attempts later on the Gold Coast because the Africans, caught up in the process of modernization, wanted their schools to have the highest possible academic level.[29]

The number of pupils at the CMS Grammar School, after its birth-pangs were overcome, varied between 56 (1856) and 183 (1884). A considerable proportion of members of the modern élite in Sierra

Leone attended this school. Since numerous 'recaptives' went back again to their homeland after 1839[30] the CMS Grammar School, like Fourah Bay College, had two peculiarities: a high percentage of boarders, who in some years accounted for more than half the pupils,[31] and a variegated make-up according to the pupils' place of origin. 'The school was cosmopolitan', T. S. Johnson notes.[32] What this meant may be conveyed by a glance at the school register for the first ninety years.[33] According to this out of 3740 pupils approximately 500, almost one-seventh, came from outside Sierra Leone, most of them from Nigeria and the Gold Coast, Gambia and Liberia – from other parts of the West African coast; others came from Fernando Po, the Cameroons, Zaire (the former Belgian Congo), South Africa, and a few even from the West Indies, one from East Africa (not identified more closely) and one from Zanzibar. The wide geographical range from which the pupils of the CMS Grammar School were drawn gives a good idea of the 'horizontal mobility' among 'Sierra Leoneans' after 1839, since one may assume that the parents of most of the pupils who came from outside the colony were themselves 'Sierra Leoneans'. Even when the children were not descended from parents who as 'recaptives' had been to the great school of Sierra Leone, as was the case with those from the Gold Coast or the Niger delta (Bonny, Brass, Opopo, Calabar), the effect this had upon the gradual development of a Pan-African consciousness may not have been less but rather the reverse.

Political effects of the missions and schools

The CMS Grammar School in Freetown spread among its pupils the knowledge that there were Africans in other parts of the continent and Afro-Americans in the New World. This enabled a feeling of their common destiny to grow almost of its own accord. Thus this school produced one of the first exponents of African proto-nationalism and 'Ethiopianism',[34] James Johnson,[35] who also taught there for some time. In 1873 its headmaster edited a bimonthly periodical, the *Ethiopian*.[36] At this time James Johnson was collaborating on a proto-nationalist and proto-Pan-African journal in Freetown, which for the first time had in its title the word 'negro', which hitherto the Africans had so despised[37] – all this half a century before the Négritude movement began.

The significant contribution made by Sierra Leone in the early nineteenth century in creating the conditions for the rise of Pan-Africanism may be explained by the early date at which the colony was founded, almost a century before the classical age of colonialism. It was a product of abolitionism and the Evangelical missionary movement that it sponsored. For the humanitarian abolitionists of the pre-Victorian and early Victorian era were indeed primarily concerned with the prosperity of the Africans who had settled in Sierra Leone. In addition the settlers who had arrived from the New World before 1800 brought with them at least the rudiments of modern ideas and practices and with this a considerable degree of self-awareness. The missionary activities, together with the logic of development, made Sierra Leone a kind of laboratory for incipient modernization in West Africa: the slaves who were freed by the British navy were settled in Sierra Leone where they quickly became modernized, and after 1839 some of them moved on elsewhere along the coast. Those who graduated from the CMS Grammar School and from Fourah Bay College in Freetown, the artisans and merchants of Sierra Leone, were a living refutation of the prejudice about the supposed racial inferiority of Africans and Afro-Americans, for they proved clearly that they, too, even in a tropical surrounding, were capable of acquiring a modern education so long as they were given the chance. Since they were relatively quick to accept modernization it was impossible to treat them as semi-barbaric savages. Until quinine was in general use the tropical climate helped to afford them greater scope than later, at the height of colonial rule, for the tropical diseases to which so many missionaries fell victim in the early years inevitably reduced the number of Europeans in the country. The Creoles of Sierra Leone,[38] like the ruling class of mulattoes in Liberia, were therefore able to develop a self-awareness which to some extent already displayed quasi-racial features vis-à-vis the 'native tribes' of the region. Their pride in the possession of European names and education explains why around 1900 the 'Sierra Leoneans' were not very popular on the west coast of Africa. To Europeans in the colonial era they seemed ridiculous feeble imitators of their own culture, whereas Africans regarded them as arrogant tools of the colonial power.[39]

The Creoles of Sierra Leone at first found greatest scope for their talents in the ecclesiastical field. To save expense and the lives of White missionaries, Fourah Bay College was founded as early as 1827 with the purpose of fostering a new generation of mission teachers and clergymen.[40] The Rev. Haensel from Bavaria,[41] the first rector, was a German, and not a 'coloured American'.[42] When the college, after years of virtual lethargy, was re-opened in 1848 in a new four-storeyed building (the rafters were taken from a wrecked slave-ship seized by the British navy), the Rev. Edward Jones, an Afro-American, was appointed rector,[43] evidently with an eye to the awakening racial feeling in Sierra Leone even if this was manifest only among the surrounding tribes.[44]

Growing African self-consciousness in Sierra Leone blended easily with the outlook of the Rev. Henry Venn, who as principal secretary of the CMS in London from 1841 to 1874 was responsible for its missionary activity. Venn was the son of the Rev. Venn, mentioned above.[45] His sympathy for Africans dated back to his childhood at Clapham Common, when he used to play with the children of the African Academy from Sierra Leone.[46] For practical and ideological reasons Venn sought to turn the missions into native churches in Africa and Asia as soon as was feasible. Once the young Christian community had enough money and personnel to establish a church of its own, the European missionary was to change his role for that of a pastor, and later to yield his place to a local clergyman. His idea of a 'self-supporting, self-governing and self-extending' missionary church[47] met with opposition from sceptical European missionaries on the spot, but especially in Nigeria and Sierra Leone.[48] His dogged pressure led to the setting up of the Native Church Pastorate on 1 November 1861, the first step in the establishment of an independent church in Sierra Leone. Three years later Samuel Crowther was appointed bishop in the mission field that was opened in 1857 in the Niger delta.[49]

In the ecclesiastical area the young modernized classes of West African society took their first steps at independent action, first within the framework of the mother church, and then after the turn of the century either in open protest or in secession.[50] After Venn had died, the CMS in London was surprised to learn in 1873 that the campaign led by the *Negro* in Sierra Leone in favour of transforming Fourah Bay College into a comprehensive modern secular university was the work of their own protégés in Freetown, who were frequently graduates of Fourah Bay College maintained by the CMS.[51]

This event alone illustrates the dialectical impact of the Christian missions in West Africa in encouraging pressure for West African independence. At the same time the missions offered a field in which the new élite could satisfy their ambitions, for in the missionary field they could rise from the rank of catechist and teacher to that of missionary, parson or even higher; in ecclesiastical bodies it was possible for zealous laymen to exert an influence in society.[52] Hence it was possible for a Nigerian historian who was basically critical of the European missions to praise Venn highly for his work:

> If any individual is to be credited with originating Nigerian nationalism, ideologically, then that individual is unquestionably the Reverend Henry Venn. . . . Singlehanded and deliberately, he urged Africans to be prepared to assume the leadership of their countries.[53]

The 'Sierra Leoneans' as the first missionaries and modernizers in Nigeria

Figures such as Samuel Crowther and James Johnson lead us directly from Sierra Leone to Nigeria. The historical link between the two countries from the mid-nineteenth century onwards were the 'Sierra Leoneans',[54] whose activities combined abolitionism and missionary work in an almost inseparable way.

Afro-Americans returned from the New World to Sierra Leone (and from 1822 also to Liberia which we have not yet mentioned) at first only in small numbers. In a corresponding movement a large number of ex-slaves from Brazil (especially Yoruba), the so-called 'Brazilians', returned to the West African coast, with their centre in what are today Togo and Nigeria. In Brazil the Yoruba had the practice of helping one another to buy their freedom from slavery and subsequently returned to Africa in groups. Here they continued to keep in touch with those left behind on the other side of the Atlantic, in particular with those in Bahia, where even today the Yoruba are clearly distinguishable as a distinct cultural group.[55]

A shorter distance had to be covered by those ex-slaves liberated by the British navy on the high seas after 1808 who were settled in Sierra Leone. Whereas some of them quickly became prosperous and tended to remain in Sierra Leone, others were anxious to return to their old homeland.[56] The Yoruba, who at that time provided the largest single contingent of slaves on account of the civil war which went on for decades in Yorubaland,[57] were especially keen to return, as were the

Ibo who had been taken to Sierra Leone. Contrary to the original hope of making Sierra Leone a colony of peasants, many recaptives turned to trade which conformed to traditional African concepts as well as to the modern capitalist principles which many Africans had become familiar with in Freetown. From 1839 onwards they carried on trade on former slave-ships which they were able to acquire relatively cheaply at auctions in Freetown, sailing along the West African coast as far as Badagry and Lagos. One of the first ships characteristically enough was called *Wilberforce*, and another *Queen Victoria*.[58]

At Badagry and Lagos – notorious slave markets since the eighteenth century – a number of Yoruba were able to recognize the place whence they had been shipped overseas and learned about the political changes that had taken place in the meantime. There were, however, risks attached to 'the return of the exiles'[59] to a country still shaken by civil wars and slave-hunting expeditions. Actually the first Yoruba to arrive from Sierra Leone, the 'Sierra Leoneans' (called 'Saros' or 'Emigrants'), were received in a different way in the two ports. In Lagos they were robbed and were lucky if they were not enslaved again and could make, even without any means, for the interior of the country to Abeokuta, the new centre of the Egba, the most important Yoruba tribe. On the other hand Badagry, which maintained good relations with Abeokuta, received the returned exiles amicably.[60] In a similar way the Ibo reached Calabar.[61]

The extent of this re-emigration was not large in absolute terms, particularly since it was spread over several years and regions. Exact figures are not available and contemporary estimates vary considerably. In 1842 government agencies in Freetown put the figure at more than 500. The Rev. T. B. Freeman, who visited Abeokuta by way of Badagry in 1842 as the first missionary, estimated their numbers to have been 2000–3000 in the same year in Abeokuta alone; according to Ajayi this was probably too high. In 1844 the governor of Sierra Leone put the figure for Yorubaland at 600–800, possibly an underestimate for tactical reasons. The British consul Beecroft, who visited Abeokuta in 1850, and the following year a British naval officer estimated that 3000 Saros lived there.[62]

Sierra Leoneans settled in Lagos, Ibadan and even in Ilorin in towns and villages both large and small. Re-emigration received a new boost in 1853 when a permanent British consulate was set up in Lagos (after the British had compelled Lagos to close down the slave market in

1851) and when regular steamship connections were established between Liverpool (formerly the most important port for the slave trade) and the West African coast as far as Lagos, one mail steamer arriving each month.[63] The consul brought a certain degree of protection; as early as 1843 George Maclean, the governor of the Gold Coast, had posted a sergeant in Badagry to protect emigrants against the danger of re-enslavement.[64] The steamship line increased the horizontal mobility of the modern élite on the West African coast, not only of emigrants but also of élite groups on the Gold Coast whose origins were different.[65] Regular postal and shipping links resulted on one hand in closer ties with the United Kingdom but on the other hand facilitated the tendency of the West African élites to coalesce into a homogeneous urban class along the coast from Gambia as far as Cameroon; this process was also aided by their common experiences at school at Freetown, later on the Cape Coast and at Lagos, and by intermarriage; it led eventually to the development of a feeling that the whole of West Africa shared a common destiny.

The Sierra Leoneans, most of whom had become Christians in Sierra Leone, rarely forgot their religion in their new (or old) homeland and invited missionaries from Sierra Leone to come to Yorubaland. Their appeal was first widely publicized by the Rev. T. B. Freeman. At the end of September 1842 this first Christian missionary in the region landed in Badagry, where he learned about the re-emigration that was just then beginning. In December he came to Abeokuta, again as the first missionary there, met the first Sierra Leoneans and later in conversation with them discovered more about their fate. Freeman described their reaction to his visit in the style of Christian devotional literature, to which his diary (published in England) made its contribution:

> After a long absence from their fatherland, they had returned, bringing the grace of God in their hearts, and had for some time been anxiously looking for a visit from a Christian missionary.[66]

Freeman was also the first to give an account of the modernizing impact the emigrants had within traditional African society. The ruler of Abeokuta exempted the re-emigrants from the obligatory kowtow and encouraged them 'to wear European clothes, and to cultivate the manners and customs of that country, which they brought with them from Sierra Leone'.[67] Re-emigrants who had learned a trade tried to apply their practical knowledge in Abeokuta, but at first had little opportunity; as a result most of them turned to trade and agriculture, cultivating yam, maize and cotton. The ruler of Abeokuta was 'pleased with their conduct, and wished his subjects to follow their example. This is honourable to both parties; and will surely be gratifying intelligence for the British Government, and all who are interested in the regeneration of Africa.'[68]

One man who was particularly gratified at this news was the venerable Thomas Clarkson, comrade-in-arms and friend of Wilberforce (who had died in 1833) and Granville Sharp. In a moving review of Freeman's *Journal* Clarkson acclaimed the Sierra Leoneans as a living testimony to the success of the Abolitionists' efforts to suppress the slave trade and slavery and to Christianize Africa.[69] They also appeared well suited to play the role mapped out for them in the 'grand design' of Wilberforce's successor in the abolitionist movement, Sir Thomas Fowell Buxton. Like Cugoano and Equiano half a century before, he worked out a detailed plan for an active struggle against the slave trade.[70] By spreading Christianity and encouraging legitimate commerce, especially in palm oil, Buxton sought to deprive the slave trade of its material basis; he hoped that the African rulers would become interested in this legitimate commerce which offered them a greater opportunity for profit. Africans themselves were to serve as Christian missionaries – and also as agents of technical progress, so giving an impetus to modernization.[71] Such ideas accorded with Venn's missionary concepts,[72] which derived from the same source. Buxton's expectations were in fact brought to fulfilment perfectly by the re-emigrants, supplemented by 'Brazilians', 'Cubans' and 'West Indians'. The two best-known illustrations of the role played by Sierra Leoneans as missionaries in Nigeria are Samuel Crowther, who in 1846 came to Abeokuta as CMS missionary together with the British minister Townsend, and in 1864 became bishop of the Niger Mission, and James Johnson, the Freetown clergyman transferred to Lagos who in 1900 was appointed Anglican assistant bishop. Crowther had a great many sons (who were educated in England) and sons-in-law, and founded an entire dynasty. Several less well-known missionaries, catechists, teachers and artisans from Sierra Leone worked under Crowther and Johnson.

The need to expand the missionary apparatus to meet the great demand overcame the resistance which European missionaries in Nigeria had originally put up against the provision of an academic education for Sierra Leoneans and their children. The Rev. T. B.

Macaulay, a Sierra Leonean and also a son-in-law of Samuel Crowther, initially had to overcome such resistance when in 1859 he founded a CMS Grammar School in Lagos[73] as an offshoot of the CMS Grammar School in Freetown.[74] Of the forty African clergymen from Nigeria who were ordained before 1890, only two were neither emigrants nor the sons of emigrants. Six received their theological training in England, fourteen at Fourah Bay College, and two at the CMS Grammar School in Freetown; six of them had an elementary education, two had only attended Sunday school.[75] What is most important in our context is that until 1890 most of the Anglican missionaries and clergy were Saros; moreover, it was at Fourah Bay College in Freetown that most of the African clergy on the coast obtained their theological training.[76] The second generation of Saros provided, in the person of the Rev. Samuel Johnson at Oyo, the first modern historian of the Yoruba, who recorded precious oral traditions about their history and so preserved them for posterity.[77] His work is also an expression of Yoruba cultural and historicizing nationalism which developed at the turn of the century.

A third-generation Sierra Leonean on his mother's side (she was a daughter of Crowther), but a second-generation one on his father's side (T. B. Macaulay), was Herbert Macaulay, the first full-blooded modern politician in Nigeria, and at his death in 1946 the 'grand old man' of Nigerian nationalism.[78]

The humanitarian and liberal tradition of Sierra Leone which Sierra Leoneans brought to Nigeria, and which Venn transplanted into the new mission field by appointing Crowther, accounted for the growth of a strong African self-awareness vis-à-vis the Europeans, especially in the field of church relations. This was to take a separatist form in the era of colonial imperialism, when European racism encroached upon what had hitherto been the predominantly liberal Nigerian mission. The desire for ecclesiastical autonomy was, as it turned out, the precursor of political nationalism.[79] The re-emigrants from Sierra Leone also had a modernizing effect in other fields, especially by their innovations in building and architecture, book and newspaper printing, and medicine.[80] The construction of solid mission buildings and of churches, schools and houses around the mission could not help but influence architectural styles in the country generally. Sierra Leoneans, Brazilians and West Indians worked as tailors, masons, joiners and cabinet-makers. CMS missionaries set up the first local printing presses; the technical knowledge gained thereby was to prove of benefit later when the first newspapers were produced in Lagos. Finally, missionaries introduced the beginnings of modern medicine into Nigeria. Some re-emigrants, including Samuel Crowther junior, acquired medical knowledge and worked first as medical auxiliaries at the mission before changing to a career in trade or administration. Others went on to study medicine in Europe and to practise their profession on a regular basis in Nigeria; among such men was Obadiah Johnson, a brother of Samuel Johnson, the historian of the Yoruba.[81] With the first generation of Christians and their direct descendants the re-emigrants from Sierra Leone, Brazil and Cuba quickly coalesced to form a relatively homogeneous and modern leading class,[82] the seedbed of Nigerian nationalism. True, it was at first restricted in the main to southern Nigeria, primarily to Lagos and to Abeokuta, Ibadan and Calabar; but similar trends were occurring in Sierra Leone and on the Gold Coast, and their combined result was to create the conditions for the development of Pan-Africanism in West Africa.

Sierra Leone and Nigeria 57

5 The Gold Coast:
Methodism and
early nationalism

Ghana, until 1957 known as the Gold Coast, lies between Sierra Leone
and Nigeria. It was mentioned in the last chapter in connection with
the CMS Grammar School in Freetown and Freeman's arrival in
Badagry and Abeokuta.[1] Chronologically, too, the course of development on the Gold Coast was closely linked to that in Sierra Leone and
Nigeria. European missionary activity commenced earlier on the Gold
Coast than elsewhere, but did not begin in earnest until the nineteenth
century – later than in Sierra Leone but earlier than in Nigeria. On
the Gold Coast events in the Church were quicker to produce political
consequences and thus to point the way towards the twentieth century.
The proto-nationalism of what is today southern Ghana belongs
directly to the prehistory of Pan-Africanism, not only because some of
its most determined African protagonists came from the Gold Coast but
also because a firm historical tradition developed there on which Pan-
Africanism could build.[2] In retrospect one can see an almost smooth
line of development from Christian missionary activity through early
African nationalism to Pan-Africanism.

Early missionary attempts

The Portuguese appeared on the coast in 1471 and built a strong castle at Elmina in 1482. Despite the official missionary ideology[3] the first permanent mission at Elmina was not initiated until ninety years later in 1572, and then lasted only a few years.[4] As was generally the case later, the mission in the castle had a school in which mulatto children as well as Whites were taught the catechism; this school lasted until the period when Elmina became a Dutch possession. To the west of the Gold Coast French priests of the Capuchin order were active in Assinie from 1633 until 1738, when they were obliged to flee to Axim at the western extremity of the Gold Coast. The Protestant mission was of a later date, for the early British and Dutch slave-dealers did not have even the formal obligation to carry on missionary work that the Portuguese had. Not until the Dutch took Elmina from the Portuguese in 1637 did the charter of the Dutch West Indies Company, renewed in 1640, require the setting up of Christian schools for African children, in accordance with the teaching of the Dutch Reformed Church. Like other schools, it was short of teachers and led a precarious and episodic existence. The longest known period during which it functioned continuously was between 1742 and 1746 when Capitein, a Fanti educated in Holland, was in charge of it. The schools run by the British in the Cape Coast Castle and by the Danes in Christiansborg suffered a similar fate.

Equally unsuccessful was the first missionary attempt in the eighteenth century, which resulted from the Pietist revival. In 1735, during a visit to Copenhagen, Count Zinzendorf, the founder of the Moravian Brethren, made the acquaintance of a Christian Protten, a mulatto whose father had been a Danish soldier in Christiansborg. In 1737 Protten and one of the Brethren went out to the Gold Coast as missionaries for the sect, but they soon returned to Europe. From 1757 to 1761 Protten ran the school for mulatto children in Christiansborg Castle, and then from 1764 to 1769 made a third and last attempt to resume his missionary work, but again in vain.[5]

Better fortune attended the missionary attempts of the Society for the Propagation of the Gospel, founded in England in 1700, which made a point of recruiting chaplains for the British trading forts along the west coast of Africa. In 1751 it sent out a theologian, the Rev. Thomas Thompson, to the Gold Coast where he was the first to preach,

teach and baptize outside the walls of Cape Coast Castle. As early as
1756 he was obliged to return to Britain owing to illness, but in the
meantime he had sent Philip Quaque, a talented young Fanti, to
England for further education. After Quaque returned to the Gold
Coast he took charge of the Cape Coast Castle School from 1766 until
his death in 1816, and thus laid the basis for regular missionary and
educational work on the Gold Coast.[6] His school produced a group of
young men who after his death continued their education by private
study and made the Bible the basis of their religious life, for which
reason the group became known as the 'Bible Band' or 'the Meeting'.

With the aid of European teachers and chaplains, and then of
African ones, Quaque's school continued to expand, *inter alia* providing
evening instruction for adults aged between twenty and forty-five.[7] To
satisfy local needs Governor MacCarthy ordered bibles, prayer books
and psalters, which after his death in the Ashanti War in 1824 were
distributed among those interested. The bibles were dispatched by the
Society for Promoting Christian Knowledge in London, and the Bible
Band in Cape Coast developed into a local society with the same name,
which maintained contact with similar groups at Dixcove and
Anomabu.[8] In 1834, the year of the general emancipation of slaves in
the British Empire, Methodists in London heard about the Bible Band
on Cape Coast. Among the leaders of the Methodist missionary society
was Thomas F. Buxton, the great abolitionist, who wanted to continue
the impulse generated by the emancipation of the slaves by developing
the missionary movement.[9] On 1 January 1835 the first Methodist
missionary landed on Cape Coast. He was well received both by the
governor, Maclean, and by the local Society for Promoting Christian
Knowledge, which provided a bridgehead on which the mission could
build. Although the first missionaries soon died, like most of their
predecessors, at least a beginning had been made.

1835 was also an important year in the history of another missionary
attempt, that of the Basel Mission further east. In 1828 the first missionaries of the Basel Missionary Society landed in the Danish trading-
post of Christiansborg (near Accra). After some casualties, as were
only to be expected in those days, in 1835 the sole survivor withdrew to
Akropong, in the cooler hills north of Accra, where he started afresh.
The Basel Mission adopted very different techniques from the Methodists. They concentrated upon a limited geographical area, were careful
in their selection of new members, taught and preached in the verna-

cular and gave a type of instruction that emphasized practical and manual pursuits. These methods reinforced the traditional social structure and contributed less to the formation of a mobile modern élite on the Gold Coast (and indirectly to the development of Ghanaian nationalism) than was the case with the Methodists, whose missionary principles were exactly the reverse. The Basel Mission's contribution was in essence confined to a single book about the history of the Gold Coast, though one of real importance, by Carl C. Reindorf, a native minister of the Basel Mission.[10] As a counterpart to *The History of the Yorubas* by Samuel Johnson, the CMS pastor,[11] it provided a certain basis for historicizing nationalism on the Gold Coast.

The Methodist mission

The Methodists quickly became the leading religious community on the Gold Coast, and later also in Ashanti. They did not face serious competition until the close of the nineteenth century with the appearance of the Catholic mission, which even today is more powerful than the Methodists in northern Ghana. On the Gold Coast as elsewhere missionary activity created a strong sense of self-awareness among the new élite. This was fostered by the fact that the ground had been well prepared beforehand by the Bible Band on Cape Coast, by the democratic character of Methodist church organization, and by the strong emphasis placed upon independent initiative by the parishes. The immediate antecedents of the Methodist mission on the Gold Coast show clearly enough that there was ample individual initiative waiting to be tapped. Later chapels, churches and schools were financed, built and maintained on an extensive scale by the African communities themselves. Even more than in Sierra Leone and Nigeria, where the young churches had been shaped by the CMS, members of the new African élite were invited to collaborate in parish meetings, synods, committees and school boards. This prepared the way for political activity later, so that it may be said that the Methodist mission had a politicizing effect and prepared the way for African nationalism. All the leading intellectuals and politicians on the Gold Coast during the nineteenth and early twentieth centuries were Methodists and among the first and most vigorous propagators of nationalism were Methodist periodicals.

The Methodists not only had a flying start as a result of the activities of the Bible Band on Cape Coast and its environs, but also had an incalculable advantage in the services of the Rev. T. B. Freeman who for half a century influenced every kind of Methodist activity on the Gold Coast. Freeman was born in England, the offspring of an English mother and a coloured man, possibly one of the slaves who were freed as a result of Lord Mansfield's ruling of 1772, or else a son of one of these ex-slaves. Freeman, although a mulatto, had such a light complexion that he could always pass as a White in Africa. At the same time, conscious of his part-African ancestry, he showed sympathy and understanding for African peculiarities and customs. On 3 January 1838 Freeman landed at Cape Coast. With the aid of some young native assistants from the Bible Band, whose names suggest that they were descended from European fathers or grandfathers (William de Graft, John Martin, John Mills, George Blankson, Joseph Smith), he energetically promoted the Christian cause. In contrast to the Basel Mission, Freeman chose to work extensively over a wide geographical area. An indefatigable traveller, he did not confine himself to the Gold Coast proper but in 1839, 1841 and 1842 undertook three journeys to Kumasi, so entering into closer relations with the Ashanti Empire, which after its conquest by the British at the turn of the century became another centre of Methodism.[12] Freeman also journeyed to Dahomey, which at that time, like Ashanti, was an awe-inspiring empire that flourished on the slave trade; from here he went all the way to Abeokuta via Badagry, as a result of which he became the pioneer of the Nigerian mission.[13]

William de Graft accompanied him on these journeys and for some time took up residence at Badagry. Like his predecessors, Freeman attached great importance to introducing the English language and European (predominantly British) customs, clothing etc. In 1839 he arranged for the centenary of the foundation of the Methodist Church to be commemorated by a private tea-party for about 400 Africans and a handful of Europeans, including Governor Maclean, although tea-drinking was at that time still a novel habit in England.[14] Freeman deliberately emphasized the breach with traditional society by causing those who wanted to become teachers to spend some time isolated from their African environment. Through the local ministers and teachers he urged Africans to abandon their traditional dances, polygamy and fetishism.[15] The fight against fetishism and efforts to win over local rulers are in some respects reminiscent of the Christianization of the Teutonic tribes – for example, in the exposure of Nanaam, the powerful tribal oracle of the Fanti, by native Methodists or in the dramatic conversion of one medicine-man to Christianity.[16]

On the Gold Coast or elsewhere the appearance of the missionaries had a modernizing effect upon African society even merely through their construction of churches, schools and houses. Farsighted chiefs recognized the value of the material progress which the missions introduced and for this reason welcomed them,[17] although they did not hasten to send their own children to the new schools; at first they usually only allowed the children of slaves to go to them.

The role of missionary activity as a factor in acculturation and modernization is clearly apparent from one bizarre episode. On his first visit to Britain in 1840 (when he took along William de Graft and presented him to Victorian audiences at lectures and sermons as a living example of African receptivity to Christian teaching) Freeman hit upon the idea of offering the king of the Ashanti (the Ashantehene), on his next visit to Kumasi, a special gift from Queen Victoria – a state coach. On his second journey to Kumasi he took the coach with him, transporting it for about a hundred miles through the jungle, up hill and down dale, across rivers and streams. The result was that, in a land devoid of horses (on account of the tsetse fly), the Ashantehene had politely to accept a coach which could not be driven anywhere. But for the first time a broad road replaced the narrow path from Cape Coast to Kumasi and the first, very makeshift, bridges had been built across the rivers.[18] What at first seems to be an absurd idea of providing the Ashantehene with a coach even though there were neither horses nor roads (apparently just as out of place as the Soviet snow-ploughs sent to Guinea in the guise of foreign aid) turned out to be an effective means of opening up the interior, and literally pathbreaking in stimulating internal trade. Another indirect contribution towards modernization was made by Freeman by his introduction of mosquito-nets, with which he was able to sleep without being bothered by mosquitoes – and, without realizing it, to keep himself astonishingly free from malaria.[19]

Freeman's extensive missionary activity, however, strained the limited financial means of the Methodist mission and led to tension with London. In 1857 he resigned from the missionary service to take up work in colonial administration. In 1873 he returned to the Methodist mission and became superintendent of the second most senior district, Anomabu, which with 1400 members was at that time the largest parish on the Gold Coast.[20] Freeman lived to celebrate the fiftieth jubilee of his mission in 1885 but retired the following year. Ten years later he died, as 'Father Freeman' venerated by African fellow-Christians, several generations of whom had benefited from his activities.

Schools and scholars

Out of early castle schools at Cape Coast Castle, Elmina, James Fort and Christiansborg there developed, with the arrival of the Methodists, the basis of a modern educational system on the Gold Coast. Freeman maintained close relations with Governor Maclean, who authorized government grants to be paid to schools recognized by the colonial authorities.[21] Elementary education was sporadic; in the case of village children it was repeatedly interrupted, often for months, by work in the fields. But a start had been made, and those who gained most from this were the inhabitants of the towns. Except for a theological institute in Accra, secondary education was slower to take root on the Gold Coast than in Sierra Leone or Nigeria. The first such school was the Wesleyan High School on Cape Coast, founded in 1876; in 1905 it was renamed Mfantsipim, and is today the most famous as well as the oldest high school in Ghana.[22] Its social function was similar to that of the CMS Grammar School in Freetown: the creation of a cultural centre and the training of a modern élite. As in the latter establishment, the careers of the 'old boys' were noted with great pride.[23] Graduates from Mfantsipim went to Fourah Bay College or to England to study law, or entered the civil service, sometimes outside the Gold Coast. Mfantsipim had its counterpart in a girls' high school, the Wesley Girls' High School on Cape Coast, founded in 1884, which developed out of the Wesley Girls' Primary School.[24] These two schools supplied their own teachers.

The newly developing élite soon began to defend its interests by forming local associations and by founding organs of opinion. In this way there gradually developed on the Gold Coast an African proto-nationalism which was by no means automatically or blindly opposed to colonial power, but quite the reverse. As in Sierra Leone and Nigeria the missions were the pacemakers for the colonialism that was to come – not as the consequence of some hidden imperialist conspiracy but simply because they sought to protect the modern elements against the threat of slavery. This is clear from the fact mentioned earlier that at Freeman's suggestion Maclean posted a sergeant in Badagry in 1843 to prevent emigrants from falling once again into slavery.[25]

The early African Methodists welcomed the expansion of British influence under Maclean, just as most Fanti tribes voluntarily accepted British jurisdiction from Cape Coast in settling their internal conflicts. Accordingly, after Maclean had left and the British government returned to the Gold Coast in 1843, they joined in giving a formal character to the state of affairs that had prevailed under Maclean by agreeing to the so-called Bond of 1844.[26] The young members of the élite identified themselves with the process of modernization of which they were the product and with the expansion of the missions, to which they owed their education and in many cases also their start in a career.[27] Thus the first news-sheet on the Gold Coast, the *Accra Herald* founded by Charles Bannerman, in its third issue of 5 October 1857 made no complaint against an expansion of British influence but on the contrary lamented that this 'is daily declining' and that there was a revival of 'old and barbarous customs which had almost fallen into disuse'.[28]

In spite of this the 'scholars' enjoyed little popularity among British civil servants, who described them as 'half-educated' or 'mulattoes'.[29] By about 1850 a remarkably large number of Africans with European names, i.e. probably mulattoes, held administrative jobs on the Gold Coast.[30] But it was another matter when they began, as in Yorubaland at this time, to establish themselves as advisors to a number of chiefs and to become politically active, for this led them into conflict with the colonial authorities. One of the first representatives of this new type of political activist was Thomas Hughes from Cape Coast, apparently the first African to attempt to mine gold by employing modern methods (his project failed because of opposition by the chiefs). Hughes was a member of the municipal council of Cape Coast,[31] elected for the first time in 1858, and corresponded with Dr Thomas Hodgkin, the British Quaker, radical abolitionist and philanthropist.[32] At the end of July 1866 Thomas Hughes was chosen as 'Representative of King and people of Cape Coast' and thereby attained an influential position.[33]

First stirrings of Fanti nationalism: Aggery and the Fanti Confederation

The first major conflict between the colonial authorities and African proto-nationalism, as yet barely articulate, broke out in 1865–6 on

Cape Coast, as a result of Hughes's influence in his capacity as advisor to King Aggery. It had no immediate consequences of any significance but is of some interest on account of its historical context.[34]

The choice of Joseph Aggery as the first Christian king of Cape Coast in January 1865 was welcomed by the British government. But that year witnessed two events which promptly had repercussions upon the Gold Coast. A Select Committee of the House of Commons, to the public sessions of which Aggery had sent a representative, recommended that most British colonies should be given up as soon as possible and that they should be prepared for independence.[35] In Africa this was misunderstood as a promise by the British to give independence to the colonies forthwith. In October 1865 unrest broke out in Jamaica; Eyre, the British governor, brought in troops who perpetrated a massacre among the so-called rebels and without compunction hanged Gordon, spokesman for the opposition in the Legislative Council.[36] At Cape Coast the colonial authorities became nervous when in the course of a local dispute Aggery insinuated that they wanted to provoke the inhabitants of Cape Coast to commit acts of violence in order to impose a state of emergency and re-enact the events that had taken place in Jamaica.[37] In 1866 Aggery was arrested and deported to Sierra Leone, but in March 1869 was allowed to return to Cape Coast, where he died in the same year. With Aggery there emerged, indirectly and as yet not clearly formulated, the idea of self-government and the hint of violent rebellion.

The Aggery incident was a confused episode of local significance, altogether untypical of the situation on the Gold Coast as a whole. Much more important was the Fanti Confederation of 1868–71 which marked the first appearance of a semi-modern, semi-traditional form of proto-nationalism. A new conflict arose out of the uncertainty of British colonial policy which at this juncture, before the onset of classical colonialism, still vacillated between abandoning the colonial empire and expanding it further. On the Gold Coast the recommendation of 1865 was regarded not only as a grant of independence but also as an unwelcome retreat by Britain whereby the Fanti and Ga, the two most important tribes along the coast, were left at the mercy of the Ashanti Empire, which since 1803 had been encroaching upon the territories lying nearer the coast.[38] The uncertainty and nervousness on the Gold Coast increased when in 1867 the news leaked out that the Dutch and British were planning to exchange their forts in order to eliminate the intermingling of their possessions and to facilitate the collection of customs duties.[39] Since the towns that had grown up near the forts were always regarded as indirectly subordinate to them, the transaction seemed to herald a territorial exchange, all the more un-popular in that the tribes concerned had not been consulted before-hand. The tribes which were to come under Dutch rule were by no means happy at the idea because the Dutch maintained notoriously good relations with Ashanti, especially through Elmina. Moreover, the Dutch had the reputation of adopting what we would today call a reactionary attitude in the questions which the Fanti of that period regarded as all-important, those concerning social progress: 'No mis-sionary is allowed to live among them and there is no school worthy of the name for the rising generation.'[40]

In their despair the Fanti representatives assembled spontaneously in their traditional 'national' centre, Mankessim, and elected three chiefs as 'Presidents of the Fantee Nation'. Shortly thereafter the inhabitants of Komenda refused to accept Dutch rule, whereupon the town was fired upon by Dutch men-of-war. Members of several Fanti tribes rushed to prevent the Dutch from seizing Komenda, to the great embarrassment of the British, who saw their agreement with the Dutch endangered. Kennedy, the governor-in-chief at Sierra Leone who was responsible for the Gold Coast, went so far as to say that the Fanti were inspired by a 'strong national sentiment'.[41]

The new 'national' ideas were first articulated by Horton, a Sierra Leonean of Ibo origin. He had studied medicine in Edinburgh, at that time one of the best medical faculties in the United Kingdom, and had served for several years as an army surgeon on Cape Coast. Horton managed to combine his professional studies on the West African coast with the role of a political observer.[42] On account of his studies in Europe he was far superior to all the 'scholars' on the Gold Coast, who often possessed no more than an elementary educa-tion, although this was enough to give them a privileged position in traditional society.

Although many of his proposals proved impracticable, Horton brought a modern rational element into the thinking of those who had been aroused by these events but whose minds were basically still traditionally oriented. He took as his starting-point the report of the select committee of 1865, to which he attributed a concern with the 'great principle of establishing independent African nationalities'.[43]

The difference in the political conditions of the western Gold Coast (Cape Coast) and of its eastern part (Accra) led him to propose the setting up of two states: a monarchy in the west and a republic in the east, both of them closely linked to Britain, to be represented by a consul. In domestic affairs he sought to attain a measure of social homogenization by weakening or even eliminating the large number of village 'kings'; in foreign affairs he called for strong measures to ward off the Ashanti. Horton regarded a British presence as indispensable, since it provided an element of stability, modernization and protection. He suggested creating two autonomous states on the coast under a British protectorate 'until such time as the country is mature for a transition to self-government'. Horton's conception was realistic in so far as he imagined that national independence could only come about as a product of the modernization of traditional society, in a close and voluntary relationship with Britain, as the most liberal of the colonial powers – then as later. For as Horton asserted two years afterwards: 'On this coast the English element is unquestionably the best civilizing agency.'[44]

Horton's ideas had an immediate effect on the Gold Coast. In the eastern part of the country the wealthy merchants of Accra, who likewise were 'educated natives', seized the initiative to defend themselves against the Ashanti threat, since the traditional rulers, especially those of the Ga, had no forces of their own and the Colonial Office adopted an attitude of restraint. In a manner reminiscent of the emergence of estates of the realm during the late Middle Ages, they raised funds to purchase munitions and formed independent companies. A group of about thirty merchants passed a resolution in which they formulated the principle that in future chiefs should not be permitted to take any important decisions about war or peace without the consent of the educated natives and their council, the Accra Native Confederation.[45] Admittedly, these efforts soon came to nothing, but the episode does illustrate the significance and the growing self-awareness of the new élite.

Horton's ideas had a more direct and far-reaching impact on the western Gold Coast, among the Fanti. The spontaneous meeting at Mankessim[46] and Horton's ideas led to the formation, under Ashanti pressure in the north, of the Fanti Confederation of 1868–9, at first as a loose union of the most important Fanti chiefs. To execute their designs they drew upon 'educated natives' such as R. J. Ghartey and George Blankson Jr. The latter was a son of the Methodist preacher of that name who had collaborated with Freeman at the beginning of the

Methodist mission;[47] Ghartey was a merchant and prominent Methodist.[48] In 1871 the Fanti Conderation acquired a formal constitution, formed a ministry, and appointed Ghartey as president; one year later he was elected king of Winneba, Ghartey IV. The objects of the constitution revealed an interest in the general development of the country, for example 'to make good and substantial roads'. Provision was made 'for the education of all children within the Confederation' for which, however, sufficient teachers had first to be obtained. Finally, agriculture was to be modernized and mining developed. The close links with England were emphasized in the last article of the constitution.[49]

When at the beginning of December 1871 representatives of the Confederation attempted to submit the constitution for approval to the governor at Cape Coast they were immediately arrested, as were all the members of the ministry except one, F. C. Grant. Governor Pope Hennessey in Freetown was not prepared to back this panicky reaction by Salmon, his representative at Cape Coast, and ordered that the arrested men be freed. Nor did he endorse Salmon's opinion that 'this dangerous conspiracy must be destroyed for good, or the country will become unmanageable'.[50] However, there was no longer any hope of the Confederation becoming the centre of further activity. A final attempt to negotiate with the British in 1872 was thwarted. All attempts to establish internal autonomy under a British protectorate were cut short when the Gold Coast was declared a Crown Colony in 1874.

The Fanti Confederation became the starting-point of modern nationalism on the Gold Coast (and later that of Ghana), and was an important component of the tradition repeatedly invoked by the nationalists. Ghartey, the president of the thwarted Confederation and a prominent lay Methodist, became a symbolic figure for the cautious, pragmatic wing of the emerging national movement. In 1897, when the Methodist-led Aborigines Rights Protection Society (ARPS) was formed in opposition to legislation planned by the colonial authorities of Cape Coast, it received a letter from Ghartey on his deathbed exhorting them: 'Be constitutional'. These two words became the motto of West African nationalism, at least of its conservative wing.

Europeanization and the romantic reaction

Between the end of the Fanti Confederation and the beginning of the Aborigines Rights Protection Society lies a quarter-century of peaceful development. The foundation of the Wesleyan High School at Cape Coast (1876) marked the beginning on the Gold Coast of secondary education capable of creating a modern intelligentsia. Graduates from this school, such as John Mensah Sarbah and Casely Hayford, along with teachers such as Attoh Ahuma and F. Egyir Asaam, are numbered among the pioneers of Gold Coast nationalism.

Although in 1874 Accra became the administrative capital of the newly founded Crown Colony, Cape Coast remained the main cultural and political centre for several decades. This was the Methodists' stronghold; it was the site of the Wesleyan High School and the place where most of the periodicals appeared. As the educated class expanded, so too did the number of readers of local periodicals. These latter were mostly fortnightly or monthly publications with four to six pages of close print. The most important papers were the following:

1 The *Gold Coast Times*, edited by James Hutton Brew in 1874 and 1881–4. Brew was a member of a family which had many branches and could be traced back into the eighteenth century.[51] As assistant secretary of the Fanti Confederation he was a member of the delegation that had been arrested in 1871 when they tried to hand its constitution to the government's representative at Cape Coast.[52]
2 The *Gold Coast People*, founded by John Mensah Sarbah in 1891. Sarbah was one of the first lawyers on the Gold Coast; in 1888 he was the second African to become a member of the Legislative Council and considered one of the fathers of Ghanaian nationalism.[53] He was – it almost goes without saying – a prominent Methodist.
3 The *Gold Coast News* (1887).
4 The *Gold Coast Independent*.[54]

The first newspapers were never really successful since they only had a limited readership and most of them soon folded up, often after only a few issues.[55] The contents were mostly non-political and there is little trace of militant opposition. Attention is centred upon local problems, which soon also included events in neighbouring Togoland. When the government was criticized, this took the form outlined by Charles Bannerman in 1857, in his manuscript *Accra Herald*:

> The plan we have laid down for our own guidance is simple: We sincerely respect the authorities, and for that reason we shall keep our eye on them, so that we may, wherever they slip from the right path, humbly endeavour to point the road.[56]

With this cunning device, and thanks to a large measure of press freedom, these newspapers, along with the church and from the close of the nineteenth century the Legislative Council, became the great nurseries of nationalism. In September 1883 the *Gold Coast Times* took as its motto: 'As long as we remain we must speak free.' Despite its loyal stance it criticized measures taken by the governor, occasionally at a later stage with a pungency that cannot but astonish a Continental European historian whose concept of colonial Africa is unconsciously coloured by conditions prevalent in the former German colonies. For example, on 7 January 1882 the *Gold Coast Times* reproached Sir Samuel Rowe, the governor, for neglecting the administration. The criticism culminated in the sentence: 'Every branch of the public service appears to be in a state of disorganization and inefficiency.'[57]

The content as well as the style of these publications is of interest. Prominence was given to everyday problems: events in church life and in government circles at Accra, demands for provision of sewage facilities, street-lighting and schools, and better protection against burglars and thieves (still a chronic evil during the last years of Nkrumah's rule!). Occasionally such fundamental subjects came up for discussion as equality of rights for Africans and persons of African descent.[58]

The press on the Gold Coast, at least from the turn of the century, maintained contact with similar newspapers in Nigeria and Sierra Leone. These were sometimes quoted and items of news from them reproduced, which intensified the sense of homogeneity of the whole of the West African coast as well as that of the Gold Coast itself. One newspaper at least, the *Gold Coast Times* of 1874 and 1881–4, stated on its masthead the prices for subscribers in England, West Africa, the West Indies and the USA. It does not matter very much how many copies were in fact [sold in these countries or whether there were any subscribers at all outside Africa. Much more important is the point that the editors sought to extend their influence to an area identical with the scope of Pan-Africanism.[59]

The claim that Africans should have equal rights implied that their social and cultural development should progress along with that of the rest of the world, especially Europe. The generation on the Gold Coast between the Fanti Confederation and the Aborigines Rights Protection Society, i.e. between 1872 and 1897, understood and accepted this implication. The educated natives of that period went a long way in adapting their way of life and ideas along European lines. The wearing of European clothing was an external sign that one belonged to the educated native class. In the burgeoning towns there sprang up unions and associations of the most varied kind, such as temperance societies and debating clubs, in which African gentlemen cultivated the ideals and social forms of Victorian England. In one debating club such world-shaking themes were debated as the lawfulness of Charles I's execution and whether the invention of gunpowder had been a blessing or a curse for mankind.[60]

Most societies were, like the newspapers, short-lived and non-political. Of a quasi-political character was one society whose objective it was to bring together the 'educated natives' as a class: the Gold Coast Union Association, founded on 1 September 1881.[61] In order to promote the development of the country, it argued, it was not enough to exchange ideas among the 'educated natives' or to imitate the Europeans externally. It was necessary also to copy European methods, especially by organization. As the president of the association put it in his opening speech:

> If we will imitate the civilized European in his mode of life and his leisure and copy him in his customs and manners, . . . if we will put on European clothing, why can we not clothe our minds with European ideas and thoughts, so far as they are necessary to our advancement? – if we will endeavour to erect buildings like theirs, why can we not follow them in that system of co-operation which runs through their social fabric? Why, in one word, can we not imitate them in the one grand requisite – unity of purpose and action?[62]

When mention is made of the opening up and development of the country, there is a hint of the ideas of Horton and the Fanti Confederation[63] – and also of the grievous experiences suffered by the latter when the warning follows that one must not attempt too much,[64] or when J. H. Brown pleaded for 'moderation'. It is of interest that in the same breath it is said that tolerance is necessary 'towards less cultured members'. Previously the president of the association had declared: 'It seeks to unite all classes of us together, and by establishing branches in the different centres of commerce, where the aggregates of the educated community are to be found, to enable us to exchange ideas among ourselves. . . .'[65]

The proposal to discuss later the need for communal self-government encroached on what was then a political theme. At a meeting on 22 December 1881, at which, besides F. C. Grant, the former treasurer of the Fanti Confederation, and J. H. Brown thirty other people were present, a further step was taken. It was resolved 'to agitate for the reform of the existing laws of the colonies and their better administration, and for the codification of the native laws'.[66] Here the political element is obvious. At the same time one can detect a sign of the return to native traditions by the 'educated natives', which during the last few years of the nineteenth century represented a cultural renaissance as well as a reaction to thorough-going Europeanization.

In 1889 this initiative at Cape Coast was followed by the formation of a new society, the Mfantsi Amanbuhu Fékuw (Fanti National Political Society) whose name alone indicates a conscious turn towards a political form of nationalism on a tribal basis, that of the Fanti tribe. It resolved to collect and record the traditions of the people; Mensah Sarbah's fundamental works on the Fanti judicial system were a product of this new movement.[67] Mensah Sarbah also played a leading part in the movement to return to traditional clothing.[68] Towards the end of the century the tendency spread to discard European or Europeanized names and to revert to African ones; such changes were occasionally publicized by advertisements in the press, an act which had quasi-political overtones: 'Two gentlemen of intelligence having pluckily dropped their foreign names, have encouraged me to do the same. . . . I am no slave, so nobody must call me Ebenezar Weldu Cole Eshun any more. My real name is Esuon Weldu.'[69] Thus the period of conscious and consistent Europeanization on the Gold Coast was quite brief; it lasted for barely a generation, and was quickly replaced by a romantic reaction.

In this new development an outstanding part was once again played by African Methodists, laymen and clergy alike. In addition to the secular press, which was largely the creation of Methodist laymen, there were also from time to time periodicals officially published by the Methodist Church: the *Gold Coast Methodist* (1886) and the *Gold Coast Methodist Times*. The *Times* it is true was published by British missionaries, but the editors were two native ministers, Samuel Richard Brew Solomon and Egyir Asaam. Solomon was the son of an African Methodist missionary and belonged to the great Brew family. He published in the *Gold Coast Methodist Times* the results of an inquiry which finally made it socially acceptable to revert to African names. He drew the logical conclusion himself by adopting the name of Attoh Ahuma, by which he is known in the pantheon of Ghanaian nationalism.[70] Attoh Ahuma, who occasionally acted as superintendent of Anomabu, was a sharp-tongued journalist who engaged passionately in the agitation against the Lands Bill and in favour of the Aborigines Rights Protection Society, founded in 1897. At the close of that year the Methodist Synod yielded to the pressure of its European critics and dismissed Solomon, whereupon the *Gold Coast Methodist Times* soon ceased publication. But before his departure Solomon once again defended energetically his political commitment:

> . . . as if there is any sin in taking a deep interest in the political development of one's own native land. . . . We have been indoctrinated as to how a religious paper should be conducted . . . The Methodist Times should content itself with the chronicling of sermons, missionary reports and other ecclesiastical matters. . . . Nothing that has to do with oppressed humanity should be foreign to our ministers. Take the Land Bill as a case in point. Putting aside for the moment the fact that the majority of the Wesleyan Clergy are themselves Landowners, no one should attach any blame for displaying more than a passing interest in the constitutional means and methods employed by the peoples of the Colony and Protectorate, with a view to protect their property from being tampered with and from possible confiscation.[71]

On 1 January 1898, in collaboration with Asaam at Cape Coast, he started a new periodical, the *Gold Coast Aborigines*, as the organ of the Aborigines Rights Protection Society (ARPS) in which the Methodist element was prominently represented. In 1900 we find him featured in a group photograph together with other West Africans in London;[72] later he spent some time in the USA.[73]

The ARPS is of concern to us here only in so far as it contributed directly or indirectly to the development of Pan-Africanism and in so far as it illustrates the political effect of the Methodist mission. Out of the opposition to the Lands Bill defended by the colonial authorities in Accra, an opposition that was supported above all by Methodist groups, there was formed in 1897 a small group which included such men as Mensah Sarbah and J. W. de Graft-Johnson, who first met in J. P. Brown's house. The latter had already served as a teacher of the

Methodist mission in the early 1860s and was to die in 1932, at the age of eighty-seven, as one of the most venerated Methodist leaders on the Gold Coast.[74] Jacob W. Sey, a well-to-do merchant and prominent Methodist, became the president of the new organization, and the vice-presidency fell to Brown. In the first years the secretaries included A. M. Wright, a teacher of the Wesleyan High School (meanwhile renamed the Collegiate School) and James E. Kwegyir Aggrey, whom we shall have cause to mention later.[75] The ARPS held its first protest meeting on 17 April 1897 on Chapel Square at Cape Coast, the centre of the Methodist mission. The superintendent of the Methodist mission, an English clergyman named the Rev. A. W. Parker, said prayers before the assembled crowd.[76] Two Methodist ministers acted as editors of the central organ. They had just fallen out with the mission (probably mainly for political reasons)[77] but were of Methodist origin.

The Aborigines Rights Protection Society scored a political success in 1898 when it sent a deputation to London which brought the views of the bill's opponents directly to the notice of Joseph Chamberlain, Secretary of State for the Colonies, with the result that the governor at Accra had to withdraw the bill. From then onwards the ARPS was regarded as a socially acceptable organization; for decades it lived off the credit won by its first success, which it repeated in a similar situation by sending another deputation in 1912.[78] On this occasion it exceeded for the first time the limitations set by the Fanti Confederation and by nascent Fanti nationalism, to become the mouthpiece of the new nationalism of the entire Gold Coast, both west and east (although not Ashanti, which was annexed in 1901). Its significance remained un-challenged until Casely Hayford, with his National Congress of British West Africa founded in 1920, initiated a new phase in the development of nationalism.[79]

When in 1925 the governor, Gordon Guggisberg, considerably strengthened the position of the paramount chiefs by entrusting them with legislative powers and by setting up provincial councils, this dealt a death-blow to the ARPS. At Sekondi near Cape Coast a rump organi-zation survived under the old name, led by Kobina Sekyi, who later indirectly gave a stimulus to the organization of the Pan-African element in England.[80] A second line of development derives from Attoh Ahuma, who after periods of residence in Britain (around 1900) and the USA took charge of the new publication the *Gold Coast Leader* (later the *Gold Coast Nation*), which appeared from 1912; as the official newspaper of the ARPS it was the successor to its old paper, the *Gold Coast Aborigines*. In both papers Attoh Ahuma propagated a militant form of nationalism which went beyond the narrow confines of the Gold Coast and had a Pan-African flavour.[81] A third channel of influence can be detected in the case of Casely Hayford who, together with Mensah Sarbah his coeval and school friend, represented the ARPS legally and became one of the most important leaders of West African nationalism until his death in 1930.[82] Finally there is Aggrey, who with his many decades of activity in the USA prior to his return to Achimota represented a moderate variant of Pan-African ideas in the widest sense. All of these trends, directly or indirectly, bore the imprint of Gold Coast Methodism.

6 Afro-American emigration from the USA

The interest which Afro-Americans took in Africa and in Pan-Africanism arose out of the tension that existed between their desire to be treated as equals in American society and their constant rejection by that society (slavery, segregation and racial discrimination). Torn between the attractions of American democracy and high living standards and their rejection by White racism, there were two possible courses for them to take (apart from apathy): either to retreat into the separate existence of the ghetto, and to try to establish a kind of micro- or sub-society, with its own schools, churches, welfare institutions etc., or else to try to emigrate from the USA. From the late eighteenth century onwards Afro-American history oscillated between the two poles of complete integration and voluntary segregation (i.e. emigration). Since these two extreme objectives were only attainable in part, most Afro-Americans had to put up with a ghetto-like existence, discrimination and segregation.

These two extreme solutions could lead to an active interest in Africa, although this was not invariably the case. All ideas of emigration centred upon Africa. But integrationists, too, sometimes also turned to Africa as a means of improving their own standing in America. When

Whites referred humiliatingly to the negroes' historical roots in a continent that had been subjected to colonial rule, the latter might claim solidarity with Africa, indeed with the whole non-White part of the world, as a means of enhancing their position in the USA. They strove not to return to Africa physically but to establish cultural, economic and political links with that continent.[1]

The main content of Afro-American history in the USA is the adjustment to ghetto-like conditions and the repeated efforts to escape from them by integration into White American society.[2] Here we can only deal with Black history in the USA in so far as it is relevant to the evolution of Pan-Africanism. Reference must be made to the negro churches, especially the Methodist, since in all of them the three main tendencies are to be found: adjustment to the ghetto, the quest for integration and equality, and the idea of re-emigration to Africa, or at least of establishing contacts with that continent. The negro churches are also important because they played a prominent role in developing Afro-American education. They set up colleges and universities in which there developed an intellectual élite that later became actively involved in Pan-Africanism. In this chapter we shall try to illustrate the evolution of the third component, the emigration movement, within the context of Afro-American history. This is an essential part of the background to early Pan-Africanism (before 1900),[3] for the attempts to justify emigration from the USA gave rise to the first statements with a Pan-African or proto-Pan-African content.

Effects of the American War of Independence

The American Revolution, which literally threw thousands of Afro-Americans into turmoil, was the central event in their lives for long to come. The new ideas in American society reached down to them also. They were to be found among the followers of those Whites who wanted the principles of freedom and human dignity to be extended to slaves and free negroes, such as Thomas Paine,[4] James Otis,[5] Mrs John Adams,[6] Benjamin Franklin and the abolitionist wing of the Quakers.[7] It was during the Revolutionary period that slaves addressed their first petitions to provincial assemblies asking to be emancipated.[8] In 1780 a group of free slaves from Dartmouth, Massachusetts, among them Paul Cuffee, protested at being obliged to pay taxes without having the right to vote ('no taxation without representation') and in 1783 their case was upheld in court.[9] Prince Hall, the founder of negro freemasonry in the USA, signed a similar petition.[10] For Richard Allen, the founder of the African Methodist Episcopal church,[11] the American Revolution was together with Methodism the decisive event in his own biography.[12] As we have seen, the first organized protest by free Afro-Americans took place in Philadelphia, then the provisional capital of the young state, in the very year 1787 when the American Revolution reached constitutional fulfilment.[13] In the same spirit one year later a group led by Prince Hall protested to the Massachusetts legislature against the kidnapping of free negroes and their abduction into slavery; and in 1791 Benjamin Banneker wrote an important letter to Thomas Jefferson in which he applied the principles of the American Revolution to the coloured population.[14]

To these rousing ideas were added active engagement during the Revolutionary War. Afro-Americans fought on both sides, and their motive was invariably freedom. Hundreds of slaves were prepared to fight for the American Revolution, especially in the North, if thereby they would be granted their liberty. Thus in one Connecticut regiment we find coloured soldiers with names such as Pomp Liberty, Sharp Liberty, Cuff Liberty, Dick Freedom, Ned Freedom, Cuff Freedom or Peter Freedom.[15] Besides volunteers there were negroes who were drafted into the army after the introduction of quotas for individual states and others who served as substitutes for wealthy Whites who were unwilling to fight themselves. Moreover, apart from serving as soldiers – approximately 5000 of them – Afro-Americans made themselves useful to the cause of independence as servants, cooks, workers, spies, messengers and scouts. Active service in the Revolutionary army signified a massive advance towards emancipation, since all the slaves who served in the army automatically obtained their freedom. Another result was a military tradition to which Afro-American leaders time and again referred: Prince Hall fought at Bunkers Hill; James Forten, a negro leader in Philadelphia, served in the US fleet; a grandfather of Du Bois was a soldier in the American Revolutionary army.

On the other hand thousands of slaves, especially in the South, sided with the British.[16] In Virginia and South Carolina a particularly large number of slaves fled from the signatories of the Declaration of Independence, whereas other slaves hesitated to join the British army since many Tory loyalists were still slave-holders. Fugitive ex-slaves mainly served the British as non-combatants. When the British withdrew after the war at least 14,000 men, women and children followed them from Savannah, Charleston and New York, evacuated in 1782–3, and another 5000 before the decisive battle at Yorktown.[17] Others remained with the French, who although allies of the American revolutionaries refused to hand these slaves over to them; this led to a conflict between the French and Americans. At least 20,000 ex-slaves probably left the USA after the War of Independence in the hope of preserving a newly won freedom which according to American law was 'illegal'. These emigrants in the main went either south or north: to Jamaica and the Bahamas or to Canada, especially to Nova Scotia, from where, as we have seen, in 1792 almost 1200 re-emerged in Sierra Leone as 'Nova Scotians'.[18]

The American Revolution had a particularly strong impact upon Haiti. During the siege of Savannah a French auxiliary corps fought on the side of the American besiegers; one of the detachments comprised 545 mulattoes from San Domingo. Among these soldiers were some of the men who were to lead the revolution in Haiti, notably Henri Christophe. At a critical moment in the action the detachment covered the Americans' retreat from Savannah with great bravado and suffered heavy losses.[19] Just twelve years later, under the direct influence of the French Revolution, Haiti carried through its own revolution under the leadership of Toussaint l'Ouverture. This in turn had repercussions in America: on one hand the successful slave rebellion in Haiti intensified the ever-latent fear of the southern slave-holders that similar events might occur in their own states;[20] on the other hand Haiti and Toussaint l'Ouverture personally acquired an almost legendary reputation among Afro-Americans, and later among Africans as well.[21] In the struggle for Latin American independence the young republic of Haiti gave the defeated Simon Bolivar asylum and material aid which contributed to his final victory over the Spaniards.[22] Moreover the Haitians repeatedly endeavoured to establish close contact with Afro-Americans in the USA. Haiti was also the destination of many would-be emigrants, some of whom actually made the journey.[23] The defeat of the French troops by the Haitians in 1803 also had spectacular results of a different order: deprived of his base in Haiti, Napoleon I gave up his ambitions in America and in the same year sold Louisiana to the USA, which hereby at little cost gained a vast territory into which it could expand; initially this also meant an expansion of cotton-growing and thus of the slave system in the South: where King Cotton reigned supreme, slavery was absolute.

Liberia and compulsory deportation to Africa

The American Revolution also affected the relationship between Afro-Americans and Africa. Some Whites interpreted their newly won freedom as the right to treat negroes as they thought fit, and *inter alia* to send them back to Africa, since at the time they made up almost a quarter of the population and were regarded as a threat to the United States' social cohesion. At the same time some Afro-Americans now envisaged the possibility of returning to Africa. Thus from the first there were two contrasting principles: enforced resettlement and voluntary return to Africa. In 1773 the Rev. Samuel Hopkins, a White Congregationalist minister from Newport, Rhode Island, still pleaded for voluntary negro emigration – but soon afterwards Thomas Jefferson, author of the Declaration of Independence (1776) and a Virginia slave-owner, suggested in his *Notes on the State of Virginia*, which appeared in 1787, that they be deported. He summed up his proposals in the sceptical question: 'What further is to be done with them?'[24]

At the beginning of the nineteenth century Jefferson's ideas were taken up again. At the end of December 1816 they led to the foundation of the American Society for Colonizing the Free People of Color in the United States. The constituent meeting of this body took place in the Congress building; among its founding members were such prominent members as Bushrod Washington, the brother of George Washington, Henry Clay and the wealthy lawyer Francis S. Key (author of *The Star-Spangled Banner*), which gave the organization an almost official character.[25] Among them were naïve philanthropic idealists who honestly believed that the Afro-Americans' interests would best be served by resettlement, since equality in American society was unattainable, as well as men who sought to consolidate the slave system in the South by deporting the free Afro-Americans. The philanthropic element in the North took as its model the colony of Sierra Leone, also inspired by correspondence with Wilberforce and Clarkson. An initial colony was planned on Sherbro Island, not far from Freetown, where in 1820 a ship did actually land with more than eighty would-be settlers. Malaria quickly put an end to this experiment; the survivors went on to Sierra Leone and settled temporarily at Fourah Bay. In December 1821 a second expedition went to Cape Mesurado which Peter, king of the local tribe, at first refused to sell to them. He was persuaded to change his mind by a loaded pistol held to his head by

Lieutenant Stockton of the US Navy, who accompanied the expedition, by a sudden break of sunshine through the thick clouds and by various promises. In return for goods (muskets, beads, tobacco, rum etc.) valued at $300 Peter sold the land which the settlers wanted. In this way the basis was laid for what was to become Liberia: by 'dexterity at mixing flattery with a little well-timed threat',[26] as Stockton's colleague, Ayre, admiringly described the transaction. The few original settlers were subsequently reinforced by the arrival of most of the survivors of the first expedition who had gone to Fourah Bay. During the later years up to the American Civil War there followed some 12,000–15,000 settlers, mostly slaves from southern states, who were often set free on the condition that they emigrated to Liberia. Some southern advocates of forced emigration even packed their slaves into ships bound for Africa without having previously obtained their consent. In addition more than 5000 of the slaves freed by the US Navy off the west coast of Africa settled in Liberia.[27]

The Libero-Americans, as they called themselves, like the re-emigrants in Sierra Leone but even more rapidly than they, evolved into a small, almost parasitic upper class which exploited and oppressed the African tribes to the extent of introducing conditions akin to slavery.[28] Even after the republic of Liberia had been formally founded in 1847 the new state did not have much attraction for Afro-Americans or Africans, although Blyden emigrated from the West Indies to Liberia by way of the USA and engaged in eloquent propaganda on its behalf.[29] For the development of Pan-Africanism Liberia remained solely of indirect significance, negative rather than positive. Nevertheless it temporarily provided a platform for Blyden, the most important Afro-American or African intellectual in the nineteenth century.[30]

The first re-emigration projects:
Africa, Haiti, Canada

Spokesmen for the coloured people vigorously rejected the compulsory deportation propagated by the American Colonization Society. Through their prompt protest, repeated from 1830 in irregular meetings of the Negro Convention movement,[31] they succeeded in detaching the truly philanthropic element from the American Colonization Society and in enlisting its support for abolitionism. Gerrit Smith, the Lewis brothers and Arthur Tappan, all of them from New York State, and particularly

William Lloyd Garrison, were among those won over in this way to the cause of militant abolitionism, which reached its active phase in about 1835.[32] From this point the course of events led to the Civil War and the abolition of slavery in 1863–5.

Another consequence of the protest against the Liberia project was the fact that the free coloured people developed a political will, to which the newly founded Negro Convention movement was the first to give continuous expression. In search of constructive alternatives to Liberia they developed two possible solutions of their own: either to hold fast to the 'land of our birth', i.e. to the USA, or to recommend voluntary emigration to the country of each one's own choice. The first alternative was more acceptable to the relatively wealthy and successful Afro-Americans, whereas the second was more readily accepted by numbers of the poorer classes. Despite this the two solutions were not mutually exclusive. True, one of the earliest and most determined opponents of compulsory return to Africa, Richard Allen, pleaded that the negroes remain in the USA, but he also supported an early project for emigration to Haiti on a voluntary basis.[33] Out of such considerations grew the idea of 'Back-to-Africa'.

The question of Africa, their land of origin or that of their fathers and ancestors, was always close to the hearts of Afro-Americans, because a fundamentally racist society at every turn reminded them of the fact in a negative way by referring to their physical features. During the era of slavery they sought consolation in their suffering in the idea of returning to Africa, expressed in the semi-religious form of the slave songs.[34] The notion that men's souls returned to Africa after death in America also illustrates the existence of an elemental bond with Africa. This was probably strongest among those who had actually made the journey across the Atlantic and weaker, if existing at all, among those born in the New World. Some slaves did seriously contemplate a return to Africa. One of the first slave petitions to become known, dating from 1773, called for manumission so that the slaves concerned might emigrate to Africa. For at the end of the petition we read that after emancipation they intended to save enough money 'to transport ourselves to some part of the coast of Africa, where we propose a settlement'.[35] One year later other petitioners requested a land where 'each of us may there sit down quietly under his own fig-tree',[36] which of course may not necessarily mean a location in Africa.

Two years after the Free African Society had been founded in Philadelphia,[37] in October 1789, forty members of the Free African Society in Newport, Rhode Island, proposed to its parent body 'the return of Africans to Africa'. The answer from Philadelphia is both typical of the prevalent cosmopolitan spirit of the time and of Richard Allen's attitude to the question of Back-to-Africa: 'They would say little with reference to emigration to Africa since they were of the opinion that "every pious man is a good Citizen of the world". They would pray on the contrary that every yoke would be broken and that "the oppressed go free".'[38] The opinion of the Philadelphia group is summarized thus by Richard Allen's biographer:

> It is evident that many of the free Negroes in Philadelphia were not in sympathy with the proposal to return to Africa, but they would agree not to interfere with those who desired to return there, and would wish them well.[39]

Despite this the Newport group turned to the Rev. Samuel Hopkins, their Congregationalist minister, who had already proposed emigration to Africa at an earlier date.[40] In 1795 they sent a delegate to Freetown, Sierra Leone, to reconnoitre the situation, but decided to stay in America.[41] After these early efforts the settlement of American ex-slaves and Maroons (by way of Nova Scotia) in Sierra Leone in 1792 and 1799[42] amounted to an initial wave of re-emigration from the New World to Africa.

Sierra Leone was also the goal in the first concrete project for re-emigration directly from the USA, which originated with Paul Cuffee. The latter had an African father and an Indian mother; he joined the Quakers as a grown man, which in itself was unusual.[43] In 1780 he was politically active in his native state of Massachusetts;[44] in 1788 he is said to have proposed emigration to Africa and to have belonged to the group in Newport, Rhode Island.[45] After he had attained some prosperity as captain of his own ships he determined with missionary zeal to spread Christianity in Africa and to make it possible for his Afro-American countrymen to return there. Perhaps because he was a Quaker, he heard at a relatively early date about Sierre Leone and the African Institution.[46] In 1810 he sailed a brig manned by a crew composed entirely of Afro-Americans across the Atlantic to Freetown, whence he was invited to England. In London he carried on negotiations with the African Institution. In 1811, back in Freetown, he gave the stimulus to the foundation of the Friendly Society of Sierra Leone, a kind of co-operative society designed to break the monopoly of the European merchants. After his return to the USA the British–American War of 1812 caused Cuffee to delay the second journey he had planned to Sierra Leone until 1816. In February of that year he arrived back in Freetown with about three dozen Afro-Americans who were prepared to settle there,[47] some of whom travelled at their own expense. His death in the following year prevented another 2000 Afro-Americans who were by then on his waiting list from going back to Africa.

In 1816 Paul Cuffee was in touch with the Rev. Robert Finley of New Jersey, who founded the American Colonization Society at the end of December 1816.[48] Since Cuffee's plans tended in a similar direction (although they had a voluntary basis), Finley thought that Afro-Americans would react positively to his own settlement project, especially as James Forten of Philadelphia, one of the leaders of the free Afro-Americans and a collaborator with Richard Allen, had welcomed and supported Cuffee's initiative in the same year (1816).[49] All the greater was the surprise of the organizers of the American Colonization Society at the hostile reaction of the free Afro-Americans, which found expression as early as January 1817. At a meeting in Richmond, Virginia, it was stated that the free people of colour 'prefer being colonized in the most remote corner of the land of our nativity [i.e. the USA], to being exiled to a foreign country [i.e. Africa]'.[50] Another meeting, convened and presided over by Richard Allen at Bethel church, the mother church of the African Methodist Episcopal church (AME) which had been founded just a year before, likewise condemned the idea 'to ban us from the land of our nativity' and 'resolved, that without art, without science, without a proper knowledge of government, to cast into the savage wilds of Africa the free people of color seems to us the circuitous route through which they must return to perpetual bondage'. At the same time the meeting declared its solidarity with the slave population in the USA. It resolved 'that we never will separate ourselves voluntarily from the slave population in this country; they are our brethren by the ties of consanguinity of suffering, and of wrong; and we feel that there is more virtue in suffering privations with them, than fancied advantages for a season'.[51] In the summer of 1817 a further protest meeting took place in Philadelphia with 3000 participants; on this occasion the Colonization Society was again vehemently attacked.[52]

In 1824 Boyer, the new president of Haiti, invited free negroes to immigrate into his country. This led in the same year to the formation of the Society for Promoting the Emigration of Free Persons to Hayti, under the chairmanship of Richard Allen.[53] Until 1825 about 2000 Afro-Americans emigrated to Haiti, among them numerous members of the AME church in Philadelphia. The undertaking soon failed for a variety of reasons: embezzlement of money by agents of the emigration organization; President Boyer's fear lest he should lose control of his country if immigration took place on too large a scale; and finally tension between the immigrants and the native inhabitants over differences of religion, language, customs and mentality. 'Sharp class lines wrecked dreams of equality' (Staudenraus), with the result that some emigrants preferred slavery to life in Haiti. American Quakers who visited the emigrants there wrote a report which had a dampening effect upon the enthusiasm for the scheme. In 1825 200 emigrants returned to the USA, and others followed in subsequent years. Nevertheless sufficient Afro-Americans remained in Haiti to form the nucleus of the AME church in Haiti, which however always remained small.[54] In spite of this fiasco a certain interest in Haiti remained, which was renewed a generation later.[55]

In the following years would-be emigrants from the USA, spurred on by discriminatory measures and racial riots like the one in Cincinnati in 1829,[56] concentrated their interest on Canada. This country was closer to the USA and offered living conditions similar to those they had meanwhile become accustomed to in the USA. From this period onwards Canada became for many ex-slaves the terminus of the well-known 'underground railroad', once the North of the USA was no longer safe for escaped slaves from the South. Their situation worsened with the Fugitive Slave Law (1850), according to which every fugitive slave on American soil was to be captured and returned to his 'lawful' owner. Thus it becomes understandable that although the Negro Convention of 1832 in Philadelphia condemned all colonization projects in Africa, it sanctioned voluntary emigration to Canada.[57]

Delany's re-emigration plan (1854–60)

The early 1830s saw the beginning of the next most important of all re-emigration projects, initiated by Martin R. Delany. Delany came from the South, where he learnt how to read and write illegally and secretly from his mother and from northern dealers.[58] His family was on this account compelled to leave Charleston and moved to Pennsylvania, where schools for coloured children had already existed for decades.[59] Later he went to Pittsburgh where he worked his way through school; his favourite subject was history. He was impressed by Nat Turner's attempt at rebellion in 1831 and by Garrison's vehement polemics against the American Colonization Society.[60] In Pittsburgh he organized the Philanthropic Society, which was predominantly concerned with the 'underground railroad'; he also took part in public activities of the abolitionist movement. Between 1843 and 1846 he published quite successfully in Pittsburgh a paper, *Mystery*, where in one article he touched on a theme to which he was later to return: the numerical preponderance of the coloured peoples vis-à-vis the Whites.[61] Later he collaborated with Frederick Douglass (1817–95), the most important nineteenth-century negro leader, on his weekly *North Star*, which later became the *Frederick Douglass Paper*. He studied medicine at Harvard and went on a lecture tour, during the course of which he propagated the political ideas that were later formulated in detail in two books. The first one was devoted to propaganda on behalf of emigration from the USA;[62] the second provided as well an account of the first (and only) concrete result of his endeavours up to that moment.[63]

Delany was no mulatto but the first full-blooded negro among the Afro-American leaders in the USA. In contrast to most of his coloured fellow-countrymen he was proud of his black complexion and for this reason he always rejected vehemently the doctrine of the inferiority of coloured people. His historicizing racial consciousness was reflected in the names he gave his children, which included Toussaint l'Ouverture, Alexander Dumas, Saint Cyprian, Faustin Soulouque (emperor of Haiti), Ramses Placido (after both the pharaoh Ramses II and a Cuban poet and hero of the struggle for liberation) and Ethiopia Halle Amelia.[64] In a way he was the herald of the later Négritude movement, as was Blyden, twenty years his junior, who was also proud of his full-blooded Black descent.[65]

In the winter of 1831–2, during the months between Nat Turner's revolt and the appearance of Garrison's polemic against the American Colonization Society, Delany decided to go to Africa, 'the land of my ancestry',[66] together with a sympathizer, Molliston M. Clark – Clark as a clergyman, Delany as a physician. In 1850, the year of the Fugitive Slave Law, he revealed his plans to a select group of Afro-American 'intelligent gentlemen' who gave their consent to them. Two years later he published his call for Afro-Americans to emigrate from the USA, which we have already mentioned. After a general introduction in which – already following a literary tradition[67] – he rejected the arguments for the alleged racial inferiority of the Africans and Afro-Americans, he turned to the practical question of 'where shall we go?'[68] Delany concealed his preference for Africa for tactical reasons, because most Afro-American spokesmen were opposed to emigration to Africa. This led to contradictions in his argument. 'Our common land is the United States. We are Americans and have civic rights by virtue of our birth', he wrote.[69] Or more sharply: 'We are determined to remain on this continent in spite of all the difficulties.'[70] On the other hand he called for emigration from the USA and referred to Africa as the 'father-land'.[71] He dissociated himself emphatically from the Liberia settlement project[72] and also condemned emigration to Canada,[73] although he may have known from personal experience the practical advantages of the latter country as an asylum for fugitive ex-slaves.[74] His final choice apparently fell unequivocally upon Central and South America, including the West Indies – 'evidently the ultimate destination and future home of the coloured race on this continent'.[75] Delany's true intentions only became clear in the appendix, where he proposed an expedition to the eastern coast of Africa; to prepare for this a 'national meeting' would have to be convened and a body of commissioners especially appointed.[76]

At the next general convention in Cincinnati (Ohio) in 1852 the first straw votes were taken on the emigration question. Most members of the steering committee decided in favour of emigration, but the delegates to the plenary assembly voted four to one against it.[77] Thereupon the defeated advocates of emigration split off and called a separate convention of their supporters at Cleveland (Ohio), the National Emigration Convention of Colored Men. This assembly met from 24 to 26 August 1854 under Delany's chairmanship. He also delivered the main report, approved as the 'Report on the Political Destiny of the Colored Race on the American Continent'.

In a public appeal the eastern hemisphere, i.e. Africa, was explicitly ruled out as a possible destination for emigrants; but as Delany made clear later this was

> a mere policy on the part of the authors of those documents [the appeal and the invitation to the conference] to confine their

scheme to America [including the West Indies], whilst they were the leading advocates of the regeneration of Africa, lest they compromised themselves and their people to the avowed enemies of the race. The Convention, in its Secret Session made Africa, with its rich, inexhaustible production, and great facilities for checking the abominable Slave Trade its most important point of dependence, though each individual was left to take the direction which in his judgment best suited him.'[78]

Delany occupied a leading position in the new organization and was appointed one of the commissioners who were to explore the possibilities for settlement. James T. Holly was sent to Haiti;[79] Delany, together with Robert Campbell, went to West Africa. Holly travelled to Haiti as early as 1855 and was able to announce to the next Emigration Convention at Chatham (Ontario) that the Haitian government had commissioned him, at a fee of $1000 per year plus travel expenses, to recruit immigrants into that country.

Delany and Campbell took more time. It was not until July 1859 that they arrived separately in Liberia. In Monrovia, the capital, Delany was welcomed with an address signed *inter alia* by Blyden: the latter honoured Delany enthusiastically at a public meeting as the 'Moses' who would lead his people out of servitude.[80] After a lecture in the Methodist church in Monrovia Delany met Alexander Crummell, an Afro-American who had worked in Liberia for twenty years and who later still played an important part in Afro-American affairs after he returned to the United States towards the end of the century.[81] By way of Lagos Campbell travelled to Abeokuta, already at that time the stronghold of the CMS mission; Delany followed in September 1859. During their stay in Abeokuta they probably lived with Samuel Crowther Jr.[82] In December 1859 the two delegates, supported by Samuel Crowther Sr who happened to be staying in Abeokuta too, signed an agreement with the *alake* (king) of Abeokuta whereby Afro-Americans were to be settled on Egba land that was not being cultivated.[83] The sole witnesses to the signing of this agreement were the two Crowthers. Afterwards Delany and Campbell travelled across Yorubaland until April 1860.[84]

Satisfied with what seemed to be a successful conclusion to their mission, Delany and Campbell returned to the coast, arriving in Liverpool on 12 May 1860. During their stay in London they were able to make several contacts, especially with philanthropic and humanitarian groups that took an interest in Africa. One of the consequences of their visit seems to have been the foundation of the African Aid Society, presided over by Lord Alfred Churchill (no relative of Winston Churchill).[85] Their newspaper was the *African Times*, which appeared from 1861 onwards. After their return to the USA the two men gave an account of their journey, but their endeavours were soon overtaken by events: the outbreak of the American Civil War directed men's attention and energies to problems closer at hand; Delany joined the US Army and became the first coloured army surgeon in the States.

But this was not the only reason why the project failed. In Abeokuta Henry Townsend, the CMS missionary, wrecked the settlement plan by putting pressure on the *alake*, for he feared that the Afro-American settlers would keep aloof from the CMS mission and develop into an *imperium in imperio*. At the beginning of February 1861 the *alake* withdrew his signature and issued a declaration denying that he had promised to allot the would-be settlers any land.[86] Moreover, Delany's and Campbell's unexpectedly long stay with British humanitarians seems to have caused some antagonism and to have dampened the enthusiasm for their cause. According to Delany, for whom the whole business later seems to have become embarrassing, their stay in London lasted only five days, from 16 to 20 May 1860; but at the end of June 1860 Thomas Hodgkin, a patient and meek man, criticized them for spending such a long time in the capital. They were said to have had a better reception than if they had been Whites; now they should go back to America to inform their brothers about the results of their journey. 'Expenses of their stay may cause them difficulties. My friend Bourne is still labouring for the cause that brought them here.'[87] The last item of information about the emigration project comes from Canada by way of F. Fitzgerald, the secretary of the African Aid Society. In August 1861 he wrote that Delany intended to go straight from the USA to Lagos with two or three coloured families who were to be settled in Abeokuta.[88] Even this modest offshoot of the planned wave of emigration probably fell victim to the American Civil War: Delany remained in the States, and nothing is known about the arrival of Afro-Americans in Lagos or Abeokuta.

Offshoots and effects of the Delany project

Although the National Emigration Convention's re-emigration project was thus a downright failure, the episode was nevertheless of historic importance. On the western side of the Atlantic it demonstrated that there did after all exist a far from negligible minority which was interested in returning to Africa. It also produced the clearest and politically best-founded statement of Pan-African ideas to be made during the nineteenth century.[89] Finally, if one disregards the blind alley of Liberia, this was the first time since Cuffee that a purposeful contact had been established between Afro-Americans and Africans. Even though nothing came of the massive emigration movement, the propaganda in favour of it by Delany and the National Emigration Convention had a greater effect than Cuffee's solitary action. Campbell's activity was particularly important. Born in Kingston, Jamaica, in 1829, he was a teacher at the Institute for Coloured Youth in Philadelphia from 1855 to 1859 before going to Africa with Delany. His account of their trip contributed towards the deepening of emotional ties with Africa.[90] In 1862 he returned to Lagos where he was active until his death in 1884; at the end of his life he was a leading member of the masonic lodge in Lagos and president of the Lagos Mutual Improvement Society.[91] He also published from 1863 to 1867 the first periodical in Lagos; besides his skills as a printer (the craft he had originally learned) he brought from America the title of a new journal, the *Anglo-African*, modelled on the *Anglo-African Magazine* which had appeared in the USA around 1860. The *Anglo-African* in Lagos featured several items of information about the New World, especially during the American Civil War; a whole number was devoted to events in his native Jamaica (October 1865). [92-3]

The foundation of the African Aid Society and its periodical the *African Times*, which at least indirectly resulted from Delany's and Campbell's visit to England, likewise had a 'Pan-African' impact. The periodical served as a substitute for the central organ which the young élite on the west coast of Africa lacked and also as a link with America and British humanitarian groups. The *African Times* kept up this function after the African Aid Society had ceased to exist and survived until 1900, long after the death of its editor and publisher, Fitzgerald.

Although the American Civil War finally put an end to Delany's and Campbell's settlement project in Abeokuta, it did give a new impetus

to emigration to Haiti, which had been reconnoitred at least superficially by the National Emigration Convention. Whereas most Afro-
Americans emphasized their desire to stay in the USA by their commitment to the cause of the Union, a minority felt disgusted by the North's
continuing animosity towards the coloured element. The idea of emigration was reinforced by the fact that President Lincoln was in favour
of deporting the Afro-Americans from America to Africa or alternatively to Haiti.[94] In mid-January 1861 a Haytian Emigration Society
was formed in Toledo (Ohio) which adopted a resolution printed by the
Anglo-African Magazine. Redpath, the agent of the Haytian Emigration
Bureau, even published a periodical of his own, *Palm and Pine*, as
well as a handbook to encourage emigration to Haiti.[95] In 1860 he
initiated a settlement project in Haiti. He was assisted by James T.
Holly, who several years before had gone to Haiti to explore conditions
there on behalf of the National Emigration Convention,[96] by Henry
Highland Garnet (1815-82), one of the most militant Afro-American
leaders of the nineteenth century, and by William W. Brown, the first
Afro-American amateur historian.[97] Frederick Douglass and Garrison's
Liberator, however, launched a violent polemic against this project.
Garnet even undertook a parallel mission to Jamaica to explore the
situation there, apparently without any real success.

The settlement movement in Haiti seems to have flourished at first.
Between December 1860 and October 1861 about 2000 settlers arrived.
As in 1824[98] the enterprise proved abortive as a result of disease,
inadequate organization and tension between the native population and
the immigrants. Several of the latter died, while others went back to
the USA, so that in 1864 no more than 200 remained in Haiti. In
October 1862 Redpath suspended publication of *Palm and Pine* and
gave up his post as agent of the Haytian Emigration Bureau.

Despite this fiasco Lincoln adhered to the idea of supporting a mass
emigration after the emancipation of the slaves, although without the
use of force. On 14 August 1862 Lincoln summoned to the White House
a group of leading coloured people to whom he stated his proposals.
Despite bitter opposition, by Frederick Douglass among others, Lincoln
proceeded to execute the project, for which $600,000 had already been
assigned. From time to time Lincoln also thought of settling Afro-
Americans in modern Panama, where they would be put to work in
the new coal mines. Finally, at the end of December 1862 a business
man received a commission from the government to transport 500

negroes at $50 per head to the Ile de Vache near Haiti. This time failure was registered even sooner than with the earlier projects, for the entrepreneur concerned turned out to be a swindler. Thus the idea of settlement in Haiti remained just a dream.

The historical importance of the plans for emigration to Haiti lies in the fact that its advocates used the same arguments in their propaganda as in the case of emigration to Africa. It would, they thought, prove the falsity of the theory of racial inequality by showing that the Afro-Americans were able to exercise self-government and to form a national entity of their own. The Haytian Emigration Society even went so far as to declare Haiti 'the main corner-stone of an Ethiopian empire', a stepping-stone, as it were, in the establishment of a Black belt in the tropics.[99]

Chief Sam and Back-to-Africa, 1914–15

After the Civil War the idea of emigration generally lapsed among Afro-Americans. It was upheld only by the American Colonization Society, which had less success than ever before even though it boasted such prominent advocates as Blyden and Henry Turner, a bishop of the AME church. A coloured spokesman of the society even took up the slogan 'Africa for the Africans'.[100] Turner maintained that a great interest in Africa was to be found among all coloured people.[101] Another spokesman claimed in 1895 that the society held the documents of more than 100,000 would-be emigrants to Liberia.[102] He stated:

> The thousands of letters received by this Society from Negroes in the United States show conclusively that a very large number of these feel that they are and must continue to be at a great disadvantage in a country dominated by the white race, that they are engaged in a hopeless conflict and they desire, more especially for the sake of their children to escape from this hostile environment.

There was, however, no extensive emigration either to Africa or to the West Indies. A latent interest in Africa seemed to live on among the poorer classes, as is illustrated by the astonishing reaction to Chief Sam's settlement project just before the outbreak of World War I.[103]

This episode, in itself insignificant, affords an instructive insight into the attitude of Afro-Americans who returned to Africa, their long sought-after 'fatherland'. At the end of August 1913 one who claimed

to be 'Chief Sam', an African from the Gold Coast, appeared in Okfus-
kee County, Oklahoma, and sold shares worth more than $25 each in
a company to promote trade and emigration, in return for which he
generally offered a free crossing to Africa. The enterprising business
man apparently had an excellent response among Afro-Americans.
The reason for this is self-evident: for some years lynching had been
practised in this part of Oklahoma, and the Afro-Americans felt themselves more insecure than ever. On the other hand the Whites did not
want to lose their cheap labour (a dilemma which was to be repeated
on a more extensive scale in the South during the war years), so that
some newspapers, possibly exaggerating the matter, lamented 'that
many of the local Negroes were buying shares in the company and
making no provisions for winter, so confident are they of going to
Africa'.[104] After several difficulties had been overcome the liner *Liberia*
with the emigrants on board set sail for Africa on 20 August 1914.
After being compelled to spend forty-five days in Freetown, and being
made by the colonial authorities to pay a special tax of £25 per head,
the *Liberia* arrived in Saltpond on the Gold Coast on 13 January
1915.

The returning Afro-Americans were indeed given a friendly reception by the local Africans. But already at the emotional climax of the
journey they must have experienced an embarrassed disenchantment,
as they suddenly realized, at least subconsciously, that they left behind
them an industrialized society with a higher standard of living, and
that material considerations weighed more heavily than sentimental
bonds to 'Mother Africa'.

> Not one of the [Afro-American] speakers mentioned the benefits
> which members of the movement might derive from their stay in
> Africa. . . . No syllable touched on the possibility of African custom
> intruding in their way of life. It was a significant omission, and
> certainly betrayed a sudden awareness on the part of the Americans
> that their fatherland was historically a long way behind them, and
> that what emotional ties they fancied they had with it were some-
> what vapid. Despite their obvious delight at being on the con-
> tinent of their origin, they reacted as would have any European
> on being confronted with barefooted, gaudily dressed men and
> women of tribes little distant from outright savagery. The psycho-
> logical dissociation of the emigrants from their brethren was almost
> immediate.[105]

When, after overcoming their first disappointment, they finally settled at Akim some way inland, their unwillingness to let themselves be reduced to African standards led them to live in groups apart from the rest of the population. Having emigrated to escape segregation in the USA, on arrival in the 'African fatherland' they segregated themselves from the other members of their 'race' whom they regarded as inferior:

> They were much too used to living conditions in the United States, and despite their voluntary segregation, they were unwilling to settle for the standards of the Gold Coast, however much their own Jim Crow status might be alleviated. They did not want to be Americans, but now they found that they did not want to be Africans either.[106]

The same conflict between racial sentimentality and a drop in living standards appeared time and again when Afro-Americans, full of high ideals and romantic concepts about Africa, were brought abruptly face to face with harsh reality. This often led to psychological catastrophe. Either they developed a superiority complex with quasi-racist overtones or else they indulged in a romantic emotionalism, as was the case with W. E. B. Du Bois.[107]

The settlement of Afro-Americans on the Gold Coast turned out to be a failure, as was to be expected under such conditions. Having been decimated by death and illness, the usual fate of re-emigrants, most of the survivors returned to America. So far as the history of Afro-Americans in the USA is concerned, the 'Chief Sam' episode had one particular result: in Oklahoma at least it apparently promoted a feeling of solidarity, and the co-operation[108] which resulted helped the Afro-Americans to acquire fresh self-confidence. Only a few years later Marcus Garvey produced the same impact on an even greater scale with his spectacular 'Back-to-Africa' movement, which at the same time was of great importance in the development of Pan-Africanism – perhaps because Garvey was spared the sharp confrontation with African reality that had been experienced by the emigrants on the *Liberia*.[109]

The demand for equal rights

The basic elements of a literary tradition

Pan-Africanism as an ideology of emancipation maintained the principle that all men and all races are equal and therefore should enjoy equal rights. This idea derives from an older tradition of European origin.[1] The claim to equal rights was formulated in the course of a polemic against all those who postulated that the White races were superior and the coloured races inferior, i.e. against all theories on racial superiority. Like the racists themselves, the anti-racists made use of various arguments which on the surface changed little in the course of nearly two centuries,[2] but which actually underwent a certain elaboration and modification. The main points were the following: rejection of the doctrine that the races were unequal; reference to the history of Africa, especially of ancient Egypt, as proof that Africans were able to produce an advanced culture, even if only in the past; and emphasis on individuals of African descent who had achieved success in various fields. To this may be added the demand that Africa should have a political existence of its own in the modern world, the 'regeneration' or 'redemption' of Africa, a demand which was often put forward with a quasi-religious fervour. Taken together, these ideas produced a new self-awareness based upon a feeling of solidarity among all men of African descent.

In the fight against racist theories the forerunners of Pan-Africanism were able to draw upon the work of European authors, who advanced most of their standard arguments. Most of these men were eighteenth-century abolitionists such as Benezet,[3] Abbé Raynal, Granville Sharp[4] and the Rev. James Ramsay, who after spending nineteen years in St Kitts (in the West Indies) wrote 'the best anti-racist tract of the eighteenth century'.[5-6] The writing of Johannes Blumenbach, the distinguished anthropologist from Göttingen, had only an indirect impact.[7] Much more important were the works of two French authors: Abbé Henri Grégoire, leading light of the Amis des Noirs during the French Revolution and the leading French abolitionist,[8] and C.-F. Volney, who travelled in Egypt.[9] To complete the list there was the English author, Armistead, with his large collection based upon Grégoire of brief biographies of important Africans and Afro-Americans.[10]

Benezet early on pointed to the historical dynamic of the civilizing process, and in opposition to the doctrine that the Africans were permanently inferior showed that the Europeans' ancestors had themselves been barbarians in antiquity.

> It was by these means [fair and honourable commerce] that the inhabitants of Europe, though formerly a barbarous people, became civilized. Indeed the account Julius Caesar gives of the ancient Britons in their state of ignorance, is not such as should make us proud of ourselves, or lead us to despise the unpolished nations of the earth; for he informs us that they lived in many respects like our Indians. . . . Nor doth Tacitus give a more Honourable account of the Germans.[11]

Grégoire's contribution was to record the biographies of leading Africans. Volney claimed that the achievements of ancient Egypt were the work of the negroid element.[12] This idea was later taken up in the USA; we are told by an anonymous author that the Africans, far from being inferior, had been 'for more than a thousand years . . . the most enlightened on the globe'.[13] Since Afro-American and African authors very rarely indicate the sources they use, it is not possible to prove that there was a direct connection between the two statements.

Two groups may be distinguished according to the form and content of the arguments they employed, a distinction which continues right down into the twentieth century. On one hand are the writers who make use of biblical arguments (Ham's curse not applicable to negroes; Man's descent from a single couple; evolution of the races, according to the Old Testament account, due to the dissemination and differentiation of Noah's descendants). On the other hand are those who refer to ancient history (Herodotus in particular) and, following Benezet, emphasize the role of cultural contact in fostering historical change.

So far as the content of the arguments is concerned, we may distinguish one group of writers who sought to show the equality of Africans and people of African descent but nothing more from others who, reacting against White racism, went on to develop an inverted Black racism and tried to trace back to Africans or those with a mixture of African blood every achievement in world history. Those who argued in biblical terms are frequently, but not invariably, identical with the Black racists. For many self-taught writers the Bible was at first the only or the chief source of their knowledge.[14] Moreover, these early Afro-American authors were often ministers.

Eighteenth-century African authors : Capitein, Sancho, Cugoano, Equiano

The first written comment on these questions by an African, even before the beginning of the discussion about race, was made by Jacobus Capitein, who in 1742 submitted a doctoral thesis to the University of Leyden.[15] Considering his personal situation and the historical conditions in which he wrote, it was quite understandable that he should have defended the concept of his Dutch benefactors that slavery could very well be reconciled with the Scriptures.

More influenced by the spirit of the new age was Ignatius Sancho, who lived in London a generation later. After his death his letters were published by his English benefactors to prove 'that an untutored African may possess abilities equal to an European'.[16] In two letters Sancho signed himself as 'Africanus', in three others as 'Blackamoor'.[17] In a letter dated July 1776 to Laurence Sterne thanking him for having supported Abolition, we can discern the probable intention of Sancho's choice of the word 'African', for he protested against the term

'negro', which was then coming into more frequent use, as discriminatory and derogatory.

> I am one of those people [he writes] whom the vulgar and illiberal
> call 'Negurs' . . . 'Consider slavery – what it is – how bitter a
> draught – and how many millions are made to drink it!' [quoted
> from Sterne]. Of all my favourite authors, not one has drawn a
> tear in favour of my miserable black brethren – excepting yourself,
> and the humane author of Sir George Ellison. . . . Dear Sir, I
> think in me you behold the uplifted hands of thousands of my
> brother Moors. – Grief (you pathetically observe) is eloquent;
> and figure to yourself their attitudes; – hear their supplicating
> addresses! – alas! – you cannot refuse. – Humanity must comply –
> in which hope I beg permission to subscribe myself, Reverend Sir.[18]

It is noteworthy that, although Sancho was a petty greengrocer
who could not claim high social status, he dared to say proudly: 'I am
not sorry I was born in Africa.'[19]

Cugoano, whose book appeared only seven years after the publication
of the Sancho letters, broached a standard theme of later literature on
the subject. He came to grips with the Old Testament argument that
Africans, as descendants of Ham, were eternally condemned to a subordinate position by Noah's curse (Genesis 9: xxv–xxvii). Cugoano,
like many other writers after him, protested that the curse was intended
not for Ham but for his son Canaan.[20]

Considerably more rational were the arguments advanced by Equiano
only two years later. The author, born in 1745, kidnapped at the age
of eleven and taken to England the following year, was a widely
travelled man since from time to time he earned his living as a sailor.
In 1766 he was in Philadelphia where he attended a Quaker meeting.
In 1779, back in London, he was asked to go to Africa as a missionary.
After first declining the invitation he then accepted, but nothing came of
the idea. In 1785 he reappeared in Philadelphia where he said that he
was impressed by the work done by the Quakers on behalf of Afro-
Americans.[21] In the following year he heard in London about the
project to colonize Sierra Leone and at first wanted to go there as a
commissioner but withdrew before the expedition left because of differences of opinion with the organizers. On 21 March 1788 he submitted a petition to the Queen asking her to abolish slavery in the
West Indies.[22]

Equiano observed that there was a remarkable similarity between the Africans and the Jews before they entered the promised land; this is indeed correct in so far as in both cases their societies were semi-nomadic and semi-agrarian. He becomes abstruse, on the other hand, when he goes on to argue that the Africans were descended from the Jews, and had only become black under the influence of the climate.[23] The argument again acquires a rational character where the author turns to slavery and its effects: Africans are not inferior but slavery humiliates them as human beings. Finally, the ancestors of the Europeans had once been uncivilized, although they could not for this reason be called inferior.[24]

The first Afro-American authors: Easton and Pennington

The first Afro-American author almost half a century later combines the biblical story with rational arguments to explain the current superiority of Europeans and inferiority of Africans.[25] Easton touches upon most of the themes employed by his successors: 'Ham was the son of Noah and founder of the African race', he states in a lapidary fashion. His brief sketch of the history of Egypt, allegedly founded by Misraim, the son of Ham, in 2188 B.C., is based completely on the Old Testament. Besides ancient Egypt, Ethiopia and Carthage are cited as testimony to African achievements.[26] Noteworthy is the historical dimension of Easton's work: basing himself on a historian he does not identify (this was Niebuhr), he points out that the Egyptians transmitted their knowledge to the Greeks, and the latter in turn passed it on to the Romans, to whom modern Europe owed so much; this concept of the importance of cultural contacts and of a succession of cultural centres was apparently more widespread in medieval Europe than it was in later centuries.[27] Nor is the converse argument forgotten: the ancient Greeks were 'a race of savages' before they had been influenced by Egypt; the tribes of Germans were barbarous at the time of the great migrations.[28]

> Africa never will raise herself, neither will she be raised by others, by warlike implements, or ardent spirits; nor yet by a hypocritical religious crusade. But when she rises, other nations will have learned to deal justly with her from principles. When that time

shall arrive [incidentally, without the use of arms], the lapse of a few generations will show the world that her sons will again take the lead in the fields of virtuous enterprise, filling the front rank of the church, when she marches into the millennial era.[29]

Easton's position anticipated the rational arguments of later writers. The next representative of this school of thought, James W. C. Pennington, was likewise a minister as well as a leading abolitionist. In his view Noah's curse could not apply at all to the Africans, since they were the descendants not of Canaan but of Kush and Miraim.[30] Pennington was the first Afro-American author to note Herodotus's references to the negroid features of the ancient Egyptians, which he reproduced in detail.[31] Since he took literally the statements in the Bible about the origin of Egypt and Ethiopia, the first-generation Egyptians and Ethiopians were in his view cousins who had at first been ruled in common.[32] His attempt to distinguish between Africans and Ethiopians was instructive, for generally 'Ethiopia' and 'Ethiopian' were at that time regarded as synonymous with 'Africa' and 'African'. The ancient Carthaginians, he pointed out, were Africans, but not Ethiopians. Thus for Pennington Africa, unlike 'Ethiopia', was a geographical unit.[33] He was the first to try to connect Africa's past glory and its undoubted present backwardness by asking how this decline might be accounted for. Although the answers he gave were unsatisfactory[34] his historical approach is proof of a rational mode of argumentation. It was by the same critical reasoning that Pennington explained the development of slavery in the New World: 'Slavery on this continent did not originate in the conditions of Africans. . . . It is commonly asserted that the Africans have been enslaved because they are fit only for slaves.'[35]

On the contrary, he pointed out, slavery had already been introduced into America for economic reasons under Emperor Charles V. From this position Pennington arrived at the heart of all Pan-African thinking, later expressed in the most varied turns of phrase: 'Are colored Americans, in point of intellect, inferior to white people? . . . My position is that the notion of inferiority is not only false but absurd and therefore ought to be abandoned.'[36]

To prove his doctrine he mentioned the migration of cultures from their origin in Africa, the African character of ancient Egypt, and the cases of Africans who had managed to hold their own in the modern world despite slavery. In particular he mentioned Cugoano, Amo and Capitein as living examples of how receptive the Africans were.[37] As Pennington put it, 'I have been the more confined in this selection to native Africans, because my opponents of the Jefferson school always pitifully reply to the argument when pressed with cases, by answering that they are either whites or so intermixed as to have the benefit of white intellect. Thus they beg the question.'[38] In brief Pennington's position was 'that intellect is identical in all human beings, and that the contrary opinion is an absurdity'.[39] He ended by examining American racial prejudice and came up with some devastating statements:

> It is supreme selfishness. It is emphatically ill will . . . Insubordination, bloodshed and murder are its legitimate aim . . . It tends to blindness of mind . . . It established in the whites a character for injustice . . . Hypocrisy is copiously gendered by this prejudice . . . Brutish and uncivil manners are the fruit of this prejudice . . . The tendency of this prejudice is to blasphemy . . . This prejudice hates the truth . . . Finally it is carrying the total nation down to a state of refined heathenism.'[40]

The irrational-racist tendency from Lewis to Osei

The group of writers who used rational historical arguments were very definitely in the majority – so much so that it is worth while breaking off here and dealing next with the irrational-racist minority, which employed biblical arguments extensively right up to the early twentieth century, before we return to consider the majority group.

The next author to be mentioned here introduced digressions – and did so with breath-taking *élan*. Robert B. Lewis, likewise a minister, was, with Cuffee, one of the few men who could claim both Afro-American and Indian descent; this helps to explain his interest in Indian history. His book[41] is a vast compilation taken from the Bible, classical mythology, and authors both ancient and modern. Lewis was the first to claim for Africa all the achievements of great nations and great men. According to him the Greek barbarian tribes and the Roman Empire were colonized by Phoenicians and XVIIIth Dynasty Egyptians; Athens was founded by an Egyptian in 1556 B.C. and Macedonia by a descendant of 'Hercules, an African'; Greece, Europe and the whole of America were originally settled by descendants of the Egyptians; the

Indians were related to the Israelites of Egypt; Syrians, Greeks, Phoenicians and Romans were all negroid. No less imposing is the list of those who, according to Lewis, were either Africans or of African descent: from Plato the line extends to Pompey, Euclid, Caesar, Cicero and Cato, by way of the great kings of the ancient Near East, and from David to Solomon and Christ. Art and science, the first discoveries and inventions, are likewise attributed to Africans. Lewis ends with the by now traditional enumeration of outstanding coloured personalities, whose importance was greatly exaggerated, as it was to be so often by later writers.

Even more inadequate in intellectual substance are the three books by Joseph B. Hayne, a pastor of the AME church.[42] In his first book Hayne opposed the colonization of Africa and racial intermingling because this was an admission that Afro-Americans were inferior and Whites superior; he demanded that the former manifest a racial pride of their own.[43] His argumentation was still quite biblical. His second book was a pseudo-anthropological treatise which has only curiosity value today; the third, whose title alone divulges the whole doctrine, was dedicated 'to the Hamitic people, the authors of the ancient culture, and to their descendants'.

The same argumentations were advanced in a similar style as late as 1910 by James M. Webb, an evangelist of the small Church of God sect. That one of Solomon's numerous wives was an Egyptian princess of dark complexion, that Mary and Joseph with the infant Jesus fled to Egypt, whence civilization in any case originated, are two of the 'facts' pressed into support of the doctrine that the Africans are racially superior. According to Webb Jesus had curly hair and 'Ethiopian blood' in his veins and would be classified as a 'NEGRO' in America.[44] 'So there is nothing remarkable in the fact that Dr Booker T. Washington, W. E. B. Du Bois, W. B. Scarborough and many other Negroes or black men [allegedly] occupy places among the foremost and most eminent educators of the world' because 'they are descended from fathers who ruled Egypt centuries ago and with their wisdom layed the foundation of learning.'[45] Other figures whom Webb claimed for his doctrine included Toussaint l'Ouverture, Alexander Dumas, Pushkin and Hamilton.

In more recent times J. A. Rogers, an autodidact born in Jamaica and living in the USA, has continued in this tradition, involving himself in a vast amount of detailed research. Rogers, who in 1967 was almost ninety years of age, with his unquenchable ambition to trace African fathers or mothers of important people throughout world history,[46] seems to be trying to compensate for some psychological complex. He is of such light complexion that from time to time he apparently tried to pass for White and to write for the White market, but had so little success that he turned again to the coloured community.[47] The infatuation with which this amateur historian collected facts from all over the world and from all epochs is adequately conveyed by a popular brochure which has been repeatedly re-issued since it first appeared in 1934, and which gives an idea of the value of his larger books. Referring to a mass of literature Rogers succeeded in 'proving' that both Haydn and Beethoven were of African descent.[48] This may explain why in an antique shop on Lenox Avenue in Harlem one can buy an engraving of Beethoven with pronounced negroid features and with an appropriate caption.[49]

Rogers's obsessions are at least supported by a considerable background of reading; Gabriel K. Osei, a young Ghanaian follower, has reduced his to the credit-worthiness of flimsy pamphlets.[50] Osei is not taken seriously by reputable African historians, but represents the last stage of an older irrational-racist tradition, a reaction to White racism. His propaganda 'that Africa must unite under one strong central government' is in accordance with Nkrumah's ideas but so far is unrealistic.[51]

It is worthwhile knowing about Rogers's notions since they have apparently found a response among certain Afro-Americans.[52] Under his influence Earl Sweeting, an Afro-American artist, executed a dozen colossal paintings extolling African history in the newly built headquarters of the Convention People's Party in Accra after Ghana obtained her independence. The main themes include a glorification of ancient Ghana and the supposed former cultural superiority of the Africans vis-à-vis the White barbarians.[53] These paintings could hardly have been executed without the approval of Nkrumah, who probably came across Rogers's works while he was a student in America. One therefore should not underestimate the significance of this exaggerated reaction to White doctrines of racial superiority. Such efforts to compensate for the Africans' inferiority complex represent a subordinate current in the movement for equal rights, which has at times exercised an indirect impact upon the main current.

Writers employing biblical arguments

Among the writers in the more important majority group who demanded no more than equal rights with the Whites, only the earlier ones based their arguments upon the Bible, deriving the Africans' descent from Noah, his sons or grandsons. In the twentieth century the arguments of this school became secularized. But all these men shared an astonishing sense of the dynamic of change at work in history.

With the staunch confidence of a clergyman who was well read in the Bible, Henry H. Garnet, one of the most militant coloured abolitionists (he agitated from time to time for armed action to abolish slavery), declared: 'Ham was the first African.'[54] In his view the role played by ancient Egypt was particularly important. Garnet was apparently the first to make use of a passage from psalm 68 which later was to be repeatedly cited: 'Princes shall come out of Egypt and Ethiopia shall soon stretch out her hands unto God.'[55]

After enumerating significant personalities in antiquity who were of African descent, from Hannibal to St Augustine by way of Cleopatra, he drew a particularly daunting picture of the way the barbaric ancestors of the Anglo-Saxons had lived at that time:

> When these representatives of our race were filling the world with amazement, the ancestors of the now proud and boasting Anglo-Saxons were amongst the most degraded in the human family. They abode in caves underground, either naked or covered with the skins of wild beasts. Night was made hideous by the smoke which arose from their bloody altars, upon which they offered human sacrifices.[56]

Of no particular interest in themselves are the three pamphlets by B. T. Tanner, in which he refutes the significance of Noah's curse by reference to the Old Testament and Herodotus, and also makes use of Herodotus to demonstrate the negroid character of the 'Ethiopians'.[57] What is important about Tanner is the fact that he was a bishop of the AME church, and that his intellectually barren writings were still read in the early twentieth century.

Also disappointing is the ambitious and grandiose late work by Martin R. Delany,[58] to whose earlier contribution to the development of proto-Pan-African traditions we shall have cause to refer on another occasion.[59] Precisely because of its political significance, one is struck by the inadequacy of this work, which was intended to be a fundamental treatise. In the first section, the only one of any interest here, he follows closely the biblical account in trying to explain the evolution of the races of mankind. So utterly does he rely upon this source that he identifies the Old Testament figures of Ham, Misraim and Kush with the Egyptian pharaohs Ramses I, II and III.[60] In the second section he repeats in essence his earlier observations to the effect that the Afro-Americans' salvation lay in taking the road of emigration from the USA.[61]

On the same level is a small popular work, dating from 1905, whose title, *Primer of Facts Pertaining to the Early Greatness of the African Race and the Possibility of Restoration by its Descendants*, gives a sufficient idea of its content.[62] Here, too, the argument is still wholly biblical.

Crummell, Brown, Blyden

Of a different quality are two earlier works which show that already in the mid-nineteenth century some writers had a modern outlook. Alexander Crummell, who spent twenty years in Liberia working as a minister and teacher, published an article in 1850 in London attacking the widespread view that slavery had resulted from Noah's curse.[63] He reasoned that the phenomenon of slavery could be found almost throughout the whole of human history, so that logically the Turks, Poles and Russians, on account of serfdom, and even the medieval Anglo-Saxons, should be numbered among the 'races' which White authors so readily condemned to slavery. Slavery in the New World had originated in modern times, and was due to the discovery of America and the desire to exploit its economic riches. It was confined to a brief span of time and could not serve as the basis for generalizations about Africans.[64] In a sermon preached in England in 1852 or 1853[65] he introduced for the first time a thoroughly modern argument by pointing out that Africa had been to a large extent isolated from the rest of the world by the Sahara and by the oceans.[66] In a lecture which Crummell delivered in 1861 before audiences in several American cities he repeated this point and, referring to Niebuhr, added that progress in civilization was always based on contact between peoples.[67] For this reason Crummell could refute calmly the charge that the African negroes were inferior because they were backward. Towards the end of the century Crummell reverted to the cultural contact argument in his apologia for the negroes:

Civilization is always in its first outgrowth, among rude peoples, an exotic. It never springs up spontaneously, in any new land. It must be transported from an old to a new soil. Archbishop Whateley says: 'There is no one instance recorded of any of them rising into a civilized condition, without construction and assistance from people already civilized.'[68]

Equally modern and rational are the arguments employed by William W. Brown, a leading coloured abolitionist and the first autodidact among Afro-Americans who attempted to write a comprehensive (and quite respectable) history of the Afro-Americans.[69] In an earlier work which appeared at the height of the American Civil War, Brown proceeded expressly from the prejudice that negroes were inferior because they were slaves. He admitted

> that the condition of my [his] race, whether considered in a mental, moral or intellectual point of view, at the present time cannot compare favorably with the Anglo-Saxon. But it does not become the whites to point the finger of scorn at the black, when they have so long been degrading them. The negro has not always been considered the inferior race. The time was when he stood at the head of science and literature. Let us see.[70]

This led Brown to repeat the by now familiar pattern of historical argument, referring to Ethiopia and Egypt, varying this a little by claiming Minerva, Atlas and Jupiter (Amon) as Africans. Brown – and it is here that one notices the amateur's lack of detailed historical knowledge – ended by throwing all chronology overboard when he confused Hengist and Horsa with William the Conqueror, who 'completely annihilated the nationality of the Britons' and caused thousands of the latter to be sold in the slave markets of Rome. Quoting from the letters of Caesar and Cicero about the inferior quality of British slaves, he managed to confuse the chronological sequence of events actually one thousand years apart. For all this Brown was apparently the first coloured author to introduce an argument which one comes across right up to the present day. Caesar, in writing to Rome from Britain, had said of the Britons: 'They are the most ignorant people I ever conquered. They cannot be taught music.' Cicero warned his friend Atticus not to buy British slaves, 'because they cannot be taught to read, and are the ugliest and most stupid race I ever saw'.[71]

Both quotations illustrate the point that mattered most to the author: that civilization could develop out of barbarism, and that therefore such concepts as 'superior' or 'inferior' were historically relative. Finally – probably basing himself upon Crummell (but no doubt also on Blyden) – he gives what is probably the most impressive formulation of the argument that cultural contact played an important part in human progress by stressing the role of social development.

> No nation has ever been found, which, by its own unaided efforts, by some powerful inward impulse, has arrived from barbarism and degradation to civilization and respectability. There is nothing in race or blood, in color or feature, that imparts susceptibility of improvement to one race or another. The mind left to itself from infancy, without culture remains a blank. Knowledge is not innate. Development makes the man. As the Greeks, and Romans and Jews drew knowledge from the Egyptians 3000 years ago, and the Europeans received it from the Romans, so must the blacks in this land rise in the same way. As one learns from one another, so nation learns from nation. Civilization is handed from one place to another . . . Already the blacks in this continent though kept down under the heel of the white man, are fast rising in the scale of intellectual development, and proving their equality with the brotherhood of man.[72]

In the introduction to his second book Brown comes back once more to ancient history: Ethiopia and Egypt were flourishing cultures at a time when the Britons and Teutons were still barbarians; culture had migrated from Ethiopia to modern man by way of Egypt, Greece and Rome.[73] The main section of the book consists of a rather detailed though still readable survey of the historical development of Africa and of the Afro-Americans in the New World – an account written from a Pan-African viewpoint. Quoting Blyden, Brown refers to the contemporary example of Bishop Crowther.[74]

In the article which Brown cited from the *Methodist Quarterly Review* of January 1869,[75] Blyden reproduced the traditional mixture of quotations from the Bible, classical authors and Volney about ancient Egypt. He also advanced an explanation why the Africans had declined: in advancing into the interior of Africa, the Ethiopians had degenerated from beauty to barbarism.[76] In Blyden's view the permanence for centuries of the social and political status of the African at home must be attributed first to the isolation of the people from the progressive portion of mankind; and secondly, to the blighting influence of the traffic introduced among them by Europeans. Had not the demand arisen in America for African laborers, and had European nations inaugurated regular traffic with the coast, the natives would have shown themselves as impressible for change, as susceptible of improvement, as capable of acquiring knowledge and accumulating wealth, as the natives of Europe. Combination of capital and cooperation of energies would have done for this land what they have done for others. Private enterprise (which has been entirely destroyed by the nefarious traffic) encouraged by humane intercourse with foreign lands, would have developed agriculture, manufactures and commerce; would have cleared, drained and fertilized the country and built towns; would have improved the looms, brought plows, steam-engines, printing-presses, machines and the thousand processes and appliances by which comfort, progress and usefulness of mankind are secured.[77]

Proceeding from the view that the Black race was by nature irrevocably inferior, Blyden rejected the well-known interpretation of Genesis 9: xxv–xxvii (Noah's curse), referring incidentally to the fact that this biblical passage had only been interpreted in this way after the 'awful trade with African slaves' had commenced.[78] He appealed to all Africans to teach their children that they were not under any curse, but 'that it was [only] the force of circumstances that held them down'.[79] Blyden concluded his appeal for a new self-awareness, written in 1857 when he himself was only twenty-five years old, with a postscript in which for the first time the word 'negro' was given a value-free interpretation: he even proudly avowed himself a negro. Later Blyden made the word 'negro' the key concept of his programme to instil a new racial consciousness into the Africans and their descendants throughout the world.[80]

Blyden died in 1912 at the age of eighty, an esteemed and commanding figure[81] who towers over the history of modern Pan-Africanism. By many of his followers he is acclaimed as a great teacher.[82] Blyden's influence upon Africans and Afro-Americans was undoubtedly important,[83] although not necessarily in a positive sense because of his hatred of the mulattoes and his contradictory ideas.

T. E. S. Scholes

Theophilus E. Samuel Scholes deserves to be better known, since he was an active spokesman for Pan-Africanism during the first half of the twentieth century. He was born in Jamaica where he received his primary education, and went on to study medicine in London and Edinburgh, where he was trained to be a missionary physician. After spending five years in the Congo he visited the Colwyn Bay Institute, on the north coast of Wales, which endeavoured to combine Christian missionary work with training in modern practical skills.[84] In 1894 Scholes went on behalf of Colwyn Bay Institute to New Calabar, in what is now Nigeria, where he took over the Alfred Jones Institute.[85] Shortly before the turn of the century he returned to England, settled down in London as a freelance writer, and wrote three large books which account for his importance in the history of Pan-Africanism,[86] It is true that Scholes did not participate in the later Pan-African congresses, but prior to World War I he was in contact with Afro-Americans in the USA, especially with Arthur A. Schomburg.[87] Before World War II his books seem to have exerted an indirect influence upon Padmore's group; in any case in the 1930s Kenyatta and Makonnen called on Scholes in London to thank him for the great stimulus they had derived from reading his books.[88]

Scholes belongs unmistakably to the twentieth century, for his arguments are quite modern; there is no further mention of the Bible. Although he scarcely ever identifies his sources, he must have been familiar with the preceding literature. After Blyden he was the first West Indian author to make an important contribution to the emergence of Pan-Africanism. Residing as he did in the capital city of the British Empire, he accepted the latter as a fact of life, and although critical of many details of colonial rule did not want to destroy it. His objective was to transform the Empire into a free association of equals drawn from all races – something like the British Commonwealth after World War II. Scholes put his ideas down in writing, and they underlie his entire criticism of British colonialism, especially where he demands equality for the colonial peoples. In his controversy with the English historian Froude he says:

> Mr. Froude viewed the idea of an English Governor having a Negro Premier to prepare his speech, which he would have to read in the presence of a black Ministry and before a black Parlia-

ment, as supremely ridiculous . . . But from the standpoint of reason . . . that spectacle would neither be ridiculous nor outrageous.[89]

Already in his first book he went into a fair amount of detail in refuting the standard charges against the Africans, developing the traditional argument about the role of cultural contact. Against the assertion about 'the apparent incapacity of the full blood African Negro to make any permanent advance beyond his present normal condition without extraneous aid', he put the rhetorical question whether this shortcoming was confined to Africans:

> With the exception of the ancient Egyptians, what race, either in ancient or modern times, has shown any capacity to make a permanent advance 'without extraneous aid'? Did the Greeks, the Romans, or the modern nations of Europe?

In a controversy with the historian E. A. Freeman, of Trinity College, Oxford, he maintained that Freeman, instead of stressing the present heights reached by the White race, ought to have asked 'whether the progressive races have always held their present position; and if not, whence did the means of their progress come to them?'[90] Referring to Volney, he maintained: 'The corner-stone of the world's civilization was laid by the Negro.'[91] Noteworthy is his opinion that even without any contact with Europe the present-day African tribes would have attained the level of the ancient Romans in pre-Hellenistic times – a comparison which may be regarded as more or less valid. He stressed this idea once more in the context of ancient Egypt: 'The most forward nations of today were in a condition precisely similar to that in which most African tribes are now found.'[92]

Some years later Scholes dealt with the same problem in two massive volumes which, despite the somewhat baroque title, reflect a wholly modern approach and are still readable today. To indicate his acute intelligence it is enough to say that – amidst the security of Edwardian England – Scholes predicted that war and revolution would be the motive forces of social change in the near future.[93]

Scholes sought 'to review the arguments adduced in support of the alleged superiority of the white race, and the alleged inferiority of the coloured races'.[94] He set forth in detail the arguments in support of the alleged inferiority of the coloured people,[95] and then countered these prejudices with arguments from history, adding the ironic touch that the 'pale' races had not always been progressive and the coloured ones not always backward. 'The records of Caesar, Tacitus, Polybius and others [about the Teutons and Celts] are in their substance the same as those we read about the Indian, the Chinaman, the African and the Australian.'[96] Scholes even ventured into the difficult question of the primary causes of the development of civilization.[97] Such factors as the quality of the soil and climate he rejected as inadequate; instead he stressed the importance of cultural contacts: 'Real or characteristic differences are to be found, not in races, but in communities or nations, for the differences between race and race are only apparent.'[98] . . . 'Modern civilization is a continuity, and not a creation.'[99] Accordingly the lag in the attributes of civilization over the greater part of Africa did not prove ' "the Negroes' " incapacity for civilization'.[100]

In the second volume Scholes turns to a detailed critique of the British Empire and of imperialism, as in *Chamberlain and Chamberlainism*.[101] This is preceded by an inquiry into 'the real reason that accounts for their [the negroes'] backwardness' – the poor opportunities afforded them to develop, in the course of which he mentions the fact that there was racial discrimination even in England.[102] The basic mistake on Britain's part he sees in the indulgent attitude taken by the essentially liberal mother country towards the White settlers; i.e. the strong influence exerted upon British politics by racists on the periphery of the Empire. Similarly he sees the new Anglo-American friendship as rooted in a concept of racial solidarity that owed much to the influence of the southern states of the USA.[103]

> Thus is the policy of coercion of coloured British subjects, in which England has now openly joined with her white colonies; she and they are engaged in the enterprise of sowing the wind. . . . Alienation, then, between the governing and the governed races of the Empire, with the increased oppression and impoverishment of the latter, and its desperate attempt to regain its freedom by means of rebellion, are the actual and possible political and economic results of spoliation. . . . Alienation and separation of the two great units of the Empire, leading up to (unless there be a radical reform) a great rebellion of the governed unit against tyranny and oppression of the governing unit.[104]

This recalls a doctrine developed by Padmore in his later years.[105]

Twentieth-century Afro-American writers

William H. Ferris leads us into the heart of the Pan-African problem. His two-volume work is admittedly influenced by his personal experiences, but it is intellectually quite respectable.[106] In Afro-American 'domestic politics' – in the conflict between Booker T. Washington and Du Bois[107] – Ferris sided with the latter.[108] Later, in the Du Bois–Garvey controversy,[109] he backed Garvey, serving as editor of Garvey's *Negro World*. In his book Ferris analyses in detail the tensions among Afro-Americans and then turns to give a detailed survey of the historical development of Africans and Afro-Americans (entitled 'An Epitome of Deeds, Achievements and Progress of the Coloured Race in Africa, Europe, Hayti, the West Indies and America').[110] Dealing with ancient history, he makes use of the well-known mixture of arguments, with the difference that in addition to such authorities as Volney, Grégoire and Blumenbach he also mentions Franz Boas, the important contemporary American anthropologist (of German descent) who has made such a great contribution to the discrediting of racial theories, at least in American scholarship. Ferris discusses in particularly rich detail the negroid character of the ancient Ethiopians, relying heavily upon Herodotus, and claims that they transmitted the seeds of civilization to the ancient Egyptians.[111]

In the second volume Ferris describes unemotionally and without any romantic exaggeration the historical position of Haiti and enumerates the most important Afro-Americans of past and present. Between these sections is a chapter called 'Some Distinguished Foreign Negroes', in which his Pan-African viewpoint again comes to the fore: he mentions some African personalities who are of significance for Pan-Africanism, such as Casely Hayford and Mojola Agbebi.[112] Ferris quotes from the *African Times and Orient Review* and includes its publisher, Mohamed Ali Duse, among 'the 40 greatest Negroes in history and in the Who's Who in the Negro pantheon – among the 40 coloured immortals'.[113]

Of narrower scope is a book by Ellis which appeared one year later.[114] For him ancient Egypt also played a part, but this time as a stimulus, as a cultural centre whence influences radiated to the rest of Africa. For the first time we find an allusion to the existence of the ancient kingdoms in the western Sudan, especially Ghana: 'When England, Germany and France had just worked their way up out of barbarism, some of these dynasties had already attained a relatively high standard of culture.'[115]

Du Bois represents the climax of achievement among Afro-American writers. He attained a creditable level of scholarship and provided material that was of political value to the Pan-African movement. For Du Bois it was a great intellectual experience to hear a lecture by Franz Boas in Atlanta in 1906, in which the latter spoke about the great kingdoms of the western Sudan during the Middle Ages. Boas's introduction to African history inspired Du Bois to publish in 1915[116] *The Negro*, a slender volume but important for its content, which he expanded considerably under a new title in 1939.[117] The two editions of this work provide a modern and still readable survey of the history of Africa and the Afro-Americans. Particularly in the later book one finds the most mature version of the argument about the cultural achievements of the ancient Ethiopians and Egyptians, as well as the most balanced formulation of the traditional claim to equality of rights and social equality.[118]

After Du Bois most Afro-American historians only mentioned the African past as background material or to demonstrate their solidarity with the new national states in Africa.[119] He himself, as the most important contemporary Afro-American historian, made an attempt to explain the evolution of ancient Egyptian culture in a rational and mature way, superseding the forced emphasis prevalent till then on the dominant role of the African (negroid) element.

For John H. Franklin, too, ancient Egypt was 'a cradle of civilization', but the intermingling of races – White, Semitic, Brown and Black – was 'so extensive . . . that it is almost impossible to ascribe the civilization which emerged to any particular group'.[120] Instead one would have to assume that in the course of Egyptian history sometimes one element, sometimes another dominated; this depended on the pattern of immigration, which varied considerably from one age to another. This explanation is no doubt the most rational one and seems to fit the facts best. It avoids the awkward apologetic tone, almost amounting to an inverse racism, found among earlier writers, without in the least diminishing the credibility of the main argument, designed to prove that in principle all races are equal.

Twentieth-century African writers:
Casely Hayford to Nkrumah

If one discounts the ex-slaves who lived in Europe during the eighteenth century, and also Horton,[121] it is not until around 1900 that African writers emerged to help carry on the literary tradition begun and sustained by Afro-Americans. In Africa the new ideas were usually formulated first in West African newspapers and journals, and then in pamphlets and books. In view of Africa's lag in the technological skills of modern civilization, it is not surprising that this literature should have laid particular stress on Africa's capacity for development, utilizing most of the arguments mentioned above, especially the historical one. Already in 1870 Horton had pleaded for the conscious modernization of Africa by furthering industrial development. Western Europe had obtained its culture from Rome and had taken 1100 years to attain its present cultural level, and the same process could now be repeated in Africa, although in a much shorter span.[122] Like Crummell,[123] Horton emphasized

> the existence of the attribute of a common humanity in the African or negro race: that there exist no radical distinctions between him and his more civilized confrère; that the amount of moral and intellectual endowment exhibited by him, as originally conferred by nature is the same, or nearly so, as that found amongst the European nations, and it is [an] incontrovertible logical maxim that the differences arise from the influences of external circumstances.'[124]

At the same time he warned that Africans

> must remember that no legislative changes could be made without producing some inconveniences, and it is only by these means that they can make great progress in their political history, and an advancement in civilization; that the world would have been stationary through successive generations had no changes taken place; and that the greatness of England is dependent on the gradual and successive changes in her political economy.[125]

One generation later a writer in a Sierra Leone newspaper expressed the hope that Africa might rise to greatness in the future since it had known such greatness in the past at a time when Europe had been backward; in a restrained manner he rejected the doctrine that Africans were destined to remain permanently inferior.

> Believing as we do [he wrote] that notwithstanding our tardiness in the march of Western Civilization, we have a destiny, and may therefore without presumption anticipate for her a bright future analogous with the growth and maturity of peoples and nations under more favourable circumstances. Looking today at the wonderful progress which Great Britain has made in literature, arts and sciences, the description given by Atticus of several fine British youths exposed for sale as slaves in the market place at Rome as stupid, and that it was not advisable to purchase them, seemed almost incredible, though never contradicted. This being the case, our hopes and prospects in future must be very bright indeed. For already there are indications, that there is no normal inferiority in the Negro Race, which should render their elevation to an equality with other Races an impossibility. Africa, no doubt, has an important part to play once more in the world's great drama. That she has played such a part in the past, as the nursery of science and literature, the emporium of commerce and the seat of an empire which contended with Rome for the sovereignty of the world, there is an abundant testimony in history . . . .[126]

In this way the leader writer expressed his confidence that Africa would experience appreciable material progress during the twentieth century.

In the following year a Gold Coast periodical took Horton's argument further. In a survey of Africa's future, prompted by the completion of the first twenty miles of railway on the southern Gold Coast, it was stated that railways would now have to be driven further into the interior of the country in order to open up its riches, such as precious metals, rubber and timber. Like Delany half a century before,[127] the author dreamed of a line running right across Africa from west to east and intersecting a Cape to Cairo railway: 'The future of the once Dark Continent like the future of the United States a hundred years ago, depends upon the opening-up of the the country by roads, railways, and cultivation, and, now such a healthy beginning has been made, progress in the future will be made with accelerated steps.'[128]

The vision of a Cape to Cairo railway and of Kumasi becoming the centre for converging lines in West Africa is to be found in the final passages of Casely Hayford's well-known book.[129] It is a strange mixture of a political educational novel, a description of contemporary society in Sekondi (Gold Coast), a critique of European colonialism (but also of Afro-Americans), and an outline of an African utopia.[130] Among other things the book contains an imaginary history of the Gold Coast's political development written from an unspecified vantage point in the future. Casely Hayford dreams of a national university for the Gold Coast at Kumasi (the Ashanti capital which at that time was still largely isolated from the Gold Coast) attended by students from the USA and the West Indies, British West Africa and Liberia – from the whole area to which Pan-Africanism exerted its appeal. In 1905 the author imagines a Pan-African conference being held in his homeland at the invitation of the APRS.[131] In the context of 'mighty changes' on the Gold Coast he dreams of two periodicals appearing in 1925: the *Gold Coast Nation* (which did indeed appear in 1912) and the *Ethiopian Review*.[132]

The concept of 'race emancipation' also comprises the development of an 'African nationality', a national identity for Africans which would enable them to implement the ideal of equality of rights. For this purpose Hayford hoped to mobilize the Black races throughout the world[133] and to modernize African society while retaining its specifically African peculiarities:

> Knowledge is the common property of mankind, and the philosophy which seeks for the Ethiopian the highest culture and efficiency in industrial and technical training is a sound one. It is well to arouse in favour of the race public opinion as to its capabilities in this direction. . . . Knowledge, deprived of the assimilating element which makes it natural to the one taught, renders that person a bare imitator.[134]

Hayford thus combines the tradition of Horton *and* Blyden.[135]

Hayford was also the first to use another argument: the spectacular victory won by Japan over Russia in 1904–5, which had a galvanizing effect upon Africans and Afro-Americans. By adopting Western technology and forms of organization a 'coloured' nation, until recently still backward, had caught up on Europe's lead so rapidly that she was even in a position to defeat a White great power. The idea of an accelerating process of evolution, which had hitherto been formulated only in the abstract and with reference to antiquity, now received striking proof on the battlefields of Manchuria. African and Afro-American spokesmen on either side of the Atlantic immediately took note of the Japanese model.

Casely Hayford deals in detail with Japan's experience in swiftly and successfully assimilating modern techniques.[136] Seeing the Japanese as members of a 'coloured' race and companions in misfortune, Hayford does not let himself be influenced by the 'yellow peril' slogan.[137] Through the words of his hero Kwamankra, in whom it is not difficult to recognize Hayford himself (who regarded himself as the teacher of the modern African nation), the reader learns that the Japanese, 'those brave fellows', are hostile to the Whites' claim to a world monopoly of wealth and power. The Japanese are brave not only because they resisted the Russians but because they have also promised to give aid to other coloured nations.

Naturally in Hayford one finds the usual historical references, this time in a religious form. At the beginning of the novel the hero Kwamankra, a student in London, has a conversation about religion with Whitely, an English theology student, in which he concedes that his people on the Gold Coast had borrowed the idea of God from the Romans (proof is of course lacking), but is quick to point out that the Romans were originally pagans 'like ourselves', who 'indeed had much to learn from the Ethiopians through the Greeks';[138] this time Hayford skipped the Egyptian link in the historical chain of argument, perhaps on account of the title of his book. Thereupon Kwamankra asks the question whether, if Christ had been of African (Ethiopian) descent, this would have altered the influence he had exerted upon mankind.[139] A little later the author claims proudly that civilization originates from Africa: 'Ours was the cradle of civilization, and that it had not the permanence that the Christian civilization is likely to have does not make it any the less a civilization.'[140]

The influence of Hayford's ideological novel should not be underestimated, if only on account of the symbolic name of Ethiopia in the title and its poetic language. Even in 1963 Quaison-Sackey, then Ghanaian representative at the United Nations, gave his own book a title which owed much to the spirit of Casely Hayford.[141]

Unobtrusive in form is the contribution made by a South African student in the USA to the literary tradition we are discussing: the prize-winning address by P. K. Isaka Seme, delivered on 5 April 1906 at Columbia University in New York. The text was published for the first time in the *Colored American Magazine* and then reprinted in two books analysed here.[142] The style of the short address is, in accordance with the occasion, full of flowery rhetoric and devoid of scientific precision or care in the use of evidence. The historical claim to ancient Egypt ('All the glory of Egypt belongs to Africa and her people') and to Ethiopia leads on to a poetic description of the future resurgence of Africa: 'The giant is awakening! From the four corners of the earth Africa's sons are marching to the future's golden door bearing the record of deeds of valor done.'[143] Controverting the statement by Calhoun, the Southern writer and politician, to the effect that he would be prepared to recognize the negroes as human beings if he were to find one who understood Greek syntax, Seme points to the existence of important men in Europe of African descent, without mentioning their names. In a similar strain he describes the regeneration of Africa at the present day and in the near future, basing his argument upon its new self-awareness, modern school system and desire for industrialization:

> The African already recognizes his anomalous position and desires a change. The brighter day is rising upon Africa. Already I seem to see her chains dissolved, her desert plains with harvest, her Abyssinia and her Zululand the seats of science and religion, reflecting the glory of the rising sun from the spires of their churches and universities. Her Congo and her Gambia whitened [sic] with commerce, her crowded cities sending forth the hum of business, and all her sons employed in advancing the victories of peace – greater and more abiding than the spoils of war. Yes, the regeneration of Africa belongs to this new and powerful period! By this term regeneration I wish to be understood to mean the entrance into a new life, embracing the diverse phases of a higher, complex existence. The basic factor which assures their regeneration resides in the awakened race-consciousness. This gives them a clear perception of their elemental needs and of their undeveloped powers. It therefore must lead them to the attainment of that higher and advanced standard of life.[144]

'The regeneration of Africa', as Seme puts it, 'means that a new and unique civilization is soon to be added to the world.'[145]

This prime example of modern rhetoric derives its importance not from its intellectual substance, which is slight, but from three considerations: Seme was one of the first African students in the USA and thus demonstrates the receptiveness which such persons showed to Afro-American ideas; after returning to South Africa Seme became a leading African nationalist there;[146] finally, half a century later, he was cited in detail in an address by Nkrumah before an international audience.[147]

In the second place mention may be made of Attoh Ahuma, a former Methodist minister.[148] In the *Gold Coast Nation*, a periodical which he edited – the title alone conveys its political purpose – Ahuma attempted to lay the basis for African national feeling on the Gold Coast.[149] In 1912 he modified the doctrine about the transmission of cultural values and gave it a future-oriented twist.

> In the history of European Nations, we have only reached in many respects the threshold of the eleventh century; . . . and if in our Middle Ages our children's children unto the third and fourth generation shall become noble, heroic and vigorous as a race, we must lay the foundation at this epoch. . . . The past, however glorious, ought to be eclipsed, for the Golden Age is before, not behind us.[150]

Ahuma dedicated a whole series of articles to the biography of leading Africans and Afro-Americans, which he later turned into a book.[151] These sketches are in the tradition of Grégoire,[152] but go beyond the latter in several respects. Particular mention may be made of his sketches of persons with whom we are already familiar, Amo, Capitein, Protten (compiled by C. C. Reindorf), the Rev. Thomas Thompson, Philip Quaque, Cugoano and Paul Cuffee.[153]

With his programme of African nationalism Attoh Ahuma already belonged directly to the Pan-African tradition. The same is true of Lapido Solanke, founder of the West African Students' Union (WASU), whose first patron was Casely Hayford.[154] In a pamphlet published on behalf of WASU a number of the points mentioned above are impressively combined in a single passage. He compares the 1000 years it had taken the White race to reach its present level of development with the half-century taken by the Japanese, and suggests that Africa could do the same in a mere quarter-century. There was in his view

> no reason why we West Africans, a Negro race, should not catch up with the Aryans and the Mongols in one quarter of a century. Our education must be so directed that in a few years' time African engineers and mechanics will be able to build and operate in

African soil the necessary railways and other locomotive transport without which we cannot hope to achieve an independent West African Nationality.[155]

J. B. Danquah, the former president of WASU and publisher of the newspaper *WASU* in 1926–7, wrote a laudatory preface to Solanke's pamphlet. On his return to the Gold Coast he himself rose to be one of the young men of promise in Gold Coast political life. In the middle of World War II, which changed the perspectives of historical evolution by making the Soviet Union the second strongest world power, Danquah appealed to Africans to shorten the time-span needed for modernization still further, at least on the Gold Coast. He concluded that the Gold Coast was still undeveloped in 1943, and was not the equal of England, America or Russia. But must this state of affairs continue for ever? 'They did it in Russia in 25 years. There is no reason why we should not do it in the Gold Coast in ten years, for our population and our land are not of the larger proportions of the Socialist Soviet Republic of Russia.'[156] He went on, echoing Horton: 'Let no one make a mistake about it. We are not asking for hand presses and village machines for village industries. We are asking for a fully industrialized economy.'[157] For it would be impossible to have parity if the country remained dependent on the export of raw materials. To foster development it was necessary to borrow foreign capital.[158] An entirely new note was struck when Danquah pointed out as early as 1931 that to secure rapid development 'We must also put up a man; call him dictator or leader or whatever you may; we must have an individual at the head; one who has vision, foresight, action and intelligence – we must have a MAN.'[159]

One of the teachers who had an immediate influence upon the most recent generation of African nationalists and Pan-Africans was Nnamdi Azikiwe, president of Nigeria until 1966. During a period of almost ten years as a student and teacher at American negro colleges and universities (1925–34) he had sufficient time and opportunity to absorb the anti-racist Afro-American tradition. In the next three years, when he was engaged in political journalism on the Gold Coast (1934–7), he became one of the much-admired political teachers of 'awakening Africa'. His incisive articles appeared in book form in 1937[160] and exerted a considerable influence. He demanded as a basis of the African 'national risorgimento' a consciousness of African history: 'Let the

African know that he had a glorious past and that he has a glorious future.'[161]

In his glorification of Ethiopia, Liberia and Haiti Azikiwe followed conventional lines. He postulated the basic equality of all races[162] but later turned to a curious form of social Darwinism: 'All races are endowed equally, each according to its talents. May the fittest survive.'[163] This kind of inverted racism was not only self-contradictory but actually undermined the principle of equality. It echoed the ideas of the White racial theorists about a struggle between the races and stood in contrast to the usual egalitarian humanism. In this respect Azikiwe in his early period must be placed in the tradition of the minority group mentioned above.[164]

Particularly strong was the influence which the young Azikiwe exerted upon Nkrumah, only a few years his junior.[165] As a Pan-African propagandist Nkrumah was the heir to all the traditions outlined here and tried to translate them into political reality while he was in power until his overthrow in 1966.[166] In his writings the historical argument did not play nearly such a big role as it did with earlier writers. The reason for this is readily understandable: after World War II, and after the Asian countries had won their independence, he was able to concentrate fully upon the colonial situation in Africa and to demand independence. The politically dominant groups in the world did not call in question the Africans' rights as human beings or their right to have states of their own. Thus the old argument about the Britons' barbaric state during antiquity is to be found only in Nkrumah's first work written during his 'time of struggle' in London, and more as a distant echo than a firm statement designed to justify African claims to national independence.[167] In his later books, written at the height of his power, we are offered just a sketch of the historical background.[168] Yet this sketch introduces Nkrumah's most detailed plea for the rapid unification of Africa, which once again shows the relevance of all these questions to Pan-Africanism. It also demonstrates that the whole tradition dies out with Nkrumah, for he no longer refers to it explicitly yet utilizes its arguments.

The symbolic lands of Pan-Africanism: Egypt, Liberia, Haiti

Before we conclude this survey of literary attempts by Africans and Afro-Americans to justify the claim to equality by arguments drawn from history, it seems necessary to clarify a few more points which we have already mentioned in passing.

The great importance of ancient Egypt in the standard historical argument needs no further elucidation. It may simply be added that it appears in the works of the earliest Afro-American authors, such as in *David Walker's Appeal* . . . (1829)[169] and in those of Frederick Douglass.[170]

It would be a waste of time to follow this monotonous theme in the literature on the subject in English. In the light of all that has been said about it here it is astonishing that in the 1950s Cheikh Ante Diop, the Senegalese historian, created an immense stir among francophone Africans when he stated that pharaonic Egypt was really an achievement of Africans.[171] Apparently none of the reviewers pointed out that Diop's spectacular 'discovery' had for a long time been an almost outworn literary tradition among Afro-Americans and Africans. The fact that in French-speaking Africa such a hoary doctrine could cause a sensation, despite all the earlier literature in English, shows once again how isolated the two areas were from each other, and that one is justified in attaching only a subordinate importance to the contribution of French-speaking individuals to the development of Pan-Africanism.

On the other hand it seems necessary to add a few remarks about Liberia, for the very reason that it is constantly invoked as proof that the Africans are capable of self-government.[172] In fact Liberia's role is a most ambivalent one. Positive and negative assessments are roughly balanced, although it may be observed that the most important twentieth-century Pan-Africans were also the most enthusiastic advocates of Liberia. By contrast Afro-American authors, writing primarily for a domestic public, are in general more critical in their attitude towards Liberia.

This difference is easy to explain historically. The final phase of the abolitionist movement and the beginning of articulate politics among Afro-Americans owed their origin in part to the campaign of resistance put up by the free coloureds against the Liberian settlement scheme. In this way there developed an entire literary and political tradition among the Afro-Americans, who rejected Liberia on principle because its foundation was too openly linked with the interests of the southern slave-holders.[173] At a later stage Afro-Americans who knew Liberia from their own experience held it against the Libero-Americans that they had established themselves as a ruling class over the native

African tribes, whom they exploited ruthlessly by corrupt practices and a system of forced labour akin to slavery. Delany had already passed a devastating judgement on the 'so-called Republic of Liberia'. He was in particular perturbed by the fact that Liberia was born out of the plan of 'the slave-holders in our country to remove the free coloured people from the American continent'.[174] 'Liberia', he added, 'is not an Independent Republic, in fact it is not an independent nation at all; but a poor miserable mockery – a burlesque on a government, a pitiful dependency of the American Colonizationists . . . Liberia in Africa, is a mere dependency of Southern slave-holders . . . and unworthy of any respectful consideration from us.'[175]

It may be argued against Delany's judgement that it stemmed from the fact that Liberia was an established concern which competed with his own settlement scheme, for which he was still trying to win Afro-American support. But this argument does not apply to McCants Stewart, an author who, writing one generation later, described Liberia on the basis of lengthier observation.[176] For all his criticism he was not basically hostile towards Liberia. He conceded that it had exercised a certain useful function and in future could serve as a starting-point of a great Afro-American Republic stretching to the Congo, whereby Africa could be civilized under a stable government ruling in the Africans' own interests. 'Under a mighty African ruler there will arise a stable and powerful Government of Africans, for Africans, and by Africans, which shall be an inestimable blessing to all mankind.'[177] But his chapter on the Libero-Americans contains the most detailed critique of the social order set up by the immigrants – most of them hastily emancipated slaves, frequently without any education or special talents (from where could they have obtained them?), who wanted to lead in their new environment the kind of life that had been led by their former masters in the southern states. The motto of the republic, 'the love of liberty brought us here', Stewart suggests ironically, ought really to read 'To be free from labor we came here.'[178] The quasi-aristocratic ideals upheld in the South had been carried over to a poor society lacking the appropriate material basis, which had resulted in a caricature of the new state and its ideals. In general the author notes that until the war against the native tribes in 1875

the relations between the native and the Negro emigrant from America has been that of master and slave. The former American slave treated the African freeman as if he had no rights which were worthy of respect! . . . The natives of Liberia have been to the emigrants from America just what these ex-slaves were to the whites of the South. They have been defrauded, beaten with stripes, and made to feel that they were inferior beings.[179]

In 1930 world opinion, especially among Afro-Americans, was aroused by the news that in Liberia there existed a state of affairs virtually akin to slavery, and that the Liberian government sold or hired out native labour to the administration of the Spanish colony of Fernando Po. A League of Nations commission confirmed that the charges were substantially true, which provided new ammunition for Liberia's critics. At this time the Liberians were reproached by one Afro-American author for having failed to make use of their chance to develop into the most progressive and most modern state in Africa. Instead they had done 'practically nothing: without wanting to work themselves they had enslaved their own people and had not tried to civilize those of their own race in the interior of the country'.[180]

In 1947 an even more severe condemnation was pronounced by Leslie Buell, a (White) American author, in his centennial study of the foundation of Liberia. He set his criticism of the country within a broad historical framework, in which the principal ideas fall within our field of interest:

> Many of the problems of mankind have been due to the pressure of a higher a lower culture. Evil as it was, the institution of Negro slavery brought the transplanted African into intimate touch with a higher level of civilization. As the result, the American Negro today is centuries ahead of the African proper and the American Negro has much to offer to Africa, particularly Liberia, in return . . . . This interplay of culture, perhaps more than the negative concept of freedom, brings about the development of peoples.[181]

Buell pointed out that Liberia and Haiti were the only negro republics. Liberia's 'chief achievement has been survival'. The prevailing 12,000-strong 'oligarchy' did not possess the necessary vitality to develop the country materially. 'Liberia remains a sick country, perhaps the sickest part in Africa. Unless this sickness is soon cured, racial chauvinists will say, if unjustly, that the Negro anywhere is incapable of self-government.'[182]

Liberia's main mistake, according to Buell, is that it is not a democracy, even though its constitution is modelled on that of the USA. The oligarchy, 12,000 strong, rules imperturbably over a population of more than one million. The Liberian government had been deeply involved in the slave scandal of 1930, holds on to power by electoral fraud, and is 'incapable, arbitrary and corrupt'. The government is 'simply the cancer on the body of that unfortunate nation', writes Buell, quoting from another source.[183] He also cites approvingly the harsh words in the Chicago *Defender*, a Black periodical, of 5 June 1943, that President Barclay's twenty-eight-word speech to the United States Senate would long be remembered for its 'painful stupidity'.[184]

Opposed to this negative tradition is one of favourable comment by authors most of whom had either spent a long time in the country (Crummell), had become Liberian citizens from conviction (Blyden), or else regarded the Republic of Liberia, which was at least formally independent, as a welcome oasis in the desert of colonialism, a stepping-stone towards the coming liberation of Africa.

Alexander Crummell, one of the most impressive Afro-American figures of the nineteenth century, never lost his balance vis-à-vis Liberia. Although he gave a positive appreciation of its function, he remained cool and had 'nothing extravagant to say about Liberia'.[185] For him it was a young country which amidst great hardships and by dint of great efforts had laid sound foundations for the future. True, in another passage he criticized violently the way Liberia had neglected its civilizing mission,[186] but thirty years later he maintained his cautious optimism, stating that Liberia was not a failure but still had to contend with difficult problems.[187]

Also basically positive was the attitude taken towards Liberia by William W. Brown.[188] Blyden's commitment to Liberia, the homeland of his choice, is so self-explanatory and well-known that a brief reference to it will suffice here. Blyden appreciated Liberia's place in the modernization of Africa, for which the prerequisite was what he called 'nationality' – the claim to a national state of one's own. The slave trade, he wrote, had brought the Africans in America in contact with Christianity and some ex-slaves were now returning to their real 'fatherland' 'as though in fulfilment of a divine plan', charged with 'the blessings of Christianity and civilization'. Liberia's function was that of a base for the spread of Christianity and modern civilization. Blyden hoped that Liberia would become the model of a modern African

national state, an African power.[189] This conception gave him the
strength to call indefatigably upon sceptical Afro-Americans to emigrate to Liberia, at times not sparing his readers harsh words and
rebuking them for their lack of solidarity with Africa.[190]

During the twentieth century Liberia's advocates wholly abandoned
Crummell's relative restraint. George W. Ellis, a coloured man who
had previously served as secretary in the United States embassy in
Monrovia, wrote an intellectually unpretentious article, inferior to
Blyden's work and influenced by the tendency among diplomats to
idealize the country where they are stationed for any length of time.
This article is an uncritical eulogy of Liberia and its ideals, which
allegedly evoked 'the admiration of the Negro peoples in every section
of the civilized globe'.[191]

Of greater significance is the case of Du Bois.[192] He too praised
Liberia quite uncritically. He even went so far as to defend Liberia's
conduct in the 1930 slavery scandal,[193] although the weakness of the
Liberian government's case must have been evident to one who otherwise had such acute powers of analysis. His antagonist, Garvey, shared
his love of Liberia – as a stepping-stone towards the liberation of
Africa. He nominated the mayor of Monrovia as 'potentate for Africa',
on paper the highest dignity provided for in his scheme of organization.
But his enthusiasm for Liberia lasted only so long as that country seemed
willing to promote his plans. It gave way to boundless hatred when the
Liberian government, under the pressure of the colonial powers and out
of fear of Garvey's dynamism, withdrew the support that it had already
promised him.[194]

As followers of Du Bois the two most radical Pan-Africans in the next
generation, Padmore and Azikiwe, became sentimental and almost
blind advocates of Liberia. In his last and most influential book Padmore
devoted two chapters to the history of Liberia which were completely
uncritical and almost amounted to eyewash.[195] Azikiwe became famous
through his first book, which he wrote while he was still in the USA, during the agitation about the slave trade in Liberia.[196] This, too, was an almost unrestrained defence of the country against all slurs and criticisms.

Since 1958 the régimes of President Tubman, and his successor
President Tolbert, having swung round to a more liberal course, have
helped to promote the Pan-African cause, although not actively.

Haiti, too, with its successful slave revolt in 1791 and its winning of
independence in 1804, had a special symbolic character, along with

ancient Egypt and Liberia, for the protagonists of Pan-Africanism and racial equality. Toussaint l'Ouverture, the great central figure, and his followers have been called 'Black Jacobins' by C. L. R. James, the West Indian historian, whose views strike a somewhat ideological note.[197] In several works one finds expressions of admiration for Haiti and of veneration for Toussaint l'Ouverture; sometimes these attain an almost hymnodic pitch of ecstasy, as in 'Thou immortal Toussaint! Statesman, General, Ruler!'[198] In most cases the elevation of Haiti to the role of an ideological symbol relates to the years of struggle for national independence, whereas the subsequent century and a half of stagnation and political anarchy are understandably passed over. Only here and there does a writer refer to these facts which, if one interprets them correctly, by no means refute the doctrine that all races are equal in their capacities or potential for achievement. In this context Ferris deserves a special mention. 'Although Hayti has been nominally a Republic since 1804', he wrote, 'the rule of the majority has not been the predominating factor in Haytian history. . . . In a word, Hayti has been a republic in name only. . . . Still this does not demonstrate the inherent and innate capacity [this should probably read 'incapacity'] of the Negro race for self-government.' He went on to say that, whereas England had enjoyed independence for 2000 years and the USA had had one and a half centuries of autonomy before the revolution, 'Hayti, at the beginning of the nineteenth century, leaped at a bound from chattel slavery and barbarism to a self-governing republic. The mystery is not her revolution and counter-revolutions, but that Hayti has done as well as she has.'[199]

The mere existence of Haiti as an independent state was enough to convince Pan-African writers that Black men were capable of self-government – even though Haiti had long since sunk into a labyrinth of intrigue, corruption and permanent tension between the minority of the French-trained mulattoes and the large Black majority, who retained more affinity with African forms of life; this tension resulted in periodic pronunciamentos, revolutions and civil wars.[200]

That Haiti's sentimental symbolic value remained intact is shown by leading Afro-Americans' reaction to the American occupation of Haiti in 1915 and in the references to Haiti in Pan-African Congresses.[201]

Anténor Firmin

It is nevertheless astonishing that the chaos in Haiti should have produced the most mature refutation of European racial theories. It came from the pen of an author who nowadays has virtually fallen into oblivion except among a few intellectuals in his own country. After Toussaint l'Ouverture Anténor Firmin was the most significant personality in Haiti – 'la belle figure d'Anténor Firmin', as a later admirer called him somewhat rhetorically.[202] As a sociologist, diplomat and statesman Firmin occupied, during the two decades around the turn of the century, an honourable although not totally felicitous position in the politics of his country. For a time he was minister of foreign affairs and in 1891 negotiated with Frederick Douglass, then US ambassador to Haiti, about ceding to the USA the Mole of Saint Nicolas, where Columbus had landed. He skilfully managed to stave off claims which, had they been granted, would have delivered Haiti to American power already at that date.[203] For Firmin the establishment of a reasonable and stable order in Haiti was not just an end in itself but was 'to serve the rehabilitation of Africa' because, as he saw clearly, the charge of racial inferiority against the Africans also affected the inhabitants of Haiti. 'Haiti in particular must set the example. Have the coloured people of Haiti not provided already proof of finest intelligence and resplendent energy?' inquired Firmin somewhat optimistically.[204]

Firmin's achievement and his significance in our context rest upon his lengthy controversy with Gobineau, disclosed already in the title of his work: *L'Egalité des Races Humaines*,[205] the opposite of the French count's *Inegalité des Races Humaines*. He deals in detail with the role of ancient Egypt and the African sources, with 'the role the black race played in the history of civilization', in the course of which he also stresses the significance of Ethiopia and Haiti.[206] Up to this point Firmin has said nothing that had not been said before in the literature in English; nor is there anything new in his argument that the Black race was capable of developing an advanced culture, as it had done in bygone days.

In his conclusions, however, Firmin rises above mere apologetics on behalf of his hard-pressed race and inquires into the general implications of his doctrine about the equality of races. This section is introduced by the sub-chapter 'The Theories and their Logical Consequences'.[207] According to Firmin racial equality entails in principle the equality of all men and the dissolution of all class differences. 'Total democracy', as we might say today, would be its consequence.[208] If the doctrine of equality is the mighty weapon of democracy, then likewise the doctrine of racial inequality is a weapon in the hands of all those who aspire to a hierarchical order of society, contrary to the spirit of modern times. Firmin first made this point in the form of a rhetorical question,[209] but this was followed by clear and unmistakable references to the racists' ideas as 'the best proof of a mental aberration'.[210] To avoid any misunderstanding he comments on Gobineau's doctrine to the effect that there were two periods in human history, the second of which points 'the undeniable way to perdition',[211] by putting the annihilating question: 'Is this not the sign of a sick mind?'[212]

'All men are brothers. These are golden words.'[213] This formulation expresses the influence of German idealism[214] (in this case of Schiller) and also a basically humanist attitude towards history and politics.[215] Firmin is however no visionary. He, too, knows that there are differences within mankind but he condemns the animal, biological and non-human explanation given by racial theorists. Instead he offers rational explanations: the different level of social development determines the moral and intellectual differences between the advanced and backward elements of mankind, between civilized and barbaric societies.[216] For this reason Firmin rejects the concept of 'race' because of the 'fatalité biologique et naturelle' implicit in it, and all the more so the notion of 'superior' and 'inferior' races.[217]

This explanation of the differences between human groups with diverse patterns of social development implies a sense of the dynamic at work in history. Firmin had previously shown this in his traditional references to the bygone greatness of ancient Egypt and Ethiopia. Reverting here to the dimension of historical change, he combines it with a warning to the racial theorists: 'The world does not remain static.' Peoples and races come and go on the stage of world history, playing different roles.[218] For this reason Firmin believes in a great future for the Black race once it has taken up again, for the well-being of mankind, the torch it had borne on the banks of the Nile to enlighten the ancient world.[219] The Black race need not be discouraged by the cultural level attained by the Whites, since mankind is just at the beginning of a much greater evolution. In the course of this evolution the Black race will quickly overcome the time-lag and make its contribution, indeed play a leading role.[220] Firmin's conception is not based on an easy belief in historical determinism but implies a call to political and practical action: it is a matter of proving by deeds the belief in the equality of all races, and so bringing this aim to fulfilment.[221] In a world dominated by colonialism the ideology and the political movement which could accomplish this goal were to be provided by Pan-Africanism.

8 Ethiopianism and the independent African churches

The symbolic value of Ethiopia

Ethiopia occupied an even more important position than did ancient Egypt, Liberia and Haiti in Pan-African and proto-Pan-African concepts. The concept of 'Ethiopia' has several elements which have to be distinguished carefully. In the first place Ethiopia was synonymous with Africa, chiefly in earlier literature: witness Cugoano.[1] In a rather different way this term is employed in the entirely mystical *Ethiopian Manifesto* (1829) by Robert Alexander Young, a free Afro-American from New York. He generally uses the term 'Ethiopian', but in one passage speaks expressly of 'black African people'.[2] Apparently Young regarded only the Black, negroid African as identical with 'Ethiopian'. His linguistic usage is thus roughly in accord with that of Pennington[3] who gives evidence, although very vaguely, of a Pan-African dimension to his thought, since he envisages Africa (or at least considerable parts of Africa) as a unit.

In the second place Ethiopia denoted the actual state of Ethiopia (Abyssinia) which, however, was often used as a substitute for Africa. A distinction may be made between the symbolic value of ancient

Ethiopia (Kush) in historicizing arguments and that of modern Ethiopia, approximately since the battle of Adowa (1896). The use of ancient Ethiopia as a symbol for the demand for equality has been discussed in the preceding chapter, but this material may be recapitulated here from a systematic point of view, and some points added.

Writers like Easton and Pennington often referred to the greatness of ancient Ethiopia in the same breath as to ancient Egypt.[4] Garnet, a theologian with academic training who may have been the first to quote psalm 68: xxxii ('Ethiopia shall soon stretch forth her hand unto God'), was apparently also the first to refer to the passage in Homer where the Greek gods came to the Ethiopians to hold a banquet[5] – a turn of phrase which was later to become a *topos* in the literature on the subject.[6] Lewis dedicated an entire chapter to 'Ancient Cities and Kingdoms of Ethiopia'.[7] W. W. Brown referred to ancient Ethiopia[8] and contemporary Abyssinia.[9] Seme pointed to the massive pyramids of the ancient Egyptians and the smaller ones of the Ethiopians as proof that the Africans possessed creative capabilities;[10] Ferris and Du Bois did likewise.[11] Casely Hayford's *Ethiopia Unbound* derives much of its impact from its 'Ethiopian' pathos.[12] Here 'Ethiopian' is once again a synonym for 'African':[13] on one occasion with conscious political intention, when on Empire Day Hayford makes his hero dream about a future 'Free Ethiopian Empire',[14] just as half a century before in the USA the Haytian Emigration Society had spoken of an Ethiopian Empire (with Haiti as its corner-stone).[15]

Closely intertwined with the symbolic ideological and political value of Ethiopia is the religious one, as expressed in psalm 68: xxxii. This verse was quoted in the literature, sometimes quite directly;[16] it formed the stuff of sermons[17] and was cited in lectures and festive addresses.[18] Psalm 68: xxxii was usually quoted in the shortened version 'Ethiopia shall soon stretch out her hands unto God', omitting the previous reference to Egypt ('Princes shall come out of Egypt'). A modern German translation directly from the Hebrew varies considerably from the translation by Luther or from the King James version in what is said about Egypt, but only insignificantly in what is said about Ethiopia (in Luther: 'land of the Moors'):

Let bronze implements be brought from Egypt,
May Kush raise its hands to Yahwe!

instead of:

> Princes shall come out of Egypt
> Ethiopia shall soon stretch out her hands unto God.[19]

This passage was regarded as a biblical prophecy that Africa would be redeemed. An interpretation of this kind may seem to us today to be arbitrary and taken out of context, especially since the meaning is obscure. But this interpretation is not simply explicable in terms of the historical situation of Afro-Americans and Africans, who held fast to any ray of light, especially in the Bible. It is also confirmed by modern Protestant theology. The psalm was a triumphal song of David, probably with later insertions, which referred to Israel's political situation between the great powers of Assyria and Egypt. At least one authoritative commentator regards it as an 'eschatological hymn',[20] which would permit an interpretation valid for all time. As Kraus says, 'the Old Testament prophets also expect Kush to become a worshipper of Yahwe.'[21] The interpretation of this verse by Christian Afro-Americans and Africans thus appears understandable, especially if one considers the great role Christian missionaries and churches played in the modernization of Africa and the Afro-Americans.[22]

The origins of the AME mission in the nineteenth century

Around 1900 an ecclesiastical emancipation movement, termed 'Ethiopianism', got under way in Africa, in partial liaison with Afro-American churches in the USA and based upon psalm 68: XXXII. Religious pathos reinforced the claim to political equality; for this reason Ethiopianism and the independent African churches form part of the historical background of Pan-Africanism and also comprise part of its very substance. Ethiopianism fulfilled in African society a function analogous to that of the independent negro churches in the USA – the Baptists and more especially the African Methodist Episcopal Zion (AMEZ) church. They had initially kindled the movement for political emancipation among Afro-Americans in the USA,[23] and with their missionary work they contributed directly to the development of Ethiopianism in Africa, the influence of which was later to rebound upon Afro-Americans in the form of Garveyism.

The earlier group was the AME, which had its origin and centre in Philadelphia and was always stronger in numbers. Between 1816 and 1916 its membership grew from 400 to approximately 650,000, with 6400 local preachers, 6650 clergy and 16 bishops.[24] After the American Civil War the two churches were able to spread in the southern states and it was then that most of the negro colleges and universities were formed as the product of the drive for educational progress among Afro-Americans.[25] In 1856, after long-drawn-out preparations, the AME church had opened the Wilberforce University in Ohio;[26] it was here that W. E. B. Du Bois lectured in 1896. For the AMEZ church the educational centre was (and still is) Livingstone College at Salisbury, NC; this is primarily a theological seminary training clergy for the AMEZ, but is also engaged in important missionary work in Africa.

Although the differences between the AME and AMEZ were slight, both in externals and in theological doctrine, they were always rivals; as the smaller group, the AMEZ resisted the AME's alleged desire to dominate, and engaged in bitter polemics against it.[27] Particularly violent was the conflict over the question of historical priority, although this was clearly a matter of personal vanity and power struggles.[28] Attempts to fuse the two groups were made on several occasions, in 1846, 1864, 1868, 1886, 1892, 1918 and 1922, but without success.[29]

Despite their rivalry we may regard the two groups as a single unit so far as their missionary work in Africa is concerned. Their missionary centres, the development of which often depended on chance factors, complemented one another. The AME had relatively strong missionary churches in Liberia, and from the end of the nineteenth century also in South Africa; the AMEZ, by contrast, concentrated on the Gold Coast. The competition between the two churches had the result that the AMEZ, as the younger body, emulated the AME in the missionary field as well. The first steps in this field were spontaneous and un-organized, but later the two groups tried to institutionalize and system-atize their missionary work. In 1844 the AME set up a Home and Foreign Missionary Department which, however, did not really begin to function until 1864; after 1892 it published its own periodical, *Voice of Missions*. The AMEZ church followed in 1880 with its Foreign Missionary Board,[30] and in 1900 began to produce a missionary paper called the *Missionary Seer*. By comparison with the great European missionary societies the extent of this missionary activity was slight and the amount of money spent minimal, since both denominations were themselves small and poor. Their historical significance lies above all in their appeal to their 'racial brethren' in Africa and the West Indies.

The attitude to Africa of the two Afro-American Methodist churches reflects the same ambivalence as that of Afro-Americans generally, for they participated to a great extent in stimulating the Afro-Americans' political consciousness. Moreover, the leadership of the churches was dominated by the light-skinned mulatto element[31] whereas the ordinary members were probably mostly dark-skinned. The word 'African' in the title of both denominations does not, however, connote any ideological commitment to Africa. On the contrary it goes back to the end of the eighteenth century when 'African' was still a non-discriminatory term, free of any value judgements, used to denote Afro-Americans by contrast with the pejorative word 'negro' which was virtually equivalent to 'slave'. The titles of the Free African Society and the St Thomas African church, dating from the years 1787 and 1794 respectively, are evidence of that early linguistic usage. In 1816, when the African Methodist Episcopal church was founded, the situation had not yet changed to such an extent that it would have seemed necessary to drop the name 'African' which had by then become traditional. But at the end of that year the appearance of the American Colonization Society with its settlement schemes changed the situation completely; 'African' was now felt to be a discriminatory term, because it identified Afro-Americans by their African descent. The African Methodist Episcopal Zion church, set up in 1821, still adhered to the word 'African', possibly out of an urge to compete with the AME.

The National Negro Convention movement, which originally stemmed from or at least was promoted by AME groups, rejected the term 'African' because of the deportation to Liberia which they feared. This explanation seems to have been given for the first time at the Convention of 1833 in Philadelphia in an address by the chairman of the meeting.[32] At the fifth convention in Philadelphia (1835) negroes were even recommended in a resolution to abandon so far as possible the use of the word 'coloured' in the designations of their groups; 'and especially to remove the title of African from their institutions, the marbles of churches, etc.'[33] Most church members, however, adhered to the traditional name 'African'. One must be careful not to read into this process too much ideology of one kind or another. Neither should one speak of 'anti-African feelings' at the Convention of

1835[34] nor interpret the retention of the name 'African' as a sign of commitment to Africa, least of all in a Pan-African sense. Failing the appearance of fresh evidence to the contrary, caution is indicated: the presumption is that those who wanted to eliminate the word 'African' from the names of Afro-American organizations acted out of an understandable self-interest, whereas the majority may have kept to this term purely out of traditionalism – although it cannot be ruled out that they may have felt stronger sentimental ties to Africa.[35]

Later the AME church's existence was 'ideologized', as it were. Thus Bishop Daniel A. Payne, the official historian of the church, could say of it in the late nineteenth century:

> To aid in making the Haytian nationality and government strong, powerful and commanding among the civilized nations of the earth ought to be the desire and the aim of the AME Church. As the Haytians have completely thrown off the white man's yoke in their national affairs, so have the leaders and members of the AME Church in ecclesiastical affairs. As the Haytians have been endeavouring to demonstrate the ability of the Negro for self-government during a period of 84 years, so also have the leaders of the AME Church been endeavoring to demonstrate the ability of the Negro for self-government during a period of over 72 years.[36]

Fifty years later another official writer, already invoking the pathos of the nascent modern civic rights movement, could assert

> The African Methodist Episcopal Church has led the fight for social justice, equal opportunity and fair play for black folks for more than 150 years. Its very existence is a protest against proscription, discrimination and jim-crowism.[37]

Similarly a semi-official publication of the AME church claimed that it was especially predestined to conduct missionary work in Africa. Its battle-cry was 'Africa must be saved, for "Ethiopia shall soon stretch forth her hand unto God!" ',[38] but in reality the emotional solidarity with Africa was only superficial. We cannot accept at face value such programmatic statements which outwardly seem to fit into a Pan-African context. The situation was more complex than one might think from the combination of the slogans: 'Africa for the Africans', 'Ethiopia shall soon stretch forth her hand unto God', etc. and the common antagonism on both sides of the Atlantic against White domination. On the contrary, precisely the AME mission's inroads in South Africa in about 1900 show how dubious the official missionary ideology of the AME was. The relationship between the AME mother church and its South African mission forms part of the general problem of the relations between Afro-Americans and native Africans in the old continent.[39]

The Afro-American churches did not exist in a social vacuum. Around 1900 the AME church at least was not unaffected by the prevailing spirit of imperialism. True, some Afro-American periodicals and intellectuals protested against the Spanish-American War, and Bishop Turner came out against negro units being used in the expedition against Peking in 1900.[40] But these were minority voices. Ten years earlier the great Frederick Douglass had expressed unconditional support for an imperialist policy by the USA: 'While slavery existed I was opposed to all schemes for the extension of American power and influence. But since its abolition I have gone with him who goes farthest for such extension.'[41] In the missionary field the AME shared in its own way the new pro-imperialist mood. George Shepperson has pointed out that Bishop Turner represented the idea that it was the 'manifest destiny' of coloured Americans to redeem their unhappy African brethren.[42] He did not see the dialectic inherent in his statement, for in American history the slogan 'manifest destiny' had an expressly expansionist, indeed imperialist, character.

The beginning of the new century prompted those responsible for the strategy of the AME church to make some far-reaching observations. In its official missionary journal the Rev. G. G. Daniels appealed for each member to give his minister a dollar for the African mission:

> The best gifts we can bring to the new century are those of hearts dedicated to the Master's cause. The mandate of an imperial policy has gone forth from this great American nation. This is now according to the laws of the Medes and Persians, which cannot be altered. As a Church we have an imperial policy. We must stand by it. . . . We have sent out three bishops, with the authority to capture every son of Africa in the vast domains of Africa, Cuba, Hayti and San Domingo, Porto Rico, the Windward and Leeward West Indies and British Guiana, Canada, Nova Scotia, Bermuda and the far-off Philippines.[43]

Still more belligerent was the tone of an unsigned article in the same issue entitled 'The Twentieth Century':

The African Methodist Episcopal Church, after the march of a hundred years against the cruelties of slavery in America, superstition, vice, ignorance and hell-born caste, is called upon in stentorian voice by millions of her brethren in the Caribbean Archipelago and the land of oil, palm and mahogany, the land of ancestors, to march to the music of a world-wide evangelization that will lift from the vision of 300 millions of her ancestors the hoodwink of superstition and idolatry and enable them to see the light and glory of a crucified Saviour and move in the phalanx of the world's greatest and most useful citizens. . . . The world must be brought to Christ. Cowards and sycophants must bite the dust. Intelligence, sanctified with Christianity, must rule the world. . . . The negro must take his place as a man, like all other men, in the grand march of civilization, asking no quarter and giving none.

The negro should evangelize Africa because for obvious reasons he was better suited for the task than any other category of missionary. Mention is made of 'Christian warfare' in which there could be no neutrality, and the call goes out: 'Let the 13 living Bishops [of the AME church] send the order down their columns that the AME Church shall begin the greatest campaign of missionary endeavor in the islands of the sea, all our newly acquired territory and Africa, the world ever knew. . . .'44

In the following issue Afro-American missionary chauvinism was even more strident. The Rev. A. Henry Attaway from Cape Town, writing on the role of the negro in modern world civilization, extolled America's greatness and power, continuing:

This magnificent heritage has come to this great nation because God knows they can be trusted. We are His most favored steward. Thus far, thank God, we have proven true to our trust. Our millionaires sink their fortunes in the heads and hearts of future generations, our powerful military and naval arms are breaking the shackles of the oppressed and carrying the munificent blessings of our civilization to the lowly and oppressed. Our soldiers in blue and gray, in black and white, are foregoing the pleasures of luxury, imperilling life and limb, in rescuing humanity from barbarism . . . The millions of Africans must be saved. We must save them. This is no empty boast: We will save them . . . England has gone to Africa to stay, Germany, France and Portugal

etc. have done likewise. The natives must be civilized and christianized. We must do this. The Negro will do his part. Then ten
millions of Afro-Americans must form the nucleus of this mighty
force.
1. Because he is a favored integral part of the most powerful
   nation on earth.
2. Because it is his 'shibboleth' at the bar of civilization and his
   'sesame' at the door of eternal life. . . .
The Afro-American is today the best religious material on earth.[45]

This effusion, with its curious mixture of the most varied elements,
gives an instructive and almost intoxicating glorification of coloured
missionary imperialism in Africa.

With such attitudes as that displayed by the AME missionary Attaway in Cape Town, the leaders of Ethiopianism must have doubted
the genuineness of the AME church's claim to be working for the
Africans in an altruistic spirit. Correspondingly no Pan-African elements can be detected in the AME church's first missionary attempts
during the early nineteenth century. In what was to become Liberia,
where the AME mission was active under the Rev. Daniel Coker in
1821, it apparently only wanted to monopolize all missionary opportunities for itself.[46] In 1823 Coker went to Sierra Leone, where he is
said to have built a huge church in Freetown, but it did not develop
into a dependency of the AME in Sierra Leone.[47]

A similar fate met the first missionary attempt in Haiti, which began
in 1827. Among the two thousand-odd immigrants in 1824–5 were
several members of the AME,[48] who asked Bishop Allen to help them
to build up their own church in Haiti; in 1830 a similar letter came from
San Domingo, the neighbouring republic on the same island.[49] The
mother church did indeed send as missionary to Haiti Scipio Beanes,
who organized several AME parishes, but without trained ministers
this initiative could not prosper. Further letters asking for help did not
gain any hearing in the USA until 1879, when the AME mission in
Haiti was resumed.[50] Towards the end of the century the arguments
used on behalf of the Haiti mission had a similar ideological complexion
as those which made Haiti a symbol for the claim to racial equality.[51]
It was the duty of the AME 'to concentrate her energies upon that spot
till its two-fold republic [Haiti and San Domingo] shall have attained a
strong Christian character, and by the very force of that character shall

be able to leap upon a commanding position among the civilized nations of the earth'.[52] One does not find here the broader Pan-African perspectives which had already appeared with the second wave of immigrants in 1860–61 or in the case of Firmin.[53] Nevertheless Bishop Holly from Haiti, a descendant of the Haiti propagandists of 1854–6,[54] had a share in the preliminaries of the Pan-African Conference of 1900.[55]

In the rest of the West Indies the AME mission was of no significance. In the Bermudas and in British Guiana it did not begin until 1870–73, in San Domingo until 1874, in the Virgin Islands (after the unsuccessful attempt in 1878) as late as 1921, in Cuba in 1898, in Barbados in 1893 and in Jamaica in 1915.[56] In each case only small groups were involved which exercised little influence.

Somewhat more important were the results in West Africa – Liberia, the Gold Coast and Sierra Leone – but even here these were still only modest in scope by 1942.[57] The prehistory of the AME church in Sierra Leone is curious, for it is another example of the Pan-African triangular relationship; discounting the problematical prelude connected with Daniel Coker[58] it goes back to the sect of Lady Huntingdon. Its members came from Nova Scotia in 1792 and, more or less ignored by the mother sect in England, gained a certain importance in and around Freetown. In 1887, after a split, the larger group joined the AME which sent Dr J. R. Frederick, an Afro-Caribbean minister, to the orphaned main community of Zion in Freetown.[59]

The beginnings of Ethiopianism in South Africa and the AME mission

Up to 1891 the AME mission largely identified Africa with Liberia,[60] but after this the centre of its activity shifted to South Africa. Here within a short time it became the largest affiliated church outside the USA. However, it also faced the hopelessly complex situation produced by the beginnings of apartheid and industrialization, for just as the South African tribes were artificially split up by the ruling White minority, so also the Black Protestants were segmented into a confusing array of small churches and sects, some of them quite tiny.

Already in the 1870s isolated groups of Africans in South Africa had begun to found their own religious communities as a reaction to the growing racism among the Whites in the two Boer republics, the

Transvaal and the Orange Free State. In 1884 a Methodist minister, Nehemiah Tile of the Tembu tribe, broke with the mission and founded a separate tribal Methodist church.[61] This development was accelerated by the ruling of 1886 which for the first time obliged White and coloured ministers to hold their district meetings separately, and the coloured people to have a White chairman and secretary. In rebellion against such discrimination and White domination another Methodist minister, Mangena M. Mokone, abandoned the mission on 1 November 1892 and founded in the same month the 'Ethiopian Church' which at the start had fifty members in the Rand region, the industrial area near Johannesburg where goldmining was just getting under way. It was from this church that the Ethiopian movement took its name. Like the Afro-American independent churches, it was directed against White domination. As L. L. Berry puts it,

> The South African resents the position of subjugation to which he has been relegated by the ruling classes. He registers his protest by a tendency to withdraw from traditional denominations supervised by White Americans and Europeans, and from Separatist churches. . . . By establishing these sects the inhibited native finds an outlet for his self-expression and pent-up emotions. He is forced to resort to an escape mechanism for release of suppressed mental and emotional desires. In the separate churches the African is in absolute control and the white excluded.[62]

The Afro-American churches and most of the larger African ones were quite orthodox in their theology, if only to demonstrate their earnestness to the suspicious White churches; the more respectable they sought to be in the eyes of society, the more orthodox they were.[63] In most African churches, however, one may detect an intermingling of traditional African elements, which often led to a breach with the European missionary churches. In the case of some African sects and small churches the process of Africanization went so far as to represent God and Christ as Black – something which half a century earlier had only been hinted at ironically by coloured critics of the independent negro churches in the USA in order to discredit them.[64]

It was a general tendency for the independent churches to split up into a number of sects and tiny groups. A significant role was played by local prophets of ephemeral fame, some of whom founded new sects.

Their sermons and mass baptisms often prepared the way for systematic work by European missionary societies; this was the case with William W. Harris, who preached on the Ivory Coast and Gold Coast in 1914–15. On the other hand just after the First World War the appearance of Simon Kimbangu in the Belgian Congo led to the formation of 'Kimbanguism', a religious movement with a co-operative and pacifist slant, which is spreading in Central Africa today.[65] The sects and religious movements for their part contributed to the politicization of their followers, most of whom were illiterate. Together with their leaders, usually autodidacts or graduates of missionary schools, they formed the mass basis for African nationalism, and at times also a sounding-board for Garvey's ideas.[66]

The leaders of the nascent Ethiopian movement soon came into contact with the AME church, and its journal, the *Voice of Missions*, which appeared in the same year, appealed to them. In 1896 a conference of all independent churches in Pretoria resolved to apply for admission to the AME. In the same year James M. Dwane, likewise a former Methodist minister, was sent to the USA to put through the affiliation. The AME absorbed the Ethiopian church and so gained at one stroke an expanding establishment which already had 59 ministers, 14 parishes and 2800 members, and which almost fifty years later had increased to 400 ministers and 53,000 members.[67]

In the USA Dwane was appointed general superintendent of the South African AME church, whereupon he took the opportunity to arrange for the AME Bishop Henry Turner to visit South Africa. After his return to South Africa Dwane received formal recognition by the Transvaal government. He hoped to expand the influence of his young church into Rhodesia, and even collect funds which were to be put at the disposal of Emperor Menelik of Abyssinia to promote the mission in the Sudan and in Egypt. The audacity of these wide-ranging ideas frightened other church leaders who were aware how limited their own means and opportunities were in South Africa.[68]

Bishop Turner's visit in 1898 brought great stimulus to the AME church and for Dwane an appointment as assistant bishop. The following year he visited the USA a second time and tried to have himself promoted full bishop, but came up against the limits of obligingness on the part of the AME mother church. On his return home in October 1899 Dwane broke with the AME in disgust and made contact with the Anglican church in South Africa. In 1900 he founded the Order of

Ethiopia within the Anglican church which, however, did not prosper. True, all ministers but four followed Dwane, but most of the ordinary members remained in the AME, which in 1901 sent Bishop J. L. Coppin from the USA to Cape Town to reside there permanently. But the AME itself did not escape the difficulties besetting all non-African missionary churches at this time. It, too, had to come to grips with the opposition to non-Africans exercising leadership in the church.

In view of the missionary chauvinism of the AME mission and the predominantly mulatto leadership of the AME[69] it is understandable why radical Ethiopians were soon disappointed in the latter, and attacked it as a 'White' church. When in 1904 a conference of European missionaries in South Africa condemned Ethiopianism in every form, the Rev. Attaway sent a telegram from Cape Town to the conference dissociating the AME from Ethiopianism.[70]

After the Zulu rising of 1906, which the frightened South African Whites regarded as an outrageous manifestation of Ethiopianism and in which members of the Ethiopian movement were said to have taken part,[71] Bishop Derrick of the AME in South Africa could quote with satisfaction a statement by the local Department of Native Affairs 'that in no case a member of the AME church was accused of uproar, rebellion or of any action which might lead to condemnation by the government'.[72] This dissociation from Ethiopianism is understandable because the AME, which already in the USA attached great importance to adaptation to the prevailing society, did not wish to forfeit governmental recognition in the harsher climate of South Africa.

Thus there were soon secessions from the AME. In 1904 Brander, one of the early supporters of the AME, left it and founded the 'Ethiopian Catholic Church in Zion'.[73] From that time onwards the Ethiopian movement in South Africa became hopelessly divided.[74] It had no chance to develop out of a vague proto-nationalism into a mature and constructive modern nationalism. From the first the ruling White minority regarded it with the greatest suspicion, overestimating its strength and danger. Its slogan 'Africa for the Africans' was hardly calculated to please the Whites who were, as they thought, establishing themselves for good in southern Africa[75] and for this reason were eager to suppress all stirrings towards independence by the Africans. After the Zulu rising of 1906 and the constitution of the Union of South Africa (1910) the scope for political agitation by Africans in South Africa continued to narrow.[76]

Just before the Boer War, which led to the establishment of the Union in 1910, colonial rule had expanded northwards from South Africa, notably to Nyasaland (Malawi) by way of Rhodesia. The missions of the established churches and the non-European and American sects (Seventh Day Adventists, Jehovah's Witnesses) helped to spread new ideas from South Africa to the southern part of Central Africa; these ideas led to the development of modern nationalism in this part of the continent. Here, too, contact with Afro-Americans from the USA was especially important, as was the fact that early nationalist leaders like Chilembwe[77] and Hastings Banda went to the USA to carry on their studies. Chilembwe's career is easy to follow and may be regarded almost as a classical example of Ethiopianism, illustrating the way in which the Christian missions facilitated the development of nationalism. Afro-American influences from the USA resulted in separation from the White missionary church, in the development of a vague kind of proto-nationalism, and finally in violent risings against colonial rule at the beginning of 1915. On account of the actual balance of power at that time Chilembwe failed, but he did succeed in creating the emotional substratum for nascent African nationalism in Nyasa-land.

The AMEZ mission on the Gold Coast

The mission of the African Methodist Episcopal Zion (AMEZ) church on the Gold Coast practically amounted to the formation of a separatist church. In contrast to the AME it did not absorb a previously existing separatist church but set up a branch establishment of its own out of dissatisfied elements within the established Methodist mission. True, the AMEZ mission on the Gold Coast always remained relatively small compared to the Methodist church, but it did form a particularly virulent element within Gold Coast nationalism. Since the country was much smaller, the number of the AMEZ members on the Gold Coast was always considerably less than that of the AME in South Africa; however, its historical impact was greater because the AMEZ mission on the Gold Coast found itself in the most important centre for the development of Pan-Africanism on African soil – in a society which was already in a state of political ferment and under British rule enjoyed a relatively large measure of freedom which enabled its nationalism to develop.

PAM—F

Moreover the AMEZ leadership may have been more open towards genuine Pan-African ideas than that of the rival AME. This impression may simply be due to gaps in the sources; at any rate we find no statement comparable to those made by AME members which betray feelings of Afro-American missionary chauvinism and missionary imperialism.[78] The most important AMEZ bishop at the turn of the century, Alexander Walters (1858–1917), took a greater part than leading AME members did in Afro-American politics, e.g. the Booker T. Washington–Du Bois controversy, the anti-lynch campaign and the nascent Pan-African movement.[79]

The foundation of the AMEZ mission on the Gold Coast leads us again to the classical triangle of Pan-Africanism. The main impetus was given by Bishop John B. Small.[80] He was born on Barbados on 14 March 1845 and spent four years at Codrington College on the island, the first secondary school in the West Indies.[81] In 1862 he went to Jamaica, and in 1863, during the Fifth Ashanti War, to the Gold Coast as sergeant and company clerk in a West Indian regiment.[82] He learned the Fanti language, observed the country and people, established contact with African Methodists and came to realize what a potential field for missionary activity existed there. During his term of residence on the west coast of Africa, which lasted for three and a half years, he visited all the British colonies from Gambia to Lagos. After spending some time in British Honduras (1866–71) he went to the USA and joined the AMEZ church. In 1896 he was appointed bishop, and simultaneously the first AMEZ missionary bishop for Africa, since he had displayed interest in performing such work. As an episcopal motto he chose 'For bleeding Africa'. Still in the same year he visited the Gold Coast in a whirlwind tour that lasted several weeks, similar to that of the AME's Bishop Turner in South Africa two years later,[83] in the course of which he preached and gave lectures. In a society aroused by a new wave of nationalist agitation[84] the appearance of a Black bishop from the other side of the Atlantic – judging from a photograph he was no mulatto[85] – must have made a deep impression. One of the African Methodist ministers who was on the verge of breaking with the Methodist mission, the Rev. Fynn Egyir Asaam, established contact with Small but not until a short while before he left Cape Coast. From this first contact there developed a correspondence between the two men which finally resulted in Egyir Asaam being authorized to start an affiliate church of the AMEZ on the Gold Coast.

Small's visit in 1898 led to the establishment of the AMEZ church, at first at Keta east of Accra and on 3 November of the same year at Cape Coast.[86] These foundations at Keta and Cape Coast were the work of the Rev. T. B. Freeman Jr, the son of T. B. Freeman, the actual founder and 'grand old man' of the Methodist mission on the Gold Coast.[87] At Cape Coast several distinguished laymen also took part, including some lawyers, and Mark Hayford, a Baptist minister; Attoh Ahuma joined the new church as well.[88]

With the foundation of the AMEZ on the Gold Coast the Pan-African component came to the fore more prominently than it did superficially in the parallel process in South Africa. Our information about the former is more plentiful, since the addresses delivered at the first meeting were recorded in the *Gold Coast Aborigines*, edited by Ahuma.[89] Starting with Small's visit two years before, Egyir Asaam sketched the antecedents of the new church which he welcomed because, as in Sierra Leone and Lagos, healthy competition between churches and missionary societies was of benefit to the country's educational progress. Asaam was followed by de Graft-Johnson, who went into the origins of the Methodist mission on the Gold Coast with which his family was associated.[90] Taking up the point about inter-church rivalry, the next speaker, F. R. Fearon, a lawyer, introduced a new point of view to which other speakers responded: 'We should take a great pride in this Mission from the fact of its being composed of, and having been exclusively worked by men of our own Race since 1700 [*sic*].[91] The next speaker, Kofi Asaam, also a lawyer, put the event into a two-fold historical perspective: on one hand the events of the Gold Coast in 1898 (especially the dispatch of the ARPS deputation to England);[92] on the other hand the AMEZ mission here and now. In this passage the proto-African components were most clearly evident, in spite of certain crude formulations due to the speaker's sense of resentment at the slave trade, the dialectical effect of which he correctly indicated:

> Our fellow blacks in America who some centuries ago were entrapped by white men by being got drunk with molasses and rum and carried away packed like herrings, to slavery for the enrichment and aggrandizement of their European captors, but who being emancipated are now the equals of those very masters in intellectual attainments and in almost every way – have for the

first time in the history of our nation stretched out the hand of kinship to us across the seas, and are ready to educate and christianize us and make the land of our common ancestors a glorious habitation in the eyes of the world.[93]

After a speech by the Baptist minister Mark Hayford, who treated broadly the theme that competition gave a spur to educational progress, the meeting was brought to a close by Thomas B. Freeman Jr, who surveyed the development of the AMEZ church in the USA as stemming from resistance to racial discrimination. He concluded with a character sketch of this church, which led him back to the theme of racial kinship. 'This Church thus composed of Africans and entirely governed and worked by Africans was indeed "bone of our bones and flesh of our flesh", which would naturally take a much greater interest in their missions in the Motherland than can be possible with Missionary Boards and Missionaries of an alien race who are *not above the colour question.*'[94] Freeman immediately gave a practical example of this: the AMEZ church had already invited young men to America to be trained in the missionary college, whereas a leading Methodist in England had characterized the training of African clergy as a mistake.[95] Freeman was here alluding to the invitation to the USA by Bishop Small of two young Methodists, James E. K. Aggrey and Frank Atta Osam Pinanko.[96] Both these men studied in Livingstone at the theological college of the AMEZ church. Pinanko returned to the Gold Coast in 1903 and took charge of the Western Missionary and Church District as superintendent until 1937.[97] Aggrey, who remained in Livingstone until 1924, became one of the best-known Africans in the 1920s, respected by members of various groups within African nationalism – not only those of more conservative hue but also by his disciple, the young Kwame Nkrumah.[98]

The university controversy in Sierra Leone (1872–3)

Another important centre of independent African church activity came into being in the southern part of what is today Nigeria at the turn of the century. These churches are best seen as a specifically Nigerian form of Ethiopianism, for it was here that the movement first assumed tangible form. Its roots go back to the missionary work of the CMS in Sierra Leone and southern Nigeria. It developed at the beginning of the 1870s as a reaction against the change that was slowly setting in among the White missionaries, and partly among British colonial officials as well, whereby they forsook their earlier humanitarian and philanthropic outlook for one more paternalistic and colonialist, indeed racist.[99] It was no coincidence that this reaction among the Africans should have begun in Sierra Leone, where their Christian and modern upbringing as products of the earlier attitude[100] were most likely to lead them to protest against the change in the intellectual climate. To them it seemed a deviation from the original ideal that had been behind the foundation of Sierra Leone as well as an infringement of their interests. From the 1860s onwards the Sierra Leoneans in southern Nigeria[101] had brought into circulation the slogan 'Africa for the Africans' (based, as we know, upon an American prototype).[102] Racial ideas infiltrated into political concepts; the new self-awareness engendered by the schools and missions found expression in a new feeling of power among educated Africans in Sierra Leone. By 1871 the CMS Grammar School in Freetown[103] had a printing press of its own and in 1873 the African Rev. James Quaker, who was then headmaster, published the *Ethiopian*, a bimonthly journal of which only one copy has survived.[104] One of the graduates of the CMS Grammar School, the Rev. Johnson, was together with Horton and Blyden the most important representative both of West African Ethiopianism and of Nigerian proto-nationalism.[105]

The new developments began in Sierra Leone with the CMS native pastorate of 1861, the embryo of the first autonomous African church organization.[106] This was followed by agitation for a secular university in West Africa. At the beginning of the 1870s there was such a strong desire among Sierra Leoneans to have their own university that a conflict arose with the CMS which lasted for several years.[107] The main organ of the young intelligentsia was to become the *Negro*, a new periodical in Freetown published by the bookseller T. J. Sawyer; its permanent collaborators included Archdeacon G. J. Macaulay, James Johnson, the Rev. G. Nicol (rector of Fourah Bay College), Blyden and Horton.[108] In view of the ferment of opinion at this time it is not surprising that heterogeneous ideas should have circulated among the collaborators of the *Negro*. Most rational and consistent in his conception of modernization was Horton, who had already demonstrated his rationalist outlook during the days of the Fanti Confederation on the Gold Coast.[109] In his eyes an independent university meant having the chance 'to develop the hitherto undeveloped minds of Africa'. As subjects of instruction he had in mind botany, mineralogy, physiology, chemistry, engineering, architecture etc.[110] – all modern studies. The university was to be located in Sierra Leone but not to develop out of Fourah Bay College; it should be financed by the governments of the four British colonies in West Africa; the professors were to be well paid – on German lines – so that they could pursue 'their scholarly work in complete independence'.[111]

More ambivalent in their attitude were James Johnson and Blyden. Blyden especially spoke frequently in the accents of Negro racism, as a reaction to White racism. His racial concept was in some points identical with that of Gobineau. He thought the races were equal in principle, so that none was inherently superior or inferior, but also held that the races had such diverse inclinations that different kinds of education were necessary to develop them.[112] On top of this he idealized and romanticized Africa and its traditional society, without however drawing the logical consequences in his own personal conduct, for in his mentality and life style he remained a European or American. Towards the end of the century he even welcomed European colonialism and imperialism as a vehicle of progress for Africa.[113]

Blyden was for a time director of Mohammedan education in Freetown. He favoured Islam only because it was an African religion and oscillated between it and advocacy of an Africanized Christianity which should ward off the advance of Islam; likewise he oscillated between proclaiming that God was black and praising European missionaries – even those who, around 1890, were openly racist. His African nationalism, 'Ethiopianism' or proto-Pan-Africanism, was therefore, as Ayandele has rightly pointed out, not politically but culturally orientated[114] and therefore also more exposed to the temptations of romanticization and irrationality. With his learned romanticization of Africa he coined the slogan of the 'African personality'. His numerous lectures and publications exerted a profound influence upon all later African nationalists and Pan-Africans. All the way from Casely Hayford to Garvey, Padmore and Nkrumah, Pan-African spokesmen time and again referred to Blyden, often in ecstatic tones.[115] To a certain extent Blyden may be regarded right down to the present day as the most important progenitor of the myth of 'Négritude'. The duality in his character and spiritual background, in which European-American and learned African elements were intermingled, helps to explain why the same intellectual confusion was to be found also among his successors.[116]

One generation later Du Bois offered a parallel, with the difference that Du Bois spent only a fraction of his life in Africa.[117] On the other hand it is characteristic that Horton, who was consistently rational and modern in his outlook, apparently fell into oblivion soon after his death; it is only recently that he is being rediscovered by historians.[117a] Had he become the spiritual patron of nascent African nationalism and Pan-Africanism these two movements, which were so closely interlinked, would no doubt in many points have evolved differently.

Johnson's nationalism – by contrast with that of Blyden – was rather more political in inspiration. In ecclesiastical matters he was faithful to the CMS and to the Anglican church for all his detailed criticism of them. From about 1890 he opposed the spread of British colonial rule, as in the Ijebu War of 1892; as a member of the Legislative Council of Lagos he used his position to defend vigorously the interests of the Africans vis-à-vis the colonial administration and White business interests, with the result that he was soon dismissed from the Legislative Council of Lagos.[118]

As the first expression of cultural nationalism and racial feeling among the young intelligentsia the agitation by Horton, Blyden, Johnson and their friends for a West African university in Sierra Leone, with African and Afro-American professors, reached such a scale that the CMS headquarters in London (until 1966 located in Salisbury Square in the City of London, near St Paul's Cathedral) became anxious. The CMS leaders were disappointed that it was precisely graduates of the CMS Grammar School and of Fourah Bay College who belonged to the rebels.[119] The CMS feared that it would lose influence in such an atmosphere; a secular university, warmly advocated by the (Catholic) governor Pope Hennessey, could serve as a cover for penetration by Islam.[120] In 1873, at the height of the campaign led above all by the *Negro*, the CMS started a counter-offensive. It was aided by the heterogeneity of its foes. One year after Venn's death[121] an unsigned leading article in the CMS journal, the *Intelligencer*, attacked both Governor Pope Hennessey for favouring Islam and the *Negro*. The writer struck out against everything that was precious to early Pan-African leaders: there was no African history; Egypt was not a cultural achievement of Africa; all important Africans were of foreign descent; all major achievements in Africa were the work of foreigners. 'When we look into the history of the negro races, considered apart from their prosecutors and oppressors, all that meets us is – a blank.

There seems no possibility of escaping it, that the Africa of the negro has no past.'[122] To the view that Islam was an African religion the CMS leader writer replied that it was of Asian origin, although spread quite widely in Africa; the Arabs, the main supporters of Islam, had been the traditional suppressors of the negro Africans. In still harsher language he went on to reproach the *Negro* for propagating secular education: an independent West African university would be too expensive to maintain and there were still not enough African and Afro-American professors. Africa should indeed belong to the Africans, but it was desirable that the latter should distinguish between good-for-nothings and professional agitators on one hand and their traditional friends on the other. The *Negro*, he admitted, was well written but it was still immature, as was proved by its defence of native slavery and its approval of Islam as 'racy of the soil'. A temperate discussion would be useful but at the moment it was a question as to whether the mother church could still continue to afford sympathy and support for its affiliate in Africa.[123]

After this broadside from London the *Negro* drew in its horns – not surprisingly, since several collaborators were dependent upon the CMS. In an article and two letters published in the journal by the Rev. Nicol and the Rev. James Johnson, this group retreated before the CMS's powerful offensive. The agitation for a separate West African university died down; soon the *Negro* ceased publication; and in 1874 the rebellious James Johnson was transferred to Lagos. But as a positive measure to forestall a similar protest the CMS promoted the affiliation of Fourah Bay College to a British university. The University of Durham was thought the most suitable, since it was originally a Church of England foundation. In 1875 it had already entered into an analogous relationship with Codrington College in Barbados, so that once again a kind of triangular Pan-African link was established. In 1876 the affiliation of Fourah Bay College was carried through, after which it was possible to obtain external degrees from the University of Durham in Sierra Leone. This meant that the CMS recognized subsequent to the event that the demands for full university studies to be provided on African soil was legitimate.

Once the university controversy had been settled and Johnson had broken with the mission, the pioneering role of Sierra Leone largely came to an end. True, Fourah Bay College retained its important function as the best academic institution in West Africa, but from a political and intellectual view Sierra Leone contributed only little to the development of Pan-Africanism and African nationalism. Sierra Leone from then on occupied third place after the Gold Coast and Nigeria in the development of Pan-Africanism.

The beginnings of independent churches in Nigeria

Without realizing it, by posting Johnson to Lagos for disciplinary reasons the CMS stimulated the opposition movement within the church in southern Nigeria, for here he found himself once again in the midst of a society in ferment. Since their return from Sierra Leone the Sierra Leoneans[124] had established themselves in Yorubaland as a prosperous element aware of their strength. As in Freetown, the tensions with the CMS revolved around education, but in Lagos it was just a matter of schools. As early as 1859 the Sierra Leonean T. B. Macaulay, a son-in-law of Bishop Crowther, had founded, against the resistance of the European missionaries, a grammar school supported at first by the CMS; in its early years the level of instruction given was little more than elementary (as was only to be expected).[125] All in all the Africans in Lagos, who were keen to have modern educational facilities, felt that the CMS was neglecting them; they suspected it of not wanting the parishes to become so strong that they could develop into a 'native pastorate', i.e. into the beginnings of an independent African church. In September 1873, under the leadership of two active parish members, Charles Forsythe and Otunba Payne, those who were dissatisfied with the CMS's school policy founded the Society for the Promotion of Religion and Education. This was the first modern quasi-political organization above the tribal level in modern Nigeria; its object was to drive the CMS out of Lagos, as far as possible, by raising the level of local churches and schools through their own financial efforts. The Europeans and missionaries were opposed to this, and tried to canalize the opposition within the church into one for a 'native pastorate' by posting James Johnson to Lagos. But in so doing they unwillingly transferred the strongest force in the nascent African nationalist movement to a country with much greater potential than Sierra Leone, Nigeria.

Johnson, called by the Sierra Leoneans 'Wonderful Johnson', by the Nigerians 'Holy Johnson' and by Salisbury Square the 'pope' of Nigeria,[126] never actually broke openly with the CMS and the Anglican church. In 1900 he accepted an appointment as assistant bishop of the Niger delta. But time and again he drove his passionate commitment on behalf of African interests to the brink of a breach. He represented the African opposition within the established church, and for this reason had to reckon with continued hostility on the part of colonial authorities and European missionaries.

To the annoyance of the European missionaries, who would have rather seen him fail, Johnson quickly and successfully built up the 'native pastorate', so giving the young African intelligentsia and middle class an opportunity to gain practical experience in the exercise of individual responsibility, which could later stand them in good stead in the political field. The European missionaries saw the political consequences latent in this and issued warnings against them. They were particularly exasperated at the slogan 'Africa for the Africans' which circulated in native pastorate groups in Lagos. The fear of secession by an embryonic independent African church was never stilled.

But secession did not come about until later, and Johnson's (and Blyden's) role in it was only indirect. The conflict arose out of the growth of racism, which in the British West African colonies in particular contrasted with the earlier traditions of philanthropy and abolitionism. Thus there gradually emerged, even in the relatively mild political climate of British West Africa, a pattern of racial segregation and the much-feared colour bar, which affected even the personnel policies of the colonial governments. Thanks to the progress made in general hygiene and in tropical medicine, West Africa was no longer 'the White man's grave'; accordingly more Europeans arrived to serve in the colonial administration and in the missions. At the same time local merchants were encountering competition from European business men on the Niger, from 1879 united in the huge monopolistic combine of the United African Company under the direction of George Goldie-Taubman (later Sir George Goldie).[127] In this rivalry African missionaries and ministers took the part of the African merchants and traders, who were often related to them and many of whom came from Sierra Leone. The White missionaries backed the European business interests,[128] but in internal church controversies preferred to stress against Africans such questions as the survival of polygamy.[129]

The last offshoot of the earlier, more liberal tradition in the spirit of Henry Venn was the grant of ecclesiastical autonomy to the (small) Methodist mission between 1878 and 1880.[130] A few years later the climate had already changed to such an extent that the Baptist mission, which was also quite small, was driven to secede. This latter had only been able to survive after the Christian missionaries had been temporarily driven out of Abeokuta in 1867 as a result of stalwart efforts by the native Baptist communities, but in 1875 it had been taken over again by two American missionaries, one White and the other Afro-American. The missionary society on which they depended, the Southern American Baptist Mission, had very strong racist leanings on account of its links with the southern states, and it was no accident that the conflict should have first broken out openly here. The Rev. W. J. David, the White missionary, sabotaged the efforts of active parish members to obtain a higher education in the USA, overrode in an autocratic manner the democratic practices customary in parish matters among Baptists and treated the Afro-American missionary as a subordinate rather than a colleague.

The opposition, and later the actual secession, were led by two members of the parish, J. C. Vaughn and S. M. Harden, who had been to the USA and who attacked David for applying American racial ideas to African conditions. In April 1888 the entire parish, except for eight members, seceded and established a Native Baptist church, to the applause of nationalist groups.[131] This was the prelude to the formation of several other independent African churches in Nigeria. It was also a launching-pad for the Baptist leader D. B. Vincent (Majola Agbebi, to give him the African name he adopted soon afterwards) who rose to become the most important African church leader and nationalist in Nigeria around 1900 after James Johnson. Agbebi also became a well-known spokesman for early African nationalism on an international plane. He kept up links with Afro-Americans in the USA, especially with the well-known journalist and publicist John Edward Bruce from Yonkers, New York State; the latter was so impressed by Agbebi that he had his birthday (11 October) celebrated as Majola Agbebi Day by Afro-Americans in New York, in this way 'immortalizing the African personality'.[132] In 1911 Agbebi was the only West African to speak at the First Universal Races Congress in London; a decade later his son represented the Garvey movement in Lagos.[133]

The birth of African churches out of increased racial discrimination can be followed even more dramatically in the case of the secession from the CMS.[134] In 1889, one year after the secession by the Baptists, several young and zealous CMS missionaries arrived from England so full of the new racist ideas that even veteran missionaries were dismayed. In 1890 these young men, led by the particularly fanatical twenty-four-year-old G. W. Brooke, carried out a purge of the entire missionary field, aimed directly against the African CMS missionary agents and teachers and indirectly against Bishop Samuel Crowther. Crowther was a first-generation product of the abolitionist movement and the first wave of missionaries.[135] By contrast with James Johnson, who had been born in Sierra Leone, let alone with the first generation of young nationalists, he never showed the least spirit of opposition – although he was greatly concerned at European economic penetration of the Niger and the abandonment of the liberal non-racist principles held by the abolitionists (and by Henry Venn), to which after all he owed his position as the first African bishop. Crowther was full of gratitude towards the CMS but he was not prepared to accept without proof the accusations levelled against his subordinates. Already over eighty years of age, he no longer had the necessary combatant spirit and in any case was of gentle disposition. By the 1880s his position as bishop had been largely undermined. Once the symbol of the emancipated and modernized Africans, Crowther was systematically ousted by young missionaries from various positions in the missionary church. In August 1890 an open conflict broke out in Onitsha when British missionaries in Crowther's presence – quite arbitrarily and without substantiating any of their charges – suspended several African ministers, including Crowther's son, Archdeacon Crowther. Trembling with rage, Bishop Crowther announced his resignation from the finance committee. Ajayi comments: 'It was unlikely that they would have gone so far if Crowther had been a European. Few scenes could have been more painful to watch than the grey-haired old Bishop of 80 active years, tormented and insulted by the young Europeans, trembling with rage as he never trembled before, as he got up to announce his resignation from the committee.'[136]

No doubt there were indeed abuses in the mission, given the backwardness of the country and the relatively rapid expansion of the mission (which was usually short of funds and personnel). During these early years the quality of some missionary agents and Christian converts was doubtful, and the degree of Christianization often superficial, as is demonstrated in the case of several Christian parishioners of Brass in the Niger delta. In 1885 after violent quarrels they slaughtered their enemies and ceremoniously devoured them in accordance with ancient

tribal custom, whereupon Archdeacon Crowther simply barred them
for a time from access to the sacraments, while his father, Bishop
Crowther, emphatically defended these Christian cannibals vis-à-vis
Salisbury Square, although without actually going so far as to justify their action.[137] But on the whole the young White missionaries
carried out their purge in an excessively summary fashion, for they were
all too obviously concerned to make use of the abuses they inveighed
against, and the indulgence shown them by the two Crowthers, a pre-
text for declaring the Africans generally unworthy and incapable
of governing themselves. The virtual dismissal of Crowther in these
conditions, as part of an attack upon the position of the 'educated
Africans' as a whole, was calculated to evoke a sharp reaction among
Africans. As soon as the events at Onitsha and the humiliation of Bishop
Crowther became known, numerous protests were sent by Africans to
the CMS headquarters in London:

> National feelings ran to heights never known before in the history
> of West Africa. This nationalist outburst was universal. As James
> Johnson said, it was Africa that was on trial and it behoved all
> Africans, whether Christian or Muslim or 'pagan', to rally round
> the Bishop and the agents of the Mission. Protest upon protest
> came to Salisbury Square on a scale never known before, all
> declaring that it was not the Bishop but the Negro race that was
> insulted. Protests came from Bonny, Brass, Lagos and Sierra
> Leone and they were all signed by all the editors of the Nigerian
> newspapers.[138]

It was into this agitated milieu that Blyden stepped when he arrived
in Lagos on 23 December 1890. On 2 January 1891 he gave a lecture
there on 'The Return of the Exiles and the West African Church', in
which he spoke out in favour of constituting an independent West
African church which would be better able to ward off Islam. His
words fell upon fertile soil, and the preparations for the establishment
of such a church prospered so well in the following months that all the
African ministers in Lagos were willing to declare for the West African
church as soon as Johnson gave the signal. The latter, however, shrank
from an open breach with the CMS and refrained from giving the
signal as arranged; meanwhile the African clergy once more came to
terms with the CMS. By this compromise the successor to Crowther was
to be a British bishop, to whom two African assistant bishops would be

attached. The latter appointments did not, however, go to James Johnson and Archdeacon Crowther but to two more docile men who accordingly enjoyed less standing among the Africans in Lagos.[139] Not until 1900 was James Johnson appointed assistant bishop of the Niger delta.

Instead of the expected declaration of secession a new initiative was taken in Lagos. At the instigation of laymen, especially of Otunba Payne, a well-to-do Yoruba merchant, a committee was formed to raise funds with which to make the CMS missionary church of the Niger delta independent under Bishop Crowther. This movement had as its spokesman none other than James Johnson, but the CMS head office did not take it really seriously until to their dismay the gentle and hitherto non-political Bishop Crowther accepted aid from the African nationalists.[140] Crowther's death on 31 December 1891 put a stop to this initiative, and the Church of England marked up its experiment with an African bishop as a failure.[141]

In the meantime some laymen who felt that they had been deserted by their ministers founded their own independent ecclesiastical body, the United Native African Church (August 1891). Later, under the leadership of the lay element, secessions took place from various European missionary societies: in 1901 from the CMS with the foundation of the African Church Organization; in 1903 from the Episcopalians with the foundation of the West African Episcopalian Church; in 1917 from the Methodists with the foundation of the United African Methodist Church. In the course of time further groups split off from these African churches, so that by 1921 a total of nineteen different bodies were to be found in southern Nigeria, including two which had since merged with other groups. From 1922 a movement got under way with the object of reuniting the independent African churches, and by 1964 there were only four of them.[142]

The political implications of this ecclesiastical independence movement became apparent from 1900 onwards. The appointment of James Johnson as assistant bishop was a concession to the Africans' growing political consciousness and was immediately understood as such.[143] As had been shown by the reaction to Bishop Crowther's treatment, on the West African coast burning questions within the church could evoke an interest and a sense of solidarity which extended beyond the confines of the religious community and also beyond colonial boundaries. In 1900 the West African coast was similarly affected by

Johnson's appeal, after he had been ordained bishop, for contributions towards a fund to support his diocese, the West African Bishopric Fund.[144] Thus it becomes understandable that James Johnson and Otunba Payne, one of the leading laymen in Lagos, should have played a part in connection with the first Pan-African Association in 1900.[145]

Part II The formation of Pan-Africanism (1900–1945)

9 Nineteenth-century forerunners

The development of Pan-Africanism in the narrower sense must be seen in the context of the historical background described above, for all the elements mentioned were to become relevant again in one form or another during the twentieth century. A major turning-point was the Pan-African Conference, held in London in 1900. This was the first time the name 'Pan-African' appeared and assumed organizational form. The Pan-African Conference has a prehistory of its own which will be outlined here.

To the remoter antecedents of the conference there belong – as well as the facts analysed in Part I – all the ideas expressed and the efforts undertaken during the nineteenth century to bring about a kind of Pan-African solidarity. Judging by the documentation at present available, only a few stirrings in this direction are detectable, yet they amounted to more than is generally assumed.

Such concepts as 'African' and 'Africa', 'Ethiopian' and 'Ethiopia' – at first employed by ex-slaves who came directly from Africa like Cugoano and Equiano, but also by Afro-Americans[1] – were the first elementary preconditions for the emergence of a proto-Pan-African consciousness in the nineteenth century. For there could be no Pan-

Africanism without reference to an entity beyond that of the tribe or the immediate neighbourhood. A second stage in the formation of a Pan-African consciousness came with appeals to the solidarity of all Africans and persons of African descent, as in Walker's *Appeal*.[2] This feeling of solidarity became tangible through the action taken by newly independent Haiti on behalf of enslaved negroes elsewhere; in 1816 President Pétion at a critical moment gave moral and material support to Bolivar and the Latin American revolutionaries, whereupon Bolivar (himself an important landed proprietor and slave-owner) promised to abolish slavery immediately after the revolution.[3]

Delany's conception (1852–60)

A third stage was attained with the schemes for settling Afro-Americans in West Africa and Haiti between 1854 and 1861. One group wanted to make Haiti the 'main cornerstone of an Ethiopian empire' – a Pan-African one, as it were. The group around Delany and Campbell hoped to make a start in what was still free pre-colonial West Africa, in Abeokuta and in Yorubaland.[4] In support of his emigration projects Delany outlined, for the benefit of the National Emigration Convention of Colored People meeting at Cleveland, Ohio, in August 1854, a far-reaching panorama of global political and historical development. As early as 1852, in his programmatic publication, Delany had drawn attention to the fact that the Whites were a minority in the world: 'Thus there are two coloured persons for each White man in the world, and yet . . . the White race dominates the coloured.'[5] In his major report of 1854 he expanded this idea: 'Some day the question of black and white will decide the world's destiny.' Over the past three centuries the territorial aggrandizement of the Whites had been based upon the subjugation of the coloured peoples, the Anglo-Americans excelling in

> deeds of injustice and acts of suppression, unparalleled perhaps in the annals of world history. The imbalance could not, however, persist and every individual would soon have to identify himself with the Whites or the Blacks. The coloured races formed two-thirds of the world's population and were drawing closer together and two-thirds could no longer passively submit to the universal domination of this one-third.[6] Negroes now demanded their rights. Since they could not be acquired within the United States, Negroes would have to go elsewhere and settle in the West Indies

or Central or South America. They would have to assert their manhood, and develop a new civilization. There they would achieve also political equality and social and economic betterment. [The natives, we are told hopefully, would] encourage such development as a check to European presumption and the insufferable Yankee intrusion and impudence.[7]

There was no mention here of Africa, but Delany's silence at this point may be explained by tactical considerations.[8] He still had to persuade his fellow-countrymen of the merits of emigration. His plan to set up independent states of free negroes in the southern part of the western hemisphere could easily be translated to Africa. After he had visited West Africa he could openly say:

Africa is our fatherland and we are its legitimate descendants. . . . Africa, to become regenerated, must have a national character, and her position among the existing nations of the earth will depend mainly upon the high standard she may gain compared with them in all her relations, morally, religiously, politically and commercially. . . . I have determined to leave to my children the inheritance of a country, the possession of territorial domain, the blessings of a national education and the indisputable right of self-government.

He boiled everything down to a handy formula: 'Our policy must be . . . Africa for the African race and black men to rule them. By black men I mean, men of African descent who claim an identity with the race.'[9]

In the same context Delany was also probably the first to object to 'the utility of the custom on the part of Missionaries in changing the names of native children and even adults [on baptism], . . . as though their own were not good enough'.[10]

Delany's idea of a politically motivated re-emigration to Africa, with its strong anti-imperialist implications, certainly did not remain unknown to later generations of Afro-Americans; nor did the idea implicit in it that the Afro-Americans were marked out to civilize an Africa that was still underdeveloped. Du Bois and Garvey later put forward analogous ideas about the role of the Afro-Americans as the vanguard of the coloured people throughout the world.[11] Du Bois's famous formula of 1900 at the London Pan-African Conference, 'the problem of the twentieth century is the problem of the colour line',[12] reads like a brilliant encapsulation of Delany's ideas.

Thomas Hodgkin's Native African Association (1859–61)

The next move in the prehistory of Pan-Africanism apparently originated in London with Dr Thomas Hodgkin, one of the founders of the Aborigines Protection Society in 1837. In 1860 he established contact with Delany and Campbell during their stay in England (after their return from Abeokuta).[13] Our knowledge of his initiative comes from the correspondence in his private papers.

In 1859 at the latest the idea arose of creating an association of Africans, West Indians and Afro-Americans. In June 1859 Hodgkin informed Thomas Hughes[14] at Cape Coast that 'we have had no meeting of the projected association. . . . Indeed we know but few such now in England.' In other words, around 1860 there were still too few persons with Pan-African sympathies on British soil, which was particularly favourable for the development of the movement. Nevertheless Hodgkin regarded

> the efficient establishment of such an association on a large scale as one of the most desirable objects in the interest of the African race. – Surely, while Italians, Hungarians, Servians are bestirring themselves on behalf of their respective nationalities the long oppressed men [two words illegible] of the globe might make an effort when their eyes are opened and their attention is called to the peculiarities and dangers of their situation. If their opportunities are favourable at the present time, what I believe to be the case, the dangers that are also at hand and threatening are [not] inconsiderable. – America is reviving the slave trade, France and Portugal are solicitous to extend their African territories.[15]

England, which had produced so many friends of the African race and had done so much for their cause, was hopeless because of the poor quality of her colonial governors and her hypocrisy. Hodgkin apparently felt it necessary to calm the fears of his correspondent on the distant Gold Coast about the political implications of his idea, and this may have been why he referred to the revolutionary nationalist tendencies in southern and south-eastern Europe: 'Think not that I am wishing to stir thyself, thy friends or any African on your coast or anywhere to

wild revolutionary or democratic struggles. – By no means. – You require combinations but not to such proceedings but rather to promote
individual and general improvement – the spread of morality, knowledge, industry, the true sources of Happiness and prosperity to individuals.'[16] He made the following proposal to Thomas Hughes: 'People
if they were what they ought to be would be prepared to unite in some
federal union of which Liberia from its African material and American
type seems calculated to form the nucleus as well as the pattern. . . .
The proposed African Association would assist the execution and progress of the design but the chief part must be done in Africa by
Africans.'[17]

Three months later Hodgkin wrote to Hughes: 'No progress has
been made on the formation of an African Association of permanent
operation. . . . I attach considerable importance to the object as I
think it would promote African progress and command attention from
those who now despise or neglect the African race. . . .'[18]

If one interprets these passages with necessary caution, one arrives
at the following deduction: the two men were thinking of an organization in London, consisting in the first place of Africans and Afro-
Americans, and possibly British benefactors as well. Already *in statu
nascendi* this organization entered into contact with Afro-Americans
(Delany) and Africans (Hughes). It had as yet no established name but
almost spontaneously its founders twice used, as a kind of working title,
the name 'African Association'; this name was to reappear towards the
end of the century.[19] Its objective was the economic, social and
political development of Africa, if possible with a federal structure,
inter alia to ward off the machinations of colonial imperialism and
racism.

Two years later the organization was still not yet in existence. But in
the meantime a kind of substitute solution had been found by the
African Aid Society and its publication the *African Times*, edited by
F. Fitzgerald.[20] This had the result that Africans and Afro-Americans
were seen to a greater extent as objects of philanthropic activity than
had been intended in the plans for an African Association (as we may
call it), as is indicated by the term 'Aid' in the title. Hodgkin, together
with his Quaker friends and other like-minded persons, consciously
followed the tradition of Granville Sharp and Paul Cuffee in his work
for Africa,[21] and did not give up his plans. On 7 November 1861 the
'Native African Association and their Friends' met in his house.[22] The

names of the twelve men who attended besides Hodgkin as yet convey little, but they may become better known after further research. They were: Forster,[23] G. Ralston,[24] M. Gentze, the Haitian chargé d'affaires in London, R(obert?) Campbell, F. Fitzgerald, secretary of the African Aid Society and editor of the *African Times*, D. Chinery,[24a] Cha(rle)s Scvin, J. Fuller, L. A. Chameroozow, secretary of the Anti-Slavery Society, W. Oliver, T. C. Taylor, British vice-consul designate of Abeokuta,[25] and Lyons McLeod.

The nucleus of the group consists of British abolitionists (Hodgkin, Chameroozow; possibly also Forster) and activists of the African Aid Society (Fitzgerald). To these may be added the vice-consul appointed to Abeokuta. Of significance is the presence of the Haitian chargé d'affaires in London; his predecessor, Linstant Pradine, had in April 1860 given the Anti-Slavery Society, on behalf of his government, £100, which for that time was a not inconsiderable sum.[26] Should the R. Campbell mentioned be identical with the Robert Campbell whom we have already had cause to mention,[27] then Africans and Afro-Americans would have been represented by a West Indian who had worked in the USA, was already in West Africa and was about to settle there.

The meeting began with

a brief account of the attempt to form an association of natives of Africa and their descendants in other parts of the world . . . and the satisfaction which had occurred in the Coast of Africa when steps were taken to form an association to be in communication with one which might exist in London for the purpose of promoting African [emancipation?] by the energetic co-operation of men of African race, an interesting conversation took place.'[28]

After a discussion in which the Haitian chargé d'affaires and vice-consul Taylor were especially prominent, it was resolved

that it is desirable at this time to renew the effort for the attainment of the object described and that for this purpose the best means would be to take advantage of the existence of the African Aid Society, which, it is hoped, will kindly undertake it and that the draft and address should be prepared for submission to that Society with the view to circulation on the Coast of Africa through the medium of Journals published at Sierra Leone, Cape Coast Castle and Abeokuta and through any other available channels inviting the co-operation of the many intelligent natives known to exist.[29]

However, this initiative probably led to nothing. It is revealing on account of its Pan-African horizon and the plan for collaboration between British abolitionists, Afro-Americans, Haitians and Africans. It was still too early for the idea of a Pan-African organization to take root: there were not enough 'intelligent natives' in Africa or even among Afro-Americans in the New World. To put it differently: the class of politically alert and active intellectuals on both sides of the Atlantic was still in its formative stage; in Britain, too, there were not enough people interested in African and Afro-American problems for the venture to succeed.

A final offshoot of Hodgkin's initiative was a proposal which he made during the American Civil War in a letter to the journal *Dial*. From the time of the Fugitive Slave Law (1850) onwards a number of American negroes had arrived in Britain penniless and a second wave would come during the 'present struggle'. Hodgkin announced the foundation of an organization which, with the aid of the Anti-Slavery Society, the African Aid Society and the Quakers would take such Afro-Americans to Africa as quickly and cheaply as possible. In order to test the seriousness of the applicants' intentions, they would have to pay their passage, so avoiding disappointment and fraud.[30] The outcome of this suggestion, which recalls the settlement of the 'Black poor' in Sierra Leone in 1787, is not yet known.[31]

The social preconditions for the emergence of Pan-Africanism around 1900

After nearly half a century had elapsed the preconditions for an attempt to form a Pan-African organization were already somewhat more favourable. In the meantime there had arisen on the West African coast a relatively well-to-do African élite already in a position to send its sons to study in Britain; this class had also developed a new political consciousness.[32] In Cape Province, after the British takeover in 1815, a gradual improvement had taken place in the position of the 'coloureds' (mulattoes) and of Black Africans, especially after slavery had been abolished in the British Empire between 1834 and 1838. The constitution of the Cape Province granted by London in 1852 conceded the coloureds their first political rights on a restricted franchise. Both the coloureds and the Black Africans began to develop a middle class. This process was furthered by the industrialization of the country at the end of the nineteenth century. The South Africans, who in social progress had a long lead over the rest of the continent and who already had a relatively broad basis for modernization, were the first to be able to send students in considerable numbers to negro colleges and universities in the USA. Whereas at the beginning of the twentieth century only a few such cases were known from the rest of Africa, in 1906 there were already about 150 South Africans studying in the USA.[33]

A similar situation was to be found in the British West Indies, especially in Jamaica and Trinidad, where the prosperous mulatto element had risen to economic importance already at an early date, and the emancipation of the slaves (1834–8) had eliminated major obstacles to the modernization of society sooner than in Africa. Thus towards the end of the century an Afro-West Indian Literary Society already existed in Edinburgh – after London the most important British university for African and Afro-Caribbean students (on account of its excellent medical faculty); no details of this society are available, but one may assume that it was made up in the main of students from the British West Indies.[34]

The extension of the British colonial empire to wide parts of Africa in the late nineteenth century for the first time enabled a larger number of Africans and Afro-West Indians to come into personal and intellectual contact with one another in England; it also brought numerous tribal princes and chiefs to the imperial capital to defend their interests. The United Kingdom, and London in particular, became a centre of intellectual and political exchanges between individuals and groups from those parts of the British Empire whence Pan-Africanism drew its support.

Also among the Afro-Americans in the USA the development of an intelligentsia able to articulate Pan-African ideas had made some progress since the days of Delany and the American Civil War. The slave emancipation had directed their energies away from emigration and towards the improvement of their social and economic status in the USA, as Delany's career shows.[35] The Reconstruction period had generated new hopes which, however, were again frustrated when a new reactionary era set in from about 1877.[36] With the triumph of imperialism in the USA towards the end of the century the social and political status of Afro-Americans deteriorated: in the North this was camouflaged, but in the South it was openly recognized and constitutionally rooted in the deprivation of the right to vote, as well as in systematic segregation in all fields of life, lynchings etc. – a tendency which continued until as late as 1910.[37] In the course of some twenty years there were about 100 lynchings each year; in 1892 the number reported rose to 235.[38] Then there were the notorious race riots directed against coloured people. The first of these occurred in Wilmington, North Carolina, in 1898; later ones with historical repercussions took place in Atlanta, Georgia, in 1906 and in Springfield, Illinois, in 1908.[39]

For the Afro-Americans there were two possible reactions: to resist or to accept matters with resignation. At first the latter attitude prevailed, propagated by Booker T. Washington. He had risen from the status of a slave to the directorship of the Tuskegee Institute at Tuskegee, Alabama, which he had established with the aid of funds donated by Whites in the southern states; after the death of Frederick Douglass (1895) he quickly advanced to the position of undisputed leader of the Afro-Americans.[40] Out of concern for the White backers of his institute, if for no other reason, Washington was against the intellectual advance of the Afro-Americans since this would prepare the ground for political agitation. The Tuskegee Institute therefore provided training in handicrafts and agriculture and avoided any form of political orientation, let alone a militant posture.

Opposition was at first only found at a local level; it was greater than is usually assumed,[41] but all told had little effect. In protest against lynchings there came into being in the North an anti-lynch movement; among those who took part in it was Alexander Walters, bishop of the AMEZ church in New York. He founded a National Afro-American Council which tried to coordinate activities on a national level; however, it was not very dynamic or successful, since Booker T. Washington exerted a great influence for much of the time and this had a restraining effect.[42] In the intellectual sphere Alexander Crummell, after spending twenty years in Liberia, attempted to give young Afro-American intellectuals a platform with his Negro Academy, set up in 1897. This did indeed develop over the years as an alternative centre to that of Booker Washington. This trend laid emphasis upon intellectual and political activity, if need be in association with White liberals. Its spokesmen were William M. Trotter and W. E. B. Du Bois.

The break with Washington did not take place until 1902 (Trotter) and 1903 (Du Bois);[43] in 1900 Du Bois collaborated with Washington, whose leadership was at this time still undisputed.

New interest in Africa: B. T. Washington and W. E. B. Du Bois

For Afro-Americans the rapid decline in their status must have had a disillusioning effect, for it meant there could be no hope of freedom and equality within the foreseeable future. The triumphant racism and imperialism among the Whites made them all the more aware of their African descent, especially as that continent was partitioned among the colonial powers. Thrown back upon themselves psychologically the Afro-Americans faced an Africa which on account of its colonial status was treated with more disdain than ever.

Thus it was tempting for them to seek an improvement of their own situation in America by the roundabout way of Africa. Emigration to Africa was no longer possible since the European colonial powers would have prevented collaboration between Afro-Americans and Africans. It was now rather a matter of developing Africa economically, socially and intellectually in such a way that progress in Africa would reflect back upon Afro-Americans in the USA. Thus the appearance of Pan-Africanism among Afro-Americans in the USA was a by-product of the permanent tension between assimilation and segregation; this became particularly acute at the turn of the century with the emergence of a modern Afro-American intelligentsia which had less scope than ever for social and political activity.

In this context at the turn of the century even the conservative Booker T. Washington showed a certain interest in Africa without, however, any hint of militancy in his motives.[44] The fame which he had gained through the Tuskegee Institute brought him into contact with Africans and West Indians, some of whom asked him for advice in setting up schools for agriculture and crafts modelled upon Tuskegee. Also with regard to Africa he recommended moderation and accommodation to the existing order, which he thought could only be improved by patient and dogged work.[45] His commitment to Africa found expression in the despatch of a team to Togo which introduced the cultivation of cotton and set up an agricultural school. In 1910, during a visit to Berlin, Washington extolled German colonial policy.[46]

With hindsight one can detect the origins of the divergence between Washington and his severe and persistent critic Du Bois on the role of Afro-Americans in the modern world at a time when Du Bois still accepted Washington's leadership without reservation. In 1897, during the high tide of the lynch murders, Du Bois wrote a pamphlet called *The Conservation of the Race*, published by the newly founded American Negro Academy. In this he struck a different note from that of Washington in the context of Africa. His call to Afro-Americans in the USA to avoid mixed marriages was completely political in its motives: 'The advance guard of the Negro people – the 8,000,000 people of Negro blood in the United States of America – must soon come to realize that if they take their just place in the van of Pan-Negroism, then their destiny is not absorption by the white Americans. . . . If the Negro were to be a factor in the world's history, it would be through a Pan-Negro movement.'[47] Vague in regard to political demands but unequivocal in his historical allusions he continued: 'If in America it is to be proved for the first time in the modern world that not only Negroes are capable of evolving individual men like Toussaint, the Saviour, but are a nation stored with wonderful possibilities of culture, then their destiny is not a servile imitation of Anglo-Saxon culture but a stalwart originality which shall unswervingly follow Negro ideals.'[48]

Admittedly, Du Bois considered Afro-Americans as Americans, but only as regards their place of birth, nationality, political ideals, language and religion. At the same time they were negroes, 'members of a vast historical race that from the very dawn of creation has slept in the dark forest of its fatherland'.

'We are the first fruits of this new nation', he went on, 'the harbinger of that black tomorrow which is yet destined to soften the whiteness of the Teutonic today. . . . As a race we must strive by race organization, by race solidarity, by race unity to the realization of that broader humanity which freely recognizes differences in men, but sternly deprecates inequality in their opportunities of development.'[49]

In the same context Du Bois formulated his ideas expressively: 'Should the Negro become a factor in world history, this will be through a Pan-Negro movement.'[50] Terms such as 'vanguard' and 'Pan-Negroism', and the confident future projections of world history, were indicative of a militant, dynamic and political attitude. Thus Du Bois considered Africa and the emancipation of the negro race as a function of the efforts of Afro-Americans to improve their own position in the USA; this was the weak point in the system of segregation whereby it could be completely unhinged. Out of such considerations sprang his commitment to the Pan-African movement, and above all his participation in the London Conference of 1900.

The political constellation in 1900

In order to understand the circumstances in which the Pan-African Conference of 1900 took place, the European must realize that these years were not so idyllic for Africans or Afro-Americans as they may seem to have been for us. The disillusionment encountered by Afro-Americans in the USA[51] had as its counterpart the seeds of apartheid in South Africa.[52] A similar retrogression was experienced by the young middle class in British West Africa and the West Indies. The liberal practices in the British colonies at mid-century, which had permitted Africans to attain even senior positions in the colonial administration with relative ease after undergoing appropriate training,[53] had given place by the end of the century to the 'colour bar'.[54] There thus developed, as with Afro-Americans, a discrepancy between the expectations engendered by modern education and the reduced chances of applying its fruits.

British Africa found itself at that time in a state of mental and political ferment. In 1898 in the Sierra Leone Protectorate, in the hinterland of Freetown, a serious insurrection broke out, the so-called 'Hut Tax War'.[55] The Gold Coast was the scene of the agitation by the Aborigines Rights Protection Society on the land question and the conflict within the Methodist mission which led finally to the foundation of an affiliate of the AMEZ church.[56] In Nigeria the formation of independent African churches was beginning.[57] On the Gold Coast and in Nigeria much commotion was also aroused by the question of reverting to African names and clothing, an external symbol of the return to traditional values.[58] In 1899 in South Africa the Boer War broke out and the Ethiopian movement began to develop.[59] In Rhodesia the Matabele uprising was suppressed with much bloodshed, as was the uprising in Bechuanaland further south. The glint of light was Abyssinia's victory over an Italian invading army near Adowa in 1896, which gave a topical slant to the Old Testament prophecies about Ethiopia.[60] Another cause of disquiet was the news that slave-like conditions existed in Zanzibar and Pemba. The West Indies were stricken by twin evils: the sugar crisis and unusually severe hurricanes. The rise of the White man to uncontested world domination, with the coloured colonial peoples in a corresponding subordinate position, seemed as though it could be neither halted nor reversed.

10 The Pan-African
Conference of 1900
and the first Pan-
African Association

This was the historical moment when the Pan-African Conference convened in London in July 1900: a small handful of men and women,
Africans and Afro-Americans from the New World, who met to discuss
the position of their respective groups and the defence of their interests.
The idea sprang from the 'fertile brain' of Henry Sylvester Williams
from Trinidad.[1] The latter had studied law in London and established
contact with African students there. As a barrister in London he represented the interests of African tribal chiefs, mainly over land disputes.[2]
He was also in touch with liberal groups in Britain such as the Aborigines Protection Society. At its annual meeting on 22 June 1899
Williams was among the speakers, who included James Johnson of
Lagos and Booker T. Washington and his wife; Williams took part in
the discussion about conditions in southern Africa.[3]

If in 1897 Du Bois spoke of 'Pan-Negroism', at the London Pan-
African Conference the term 'Pan-African' was introduced for the first
time. What we know about this comes from Du Bois;[4] it was adapted
and repeated in a stereotyped manner by Padmore[5] and other writers
since have with slight variations kept to his account.[6] No attention has
been paid to the evidence of Bishop Alexander Walters. A printed

account of the conference in the Du Bois papers and three reports in *The Times* provide valuable new information, as do some other contemporary statements which have hitherto been ignored.[7]

The African Association (1897–1900)

From the beginning of 1897 Williams pursued the idea of a conference to be attended by representatives of the 'African race from all the parts of the world'.[8] The motive seems to have been dismay over most of the events summarized at the end of the last chapter.[9] Williams made preparatory journeys through England, Scotland and Ireland, visiting especially such cities as Birmingham, Manchester, Liverpool, Edinburgh, Stirling, Dundee, Glasgow, Belfast and Dublin as well as the environs of London; then on 14 September 1897 he founded the African Association[10] in London, composed of 'several representative members of the race who lived in London'.[11]

Active membership was reserved for Africans and Afro-Americans but there was also an honorary membership for White sympathizers[12] – a solution which commended itself to similar organizations later.[13] On 15 October Fox-Bourne, the secretary of the Aborigines Protection Society, spoke to a meeting of the African Association of a possible collaboration between the older and younger organizations 'in the pursuit of their common aim'. At the meeting on 22 October the constitution was passed and the executive committee elected.[14] The chairmanship fell to the Rev. H. Mason Joseph from Antigua (West Indies); his deputy was T. J. Thompson from Sierra Leone.[15] Sylvester Williams was made honorary secretary and his compatriot A. C. Durham exercised the functions of assistant secretary. The treasurer was at first Mrs A. V. Kinloch, an African from South Africa who, apart from Miss Henrietta Colenso (daughter of the famous Anglican missionary bishop among the Zulus),[16] was the first to draw the attention of the British public to conditions in South Africa; as early as February 1898, however, she returned to South Africa.[17]

The name 'African Association' may perhaps be linked with the stillborn project of Thomas Hodgkin more than a generation earlier,[18] but until further material becomes available one must beware of making such hasty conjectures. The objective of the organization was

> to encourage a feeling of unity: to facilitate friendly intercourse among Africans in general; to promote and protect the interests of

all subjects claiming African descent, wholly or in part, in British Colonies and other places, especially in Africa, by circulating accurate information on all subjects affecting their rights and privileges as subjects of the British Empire and by direct appeals to the Imperial and local governments.[19]

As early as March 1898 the organ of the Aborigines Protection Society recorded with satisfaction: 'This promising society . . . appears to be making steady progress. Frequent meetings of its increasing number of members are held, at which information is exchanged on important questions affecting the welfare of Africans, not only on their own continent, but also in the West Indies and elsewhere.'[20] On 11 January the African Association organized a 'well-attended function' for members and friends at Exeter Hall, the traditional meeting-place of abolitionists and philanthropic societies, and later of the anti-imperialist left. Speakers included the president, the Rev. H. Mason Joseph, the chief editor of the journal *New Age*, A. E. Fletcher, W. Law, the Rev. C. W. Farquhar, Isle de Los,[21] E. J. Hayford,[22] a member of the distinguished Hayford family, and Williams. The only record of these addresses is Williams's statement that efforts were made 'to obtain direct and first-hand information from various parts of the Empire', and his suggestion 'that branch societies should be encouraged in the colonies and protectorates'.[23]

The new organization soon became politically active. In the autumn of 1898 members of the Liberal party suggested that the African Association should 'endeavour to get the Whigs to consider the possibility of giving a qualified member of the Association a constituency to run for Parliament with the express object of representing the Crown Colonies and Protectorates, West Africa, West Indies etc., etc.'[24] In October 1898, on behalf of the African Association, Williams submitted a petition to the Secretary of State for the Colonies, Joseph Chamberlain, asking for a clause to be included in the constitution then being enacted for Rhodesia which would safeguard the interests of the 'natives', i.e. of the Africans, similar to that which protected the Indians in Canada.[25] The Colonial Office gave a reassuring reply: the interests of the Africans would be safeguarded.[26] This episode gave the *Lagos Standard* further cause to praise the African Association. Already on 27 June 1898 the newspaper had introduced the organization to the African public, on the occasion of the first anniversary of its foundation.[27] The article was clearly inspired from London, for the wording of its aims is much the same as that of the official report of the Conference two years later, in 1900. But this article also contains some additional information. Thus we read: 'That in order to render the Natives who are brought under the control of Great Britain better for the transaction, their customs should be respected, Industrial Schools instituted for their benefit, and a simple and true Christianity taught them.'[28] Furthermore it was stated

> That the time had come when Parliament is required to parti-
> cularly consider the welfare of the Natives, and not to leave them
> absolutely to the capricious greed of so-called Empire builders.
> The thinkers of the [Black] Race fully recognise the fact that
> British rule has been of advantage to the people, but in no wise are
> prepared to contend that a system of oppression as enforced and
> practised in the Empire today is beneficial or emulatory.'[29]

The organization sought to win influence in Parliament, for many an evil could be checked by the central legislature. To put it differently: the African Association sought to act as an African lobby, influencing the British Parliament and the imperial government by means o petitions and meetings[30] or winning the sympathy of MPs. Finally the *Lagos Standard* went on to say: 'It is significant of the times in which we live that . . . an Association of this nature should be formed in the metropolis of the Empire. We call upon our countrymen to rally round the standard of the AFRICAN ASSOCIATION.'[31] The second comment shows that this first Pan-African organization was not nearly so isolated as is generally assumed. The *Lagos Standard* gave a positive appraisal of the work that had been achieved hitherto: 'The letter addressed by the Hon. Secretary of the African Association to Mr Secretary Chamber-lain in reference to the welfare of Native races in Rhodesia . . . shows the Association to be alive and active in the interest of Africa. The Association . . . is favourably situated for doing much good work in ameliorating the condition of down-trodden races.'[32] The paper also

> would like to see a more intimate connection established between
> the Association and the different colonies by having a representa-
> tive in each. By this a closer bond of union would be maintained
> between the Association and the people whom it is their object to
> benefit, and the former would be acquainted with many matters

which would escape their notice altogether if they depended only upon newspaper reports for information.[33]

The London Conference, the actual *raison d'être* of the African Association, was intended as an important step in enlightening British public opinion and influencing both parliament and government. At a meeting convened in London on 19 November 1898 it was decided

> in view of . . . the widespread ignorance which is prevalent in England about the treatment of native races under European and American rule, the African Association, which consists of members of the race resident in England, and which has been in existence for some years, has resolved during the Paris Exhibition, 1900 (which many representatives of the race may be visiting) to hold a Conference in London in the month of May in the said year.[34]

It was intended 'to take steps to influence public opinion on existing proceedings and conditions affecting the welfare of the native in the various parts of the world, viz. South Africa, West Africa, West Indies and United States of America'.

In reply to a circular letter 'most encouraging answers' were received. On 12 June 1899 a preparatory session was held in London at which several prominent Africans and Afro-Americans were present. The report of this meeting mentions expressly: Bishop J. F. Holly (Haiti),[35] Bishop James Johnson (Lagos)[36] and Bishop Henry Turner (USA)[37] (i.e. two AME bishops and one Anglican assistant bishop); the Rev. M. Agbebi (Lagos),[38] the Rev. C. W. Farquhar,[39] August Straker, an American judge, Professor Scarborough (USA),[40] H. R. Cargill (Jamaica), Tengu Jabavu (South Africa), Otonba Payne (Lagos)[41] and Booker T. Washington (USA).[42] The other participants were probably members of the African Association resident in London or its environs.

The composition of the wider group of interested persons already deserves to be called Pan-African. Of the nine whose provenance can be determined at the present time, at least four came from Africa itself (Johnson, Agbebi, Payne, Jabavu), and no less than three from Lagos. Equally strongly represented were Afro-Americans from the USA, special importance being attached to the attendance of Booker T. Washington. The presence of Bishop Turner of the AME may be explained by his earlier interest in resettlement in Africa and in missionary work in South Africa.[43] Considerable historical significance is also attached to the presence of Bishop Holly from Haiti.[44] He was a product of the second wave of Afro-American immigrants from the USA to Haiti around 1860, and along with Turner embodies the Pan-African interests of the AME church, although without being a party to its Afro-American missionary chauvinism.[45]

The preliminary meeting was almost as representative as was the actual Pan-African Conference. About its results nothing is as yet known. It may have suggested postponing the date originally fixed from May to 23–25 July 1900, so that it could take place just after the World's Christian Endeavour Conference, which some of the clerical members who were present in such large numbers wanted to attend. The end of July was also convenient for Afro-American tourists on holiday to combine the Pan-African Conference with a visit to the World Fair in Paris.[46]

It is not yet certain by whom, when and for what reason the term 'Pan-African' was introduced. Neither in the announcement issued in November 1898 nor at the preliminary conference in the following year does the word 'Pan-African' appear. The preliminary conference of 1899 would have been the most likely place at which to discuss the title of the planned conference, which at any rate 'put the word "Pan-African" in the dictionaries for the first time'.[47] The term was apparently chosen on an analogy with other 'Pan' movements, which were so widely known by 1900 that theoretically speaking anyone might have suggested it. Du Bois may be ruled out for otherwise he would surely have mentioned the fact soon and on frequent occasions thereafter. Yet he may have given an indirect impulse since already in 1897 he had spoken of 'Pan-Negroism',[48] a term which he may have coined from his observations in Central Europe some years before, when Pan-Germans and Pan-Slavs were in the news.[49] 'Pan-African' would thus be a development of 'Pan-Negroism', which for its part may also have been coined as an analogy to the catch-word 'Pan-Americanism'. The term 'Pan-African' may have emerged during the preliminary conference held on 12 June 1899 or in the course of other discussions in London without it being possible to ascertain afterwards whose idea it was – as frequently happens on such occasions. In this case the creation of the term would have been a collective achievement The word 'Pan-African' may have originated from the 'fertile brain' of Williams (Alexander Walters) without his having left behind any evidence of the fact, for he was a modest man and up to the present has remained an almost shadowy figure. At the moment one can do no more than formulate hypotheses and weigh up possibilities.

The composition and course of the Conference

The Pan-African Conference took place at Westminster Town Hall, London S.W.1, from 23 to 25 July 1900. By modern standards the number of participants was small: the most precise enumeration of the participants, by Alexander Walters, mentions thirty-two.[50] Grouping them according to their countries of origin, we get the following picture:

AFRICA

Benito Sylvain, *ADC to Emperor Menelik, Abyssinia*
F. S. R. Johnson, *ex-Attorney-General, Liberia*
G. W. Dove,[51] *City Councillor in Freetown, Sierra Leone*
A. F. Ribeiro,[52] *lawyer, Gold Coast*

USA:

Alexander Walters, *AMEZ bishop and president of the National Afro-American Council*
W. E. B. Du Bois, *professor, Atlanta, Georgia*
J. L. Love, *professor, Washington DC*
Henry R. Downing, *ex-consul in Luanda (Angola)*
T. J. Calloway, *Washington DC*
Chas P. Lee, *counsellor, New York*
Miss Anna H. Jones, MA, *Missouri*
Miss Barrier, *Washington DC*
Mrs Annie J. Cooper, *Washington DC*
Miss Ada Harris, *Indiana*
B. W. Arnett, *chaplain, Illinois*

CANADA:

Rev. Henry B. Brown, *Lower Canada*

WEST INDIES:

C. W. French, *St Kitts*
Dr R. A. K. Savage, *delegate of the Afro-West Indian Literary Society, Edinburgh*

Mr Meyer, *ditto*
A. Pulcherrie Pierre, *Trinidad*
H. Sylvester Williams, *barrister, Trinidad (and London)*
R. E. Phipps, *lawyer, Trinidad*
John E. Quinlan, *land surveyor, St Lucia*
G. L. Christian, *Dominica*
A. R. Hamilton, *Jamaica*
Rev. H. Mason Joseph, *Antigua*

LONDON:
S. Coleridge-Taylor
Rev. Henry Smith
J. Buckle
J. F. Loudin, *director of the Fisk Jubilee Singers*
Mrs J. F. Loudin

ORIGIN NOT GIVEN:
Dr John Alcindor[53]

To these should be added others who do not appear as participants in Walters's account but who signed an address of congratulation to James Johnson on his appointment as bishop several days before the Conference began. In this document, besides some of the participants already mentioned (such as Williams, Johnson, Sylvain etc.), there also appeared the following names: Mrs. M. T. Cole, N. W. Holm (Lagos), Dr Schomerus, D. E. Tobias and J. W. D. Worrell.[54] These were probably interested persons who had to leave before the Conference began; this was also the case with James Johnson, who regretted the fact greatly.[55] Finally mention may be made of Felix Moscheles, a participant not referred to by Walters, as well as J. R. Archer, London, committee member of the permanent organization which was founded later.[56]

At the conference of 1900 Africa was less well represented than at the preliminary conference of 1899. A somewhat mysterious figure is Benito Sylvain; rumour has it that he originated from Haiti, as his surname would suggest.[57] Lagos was not represented this time, whereas Sierre Leone and the Gold Coast were. Samuel Coleridge-Taylor, a composer who was well known at the time, and who had an English mother and a father from Sierra Leone, identified himself with the aspirations of Africans and Afro-Americans; he took charge of the musical side of the programme.[58] J. F. Loudin and his wife were probably Afro-Americans then living in London, for Fisk was an Afro-American university with a well-known choir.

If one takes the participants whose origin can be identified unequivocally, then Afro-Americans from the USA and the West Indies provided the largest contingent with eleven each. In the Afro-American contingent it is striking to find a relatively large number (four) of female participants. Noteworthy is the presence of five lawyers; the number of clergymen had declined from nine to four since the preliminary conference of 1899. Du Bois's subsequent description is misleading, since the delegates did not come mainly 'from England and the West Indies with a few colored North Americans',[59] but mainly from North America and the West Indies. The African element was underrepresented but all the same worth mentioning.

As regards the proceedings of the Conference, the best information is provided by three reports in *The Times*, in addition to which one should consult the account given by Alexander Walters.[60] It was apparently hoped that the bishop of London would take the chair, for *The Times* reports that because of his absence Bishop Alexander Walters did so; he remained chairman for the three days that the Conference lasted. He was assisted by the two vice-chairmen: Johnson (Liberia) and Benito Sylvain (Abyssinia). If we add Sylvester Williams, then Pan-Africanism was represented in the first instance by one representative of the vanguard of the Pan-Negro movement (i.e. an American negro), one West Indian and delegates of the two independent African states – Liberia and Abyssinia (Ethiopia). But it was a full-blooded African who was the object of special honours on the part of some participants before the Conference: Bishop Johnson, the 'Sierra Leonean' from Lagos.[61] In a ceremonial address he was congratulated upon his recent promotion to the rank of Anglican assistant bishop for the Niger delta; this congratulatory message was combined with a survey of the situation of the Black race:

> 'Tis true, my Lord, that the present features of the history of the African race, wherever found, either in their own home, or under the flags of the known powers, are not too reassuring, but there is consolation in the unquestioned fact that there is a noticeable *esprit de corps* amongst them, encouraging us to look forward to the

future. The powers and capacity of our great men have hitherto had little scope for development, through a cruel design of time to dissociate the race from its share in the progress of the civilization of the world; but it is our firm belief that we must employ our own talent and energy to (a) educate our young minds in the prolific possibilities of the race; (b) develop our own chroniclers; (c) institute our own libraries and organisations, and thus march side by side with our more fortunate Caucasian brothers.[62]

Johnson's answer throws some light upon the participants at the Conference: 'The fact that almost all those who are taking part in this wonderful movement are still young is encouraging.' Two of the leading men (Williams and Du Bois) were aged thirty-two, Coleridge-Taylor twenty-five and Walters forty-two. In view of a certain apathy in his own country – the result of an inadequate educational system – Johnson was delighted with 'the young men from the West Indies, the USA, Liberia and Abyssinia and with their determination to represent the cause of their race to a happy end'. He predicted hopefully:

> The Pan-African Conference is the beginning of a union I long hoped for, and would to God be universal. As a people, recollect this: we are destined, despite the fallacies of many, to be recognised. Already we have morality, religion and perseverance on our balance sheet – government will come as we labour towards that end. Temper your deliberations with truth, and God will do the rest. There are good friends in England yet, and though we wade through the mire of the evil curses of civilization in the Colonies, their voices will blend with ours, that righteousness and justice be the ruling words of British civilization.[63]

After this prologue Alexander Walters opened the Conference on Monday, 23 July 1900, with a remark which took up James Johnson's ideas: 'For the first time in the history of the world black men had gathered together from all parts of the globe with the object of discussing and improving the condition of the black race.' Subsequently he gave a survey of the condition of Afro-Americans in the USA: '. . . . it was their misfortune to live among a people whose laws, traditions, and prejudices had been against them for centuries. It had ever been the policy of a certain class of Americans to keep the negro down. The real question which concerned them in America was: Was the negro to be granted equal rights?'[64] 'They [the negroes] had been able to eliminate 45 per cent of their illiterates, and today they represented $m.753 real estate and property. They were engaged in a long and severe struggle for full social and political rights, and they asked for sympathy, consideration, and encouragement.'[65]

After Walters it was C. W. French (St Kitts) who put in a claim for the coloured people to be recognized as men enjoying equal rights with the Whites. Subsequently Miss Jones (Kansas) spoke about retaining the individual characteristics of the race, but no more details about her contribution were recorded. The chairman, Bishops Walters, announced the creation in the near future of an office in London to influence the legislature in favour of the coloured race, i.e. the formal setting up of the coloured lobby.

In the meantime the bishop of London had arrived late. In his address he expressed the hope that the Conference might be the forerunner of many others; he warned against impatience but regarded it as a good omen that such a meeting could take place for the first time in the history of the world. He emphasized that

> they [the public] were well aware that the future of every race must be in the hands of that race itself – who should learn how to protect the race against the results of the too rapid contact with other and more advanced forms of civilization; and how to educate the people to a sense of responsibility of self-government. After all they must look forward in their dealings with other races ultimately to confer on them, and that as soon as possible, some of the benefits of self-government that they themselves enjoyed. How to do that wisely and well was not an easy matter.[66]

This was the highlight of his speech; it implied an indirect criticism of the prevailing imperialist ideology which was received with grateful cheers. The British public, he said, 'did not want the period of tutelage to be unduly prolonged, and they desired that the result of the tutelage should be wise, judicious, kindly and tending to the ultimate development of native races. They might rest assured of the real and deep sympathy of the English people. Any help that the delegates could give in the settlement of the problems would be most gladly welcomed (cheers).'

In the evening Benito Sylvain gave a speech on the theme 'The Necessary Concord to be Established between Native Races and

European Colonists'. He asserted that everywhere Blacks had already proved themselves worthy of freedom and criticized Britain as

> responsible for the anti-liberal reaction which had characterized the colonial policy for the last 15 years. The British Government had tolerated the most frightful deeds of colonizing companies. Before very many years had passed away the rights of the natives must be recognized by every colonial Power. Natives must be no more considered like serfs, taxable and workable at their master's discretion, but as an indispensable element for the prosperity of the colonies, and consequently must have an equitable participation in the profits, both material and mental, of colonizing. No human power could stop the African natives in their social and political development. The question now was whether Europe would have the improvement for or against her interest. The Pan-African Association, which must be the issue of the conference, would assist by all means a realization of such a desirable understanding.[67]

The evening session ended with a talk by Mrs A. J. Cooper, 'The Negro Problem in America', of which nothing is known except the title.

The second day of the Conference began with a general discussion about 'The Progress of our People in the Light of Current History'. Opening the discussion, Johnson (Liberia) referred to the example of his country and to the good qualities of the Africans who only needed time to develop a capacity for self-government. He was followed by J. E. Quinlan (St Lucia) with a complaint about conditions in the West Indies and a criticism of conditions in South Africa, where the British ought to complete their great work of sixty years ago (probably the slave emancipation of 1834-8). Meyer of the Edinburgh Afro-West Indian Literary Society attacked the assumption by some people who 'were trying to prove that negroes were worthless and depraved persons who had no right to live. It was difficult to understand this.' He appealed to the British, as a Christian nation, 'to act up to their principles and to do justice to the black race. Black children of America were making remarkable progress in the universities and colleges and competing with the child of 1900 years of civilization.'[68]

R. E. Phipps (Trinidad) complained about discrimination against coloured people in the colonial service, who received only the worst jobs and were passed over in promotion.

Subsequently the discussion turned to the general theme 'Africa, the Sphinx of History, in the Light of Unsolved Problems'. Mr D. Tobias, a participant who does not appear in any list and about whom nothing else is known, touched upon a theme familiar to us: Africa's contribution to the history of culture. He claimed that civilization had been commenced by Black men, obviously alluding to the African character of ancient Egypt. As a model in solving difficult contemporary problems he referred to Bishop Colenso, the great Anglican missionary bishop among the Zulus, and was cheered by those present. On the Boer War 'he said that they must see at the end of the war that all the vile principles that made war possible were removed',[69] by which he probably meant the beginnings of apartheid.

The chairman, Bishop Walters, indicated at this point that three things ought to be borne in mind: knowledge of actual conditions, the claim to human rights and justice, and the way in which their own objectives were to be implemented. Subsequently Du Bois, the Rev. H. Smith, chaplain Arnett and Professor Calloway participated in the discussion; the report in *The Times* unfortunately has nothing to say about their contributions. The meeting concluded with a prayer. A tea-party at Fulham Palace, the official residence of the bishop of London, was followed by further speeches in the evening; of these, too, there is no record, and we are told merely that there were musical offerings, probably by Coleridge-Taylor.

The third and last day of the conference was opened by Bishop Walters who thanked the liberal and philanthropic elements in Britain and America who had stood up for the negroes in those countries. G. L. Christian (Dominica) criticized the Boers' policy towards the natives in South Africa. In particular he gave several examples of the harmfulness of racial segregation, and then turned to the difficult conditions facing labourers in Rhodesia and the West Indies, his own homeland. The speaker characterized these conditions as a revival of slavery and demanded that the imperial government should pass legislation to protect the natives. He also called for native reservations to be set up and for chiefs to be granted a certain measure of autonomy.

H. R. Downing (USA) declared that the Black race would not accept a permanent state of slavery. It did not wish to take freedom by force, but to earn it by its own merits. 'The day will come when the world will recognize its value.' C. P. Lee (USA) thought that the Negro problem could best be solved by the acquisition of property and education, so that coloured people could compete with Whites in all fields. This meant that they would have to settle their own differences and win complete equality of rights. Sylvester Williams came back to the question of South Africa and suggested that the time had come for a public protest. The last speakers included Felix Moscheles as well as several unidentified persons.

The afternoon was devoted to questions of organization. The central issue was the transformation of the African Association into the 'Pan-African Association'.[70] Subsequently a declaration 'To the Nations of the World' was adopted and it was announced that a petition would be sent to Queen Victoria. It was probably at this session that the delegates passed several special resolutions which are printed in the report of the Conference. After a reception at the House of Commons in the afternoon, the participants met once again in the evening for a final musical entertainment, at which the speakers included C. W. French (St Kitts) and the Rev. H. M. Joseph (Antigua), who up to this point had been chairman of the African Association.

The resolutions were mostly votes of thanks to organizations which had worked for the African cause, i.e. the traditional humanitarian and philanthropic circles in England spoken of by Walters on 25 July 1900.[71] The British and Foreign Anti-Slavery Society was thanked for having brought about the abolition of slavery in the West Indies, Africa, the USA and Brazil, but regret was expressed at its survival in Zanzibar and on Pemba and other places. It was resolved 'that the same spirit which inspired that noble host, represented in the names of Granville Sharp, William Wilberforce, Thomas Buxton and William Clarkson to work for the liberation of our fathers and forefathers, will continue to inflame the lives of the present generation for the achievement of like, if not greater, heroism for Christ and humanity'.[72] The same initial and concluding phrases[73] were employed in another resolution on 'The Native Races and the Liquor Traffic United Committee', which thanked it for having opposed the import of cheap alcohol into Africa. Briefer and less emotional was the resolution on the Aborigines Protection Society. This expressed gratitude for its efforts on behalf of the 'aboriginal inhabitants' of the British Empire and elsewhere. Finally, a lengthy resolution was passed thanking the Quakers for the part they had played in the emancipation of the slaves and for their present endeavours in Zanzibar and East Africa to win 'the freedom of the underprivileged members of the race who are enslaved under

British rule'. The hope was also expressed that the Quakers would continue to help members of the Black race in their demand for human and civil rights during the transitional period when they still had to suffer from prejudice and greed.

The petition to Queen Victoria, signed by the chairman of the Pan-African Association, directed the British government's attention to conditions in southern Africa. The grievances listed included the following: the 'compound system' of enclosed and controlled barracks for African workers in Kimberley (South Africa) and Rhodesia; the system of indentured labour, a camouflaged means of enslaving Africans to White settlers; the use of forced labour in public works; special passes for coloured people; rules enforcing segregation; and obstacles put in the way of Africans obtaining land and voting rights.[74] Joseph Chamberlain later replied with a general and vague statement, frequently quoted in the literature, to the effect that Queen Victoria would not 'overlook the interests and welfare of the native races'.[75] Neither the petition nor the reply exerted any influence upon subsequent developments in South Africa or Rhodesia.

The appeal 'To the Nations of the World' will be well known to those who have read the literature in English. In this Du Bois predicted boldly: 'The problem of the twentieth century is the problem of the color line.'[76] Today, now that decolonization is almost complete,[77] it is well worth going into the details of this declaration of 1900; those familiar with the background material discussed above in Part I will find that some of its points stand out in high relief. It begins with a brief indication of the geographical, political and historical significance of the conference's meeting-place: 'In the metropolis of the modern world, in this the closing year of the nineteenth century, there has been assembled a congress of men and women of African blood, to deliberate solemnly the present situation and outlook of the darker races of mankind.'[78]

Then follows the sentence which makes this one of the most important documents of our century: 'The problem of the twentieth century is the problem of the color line, the question as to how far differences of race, which show themselves chiefly in the color of the skin and the texture of the hair, are going to be made, hereafter, the basis of denying to over half the world the right of sharing to their utmost ability the opportunities and privileges of modern mankind.'[79]

The next passage combines a realistic insight into the situation as it existed at the time with praise for the cultural achievements of the past, entirely in the sense of the tradition analysed above:[80] 'To be sure, the darker races are today the least advanced in culture according to European standards. This has not, however, always been the case in the past, and certainly the world's history, both ancient and modern, has given many instances of no despicable ability and capacity among the blackest races of men.'

After this sober assessment of the present and comforting glance at the past, the authors of the document look forward to the future with confidence, coupled with a warning:

> In any case, the modern world must needs remember that in this age, when the ends of the world are being brought so near together, the millions of black men in Africa, America, and the Islands of the Sea, not to speak of the brown and yellow myriads elsewhere, are bound to have a great influence upon the world in the future, by reason of sheer numbers and physical contact. If now the world of culture bends itself towards giving Negroes and other dark men the largest and broadest opportunity for education and self-development, then this contact and influence is bound to have a beneficial effect upon the world and hasten human progress. But if, by reason of carelessness, prejudice, greed and injustice, the black world is to be exploited and ravished and degraded, the results must be deplorable, if not fatal – not simply to them, but to the high ideals of justice, freedom and culture which a thousand years of Christian civilization have held before Europe.[81]

In the name of these high ideals the Conference appealed to the world not to allow any retrogression in human development, not to make race a barrier between men and not to accept the exploitation of Africa, least of all in the disguise of Christian missionary activity. The British were reminded of Wilberforce, Clarkson, Buxton, Sharp, Bishop Colenso and Livingstone and were called upon 'to provide as soon as possible the rights of a responsible government for the Black colonies in Africa and in the West Indies', i.e. at least autonomy within the framework of imperialism. In the name of abolitionists such as Garrison, Wendell Philips and Frederick Douglass the USA was called upon to grant full equality to Afro-Americans. The German Empire and the French Republic were reminded that justice was the elementary condition for the prosperity of their colonies. The Congo Free State should become a great negro state. Finally the world was called upon to respect the integrity and independence of the free negro states of Abyssinia, Liberia, Haiti, 'etc.',[82] while 'the independent tribes of Africa, the Negroes of the West Indies and America and the Black subjects of all nations should take heart, try unceasingly and fight bravely' in order to 'prove to the world that they were indisputably entitled to belong to the great brotherhood of mankind'. The appeal was signed by Walters, Henry B. Brown, Sylvester Williams and Du Bois.

With its mixture of realism and idealist pathos, rationalism and romanticism, élitist cultural consciousness and appeal to the African tribesmen, the declaration is wholly in the spirit of Du Bois, who was also its main author.[83] To some extent it brings together various elements of proto-Pan-Africanism, as the preceding reports and contributions to discussions had done,[84] but here the language is more literary, combining elegance with a stylized pathos.

Although the provenance of the participants to the Pan-African Conference gave it the character of a Pan-Negro movement, in the sense of Du Bois's formula of 1897,[85] the practical demands contained in the petition to Queen Victoria were restricted to Africa, indeed to the southern part of the continent. The declaration 'To the Nations of the World',[86] by contrast, saw the problem as one affecting coloured people the world over, and so took up Delany's ideas.[87]

The first Pan-African Association

One result of the Conference was the transformation of the provisional African Association into a Pan-African Association. In London it broadened its organizational foundations, at least on paper, and changes were made in the leadership. Alexander Walters was elected chairman and the Rev. Henry B. Brown his deputy. The following officers were appointed: Dr R. J. Colenso as general treasurer,[88] Benito Sylvain as general delegate for Africa and Sylvester Williams as general secretary. There was also a six-man executive committee: Henry R. Downing (USA), S. Coleridge-Taylor (London), F. J. Loudin (London), J. R. Archer (London), Mrs Jane Cobden-Unwin and Mrs Annie J. Cooper (USA).[89] As a whole the Afro-American element was thus predominant.

The Pan-African Association had no wish to restrict its activities to those of its central organization. It sought the corporate affiliation of existing regional and local organizations with analogous objectives and the establishment of regional branches throughout the area to which Pan-Africanism appealed – in conformity with the ideas aired earlier in the *Lagos Standard*.[90] The geographical distribution of these projected branches gives an impression of the Association's ambitions and confirms its character as a Pan-Negro movement, for no branches were foreseen in Asia or North Africa, whereas full coverage was provided for areas with a Black population: USA, Haiti, Abyssinia, Liberia, South Africa (subdivided into Natal, Cape Town, Rhodesia), West Africa (Sierra Leone, Lagos), Gold Coast, British West Indies (Jamaica, Trinidad), Canada and finally the Orange River Colony and the Transvaal. Only for about half the regional branches could vice-chairmen or secretaries be found in London. The concluding sentence invited interested parties to report to the general secretary, so that the gaps might be filled.

A list of those whose names were put forward in this connection provides an insight into the strengths and weaknesses of early Pan-Africanism, and also shows the range of personal contacts that had been made. The report of the Conference gives the following picture:[91]

USA:	W. E. B. Du Bois; T. J. Calloway
Haiti:	M. A. Fermin; Bishop Holly
Abyssinia:	Benito Sylvain; Dr. A. K. Savage
Liberia:	F. S. R. Johnson; S. F. Dennis
Natal	Edwin Kinloch; N.N.
Sierra Leone:	J. A. Williams; M. Lewis
Lagos:	J. Otonba Payne; N. W. Holm
Jamaica:	H. R. Cargill; N.N.

One of the most notable gaps is the Gold Coast, a traditional centre of nationalist activity, although in 1900 several Africans from the Gold Coast lived in London;[92] another is Trinidad, although besides Williams three other delegates (Pierre, Phipps and Alcindor) came from that island.

We may restrict our comments to the less well-known personalities. M. A. Fermin is probably identical with Anténor Firmin, the most important intellectual and statesman of Haiti.[93] If this is so, 'M' is presumably an abbreviation for 'Monsieur', and the 'e' in the surname a mistake in the transcription or a misprint. Dr A. K. Savage, secretary of the Abyssinian organization, had participated in the Pan-African Conference as a delegate of the Afro-West Indian Literary Society;[94]

from this, and from his English name, it may be inferred that he was of British West Indian descent, so that his appearance in this new position is something of a surprise. About S. F. Dennis (Liberia) nothing is as yet known. Edwin Kinloch (Natal) was presumably related or married to Mrs A. V. Kinloch, the first treasurer of the African Association.[95] J. A. Williams is probably James A. Williams, a prosperous merchant from Freetown.[96] M. Lewis may be a member of the family of Sir Samuel Lewis, the most eminent lawyer in Sierra Leone at the turn of the century;[97] in his monumental *History of Sierra Leone* C. Fyfe does not refer to any Lewis with this initial, so that the question must still remain an open one. Payne (Lagos) had participated in the preliminary conference in London in June 1899, and Holm (Lagos) had signed the congratulatory address to Bishop James Johnson just before the Conference opened.[98]

For practical reasons London remained the seat of the Pan-African Association, with an address at 61–2 Chancery Lane. Since this is close to the Law Courts, it may have been Williams's chambers. The building was destroyed during World War II, so that there is no chance of finding any documents about the Pan-African Association in some dusty attic.

What actually became of the planned regional organizations cannot as yet be determined. Probably most of them existed only on paper. At present we have only a little information about the branch in Jamaica, and this may simply be because Sylvester Williams himself pushed ahead with it during a trip through the West Indies at the beginning of 1901. In March 1901 a meeting took place at St George's School, Kingston, 'to found a local branch of the Pan-African Association'. The chair was taken by Sydney Olivier, the British governor, who in a lengthy address showed himself rather sceptical about the necessity for a Pan-African Association but otherwise defended negro interests in a completely loyal way. The participants in the meeting included 'many well-known natives' whose names, however, are not recorded.[99]

To maintain the unity of the organization and to develop the Pan-African movement it was planned to hold a Pan-African conference every two years; the meetings were to take place in the USA in 1902 and in Haiti in 1904. Nothing is known about any preparations for such a meeting except for the information, printed in bold type in the report, that persons interested in attending the next conference should report in writing as soon as possible.[100]

The same purposes were fulfilled by the newspaper of the Pan-African Association, which was intended to be a monthly and bore the title the *Pan-African* to indicate its programme. It appeared in London under the editorship of Sylvester Williams; each issue cost sixpence and had eight pages with two columns to a page. The first number (October 1901) was probably also the last, for the newspaper collection of the British Museum has only this single issue.[101] The address of the editor was given as 26a Tudor Street, London E.C.; its motto was 'Liberty and Light', to which was added: 'Issued for the express purpose of diffusing information concerning the interests of the African and his Descendants in the British Empire.'[102]

The leading article which inaugurated the *Pan-African* was accordingly not Pan-African in the strict sense of the term, but spoke of 'the educated British Negro', about whom the British public knew so little. 'The whole members of the race are clubbed together, indicating so many helpless subjects fit for philanthropic sympathy. They are not considered as independent thinkers and doers.'[103] This ignorance it was the task of the *Pan-African* to rectify. On the other hand it regarded itself as 'the spokesman of millions of Africans and their descendants' and promised to represent their interests 'fearlessly and impartially'. The leading article concluded:

> Having disclosed in a brief outline the policy of the paper, we apprehend difficulties, but these have always stood in the path of progress. At times they have been scaled and at others succeeded in crippling a beginner. Whatever may be the future of this attempt, we are convinced that no other but a Negro can represent the Negro, and the times demand the presence of that Negro, to serve the deserving cause of a people the most despised and ill-used today.[104]

In conformity with this principle of solidarity, news was published about abuses in various parts of the British Empire, ranging from a draft bill on corporal punishment in Jamaica to the ambiguous position of Africans during the South African War. Sometimes items were accompanied by brief comments. The briefest one was appended to a Reuter report that the Australian parliament had passed a law prohibiting mail ships from signing on Black seamen, whereupon members gave 'three cheers for White Australia'. The comment: 'Oh!!'.

A report about the discourteous treatment of a coloured missionary on a liner owned by Elder, Dempster & Co., which had for decades run the passenger service between Liverpool and West Africa, drew from the *Pan-African* the remark that the shipping line should realize 'that West Indian Negroes who paid for their passage would not tolerate that persecution by its servants should go unpunished.'

Of particular historical interest is a letter written on 10 October 1901 by Keir Hardie, the first leader of the newly formed British Labour party, to Sylvester Williams:

> Dear Sir, I am much interested in your proposed new venture, THE PAN-AFRICAN, and cordially wish it success. I know that apart from a few interested parties of the South African millionaire type, the wrongs done to your people under British rule are more due to ignorance than to any desire to act unjustly. Such an organ as THE PAN-AFRICAN will do much to remove this ignorance; and this, if backed by temperate yet strenuous action on the part of your own people, will, in course of time, lead to the redress of those wrongs, the continuation of which is a disgrace and a source of weakness to the British Empire. Again wishing the venture success, I am, yours faithfully . . .[105]

From the start the *Pan-African* had no illusions about the difficulties of the new enterprise and fully appreciated that the Pan-African Association might collapse.[106] That these fears were justified is proved by a notice in the first issue about the internal life of the association. Under the heading 'The Pan-African Association Exists' the journal noted in a somewhat desperate tone that certain unidentified members had taken advantage of Sylvester Williams's absence from London (when he stayed in the West Indies at the beginning of 1901) to carry out a kind of palace revolution – not in order to seize power but to dissolve the association on the grounds of shortage of funds, and to report the fact to the press. No names were mentioned, but apparently at least the London-based members of the executive committee were involved, as they were fired later on for their move.

The move was made without the knowledge of the chairman (Alexander Walters) or 'all the members of the committee'. On 4 September 1901 Bishop Walters and Sylvester Williams returned to London and convened a meeting for 13 September. This took place in the South Place Institute, Finsbury Pavement, London E.C., and announced that the Pan-African Association was still in existence. The members of the committee who had backed the move to dissolve the association were considered to have disqualified themselves. In their place six new members were appointed: Bishop Small of AMEZ (USA),[107] Dr R. N. Love (Jamaica), Lieutenant Lazare (Trinidad), the Rev. Henry Smith (London), Tengu Jabavu (South Africa) and J. Otonba Payne (Lagos);[108] until the next conference, to be held in the States in the following year, Sylvester Williams was to remain general secretary.

The newly constituted committee had a stronger African representation. But the change remained an academic matter, for the Pan-African Association had apparently reached the end of its tether and was unable to bring off any further conferences.

Some time during the following months, unnoticed by contemporaries and historians, it ceased to exist. After a brief spell in South Africa, where he was not allowed to practise as a barrister,[109] Sylvester Williams returned to his native Trinidad and disappeared into obscurity. In 1911 he died there, without having committed anything to print about the Pan-African Association. Alexander Walters mentioned the foundation of the Pan-African Association; he also named its inner circle of leaders and the members of the committee;[110] but Walters, too, virtually fell into oblivion. Du Bois with his vast literary output would have been in the best position to speak about this first attempt to set up a Pan-African organization, but his lips remained sealed until 1945–7, when he made a few rather vague remarks[111] – possibly because the Pan-African Conference was not his idea, as one Afro-American author suggests rather harshly; this view is strengthened by what we know about Du Bois's character, which was notoriously egocentric and narcissistic.[112]

Whatever the case may be, the first attempt to give organizational form to the disparate forces of Pan-Africanism was a failure. It was premature and over-ambitious; nevertheless the endeavour was not in vain. A beginning had been made in the task of uniting, on a common Pan-African basis, elements situated at the three corners of the 'Pan-African triangle': the modernized Afro-American, South African and West African élites; the abolitionist tradition; and opposition to imperialism and racism throughout the world, especially in South Africa and the USA. Moreover, in the person of Du Bois, Pan-Africanism had found an eloquent propagandist with a powerful imagination, who embodied the intellectual continuity of the entire Pan-African movement.[113]

Furthermore it may be said that the London conference of 1900 was by no means an isolated episode, as has been assumed hitherto in the light of Du Bois's remarks.[114] Not only was Williams in contact with humanitarian anti-imperialist elements in England, but also the links with Africa were stronger than has been assumed: Sierra Leone, the Gold Coast, Nigeria and South Africa were all represented in the Pan-African Association and at the Pan-African Conference.[115] The *Lagos Standard*, which had welcomed the establishment of the association,[116] concluded its relatively detailed report on the Conference with the following comments:

> Such an organization cannot but be a powerful agency in the work of the amelioration of the condition of Native Races, and the solution of the Negro Problem, and we look for substantial results from its permanent operation. Whilst congratulating the founders and supporters of the 'African Association' for the success which has attended their efforts, we take this opportunity of appealing to members of the Race the world over to extend their hearty co-operation to an institution which in its great and noble aspirations is so very deserving of their help, sympathy and encouragement.[117]

In spite of all the interest shown, social and political conditions were not yet mature enough for success to be permanent. The intelligentsia in Africa, the USA and the West Indies was still too weak in numbers and economic power, and at the beginning of the twentieth century colonial imperialism still stood unshaken.

11 Developments prior to World War I

After the break-up of the first Pan-African Association shortly after 1900 almost two decades passed before a second Pan-African Association developed after World War I. From 1919 onwards Pan-African meetings were again held, this time as congresses rather than merely a conference as in 1900. Until 1945 the Pan-African movement was thought to have begun in 1919; no reference was made to its antecedents in 1900 – partly, it seems, due to Du Bois's long silence.[1]

After 1900 came a period of preparation, a breathing-space. It is no simple matter to deal in a single chapter with developments in areas situated so far apart from one another. The most important events took place in Africa, the West Indies, Britain and the USA – in that chronological order, but we also have to keep in mind the interconnections between the terminal points of the Pan-African 'triangle'.

Simultaneously at all these three (or rather, four!) points we can follow the further development of that sociological process which had been under way since the late eighteenth century and had created the conditions for the emergence of Pan-Africanism. The formation of a privileged bourgeois intelligentsia was accelerated by modern economic development. The spread of democratic ideas heightened the self-awareness of these men and made them feel twice as painfully the iniquities of racism and colonialism. They demanded the removal of the social and political barriers which impeded their further ascent up the ladder of success, in rather the same manner as the rising French bourgeoisie confronted and absolute monarchy under the *ancien régime*. For them the *ancien régime* comprised the European colonial oligarchy headed by a governor who wielded absolute power[2] or, in the case of the southern states of the US, the White majority.

The young urban Afro-American intelligentsia in the USA was perturbed at the growing number of lynch murders and race riots in the cities and was provoked to political activity.[3]

The struggle for elementary human rights and equality acquired in their eyes a new urgency and ceased to be merely an abstract issue. Conditions in Britain, for all the latent racism (as it affected negroes looking for accommodation etc.), were almost idyllic by comparison with the United States and afforded Afro-West Indians and Africans from the colonies more scope for individual and political development than they enjoyed in their own homelands. In Africa the most important centres in the development of Pan-Africanism were, as before, the Gold Coast and Nigeria; the significance of Sierra Leone and South Africa declined, but in Nyasaland there developed a new secondary centre; Chilembwe was in contact with the United States by way of South Africa.[4]

In the three West African colonies the events of the turn of the century, once the initial turmoil had subsided, brought about a new stability which in turn facilitated an economic boom and the spread of education. In Nigeria Lugard subjugated the Fulani emirates; on the Gold Coast Ashanti was conquered and annexed, which put an end to decades of pressure upon the coastal tribes from this quarter; in Sierra Leone the colonial authorities consolidated their hold on the hinterland. Economic structures on a larger scale than those known hitherto came into being. The cocoa crop quickly gained in importance among the Yoruba in Nigeria, as it did also on the Gold Coast (in Ashanti and also in the hilly area between the coast and Ashanti). Cocoa brought great prosperity to a relatively broad segment of the population. The railways to Kumasi and Kaduna (the new administrative capital of northern Nigeria) and the building of roads into the interior of the country facilitated economic development. In both countries mining with modern production methods was introduced, on the Gold Coast especially the mining of gold. Another source of prosperity was the import of consumer goods; advertisements appeared in the native press for high-quality products such as European clothing, pianos and soon also cars. The old nineteenth-century families with their European names (and ancestors) had an advantage over their more recent native competitors. So far no detailed investigations have been made into this burgeoning class of merchants and even managers. Only a few points can be made here by way of illustration.

More and more frequently African merchants travelled to London to do business. This practice was noted by Ferris with regard to merchants from the Gold Coast, but only from afar and at second hand.[5] He mentions a custom which is almost reminiscent of those practised by the great merchants of the Middle Ages. Those who went to London from the Gold Coast met there once a year for a ceremonial dinner at the Holborn Restaurant, High Holborn (the same restaurant in which the African Association held its farewell party for Mrs Kinloch in February 1898 before she went back to South Africa).[6] Apparently tribal princes who were staying in London occasionally also invited merchants from the Gold Coast and their friends to dinner. One of these occasions was attended by Ferris's Afro-American informant, who said that 150 people were present; if this is true, it is an astonishingly high number.

A 1920 handbook about West Africa contains photographs of 'some representative native business men of Accra' in faultless European dress; it mentions twenty-one African firms in Accra and reproduces 'some of their imposing buildings'.[7]

Finally, an example from Cape Coast. After the turn of the century, the removal of the capital to Accra in 1874 began to have an effect on this town and according to the official census data (which must be treated with caution) the population diminished from barely 29,000 (1901) to 11,269 (1911).[8] Nevertheless, although the economic life of the Gold Coast came to focus increasingly on Accra, there was apparently so much prosperity in Cape Coast that an 'Automobyle Club' was founded there in 1911. Since its members could read and write (in Cape Coast, too, education went hand in hand with material property), they found they needed a library. This was formally set up in the summer of 1912 with the Rev. F. Egyir Asaam of the AMEZ church in the chair.[9] In 1920 there were already more than 200 African car-owners on the Gold Coast.[10]

This relative economic boom brought about an undramatic but steady educational expansion. Between 1901 and 1920 the number of government-aided schools on the Gold Coast rose from 135 to 218 and the number of pupils from 12,018 to 28,622; that of non-grant-aided schools (mostly inferior in quality) increased from 120 to 309. In 1920, the only year for which the information is available, the number of pupils was 13,717.[11] Thus in the better schools the attendance rate more than doubled. To these pupils may be added those who attended those secondary schools in West Africa which still enjoyed the greatest prestige: the CMS Grammar School and the Wesleyan Boys' High School in Freetown.[12] A growing number of Africans from all four colonies could afford to send their sons to study law and medicine in Britain. The spread of cocoa cultivation gave a living to an ever-growing number of lawyers, who were needed to settle the frequent disputes about land. As was the case in France under the *ancien régime*, lawyers were along with liberal-minded clergymen the main exponents of the new political trends.

Increasing prosperity and the growth of the educated classes brought stability to the press. The new periodicals which served to articulate the keener political consciousness of these men lasted longer than their predecessors. Journals such as the *Sierra Leone Weekly News*, the *Lagos Standard*, the *Lagos Weekly Record*, the *Gold Coast Leader* and the *Gold Coast Independent*, which came into being at the turn of the century, all survived for more than a decade. They were more or less nationalist in outlook, and most of them were strongly oriented towards British West Africa.[13]

Nationalism in West Africa prior to 1914

The *Gold Coast Nation*, founded by the Rev. Attoh Ahuma in 1912, was expressly a political organ, as implied by the word 'nation' in its title; in it were to be found the clearest formulations of the new nationalism. At an earlier date and most recently in his journal the *Gold Coast Leader* Ahuma had consciously sought to develop a 'national' consciousness on the Gold Coast. In his zeal he treated as 'national' phenomena even such trivial occurrences as the erection of a new Baptist chapel. 'Dr. Mark C. Hayford's Baptist Chapel' was hailed as 'his single-handed enterprise, strenuous activity . . . a valuable national asset'.[14] In the following issue Ahuma justified his attitude by referring to 'Our

National Crisis', which made it necessary 'to lay hold of every sentiment that makes for self-reliance in the struggle before us'.[15]

The paper printed an enthusiastic report of a lecture by Casely Hayford in the Wesleyan chapel at Cape Coast; the speaker, 'in his native costume, presented a picturesque appearance and was attended with enthusiasm'; it was apparently not found disconcerting that the African nationalist Hayford should have spoken in English and that an English missionary should have had to translate his lecture into Fanti.[16] Shortly afterwards, reviewing the book *West African Celebrities* by Attoh Ahuma, Casely Hayford spoke out against the 'new vile importation in terms of "Negro" and "nigger" ', invoking the authority of Ignatius Sancho:[17] 'No race that is self-respecting ought to suffer itself to be called by approbrious names. . . . We are Ethiopians – Africans. As such we have been known from the days of Herodotus and Homer.'[18] Naturally enough, the journal engaged in propaganda on behalf of the Fanti National Educational Trust,[19] which was set up to finance new secondary schools but never got beyond founding one of them, at Cape Coast in 1905.[20]

It was during these years that Mensah Sarbah published his book on the Fanti *national* constitution;[21] three years earlier Casely Hayford had still spoken of 'Gold Coast *native* institutions'.[22]

As part of this development of national consciousness these intellectuals rediscovered and re-evaluated their own history, taking as their motto: 'We have a past'.[23] Reindorf's *History of the Gold Coast* . . . had already appeared,[24] and in 1898 Ahuma's *Gold Coast Aborigines* used history as an instrument of political agitation. 'The primary object of the *Gold Coast Aborigines*', he wrote, 'is to instruct the rising generation of the Protectorate in the history of the country. . . . We do not know of a better weapon to be wielded in any political struggle for existence than a smart acquaintance with the history of a country, backed by a clear intelligence of the laws of the land.'[25] In the same year the journal published a series called 'Sketches of the Lives and Labours of our Great Men', in this way taking up a literary genre fostered by Afro-Americans.[26] In the *Gold Coast Leader* Ahuma contributed a new series mainly dealing with eighteenth-century figures,[27] whose historical importance he exaggerated considerably, calling them 'intellectual giants'. Ahuma turned the series of articles into a book,[28] and in this form it had a considerable impact. Afterwards several other accounts of the lives of these men were written to provide proof of African achievements; later twentieth-century contemporaries, too, were incorporated into this literary genre, among them Attoh Ahuma himself.[29]

Finally Ahuma made a book out of a series of leading articles which he contributed to the *Gold Coast Leader*, under the title of *The Gold Coast Nation and National Consciousness*, which was similar to the heading of one of the articles.[30] The title was both a programme and an act of auto-suggestion. To the question of whether the Gold Coast was a nation, the militant minister replied with the faith that can move mountains: 'WE ARE A NATION.' He went on: 'We have a nation, and what is more, we have a Past – "though ungraced in story". We own a Political Constitution, a concentric system of government, of one Race, born and bred upon our soil.' There followed references to the spreading of the Akan language and to the Gold Coast's allegiance to the British Empire.[31] The definition of the new nation was at best additive, eclectic and scarcely consistent. The nation is a modern phenomenon, yet early nineteenth-century African nationalists dreamed of reviving the cultural and political status of West Africa before the coming of the Europeans.[32] On the other hand, Casely Hayford, who was among the exponents of a cultural renaissance oriented to the past, thought quite naïvely that:

> If the Gold Coast were a country with free institutions, free from the trammels of Downing Street red-tapism, we should soon have good wharves and harbours, gas works, water works, and railway communications all over the country. Prosperous cities would grow up, knowledge would spread among all classes of the people, producing a willing and an efficient body of workmen for the material development of the vast wealth and resources of the country.[33]

Hayford thus combined in his outlook, as did Du Bois and Nkrumah, two tendencies that were opposed to one another: the modernizing rationalism of Horton and the romantic irrationalism of Blyden.[34] The fact was, as David Kimble has pointed out,[35] that 'the difficult art of thinking nationally'[36] had yet to be learned. It was not made any easier by the fact that Ahuma projected national aspirations on to the entire continent and backwards into the past as well: 'Africa shall rise, but only when we begin to think continentally and nationally. . . . In prehistoric days, Europe looked to Africa for new ideas. . . . The most difficult problem of our times is how to think so that Africa may regain her lost Paradise.'[37]

On closer inspection the prescription for a national renaissance proves to be an empty phrase, with glimmerings of a neo-African *Blut und Boden* ideology.[38] Ahuma writes: 'The easiest way to become civilized, refined and enlightened is to endeavour at all times, in all places and circumstances to remain a true-born West African – nothing more and nothing less, and that Grand Reformation, which is after all an intelligent Backward Movement should begin here and now.'[39]

To leave no doubt as to the logical consequences of such postulates, Ahuma began his article by denouncing Western influences: 'As a people we have ceased to be a THINKING NATION. . . . Western education or civilization undiluted, unsifted has more or less enervated our minds and made them passive and catholic.'[40]

Several months later Ahuma took his intellectual self-annihilation to the ultimate stage. Seeking the deeper causes 'of our national decline', he considered the historical roots of his own social class and argued that the missionaries as such would not have done such harm if they had not so over-hastily held everything African to be bad. The main evil was 'the manufactured West African "Scholar" – a cross between a European and a Baboon – [who] has carried on the Vandalism of his misguided masters.'[41]

Here Ahuma employed the language and arguments of those Whites hostile to the Africans for whom the 'educated native' and the 'scholar' were 'the curse of the Coast'.[42] Moreover, he himself was a product of Western influences and a 'scholar', for his father, an unlearned Methodist pastor, would have been seen by Europeans prejudiced against the Africans as a member of the class they despised (yet secretly feared). The tension between modernization and tradition which afflicted early twentieth-century African nationalists was evidently already so acute that they could no longer endure it. Lacking a clear rational conception, such as might have developed out of the Horton tradition, they broke down emotionally and decided to return to traditional ways, albeit in modified form. This flight into a romanticized past, the search for a 'lost paradise' in Africa before the arrival of the White man, was a means of compensating psychologically for the inferiority complex induced by colonialism and racism; in Gold Coast society, still largely tradition-bound, it was the easiest way of resolving the tensions which had been building up for decades. But the Backward Movement had disastrous consequences, for it caused the nascent Pan-African movement to take on an increasingly eclectic, irrational and romantic character.

In his new journal, which bore the programmatic title the *Gold Coast Nation*, Ahuma continued to stress national themes, now with Pan-African accents. His stay in England and in the United States, if not already the AMEZ mission, had taught him to appreciate the value of the Afro-American link. In the struggle for national self-assertion he therefore sought 'the practical sympathy and cordial co-operation of all Africans in whatever part of the world found'.

He expressly welcomed

> the enlightened aid of our Afro-American brethren in matters industrial and economic.[43] For a wise purpose some of our brethren in the historic past were allowed to suffer the pains and penalties of servitude in foreign countries only to be able in the twentieth and following centuries to pour into the lap of Ethiopia the wealth and resources of highly favoured nations. . . . We welcome all and sundry in the name of a common ancestry, a common fatherland, and the common God of our Race.[44]

In conformity with Ahuma's emphasis on the need to think 'continentally', British West Africa also found a place in his nationalism. He rejected organization as an end in itself, but inquired rhetorically:

> Are there not a dozen inspiring leaders ready to fuse into one indivisible whole matured thoughts and ripened judgements for counsels or for fight in Gambia, Sierra Leone, the Gold Coast and Nigeria? . . . The leaders themselves must fall into line; come together; think out things as an organic body. West Africa clamorously calls for them, for we are within hail of revolutionary eras and epochs in the land of our fathers and may yet be saved, if our faith fail not.[45]

We should not underestimate the influence of Ahuma, who worked for over thirty years on the Gold Coast as an active minister, teacher and political journalist, a controversial but respected figure. Rather we should take him as representative of the ideas and aspirations of the class from which he sprang and to which he addressed himself. With his cautious plea for West African collaboration, and despite all his criticism of the mess in which West African organizations found themselves, he kept in touch with Casely Hayford's group, which pressed for 'national' unity with Ashanti and a West African union in one form or another.[46]

Finally, two ecclesiastical matters were relevant to West Africa. One of these goes back to the last years of the nineteenth century and is connected with missionary work. As early as 1888 there was founded at Colwyn Bay in North Wales the Congo Training Institute, generally called the Colwyn Bay Institute. It sought to give African missionaries training in industrial subjects as well as in the standard curriculum, in order both to save money and to encourage the missionaries to act as modernizing elements in African society. The number of students sent for training to Wales was never high – in 1899 there were eighteen of them. They came in the main from the West African coast (from the area between Gambia and Angola); at least one was from Charleston, South Carolina, and another, Scholes, from Jamaica.[47] To support the institute committees were formed in all four British colonies; their work was publicized in the local press, so that even this modest kind of activity contributed something to the creation of a West African consciousness in the area between Gambia and the Cameroons.

The second ecclesiastical matter involved James Johnson's appointment by the CMS as Anglican bishop in February 1900,[48] on condition that he raised the sum of £8000 to support his diocese. On his return from England Bishop Johnson began to collect funds on the West African coast, receiving an especially enthusiastic response at Freetown and Cape Coast. Later he extended his campaign to Fernando Po, Benin, Calabar and Douala – to places where 'Sierra Leoneans' had settled and formed nuclei of Christian missionary activity. His fund-raising suddenly became much less successful in 1901, when Johnson refused to go along with those members of his own parish of Lagos, two-thirds of the community, who seceded to join the 'Ethiopian' independence movement and proclaimed a separate, independent African diocese.[49] Despite this apparent failure the campaign for the West African Native Bishopric Fund is worth mentioning for its effect in bringing West Africans together.

Nationalism in South Africa

In South Africa on the other hand the nationalist movement found itself in a blind alley almost as soon as it got under way. For Africans in 1900 the Cape Colony was still the most modernized part of the continent and apparently the best suited for further progress, so that South Africa might have played a significant role in the Pan-African movement if the African population had been allowed to develop freely.

Shortly before the end of the nineteenth century contact was established with Afro-Americans in the United States through the intermediacy of the AME mission. South African students left for that country in growing numbers to obtain a modern education, while others went to Britain.[50] The Boer War seemed to hold out the prospect that the liberal principles observed in the Cape Province and Natal would also be extended to the Transvaal and the Orange Free State after the Boers' defeat.[51] However, all such hopes came to nothing with the capitulation of Vereeniging in 1902, when the victorious British gave their enemies full power over the Africans. With the re-establishment of Boer rule, and its *de facto* expansion to Natal and Cape Province on the foundation of the Union of South Africa in 1910, there was less and less scope for Africans to engage in political activity.

The first serious breach in their rights came with the Lands Act of 1913, whereby all Africans in the Union were virtually expropriated and allotted 13 per cent of the land in the form of native reserves. To protect their political interests, members of the growing African middle class had united on a local and provincial level, at first in Natal, as early as 1901 – emulating Gandhi's organization of the Indian minority in Natal. Miss Henrietta Colenso acted as the link between the various groups.[52] To ward off the threats of the Lands Act, these groups merged to form the South African Native Congress, later renamed the South African National Congress. Until it was banned under Verwoerd it was moderate in its political demands. For decades it represented only the educated bourgeois element among the Africans, but it also sought from the very start to forge a link with the tribal princes; the importance of the latter was, however, less than in West Africa, because of the greater degree of urbanization and the fact that they were restricted to the reserves. Most of the early leaders of the congress came from Lovedale missionary school; almost half of its committee had studied either in the United States or in Britain, and Seme had been to both countries.[53]

A symptom of the Native Congress's lack of radicalism is the strong participation of clergymen in the committee (four members out of eleven), as well as the fact that three of the leading men in the organization – the Rev. Rubusana, Jabavu and Chief Dalindyebo of the Tembus – had participated in the First Universal Races Congress, held in London in 1911.[54] The initiative in founding the Native Congress was taken by four young lawyers who had returned after completing their studies in Britain. Among them was Seme, who had gone from New York to Oxford and who held the position of treasurer in the congress. Dube, the first president, had studied in the United States and was in contact with B. T. Washington. He set up an educational institute, the Ohlange School, modelled upon Tuskegee College. In the note accepting election as president of the congress Dube proclaimed his motto to be *festina lente* and referred expressly to B. T. Washington as 'the best living example of our Africa's sons'; he also professed his 'deep and dutiful respect for the rulers whom God has placed over us'.[55] The congress wanted to win help and sympathy from European organizations in its struggle against racial barriers in the schools and in economic life and for a 'proper representation of natives in Parliament' and other elective bodies. Its ideal was the restricted franchise, based on a property census, of the Cape Colony, which did at least grant the vote to coloureds and prosperous Africans. Its objective for the distant future was to create a South African nation which would be interracial in its composition.

In view of the relatively close links between leading congress members and Afro-Americans in the USA, and also with England, the congress naturally had a Pan-African outlook. South Africans participated actively in the Pan-African Association and in the Pan-African Conference of 1900. Sylvester Williams's tour of South Africa[56] probably reinforced the latent Pan-African tendencies there. In Cape Town F. Z. S. Peregrino, an African from the Gold Coast who had spent some time in the United States, provided an additional Pan-African element. As a journalist he was in contact with Seme, whom he interviewed in 1916. In the preamble to the constitution of the congress, which was formally passed as late as 1919, we are told that it was planned to invite various organizations and associations to create 'a federation of a single Pan-African association'.[57] The South African Native Congress was undoubtedly the first African organization to adopt officially in its programme the key term Pan-African and therefore to form part of the Pan-African movement. It does not say much for the strength of Pan-Africanism that this first allegiance came from an organization which was condemned to political impotence. For this reason the South African National Congress could not give Pan-Africanism any assistance but became itself the object of a sympathy that verged on charity. Africans and Afro-Americans continuously protested against the growth of racism in South Africa, from the London Conference of 1900 to the founding of the Organization of African Unity in Addis Ababa in 1963 and ever since. South Africa became a negative symbol of Pan-Africanism, a permanent admonition not to let matters come to such a pass in other parts of the continent.

During the time of relative freedom between the Boer War and World War I South Africa still exerted a certain influence upon the less developed territories to the north, Rhodesia and more especially Nyasaland (modern Malawi). The Cape Province and Natal were the chief channels through which these influences were transmitted; the ecclesiastical and proto-political organizations formed there gave rise to John Chilembwe's rebellion in Nyasaland at the beginning of 1915. Chilembwe, too, was a European missionary product, who had had contact with Afro-Americans in the USA (later with Afro-American missionaries) and with Ethiopianism[58] in southern Africa. His mentor Joseph Booth imprinted deeply upon him the slogan 'Africa for the Africans' and the need to rely on one's own resources,[59] so that after his attempted rising Chilembwe became the martyr and father of African nationalism in Nyasaland.

Developments in the West Indies

Our survey of the West Indies can be relatively brief. In lieu of dramatic events there was the significant fact that Pan-African leaders had to leave their homelands in order to play a major historical role. After the emancipation of the slaves (1834–8 and 1848) the initial situation was at first similar to that in the Cape Colony, where the negro and mulatto elements became quite rapidly modernized under White supremacy. But whereas in South Africa the White ruling minority increased in number and its rule became harsher, in the West Indies, on account of the decline of sugar production and the general economic stagnation, it diminished in size and was reduced almost to the status of a ruling colonial oligarchy such as existed in most other colonies. The liberal impulses of the nineteenth century facilitated the rise of a native bourgeoisie, composed mostly of mulattoes, which clamoured for modern education. Codrington College on Barbados, which was affiliated to the University of Durham in 1875,[60] catered for local and regional needs. From the end of the nineteenth century onwards West Indian students came to England in increasing numbers. Personified by Sylvester Williams, they played a leading role at the Pan-African Conference of 1900. The initial *élan* gave way to a period of quiet undramatic preparation which lasted until World War I. At that time most of the men and women were born or grew up who later, after the two World Wars, gave Pan-Africanism such a powerful impetus – Marcus Garvey and Claude McKay (both born in 1887), the former's two wives, Amy Jacques and Amy Ashwood Garvey, Dr Harold Moody (all from Jamaica), George Padmore and C. L. R. James from Trinidad and the leaders from the French Antilles.[61]

The Washington–Du Bois controversy and the beginnings of the NAACP

Far more dramatic were the developments among Afro-Americans in the States, where shortly after 1900 the tensions which had been building up during the preceding decades, through the hardening of racial segregation, finally snapped.[62] The modern civil rights movement in the USA developed out of this conflict between the moderate conservative wing, which was ready to accept the long-term subjection of the Afro-Americans, and a militant wing which revolted against this prospect. On the surface the problem was the character and content of the education that Afro-Americans should receive, but in reality it was a question of their social and political status. In contrast to the moderates, the militants claimed full equality of rights at once. The protagonists in this conflict were Booker T. Washington and his former follower W. E. B. Du Bois. Washington represented those Afro-Americans who after the Civil War had worked their way up to a certain prosperity from modest beginnings, usually straight from slavery. Since they were often dependent upon benevolence and financial aid from the Whites, as was Washington with his Tuskegee Institute, they did not want to jeopardize once again their in any case precarious status by political agitation for equality.

Washington's militant critics were composed of young intellectuals who had studied at negro colleges and universities and were soon also to teach there. From 1903 onwards their chief spokesman was W. E. B.

Du Bois.[63] His long career – he died at the age of ninety-five – spans the entire history of Pan-Africanism proper, and even part of its nineteenth-century prehistory;[64] it is therefore worth sketching in some detail.[65]

William Edward Burghardt Du Bois was born in Great Barrington, a small town in Massachusetts, on 23 February 1868. If one can believe the record of an interview which he gave in old age, he was by no means descended from a family who 'had come to enjoy bourgeois prosperity'.[66] His grandparents on his mother's side, the Burghardts, were simple poor farmers. His father, a West Indian mulatto of light complexion,[67] led a restless life mostly as a barber which took him to Great Barrington. After a few years of marriage he disappeared without trace, driven away in part by the aversion of the dark-skinned Burghardts for the light-complexioned intruder.[68] Du Bois grew up in his grandparents' home, while his mother earned her livelihood as a servant, although she was never referred to as such.[69] Only with the aid of scholarships did young Du Bois succeed in attending secondary school, and later Fisk University (one of the great negro universities) and finally Harvard. He won a special grant to study abroad which enabled the ambitious young student to spend two years in Berlin, the most distinguished German university at the time, where in 1892–4 he studied under Treitschke and Schmoller among others. He learnt German quickly and later garnished many of his works with quotations in German, especially from classical authors. From Berlin he undertook study trips during the summer vacations through Germany and Central Europe. A keen observer of his surroundings, he noted the rise of Social Democracy and the Pan-German movement, as well as the national tensions in Bohemia and East Prussia.[70] Originally Du Bois wanted to take his doctor's degree in Berlin. Since, however, his studies in Harvard were not taken into account there, he returned to the United States without a German degree.[71] In 1896 he gained his Ph.D. at Harvard with a thesis on the suppression of the slave trade to the United States which more than seventy years after it was published is still a standard work. Its quality may be judged from the fact that it appeared as the first volume in the Harvard Historical Studies series and that several editions have since appeared.[72]

In 1895, after Du Bois had completed his studies, he went as professor of classical languages to Wilberforce, the university of the AME church.[73] In the following year, as a young sociologist at Pennsylvania

University in Philadelphia, he was in charge of a research project on the negroes in that city, of which he provided a comprehensive study.[74] To Du Bois therefore falls the merit of having initiated historical and sociological scholarship on the Afro-Americans in the USA. From 1897 to 1910 he was professor of sociology at Atlanta University in Georgia, in the deep South, where he took his sociological studies further. Each year he arranged a university conference and in his *Atlanta Studies* endeavoured to examine systematically all the major aspects of his topic.[75]

His personal experiences and scholarly work led Du Bois to adopt an increasingly critical attitude to the problem of the Afro-Americans' status in American society – a question that concerned them all. In 1895 he was still prepared to agree with Washington's so-called Atlanta Compromise, which favoured the formula 'separate but equal'. As time went on, however, Du Bois realized that in this formula only the word 'separate' had any reality, while 'equal' was just a fiction, the more oppressive the longer it lasted. Thus he gradually came to oppose Washington. In 1903 he gave a clear sign of the impending breach by publishing two essays, 'Of the Dawn of Freedom' and 'Of Mr. Booker T. Washington and Others', in his famous volume *The Souls of Black Folk*.[76] In these he was still discreet in his criticism of Washington's strategy of adaptation as it applied to the question of the kind of education that was best for Afro-Americans. Du Bois did not doubt the value of an industrial and agricultural training for most Afro-Americans, as propagated and practised by Washington. At first he only condemned the idea that such schools should have a monopoly and that an academic education was contemptible – an idea shared by Washington, a 'self-made man' from a slave hut. Instead Du Bois also demanded that talented young Afro-Americans, the 'talented tenth' as they were later called, should have the possibility of an adequate education. He proceeded from the point that a one-sided industrial and agricultural training would condemn Afro-Americans to a permanent position of subjugation. On the contrary, he thought it necessary that Afro-American intellectuals should take up posts in all modern professions in order to promote the economic and social progress of their fellow Blacks, accelerated as it was by the agitation for political equality.

Since Washington possessed considerable power and maintained it by autocratic methods,[77] he reacted negatively to this open criticism. Publicly he said hardly anything about the matter, but secretly he got his numerous friends and supporters, many of whom were dependent upon him materially, to defend his position, while he himself made difficulties for Du Bois behind the scenes. In the so-called Washington–Du Bois controversy one salvo followed another. At first the divergence extended only to educational matters; but Du Bois expanded it into a fundamental attack both upon Washington's position of power, the 'Tuskegee machine' as Du Bois called it polemically, and upon Washington's conception of a non-political attitude of resignation and adaptation to prevailing conditions.

Du Bois split the American negroes into two camps. Since he and his intellectual followers were in the minority, he sought to strengthen his position by founding in 1905 the Niagara movement, called after its place of foundation on Lake Niagara. In numbers it always remained small: on Lake Niagara there were hardly two dozen members, including Trotter who had started the revolt against Washington before Du Bois,[78] and Carter G. Woodson who became the most important Afro-American historian after Du Bois.[79] By 1907 the number of registered members had barely reached 400. But the impact which the small group exerted was considerable. In 1906, in a manifesto headed 'An Address to the Nation', on the occasion of its second annual meeting at Harper's Ferry where John Brown had undertaken his vain attempt at rebellion in 1859, the Niagara movement protested against discrimination, segregation, exploitation and political lawlessness and demanded immediate political and social equality. The language of the appeal had that unmistakable pathos that one associates with all such statements, manifestos and declarations by Du Bois.[80]

The Niagara movement was never able to overcome its organizational weakness, so that after a few years it stagnated and found itself on the verge of collapse. In this situation the White racists involuntarily came to its aid when they shocked the conscience of White liberals in 1908 by staging a race riot at Springfield, Illinois, Abraham Lincoln's town. In reply to this Oswald Garrison Villard, a grandson of William L. Garrison,[81] together with a group of prominent personalities drew up an appeal for solidarity with the Afro-Americans which was published on 12 February 1909, the hundredth anniversary of Lincoln's birth. The signatories included AMEZ Bishop Alexander Walters, Mrs Ida B. Wells-Barnett, a pioneer in the fight against lynchings, and Du Bois. A public conference held in New York from 30 May to 1 June 1909 led to the emergence of a new organization, the National Negro Committee, which in 1910 definitely assumed the name of the National Association for the Advancement of Colored People (NAACP).[82] At first its top leadership consisted almost entirely of White liberals except for Du Bois, who as 'director of research' published the new organization's journal, *Crisis*. Du Bois brought virtually the entire Niagara movement into the NAACP, which for its part adopted the methods of agitation which this body had developed: systematic presentation of the facts about lynch murders and racial disturbances, the defence of victims of racial violence in the courts, etc.

As the herald of Pan-Negroism in 1897 and a leading participant in the Pan-African Conference of 1900, Du Bois was at the same time a forerunner and prominent exponent of Pan-Africanism.[83] He implanted his Pan-African interests upon the organizations which he led or influenced. *Horizon*, the journal of the Niagara movement published by Du Bois between 1907 and 1909, which he largely wrote himself, by no means confined itself to pungent polemics against Washington or to problems of internal politics.[84] As well as news and comment about events in Europe it featured information about Africa.[85] Du Bois familiarized his readers with Scholes, Mensah Sarbah and Casely Hayford.[86] In the miserable office occupied by the Niagara movement there is said to have been a Pan-African desk;[87] but probably his Pan-African activity at that time ran only to the collection of information about Africans and correspondence with them. In *Crisis* Du Bois continued to provide news about Africa, and after World War I the NAACP gave important financial backing to the two first Pan-African Congresses of 1919 and 1921.[88]

The Universal Races Congress of 1911

Further possibilities for obtaining information about Africa and establishing contact with Africans were offered by the first Universal Races Congress, held in London in July 1911. This was not a Pan-African event but rather a well-meant sentimental attempt to contribute towards a better relationship between the various races by means of personal contact and scholarly discussion. The initiative came from the International Union of Ethical Societies, whose chairman was Felix Adler of New York, an association of pacifist and humanitarian character in which Friedrich Wilhelm Foerster was a leading German participant. The idea first emerged at a meeting of this organization at

Eisenach in July 1906, and the first stages towards implementing it were taken at the end of 1908. The guiding spirit behind the enterprise was apparently a German, Gustav Spiller, who also edited the report of the conference.[89] At that time Spiller apparently lived in London, for it was here that he tried desperately throughout 1909 to assuage the scepticism of the Aborigines Protection Society about the intended congress.[90] According to Arna Bontemps the idea of the congress originated with Du Bois.[91] The atmosphere of 'embrace, o ye millions' which prevailed at the congress would befit Du Bois well; and its main financial backer was John E. Milholland, a wealthy American philanthropist who had just lent support to the recently founded NAACP; however, in the absence of further evidence this must remain a hypothesis.

The congress took place in London from 26 to 29 July 1911 and was attended by a large number of participants from all over the world. Illustrious names in society and scholarship adorned the long list of members of its committee and its supporters, from which it is not quite clear who actually took part in the congress. Most of them came from the USA. From Germany alone eighty-one names were listed, including C. H. Becker (later Prussian minister of education in the Weimar Republic), Luju Brentano, Hermann Cohen, Matthias Erzberger, Rudolf Eucken, Ernst Haeckel, Georg Jellinek, Wilhelm Kaufmann, Franz v. Liszt, Felix v. Luschau, Friedrich Meinecke, Hermann Oncken, Ludwig Quidde, Walter Schücking, Georg Simmel, Werner Sombart and Ferdinand Thönnies.[92] Among the names from India one is today particularly struck by Mohandas Karamchand Gandhi, at that time still a lawyer in Johannesburg and leader of the Indian minority in South Africa.[93]

Apart from India, few of the lands inhabited by coloured peoples were represented. The participants from Africa included Mojola Agbebi, who also gave a paper, and three South Africans, among them Jabavu.[94] One of the most active and enthusiastic participants was Du Bois. The tensions with Washington followed him to the Universal Races Congress, for Washington had sent his personal secretary, Moton, to London as a kind of watchdog, and he took the floor immediately after Du Bois. But the Washington–Du Bois controversy was not paraded before this world forum, since Du Bois referred to his opponent in a restrained and unbiased manner, as Moton was able to report with satisfaction to Washington in the USA.[95] Otherwise the congress evoked little echo among Afro-Americans and Du Bois alone made propaganda for it in *Crisis*.[96]

At the London congress Du Bois seems to have been in an idealistic and exuberantly happy mood. His paper on 'The Negro Race in the United States of America' was restrained and academic[97] but during a plenary session of the congress he delivered a 'Hymn to the Peoples' which he had composed himself in his best hyperbolic style.[98] He evidently enjoyed the 'cosmopolitan atmosphere' of the congress. His 'life-long search for human fraternity' was fulfilled. He believed 'quite naïvely but sincerely that, if members of all races and nationalities assembled and exchanged ideas, a "spiritual" bond would grow after the delegates departed from London'. And from his 'ecstatic reports' (Rudwick) sprang the hope that 'this reunion between East and West would lead directly to world peace'.[99] This hope of course came to nothing in the summer that witnessed the second Morocco crisis, and perhaps such illusions were more typical of Du Bois than of the congress. The fundamental problems of colonialism and imperialism were not discussed thoroughly or consistently, in spite of the active participation of John Hobson; this was keenly regretted by at least two female participants, Mary White Ovington, a White welfare officer from New York and co-founder of the NAACP, and Annie Besant, theosophist and vehement critic of British colonial rule in India.[100]

Besides Du Bois a Pan-African ingredient was supplied by Jabavu and Agbebi, who also gave papers to the congress. In his survey of 'The Native Races of South Africa' Jabavu gave an idealized description of traditional African society, emphasizing the exploitation brought by the Europeans. He mentioned the restricted franchise in Cape Province and deplored the fact that Christian missionaries were the only philanthropic element in South Africa. Jabavu stressed the need for a college for Africans[101] and appealed to the congress to aid him in founding one.[102]

Agbebi, announced as 'director of the Niger Delta mission', discussed 'The West African Problem'. Matters which Jabavu had only touched on in passing he treated in detail: the dissolution of the native social structure through contact with Europe. He deplored the scanty knowledge Europeans had about conditions in Africa. In the tradition of Blyden[103] Agbebi was against modernizing influences, while on the other hand he described the 'vogue of segregation' as not too dreadful for non-Europeanized Africans. Agbebi appealed for an understanding of certain aspects of traditional African society: the secret societies, he argued, were comparable to those of the freemasons; human sacrifice had had religious motives, namely a readiness for self-sacrifice; dealing with ancestor- and hero-worship, magic, polygamy and cannibalism, the African nationalist minister delivered the following eloquent words in justifying them to his cosmopolitan public:

> The eating of human or non-human flesh differs only in kind, and human flesh is said to be the most delicious of all viands; superior in culinary taste to the flesh of either bird, beast, fish or creeping things. Christianity itself is a superstructure of cannibalism. . . . In administering the Lord's Supper to converts from cannibalism I have often felt some uneasiness in repeating the formula 'Take it, this is my body', and the other, 'this is my blood'.[104]

Rarely have Africa's modern spokesmen expressed so strikingly in a single passage the tremendous tension set up by the drive for modernization, the clash between traditional and modern elements in their culture. Due to the absence of a clearly defined and rational conception of modernization a desperate attempt was made to save and rehabilitate as much as possible of ancestral traditions.

The value of the first Universal Races Congress for the historian of Pan-Africanism is particularly well conveyed by this suggestive incident. The practical return from the congress was otherwise small. The attempt to create a permanent organization failed even while the congress was still in session;[105] a second gathering, due to be held in Paris in 1915, fell victim to World War I.[106] The 1911 meeting did, it is true, provide an impulse to the founding of the South African Native Congress,[107] but this new body soon found itself in the blind alley of apartheid. The most important result of the first Universal Races Congress, however, was the rise of Mohamed Ali Duse and the appearance of the *African Times and Orient Review*.

Booker T. Washington's International Conference on the Negro (1912)

First, however, let us still consider the International Conference of the Negro, convened at Tuskegee in 1912 by Booker T. Washington. The latter's interest in Africa was expressed by his journalist ally T. T. Fortune, editor of the *New Age* in New York, and also by his participation in the preliminary conference in London (1899) of the African Association, as well as by his activity on behalf of Africa.[108] Washington and Fortune are said to have planned a Pan-African conference for 1906, presumably in the USA, whereupon Fortune complained that Sylvester Williams had stolen his own ideas with the Pan-African Conference of 1900.[109] Whatever the truth may be, Washington held his conference in 1912; it was admittedly not Pan-African in its claims or designation, but was so indirectly in the theme to which the delegates addressed themselves, and to some extent also in its composition.[110]

The original idea sprang from the suggestion that a conference be held, in collaboration with missionary societies and colonial governments, on the extension of the Tuskegee model to Africa. In conformity with his whole temperament, Booker T. Washington avoided political themes such as racial questions and nationalism in his invitation, and concentrated upon the educational activities of missions and governments. The invitation, which was also published in the press, was addressed to all who worked as missionaries or in any other way for the progress of the negro. The aim of the conference was to be the study of the methods employed in the USA to promote the negro cause, in order to decide to what extent the methods of Tuskegee and the kindred Hampton Institute (likewise situated in the South) could be applied in Africa and the West Indies.[111] The conference was held at the Tuskegee Institute from 17 to 19 April 1912. As befitted the theme, most of the participants were missionaries and theologians, twenty-five in number, mostly Whites; three Afro-West Indians and some Afro-Americans and Africans also attended. Of the well-known figures one should mention AME Bishop Henry Turner, 'the well-known apostle of Back to Africa' (*African Times and Orient Review*), AMEZ Bishop Alexander Walters and Mark C. Hayford, the Baptist minister from Cape Coast.[112]

Blyden and Casely Hayford sent greetings to the conference by mail. In his letter Casely Hayford struck a political note which was otherwise taboo at the conference when he spoke of 'an African nationality': 'when the Aborigines of the Gold Coast and other parts of West Africa have joined forces with our brethren in America in arriving at a national aim, purpose and aspiration, then indeed will it be possible for our brethren over the sea to bring home metaphorically to their nation and people a great spoil'.[113] This was Pan-Africanism without the name, and recalled the speeches delivered when the AMEZ mission was started on the Gold Coast in 1898 and *Ethiopia Unbound*.[114] Other letters also arrived from Africa, one written in clumsy English from the Ethiopian church at Klipsruit, Johannesburg, welcoming Washington's work and hoping that he would soon extend his activity to South Africa as well:

> Your scheme and attitude to raise your countrymen, we hail for it, in this country. We are looking forward for the day that you would deem wise and fit to convey your scheme of raising the Negroes in that country to this country of aboriginal natives, since a very limited number could come over to that country. We believe that it was God's hand that touched and aroused such feelings in your breast and mind. . . .[115]

In conformity with the composition of the conference most papers were read by Europeans and Whites from North America. The address of a certain Dr Patton is of interest because it forms a counterpart by a White man to Agbebi's paper of 1911.[116] With the aid of a huge map he demonstrated the spread of railways and modern technology in Africa. Patton thought that the pagan tribes had either to adapt to Western standards or otherwise face destruction.[117]

One source mentions a lecture by Casely Hayford, 'Progress of the Gold Coast Native', which is probably a misreading.[118] The Rev. Mark C. Hayford's theme was 'Educational Conditions on the Gold Coast', but he treated the historical background in such detail that he had to break off his lecture before finishing it.[119] The British colonial reformer E. D. Morel addressed the conference 'On the Preservation of Native Rights and Customs in Tropical Africa' and J. W. E. Bowen, an Afro-American theologian who had already played a leading role at the missionary conference on Africa of 1895[120] spoke about 'The False and the True in Mission Work in Africa'.

On the last day representatives of the Afro-American missionary societies reported about the difficulties they had experienced in Africa, particularly the mistrust of the Whites in southern Africa.[121] The main persons giving papers were Alexander Walters for AMEZ and Dr W. W. Beckett for AME. A certain M. C. B. Mason for the Freedmen's Aid Society of the Methodist Church spoke on 'Africa in America and Africa beyond the Seas', a topic about which it would have been valuable to know more than just the title.[122] The Afro-American missionary societies assured the audience of their non-political intentions and urged Booker T. Washington himself to travel to South Africa, hoping that with his reputation as a moderate he might convince the South African government of the harmlessness of their missionary work. This journey by Washington did not take place, since two years later World War I broke out and a year after that Washington died. This also frustrated the plans for a second conference of this kind.[123] The entire conception was so bound up with the person of Washington that it did not survive his death.

Washington's demise also cut short the initiative of West Indian teachers and students at the Tuskegee Institute who had suggested in passing at the conference that a school based upon the Tuskegee model be founded in the British West Indies and that B. T. Washington be invited to visit Jamaica and the other islands.[124] At the end of 1914 or beginning of 1915 Garvey took up this suggestion.[125]

Duse and the 'African Times and Orient Review'

Garvey's contact with Washington and the *African Times and Orient Review* takes us back to Mohamed Ali Duse, and at the same time to London, the locale of the First Universal Races Congress. Here in 1911 the first important contacts had been made between Africans and Afro-Americans on one hand and Asians on the other; they were still tenuous and rested upon a rather sentimental and non-political basis. Duse developed these initiatives by the medium of his journal the *African Times and Orient Review*. Its title marks it out as the first paper to work for Afro-Asian interests and solidarity, a kind of journalistic forerunner of the Bandung movement.

With Duse one of the most colourful Pan-Africans appears on the stage of history. His long life (1867 to 1944) clearly falls into two different parts. The first was passed in almost complete obscurity, whereas in the second he displayed great journalistic and political activity. Except for cursory references in the literature on the subject, he has hitherto been virtually ignored. Although a biography is now being written about him,[126] it is worth giving an outline here of his career, which abounds in episodes of Pan-African interest.

Mohamed Ali Duse called himself an Egyptian of Sudanese descent. With his distinctly negroid features he always regarded himself as an African. His father was farsighted enough to send him to England at the age of nine to learn the language of the future, apparently with such success that Duse later forgot his Arabic. A French captain by the name of Duse who looked after him at that time gave him his own surname in addition to his Arabic one, so that he should stand out better from the large number of Muslims who went by the name of Mohamed Ali. For Mohamed Ali Duse the bombardment of Alexandria by the British navy in 1882, a prelude to the occupation of Egypt, was a personal catastrophe, for in it his father and brothers lost their lives. His mother and sisters withdrew to the Sudan and were not heard of again. As an orphan aged fifteen, Duse scraped through somehow, for the most part as an actor with a travelling company and also as playwright, freelance journalist and theatre critic. For the greater part of the time he lived in England, but his itinerant way of life also took him to the European continent, India and the United States.

His Pan-African career began as late as 1911, at the age of forty-four. Provoked by some incorrect assertions by Theodore Roosevelt about Egypt made when the American ex-president was on a visit to London, Duse wrote and published within three months his first (and only) book, which the British press immediately praised as the first rendering of modern Egyptian history by an Egyptian.[127] His sudden new fame brought him a contract to organize the artistic programme to accompany the First Universal Races Congress, which he apparently carried out with great gusto. Duse made a particular impression with the performance of one act from *Othello*, in which he himself appeared in his favourite role, that of the principal character.

During the congress, or as a result of it, Duse seems to have come into contact with J. Eldred Taylor,[128] an African entrepreneur resident in London. Taylor invited Duse to produce for him a journal, the *African Times*, which was also intended to further his commercial interests in Africa. With this title the newspaper of that name which had formerly enjoyed such prestige in Africa would have been reborn.[129] Duse agreed, but extended the journal's coverage, so that in July 1912 the first issue of this monthly could appear under the somewhat exotic title of the *African Times and Orient Review*.

The make-up and style are surprisingly reminiscent of Sylvester Williams's *Pan-African* of 1901, even down to the predilection for providing news items with brief comments;[130] as had been the case with the *Pan-African*, these were set in the same type and placed in square brackets. The format and volume, however, were a little larger. The external and internal similarities suggest that Duse may have been familiar with the newspaper of the Pan-African Association or that he consciously took it as the model for his own journal. To secure publicity and recruit subscribers Duse got Gustav Spiller to give him a list of those present at the First Universal Races Congress. The connection, which was at least indirect, between the Universal Races Congress and the *African Times and Orient Review* was documented by Duse in the first issue, which published a detailed report on the congress, albeit a whole year late. Duse's first leading article also referred expressly to the congress. Even if he actually remained in ignorance of the *Pan-African*, at least he reintroduced this key-word after the lapse of a decade: 'The recent Universal Races Congress . . . clearly demonstrated that there was ample need for a Pan-Oriental, Pan-African journal at the seat of the British Empire which would lay the aims, desires and intentions of the Black, Brown and Yellow Races – within and without the Empire – at the throne of Caesar.'[131]

Duse's journal devoted its attention in particular to British West Africa, the German colonies in Africa, the West Indies and Afro-Americans in the United States; it also paid some attention to Egypt, Morocco, Turkey, Persia, India, Japan and China. Thus with Duse new horizons opened up for the Pan-African movement. But the *African Times and Orient Review* was primarily focused upon British West Africa. This orientation was intensified soon after the first issue appeared. According to Duse's autobiographical account the journal immediately encountered financial difficulties when Taylor (allegedly or in fact) refused to pay the bill for printing the first issue. From this embarrassing situation Duse was saved by some West Africans who happened to be staying in London. Among them were Casely Hayford, who had come to London with the deputation of the Aborigines Rights Protection Society to protest against the Forest Bill of 1911,[132] Dove and C. W. Betts from Sierra Leone, and Dr O. Sapara from Lagos. At the suggestion of Rotimi Alade, a lawyer from Lagos, this group met to discuss the new journal. They were particularly pleased at a report of an incident in Zaria (northern Nigeria) in which two African employees had been whipped by a British colonial official for some trifling misdemeanour. The group came to see Duse, congratulated him on the appearance of his journal, but at the same time warned him of the bad reputation enjoyed by Taylor, his backer (a dilatory one according to Duse). The West African group offered to take over the debts of the *African Times and Orient Review*, so putting the journal upon a sound financial basis. Duse jumped at the idea; Taylor was bought out against his protests; and the journal became a limited company with shares issued to the public.

The West Africans promised to publicize the *African Times and Orient Review* after they returned home, which apparently they did. At least Attoh Ahuma's *Gold Coast Nation* took an emphatic stand on behalf of the journal. Among other things he wrote an article, 'Help the *African Times and Orient Review*', in which he introduced it as 'the organ of the Coloured Races throughout the World, and especially for the African, in every part of the great Continent of his origin, as well as in America and the West Indies, the lands of his sojourning'. In his argument that the periodical was necessary he took up some ideas from Delany and Du Bois:[133] 'The White and the Coloured Races now stand face to face at the crisis of their mutual relations . . . The Black Races are arousing from their slumber, casting off the glamour of white "superiority", feeling within themselves the power of standing alone and claiming and demanding the right of a MAN.' 'Upright men' in England made a practice of reading the journal and were influenced by it, and questions were put in the House of Commons about Sierra Leone, the Gold Coast and Nigeria – thus the *Gold Coast Nation* appealed to its readers' patriotism, calling on them 'to render substantial financial support to what we are sure will be of the greatest service to your country, and assure you that our friends are doing all in their power in connection with it, to fight the battle of our country'.[134]

Shortly afterwards an advertisement appeared offering 2500 shares priced at ten shillings each in The African Times and Orient Review Ltd, a company with a capital of £3000. Mohamed Duse of London and C. W. Betts of Freetown were named as directors of the company.[135] When it first appeared the *African Times and Orient Review* had 200 subscribers and in September 1912 it claimed to have 5000, but it aimed at 25,000,[136] a number which it probably did not reach. In March 1914 the journal appeared weekly, but at the end of August 1914 it had to cease publication until January 1917 when it reappeared as a monthly, lasting for two years. In 1920 Duse published the journal under a slightly modified title, the *Africa and Orient Review*, but only for a brief period.

The *African Times and Orient Review* is a real mine of information for the historian, both in its report on events in the Afro-Asian world at that time and for its moderate critique of colonialism. It specialized in exposing abuses in the British colonies. Duse provided material for Labour MPs who subsequently put awkward questions to the government in the House of Commons. Also in this point – consciously or unconsciously – Duse revived Sylvester Williams's line.[137]

By November 1912 the journal claimed that it had representatives in charge of distribution in Egypt, the Gold Coast, Nigeria, Sierra Leone, England, Malaya, Japan, British Guiana, the USA, Australia and Canada. Its general agent in the US was the Afro-American journalist John Edward Bruce (equally well known by his pseudonym 'Grit'); later he was aided by J. E. K. Aggrey.[138] Also employed in distributing the journal under Bruce's direction was Richard B. Moore, later a Garvey supporter and a leading member of the communist-sponsored Negro Labor Committee; he is now the owner of one of the two bookshops in Harlem, the Frederick Douglass Bookstore.[139] To ensure better distribution the journal was placed in the first and second-class saloons of ships belonging to as many as twenty-one shipping lines.[140] Those who wrote for it were a motley crowd: Africans, Afro-Americans, liberal Whites, Indians, Chinese and Arabs. Readers' letters also reflect this heterogeneous composition. Let us single out one issue (that of September 1913), as a sample: this contained readers' letters from South Africa (by a White liberal), Wales, Lagos, Winneba (Gold Coast), Paraguay, London (by an Indian), Freetown, the Bahamas, Cuba, Birkenhead (England), Sierra Leone, Nigeria and Kumasi (Ashanti).

Due to the variety of interests represented, as of collaborators and readers, a medley of views was presented in the journal. With his heavy stress on Islam, Duse introduced a pro-Turkish orientation during the Balkan Wars; he also played a leading part in founding the Anglo-Ottoman Society to support Turkey in 1913.[141] He was opposed to German colonial rule, as is shown by articles on Togo and the Cameroons, some by Africans and others by German critics.[142] On the question of race relations one could read pleas for miscegenation.[143] Hopes were placed upon both Japan and China; after the first Chinese revolution in 1911 an Indian writer hopefully and with astonishing foresight predicted that country's political regeneration,[144] while a Chinese indulged in prophecies that have a highly topical ring.[145]

Avidly the journal registered all political stirrings among Africans and Afro-Americans: for example, Booker T. Washington's International Conference on the Negro, reports on the National American Negro

Academy, or the deputation of the South African Native Congress to London in 1914 to press for withdrawal of the Native Lands Act of 1913.[146] The defeat of Turkey served as a warning to the Afro-Asian peoples to unite against European oppression.[147] The same impulse led Duse to criticize the Anglo-German agreement on colonial questions that was in the making in the middle of 1914.[148] After the outbreak of World War I Duse immediately took Britain's part, chiefly because he disapproved of German colonial methods, which he had already attacked in his journal.[149] On the other hand, he made ironic remarks about Belgium, which he thought should not be idealized: the German attack was but a punishment for Belgian atrocities in the Congo.[150] World War I pushed into the background an earlier sombre vision of a possible struggle between the White and coloured races:

> Can anyone believe that such a state of things will last forever? Have they an ideas of the crop of hatred that is being sown, hatred that will be harvested sooner or later? No race or people will for ever remain quiet under the load of contempt and of injustice that is the universal lot of non-European peoples all over the world. And yet there are Peace Congresses and people who believe in Universal Peace. Do they mean by Peace the tame acceptance by Asia and Africa of the perpetual domination of the Whites! Such a compliance would justify the contempt held by Europe and white America for Asiatics and Africans.[151]

In other respects, too, there were hints of things to come. The journal reported the speech given on 2 May 1914 by Arthur Creech-Jones, secretary of the Dulwich branch of the Independent Labour party and of the local trade-union organization, to the Egyptian Debating Society on the theme of 'Socialism and Nationalism'.[152] Between the two World Wars Creech-Jones was one of the Labour party's colonial experts and favourable to the African and Asian viewpoint; after 1945 he was for a time Secretary of State for the Colonies and directly responsible for the first step towards decolonization. W. E. G. Sekyi, one of the most militant West African nationalists, published his first articles in Duse's journal, at a time when he was a twenty-year-old law student in London.[153] Before 1914 Duse's circle in London included one of the future celebrities of Pan-Africanism, Marcus A. Garvey. Even before the outbreak of the war the latter was able to present his ideas for the first time, at least to a worldwide public.[154]

Duse shared his pupil Garvey's admiration for Booker T. Washington. His business sense made the editorial office of the *African Times and Orient Review* in Fleet Street a clearing-house for Africans who maintained or sought commercial relations with British firms.[155] In 1920 Duse moved to the United States to look after his new commercial interests, and also to collaborate with Garvey on the *Negro World* – a fact which Duse later shamefacedly concealed in his autobiographical sketch. After the Garvey movement collapsed in 1925 we find Duse in the following year acting as general secretary of the American-Asia Association Inc., which had its head office in New York. This sought to familiarize America with Asian culture; other objectives included the study of Oriental languages, the promotion of trade and the supply of high-quality textiles to members of the association. Among the patrons were the mayor of Detroit, John Smith, and the Persian chargé d'affaires in the United States.[156]

Despite this return to his Asian and Oriental interests Duse did not neglect the African aspect. He lent his name as patron to another association, the Native African Union of America, founded on 6 February 1927 and entered in the register of societies on 9 February 1928. This society's aim was to uphold the interests of Africans in America, and it thus fulfilled a kind of Pan-African function. Finally in 1928 Duse was commissioned by the Continental African Publishing Corporation to publish a lavishly illustrated and expensive-looking monthly entitled *Africa*, evidently one of the numerous ephemeral journals which adorn the fringes of Pan-Africanism.[157]

In 1931 Duse left the United States and went to West Africa. Refused permission by the colonial authorities to land on the Gold Coast,[158] he and his wife settled in Lagos. It was here that he published in 1933 his last paper, the *Comet*, which was later to play a far from insignificant role in the history of Nigerian nationalism. At first, however, it had no particular political angle and tended to emulate the British popular press. The most valuable element for the historian of the pre-war decades is Duse's autobiographical sketch, published in instalments.[159] Towards the end of his long and colourful life Duse again plunged more deeply into the politics of Nigerian nationalism. Shortly before his death in 1944 he took the chair at the great meeting in Lagos on 26 August 1944 at which was founded the National Council of Nigeria and the Cameroons (NCNC), the first mass nationalist party in Africa south of the Sahara.

228 The Pan-African Movement

This glimpse into Duse's later career is intended to underline the fact that with his *African Times and Orient Review* Duse fulfilled a Pan-African function, in regard to the range of his collaborators and readers as well as the themes chosen for treatment in the journal. By virtue of its relatively long and continuous appearance, as well as its world-wide connections, it propagated and promoted ideas of which many were to become practical politics after World War I.

12   Du Bois and the
Pan-African
Congress movement

The politicizing effect of World War I

World War I was of extraordinary importance in the development of
African (and Asian) nationalism in general and Pan-Africanism in
particular. It accelerated and promoted tendencies which had been in
existence previously, but more particularly it struck the first blows that
shook the colonial system. Initially, however, the outbreak of the war
hampered nationalist and Pan- African activities.At the end of August
1914 Duse's journal, the *African Times and Orient Review*, had to dis-
continue publication for over two years. Its endeavours to secure
representatives in British West Africa came to a halt, as people wanted
first to wait and see how the war was going and how it would end.[1]

The accelerating effect of World War I set in before the war ended.
As early as 4 August 1914 Duse jubilantly contemplated the possibility
that all the ruling White nations would be exhausted by the war, to
the profit of the coloured peoples:

> We can only watch and pray. Unarmed, undisciplined, disunited
> we cannot strike a blow, we can only wait the event. But whatever
> that may be, all the combatants, the conquerors and the conquered

alike, will be exhausted by the struggle, and will require years for their recovery, and during that time much may be done. Watch and wait! It may be that the non-European races will profit by the European disaster. God's ways are mysterious.[2]

On a higher theoretical level Du Bois in 1915 gave the first analysis of Africa's position in the war.[3] Proceeding from the Berlin colonial conference of 1884–5, he achieved results similar to those of Lenin in his *Imperialism as the Highest Stage of Capitalism* (published in 1917). Du Bois saw the profounder causes of European colonial imperialism and the division of Africa in economic motives and thought that the war was being fought to achieve domination over tropical Africa. In a particularly striking parallel to Lenin, he wrote of the 'aristocracy of labour' as a force uniting the capitalists and the working class against the coloured proletariat, determined to frustrate the progress of the Chinese and negroes.[4] Du Bois demanded that the land be returned to Africans wherever they had been deprived of control over it (as was the case in southern and eastern Africa). The colonial peoples should be introduced into modern civilization and granted home rule.

> The principle of home rule must extend to groups, nations, and races. The ruling of one people for another people's whim or gain must stop. This kind of despotism has been in latter days more and more skilfully disguised. But the brute fact remains: the white man is ruling black Africa for the white man's gain, and just as far as possible he is doing the same to colored races elsewhere. Can such a situation bring peace? Will any amount of European concord or disarmament settle this injustice?[5]

For the future he foresaw three risks to world peace: European discontent at the new partition of Africa; a revolt of the poorer elements among White workers; and a general rising of the coloured peoples leading to a race war.

> The colored peoples will not always submit to foreign domination. . . . These nations and races, composing as they do the vast majority of humanity, are going to endure this treatment just as long as they must and not a moment longer. Then they are going to fight and the War of the Color Line will outdo in savage inhumanity any war this world has yet seen. For colored folk have much to remember and they will not forget.[6]

To such theoretical considerations was added, for tens of thousands of Africans, a direct experience of war. A number of factors contributed to the politicization of broad masses of the population in Africa and Asia: their introduction to modern technology as soldiers or as construction workers employed by European armies; the criticism of harsh German colonial methods (now enthusiastically taken up by Allied propaganda); the relative lack of racial prejudice in France (which made a particularly profound impression on coloured US soldiers posted to that country); President Wilson's proclamation of the principle of national self-determination; and the Russian revolution of October 1917.

Service in the British or French army meant for tens of thousands of Africans a widening of their hitherto narrow horizons, regardless of whether they returned to their homelands immediately after the end of the war or stayed on in Britain or France. In his memoirs Claude McKay, the distinguished Afro-American poet and political journalist from Jamaica, describes two London clubs in the winter of 1919–20. One of them, in a basement in Drury Lane, enabled coloured people to make contact with one another, to read journals (*inter alia* from the United States) supplied by McKay, and to discuss political problems. The second one, the International Club, provided the possibility of contact with British intellectuals, artists and left-wing groups; it was here that, for example, McKay first became acquainted with Marx and Marxism.[7]

In this milieu an intellectual ferment was generated which could not but accelerate the pace of political development. Similarly ex-soldiers of the French colonial army, especially the Tirailleurs Algériens and others from Senegal and Dahomey, played a major role in the early stages of the national movement in these countries.[8] In the capitals of the two West European democracies with large colonial empires Africans absorbed more intensely than they had before the war the political ideas of a Europe that was rapidly changing. Here it was also easier for simple but politically conscious soldiers to come into contact with African intellectuals and students than in their own homelands. Many Africans and Afro-Americans became acquainted with one another for the first time in London and Paris.

World War I had a similar influence upon Afro-Americans, since the worldwide struggle for democracy raised their hopes for social and political equality at home and gave them a new self-awareness. During the period of reaction directly after the end of the war this self-aware-ness and the demands to which it gave rise provoked a wave of lynch murders and race riots, of which there were twenty-five in the USA, one of the most serious occurring in Washington DC. The 'red summer' of 1919, so called after the blood which was shed in the States, created a mood of profound disillusionment and bitterness; but it also forged a determination to win equality of rights. One result of World War I was the Pan-African Congress movement.

Sources

The Pan-African Congress movement has hitherto always taken up most space in literature on the subject, although a more comprehensive analysis shows that its importance was less than is generally thought. There are two reasons for this overemphasis. Firstly, the five Pan-African congresses, if only by virtue of their name, put Pan-Africanism on the map, as it were, and gave it a certain tradition and continuity, embodied in Du Bois's long career. Secondly, Du Bois engaged in some exceptionally clever self-advertisement in his numerous autobiographical and other works.[9]

The high evaluation which Du Bois gave to his handiwork, the Pan-African Congress movement, has so far been accepted uncritically by other writers; it stands in contrast to the scantiness of the sources available to anyone seeking to reconstruct what actually happened. This scarcity to some extent reflects the weakness of the movement, for in some points it even represented a step backwards by comparison with the Pan-African Conference of 1900 and the first Pan-African Association. There is no comprehensive, let alone printed, report (even if only for internal use) of the proceedings of any of the four Pan-African congresses which Du Bois organized; nor do we have such a detailed account as was given in the London *Times* of the 1900 conference;[10] nor is there available a complete list of those who participated in the congress; nor did the second Pan-African Association get beyond a resolution to publish a journal of its own. The information given by Du Bois is vague and the press reports, although numerous, provide only summary accounts. Even Du Bois's personal papers contain only a few items which could yield fuller information, and despite the wealth of material in them they are rather disappointing on more important matters.

Except for reports in *Crisis* which have hitherto been neglected by scholars, Du Bois's autobiographical statements consist mostly of quotations from reports on the congress by American correspondents which largely reflect its snob appeal as a social event instead of satisfying the historian's curiosity.[11] Du Bois's own comment, 'the Congress influenced the Peace Conference'[12] is an obvious exaggeration, as is also his assertion that the introduction of the League of Nations mandatory system was attributable to the Congress movement and thus in the last resort to himself.[13]

In its content, too, the Pan-African Congress movement is by no means what one might expect, given the great emphasis it has received in the literature. The speeches contained more in the way of declamatory pronouncements than solid intellectual analysis of the actual situation. Owing to the unsatisfactory state of the sources, the following account of the Pan-African Congress movement between 1919 and 1927 is somewhat unsatisfactory and relies to considerable extent on published material (of which most, however, has hitherto been as good as ignored). It diminishes the importance of Du Bois's Pan-African congresses, and also of Du Bois himself and his contribution to Pan-Africanism. This is done with some reluctance, for even so Du Bois remains an important figure in the Pan-African movement, quite apart from his great achievement as an Afro-American leader, journalist, historian and sociologist. But the respect due to this almost patriarchal figure, which extends right up to the present time, should not reduce scholarly critics to silence.

First, however, let us return to the subject of Du Bois's biography.[14]

Du Bois's career from 1910 to 1963

After 1910 Du Bois kept up his Pan-African interests from his position on the committee of the NAACP and on its journal *Crisis*, which he edited independently and not always in complete agreement with that organization. In 1915 he published a small volume, still worth reading today, on the history of Africa and Afro-Americans, which he was to expand twenty-four years later.[15] In 1920 there appeared the first of several autobiographical accounts which he wrote.[16] During the great depression Du Bois gradually lost his belief in the possibility of racial integration in the USA, which led to differences with the NAACP. In 1934 a conflict broke out when he swung towards the position taken by Garvey, whom he had fought bitterly in the early 1920s, and came out in favour of Afro-Americans pursuing their own advancement in voluntary segregation. With a flourish Du Bois left the NAACP executive committee and his editorship of *Crisis*, and went back to the University of Atlanta. Here he wrote a great pioneering work on the history of the Reconstruction period,[17] *Black Folk, Then and Now*, as well as his second autobiography.[18] In 1944 Du Bois, then seventy-six, rejoined the NAACP executive and participated in the fifth Pan-African Congress of 1945.

As the cold war got under way Du Bois became more and more involved in the left-wing World Peace Movement and found himself again in conflict with the NAACP. He was the object of proceedings for alleged 'un-American activities' and experienced all manner of other difficulties, which he related vividly in another book.[19] In 1961 he joined the American Communist party, more out of spite than from truly communist convictions. In the same year he moved to Ghana, where at the invitation of Nkrumah he took over the management of the *Encyclopaedia Africana*. This is a scholarly enterprise on a grand scale with a Pan-African horizon, sponsored by Nkrumah; it developed out of an idea which Du Bois had in mind as early as 1909, namely to produce, with the collaboration of scholars from many countries, an *Encyclopaedia on the Negro*. At the beginning of 1963, shortly before his death, Du Bois acquired Ghanaian citizenship, so giving personal effect at the biblical age of ninety-five to the 'Back to Africa' ideal for which he had fought in his earlier years. On 27 August 1963, on the eve of the great civil rights demonstration in the USA, the march to Washington, Du Bois died in Accra, highly venerated by Africans as the 'Father of Pan-Africanism', respected at least by the NAACP, which in the meantime had become the conservative wing of the modern civil rights movement, and honoured by the latter's militant wing.[20]

The first Pan-African Congress: Paris, 1919

In December 1918 Du Bois was commissioned by the NAACP to travel to Paris together with Moton, its former secretary and now the successor to Booker T. Washington. He was given two tasks: to investigate the complaints about discrimination and maltreatment of negro troops in the US army stationed in France, and to look after African interests at the impending Peace Conference. According to his own subsequent account he arrived in Paris with the intention of holding a Pan-African conference.[21] This assertion seems plausible in view of the fact that he had been interested in Pan-African problems for nearly two decades. In Paris at any rate he seized the opportunity and improvised a Pan-African congress, the first in a series of five.

Du Bois began to make useful contacts shortly after his arrival in Paris. At the beginning of January 1919 a letter reached him from the African Progress Union in London founded in 1918, in which Mohamed Ali Duse played a leading role. Its secretary, Robert Broadhurst, welcomed Du Bois, wished the planned congress success and reminded him that they had already met at the Universal Races Congress in 1911.[22] Through its secretary, the Rev. Harris, the Anti-Slavery and Aborigines Protection Society likewise expressed interest in the projected Pan-African congress. It could not, however, send a delegate or observer to Paris since the British military authorities would not allow a representative of the society to go there[23] – an indication of the kind of technical difficulties Du Bois had to overcome. In another instance an Afro-American officer stationed with his unit in France was obliged to inform Du Bois that he had not been given leave to participate in the congress since his unit had been posted back to the United States.[24]

In the course of preparing for the congress Du Bois established contact with Blaise Diagne, who in 1914 had been elected deputy for Senegal[25] and as commissioner of recruiting in 1917–18 held an important political position in Paris directly after the war. It is not yet clear when and why Du Bois hit upon the idea of collaborating with Diagne. It may have been because Du Bois witnessed the ceremony at which Diagne was awarded the cross of the Legion of Honour, on 28 December 1918, as he relates full of ecstasy in his periodical: 'Vive la France!: "Mine eyes have seen" and they were filled with tears. . . . Men of Africa! How fine a thing to be a black Frenchman in 1919 – imagine such a celebration in America!'[26]

In an undated memorandum, available in English and French, which must have been drawn up before 8 January 1919, Du Bois turned to Diagne and others[27] suggesting the following. The congress was to be held from 2 to 4 February (this date, however, could not be kept to); an organization committee was to be formed; personal invitations were to be sent to representatives of the negro race who might be able to attend, as well as to the Abyssinian, Liberian and Haitian governments. Other representatives were to be invited from the French, British, Spanish, Italian, Belgian, Dutch and former German colonies, from the negroes in North and South America as well as the West Indies; yet other invitations were to go to all governments which had negro citizens and subjects, and finally to China, Japan and India. Du Bois also proposed inviting to the open sessions 'representatives of organizations engaged in the advancement of darker races', i.e. philanthropic and humanitarian groups. The range of prospective participants was typical of Du Bois's breadth of vision; he was fond of addressing appeals and manifestos to the entire world.

The agenda outlined by Du Bois was no less ambitious. It comprised an analysis of the present situation and the formulation of the negroes' demands, including economic development primarily in the interest of the natives and general modern education; 'full recognition of the independent governments of Abyssinia, Liberia, and Hayti, with their full natural boundaries, and the development of the former German colonies under the guarantees and oversight of the League of Nations'[28]. It was also intended to organize another congress in 1920. There were to be alternate open and closed sessions, with mass meetings in between.

Du Bois envisaged a permanent secretariat with its seat in Paris, whose task it would be 'to compile the history of the Negro race, to study the present situation of the race, to publish articles, pamphlets, and a record of the congress, and to promote literature and art among the Negroes'.[29] Finally Du Bois suggested holding a small preliminary meeting on 8 January at a place yet to be fixed.

Apparently it took several meetings to reach a decision to hold the congress from 19 to 21 February 1919. The interested parties present in Paris formed a provisional organizational committee, composed of Diagne, Du Bois and E. F. Fredericks, a lawyer from Freetown, Sierra Leone.[30] This committee took charge of further preparations, Du Bois presumably acting as the driving force, while Diagne's political connections as a deputy befitted him to undertake the practical side. The role which Fredericks played still remains obscure; his name appears here for the first time, and as yet nothing is known about him.[31] In any case his participation was at least of symbolic value in view of the important part Sierra Leone had played in the past.

The second memorandum, likewise undated, which may have served as a working paper for negotiations with French political circles or to win their interest in the congress, mentioned two objectives: securing proper regard for the interests of 'la race noire' and the taking of measures to unite all people of African descent, without prejudice to their loyalty as French, British, Liberian, Haitian or American subjects, in order to give them a new sense of self-awareness.[32] Finally the memorandum emphasized the value of the congress as a means of making the voice of 'the children of Africa' heard during the Peace Conference. Regret was expressed at the need for improvisation, which may have been a reaction to criticism of the projected gathering.

It did not suit American policy that a Pan-African congress should be held in Paris on the fringe of the Peace Conference. Although President Woodrow Wilson had proclaimed during the war the right of peoples to determine their own fate, as a southern Democrat he had deeply disappointed Afro-American intellectuals (including Du Bois, who had supported him) by clinging to traditional segregationist policies at home. Wilson did not intend to apply the principle of national self-determination to non-European peoples, let alone guarantee such rights to the inhabitants of the African colonies.[33] The US government therefore tried, as best it could, to prevent the congress taking place. Nothing could be done about Du Bois and the not very militant Robert Moton, Washington's successor at the Tuskegee Institute, who were already in France, but the government refused passports to other Afro-Americans and White sympathizers who wanted to participate. Among these latter were Monroe Trotter of the *Boston Guardian*, the first intellectual to criticize Washington. The New York socialist journal the *Messenger*, one of the keenest rivals of Du Bois's *Crisis*, uttered the reproach that apparently only 'good niggers' would be allowed to travel to Paris. This slur could not apply to Du Bois since he had gone to Paris without informing the US government of his ultimate intentions. Similarly the government in London refused to allow Africans to travel from British colonies to Paris for the congress. The US authorities intimated that the French government would in any case prevent the gathering being held.[34]

It is a well-known story, often related, how Du Bois with the aid of Diagne overcame the resistance of the American government and its delegation to the Peace Conference. Diagne won the discreet support of Clemenceau who gave permission with the following words: 'Don't advertise it, but go ahead.'[35] Walter Lippmann, then still a young man, took an interest in Du Bois and offered him moral support.[36] The short period of time available for organizing the congress, the numerous administrative and political obstacles created by immediate post-war conditions, the vast distances that mail had to travel, and finally financial difficulties all help to explain why Du Bois's grandiose original plans had relatively modest results. When the First Pan-African Congress opened on 19 February 1919 fifty-seven 'delegates' were present. They had in fact not been delegated by anybody to attend the congress but came of their own accord, as was only to be expected in the circumstances.

About the composition of the congress and the papers read there we do not have much information to go on. The report on the assembly signed by Du Bois and Diagne does not mention any of the participants' names but only provides a general classification by country of origin.[37] According to this account sixteen of them came from the United States, thirteen from the French West Indies, seven each from Haiti and France, three from Liberia, two from the Spanish colonies and one each from the Portuguese colonies, San Domingo, Britain, British territories in Africa, French territories in Africa, Algeria, Egypt, the Belgian Congo and Abyssinia. The British West Indian element, which played such a vital role in the development of Pan-Africanism, was wholly absent and there were scarcely any representatives from West Africa. In the circumstances the congress was as representative as possible. A sympathetic French observer, M. Delafosse, drew attention to this point, explaining that the representatives of the still underdeveloped tribes of the interior would not have been intellectually capable of taking a meaningful part in the deliberations of the congress. Finding themselves in an atmosphere to which they were utterly unaccustomed, they would probably have raised questions of local significance which would not have fitted at all into the framework of the discussions.[38]

The provisional organizational committee was expanded into a presidium, in which Diagne acted as president and Du Bois as secretary; the other members were Fredericks and Mrs Ida Gibbs Hunt (USA). So few participants in the congress are known by name that it is worth while enumerating them individually. Besides the four just mentioned we may list the following: C. D. B. King, who had just been appointed President of Liberia but had yet to assume office, and who at that time was a member of the Liberian peace delegation in Paris; Gratien Candace, a representative in the Chamber of Deputies in Guadeloupe; Plaatje from South Africa; and two other deputies from the French Antilles, Boisneuf and Lagrosillière. The White sympathizers included William E. Walling (USA), one of the initiators of the appeal of 1909 which led to the foundation of the NAACP.[39]

The congress took place in the Grand Hôtel, Boulevard des Capucines and another office was installed at the Hôtel de Malte, 63 rue de Richelieu. The languages used in the proceedings were English and French. The chair throughout was taken by Diagne, who opened the congress with a speech extolling French colonial rule.[40] He went on to express his hope that the ideal of solidarity might inspire men of African descent all over the world. After him Candace, Boisneuf and Lagrosillière vigorously criticized the United States for its racial policy, as a result of which equality of rights was denied to men who had nevertheless given their lives for democracy and justice during the war. King emphasized the role played by Liberia and called for support from his fellow-negroes for Liberia 'as the home for the darker races in Africa'.

The White representatives from France, Belgium and Portugal gave speeches more or less in favour of the colonial policy of their respective countries; Walling (USA) at least indirectly stood up for his homeland, arguing that a change was on the way since America would have to bow before the world opinion on the question of racial discrimination. Other delegates threw light upon the situation in specific countries without calling in question the basic principle of European colonial rule. It was hardly conceivable that they should have adopted a different attitude. For this reason the chief resolution passed by the congress, quoted frequently and in detail in the literature,[41] turned out to be a moderate one. It demanded international supervision of Africa and peoples of African descent through the League of Nations and an improvement of living conditions (abolition of slavery, corporal punishment and forced labour, general access to modern education, and protection from expropriation of land and economic exploitation). The principal political demand was that Africans be permitted to participate in governing their countries as soon as their level of development enabled them to do so, at first by retaining traditional forms on the local and regional level. This participation should gradually be extended until in the last resort 'Africa is ruled by consent of the Africans'.[42] Such aspirations were not 'indirectly revolutionary'[43] for the time, for the London Conference of 1900 had already spoken of 'responsible government' for Africa,[44] so that the Paris resolution of 1919 was tantamount to a retreat from the principle of self-government. Thus American and French observers were able to comment with satisfaction that the demands had been reasonable and moderate.[45]

Also in the field of organization the first Pan-African Congress took a retrograde step by comparison with its predecessor of 1900. It was not even found possible to set up a new Pan-African Association, but merely a permanent committee of which Diagne was president and Du Bois secretary. The *Black Review*, an international quarterly which Du Bois announced was to appear in English and French and possibly also in Spanish and Portuguese,[46] did not get beyond the stage of inquiries by Du Bois – to which at least one reply was received, from Isaac Béton[47] – and the premature proclamation: 'The world fight for black rights is on!' With astonishing naïveté and a characteristic belief in the power of money Du Bois added: 'If the Negroes of the world could have maintained in Paris during the entire sitting of the Peace Conference a central headquarters with experts, clerks and helpers, they could have settled the future of Africa at a cost of less than $10,000.'[48]

The second Pan-African Congress : London – Brussels – Paris, 1921

Even the question of holding future congresses was by no means clarified unequivocally in Paris in 1919. In his first memorandum of January 1919 Du Bois had thought of holding the next congress in 1920.[49] But in the second memorandum the idea emerged of arranging further sessions of this congress in London in 1919 and then in New York to prepare for the next congress in 1920 or 1921.[50] Apparently the first Congress did not come to any final decision about the future of the movement, for in the autumn of 1920 Du Bois had to take the initiative for the next gathering. He wrote to Diagne and Candace, who agreed in principle to holding the meeting in 1921 but suggested different months. Diagne proposed that this time the position of Afro-Americans in the States should be placed properly on the agenda. He thought that the congress could only succeed if the American delegation was homogeneous and united[51] – which suggests that this had not been so in Paris.

To ensure that Africa should be better represented, Du Bois (according to his own information) wrote to certain personalities,[52] but the only reply that has survived in Du Bois's papers is that from Casely Hayford. Already in March 1919 the latter had manifested his interest in the congress and regretted that no representatives from British West Africa could be present in Paris. In reply to a letter from Du Bois of 10

December 1920, in which he desired 'to have a strong representation of the West Africans at the next Pan-African Congress in Paris meeting in August next', Hayford gave an encouraging answer (29 December). He did, however, advise Du Bois 'to address our Congress [National Congress] officially in my care [in Sekondi, Gold Coast], when I shall use all my influence in recommending the proposal, which I personally think is a good one'. He went on to assure Du Bois that 'I have always looked forward to the time when representative and responsible members of our race could meet together upon a common platform for the discussion of common problems affecting us all, and I am sure I am not singular in this wish. . . .'[53]

All in all Du Bois's endeavours seem to have been successful, for this time more than one-third of the participants came from Africa; 41 out of a total of 113 originated from the States, and only 7 from the West Indies; 24 were Africans and Afro-Americans living in Europe.[54] A list of names is available only for 24 participants from the States including four wives accompanying their husbands.[55] Of these it is worth noting Florence Kelley and Jessie Fauset (both from New York), the latter at that time still a young and quite well-known Afro-American author and also Du Bois's collaborator in the NAACP and on *Crisis*. Three bishops are of interest, more for their social position than for their personal importance: C. H. Phillips (Nashville, Colored Methodist church), John Hurst (Baltimore, AMEZ) and Cary (Chicago, AME). The other participants included another theologian, one professor and three graduates, and Rayford W. Logan. The latter was an Afro-American ex-officer who had served with the US army in France during World War I and had later returned to Paris, where he acted as a contact man for Du Bois; from 1938 he was for many years professor of history at Howard University in Washington DC.[56] The following are known to have participated from other countries: Diagne, Candace and Béton; Dantès Bellegarde, Vilius Gervais (both from Haiti); Jose de Magalhaens (Liga Africana, an association of *assimilados* in the Portuguese colonies founded in May 1921; it tried to cultivate good relations both with Du Bois's Pan-African Congress movement and with the Garvey movement[56a]); Louis Hunkarin (Dahomey), Max Bloncourt (French Antilles); Davies (South Africa) and the participants in the discussion mentioned below.[57]

Before the congress began Du Bois held talks with leading representatives of the Anti-Slavery and Aborigines Protection Society and the

Labour party, including Beatrice Webb, Leonard Woolf and Norman Leys, an expert on Kenya. About these talks Du Bois gives only a brief and cautious account,[58] which may suggest to the average reader that they were important and successful. In reality they seem to have taken a less gratifying turn which goes far to explain Du Bois's later reserve. In any case he left a most unfavourable impression upon his opposite numbers in London (who were themselves open-minded), especially on account of his personal abruptness and his pronounced anti-British and pro-French attitude.

Irritation was already manifest in London before the congress when Du Bois, against the advice of the Rev. Harris, secretary of the Anti-Slavery and Aborigines Protection Society, insisted at all cost on holding the meeting in August. Harris agreed to support the venture but refused to identify his organization with it formally. He did not think a vast congress would be useful but preferred a small private working conference in London which would keep away 'persons with impractical ideas'[59] – presumably meaning Garvey's supporters. Du Bois agreed to this, but not to the date proposed by Harris because, as he wrote to Robert Broadhurst, secretary of the African Progress Union, a month later, the locale of the meeting could no longer be altered. Du Bois did, however, want to invite representatives of the Labour party, the CMS and 'some of the coloured organizations in London'. In his reply Harris backed Du Bois's proposal but again warned that a congress of coloured people in London in August stood hardly any chance of success. Harris hoped to be able to invite some West Africans who happened to be in London then, and said he wanted to see the resolutions of the congress first before backing the scheme in public.[60] On several occasions after the congress Harris was critical of Du Bois. Despite all the sympathy felt in London for Africans and Afro-Americans, Harris stated, it was difficult to mobilize support for Du Bois, whose unconventional defence of French colonial practices had caused general vexation. Although fervent endeavours had been made to enlighten him about the true state of affairs in the French colonies, Du Bois had turned a completely deaf ear. When Du Bois came to Geneva to hand in a petition to the League of Nations, he seems to have behaved in such a way that even some of the best friends of the 'negro race' dissociated themselves from him.[61]

The congress of 1921 met in several sessions, first in London and then in Brussels and Paris; the composition varied accordingly. In London

Anglo-African and Afro-American elements predominated; in Brussels and Paris a francophone element was added, which led to acute tensions and eventually to virtual schism.

We do have a number of press reports about the three meetings of the congress, but only rarely do they contain concrete information. They mostly focus attention on Du Bois; there are some general commentaries reflecting the viewpoint of the author concerned or emphasizing the differences with the Garvey movement, which were felt to be beneficent.

The congress was held in the Central Hall, Westminster, on 28 and 29 August 1921. Participants came from the United States, South and West Africa, and the British West Indies. The chair was taken by Dr Alcindor, president of the African Progress Union and a participant in the London Conference of 1900,[62] and on the second day by Du Bois and J. R. Archer. In his opening speech Alcindor expressed regret at Diagne's absence. The aim of the meeting, he said, was to promote mutual understanding about the Africans' problems and to articulate some of their grievances. Contrary to a common opinion, the governments were not enemies of the Africans; often the latter's worst enemies were themselves. They should fight for their cause with all their might, but always with clean weapons. After these self-critical notes had been sounded Du Bois reported on the endeavours to bring African problems before the Peace Conference and before the US Senate; apparently he gave a description of the first Pan-African Congress and his own lobbying in the States through the NAACP. It was particularly urgent, he said, for negroes with a modern education to meet and inform themselves about the negro problem as a whole throughout the world.

In the subsequent discussion on racial barriers in West Africa there were two speakers: Peter Thomas (Lagos) and Dr Olaribigbe (formerly from Sierra Leone). Thomas began by remarking that hitherto no negro organization had existed through which they could formulate their grievances, and pointed out that it was not an act of disloyalty for negroes to put forward demands. He went on to plead for wider access to modern education and economic activity, which would allow negroes to win more friends among Europeans. This attitude was in conformity with the line of Du Bois and Booker T. Washington. Thomas was followed by the Rev. W. B. Mark (Sierra Leone), L. B. Augusto (Lagos; to judge by his name a 'Brazilian'), W. F. Hutchinson, a former collaborator of Mohamed Ali Duse, J. Eldred Taylor, the original initiator of the *African Times and Orient Review*,[63] and the Rev. E. G.

Granville Sutton (formerly from Sierra Leone).[64] On 29 August the speakers were J. R. Archer, (coloured) mayor of the borough of Battersea in 1913 and 1914, for a time committee member of the Pan-African Association of 1900 and president of the African Progress Union founded in 1918; the Communist candidate for Battersea, Shapurji Saklatvala; and Albert T. Marryshaw (Grenada). Marryshaw strongly attacked the existing political system in this crown colony, which was dominated by an all-powerful governor, and described his journey to London as the climax of West Indian agitation for representative government.

The customary major resolution passed at the end of the congress is well known and frequently quoted.[65] The title alone, 'Declaration to the World', betrays Du Bois's hand. Some of the principal sentences, too, have the pathos so characteristic of the man. In some respects the new declaration brought greater precision and showed that his political ideas had developed since the Paris resolution of 1919. Keeping to the intellectual and literary tradition outlined above, it came out vigorously for the recognition of the principle of racial equality, without denying actual differences in the level of development:

> The absolute equality of races, physical, political and social is the founding stone of the world and human advancement and attainment among individuals of all races, but the voice of Science, Religion and practical Politics is one in denying the God-appointed existence of super-races or of races naturally and inevitably and eternally inferior. That in the vast range of time, one group should in its industrial technique, or social organization, or spiritual vision lag a few hundred years behind another, or forge fitfully ahead, or come to differ decidedly in thought, deed and ideal, is proof of the essential richness and variety of human nature, rather than proof of the coexistence of demi-gods and apes in human form. The doctrine of racial equality does not interfere with individual liberty; rather it fulfills it. And of all the various criteria of which masses of men have in the past been pre-judged and classified, that of the color of the skin and texture of the hair, is surely the most adventitious and idiotic . . .

The declaration further demanded 'the establishment of political institutions among suppressed peoples' to promote inter-racial contact. 'The habit of democracy must be made to encircle the earth. . . . Local self-government with a minimum of help and oversight can be established tomorrow in Asia, in Africa, America, and the isles of the sea. . . .'[66] In eight points the declaration comprised the demands of the 'Negro race through their thinking intelligentsia': that the criterion of achievement should be the level of civilization, not race or colour of skin; that access be granted to education in the widest sense;[67] freedom of religion; tolerance of all forms of society, however different from one's own; collaboration with the rest of the world on the basis of justice, freedom and peace; return of negroes to their own countries and protection from investment capital; establishment of two institutions under the League of Nations to study the negro problem and to protect native workers, as had been demanded in 1919.[68] Of the greatest political significance was the second of the points listed above, on 'local self-government for backward groups, deliberately rising as experience and knowledge grow to complete self-government under the limitation of a self-governed world'.[69] With this formula, providing for future sovereignty ('self-government'), the second Pan-African Congress of 1921 went beyond its forerunner in 1919 and took up again the lead given by the Pan-African Conference of 1900.

After passing this resolution the congress moved to Brussels, where it resumed its sessions in the Palais Mondial from 31 August to 3 September. Here the francophone element came into the picture, most prominently represented by Diagne, who now took the chair. A kind of intellectual patronage was provided by Professor Paul Otlet and Senator La Fontaine, two well-known spokesmen for the League of Nations idea in Belgium, with whom Du Bois was in vigorous correspondence. Because of their prestige they were able to ward off some sharp political attacks against the congress, in which it was alleged that it was under communist control or was identified with the Garvey movement. Otlet apparently also saved the congress by advancing a compromise formula when deep differences of opinion appeared, whose nature Du Bois only hints at.[70] According to the latter one of the London resolutions, which were voted on again in Brussels, contained a passage criticizing Belgian colonial policy. When the attempt to water it down was rejected by a majority of those present, Diagne simply declared that the amendment had been carried. According to a newspaper report Diagne explained his attitude by referring to the attacks on the congress in the Belgian press; if the resolution were accepted, this would only confirm the suspicion that the congress was a Bolshevik front organization for Africa. Thus for Diagne, who one year later was to make his peace with the French establishment in Dakar, even cautious criticism of the colonial rule of a neighbouring country went too far in the direction of radicalism. Thereupon Otlet got an innocuous compromise resolution passed which called for common efforts by Blacks and Whites to develop Africa.[71]

Another conflict revolved around Garvey and his movement. Du Bois admitted in general terms that at this time he had to contend with Garvey's rivalry,[72] but he concealed the fact that, at least in Brussels, violent dissension broke out between Garvey's supporters and his own adherents. In London Du Bois had already had to endure questions from White visitors and journalists about his attitude to Garvey. To at least one journalist he explained that he agreed basically with Garvey's programme but could not approve of the methods he employed, especially economic enterprises of doubtful soundness such as the Black Star Line. The journalist gained the impression (doubtless not incorrect) that although Du Bois rejected Garvey's crude methods, he was in his way just as determined to help the Africans attain their rights by peaceful and constitutional means.[73]

In Brussels and Paris the leading delegates to the congress, and finally the majority, unequivocally condemned Garvey and his slogan 'Africa for the Africans'. This decision was preceded by a violent debate. In this a participant from Jamaica, without identifying himself completely with his compatriot Garvey, delivered a speech full of bitterness about the situation in his country, confessing that he himself had occasionally thought of resorting to murder as a weapon in the struggle. Apparently other defenders of Garvey also intervened, among them Alcandre, whom Le Petit Parisien described as 'un noir français à la parole souple et mordante'.[74] He demanded that Garvey be invited to the next Pan-African Congress so that he might have the opportunity to expound his views; he himself was anxious to hear 'this Black man with red ideas'. Du Bois argued strongly against this and was seconded by Bellegarde and Candace, who assured the congress that they were not thinking of returning to Africa. Diagne, from the chair, succeeded in preventing a vote being taken on this point, but there is evidence to suppose that, as the session proceeded, a majority of the delegates were in favour of Garvey's being invited to the next congress and being allowed to defend his views.[75]

In Paris, where the debate about Garvey was apparently continued, the congress convened on 4 and 5 September in the Salle des Ingénieurs civils, rue Blanche. It was again chaired by Diagne; on the presidium he was flanked by Du Bois, Candace, Magalhaens, Judhava (British West Indies), Senator Aubert (La Réunion) and Félicien Challaye, agrégé de l'université, as well as 'many other notables'.[76] In his opening address Diagne emphasized the absolute freedom which the congress enjoyed on French soil. He concluded with a reference to the vigour of 300 million coloured people[77] who could no longer be ignored and despised: 'An appeal was made to our solidarity during the war and we never refused it. Have we now not also the right to demand it for ourselves in peacetime?'[78]

Subsequently Bellegarde spoke about an international office to maintain contacts between the individual groups, by which he apparently meant the (second) Pan-African Association, founded at the second Pan-African Congress. In a passionate address Candace attacked Garvey and pleaded for trustful collaboration with the Whites. Other participants in this discussion included Senator Aubert, Judhava and Magalhaens.

During an interval between sessions the delegates visited the Tomb of the Unknown Soldier. *Le Temps* records the remark of one of them, not identified, who said that the unknown soldier 'may be a coloured person, because the death which struck the defenders of France made no distinction between soldiers according to the colour of their skin'.[79]

During the afternoon session Du Bois presented the Pan-African programme of Afro-Americans from the USA. He called for absolute racial equality; the development of the masses, without whom the leaders could not make any progress; political power for all coloured people; self-government for the Africans in Africa; and the return of expropriated land.[80] He was against racial separation but said that if the colonial powers refused to make the Africans full citizens under their rule there would be no alternative but to separate the Whites from the Blacks.

Du Bois apparently also struck some socialist notes, reproaching the leaders of his own race for being closer to White capitalists than to the Black proletariat. Candace, who as a deputy probably felt offended at this, protested and rejected the patronage of the Labour party because in his view it was linked with the Third International – i.e. with Communism.[81]

In Paris the resolutions which had been discussed in Brussels were carried and a petition adopted for submission to the League of Nations. The latter, referring to the London and Paris resolutions, emphasized the point about setting up a special section for Africa in the International Labour Office, and called for an African or Afro-American to be appointed to the Mandates Commission as soon as there was a vacancy, since in the last instance the world was moving towards the principle of self-government for all men. Finally the petition to the League appealed for an end to racial discrimination.[82] Du Bois and Bellegarde represented the Pan-African Congress when the petition was handed over in Geneva. According to Harris's letter mentioned above, when in Geneva Du Bois does not seem to have kept to the deferential tone in which the petition was couched.[83] It may be that his polemical temperament got the better of him when he found the League of Nations more reserved than he had expected.

The second Pan-African Association of 1921

The most important result of the second Pan-African Congress, besides the dissociation of the movement from Garveyism, was the establishment of a new Pan-African Association (no express reference being made to the first one of 1900–1). The office of president fell to Candace and that of general secretary to Isaac Béton, a young schoolmaster from Martinique who taught at a lycée in Paris and published his own Journal, *Imperium, Revue Coloniale Française*. It was planned to set up branch organizations in different countries and regions, but it is not known whether they were actually founded. In his report on the congress Candace spoke of 'sociétés des amis des noirs'[84] which were to be founded everywhere; the name was purposely evocative of the Société des Amis des Noirs which had been active at the time of the French Revolutions of 1789 and 1848, and which was held in high esteem among francophone Afro-Americans and Africans.[85]

According to a Portuguese account the association's official name was 'International Pan-African Association' ('Associaçaõ Internacional Pan-Africana' in Portuguese) and it had a constitution very similar to that of the Liga Africana in Lisbon, explained by the influence of Dr Jose de Magalhaens of the Liga Africana on the special committee for drawing up the constitution.[86] The constitution which is, to the best of my knowledge, so far known only in its Portuguese version, defined the aim of the association as being the improvement of the position of negroes all over the world by developing their economic, political, intellectual and moral faculties through co-operation and organization. The Congress Board of Directors and a permanent Bureau in Paris were to be set up under its auspices; and branches of the association with more than 250 members would be able to send one delegate to the congress, those with up to 5000 members could send two and between 5000 and 10,000, three. The Pan-African Association clearly had tailored itself a mantle far too wide to be filled. The reality must have been sobering indeed.

The organization of the new body was almost wholly in the hands of Du Bois, and to some degree of Béton, and for this reason it was weak, as one might expect. It suffered from a chronic shortage of money and from the tensions that existed between its francophone and Afro-American elements. The extensive correspondence between Du Bois and Béton provides an instructive insight into this state of affairs. It is almost embarrassing to see to what extent these men were preoccupied with petty intrigues, quarrels about a few dollars' worth of membership fees, and various trivial misunderstandings, all of which took up a great deal of their energy and time.

On one occasion the deeper causes of these disputes came to the surface. At the beginning of 1922 Béton turned to Du Bois with a suggestion that he should raise some money from Afro-Americans in the USA in order to relieve the organization's penury. Two thousand francs were required to get its constitution printed at long last and to set up a permanent office. This move led to acute tension between Candace and Béton. No details of the matter are available, but in January 1922 Candace offered to resign. Du Bois's reply to Béton's suggestion left nothing to be desired in the way of clarity. It showed that there must have been some personal friction between the two main groups in the association during the second Pan-African Congress, probably while it was meeting in Brussels or in Paris. According to Du Bois the Afro-Americans felt that they had been so badly treated by the francophone element that none of them had any desire to help raise more money for the organization. The NAACP, which had already raised $4000 for the two congresses, was only prepared to provide further funds if other negro organizations did so as well.[87] To this letter, which Du Bois himself in a remarkable understatement described as 'not encouraging', Béton replied by return of post in a mood of resignation and disappointment. He took comfort, however, in some pathetic flourishes about his desperate straits: 'The blow is a harsh one and here I am condemned (me voici condamné) to an increase of efforts without the least of hope in my soul. Well! So much the worse. The cause is glorious enough! She deserves we face the . . . [word illegible] of dangers for her.'[88]

In his next letter, written in French, Béton conceded that the American delegates had been badly treated by 'our Black parliamentarians', which tells us where the responsibility for the tension lay on the francophone side, but he warned the Afro-Americans not to lose sight of the wood for the trees. It was their duty to give financial aid to the 'Association Pan-Africaine' in its early stages if only because they were better organized than all the other groups. Although the French had not yet raised any money, it would be 'noble, généreux, élégant et surtout intelligent' if the negroes of America could provide $5000 as an initial grant.[89]

Du Bois would have been willing to help, but in view of his own limited resources he saw no way out but for the francophone element to bear the financial burdens of the association and to take the initiative in its affairs.[90] Béton appreciated the significant contribution made by the Afro-Americans in the past but once again pointed to their greater organizational strength. He drew attention to the basic difficulty with which Pan-Africanism had constantly to struggle, the lack of contact between the anglophone and francophone elements. He, Béton, was supposed to organize the next Pan-African congress without any money, without knowing a single anglophone negro or even one of their journals. His complaint illustrates the lamentable lack of coordination within the Pan-African Association (for Du Bois did have good contacts) and also to a lack of initiative on Béton's part, for after all he had been present at the second Pan-African Congress and could have made the acquaintance of the anglophone West Indians and Africans there. It was at this point that Béton indirectly threatened to resign as general secretary or to obstruct the next congress should there be no improvement in its financial or organizational state. At no cost did he wish to appear empty-handed before the next congress to be held in two years' time, or to send out invitations for a meeting which would be taken up with idle chatter and vain threats.[91]

Under such conditions there was little hope that the congress, fixed for Lisbon in 1923, could be a success. As late as 8 May 1923 Béton wrote to Du Bois that he was keeping to the plan to hold the meeting during the last two weeks of September. But at the beginning of August he cancelled the congress at short notice, reproaching Du Bois for having sabotaged it in favour of his own plans in the West Indies, and for failing to make any propaganda for it in *Crisis*. For the collapse of the Pan-African Association he blamed Diagne, Candace and Du Bois, in equal measure. Its financial and organizational weakness is also evident from the fact that during the first year of its existence only twenty-three members of the association had paid their membership dues, amounting to 1157 francs, and during the second year only nine members, who together raised 636 francs. Having put approximately 15,000 francs of his own money into the organization over two years, he felt he could no longer afford to continue.[92]

The third Pan-African Congress: London – Lisbon, 1923

After Béton had resigned from his office in dark despair and had cancelled the third Pan-African Congress, which he was supposed to have prepared, it was nevertheless rescued by Du Bois in New York, who displayed superhuman energy, despatching numerous letters and telegrams over a short period of time which apparently created a great deal of confusion, however, in Lisbon with the Liga Africana.[93] In November 1923 the congress met in London and Lisbon. Its scope was narrower than that of its predecessors, and its programme was even less precise, as was noted in an unsigned article in *West Africa*.[94] In *Crisis*, where Du Bois combined an explanation of the débâcle with an announcement that the congress had been postponed until November, he remarked that Béton's mistake had been not to realize that he was not dealing 'with an established institution, but only with a great dream'[95] – a remark which might equally well have been applied to himself.

About the composition of the congress the sources tell us even less than usual. According to Du Bois eleven countries were represented.[96] One commentator notes that the Africans came mainly from Sierra Leone, the Gold Coast and Nigeria.[97] A list in the Du Bois papers only mentions the participants from Britain and France, most of whom were natives of these countries; they included Leys, Professor Gilbert Murray, vice-president of the Anti-Slavery Society, and Sir Sidney Olivier, former governor of Jamaica.[98] Of the Africans and Afro-Americans present we know of Mrs Ida Gibbs Hunt, from the US consulate at St Etienne, Rayford Logan and Isaac Béton. To these may be added Harold Laski, the left-wing socialist political thinker, and the social historian J. H. Tawney; Ramsay Macdonald, whose attendance had been announced, was preoccupied with his election campaign and contented himself with a written message of sympathy.

The congress convened on 7 and 8 November in Denison House, Vauxhall Road, the headquarters of the Anti-Slavery Society and other similar groups. On the printed invitation to the London meeting Candace and Béton were still listed as president and general secretary of the Pan-African Association, but they had virtually already withdrawn; Diagne had left inconspicuously as early as 1921. The leadership was now quite unequivocally in the hands of the Afro-Americans. Three of their representatives comprised the presidium of the congress: Du Bois, Logan and Mrs Hunt. They were also mainly responsible for its programme.

Du Bois opened the congress at about ten o'clock with a topic which from then onwards was to be one of his favourites: 'The History of the Pan-African Movement'.[99] On this occasion he mentioned for the first time the London Pan-African Conference of 1900, without referring to Sylvester Williams (Du Bois evidently forgot the name of the young coloured lawyer who had been secretary of the conference), but mentioning the presence of Coleridge-Taylor and his wife and the support given by the Colensos; he also stated that Bishop Alexander Walters had attended, but did not indicate the leading part he himself had played or the foundation of the first Pan-African Association. He went on to note the importance of the Universal Races Congress of 1911 and gave an account of the way in which the first Pan-African Congress of 1919 had come to be held. After this Logan outlined the organizational difficulties of the Pan-African Association and called for its activities to be stepped up, especially in Europe.

The evening session, too, was dominated by Du Bois, who gave a talk on 'The Black World at Present'. With the aid of diagrams he had drawn himself he described the dissemination of the races throughout the world. Taking Nigeria as an example,[100] he attacked the Whites' concept of race and underlined the need for a better school system in Africa. The next person to speak after Du Bois was Mrs Hunt, who chose the subject of 'The Colonial Races and the League of Nations'. The original hopes pinned on the league were now much subdued after four years of disappointment. Despite this Mrs Hunt still regarded it as the best instrument for preserving world peace, which she apparently saw as closely interlinked with the racial question. On the second day the morning session was taken up for half the time at least, by Du Bois who gave a speech on 'The American Negro'. With the aid of blackboard and chalk, he analysed the USA from an Afro-American point of view, a task for which he was very well qualified by his scholarly and journalistic activities. Starting with the lynchings in the southern states and the mass migration to the large cities of the north, he warned against what would nowadays be called the 'ghetto situation' of Afro-Americans in the States,[101] i.e. their political and psychological confinement within the 'negro community'; the 'spiritual and racial provincialism' building up in America was 'a peculiar danger, making it difficult for the coloured people to see the world's problems in a large way'. It was here that Du Bois made clear the driving force behind Afro-Americans' interest in Pan-Africanism: 'because of their experience the coloured people of the United States had gradually become interested in other coloured groups in all parts of the world'.[102]

According to Du Bois, Harold Laski then took the floor and gave a critical evaluation of the mandate system. He praised Lugard as a colonial theorist but contrasted his achievement with his practical policies as the conqueror of modern Nigeria. Laski was followed by an African from the Portuguese colonies, Kamba Simango, who spoke about the situation in Portuguese Angola. During the evening session Du Bois gave another speech on 'The Future of Pan-Africa'; we know little about its contents, or those of another paper delivered by John Alcindor on Uganda.

Altogether the whole proceedings were more subdued than those of earlier congresses. After the secession of the francophone element Du Bois was almost the sole performer. One observer noted that 'much of the enthusiasm that distinguished the last gathering in London had evaported. The many eloquent speakers from America and other parts of the world who came to the former gathering were sadly missed, and although Dr Du Bois again proved that he could talk, and talk well, for hours without a note, he was not able to rouse the fire again in a much diminished audience.' He went on to mention the main reason for this: 'The grip which knowledge creates is therefore absent at these meetings.' The Afro-Americans knew too little about the actual state of affairs in Africa, so that they could not arouse much interest, especially in an audience which included men who came from that continent and knew more about it than they did.[103]

Everything was very vague and non-committal, as Du Bois conceded.

When in the discussion on the first day Alcindor asked about the constitution of the Pan-African Association, Du Bois spoke as if Candace and Béton were still president and general secretary, without alluding to their resignation. Making a virtue out of necessity, he claimed that the organization's weakness was offset by its flexibility – not a very convincing argument. He added ingenuously that he had tried 'to keep the thing [i.e. the constitution] fluid'[104] and for this reason had relatively few officers – an elegant way of describing the desolate condition of the association. As the report put it,

> They had no stated definite objects beyond the fact that the Congress is 'an attempt to unite in periodical conference representatives of the main groups of peoples of African descent for purposes of information and cooperation'. So they were charged with 'a certain vagueness', to which they [Du Bois] pleaded guilty. 'But their objects would be less vague presently as they got to practical things', he added smilingly.[105]

Earlier in the discussion Du Bois had expressed hope that the Pan-African Congress would become a kind of clearing-house for various African movements.

The vague prospects that lay ahead could not gloss over the fact that the association's present situation was unsatisfactory. In practical terms it was a failure. The second session, held in Lisbon in late November and early December 1923, was a feeble echo of the first. It was not, however, as Padmore maintains, 'hastily improvised at the improvised congress in London' in response to reports about abuses in the Portuguese colonies.[106] On the contrary, it had been planned from the first that the congress should be held in Lisbon.[107] Preparations had been made by the Liga Africana for the congress to take place in August. But when Béton brusquely cancelled it at the last moment, Du Bois insisted on its taking place at least in November. The reason he gave later on was that he wanted to give a moral boost to the Liga Africana. Our knowledge about the second session is even slighter than about the first. In his bombastic report in *Crisis* Du Bois did not give any precise information about the participants and the course of their deliberations, but instead described the interior aspect of the convention hall, taking an evident delight in status symbols, and proudly giving the names of two ex-ministers for the colonies who had honoured the congress with their presence.[108] From Du Bois's hints it may be assumed that he touched on virtually all the topics that had been discussed in London: the history of Pan-Africanism and the position of Afro-Americans in the United States. The participants came from all the Portuguese colonies including Goa, as well as from Nigeria, Portugal and the USA. The Portuguese account, however, has it that no 'congress' took place at all in Lisbon. The leaders of the Liga Africana had protested against the postponement to November, giving technical reasons – it was impossible to inform Africans in the Portuguese colonies in time.[109] The congress 'sessions' at Lisbon would thus turn out to be no more than a visit by Du Bois, which, if true, would easily explain the latter's odd silence on concrete details about his alleged 'congress' at Lisbon, such as participants, proceedings, results etc.

The political reason behind the restraint, even the apparent embarrassment of the Liga Africana, seems to have been, according to the same account, criticism from British Quakers against the use of forced labour in Portuguese colonies. The Portuguese took this as an unjustified slander to cover up new plans for partitioning Portuguese colonies between Britain and Germany (Sao Thoma allegedly earmarked for the Quaker chocolate firm Cadbury, because of its richness in cocoa), while Du Bois apparently must have been suspected because of his well-known links with British Quakers and philanthropists.[110]

The Lisbon session could neither save the congress idea nor give support to the *assimilados* in the Portuguese colonies. Here, as in South Africa, they found themselves heading down a political blind alley. The hopes for a liberal epoch in Portuguese history came to grief only a few years later, when Salazar came to power, imposing a harsh colonial régime and destroying any prospect for the Africans' political advance – and ultimately producing the violent revolutions of recent years.

Another reason for his insistence on Lisbon as a venue may have been Du Bois's appointment as American envoy extraordinary (and plenipotentiary representative of the US president) on the occasion of the installation of the new Liberian president. Portugal lay conveniently on the way from London to Monrovia. Two weeks after the third Pan-African Congress was over, Du Bois left Lisbon on a German liner for Liberia, and at the end of December 1923 set foot on African soil for the first time in his life. This initial confrontation with African reality did not, however, do much to dispel the ignorance about conditions in that continent which had been such a disturbing factor in London, let alone fortify the rational element in Du Bois's thinking. Quite to the contrary: Du Bois seems to have worked himself into unparalleled paroxysms of ecstasy when he finally reached the destination of his sentimental pilgrimage – Africa. His romantic mood got the better of his reason.[111]

The fourth Pan-African Congress: New York, 1927

The *tour de force* with which Du Bois saved the 1923 congress exhausted his energies and those of his Pan-African Congress movement. Without an organization the principle of holding periodical meetings could not be maintained. No congress was held in 1925. Du Bois wanted to arrange one in the West Indies, as Béton suggests he had intended in 1923.[112] He planned to sail from one island to another in a chartered ship, in the hope of arousing as much interest as possible in his movement, and possibly also of taking some of the wind out of Garvey's sails in the latter's own territory. The plan evidently failed owing to exorbitant rates demanded by one of the shipping lines. Du Bois suspected that behind this lay some move by the colonial powers,[113] but probably the congress movement was in any case too weak to have organized another meeting two years after the last.

Nevertheless Du Bois still did not give up, and the movement dragged on until 1927 when he succeeded in arranging a fourth Pan-African Congress in New York. The initiative for this meeting came from Du Bois, as indeed it usually did. At the beginning of 1926 he had tried to obtain the support of Afro-Americans in Philadelphia, but in vain. In April of that year he had then turned to Mrs A. W. Hunton, president of an Afro-American women's organization, The Circle of Peace and Foreign Relations, which had its headquarters in the Bible House in New York.[114] To judge from the letter-heading, this group consisted all told of only twenty-one ladies; among them were Mrs Du Bois, Miss Jessie R. Fauset, Mrs Casely Hayford and Mrs Ida Gibbs Hunt, who had occupied a leading position since the first Pan-African Congress. This women's group was more or less responsible for organizing the fourth congress; they supplied the thirty-six members of the presidium, as well as the bulk of the nine committees (Education and Exhibits, Finance and Registration, Publicity and Press, Entertainment, Courtesies, Reception, Foreign Relations, Programme, Housing), which had a total of fifty-two members. Du Bois acted as general secretary and Logan as secretary and interpreter.[115]

The congress, held from 21 to 24 August 1927, was attended by 208 delegates from eleven countries and twenty-two US states (according to Du Bois), but Afro-Americans must have comprised the overwhelming majority. Du Bois himself admitted that Africa was only sparsely represented, with no more than a few delegates from Liberia, Sierra Leone, the Gold Coast (including a genuine chief, Amoah III) and Nigeria. In addition to these men there were delegates from Haiti, the (Danish) Virgin Islands, the Bahamas, Barbados and South America (not specified more closely). Among the White sympathizers were the outstanding American Africanist Melville J. Herskovits and Pastor Wilhelm Mensching, a member of the German pacifist movement.

In the absence of any new ideas or impulses, the conclusions of the congress were slight. The resolutions, of which Du Bois reproduces the main points, merely repeated earlier demands.[116] On the congress agenda were, *inter alia*, the by now traditional survey of the history of Pan-Africanism (probably by Du Bois). Messages of greeting from West Africa and the West Indies were read out. William Pickens (NAACP) reported on the congress of the 'League Against Imperialism' held in Brussels, in which he had intended to participate.[117] There was also a discussion of such questions as missions in Africa; the history of Africa and the West Indies; the economic development and political division of Africa; educational problems in Africa; and African art and literature. An exhibition arranged by Du Bois, with fifty-two charts and diagrams, provided information about the situation of the peoples of African descent.

Among the most important speakers were Dantès Bellegarde (Haiti), the Afro-American historians Charles H. Wesley and Leo W. Hansberry (both from Howard University), Herskovits, Chief Amoah III (Gold Coast), Mensching and John Vandercook (Netherlands). In New York a committee was formed whose members included Du Bois, Mrs Hunton, Bellegarde, Logan, Bishop R. C. Ransom and others. Its task was to work out proposals for a solidly based organization and to prepare the fifth Pan-African Congress.

The external display and technical perfection of the organizational arrangement for the New York meeting could not conceal the movement's inner weakness. To escape from these desperate straits Du Bois put on a brave front and decided to hold the next congress on African soil. The site chosen was Tunis. 'Extensive preparations' are said to have taken place[118] of which, however, no traces are left either in that part of the Du Bois papers kept in Accra or in the literature on the subject. In view of the movement's weakness one may legitimately doubt whether the first Pan-African congress on African soil would have been a success. A kind fate spared Du Bois's scheme from being put to the test because the French government withdrew its permission to hold the gathering in Tunis or in any other city in French Africa (Marseille was offered as a substitute). The effect of the great economic crisis which began in October 1929 was as usual felt first and most seriously by the Afro-Americans; this put a temporary halt to the Pan-African Congress movement. During the 1930s both Afro-Americans and Africans became more preoccupied with their own problems, although simultaneously they were more intensely involved in general problems of world politics owing to the rise of fascism and the Third Reich. For purely Pan-African activities they had for the time being little time and energy to spare.

Inner weakness of the Pan-African Congress movement: Du Bois as a Pan-African romantic

The moment for Pan-Africanism had not yet matured. Surveying the outward course of the four Pan-African congresses held under Du Bois's aegis, we must add that Pan-Africanism, too, had not yet matured either. Apart from the rejection of racial discrimination and a general vague resentment against the ruling White minority, there was no common denominator on which to unite the political interests of the various parts of Africa and of the Afro-Americans scattered throughout the New World. Even rejection of colonial rule was not universal, as is illustrated by the examples of Diagne and Candace.

The Pan-African Congress movement could have made a great contribution to the political education of Africans and Pan-Africans. In this matter, however, it was an almost complete failure, at least after the first steps had been taken in 1919. The tangible results of the congresses were meagre and their impact slight in every respect. They did not develop a clearly defined self-sufficient concept which might have helped to give Pan-Africanism greater intellectual discipline. Instead the congresses were mainly restricted to emotional laments about the oppression from which Africans and Afro-Americans suffered. In the conditions of that era one could not expect much else, but one might have expected more from W. E. B. Du Bois himself – a man with first-class academic training, who had a reputation as the leading intellectual in the Pan-African movement.

Du Bois missed his opportunity to give Pan-Africanism a rational basis. Although Padmore, in his influential book, describes him as a great rationalist and the supremely modern theorist of Pan-Africanism, he was in reality a hopeless romantic, incapable of imposing upon Pan-Africanism the necessary intellectual rigour. His failure reflects once again the fundamental dilemma of Pan-Africanism, which was apparent with some of its forerunners, especially with Blyden. Moreover Du Bois personally was inclined to be carried away by romantic enthusiasms. He was fond of sentimental hyperbole and was almost obsessed with the racial problem – in part, it seems, because his personal pride had been hurt. 'My African racial feeling', he writes, 'was then purely a matter of my own later learning and reaction, my recoil from the assumptions of the whites.'[119] Thus Du Bois may be regarded as a typical product of the confrontation between the old and the new, between traditional Africa and the modern world, out of which Pan-Africanism, along with other political movements, sprang. In this respect, for all his personal weaknesses, he is nevertheless representative of Pan-Africanism and it is no coincidence that Padmore gave him the honorary name of 'Father of Pan-Africanism'.

Du Bois embodied its two main components: on one hand the rational, modernizing element, personified in its purest form by Horton in the nineteenth century and above all by Padmore in the twentieth; and on the other hand the irrational, romanticizing element, which had its first great representative in Blyden and left a deep imprint upon all later Pan-African leaders. Du Bois emphasized sometimes one and sometimes the other aspect. He was quite modern in his work as an academic and as a political journalist. His aggressive advocacy of equality, of educating the 'talented tenth' as a precondition of moderniz-ation, and of active political commitment by Afro-Americans in the USA – all this was thoroughly rational. He was also quite modern in his attitudes on issues in American domestic policy: he pledged himself to the Democrats at the beginning of the twentieth century and so established a voting pattern that has since become traditional for most Afro-Americans; furthermore he supported a form of socialism which, without being directly influenced by Marxism, had some affinities with it.[120]

Du Bois was ambiguous in his attitude towards Africa. On one hand, through the journal of the Niagara movement, *Horizon*, he transmitted information about contemporary Africa which in itself was a rational form of activity, and at the beginning of World War I he saw the solution for African problems in a determined and consistent modernization of African society by fostering industrial growth.[121] On the other hand it was in *Horizon* that he published one of his worst poems, 'A Day in Africa', pure neo-romantic trash which cultivated a disastrously mystical and irrational vision of that continent.[122]

At the Pan-African congresses held on European soil and before a mixed audience, Du Bois behaved wholly as a modern intellectual, but at the end of 1923 he was bowled over emotionally by his first visit to Africa. Until that point he knew Africa only from books, journals and oral descriptions. Now, in physical contact with that continent for the first time, the irrational and romantic aspect of his nature broke through with irresistible force. His reports about this trip have an ecstatic quality and provide an instructive insight into his snobbism: he clearly enjoyed the honours bestowed upon him, the light-skinned mulatto representing the United States, by European colonial officials.[123] Even before then he had indulged in a virtual ancestor cult, as a means of justifying his commitment to Africa – or as he was fond of calling it, 'Pan-Africa'.[124] But now he virtually threw himself into the arms of an African mysticism, expressed in high-flown prose as bad as his poetry fifteen years earlier.

> The spell of Africa is upon me. The ancient witchery of her medicine is burning in my drowsy, dreamy, blood. This is not a country, a universe of itself and for itself, a thing Different, Immense, Menacing, Alluring. It is a great black bosom where the spirit longs to die. It is life so burning, so fire encircled that one bursts with terrible soul inflaming life. One longs to leap against the sun and then calls, like some great hand of fate, the slow, silent, crushing power of almighty sleep – of Silence, of immovable Power beyond, within, around.[125]

The sight of a dark-skinned bourgeoisie on African soil so encouraged him that he forgot all his socialist principles and was blinded to the truth about class relationships in Liberia.[126] His partiality for that country, now given emotional underpinnings, became an uncritical admiration which led him to defend Liberia over the question of the forced labour discovered there in 1930.[127] A visit to a village near Monrovia cast him back almost two centuries, into worshipping the 'noble native', pure and unspoilt by European civilization: 'Neither

London, nor Paris, nor New York has anything of its delicate precious beauty...' Du Bois goes on to ask: 'Therefore shall we all take to the Big Bush?', to the 'simple life' of traditional Africa?' He replies: 'No, I prefer New York. But my point is that New York and London and Paris must learn of West Africa and may learn.'[128]

Strangest of all, however, is the sight of the productive journalist and professor, the prophet of the 'talented tenth' and modern education for Afro-Americans, overcome by his own emotions, suddenly singing dithyrambs of praise to laziness and vehemently condemning modern civilization[129] – that same modern civilization of which he himself was a product, which represented the basis of his entire existence, and which must also provide the basis of any meaningful Pan-African movement. Rarely can the schism within Du Bois's character, and at the same time within Pan-Africanism, be seen so vividly as here. This was not a transitory episode in Du Bois's life, a forgivable youthful peccadillo, a lapse made under the emotional weight of his first physical encounter with Africa. After all Du Bois was then at an age of maturity, almost fifty-six. Moreover the romantic vein in his writing about Africa can be traced back at least to the beginning of 1908 ('A Day in Africa'), and in 1940, aged seventy-two, he continued to pay a romantic homage to that continent.

If one tries to form an appreciation of the Pan-African Congress movement between 1919 and 1927–9, taking into critical consideration Du Bois's contribution, almost its only merit is to have taken up again the idea of Pan-Africanism, however vaguely and loosely. For the first time the anglophone and francophone elements co-operated, notably in Diagne's active part in the congress of 1919. But this success was deceptive and short-lived. Most of the participants on the French-speaking side came from the West Indies, above all from Guadeloupe and Martinique, and only a single individual, Diagne, was actually an African. Besides, Diagne was the first to leave the movement in 1921, the French and West Indian element following in 1923. Diagne and Candace were representatives of the colonial establishment, and the young radical proto-rationalists and nationalists from the Antilles, Dahomey and Senegal who congregated in Paris after the war heartily despised such notables of their own complexion.[130] Du Bois's partners in France were thus a liability rather than an asset in the eyes of the real exponents of Pan-Africanism.

The most important result of the four Pan-African congresses was perhaps simply the fact that they took place at all. They established a certain tradition which gained an intellectual standing with the passing of time, thanks also to Du Bois's academic reputation. They offered a point of reference for the Pan-African movement when it regained momentum towards the end of World War II, and Du Bois, at the ripe old age of seventy-seven, then became a symbol of its historical continuity.

Du Bois himself also felt that the results had been sparse. 'What has been accomplished? This: we have kept an idea alive; we have held to a great ideal, we have established a continuity, and some day when unity and co-operation come, the importance of these early steps will be recognised.'[131] His justification of the Third Congress, with its uncertain hopes for the future, reads like a swan song for the Pan-African Congress movement as a whole.

13 Garvey and imperial Pan-Africanism

At the beginning of the 1920s there developed, as a rival to the Pan-African Congress movement led by Du Bois, the movement known as Garveyism. Its Pan-African aspects, as distinct from Garvey's biography, have yet to be examined.[1] Assessments of it have wavered between such terms as 'messianic', 'racist', 'pseudo-fascist' or 'Black Zionism'.[2] In our view its chief trait is a curious predilection for the imperial idea, which corresponds to the general romantic mood of Pan-Africanism. For this reason our term, 'imperial Pan-Africanism', seems the most appropriate for Garveyism, even if it does not do justice to all aspects of this complex phenomenon.

Garvey's development up to the foundation of the UNIA in Harlem

Marcus Aurelius Garvey was born in Kingston, Jamaica, on 17 August 1887. He was very black-skinned and was regarded as a 'full-blooded negro'. His father is said to have been a descendant of the Maroons, the rebellious ex-slaves in the mountains; Padmore called Garvey a Koromantee negro.[3] Garvey's father rose into the middle class and attained prosperity, but then became involved in a lawsuit over some trifle, adhered doggedly to his case, and as a consequence lost all his property; at the end of his life he dedicated himself solely to his books. Garvey's father seems to have occupied a respected position in Kingston society, as is indicated by the fact that his son for a long time styled himself Garvey Jr. The son learned the printer's trade and soon rose to a high position in it. In 1907 he took a leading part in a strike in Kingston; subsequently he was discharged and blacklisted, an experience which for the rest of his life made him suspicious of trade unions which employed the strike weapon. Three years later he began to publish *Garvey's Watchman*, the first of a large number of journals which he founded. When it failed he went to Central America and then to the northern part of South America, where he studied at close hand the miserable conditions of his fellow-Blacks. Along the way he left behind traces of other ephemeral journals: *La Nacionale* in Costa Rica, *La Prensa* in Panama. Only during his stay in Ecuador was he unable to publish a new periodical.

In 1912 Garvey went to London, from where he also made tours on the Continent. In London he joined Mohamed Ali Duse's circle, earning his living by running errands in Duse's editorial office. In his spare time he dedicated himself wholeheartedly to study. The books he read included Booker T. Washington's autobiography, *Up from Slavery*. It would have been logical that with his passion for producing newspapers he should have assisted Duse in his editorial functions, but there is no record that this was the case. At any rate Garvey published his first article in the *African Times and Orient Review*, a periodical which enjoyed a greater international reputation than his own three short-lived journals. Garvey outlined the history of Jamaica and present conditions there, concluding with a survey of future prospects in which one may already discern his far-reaching ambitions. Still unpolished, and with the predilection for hyperbole and the imperial idea which were characteristic of him, he described his vision of the future of the Black races.[4] In London Garvey widened his intellectual horizons and absorbed notions of African nationalism. Perhaps already then one might apply to him the words used later about himself: 'I know no national boundary where the Negro is concerned. The whole world is my province until Africa is free.'[5]

Early in the summer of 1914 Garvey went back to Jamaica, from where he sought to carve out a basis for his future career. On 1 August

1914 he founded the Universal Negro Improvement and Conservation Association and African Communities League, generally known by its abbreviated title as the Universal Negro Improvement Association (UNIA). In a manifesto he proclaimed it his objective.

> to establish a Universal Confraternity among the race; to promote the spirit of race pride and love; to reclaim the fallen; to administer to and assist the needy; to assist in civilizing the backward tribes of Africa; to assist in the development of independent Negro nations and communities; to establish a central nation for the race; to establish commissaries or agencies in the principal countries and cities of the world for the representation of all Negroes; to promote a conscientious spiritual worship among the native tribes of Africa; to establish universities, colleges, academies and schools for the racial education and culture of the people; to work for better conditions among Negroes everywhere.[6]

At first Garvey was preoccupied with his regional base and sought to improve mass living standards in Jamaica. Emulating his great model Booker T. Washington, he wanted to establish a kind of Tuskegee Institute and to mobilize the Afro-Americans to help him. He established contact with Washington and was invited to Tuskegee for a visit. But all these projects came to nothing with Washington's death in 1915.[7] Thereupon Garvey decided to go to the USA on his own. On 23 March 1916 he arrived in Harlem, which at that time was harbouring the mass of coloured people who had been pouring in since 1915 from the southern states of the USA and the West Indies, Jamaica in particular. World War I accelerated the social process which between 1900 and 1930 turned Harlem from an elegant White residential area into one of the best-known negro ghettoes in the USA.[8] Among these new arrivals, who felt cut off from their rustic homelands and disoriented in the alien capital, Garvey found a receptive audience for his own ideas, which were still only half formulated.

In New York Garvey made contact with well-known Afro-Americans. One of the first was the journalist John Edward Bruce, who for years had published a column in the Afro-American press under the *nom de plume* of 'Grit'.[9] Garvey heard of him through the *African Times and Orient Review*, of which Bruce had been general representative in the United States.[10] Bruce was also president of the Negro Society of Historical Research, of which Duse had given a detailed account.[11]

With the sweep characteristic of him Garvey told Bruce of his concern for the grievances of West Indians in New York, giving Bruce the impression that he was a young man with a sense of mission. Garvey was given the addresses of leading Afro-Americans whom he then went to see. One of these men was Du Bois. Garvey would have heard of him through the *African Times and Orient Review* unless – and this is more likely – he had already learned that Booker T. Washington, whom he venerated highly, had a sharp-tongued opponent; he must have heard of their controversy.

The first fleeting and indirect contact between the two protagonists in the Du Bois–Garvey controversy, which followed that between Washington and Du Bois, had already taken place in Jamaica one year before when Garvey had sent Du Bois, who was visiting the island, a hand-written note written in the third person and welcoming him in a manner befitting a sovereign receiving a foreign guest. 'Mr. Marcus Garvey presents his compliments to Dr E. B. Du Bois and begs to render to him, on behalf of the Universal Negro Improvement Association, a hearty welcome to Jamaica and trusts that he has enjoyed the brief stay in the sunny isle.'[12] Now Garvey was lost in the vastness of New York and came as a petitioner to Du Bois, a professor who had already achieved high status and apparently did not think much of his visitor's ideas. Garvey, however, was tenacious. After making a round trip through several American states he returned to Harlem and began to agitate in the streets as a soapbox orator in the style of Speakers' Corner in London's Hyde Park. At a gathering on the corner of 135th Street and Lenox Avenue he won over Bruce, who had apparently at first been too sceptical to attack him in public. According to Bruce's later report, couched in the tone of a repentant convert, Garvey at that time unfolded his 'plan of an Organization which was to draw all Negroes throughout the World together, to make one big brotherhood of the Black Race for its common good; for mutual protection, for commerce and industrial development and for the fostering of business enterprise'.[13]

His first public appearance at an indoor meeting before the respectable public took place on 12 June 1917 at a mass meeting in the Bethel AME church in Harlem. The purpose of the event, attended by thousands, was the establishment of a new organization, the Liberty League. On this occasion Garvey was also introduced and received permission to give a short address. Apparently a little later the Jamaican

Club of New York City rented Ark's Hall in 138th Street, near Lenox Avenue, for an evening meeting with Garvey as speaker; the tickets cost five dollars each. According to Bruce, Garvey by this time seems to have outgrown his provincial limitations and to have established himself as spokesman for all Afro-Americans.

Despite this Garvey at first recruited most of his supporters among the West Indian element. He succeeded in founding in New York a branch of the UNIA, the organization based in his homeland of Jamaica. In December 1917, however, a schism occurred when an opposition group appeared which wanted to transform the UNIA into a political club. Garvey's influence was not helped by a letter from Duse in London in which the latter made some disparaging remarks about his character. In January 1918 the New York branch of UNIA was reorganized. At the request of those members who had remained loyal to him, mostly fellow-countrymen from Jamaica, Garvey took over the presidency. In the same month there appeared, as the journal of the UNIA, the *Negro World*, the fourth journal which Garvey had published within eight years. This periodical was designed to appeal to Africans and Afro-Americans throughout the world. In order to reach the new immigrants from non-English-speaking parts of the West Indies, the main English edition soon added several pages in Spanish and French. Garvey succeeded in winning for his journal the collaboration of several able journalists, including Thomas T. Fortune,[14] H. Ferris[15] and J. E. Bruce. Even Mohamed Ali Duse left London in 1920 to enter the service of his former pupil.[16] The *Negro World* became the most important vehicle for disseminating Garvey's influence. It was later replaced by *Philosophy and Opinions*, a collection which contains several of his articles from the *Negro World*.[17]

The UNIA as a Pan-African organization

Thanks to his magnificent eloquence, organizational talents and wealth of ideas, Garvey was able within a few months to expand the UNIA's influence beyond Harlem and to build up local associations in the large industrial cities of the North into which Afro-American labour had been pouring during the wartime boom – above all Chicago, Detroit, Pittsburgh, Cleveland and Philadelphia. At the end of July 1919 Garvey opened Liberty Hall in Harlem, with 6000 seats, which served as the centre of his agitational activity. With the UNIA as his chief stronghold,

Garvey created one new subordinate organization after another. The Black Star Line, started in 1919, more than any other caught the imagination of Africans and Afro-Americans. This new shipping company was to be operated only by Blacks. It was founded as a limited company, with an initial issue of 100,000 shares priced at five dollars each. The shares were also sold in Africa – e.g. in Lagos, where Agbebi's son served as an agent for the company.[18] As early as July 1920 the first meeting of the Black Star Line's shareholders took place in Liberty Hall. Garvey took bad advice when purchasing ships for his company. In September 1919 he bought for $165,000 a ship weighing 1424 tons built in 1887, just as old as Garvey himself, which had previously been used as a coal carrier. The *Yarmouth*, renamed the *Frederick Douglass*, only managed to make two trips to the West Indies. The second ship, a small excursion steamer weighing 420 tons, had been built in 1873 and was therefore only five years younger than Du Bois. It sank on its first excursion trip on the Hudson. Garvey was hardly any luckier with a third ship, a little steam yacht which he bought for $60,000. In 1919 he also set up the Negro Factories Corporation, designed to put his dreams of a negro empire upon a solid economic basis. However, this never really became a flourishing concern.

Although he had originally been a Catholic, Garvey endowed a new church, the African Orthodox church, with its own patriarch, Alexander McGuire, a 'brilliant theologian' (Padmore) from the West Indies. To a modern European this new sect, taken out of context, may seem absurd with its worship of a Black Christ and a Black Madonna, but as a logical continuation of Ethiopianism[19] it was not so misplaced. Garvey's predilection for bizarre forms and external pomp gave rise to such organizations as the Universal African Legion, devised as the nucleus of a shadow army to liberate Africa, Universal Black Cross Nurses, Universal African Motor Corps and Black Eagle Flying Corps – each with its own fanciful uniform, ceremonial etc. At the height of his power Garvey arranged colourful and noisy annual parades in Harlem during the meetings of the UNIA, which lasted throughout the whole month of August. These parades satisfied a widespread emotional need among Afro-Americans, especially the poorer elements, by offering them psychological compensation for the tremendous inferiority complex from which they suffered as a result of their history and the social oppression they had to endure.

The same psychological purpose was served by the proclamation of a shadow empire upon the soil of the African continent which Garvey aimed to liberate. With a Napoleonic gesture he had himself unanimously elected 'Provisional President of Africa' at the first UNIA convention in August 1920; the mayor of Monrovia, Gabriel Johnson, was elected 'Potentate of Africa', and formally held a higher rank in Garvey's organization than he did himself. Subsequently Garvey conferred upon his closest supporters imaginary decorations and aristocratic titles, such as 'Knights of the Distinguished Service Order of Ethiopia, Asanti and Mozambique', 'Duke of the Nile', 'Earl of the Congo', 'Viscount of the Niger', 'Baron Zambezi'.[20] This pseudo-feudal mummery reached its climax with splendid 'court festivities' – all this amidst the shabby reality of Harlem.

These superficial phenomena, whose importance was merely psychological, were less significant for the history of imperial Pan-Africanism than the annual conventions of the UNIA in Harlem. These began on 1 August each year, a symbolic choice of date readily appreciated by Afro-Americans, since this was the day on which, in 1834, the emancipation of the slaves had come into force in the British Empire.[21] In the middle of this month, on the 17th, came Garvey's birthday. About the composition of these conventions, which served as a kind of UNIA parliament, we have little information. Delegates came from twenty-five countries. Among them particular attention was given to an African 'prince', several chiefs and their successors – although there was no shortage of genuine native aristocrats in Africa, where the social structure was so fragmented that each village of any size had its own chief and 'royal family'.

With his appointment as 'Provisional President of Africa' Garvey acquired the services of a continental government in exile, which boasted its own green, black and red flag.[22] The UNIA also had its own national anthem, 'Ethiopia, Thou Land of Our Fathers!', completing the illusion that the dream of an independent and united Africa in the future was already becoming reality. At a mass demonstration in Madison Square Garden, attended by an enthusiastic 25,000-strong audience, Garvey cried: 'We shall now organise the 400 million Negroes of the world into a vast organization and plant the banner of freedom on the great continent of Africa.'[23] With equal pathos he put forth a 'Declaration of the Rights of Negro Peoples of the World'.

Garvey also utilized the annual conventions as a platform to air his differences with Du Bois and the latter's fair-complexioned intellectual supporters. In 1921 he caused Du Bois and the second Pan-African Congress to be formally condemned.[24] The controversy between Garvey and Du Bois quickly took on a personal form, partly due to racial differences. Garvey had brought with him from his West Indian homeland a deep-rooted mistrust of mulattoes, who had formed a privileged class there from the time of slavery onwards,[25] whereas Garvey himself was always very conscious of his own negro descent. His animosities were in no way lessened in North American conditions.[26] It may have been true that for White Americans, at least in Garvey's era, all colonial people were no more than 'darned niggers' (as Padmore said), whether their skin was light or very dark, but this subjective reaction by the Whites must be distinguished from the reality that the Afro-American élite was in the main hybrid; and this state of affairs naturally inflamed Garvey's feelings of resentment. In this way he came into sharp opposition to more powerful elements in the Afro-American leadership which finally brought about his downfall.[27]

Garvey's main objective was to liberate Africa. Except for a few generalities he never explained how he expected to do this. For all his verbal bombast Garvey was sufficiently practical and a disciple of Booker T. Washington to recognize the value of proceeding pragmatically. He therefore sought to secure a foothold on African soil, in Liberia. The election of the mayor of Monrovia as 'High Potentate' of the UNIA was not merely a tribute to Liberia's historical role,[28] but also gave a clue to Garvey's strategy. In 1920 he sent a delegation to Liberia to investigate the possibility of settling Afro-Americans there. The leader of the delegation, Elie Garcia,[29] gave a positive assessment but vigorously condemned the ruling Libero-American class 'as the most despicable element in Liberia' since they treated the natives like slaves.[30] Garvey apparently identified himself with the views contained in Garcia's report. Despite this he tried to collaborate with the ruling oligarchy. At the end of 1920 he launched a campaign to raise two million dollars for his Liberia project. In February 1921 and December 1923 two groups of experts went to Liberia to prepare the settlement scheme, at first with the approval of the Liberian government which, however, made it quite clear that not too many members of the UNIA should come to the country. By the time a further UNIA delegation arrived in Liberia in June 1924 the wind had already changed. The Liberian government had been informed about Garcia's report of 1902 and feared that the Libero-American oligarchy might be overthrown by the more radical UNIA, perhaps in league with the subjected and exploited tribes of the hinterland. There was also some pressure by the colonial powers, which never bothered to conceal their animosity towards Garvey. Finally, Du Bois's official mission to Monrovia at the end of 1923 and the beginning of 1924 for the inauguration of President King after his re-election may have been another reason why the Liberian government changed its mind. By utilizing Du Bois's personal weaknesses (his vanity and eagerness to be accepted socially) and his personal connections with King (who had participated at the first Pan-African Congress held in Paris),[31] the US government helped to prevent Garvey from extending his influence to Africa.

To this may be added distrust on the part of the Africans. In an open letter to Garvey Diagne condemned the idea of handing over the French possessions in Africa to the Africans alone.[32] The slogan 'United States of Africa' evoked the suspicion among African nationalists who were in principle not hostile towards Garvey that his movement sought to set in train a kind of Afro-American colonization of Africa or to give the colonists a position of hegemony there. At any rate Mohamed Ali Duse had to reassure Sekyi:

> ... I think, however, that you take the wrong view of the matter of the intentions of the Americans. I do not think that they are disposed to impose a new kind of European or American civilization on a Government which antedates the so-called white civilization. You should know by this time how reckless words are used and I do not think the term 'United States of Africa' would possibly mean a bulk reproduction of the United States of America. That would indeed be a bastard civilization. It is because the Negroes of the New World are anxious to co-operate with those of Africa that you among others are invited to contribute your viewpoint. . . .[33]

The Liberian government had the UNIA delegation arrested as soon as it arrived in the country. The UNIA convention of 1924, which was to have put the final touch to the scheme, protested and petitioned in vain. The Liberian government withdrew its permission and Garvey's grandiose plan failed.

On top of this fiasco in Liberia came the fiasco of the Black Star Line. With the active participation of Du Bois and other NAACP activists, Afro-American intellectuals launched a campaign against

Garvey, accusing him of irregularly issuing Black Star Line shares through the mail. Garvey was arrested, freed on bail, but on 2 February 1925 sentenced to several years' imprisonment. He served his term in the prison at Atlanta (Du Bois's university town). His second wife, Amy Jacques Garvey (like the first, Amy Ashwood Garvey, from whom he was divorced, of Jamaican descent and linked with the UNIA from the start), kept the organization together as best she could and published Garvey's *Philosophy and Opinions*.[34] In spite of much dissension the annual conventions continued to be held. At the end of 1927 Garvey was reprieved and expelled from the USA.

Attempted revival and failure

Garvey returned to Jamaica to create a new base for the movement in his homeland. A triumphal trip through the West Indies at first made him forget the humiliations he had suffered in the United States. In May 1928 he went to England to open a UNIA headquarters for Europe in London; there was also to be a branch in Paris. In an address he gave in the Royal Albert Hall, which was sparsely filled with no more than twenty people in the audience, Garvey reverted to his plans for Africa but this time with greater restraint. He no longer demanded that Africa be completely free, but urged the colonial powers to relinquish certain areas at present in their control and to place them under African rule. For all his caution Garvey concluded on a defiant note: 'But we are going to have our part of Africa, whether you will it or not.'[35] Despite its apparent failure Garvey's visit to London was not without effect. At that time he established contact with Lapido Solanke of the West African Students' Union (WASU) and apparently had sufficient money at his disposal to lease a house for WASU in London for one year.[36]

A friendly reception was given to Garvey in Paris in the Club du Faubourg,[37] since he exerted a certain influence among French-speaking African and West Indian nationalists through the French supplements of his *Negro World*. In September 1928 he handed over to the League of Nations in Geneva a petition in which he declared: 'We believe that as a people we should have a Government of our own in our homeland – Africa.' He put forward two alternative proposals: either 'that the mandates of former German colonies in Africa should be given to Negroes so that they could prove their ability to govern themselves (an idea which was no longer quite original, since it had been formulated earlier by Duse and Du Bois) or, failing this, 'he asked that parts of West Africa be brought together into a United Commonwealth of Black Nations, and placed under the government of black men as a solution of the Negro problem both in Africa and the Western World'.[38]

By way of London and Canada Garvey returned to Jamaica, where he tried to establish himself in the domestic politics of his homeland. He was elected town councillor in Kingston but failed dramatically in the elections to the Legislative Council. His Jamaican People's party had a modern-sounding programme, but never really got off the ground. In August 1929 he held the UNIA's sixth convention in Kingston, Jamaica. The climax of this was a gala reception given by the UNIA for 10,000 guests, in an endeavour to re-enact in modern form the feudal pageantry of ancient Africa (Ethiopia) as Garvey imagined it.[39]

In about 1930 the UNIA in the USA finally collapsed. The *Negro World*, however, did not cease publication until 1933. Indefatigably Garvey set out to publish his fifth journal, the *Black Man*, which appeared at irregular intervals from 1933 to 1938 or 1939, and was to all intents and purposes written wholly by Garvey himself. In August 1934 Garvey tried once again to rebuild the UNIA, this time by holding the seventh convention, which was given a bombastic title out of all proportion with reality: the International Convention of the Negro Peoples of the World. For a five-year plan to develop the Black race he called for no less than 300 million dollars, which of course he could not obtain. The 17th of August, Garvey's birthday, which many Afro-Americans already celebrated as a private festival, was declared an international negro holiday. The convention suggested that an African language be chosen to serve as lingua franca, but apparently without deciding which one.

The *Black Man* appeared in London from November 1934, and in the following year Garvey, now no more than a shadow of his former self, went to London without his family. After the Italian invasion of Ethiopia he returned to his Harlem beginnings and spoke out in public at Speakers' Corner in Hyde Park, but was not taken seriously. He thought of becoming a candidate in the parliamentary elections, standing for the coloured people of the Empire – a move reminiscent of the days of the African Association[40] – but this idea failed since nobody wanted to see Garvey in parliament. Still pursuing his dream of a renaissance of the UNIA, and nourishing his animosities against

Du Bois and the light-skinned 'traitors' to the Black race, he made many sound remarks about the course of world affairs in his organ, and in particular predicted indefatigably the outbreak of a new world war. Garvey still lived to see this, for he died on 10 June 1940, in the end almost completely paralysed, but fully conscious. He had the ill fortune to read in the papers the premature news of his own death, accompanied by generally malevolent and unsympathetic commentaries.

Garvey's historical impact

What remains of Garvey? To judge by externals, not much: the UNIA scattered to the far winds, except for small remnants in Harlem and Jamaica; many members and supporters lapsed into disillusionment and apathy; the more active elements disintegrated into the two main components of Garveyism. Some joined the bourgeois-capitalist establishment of the Afro-American sub-society; others joined the Communists.[41] But Garvey's indirect historical effect was not insignificant. He was the first to mobilize the Afro-American masses and to give them a new sense of self-awareness by teaching them not to be ashamed of their descent. His attempt to overcome the century-old inferiority complex which sprang from slavery and his emphatic commitment to Africa had a fascination for young intellectuals in Africa as well as for students at American negro colleges and universities who came from Africa (Azikiwe and Nkrumah) or from the West Indies (Padmore). Finally he influenced the African masses to an extent which Du Bois could never have dreamed of.[42] That Garvey was able to win over men like Duse, Johnson, Bruce, Fortune, Ferris and McGuire, besides apparently fraudulent elements, points to the attraction of his personality and his programme. Apparently he not only appealed to the broad masses but also to at least part of the articulate élite. In Africa Sekyi, who had written for the *African Times and Orient Review* in his London student days,[43] was sufficiently interested in Garvey's movement to remain in contact by correspondence with Duse during his UNIA period.[44] He criticized one defect of Pan-Africanism in the New World which was already noticeable in Du Bois – the sparse knowledge of what conditions were really like in Africa. In this respect Duse in particular was able to play the role of intermediary, on account of his wide-ranging contact with Africans and his first visit to Black Africa in 1920. At the convention of 1922 he had Sekyi's article in the *African Times and Orient Review* on 'Education in West Africa' 'read before the Convention as a matter of enlightenment . . .' because, as he wrote to Sekyi, 'the opinion you have expressed in regard to the UNIA . . . represents my view, and in my humble way, I have endeavoured and I am endeavouring to educate the people here as to the prevailing conditions on the West Coast of Africa as I saw them personally whilst there. . . .'[45]

Contacts with Africa were also maintained by J. E. Bruce (Grit), especially with Agbebi and Casely Hayford.[46] The correspondence with Agbebi's son provides some clues which illustrate Garvey's influence in Lagos. In this case an important medium seems to have been the sale of shares in the Black Star Line. According to Agbebi Jr the shares were such a success that Agbebi hardly knew how to cope with the demand for them and the amounts of money coming in: 'The matter of the Black Star Line has become very serious in this place. Hundreds of pounds are coming to me daily, but I cannot take them.' He also goes on to say:

> We are faring better with our local branch of the UNIA in this place . . . but we are trying to pull on, and when we have the Black Star Line, it will be better for us. . . . The people of this place are now so enthusiastic as the people in the United States, and when once I have been sent out and have got our people all over Nigeria interested, I think the work must be done.[47a]

Bruce's correspondence with Casely Hayford goes back at least as far as 1915.[48] During the Garvey period contacts with Hayford were so good that not only was Bruce kept informed about Hayford's activities, on which he reported in his 'Grit' column,[49] but that when Du Bois went to West Africa at the end of 1923 and the beginning of 1924,[50] Bruce sent a telegram warning his correspondent against Du Bois and supporting Garvey.[51] The interest which Hayford took in the movement is also indicated by the fact that he once asked for forty copies of the *Negro World*, although Bruce exaggerated when he acclaimed the National Congress of British West Africa as an African equivalent of the UNIA.[52]

Another testimony to the geographical extent of Garvey's influence, which reached even to the interior of West Africa, comes from Ibadan (today the capital of the western region of Nigeria) in the form of a diary kept by Jacob Akinpelu Obisesan, a lay churchman in one of the independent African churches.[53] Obisesan, at that time still a young man, met Mohamed Ali Duse in Ibadan in July 1920 during the latter's first tour of West Africa[54] and discussed with him and other friends the possibilities of developing trade.[55] At the end of December he received – possibly through the intermediacy of Duse – two copies of the *Negro World*, which he found 'very stimulating, instructive, amusing and interesting'. He immediately became a most enthusiastic supporter of the Garvey movement, which it is interesting to see he identified completely with America:

> I must confess I am greatly infused with the spirit of Americanism and were I to express my mind to the general public I am afraid I would be charged for disloyalty. The Aliens who rule us would indict me, but the men of my kin would regard it a spirit of true patriotism; it is admitted the Negroes all over the world are being down-trodden, ill-treated and boycotted, this fact speaks for itself. When one looks back to the undignified discrimination of Lugardian Regime and which is still being diplomatically practised today.[56]

Whereas in the first half of 1921 his diary contains many entries about Casely Hayford's National Congress (which again shows how interconnected the different movements were although we have to treat them separately), in the later part of the year we find that most entries are devoted to Garvey and his movement; even allowing for the hyperbolic style in which they are written, they provide an idea of the effect Garvey had. Time and again there are references that Obisesan had read the *Negro World* together with some friends or discussed Garvey's programme with them.[57] In between there is a laconic note that Duse had written a letter asking him to buy some shares (probably in the Black Star Line). A few months later comes the almost jubilant decision to buy as many shares as possible for the Garvey movement: 'I read the *Negro World* throughout the day, the singing, most inspiring message of Marcus Garvey to the Negroid people of the world nearly maddens me. I feel as if I am in America, as one of the hearers of his golden speech. I am a Garveyite and wherever opportunity offers I will take shares in Black Star Line, the Convention Fund and the African Redemption Fund.'[58] On New Year's Day 1922 the pious author gave himself over to 'important meditations', reading the *Negro World* and contemplating his own existence and God: the juxtaposition is significant.

In the same year that Kobina Sekyi deplored the fact that the Garvey movement was so poorly informed about conditions in Africa, a parallel complaint appeared in Ibadan as Obisesan's sole criticism of Garveyism. His enthusiasm was, however, still so strong that he read his copy of the *Negro World* twice

> and learned some lesson from the writings of Brilliant Writers who contribute articles of great interest to the papers. The only remark I can make about Garveyism in Africa is, if Africa will be redeemed, it will be the work of providence. Garvey, though a great champion of his race's cause, does not know the aims and aspirations of Africans politically, commercially and otherwise; his plans are feasible of course. A great number of Africans of intelligence believed Europeans are demi-gods or gods-incarnate and whom no one on earth can oppose. My conviction is that Africans will be free from European bondage, but when and at what hour no mortal African [can] say.[59]

At the same time Obisesan was by no means uncritical of African society or blind towards the positive effects of British rule. Thus on 12 April 1922 he convinced his friend Babarinse, a supporter of Garvey, 'that we are very backward in civilization. I recalled the history of Ibadan's past age of terror, he was deeply moved.' And in an entry two days later we learn that Babarinse 'is a Garveyite, likewise myself and Akinyele, but we must praise the British people in our heart and soul, they are the great civilizing agency who have rescued us from woes. I confess now that we have greatly benefitted ourselves by the presence of British people in our country.'[60] Subsequently he went to Chief Balogun Sowemimo and talked to him about Garveyism and British colonial policy. Sowemimo had been invited to attend the third UNIA convention in New York. According to Obisesan he was 'a loyal friend of the British Government, a patriot who believes in Garvey's principles in Africa'.[61] Several days later a meeting took place in Sowemimo's house to mobilize Anglican support for Garvey (entry for 17 April 1922). At the end of June 1922 another entry gives an idea of the global and future-oriented outlook common at the time among politically conscious Africans and Afro-Americans: 'Babarinse and Mr. Ibaru [two friends] discuss Garveyism's possibilities in Africa, local politics and the future world conflagration, and nature of man and the application of Baxter's doctrine to perfecting them.'[62] The eclecticism in the statement is typical, but the realism with regard to the next world war ('future world conflagration'), prophesied earlier by Duse and Garvey, is depressing enough. A few days later, on 6 July 1922, we hear that the colonial customs authorities had confiscated Garvey's periodical, the *Negro World*. From then onwards references to Garvey, the UNIA and the *Negro World* disappear from the diary.[63]

Garvey's influence was not limited to members of the modern élite living on the coast or, as in Ibadan, fairly close to the coast – or even to adults. Azikiwe heard of Garvey for the first time when he was a schoolboy in Calabar; his informant was a semi-literate youth from Liberia.[64] Even deep in the interior of Nigeria men learned of Garvey and his movement to liberate Africa; if one may believe Joyce Cary, the British colonial officer and novelist, he almost became a legend there.[65]

As far as southern Africa is concerned, we have as yet only one indirect reference to the strength of Garvey's influence. When Aggrey came to South Africa in 1921 as a member of the Phelps–Stokes African Education Commission on its first tour, he was frequently questioned, both here and further to the north in Nyasaland, 'about the fleet that is coming from America' – so much so that at many places he visited, such as Lovedale, the oldest missionary school catering for Africans, he attacked Garveyism with scathing irony. Aggrey, otherwise so gentle, told them that he knew of only two ships, one of which leaked, and added revealingly: 'If you love your race tell it around that Marcus Garvey is their greatest enemy.'[66] Aggrey considered the potential effect of Garveyism in South Africa so important that, contrary to his original intention, he spent another three months in the country. He tried to bridge the ever-widening gulf between Blacks and Whites by encouraging renewed co-operation between the White liberals of the Transvaal and the moderate Africans, especially through the Joint Council in Johannesburg. In this work he could claim a certain success, although the illusions he spread set back the development of South African nationalism by several years.[67] Garvey's impact is most potent in the cases of Azikiwe and Nkrumah, neither of whom made any bones about it. Nkrumah in particular confessed that reading Garvey's *Philosophy and Opinions* during his student years in America made a deep impression upon him.[68] From Garvey he took the symbol of the black star,[69] and the name of the Black Star Line came to be given to the shipping line run by the independent state of Ghana.

Garvey: an historical assessment

In trying to obtain a just appreciation of Garvey one should not be unduly impressed by the fanciful, bizarre and frequently superficial aspects of his activity, which have caused him to be presented hitherto as a kind of melodramatic clown, a 'semi-educated' Black racist torn by feelings of resentment, more a figure of fun than a historical personage worthy of serious attention. If one takes the trouble to read Garvey's own writings and to give him his proper place in the history of Pan-Africanism, this traditional caricature must be discarded. It is true that Garvey was fond of bombastic and pungent phrases and that he preached a bold and prophetic message which sounded ridiculous in the situation he faced; it is likewise true that his romantic invocation of a dream world from the African past and his messianic or Napoleonic pose was a means of compensating psychologically for his deep-rooted inferiority complex. In this way, however, his were the weaknesses inherent in Pan-Africanism itself, which he embodied in his own person in almost caricature-like fashion.

The secret longing to go 'back to Africa' that inspires many Afro-Americans in the New World is deeply rooted in their historical and psychological experience.[70] In idealizing African history Garvey followed a long literary tradition.[71] The cult of individual heroes is another way of overcoming one's inferiority complex, and is often found among Afro-Americans and modern Africans.[72] Garvey's unsuccessful attempts to excel in business were a caricature of the ideology of Booker T. Washington, who wanted to form a class of Afro-American capitalists, but in effect produced what the distinguished Afro-American sociologist Franklin E. Frazier contemptuously calls a 'lumpen-bourgeoisie', comprised for the most part of barbers, petty shopkeepers, and proprietors of funeral parlours or beauty salons catering for negroes.[73]

Even in his imperialist inclinations Garvey was not alone. Many Afro-Americans and Africans reacted to European imperialism with dreams of an empire of their own, be it ancient Egypt or the romanticized kingdoms of the medieval Sudan (Ghana, Mali, Songhai), or the vision of a future 'Ethiopian' (one might also call it Pan-African) empire.[74] It was in vain that acute critics in their own camp pointed out to Africans and Afro-Americans that their future lay in adopting modern political structures, in democracy, and that the time was past for pseudo-feudal trivialities.[75] Even the knowledgeable Du Bois was carried away, at least temporarily, by the idea of using military force to free Africa.[76] The gentle and pious Aggrey, too, could lapse into an imperial pose when contemplating the historical record: in his doctoral thesis, which he wrote when he was more than fifty years old and intended to submit to Columbia University, he set out to prove that the Africans, too, had a glorious past and were descended from great conquerors and empire-builders.[77]

If one ignores the shrill tones which earned for Garvey the mockery of his contemporaries and of posterity, one discovers that he had a consistent, if vague, programme for Africa. It is nowhere clearly summarized in his articles and speeches, but its elements may be reconstructed by an analysis of various statements he made during his acreer. As his widow declared later, he did not imagine that all Afro-Americans should return to Africa from the New World,[78] at any rate not within a short time. He was intelligent enough to realize that there would be no room in Africa for millions of Afro-Americans, and certainly not for an African empire, so long as European imperialism existed. He sought rather to direct the Afro-Americans' attention towards Africa, politically and intellectually, in the hope that this new interest would lead them to mobilize their energies to promote the modernization of that continent. Above all he sought to establish the national basis that was a condition of political equality. 'Nationhood', he wrote, 'is the only means by which modern civilization can completely protect itself.'[79] In the circumstances his conception, too, was hardly practical politics, but it does look more practical and rational than the utopian ideal of a Black empire upon African soil, which generally gets all the limelight.

Similarly Garvey's all too obvious feudal mummery and his flirtation with fascism should not distract us from recognizing that he was striving to institute a basically modern social and political order. The ploy with a synthetic new aristocracy was apparently a psychologically necessary means of mobilizing the energies of his fellow-countrymen, even if he did not realize the fact. The assertion often made that Garvey was the first fascist,[80] at a time when Mussolini had just come to power, should not be pressed too far. It was an expression of his notorious ambition to achieve fame and his tendency to strain after originality at any cost. In statements he made later, when the character of fascism became clearer, he dissociated himself unequivocally from it as well as from its German variant, national socialism. Cynics might say that he only called Mussolini the 'arch barbarian of our times' (in October 1935) because of the Italian invasion of Ethiopia;[81] nevertheless the fact remains that two months later he spoke out clearly against the anti-semitism of the Third Reich: 'Our sympathy is with the Jews as with any other suppressed minority group.'[82] At a pinch one could describe as 'fascist' his truly bewildering eclecticism, which led him to combine reactionary, bourgeois capitalist and (quasi-) social revolutionary elements.[83] But this would be to stretch unacceptably far the meaning of this already overworked term. Garvey occasionally made statements in favour of democracy,[84] although admittedly rather vague ones; these views may have corresponded more closely to his true sentiments, especially as he wanted the oppressed peoples to enjoy freedom and equality, not alien domination – i.e. the very opposite of fascist ideals:

> The Negro has had enough of the vaunted practice of race superi-
> ority as inflicted upon him by others, therefore he is not prepared
> to tolerate a similar assumption on the part of his own people. . . .
> It will be useless . . . for bombastic Negroes to leave America and
> the West Indies to go to Africa thinking that they will have priv-
> ileged positions to inflict upon the race that bastard aristocracy
> that they have tried to maintain in this Western world at the
> expense of masses.[85]

Fresh source material and new historical perspectives make it possible to see the Du Bois–Garvey controversy in a different light. To a certain extent Du Bois and Garvey were complete opposites. Du Bois, so light-skinned that he could only just pass as a 'negro', was of humble origins but had an excellent academic education – he was on the surface a modern, rational intellectual but at heart a hopeless romantic.[86] Garvey, on the other hand, even in his external appearance, with his very black skin, stood at the opposite end of the spectrum. Of bourgeois background, he was a self-made man with a curious mixture of proletarian, bourgeois and pseudo-feudal traits. His irrationality, bombast and bizarre pretensions concealed a certain rational substance. Garvey was realistic enough to see that the Africans could not expect any aid from Europeans, a few individual exceptions apart, in accomplishing the liberation of Africa. Also in another respect he had no illusions: he saw clearly that it would be necessary to use violence.[87] Also realistic was his emphasis on national independence as a condition for self-assertion in the modern world.[88] His temporary flirtation with the Ku Klux Klan, which so enraged the NAACP and its leaders,[89] may be explained as a bold tactical ploy of doubtful validity. He couched his views in language which brought him a reputation for racism. In coming to a fair assessment, however, one must remember that thinking in Social Darwinist and racist categories was widespread in the world at that time, so that it would be surprising if a man like Garvey should not have used racist terminology in his revolt against European racism and its political consequences. In this respect Garvey's so-called 'racism' is little more than a reflection of European racism. It was basically a means of instilling into his fellow-countrymen of African descent and into Africans a new form of self-awareness without which modernization and the road to independence were unthinkable. Garvey's emphasis on race was in the last resort not destructive, not racist in the European sense, because its objective was the equality of all human beings in principle. In this point he was at one with Du Bois, who in his best moments, however, employed formulations of greater elegance, more attuned to the European ear, than did the unpolished Garvey. Garvey's racism was basically what Léopold S. Senghor has called the anti-racism of Négritude. For all his aberrations and confusion Garvey was an important figure in the Pan-African movement. What he lacked was the rationality of a Horton, which might have allowed him to master and channel more effectively his volcanic energy.

Besides Du Bois's Pan-African Congress movement and the movement
led by Marcus Garvey, there existed between the two World Wars
other groups, tendencies and movements which although they did not
call themselves Pan-African were nevertheless linked to it. The most
important of these were two West African organizations, the National
Congress of British West Africa (NCBWA) and the West African
Students' Union (WASU), its student auxiliary in England. In the
following chapters we shall discuss the proto-nationalist and nationalist
African and West Indian groups in France,[1] which were partly under
communist influence; the efforts made by the Communists to win over
the Africans and Afro-Americans, especially between 1927 and 1934;[2]
and Dr Harold Moody's League of Coloured Peoples.[3] Of only mar-
ginal significance were the two great organizations in South Africa,
the South African National Congress[4] and the Industrial and Commercial Workers' Union led by Clements Kadalie.[5]

Any account of these various groups presents considerable difficulties. The state of research into the subject is still unsatisfactory and
almost every organization would deserve a monograph of its own.[6]
Despite this it is possible to give a rough outline and to indicate the

main interrelationships between the various groups, referring back to the historical antecedents discussed in Part I. It is just as difficult to decide in what order to treat these various bodies, many of which were contemporaneous and influenced one another. In the following chapters we shall try to keep to a chronological approach, dealing with the individual organizations in the order in which they appeared.

The National Congress of British West Africa and the development of nationalism in West Africa

In the 1920s the National Congress of British West Africa (hence-forward referred to in this chapter simply as the Congress) was the leading African nationalist organization.[7] Admittedly it was confined to British West Africa, but except for the African National Congress in South Africa it had no significant competitor. Since the Congress maintained contact with the USA and England it also had a Pan-African function in the wider sense of the term. Moreover the West African nationalism it represented was the matrix from which arose one of the most important figures in Pan-Africanism after 1945: Kwame Nkrumah.

The Congress represents the third stage of organized nationalism on the Gold Coast after the Fanti Confederation of 1867–71 and the Aborigines Rights Protection Society (ARPS) after 1897.[8] It had its origins in the nationalist tendencies evident just before World War I, whose two main exponents were (after the early death of Mensah Sarbah in 1910) Attoh Ahuma, in the last instance with his journal the *Gold Coast Nation*, and Casely Hayford.[9] To some extent one can already detect the later outlines of the Congress. In 1912, even before this was formally founded, a group led by Hayford to all intents and purposes took over, at least temporarily, the *African Times and Orient Review*.[10]

The Congress emerged in part as a reaction to the decline of the ARPS, which before World War I was led by the Rev. Attoh Ahuma. The ARPS really existed only at Cape Coast, since its central body had stifled the autonomy of the organization's branches. Besides this it was still living off the glory of the success it had scored in 1898 against the governor of the colony.[11] In spite of all Attoh Ahuma's nationalist propaganda, the influence of the ARPS under his leadership became limited to the Fanti at Cape Coast, the ancient capital of the Gold

Coast. All proposals for a more comprehensive organization were regarded by the ARPS as threats to its own position, so that finally Hayford had to found the Congress in opposition to it.

Preparatory talks apparently began in 1914.[12] The persons to whom Hayford turned were in part identical with those who had taken the initiative in founding the *African Times and Orient Review*; they included W. F. Dove from Freetown and E. J. P. Brown from Cape Coast. The stimulus to create a West African organization went back to 1912 when two delegations from the Gold Coast and Nigeria had petitioned the Colonial Office in London to grant these colonies greater political rights, but in vain. The new gathering of forces was intended to attain the same objective. In 1918 Hayford pleaded for a Pan-West African conference with the support of the ARPS; in this, however, he was unsuccessful so that later he became the enemy of E. J. P. Brown, who remained loyal to this latter organization. On the other hand Hayford did manage to set foot in Accra through Hutton-Mills and thus to attain a broader national basis, even though most of the chiefs turned against the projected new organization.

On 7 March 1919 Governor Clifford in Accra received a petition handed over by an eleven-man deputation from the Gold Coast Committee of the Projected West African Conference, led by Hutton-Mills. The petition was signed by Hutton-Mills, Casely Hayford, Dr F. V. Nanka-Bruce and Wood W. Bannerman. It began with a reference to the World War recently concluded and welcomed Germany's elimination from the ranks of the colonial powers. It then asked that Africans be consulted on political matters in West Africa through freely elected institutions; that their traditional rights to the land be respected; that the import of alcohol be prohibited; and that the present petition be wired to London by the governors of all four West African colonies.[13]

The foundation meeting of the Congress took place in Accra from 11 to 29 March 1920. All four British West African colonies were represented – Nigeria with six delegates, Sierra Leone with three, Gambia with one and the Gold Coast with forty-two.[14] For the first time the modernized intellectual element dominated unequivocally, for on account of the tension with the ARPS only a few chiefs declared their support, among them those in Jamestown (Accra) and the far west (Axim). The speakers distinguished themselves by their moderation and their appreciation of the advantages which British colonial rule had conferred – as was reported to London with some satisfaction by the deputy governor, who with several European officials attended the opening meeting, held in the native club at Accra.[15]

The predominance enjoyed by the Gold Coast representatives was reflected in the composition of the executive committee. Hutton-Mills was elected president; the vice-presidency fell to Casely Hayford, the *spiritus rector* and keenest mind at the Congress. Dr F. V. Nanka-Bruce and L. E. V. M'Carthy (Sierra Leone) served as secretaries, each having equal status, and the two treasurers were A. B. Quartey-Papafio and H. Van Hein (both from the Gold Coast); five other vice-presidents reinforced the representation of the other colonies. The principal speakers included Hayford, Sekyi, Nanka-Bruce, Van Hein (all from the Gold Coast), Dove, M'Carthy, Dr H. C. Bankole-Bright (all from Sierra Leone), Patriarch J. G. Campbell (Nigeria) and E. F. Small (Gambia).[16] Several papers were read on the most diverse topics, whose content found expression in no less than eighty-three resolutions. In addition to these there was a main resolution. In line with the petition of 1919 it demanded more consultation, proposed a new constitution, criticized discrimination in the West African civil service, and called for local self-government in all the major cities of British West Africa.[17]

In his opening address Casely Hayford recalled King Ghartey IV of Winneba and his watchword, 'Be constitutional'.[18] Hayford, who had known Ghartey personally, as late as 1920 identified himself with this programme of strictly constitutional agitation. Dove from Sierra Leone endorsed this attitude, emphasizing that the Congress with its demands was by no means motivated 'by any rebellious spirit of Bolshevism or that of Sinn Feinianism'. That the Congress was no 'anti-government movement' (Patriarch Campbell) is shown by the resolution on the right of self-determination. It did not contain, as one might have expected after the end of the war, a call for independence but limited itself to a protest against the exchange of colonies without consulting the population, especially the division of Togoland between Britain and France. In conclusion it assured 'His Majesty the King and Emperor' of the participants' 'sincere loyalty and respect'.

The resolution on educational matters held that the time had come for a West African university which should work to enhance the students' West African national consciousness. To provide the necessary academic infrastructure the Congress demanded that compulsory education be introduced throughout British West Africa and that the level of instruction be raised in all the secondary schools that existed or were to be founded, so that they could train their pupils for university entrance. Of interest is the reference to Japanese experience, which it was suggested ought to be taken into consideration.

In the economic sphere the conference demanded the expulsion of the so-called 'Syrians' – merchants from the Near East who had established themselves as keen competitors of native traders. As an organizational framework for the economic development of British West Africa as a whole it suggested the formation of a British West African Co-operative Association. Finally, to meet the difficulties faced by African importers and exporters, it welcomed efforts to find the necessary tonnage of shipping by approaching every competing company engaged in overseas maritime commerce, making special reference to the Black Star Line – a cautious plea for the Garvey movement which avoided explicit mention of its leader's name.[19]

To establish West African collaboration in another field the Congress suggested the formation of a West African Press Union. In the three largest of the four British colonies there were local journals which either supported the Congress or were sympathetic to it, such as the *Sierra Leone Weekly News*, the *Gold Coast Independent*, *Vox Populi* (Gold Coast) and the *Lagos Weekly Record*. The Congress acclaimed freedom of the press as 'the birthright of every community in the British Empire' and announced the publication of an official organ, the *British West African Nation Review*, edited by Casely Hayford. Unfortunately for modern historians, no such periodical ever appeared.

At first the Congress enjoyed a measure of goodwill on the part of the colonial government. But this, however, turned to icy coolness at the end of 1920, when the Congress sent a deputation to London without informing the chiefs or the governor beforehand. In September 1920 nine delegates in all arrived in London to hand a petition to King George V. These included two men from Nigeria (Chief Oluwa, Lagos; J. Egerton Shyngle; also Herbert Macaulay as interpreter for Chief Oluwa); three from the Gold Coast (Hutton-Mills, Van Hein, Casely Hayford) and two each from Sierra Leone (Bankole-Bright, F. W. Dove) and Gambia (E. F. Small, H. N. Jones).[20] The petition referred to the select committee of the House of Commons set up in 1865 which had bound the British government to transfer sovereign power to the Africans.[21] As representatives of the West African intelligentsia and people the Congress asked for an extension of the franchise and for the establishment of political institutions which should not be mere copies of European ones but should take account of native traditions.

Although the delegation stayed in London for several months and during that time acted as a West African lobby, trying to mobilize public opinion, it had no immediate success. In Nigeria the governor, Sir Hugh Clifford, who had just been transferred from the Gold Coast, attacked the Congress with unusual pungency[22] and his successor in Accra, Sir Gordon Guggisberg, who by and large was sympathetic to African aspirations, expressed his extreme displeasure. Some of the chiefs, headed by Nana Ofori Atta, the influential Paramount Chief (Omanehene) of Akim Abuakwa (north of Accra), sharply opposed the Congress in the Legislative Council. They were joined by E. J. P. Brown,[23] who had still taken a positive attitude when the gathering had opened in Accra. In view of the negative reports from West Africa the Colonial Office saw no cause even to receive the deputation.

Despite this the deputation had a historical impact. Already in 1922 Governor Clifford gave Nigeria a new constitution which entered into force in 1923. It provided for the election to the Legislative Council of four African members, three from Lagos and one from Calabar. In the first Nigerian elections, held in 1923 on a limited franchise, there came into being Black Africa's first nationalist party, the Nigerian Democratic party led by Herbert Macaulay.[24] The latter had taken a modest part in the Congress and now profited from its indirect success.[25] In 1925 Governor Guggisberg promulgated an analogous constitution for the Gold Coast. This gave the Africans nine representatives, six of whom were elected by the newly constituted Provincial Councils and were thus representatives of the chiefs (in practice they were themselves chiefs, which was wholly inconsistent with the traditional constitution), while one representative each was elected by the enfranchised groups of the population in Accra, Cape Coast and Sekondi.[26]

Besides this Guggisberg responded to what had by now become a traditional demand for a West African university by founding Achimota College, a new educational establishment near Accra. This offered instruction at all levels from kindergarten to teachers' training. The staff consisted predominantly of White teachers. The first African teacher, who was at the same time deputy rector, was J. E. K. Aggrey whom Guggisberg appointed in 1924; since 1898 Aggrey had studied and taught at the AMEZ college at Salisbury, NC.[27] Achimota College was greatly influenced by Tuskegee and the Hampton Institute, but above all by the findings of the Phelps–Stokes Commission on Education in Africa, which toured Africa in 1920–21 and again in 1923. Its first major report[28] made such an impression on Guggisberg that the official responsible for education in Accra was sent on a study trip to the southern states of the USA, where he visited both Tuskegee and the Hampton Institute.[29] Thus Achimota College was another delayed and somewhat surprising victory for the late Booker T. Washington.

Under the personal influence of Guggisberg Achimota endeavoured to keep a balance between Western and traditional native subjects,[30] which could only have had the effect of strengthening the eclectic character of African nationalism and giving it an institutional form. Achimota College was very popular among Africans, attracting pupils and students from other regions. Among the first generation of student teachers was Nkrumah, and other leading Ghanaian nationalists were taught there. To some extent the college had a national function by the mere fact that people in all walks of life on the Gold Coast helped to build it up and expand it. Its official inauguration in January 1927 was the occasion for a public reconciliation between Casely Hayford and Nana Ofori Atta, who had often contended for political leadership on the Gold Coast during the years following the foundation of the Congress.[31]

A further historical effect of the 1920 Congress deputation is obvious: in view of the traditional connection between the modern West African element and Britain, a stay of several months in London by nine West African nationalists intensified British interest in West African nationalism, at least in left-wing circles. The African leaders gave numerous lectures and held private as well as public discussions, which contributed to the politicization of the West African colony in London, especially the students. In 1927 Casely Hayford became the patron of the West African Students' Union (WASU). This had been founded in 1925 with the participation, at least indirectly, of another member of the Congress, Bankole-Bright.[32] The Congress delegation also established contact with the African Progress Union, which for its part participated in the Pan-African Congress movement under Du Bois.[33]

The external failure of the deputation was followed, as often happens in such cases, by internal dissension. At the beginning of 1921 the deputation returned to Africa empty-handed. This failure paralysed the Congress to such an extent that it was two years before a second meeting took place, this time in Freetown. The Pan-West African character of the event was emphasized by the special commemorative service held on the opening day, 28 January 1923, which was attended by representatives of all Christian creeds and denominations in British West Africa. This ceremony took place in the Wesley (Methodist) church. The African ministers present joined together 'in a great patriotic impulse by praying for God's blessing on the Congress'.[34] Hymns written and composed especially for the event by Africans – the 'National Congress of British West Africa Hymns' – gave the service a special cachet. The commemorative sermon was delivered by the Rev. J. O. C. During, a Methodist pastor who also taught at Fourah Bay College, on the text 'I appeal unto Caesar'. He sought to impress upon his listeners that 'we as Africans and members of the British Empire have got the right to appeal unto Caesar in the same way as the old citizens of the Roman Empire had a right to appeal unto Caesar, that is unto our King-Emperor for the redress of grievances'.[35] The text chosen for the concluding service was: 'I am a citizen of no mean city'. 'The implication was that of the status of British West Africans and their right to be accorded citizens' rights and privileges.'[36]

The keynote of these religious services underlined the political flavour of the meeting. Casely Hayford, deputizing for Hutton-Mills, gave the main speech. He claimed that all the political progress attained since 1920 could be attributed to the success of the Congress. Even more sharply than in Accra he formulated a project for a (British) West African federation such as had already existed in embryonic form during the nineteenth century (from 1866 to 1874). As a dominion of the British Commonwealth this federation should have a common parliament, and as its head a governor-general as representative of the crown.[37] Ideas of this kind were endorsed by other speakers and featured in the resolution of the meeting. On the other hand Hayford's own paper the *Gold Coast Independent* did not help to clarify matters when, in reply to critics from outside the movement, it denied that the term 'elective representation' implied a cabinet with a premier and ministers, yet at the same time adhered to the ideal of a united dominion of British West Africa on a par with South Africa, Canada etc.[38] – states which had long since had cabinet government.

The colonial reforms in West Africa between 1923 and 1925[39] took much of the wind out of the Congress's sails, so that after the convention in Freetown it led a feeble existence. The conflict with some of the chiefs on the Gold Coast also sapped its strength. In a similar way its older rival, the Aborigines Rights Protection Society, virtually ceased to exist after Attoh Ahuma's death in 1921; only in the extreme west, in Axim, did a branch survive under Kobina Sekyi and S. R. Wood, who were at the same time also active on behalf of the Congress. The effect of the third convention of the Congress, held in Bathurst in Gambia, from 24 December 1925 to 10 January 1926, was diminished by the absence of Nigerian representatives; nor did this meeting have any remarkable political results, although in his ceremonial address Casely Hayford demonstrated anew the dilemma in which African nationalists found themselves. He recognized the need to modernize African society[40] but then went on to say that Africans could do without it if it hindered their political awareness.[41]

Of significance – if for the moment without any practical consequences – was the attitude taken by the Congress towards the nationalist or Pan-African trends. Officially, it took remarkably little note of them. In 1920 at Accra one resolution made a positive but indirect reference to the Garvey movement.[42] In 1923 at Freetown Casely Hayford reported proudly that 'the National Congress . . . is known throughout the entire English-speaking world and we are recognized by, and are in touch with some of the greatest world movements of the day'.[43] The specific details he provided of such contacts were somewhat sparse, for he only mentioned the African Progress Union in London[44] and Gilbert Murray's League of Nations Union, whose committee had received the Congress deputation in London. Knowing that Hayford established at least personal contact with Du Bois and the Garvey movement,[45] one might presume that he had them in mind and did not wish to mention them by name. In Bathurst at the end of 1925 Hayford took note of the 'intense activity in racial progress both in the United States and in the islands of the sea', but thought that 'we must, to a certain extent, guide and control it. . . . The right inspiration must come from the mother continent; and in no part of Africa can such inspiration be so well supplied as in the West.'[46]

Matters had not yet progressed so far, and Pan-Africanism (for all its weakness) was relatively stronger in the diaspora outside Africa. Despite this Hayford went a stage further at the fourth (and last) meeting of the Congress, which took place in Lagos in December 1929. He bolstered the West African claim to leadership of the Pan-African movement (a claim he did not explicitly articulate) by criticizing in familiar terms the ignorance of conditions in West Africa among the Afro-American élite: 'It is necessary to realise that the duty is cast upon us in British West Africa to lead the way in making suitable suggestions for the amelioration of African disabilities. The African of the dispersion, though of high cultural attainment, has yet to grasp those indigenous conditions which must command practical reforms.'[47] He also buttressed the West African claim to leadership by emphasizing the political and social advantages enjoyed by this part of the continent vis-à-vis East and South Africa: 'Our brethren in the Eastern and Southern portions of the mother continent are so distracted by the circumstances which arise from economic servitude that they can scarcely be expected to view the situation calmly and to command the constitutional solution of their immediate problems, and, in some cases, they lack the necessary machinery.'[48]

In this context there is a somewhat surprising criticism of the favourite Pan-African slogan 'Ethiopia shall soon stretch forth her hand unto God' – all the more surprising in that Hayford himself had made extensive use of it during the past.[49] 'But it will end in idle talk until the national sentiment is sufficiently strong in us to drown our petty rivalries, our petty dissensions. . . . There must be an educational awakening throughout history, and when this pentecost breaks in upon us, we shall begin to tread the sure path of national emancipation'.[50]

This appeal was at the same time Hayford's political testament. One year later he died, after which the Congress led a shadowy existence. In 1931, it is true, public ceremonies and demonstrations were held in his honour at Accra and Sekondi, his place of residence.[51] The general secretary of the Congress, Samuel R. Wood, was able to report proudly that an affiliated organization had been founded in Trinidad[52] which gave the Congress a branch in the New World, but it was fantasy to say that 'a strong chain is gradually forged between the race-conscious men on this side and at the other side of the Atlantic'.[53] Only a few days later J. B. Danquah's daily newspaper could ask with concern whether the Congress was hibernating or already dead.[54] At its central base, the Gold Coast, the Congress had indeed virtually expired.

After 1930 the nationalists of the various territories again came more into the limelight. The leading positions were held by J. B. Danquah (Gold Coast), Herbert Macaulay and Nnamdi Azikiwe (both from Nigeria), and I. T. A. Wallace-Johnson (from Sierra Leone). Danquah, as Ofori Atta's step-brother and a former president of WASU, assumed the natural role of mediator between the traditionalist tribal princes and the modern-minded notables in the towns, so that after Ofori Atta's death in 1934 he rose to become the leading personality on the Gold Coast – until, a generation later, he was pushed aside and eliminated by Nkrumah, whose social origins were completely different. Danquah's importance lies in his contribution, not to Pan-Africanism but to the domestic politics of the Gold Coast. He was a transitional figure between Casely Hayford and Nkrumah, the inventor of the name 'Ghana'.[55] The same is true of the Gold Coast Youth League which he inspired and led – the equivalent of the Nigerian Youth League and the Sierra Leone Youth League. Above these organizations, sheltering them like an umbrella, was the West African movement with its regional claims, but its relevance to Pan-Africanism is not yet apparent. It is none the less true that Azikiwe and Wallace-Johnson played a significant part in leading young Africans to the left, and ultimately both of them became well-known exponents of Pan-Africanism.[56]

Predecessors of the West African Students' Union (WASU): African students in England

One of the most important organizations in the formation of Pan-Africanism outside Africa between the wars was the West African Students' Union (WASU), which we have already mentioned. There exists as yet only one early article on this body based upon primary sources.[57] With the aid of this and some fresh material we can sketch the Pan-African function of WASU and indicate its position in the general process of development.

The pupils and students from West Africa and the West Indies who came to England and Scotland from the late eighteenth century onwards, normally as individuals or in small groups, naturally enough did not as yet show any interest in forming an organization. The first attempt in this direction seems to have been the Afro-West Indian Literary Society in Edinburgh, which sent two delegates to the London Pan-African Conference in 1900.[58] A little later African students in England also began to organize, at first on a local level. P. K. I. Seme, who had visited the Tuskegee Institute while studying at Columbia University in New York, went to Oxford to complete his studies before returning to South Africa where in 1912 he assumed a leading position in the African National Congress;[59] at Jesus College, Oxford 'he organized a club of African students'.[60] Seme sought B. T. Washington's blessing, assuring him that the organization was not concerned with agitation, let alone with gaining power, but only with the exchange of ideas. Seme expressly drew attention to what we would now call his club's Pan-African dimension when he stated emphatically: 'Here are to be found the future leaders of African nations temporarily thrown together and yet coming from widely different sections of that great and unhappy continent and that these men will, in due season, return each to a community that eagerly awaits him and perhaps influence its public opinion.'[61] Since Seme came from South Africa, whereas most of the other students were from West Africa, one may presume that the members of the club were drawn from both these regions.

In 1906 there was at Liverpool University a student association called the Ethiopian Progressive Association, which likewise established contact with Washington but was unable to persuade him to assume patronage of it.

About the number of African students in Great Britain, or even in London, we still know very little. Just before World War I an interest came to be taken in them by liberal and humanitarian groups, especially the African Society[62] and the Anti-Slavery and Aborigines Protection Society.[63] On 18 April 1913 these two groups collaborated in organizing a conference in the Westminster Palace Hotel attended among others by Thomas Fowell Buxton (a grandson of the abolitionist of that name),[64] the Rev. J. H. Harris, secretary of the Anti-Slavery and Aborigines Protection Society, Sir Harry Johnston and two MPs, J. Cathcart Wason and Sir Harry Wilson – as well as 'by about 40 African students'.[65] Since Mohamed Ali Duse also helped to prepare for this conference from June 1912 onwards, by putting forward the names of Africans who might be invited to attend,[66] it is not surprising that some people who were not students were also present. One early letter on this subject from a Mr A. B. Merriman to the Rev. J. H. Harris[67] mentioned no fewer than twenty-three law students, including Coussey,[68] Emmanuel Quist and Charles W. Bannerman, all of whom later became distinguished lawyers on the Gold Coast, as well as seventeen merchants, including J. E. Taylor and Duse.[69]

The conference was non-political, for the president, Sir Charles P. Lucas, declared it his intention 'to discover the best way of helping Africans in London'.[70] According to W. F. Hutchinson[71] it was especially a matter of giving African students a more sympathetic reception on their arrival in London, in a world that was entirely alien to them.[72] Nothing was said about racial discrimination, but this was obviously a factor, as we know from the fact that on his first visit to West Africa in 1920 Duse complained in Ibadan about unpleasant experiences of this kind.[73] Whatever the case may be, at the conference Duse supported a resolution submitted by Johnston which aimed at improving these students' conditions. Both Duse and Johnston were in favour of aiding African students in every way once they had arrived in England, although the former said he personally would have preferred them to attend an African university. A small committee set up by the conference, which included some Africans, petitioned the Colonial Office to grant financial support for an African students' club, but at the beginning of May this proposal was turned down.[74] In spite of this, at the end of July 1913 one of the MPs in the group suggested to Harcourt, Secretary of State for the Colonies, that an African club should be founded, the costs of which were to be divided as follows: the Colonial Office and the South African government (sic) £200 each; the African Society and the Anti-Slavery and Aborigines Protection Society £50 each.[75]

In June 1914 this attempt was repeated. A new list of names oi Africans in London was compiled, and on 13 July a reception was held in the House of Commons attended by several Africans then staying in the city. Plans were discussed for the establishment of a club; as usual, resolutions were passed and it was decided to send a deputation to the Colonial Office.[76] Promptly Mr Wason, the MP, received the answer: the colonial governments 'were in general against the government subsidizing the establishment' of such a club, for which reason the minister declined to receive the deputation.[77]

Despite this disappointment the conference of 1913 probably had some historical impact. It may have been the first occasion when Africans in London met, even though still under White patronage, outside the narrow framework of their professional or local interests, if one excepts the Pan-African Conference of 1900. What deductions they drew from the failure of this well-meant effort we do not know.

The outbreak of World War I at first led to worries of a bigger kind. But it accords with the general galvanizing effect of World War I as it entered its second half that the first African students' union of more than local scope emerged on British soil. So little is known about this venture that there is not even an agreement about its name. Garigue calls it the Association of Students of African Descent,[78] whereas J. S. Coleman refers to it as the Union for Students of African Descent, and says that it was founded by African and West Indian students in 1917.[79] The *African Times and Orient Review*, on the other hand, gives its name as the African Students' Union of Great Britain and Ireland.[80] According to this latter source, which was closest to the event in chronological terms, the new union held its first general meeting as early as 23 December 1916, which suggests that it had probably been founded shortly before. Duse may have acted as a catalyst, since he participated in the London conference of 1913[81] and played a key role in other fields; at any rate his journal was probably the first to report the existence of the new union, and made its address available so that readers would know where to send inquiries and applications for membership.[82]

The West Indian element was not yet represented, at least at the time when the union was founded; the membership consisted wholly of persons from Sierra Leone and the Gold Coast. The chairman was E. S. Beoku Betts (Sierra Leone);[83] the vice-chairmanship remained for the time being vacant. The role of secretary fell to K. A. Keisah, and that of assistant secretary to T. Mensah-Annan (both from the Gold Coast); the job of financial secretary was taken by C. Awoonor Renner (from Sierra Leone and the Gold Coast, we are told). According to the same source the principal figure behind the new organization was Beoku Betts; he already had a Master of Arts degree and was a Fellow of the Royal Anthropological Institute and in general 'a credit to his fatherland'.[84]

The African Students' Union, as is repeatedly emphasized, was non-political. 'The object of the Union is primarily Social, and aims at bringing together all Africans in statu pupillaris resident in England, and thus to provide a crying need.'[85] A little more specific was the statement in December 1917 that the organization was 'founded for the purpose of dealing with African history and sociology and with the avowed aim of keeping African students in London in a condition of active intellectuality, inciting investigation through its debates and lectures by members and others. . . .'[86] Betts delivered his first presidential address on 14 April 1917, on a theme of concern to every politically conscious African: the role of Africa in world history.[87] Falling back on the well-known arguments about the negroid character of the ancient Egyptians,[88] Betts handled the theme in a quite respectable fashion. To read his address is to gain the impression that its modernity and broad canvas were influenced by Du Bois's the *Negro*,[89] although there is no firm evidence that this was the case.

Not much more is as yet known about this student association. The discrepancy in its official designations may be explained by the fact that when a strong West Indian element came in the name was changed to 'Union for Students of African Descent'. In 1921 it had only 25 members, but by 1924 already 120.[90] It was in touch with Du Bois, and in November 1923 invited him to come along one evening while he was staying in London for the third Pan-African Congress. At the last moment the plan had to be abandoned because of time-table difficulties, but four delegates from the union attended the Congress.

The Union for Students of African Descent,[91] although small, is the best-known forerunner of WASU. But there were also two other African organizations in London towards the end of World War I: the African Progress Union and the Gold Coast Students' Union, about which hardly anything is yet known. The African Progress Union was presided over by Dr Alcindor and J. R. Archer, town councillor and in 1913–14 mayor of the borough of Battersea, both of whom had taken an active part in the Pan-African Congress movement since 1900.[92] The leading personalities included Mohamed Ali Duse.[93] The deputation to London despatched by the National Congress of British West Africa in 1920 established contact with it while in Britain, and Casely Hayford later called it 'a link in the heart of the Empire between the African at home and the African abroad'.[94]

The West African Students' Union (WASU)[95]

The situation changed with the arrival in London in 1922 of Lapido Solanke, a law student whose education was rich in historical associations. Solanke was born in 1884 in Abeokuta, visited the missionary school there and subsequently went to Fourah Bay College before taking up his legal studies in England.[96] In 1926 he passed his examination and remained in London, where he died in 1958. In 1924, together with some other Nigerian students, he founded a new student organization, the Nigerian Progress Union. His political ideal was a 'United States of West Africa', envisaged as a preliminary stage to a united Africa. Unity was apparently his principal maxim, for shortly after founding the Nigerian Progress Union he addressed a passionate appeal to Herbert Macaulay exhorting the older generation in Nigeria to unite, arguing that this was an elementary condition for any kind of progress.[97]

In London he won Casely Hayford's moral support for his idea of bringing students from British West Africa together in a permanent organization. Finally, with the assistance of Dr Bankole-Bright, an activist of the National Congress from Sierra Leone,[98] he managed to establish the union he had in mind. The West African Students' Union (WASU) was founded in London on 7 August 1925; its president was Bankole-Bright and it embraced students from all four British colonies in West Africa. According to Garigue there were 'approximately a dozen students of law';[99] according to an early brief account by the organization itself, the number of founding members ran to twenty-one.[100] WASU's four predecessors apparently dissolved themselves, so that this amounted to a merger. The chairman of the Nigerian Progress Union, Joseph A. Doherty, a medical student (Abeokuta Grammar School, Fourah Bay College, University of London), became treasurer of WASU;[101] in 1929 he was its fifth chairman. The president of the Union for Students of African Descent in 1923, H. A. H. Benjamin,[102] later became vice-president.[103] The first president of WASU was W. Davidson Carrol from Gambia.

As is only to be expected with student unions, membership of the committee fluctuated sharply. Every year new elections were held, as a result of which the inner executive was always changed completely. An element of continuity was provided by Solanke as honorary secretary, later as general secretary, and warden of the WASU student hostel. From 1927 onwards WASU elected a patron. The first was Casely Hayford; then, until his death in 1931, this office fell to Prempeh I, the Kumasihene, who had returned from exile in 1924. We do not hear of another patron until 1935–7: Paul Robeson, the Afro-American actor, singer and politician, who occasionally also donated money to WASU.[104] The first deputy president and the second man to occupy the presidency was J. B. Danquah (Gold Coast).[105] Originally the membership remained restricted to students from British West Africa, but after 1928 it was open to all students of African descent.[106] Even after this the West African element must have predominated, as is shown by an examination of the register of those who patronized the WASU hostel. In this list Nigerian students were by far the most prominent, followed by those from Sierra Leone and the Gold Coast.[107]

We do not have complete and precise information about the number of members. The nucleus was formed by active students in England, especially in London, to whom were added ex-students who had returned home on completing their studies. The total number of active students at any given time cannot have been very large. After beginning in 1925 with 21 founding members, the total had by 1935 risen only to 'over 170'. In 1938 the number was 227, of whom rather more than 60 were active students. In 1939 another 25 students joined so that the total number 'both past and present' rose to 252,[108] we are told in the annual report for 1939. During World War II the number of active students sank to 30, but then rose to 100[109] around 1945 when a new wave of African students arrived. To these numbers must be added those who belonged to various local branches of WASU, especially in Africa, and the supporters of the organization, whose total number can only be calculated with difficulty. At any rate there were probably considerably more of them than there were active members in Britain.

The information in *WASU*, the union's newspaper which appeared from 1926, about examination results and the return of students to Africa gives one an instructive glimpse into the students' social background and their distribution among British universities. London was the most popular, but students also went to Edinburgh, Glasgow, Liverpool, Durham, Oxford and Cambridge. Beyond this WASU was associated with local groups such as the African Races Association in Glasgow (1928) and the African Patriotic Students' Club in New York (1933).[110]

To maintain continuity and to widen its basis of action, WASU introduced several innovations. At the time of its foundation it planned to set up a permanent students' hostel of its own and in 1928–9 it had a house put at its disposal for one year by Garvey.[111] After this the committee decided to send Solanke to West Africa to publicize the organization and to raise money for a students' hostel. Solanke remained in West Africa from 1929 to 1932, mostly in Nigeria. He made several tours on behalf of WASU and succeeded in finding enough money for the projected hostel. In his campaign he appealed to the traditional élites, but also won the co-operation of the modern élite, some of whose younger members had belonged to WASU during their student years in Britain.

A by-product of this publicity campaign was the foundation of approximately forty WASU branches or 'fraternities', as they were called, extending all the way from Gambia to the Congo, over the traditional area into which the 'Sierra Leoneans' (Saros) had penetrated from the mid-nineteenth century onwards.[112] A breakthrough was the spread of its influence to northern Nigeria as far as Kano and Zaria, as well as to Kumasi, the Ashanti capital. The most important towns to have WASU branches were Accra, Cape Coast, Elmina, Sekondi, Freetown, Lagos, Ebute Metta (near Lagos), Abeokuta, Zaria, Kano, Ibadan, Ile-Ife and Enugu; they also existed in 'about 20 further towns in West Africa' not mentioned here.[113] The degree of activity displayed by these groups seems to have varied considerably. Only local sources, should any be available, could tell us how long Solanke's impulse lasted in the various places affected. At any rate both Solanke's mission and the foundation of WASU branches brought modern political ideas into areas which had not yet been affected by incipient political agitation. Since WASU also appealed to Afro-Americans in the United States and in the West Indies,[114] it acquired a Pan-African dimension at least geographically.

With the £1500 that had already been raised and other donations it was possible to open on 1 January 1933 at 62 Camden Road, in the borough of St Pancras, London, a new WASU hostel[115] which has since become an important centre of activity in London. Solanke took charge of the hostel as warden, together with his young wife whom he had met on his publicity campaign in Nigeria. Since the annual rent of £230 proved to be intolerably high in the long run, WASU bought a house of its own in 1938. Funds were obtained in response to an appeal which had the moral support of Sir John Harris, secretary of the Anti-Slavery and Aborigines Protection Society and of the Welfare of Africans Committee. Among the contributors special mention may be made of the Alake of Abeokuta (Solanke's native town), the Oni of Ife and the Ashantehene; business firms which contributed included in particular Elder Dempster Lines (the shipping company which for decades had kept up the traditional maritime links between Liverpool and the West African coast), the United Africa Co., Shell Oil, Cadbury (the large Quaker-owned chocolate firm with cocoa interests in West Africa), Barclays Bank, the Bank of British West Africa and the Rhodes Trust; also WASU branches in Zaria, Abeokuta and Minna.[116]

On 1 June 1938 WASU moved into its new house at 1 South Villas, Camden Square. 'Africa House' had twelve beds, club rooms and enough space to hold debates, social events, African folk dances etc. Receptions or dinners were given for prominent visitors such as Bourdillon, the governor of Nigeria. The group photos popular on such occasions portray serious young men and women, wearing elegant modern clothing, obviously determined to demonstrate the social acceptability of the modern African élite.

The WASU hostel was not only a social centre but also a hive of intellectual and political activity. Apart from the lectures and debates several visitors stressed its importance as a market-place of ideas. Even before the hostel had been established several personalities had addressed WASU students or visited its headquarters. Among them were Casely Hayford (1926), Nana Ofori Atta (1927), Bankole-Bright, Garvey, Dr C. C. Adeniyi-Jones (member of the Legislative Council of Nigeria), Kobina Sekyi and Alain Locke (USA); these last-named visitors came in 1928. After the hostel had been established the visitors list included the following names: the bishops and assistant bishop of Lagos, the Rev. A. G. Fraser (rector of Achimota College), Miss Margery Perham (St Hughes College, Oxford), Reginald Bridgeman (League Against Imperialism), Danquah, Dr F. V. Nanka-Bruce; professors B. Malinowski (London) and Macmillan (New York), and J. A. Rogers (New York).[117] There were also guests who stayed for a few days at the hostel either in transit or on arrival in London before finding permanent accommodation. Thus the WASU hostel expressly served both as a kind of port of call for Africans, who despite the basically liberal attitudes prevalent in Britain frequently had difficulty in finding lodgings, and also as a means of overcoming racial prejudice.[118]   The occupants of the WASU hostel were by no means confined to students; among them were Africans who had already made their name, including the following for the period between 1933 and 1936: Dr M. A. S. Margai, later the first prime minister of Sierra Leone; H. O. Davies, in 1944–5 acting warden of the WASU hostel during Solanke's second publicity campaign in West Africa and later one of the leading politicians of independent Nigeria; and J. Dube, South Africa.[119]

The WASU hostel was unable to support itself from its own resources, especially as some of its occupants were behindhand with their payments.[120] It was therefore always dependent upon contributions and subsidies. Despite this fact WASU refused a grant from the Colonial Office in 1933 to escape government control.[121] Not until 1937 did the organization accept such support, after an official of the Colonial Office, Major Hanns Vischer, had acted as intermediary. As treasurer Vischer supervised the hostel's financial affairs without infringing WASU's political independence. From 1937 onwards WASU also received for the hostel an annual subsidy of £250 from the Nigerian Colonial administration. In addition rather small but regular contributions were made by local autonomous bodies in West Africa, especially the native administrations in Nigeria, as well as by individuals such as Paul Robeson, WASU's patron.

Finally WASU published a journal of its own. This was intended to be a quarterly; from time to time attempts were made to publish it once a month, but they could not be kept up. There is a yawning gap between January 1929 and December 1932, when Solanke was away in West Africa. The journal's layout and content varied, as did its title and subtitle. The title at first ran *Wasu (preach). The Journal of the West African Students' Union in Great Britain*; from 1935 onwards the words 'and Ireland' were added to the subtitle. In 1940 the term 'Magazine' replaced 'Journal'; in 1945 it was called '*WASU Magazine, published by . . .*'; from February 1956 to April 1957 it became '*WASU News Service. Official Organ of the . . .*',[122] and from May 1957 onwards, '*The West African Students. Official Organ of . . .*'. The editors of earlier years included J. W. de Graft-Johnson[123] and Danquah.

The character of the journal changed considerably in the course of time. The issues between 1927 and 1933 were by no means of 'exceptionally high quality'.[124] The contributions, in prose and verse, were usually tinged with hyperbole, and the emotional tone sometimes made for trashiness.[125] Like most WASU members, Solanke hailed from Nigeria (he was a Yoruba) and this was reflected in the great preference given to themes about the Yoruba, their traditions and customs.[126] The numbers published between 1935 and 1937 were more modest in size and presentation, and during World War II the journal was little more than an information sheet containing official annual reports and balance sheets. From March 1945 onwards the presentation was again reminiscent of that of the first series, but between March 1945 and the summer of 1948 only five issues appeared. Thereafter the journal increasingly bore the character of an organ for the political education of African students. It adopted a strong anti-colonial and anti-imperialist line, without being blind to developments of a dubious kind in the independent Africa that was now emerging.[127]

The value of WASU's journal thus lies not in its literary quality, which is not remarkable, but in its wealth of detailed comment about the internal affairs of WASU. It occasionally gave the gist of lectures held at the WASU hostel, and during World War II of the conferences organized by WASU.[128] Moreover in the pages of this journal one may follow that process of growing politicization which finally led to African independence.

The same development is also manifest in the history of WASU itself. To a greater extent than its predecessors it soon became politically oriented and an instrument of African nationalism. Its speakers and friends ceaselessly repeated the demand for a politically independent federation embracing British West Africa. At an early date Solanke and de Graft-Johnson gave this programme literary expression.[129] They were aware of their own historical position: 'The European Great War of 1914 has let loose the spirit of Nationalism and it behoves us to conserve our energy in tune with the policy of WASU remembering that our ultimate aim and object in view being West African National Independence, we must be ready to pay its cost.'[130] On the whole they reacted negatively to the phenomena of fascism and national socialism, even though J. B. Danquah, one early leader of WASU, vacillated; in the journal he published on the Gold Coast he first adopted a pro-German attitude, but then, appalled by the excesses against the Jews, published articles by German authors directed against Nazism.[131] One should not be deluded by the admiration occasionally expressed for the 'strong man',[132] nor by the use of the swastika as an ornamental border in one issue of *WASU* published in 1929.[133] As early as 1933 the journal gave the following warning against Hitler:

> Nationalism on the lines of Mussolinism or Fascism may not be a bad thing, but nationalism on the lines of Hitlerism or Nazism is nothing less than fanaticism. Inasmuch as Herr Hitler's aim is national isolation, he is embarking on a dangerous game – the sort of game which put him and his country, so many years behindhand in politics, economics and civilisation. . . . Once a first-class civilised power, hospitable to black and white alike, Germany, under the rule of Hitler is now following the wake of the blood-hunting savage white of the Southern States of the United States of America, by murdering and tormenting Jews, and ill-treating Negroes and Indians, or rather people who have been unfortunate to be non-Aryan.[134]

The hostilities in Abyssinia intensified the general tendency to take a political stand, as it did among Africans and Afro-Americans generally.

Seen in the context of its overall political objectives the founding generation of WASU styled itself as conservative, and in particular made much of its adherence to peaceful and constitutional actions.[135] During the Italo-Abyssinian War WASU drifted into an anti-imperialist position.[136] When in 1938 it was rumoured that the former German colonies would be returned to the Third Reich, and that even Nigeria would be ceded, WASU protested against the idea and sought the backing of liberal and socialist groups.[137] During World War II WASU was recognized by the British government as a mouthpiece of African nationalism. Thus it is only logical that it participated actively in the fifth Pan-African Congress in Manchester and that after this it continued to be a focal point of Pan-African activity.[138]

15 Nationalist groups in France: the roots of Négritude

It was only from 1920 onwards that proto-nationalist and nationalist movements emerged among francophone Africans and Afro-Americans and that contacts were forged between the anglophone and francophone areas of the continent. During the nineteenth century nationalist and proto-Pan-African trends were confined to the British colonies, and the Pan-African Conference of 1900 had no French-speaking participants. Except for the Maghreb, the *African Times and Orient Review* also ignored the French territories in Africa. On the other hand in 1906 there lived in France a Senegalese called Moussa Mangoumbel who strove, with Booker T. Washington's blessing, to promote understanding among negroes throughout the world.[1]

The politicizing effect of World War I

The politicizing effect of World War I was most apparent among French-speaking Africans and Afro-West Indians. Hundreds of thousands of Africans – from Algeria, Morocco, Senegal and Dahomey – fought in the French army and played a considerable part in the defence of France. After the war recognition of the contribution they had made was symbolized by the honours officially bestowed by the French Republic upon Blaise Diagne.[2] The mass of the *tirailleurs* who survived returned to their African homelands, inspired with vague new political ideas and impressed by the relative racial tolerance of the French. Some remained in France or returned there. Besides Paris they settled in the south, especially in the harbour areas of Marseilles and Toulon; the situation was similar in Britain, where large numbers of coloured seamen arrived in the ports during the period of unrestricted submarine warfare and got stuck there after the end of the war.[3] At the same time francophone West Indians came to France from Guadeloupe and Martinique. In Paris, as in London, the newcomers (here North Africans, West Africans and West Indians) came into contact with native left-wing forces (mostly extreme and Marxist); in France the latter were better organized than in Britain and were under greater communist influence. The role of the Indians in England was played in France by the Indo-Chinese among whom Ho Chi Minh was already prominent.[4] Thus the politicization of the relatively small African and West Indian élite in France took place in closer connection with the general anti-colonial movement, which was already to some extent influenced by Communism.

Between 1920 and 1939 the West African and West Indian elements set up some organizations and journals of their own, which at first did not last long owing to chronic financial weakness and internal tensions. The latter conflicts were partly political in character, involving the attitude taken towards Communism; partly they were due to the different stage reached by West Indians and West Africans in the process of historical development. The West Indians, who had higher educational qualifications and generally a higher standard of living than the Africans, felt themselves superior in civilization; the latter for their part regarded the West Indians as arrogant and felt that they themselves knew more about Africa's problems. Generally speaking, the West Indians were more moderate, the Africans more radical. Most organizations were penetrated by informers working for the colonial power, so that the best sources on the history of these groups are the agents' reports in the French Colonial Ministry archives. These reports were frequently accompanied by specimens of incriminating journals,[5] which makes them twice as valuable, since these journals are not to be found in public libraries.

The first steps to organization in Paris: Hunkarin, Tovalou-Houénou and Lamine Senghor (1920–27)

The first attempt to organize Africans and West Indians in Paris, by Louis Hunkarin, is characterized by a curious mixture of African provincialism and (communist) internationalism.[6] Hunkarin was born in Porto Novo, Dahomey, in 1887 but studied at the famous École Normale de Saint Louis in Dakar. On his return to his homeland he came into conflict with the governor of Dahomey. Later he edited for Blaise Diagne in Dakar the journal *La Démocratie du Sénégal*. In December 1914 he was arrested in Dahomey, but escaped to Nigeria where he published an illegal handwritten periodical. When Diagne came to Dahomey in 1918 on his recruiting campaign he got Hunkarin's sentence rescinded and made him his collaborator in recruiting African volunteers for the French army; finally he worked in the French War Ministry. After the end of the war Hunkarin again broke with Diagne and in November 1920 founded in Paris the journal *Le Messager Dahoméen*, the first paper in France to serve the African and West Indian population.

With Hunkarin and *Le Messager Dahoméen* the most varied elements were closely combined. He was at least sympathetic to the French Communist party (PCF), and one of his closest collaborators, Max Bloncourt, was a functionary in it. *Le Messager Dahoméen*, however, advocated assimilation in the French colonial empire, although upon the basis of political and social equality. On the other hand in the middle of 1921 Hunkarin appealed in his journal for an all-embracing organization of West Africans and participated, as did Bloncourt, in the second Pan-African Congress of 1921. Moreover, Bloncourt made some positive though not uncritical remarks about Garvey. Finally, Hunkarin belonged to the group centred around the periodical *Action Coloniale*, out of which emerged in 1921 the Union Intercoloniale, the first association to unite intellectuals from the French colonies who had, as it were, emigrated to the metropolis. Active in this association were nationalists like the Vietnamese Nguyen Ali Quoc (Ho Chi Minh), the Algerians Hadjali Abdelkader and Messali Hadj, and the West Africans Lamine Senghor, Émile Faure and Timeko Garan Kouyauté.

A key position was occupied by Ho Chi Minh. After he went to Moscow in 1923 the Union Intercoloniale soon lost historical importance, although it continued to exist for several years. The PCF gained its greatest influence upon the members of the Union Intercoloniale by means of evening courses, from which the Africans and Asians who attended, most of whom were self-taught, frequently obtained the first elements of a modern education. Another medium was *Paria*, the Union Intercoloniale's journal, which appeared in 1922 and 1923. It is worth noting that of the 2000 copies of *Paria* published 500 went to Dahomey alone, and that the readership also included large numbers of West Indians.

Among the contributors to *Paria* was the West Indian novelist René Maran who with his novel *Batouala*,[7] set in Africa, caused a general sensation and was awarded the coveted Prix Goncourt in 1921. He set in motion the discovery of Africa by Afro-American writers, and also, by several intermediate stages, the movement known as 'Négritude'. Maran was also important as an exponent of another group, the Ligue Universelle pour la Défense de la Race Noire (LUDRN), founded by Tovalou-Houénou in 1924; its journal was called *Les Continents*.

Like Hunkarin, Tovalou-Houénou was born in Dahomey in 1887. He was related to the last king of Dahomey, although his father, a wealthy merchant in Ouidah, had contributed to the defeat of this king, Gbéhanzin, by selling supplies to the colonial authorities. At the age of thirteen Tovalou-Houénou came to Bordeaux to attend secondary school; he went on to study law and was accepted into the Paris bar association in 1911. Until 1921 his career was characteristic of the small class of those who were anxious to assimilate and who collaborated with the French authorities. In 1921 he returned to Dahomey, where conversations with veterans from World War I made him look upon conditions in the French colonies more critically.

Tovalou-Houénou was driven to politics by an incident in a Montmartre restaurant in 1923, when he was the victim of an act of crude racial discrimination. He sued, won his case, and was awarded damages; afterwards he joined the circle around the Union Intercoloniale and entered into contact with the PCF. He wrote for the journal *Action Coloniale* and organized jointly with René Maran a series of lectures for fellow-Blacks under the title of 'Le Problème de la race noire'. Finally in 1924 he founded the LUDRN and the journal *Les Continents*. Despite his profound shock at the incident in Montmartre he did not yet agitate for separate African nationalism, but continued to work for assimilation in French society and close relations with France. Thus he could write in *Action Coloniale* on 25 August 1923: 'Tous mes compatriotes aiment la France.'[8] But he reproached the French representatives for betraying the country's revolutionary and republican traditions. Thus he rejected with irony the term of subjects (*sujets*) for Africans as inappropriate to a republican system.[9] Instead Tovalou-Houénou claimed for his fellow-countrymen the right to be citizens, even if not of France on the basis of complete integration and assimilation, then of their own autonomous state.[10]

From this sprang his sympathy for Garvey, whose plans for Liberia were supported by an appeal in *Les Continents*: 'We want a country of our own, a country where we can develop as a national power.'[11] Proximity to the Garvey movement is also indicated by the name of his new organization (Ligue Universelle pour la Défense de la Race Noire; cf. Universal Negro Improvement Association), its general objectives,[12] and the fact that in August 1924 Tovalou-Houénou spoke at the UNIA convention in New York and had himself elected successor to the mayor of of Monrovia, Gabriel Johnson, as 'potentate', the most senior officer of the UNIA. There were also links between Garvey's *Negro World* and *Les Continents*. They lost importance during Tovalou-Houénou's long absence from Paris and only survived until the beginning of 1925. In that year he had to return to Dahomey under pressure from the colonial authorities, which put an end to his influence in LUDRN.

In Tovalou-Houénou's absence René Maran dominated the scene. Although he crusaded against abuses in the colonies in even sharper tones than Touvalou-Houénou, basically he adhered to the principle of assimilation. In *Les Continents* he was particularly violent in his criticism of Blaise Diagne, whom he reproached for the fact that as a recruiting commissioner he had received a monetary premium for each African he had persuaded to enlist. This led to a libel suit in November 1924; *Les Continents* lost the case, with the result that it soon ceased to exist, but the affair undermined even further Diagne's prestige among nationalist groups. From 1922 onwards (until his death in 1934) they regarded Diagne as a traitor to their race because he had come to an arrangement with the colonial establishment in Senegal.

J. S. Spiegler sees the historical significance of LUDRN and *Les Continents*, negligible and ephemeral as they were, in the fact that they anticipated practically all the later organizations and journals set up by Africans and Afro-West Indians in France between the two World Wars, whether they were moderate or radical and whether their nationalism was of the cultural or political variety.[13]

After an interval of one year the Comité de Défense de la Race Nègre (CDRN) replaced LUDRN. Its journal, *La Voix des Nègres*, however, only appeared from January to April 1927. Its leading personality was Lamine Senghor, formerly a Senegalese rifleman who had been gassed during the war and was thereafter an incurable invalid; he died at the age of thirty-eight in November 1927.[14] In contrast to Hunkarin and Tovalou-Houénou he was a complete autodidact, whom the experience of war had made politically conscious. In 1919 he was demobilized in Senegal but in 1922 returned to Paris. By way of the Union Intercoloniale he joined the PCF and Tovalou-Houénou's LUDRN. His first public political action was his appearance as a witness for René Maran against Diagne in the big libel suit taken out by *Les Continents* in 1924. After LUDRN and *Les Continents* had suddenly ceased to exist he continued his attacks on Diagne. The first issue of *La Race Nègre*, published in June 1927, contained a brutal caricature of Diagne, with the caption: 'Il y a plus de 2000 ans, la France, ma patrie, s'appelait la Gaule, et mes aïeux les Gaulois.'

The CDRN leadership consisted of three Africans and three West Indians. Of the Africans the most important were Senghor and Kouyauté, at that time still a student from the Sudan (the modern Mali); there was also another representative from Senegal, Masse N'Diaye, who like Senghor had fought in World War I. Aware of his approaching death, Senghor, who must have had an impressive personality, plunged into almost feverish political activity. He organized African dockers and seamen in French ports, whose conditions of life and political ideas are graphically depicted by Claude McKay in his *roman à clef* entitled *Banjo*.[15] The climax came with his active participation in the congress of the League Against Imperialism, held in Brussels in February 1927 several months before his death, in which he headed the commission on the negro question.[16]

After Senghor had returned from Brussels his organization crumbled. A schism developed between the West Indian and West African elements, whereupon in May 1927 Senghor founded the Ligue de Défense de la Race Nègre (LDRN), which in June 1927 published a journal of its own, *La Race Nègre*.

National independence and cultural revival : Kouyauté and Émile Faure (1927–39)

After Senghor's death in November 1927 Kouyauté took charge of the LDRN. Like Senghor, he was a member of the PCF. In the subsequent years a reunion with the West Indians must have taken place, because after a further schism at the end of 1930 or beginning of 1931 – this time already for political reasons, connected with Kouyauté's liaison with the communists – we once again find West Indians in one of the rival groups; among them was André Béton, a lawyer and elder brother of Isaac Béton.[17] From the middle of 1931 until 1936 there were apparently two journals entitled *La Race Nègre*, one published by Kouyauté and the other by Émile Faure, the representative of the more moderate group. *La Race Nègre* served to provide information and to articulate ideas. In the forefront of its interest were Afro-Americans in the USA, above all the Garvey movement, and various groups in England such as WASU, the Negro Welfare Association, etc. The ideas put forward in *La Race Nègre* already show a Pan-African content. After Tovalou-Houénou's vague appeal to set up a comprehensive organization embracing the whole Black race, while adhering to the principle of assimilation, the attempt was made to define more exactly the organization's political objectives.[18] Sharper criticism was now made of Western civilization, which was identified with the colonial system.[19] As early as 1927 one finds the demands for political independence in connection with the claim to the right of self-determination.[20]

Under the influence of the League Against Imperialism, to which Kouyauté expressly referred at the beginning of 1929, he submitted a draft programme for the LDRN. Emulating the example of the Indo-Chinese revolutionaries, with their demand for national independence, he voiced the demand for independence for Africa. Vietnamese, North Africans and negroes were to erect national states upon the débris of colonialism, taking as their watchword 'détruire et reconstruire'.[21]

The programme was intended to appeal to all Africans and Afro-Americans (except for some in Latin American states because racial prejudice was rigorously suppressed there) as well as negroid tribes in Oceania and India. Particular prominence was given to the 'peuples nègres semi-colonisés' in Haiti, the 'peuples nègres nationaux' in the USA and the 'peuples nègres indépendents' in Ethiopia and Liberia. To realize this programme the negroes should join the League *en masse* and seek the support of the oppressed peoples in Europe, Asia and America, as well as intellectual and manual workers in France: 'Racial prejudice will be overcome once a great Negro state will have been erected upon modern foundations: African Zionism. The peoples will get on together because they will live within a framework of national freedom and international equality.'[22]

Elements of the most diverse traditions are intermingled here: Afro-Asian and proletarian solidarity, Garveyism and a touching dash of optimism straight from the Enlightenment. In the wake of the cultural movement 'Back to Africa' which had begun in the United States with the Harlem renaissance, the LDRN (É. Faure's group) withdrew a few years later into the mysticism of Négritude – without of course employing the name (first used by Senghor in 1939). A major leading article in *La Race Nègre* equated the achievement of political independence with the revival of Africa's ancient civilization, quoting the popular phrase from Claude McKay's *Banjo* to the effect that by returning to the roots of one's own race one was not reverting to barbarism but giving expression to one's own culture.[23] This romantic and restorationist programme was substantiated with well-known arguments taken from the arsenal of Afro-American doctrine.[24] Outright hostility towards modern White industrialism was combined with mystical references to a specifically African humanism opposed to the vicious individualism of the West.

For Pan-Africanism in the narrower political sense the last point of the programme is important. The LDRN sought to set up a unitary negro state embracing the entire continent of Black Africa and the West Indies. It was not to be built on the basis of Black racism, because in it the racial question was to become simply an element of pluralism, promoting a healthy sense of competition.[25]

In the crisis of conscience provoked by Italy's attack on Abyssinia, the francophone groups were caught up in the surge of indignation that affected Africans and Afro-Americans everywhere. Solidarity against Italian colonial expansion led to unity between groups that had been hostile to one another for years, and even to occasional joint demonstrations being staged.[26] From 1934 onwards George Padmore had relatively close links with Émile Faure in Paris, with whom he saw eye to eye in his mistrust of the African policy of international Communism and the PCF.[27] The Popular Front government, it is true, seemed to bring some respite; but the negligible step it took benefited assimilationist forces in Algeria rather than the militant critics of French colonial policy.[28] The outbreak of World War II and the accession to power of the Vichy régime so thoroughly smashed the incipient political movements in the negro part of French Africa that after 1945 the new groups that arose there had almost no connection with earlier traditions.[29] Political continuity had been virtually broken, leaving it to the historian to rediscover the role played by francophone groups between the two World Wars.[30]

The roots of Négritude : Primitivism, the 'New Negro' movement and modern ethnology

The francophone proto-nationalists and nationalists belong to the prehistory of the Négritude movement, the most vital contribution which they made to modern Pan-Africanism. Originally this was an almost wholly literary, philosophical and cultural group which did not adopt political overtones until long after World War II. Its most important representatives were (and are) Jean Price-Mars (Haiti), Aimé Césaire (Martinique) and Léopold S. Senghor (Senegal). About Négritude and its literary exponents there already exists an extensive literature, most of which is, however, aesthetic in character and not relevant to our theme here.[31] It is not necessary for us to analyse the poems of Césaire and Senghor, but simply to outline and set in its historical context the immediate prehistory of the Négritude movement; this account will be based mainly upon the unpublished thesis of J. Hymans (Paris).

Although neither Césaire nor Senghor were members of any of the militant groups in Paris, the appearance of the Négritude movement is unthinkable without preliminary work in the field of ideas, as a result of which contact was established during the 1920s with the anglophone area, especially the Afro-American literary milieu. The immediate prehistory of the Négritude movement illustrates once again the manifold influences exerted to and fro across the Atlantic; at the same time it affords unusual evidence of the interpenetration of francophone and anglophone areas. The chief intermediaries on each side were the few bilingual leaders: in the anglophone area Claude McKay in particular[32] and on the francophone side Mlle Paulette Nardal from Martinique, who studied English philology in Paris and had a perfect command of the English language.[33]

McKay led an itinerant life which brought him by way of Berlin and

Moscow to France, where for several years he combined keen observation of conditions there with the establishment of personal contacts, so that his novel *Banjo* exerted a considerable influence upon francophone groups.[34] Paulette Nardal's influence, on the other hand, was due rather to her relatively stationary life during the years in question. In Paris she ran a literary salon where a large number of Afro-Americans and Africans could meet. It became the intellectual centre of a new journal, *La Revue du Monde Noir*, which appeared in November 1931 and which she edited. It was published in French and English, a noteworthy achievement which was only to be attained again in the 1960s with *La Présence Africaine* and various Pan-African journals published officially by Nkrumah's Ghana. Among the contributors to *La Revue du Monde Noir* were René Maran, Claude McKay, Alain Locke, Langston Hughes, Price-Mars, Delafosse, Leo Frobenius (a translation of one contribution from his pen appeared in the issue for March 1932) and Félix Eboué, who in World War II was the first French colonial governor to declare his loyalty to de Gaulle's Free France. The younger members grouped around Paulette Nardal included Léopold S. Senghor, who thus gained admittance into the literary milieu of the *quartier latin*.

These facts are insufficient to reveal the historical roots of the Négritude movement, which has to be seen against the wider background of the general crisis of consciousness in the modern world evoked by the coming of industrialism. Just as European romanticism, as a response to the challenge of the French Revolution of 1789 and the incipient industrial revolution, led some thinkers to advocate a return to the ideals of the Christian Middle Ages, so later, as the pace of industrialization accelerated at the turn of the century, a tendency emerged to evoke an even more distant past. Thus in Germany an escape was sought by cultivating the supposed values of the ancient Teutons; in France several artists, Gauguin in particular, as early as the late nineteenth century pointed the way 'back to nature' to the 'noble savage'. Shortly before World War I the discovery of Primitivism and Exoticism as new forms of artistic expression, together with Expressionism and the Youth movement, served as means of conveying the widespread sense of dismay entertained about an industrial society that was becoming ever more complex and could no longer be mastered intellectually. World War I generalized and exacerbated this European and North American 'crisis of consciousness', which previously had been experienced only by those of finer sensibilities. This spiritual crisis came into contact with another form of the same crisis in the non-White world – one which developed out of the clash between modern society and the traditional values of the Asian, African and Afro-Asian peoples who had now attained a greater degree of self-awareness and whose expectations had been stimulated by modernization.

For some elements of the Afro-American intelligentsia World War I brought a new 'Back to Africa' movement, which had been anticipated by Du Bois during the pre-war period and was unskilfully propagated by Garvey. In 1921 René Maran's novel *Batouala* introduced for the first time an (apparently) genuine African component, which went far beyond the synthetic neo-romanticism of Du Bois's poetry ('A Day in Africa').[35] Maran exerted an influence across the Atlantic and outside the francophone area. He became the catalyst of a new artistic movement, the Harlem renaissance or New Negro movement, named after the anthology published by Alain Locke in 1925.[36] Actively promoted by Du Bois, the talented young men of the New Negro movement, especially Langston Hughes, Countee Cullen and Claude McKay, celebrated their rediscovery of Africa and the African cultural heritage in Harlem, within a White industrialized world – a world which they regarded as hostile, although its open-minded intellectuals looked upon Africa and its culture as 'chic' and eagerly cultivated the representatives of the New Negro movement.[37] Harlem at that time was still a mixed area, with artistic taverns, bars and places of amusement, and became the Mecca of the exponents of this new cultural mood; it found expression in music, especially in blues, jazz and negro spirituals.[38]

The New Negro movement in the meantime had had repercussions across the Atlantic in France. Already under Tovalou-Houénou the journal *Les Continents* welcomed this literary movement, which had been inspired by one of its own prominent contributors and formed an important bridge to the later Négritude movement. In Paris in the spring of 1924 Tovalou-Houénou organized musical evenings with jazz and negro spirituals.[39] A few years later the same tradition was continued consciously and systematically by Paulette Nardal in her circle and in *La Revue du Monde Noir*. One of those who frequented her literary salon was Alain Locke, of whom Claude McKay thought very little: '. . . . a Philadelphia blue-black blood, a Rhodes scholar and graduate of Oxford University . . . seemed a perfect symbol of the Afro-American rocow in his personality as much as in his prose style.'[40] The New

Negro group visited Paris privately in 1928,[41] and on this occasion inspired the francophone group to interest itself more intensely in the findings of modern ethnology[42] as a discipline concerned professionally with the society and culture of 'primitive man'. In this way the French champion of a humane policy in the French colonies, Maurice Delafosse, likewise found his way into Paulette Nardal's intellectual milieu; so too did Leo Frobenius, the German Africanist, who may be regarded as one of the first Europeans to have shown that traditional African culture possessed an intrinsic value;[43] others in this category included Diedrich Westermann and M. J. Herskovits, the American Africanist.

Jean Price-Mars

Interest in ethnology and Africa's traditional cultural heritage accounted for the strong influence exerted by Jean Price-Mars upon the leaders of the Négritude movement. His career took him to and fro across the Atlantic following the classical route of the Pan-African triangle, and also across the English–French language barrier. Price-Mars was born at Grande Rivière du Nord, northern Haiti, in 1876. He was descended from an Afro-American family which had immigrated from the United States during the nineteenth century and had since become completely assimilated into Haitian culture. They spoke colloquial French and only their adherence to Protestantism and their English pronunciation of the name Price reflected their American origin. Price-Mars attended the Collège Grégoire at Cap Haitien, the Lycée Pétion at Port-au-Prince and the École de Médicine at Paup. He completed his medical studies in 1900 in Paris, where he met Anténor Firmin in the Haitian Legation. At first he entered upon a diplomatic career which took him by way of Berlin, where he was a secretary in the Legation in 1903, to Washington and then to Paris, where he was chargé d'affaires in 1915. Between 1918 and 1930 he taught sociology at his native Lycée Pétion.[44]

Two events, one of a political, the other of a cultural nature, proved significant for him during these years. In 1915 Haiti was occupied by the American marines, thereby virtually losing its independence for about twenty years.[45] In 1927 a group of talented poets returned to Haiti from Paris, where they had participated in the new movement of Exoticism and Negroism.[46]

The American occupation accentuated Haiti's long-standing national crisis of consciousness, to such a point that it undermined the tendency towards cultural assimilation which had been maintained since independence. At any rate some young intellectuals turned against modern civilization as such. Attempts were made by the Union Patriotique, organized by Georges Sylvain, to gather all the forces in Haiti opposed to American intervention. One of the leading members of the Union Patriotique was Price-Mars. The occupation indirectly led to the forging of new contacts with quasi-oppositional forces in the USA, especially with the NAACP (although Price-Mars may have already established such contact earlier while he was in the USA). Its secretary, James W. Johnson, visited Haiti in 1920; this was the preliminary to a campaign launched by the NAACP to enlighten people about conditions in Haiti and the drastic actions undertaken by the US marines.[47]

The collapse of Haitian independence forced the critical intellectuals back upon themselves and their African heritage. Price-Mars found traces of this heritage, greatly transformed, among the peasants and smallholders, most of whom were Black, and especially in the Voodoo cult.[48] In an ethnological study published in 1928, which is still of historical importance today, he gave a lead to his disoriented fellow-countrymen by extolling this African heritage.[49] He elevated to the rank of an independent and valuable culture the customs, hitherto despised as semi-heathen, practised by the rural population, which in their complexion and way of life were closer to their original African homeland. Under the obvious influence of Du Bois, whose two small but very important works *The Souls of Black Folk* (1903) and *The Negro* (1915) appear in his bibliography, he introduced for the first time (apart from the Frenchman Delafosse) a historical dimension into the thinking of francophone pan-Africans, by referring to the early African kingdoms in western Sudan, Ghana, Mali and Songhai.

By rehabilitating and idealizing the African substratum in Haitian society, Price-Mars identified himself with the worldwide trend that extended from European romanticism, through the Irish renaissance and the Teutonic revival, to modern Exoticism and Primitivism. The Harlem renaissance was introduced directly to Haiti[50] by writers who on their return from Paris published the journals *Revue Indigène*[51] and *Relève* in conjunction with Price-Mars.

Price-Mars's historical influence was greater in the rest of the French-speaking world than in Haiti once it became apparent that its political misery had undergone little change after the end of the American occupation under Franklin D. Roosevelt.[52] It was no coincidence that *Ainsi parla l'Oncle* also appeared in Paris. Here Price-Mars found a response among African and West Indian students and *literati*, workers and employees who, like the young Haitian intellectuals, felt 'alienated', cut off from their traditional culture and repelled by their modern environment. To them Price-Mars opened up a new world which they avidly absorbed. Twenty years later Léopold S. Senghor may have exaggerated with poetic licence the impression Price-Mars (and Locke) made upon him;[53] nevertheless the influence which the former exerted upon intelligent young francophone negroes must have been considerable, especially since it extended over several decades.

At the beginning of the 1930s Price-Mars belonged to the group around Paulette Nardal and the contributors to *La Revue du Monde Noir*, the direct predecessor of the later Négritude movement. After World War II he was a mentor of Présence Africaine, a group which continued to propagate the same intellectual impulses from Paris and is still active today. He played a significant part in the two congresses of African authors held in Paris and Rome in 1956 and 1959, and also at the great Festival des Arts Nègres held in Dakar in 1966 under Senghor's patronage. All in all Price-Mars enjoys a reputation in the Black francophone milieu equalled only by that of Du Bois among anglophone negroes; Price-Mars, however, was never involved in such bitter polemics as was Du Bois. The fact that at the age of ninety Price-Mars still wrote a biography of Anténor Firmin, the most powerful and last exponent of the modernization of Haiti on the basis of European tradition,[54] does him a dual honour: on one hand, it shows that after having exerted an almost worldwide influence, he returned to his Haitian origins; on the other hand it shows that he is well aware of the ambivalent role Haiti has played in modern history.

The beginnings of Négritude: Aimé Césaire and Léopold S. Senghor

The discovery of Africa's ancient history must have made a particularly profound impression upon the African and West Indian intellectuals who gathered in the Latin Quarter. Later Senghor himself drew attention to the tremendous consolation he received from the thought of ancient Egypt's greatness when he and his comrades felt depressed at all the difficulties that faced them.[55] This illuminates very well the function which this historical doctrine fulfilled as a means of overcoming the negroes' collective inferiority complex.[56] A generation later a detailed exposition of the same theme by Sheikh Ante Diop evoked what was almost an intellectual revolution among African students in Paris, who by then were much more numerous – although as mentioned above, this thesis was for the anglophone countries a long-standing tradition.[57]

After *La Revue du Monde Noir* and Price-Mars there was another preliminary stage before the Négritude movement actually began. This came in 1932, when the journal *La Légitime Défense* was published by some students from Martinique, among them Étienne Léro; the latter identified himself simultaneously with surrealism and the proletariat.[58]

In 1934 matters had finally reached the point where Senghor and Césaire could found a journal of their own, *L'Étudiant Noir*, in which for the first time they set out their own literary conception of Négritude – the stress on all African elements, especially the cult of Black womanhood (cf. Senghor: 'Femme nue, femme noire'), the rejection of modern civilization (Césaire: *Cahier d'un Retour au Pays Natal*) and the glorification of the wild African landscape. The quintessence of Négritude is the unlimited positive evaluation given to the fact of being Black – in the New World as in Africa. Thus the lyrical Pan-Africanism of Senghor and Césaire turns out to be just a new way of compensating psychologically for the inferiority complex induced by historical experience. In 1934 Senegalese students in Paris founded a students' union, L'Association des Étudiants Ouest-Africains, apparently conceived, as the name indicates, as a body corresponding to WASU, even though it is not yet possible to prove a direct link between the two organizations. The chairmanship fell to Senghor, and it is therefore not surprising that the union's activities included the recital of Afro-American poetry.[59]

During his time in Paris Senghor, like Césaire (they met in Paris in 1929), traversed almost the entire political spectrum from communist sympathies to fascism. This range of political and intellectual options should no longer surprise us, considering the inborn eclecticism and confusion of the heterogeneous elements that made up Pan-Africanism. The temporary communist influences may easily be explained by the link between the forerunners of Négritude and the PCF from 1920 onwards, from Hunkarin to Kouyauté,[60] as well as by the efforts of the communists between the two World Wars to win over the young African and Afro-American intelligentsia[61] by promoting a common struggle against the (White or capitalist) industrial order with all its consequences (imperialism, colonialism etc.). For those Négritude groups who were more interested in cultural matters, especially poetry, than the rigidities of politics the communist journal *Le Nouvel Âge* offered a point of contact, because from October 1931 onwards it published, as did *La Revue du Monde Noir*, French translations of Afro-American 'New Negro' verse. After many ups and downs the Popular Front period in France brought about a high point of communist sympathies – as happened at this time in Britain, too.

At first glance the temporary affinity with German national socialism must come as a surprise, if only because of the anti-negro element in Nazi racial ideology. On closer observation the affinity does, however, acquire plausibility. We have a hint of it in the fact that the Négritude movement emerged out of the study of ethnology[62] which, with its professional predilection for what is ancient and traditional, may easily foster conservative, indeed reactionary attitudes, unless approached with extreme caution. Thus Senghor eagerly seized on the fanciful discovery by Leo Frobenius that the negro soul and the German soul were related.[63] This statement by Frobenius recalls Casely Hayford's recommendation to Emperor William II at the beginning of the century that he should read the works of Blyden (venerated by Casely and regarded as the intellectual forerunner of Négritude) because (not meaning this ironically) the German emperor would find here some parallels with German thought.[64] What is correct here is the fact that German romanticism, like German *Kulturkritik* later, reacted to the challenge of the industrial revolution and its tensions by escaping into a transfigured past with its mystique of the *Volk* and folk culture; in this it had much in common with the irrational and romantic trend in Pan-Africanism from Blyden down to Senghor and Nkrumah. From this point it was not such a great leap to emphasis on race, blood and soil. Thus at this time Senghor could cite approvingly a key quotation from Gobineau in which the latter tried to prove the principle of racial inequality,[65] probably without knowing that Anténor Firmin, the political model of his idol Price-Mars, had written an anti-Gobineau tract almost half a century before in order to prove that all men were equal.[66] But Gobineau had only achieved intellectual importance because his ideas were taken up again by German racial ideologues towards the close of the nineteenth century.[67]

During the years between 1929 and 1933, when Senghor was closest to German national socialism, one could see the parallels clearly – as Senghor himself later admitted: rejection of modern industrial society, anti-rationalism, emphasis on the will, a desire to return to 'natural', 'organic' systems etc. Senghor and Césaire, the most articulate representatives of the young francophone African and West Indian intelligentsia, cultivated a kind of anti-intellectualism, became intoxicated with an African myth of blood and soil,[68] and carried on a private war against civilization – so that the German Nazi racial theorists could have found in those angry young men from Senegal and Martinique a surprising intellectual affinity, if they had ever bothered about their literary works. The establishment of the Third Reich quickly led Senghor to take a more sober view, as did the Popular Front; nevertheless traces were left behind by the irrational mystic element of the Négritude movement, which at least in theory came close to racism.

These reflections, which may seem to have taken us away from our principal theme, should make it easier to place the Négritude movement in its proper historical context. Neither in subject matter nor in content was it original. It was merely a reaction by francophone West Africans and West Indians to the universal problem of confrontation between new and old.

By comparison with the English-speaking countries involved in Pan-Africanism this reaction came about after a considerable delay, which may explain why it exploded so suddenly. The only original thing about it is the manner in which it formulated its rejection of modern civilization, its protest against White supremacy, and its poetry in French with traditional African rhythms. But even here the Négritude movement adhered closely to the stylistic forms of European surrealism and primitivism, which it developed for its own purposes.[69]

The exuberance of lyrical Pan-Africanism, of the Négritude movement, has generally met with caution, indeed open rejection, in English-speaking countries.[70] But they have not recognized that their own brand of Pan-Africanism, with its more political slant, manifested the same basic eclecticism and confusion as did the lyrical Pan-Africanism of the Négritude movement. It is simply that the former generally speaking adopted a more restrained and pragmatic tone, rooted in a literary tradition that was already a hundred years old and had acquired a venerable patina – and for this very reason may have been largely forgotten.[71]

PAM—M

16 Communist activities (1927–1934)

The almost simultaneous ending of Du Bois's Pan-African Congress movement and of Garveyism in about 1927 left a vacuum which for a time could not be filled by any of the other contenders in the field: WASU; the National Congress of British West Africa (which in any case ceased to exist in 1930); the incipient Négritude movement; or the League of Coloured Peoples, founded as late as 1931. Thus the greatest importance attaches to the communists' Pan-African efforts during an intermediary period of about seven years between 1927 and 1934, from the foundation of the League Against Imperialism (February 1927) to Padmore's break with Communism (1934), which introduced a new phase in the history of Pan-Africanism.[1]

Historical and organizational background

That the communists should have been interested in Pan-Africanism is no surprise. Both movements were opposed to colonialism and imperialism, although with a different degree of intensity and for different motives; this necessarily gave them a certain minimum of common ground. Moreover, even in Communism there is a dash of romanticism expressed in Communist states today, above all in the ostentatious cultivation of folklore, which has its analogy in the Africans' desire to revive their traditional cultural heritage. Naturally the communists were not primarily concerned with Pan-Africanism. On one hand their interest in Africans and Afro-Americans was just part of their efforts to promote world revolution, and on the other their support for national and social revolution in the colonies and underdeveloped countries has always been just a function of Soviet foreign policy. For this reason communist influence upon Pan-African movements was no more than an episode, which began during the first years after Lenin's death, when Soviet Russia was still isolated but had already consolidated its power.

Before World War I the early Pan-Africans in Britain had first found backing on the left wing of political opinion: before 1900 predominantly among radicals and humanitarians who carried on the abolitionist tradition, and then among socialists, from Keir Hardie to Ramsay MacDonald and Creech-Jones.[2] After 1917–18 some African and Afro-American soldiers acquired their first modern political ideas through contact with Marxists and communists, as Claude McKay suggests.[3]

On the other hand, after 1919 the communists, as the most radical left-wing elements, sought allies among the colonial peoples against the established order. Since the West European, especially the German, revolution, to which in Lenin's view the October revolution was but a prelude, had failed to take place, it was natural for them to hope for compensation in upheavals in the colonies, which might serve to deflect the attention of their enemies who threatened them with counter-revolution, civil war and intervention. The Communist International therefore at an early date placed the colonial revolution on its agenda. Social and political circumstances caused its interest to be focused upon those areas that were relatively the most developed – China and India, North Africa and the Union of South Africa, and finally the Afro-Americans in the New World. The most important instruments of communist influence were the Communist International (Comintern), which held its congresses in Moscow, and later the Communist Trade Union International (Profintern).

During the turbulent initial years of the communist movement, above all at the second Comintern congress of 1920, in the exchange between Lenin and the Indian communist leader N. N. Roy,[30] the discussion revolved around the question of whether Communism was already strong enough in the colonial and semi-colonial countries to play an independent role and to struggle simultaneously against both the colonial powers and the developing indigenous national bourgeoisie, or whether it should rather form an alliance with incipient 'bourgeois' nationalism. Lenin favoured the latter policy, whereas Roy was for the former. The Comintern at first agreed upon a compromise which contained an inner contradiction.[4] Both alternative solutions of the problem soon failed: Lenin's in China, when in 1927 the Kuomintang suddenly turned against their Chinese communist allies; Roy's as the result of the communists' undeniable weakness in other areas.

The University of the Toilers of the East, at which Roy and Padmore taught for a time,[5] served to broaden the organizational basis of the movement and to recruit indigenous cadres. It was through this channel that some Africans and Afro-Americans visited the Soviet Union and came into contact with Communism. It was there that many of them obtained their first access to modern higher education, as others did with the aid of the communists in France or South Africa.

At both the fourth and fifth Comintern congresses Black delegates participated, which did something to remove the question from the plane of pure theory. From 1925 onwards the Comintern gave an impulse to the creation of new organizations which also had a partial or indirect effect upon the Pan-African movement.[6] The fifth Comintern congress resolved to proceed with the organization of the Afro-American working class in the USA, whereupon in October 1925 the American Negro Labor Congress was founded, with its centre in Chicago. The sixth Comintern congress in Moscow was attended by four Afro-American delegates from the USA, several others from Latin America and three Africans from the South African Communist party. In addition a number of Africans and Afro-Americans who lived in Moscow were invited to attend without the status of delegates. After the sixth congress the Comintern established its own Negro Bureau.

The most important areas from a Pan-African viewpoint into which communist influence could penetrate were France (Paris and the major ports in the south in particular), the Afro-American urban centres in the USA, and London. The method usually employed, especially in South Africa, was to penetrate militant organizations which already existed. On the other hand in France new organizations were founded which maintained close contact with the Communist party and were led by communists, such as the Union Intercoloniale and later groups in Paris.[7]

The League Against Imperialism and the Brussels congress of February 1927

Already at a relatively early stage an attempt was made to unite organizationally these various groups and tendencies within an international framework which exceeded the limits of Pan-Africanism. This endeavour took place at the great foundation congress, held in Brussels in February 1927, of the League Against Imperialism and For National Independence (in the literature on the subject more generally known by the abbreviated name 'League Against Imperialism'). If one considers the historical situation at that time, it was a considerable achievement to have convened such a congress, attended by about 180 participants from Western Europe, North, Central and South America, the Caribbean, Africa and Asia. In accordance with Leninist strategy this congress brought about for the first time collaboration between communist and bourgeois-nationalist forces irrespective of race.[8] The organizer was Willi Münzenberg, one of the most capable brains of the German Communist party,[9] who arranged for the congress to be financed by Comintern.[10] The communist element kept in the background as far as it could. Officially it was represented only by organizations such as International Workers' Aid (one of the numerous organizations set up by Münzenberg), whose representative the latter was. Much more in evidence were pacifist organizations and left-wing socialist groups like the Independent Labour party, represented by its general secretary Fenner Brockway (now Lord Brockway), the Socialist League with Georg Ledebour, the Socialist League of Pupils of Greater Berlin, pacifist groups from various European countries, political parties, trade unions and other groups from the colonial countries and Latin America.

The Brussels congress and the League Against Imperialism which evolved out of it should neither be dismissed as a communist front organization nor inflated into part of a worldwide communist conspiracy.[11] One rather has to recognize the fact that Münzenberg and the Comintern, with their keen sense of the forces of change at work in world history, had hit upon a theme pregnant with future possibilities at a time when European colonialism was still almost unchallenged. A closer glance at the list of those who attended also prevents one from treating the Brussels congress in a disparaging or superficial way. The participants included leading intellectuals of the European left such as Henri Barbusse, who together with Albert Einstein and Mme Sun Yat Sen was elected to the honorary presidium, as well as Theodor Lessing, Fritz Sternberg and Paul-Henri Spaak. Among non-Europeans present we may single out Jawaharlal P. Nehru, Mohamed Hatta (Indonesia), Messali Hadj (Algeria) and Victor R. Haya della Torre (Peru).

At this worldwide gathering Africa and the 'negro question' (as it was called then) comprised but one theme among others. Africa was represented only on a negligible scale; but if we add the Afro-American representatives, we can say that there was a 'Black group' at the congress. From the era to which Pan-African ideas appealed the following persons came to Brussels. Three delegates were sent from the USA, of whom Richard B. Moore represented two organizations, the American Negro Labor Congress (Chicago) and the UNIA; (another Afro-American delegate, Professor William Pickens, who had been designated to represent the NAACP and the John Brown Memorial Association, was one of those who were unable to appear in time at the congress); one delegate, Carlos Deambrosis Martins, came from Haiti, sent by the Union Patriotique (curiously enough announced as Unione Patriotica); Black Africa was represented by Lamine Senghor (CDRN), J. T. Gumede and La Guma (South African National Congress); to these were added four delegates from the Union Intercoloniale (Max Bloncourt, Elie Clainville-Bloncourt, Camille Saint-Jacques, Danae Narcisse). North Africa was represented by two delegates from the Paris organization L'Étoile Nord-Africaine (Association des Musulmans algériens, tunisiens et marocains), Messali Hadj and Hadjali Abdelkader;[12] and finally by one delegate each from the Egyptian National party and the Egyptian National Radical party, Mohamed Hafiz Bey Ramadan and Ibrahim Youssef. British West Africa was completely unrepresented.

The Brussels congress served first and foremost to exchange information about conditions in various parts of the globe and to establish personal contacts. In order to be in a better position to deal with the negro question a commission was appointed, consisting of African and Afro-American delegates, which worked out a detailed resolution that was submitted to the plenary session.[13] The chairman was Lamine Senghor and the rapporteur R. B. Moore. Five members of the 'Negro delegation' (as it was officially called in the German text of the minutes) spoke in the session devoted to the negro question: Senghor, Max Bloncourt, Martins (Haiti), J. T. Gumede and Moore.[14] Senghor delivered a passionate speech against French colonial rule. At the beginning he attacked the assertion of the chairman of the session, Hafiz Bey Ramadan, that Egypt was not a colony but independent. He disposed of French colonialism with a few succinct points:

> Colonization: what is colonization? Colonization is the violation of the right of a people to be master of itself as it understands and desires. Civilization: I just told you that when the French came to us they said they were bringing us civilization. But instead of teaching us French and enlightening us about what they call civilization, they said that Negroes should not be given any education because otherwise they would become civilized and one would not be able to treat them as one wished. This is how French imperialism sees the process of civilizing the Negroes.

Senghor continued by giving examples of atrocities committed in the French colonies, quoted from a publication by a former French colonial official. He remarked: 'Who does not tremble at the thought that in the twentieth century Frenchmen could still perpetrate such cruelties, worthy of the darkest Middle Ages?' He went on to make equally poignant criticisms, substantiated by concrete figures, under the headings of 'forced labour' and 'slavery'. Slavery, he said, had not been abolished but only 'modernized'.

As one who had fought in the war Senghor launched a violent attack on Blaise Diagne, a fellow-countryman of his who had since attained social eminence, without, however, mentioning him by name. Illustrating the way in which revolutionary movements all over the world were linked by the dialectic of repression, he said: 'Negroes are sent to Madagascar, and Negroes are sent to Indochina, for it is close to China, which provides them with an excellent revolutionary model,'[15] adding: 'the Negroes have been asleep for too long. But beware, he who has slept too well and then awakes will not fall asleep again.'

Bitter personal experience inspired Senghor's remarks on the care of war-wounded. He listed crass cases of discrimination (the Whites were paid approximately six times as much as Africans) and drew the sarcastic conclusion: 'Negro youth is beginning to see matters clearly. We know and declare that we are Frenchmen when we are needed to be killed or to work. But if it is a matter of obtaining rights we are no longer Frenchmen but Negroes.'

Since negroes were denied equality and the chance to assimilate, he argued, the entire colonial system had to be destroyed. The language employed by Senghor (then with little longer to live) at the end of his speech, which was enthusiastically received, is so illuminating that it is worth quoting in detail:

> The congress assembled here has put into practice, I believe, the wish of many who, like myself, would be glad to devote themselves wholly to the liberation of the world. Those who have come here are the very ones who sacrifice all their energies to the revolutionary ideal in order to abolish the monster of imperialist oppression from the entire world. Imperialist oppression, which we call colonization and which you here call imperialism, is the same thing. It springs from capitalism. It is this that engenders imperialism among the peoples of the principal countries. For this reason those who are suffering from colonial oppression must join hands and stand together with those who are suffering from the imperialism of the principal countries. Fight with the same weapon and destroy the world evil – world imperialism. It must be destroyed and replaced by the union of free peoples and then there will no longer be any slavery.[16]

Senghor was followed to the tribune by Max Bloncourt, who spoke about the situation in the French Antilles. Although there was great misery there he feared an even greater evil than French rule: sale to the USA. Bloncourt expressly pointed to Haiti, which had been occupied from 1915 onwards, as an example of what to avoid. More detailed information about Haiti was given by Martins of the Union Patriotique, which was said to have 50,000 members. Martins accused the Americans in particular of suppressing the Haitian parliament in order to preserve their economic interests, of manipulating the government, and of suppressing the local press either by decisions of their own courtsmartial or by decrees of the Haitian government which they controlled. Finally he protested 'against the murder of more than three thousand Haitians who had been killed by Yankee forces in the course of their 11-year occupation'.

This description of the situation in Haiti was followed by a report on South Africa given by J. T. Gumede, the newly elected president of the

African National Congress. In line with the actual state of affairs in that country[17] it was dismal and depressing. Gumede combined a historical survey of developments since 1912 with a description of the present situation which left him but little hope of liberation. His concluding sentence breathed resignation rather than militancy: 'Humanity is suffering under the whip and torture of world imperialism and capitalism.'

In conclusion Richard B. Moore introduced the resolution of the 'Negro delegation'. His introductory remarks emphasized the need to forge solidarity between White and Black workers in the struggle against 'the monster of world imperialism' which threatened all the peoples of the globe. In order to do this it was necessary to fight 'against fascism, against the Klu Klux Klan movement, against chauvinism and against the doctrine of White superiority', for 'as long as European workers are still infected with these unfortunate ideas it will be impossible to free the world from the burden of imperialism'. In the light of the fact that negroes were frequently still regarded as inferior even within the labour movement, Moore quoted a historical example to illustrate the solidarity of coloured and White workers: the protest demonstration which John Bright and Karl Marx had organized during the American Civil War with the aid of the cotton-workers in Manchester, in order to prevent the British government from actively supporting the southern secessionists, even though the cotton-workers themselves were badly off at that time. Previously Moore had warned against the great war of the future 'in which race will fight against race' – an ideal suggestive of Garvey,[18] whose movement Moore represented.

The resolution on the negro question began by drawing a dismal picture of colonial imperialism and the situation in Africa, the Caribbean islands and the United States, in contrast to which the alleged absence of racial prejudices in Latin America stood out favourably. The resolution demanded complete independence for Haiti, Cuba and San Domingo, as well as all the colonies in the Caribbean region. A somewhat mystical note was struck with the wish that there should be a 'confederacy of the West Indies' and a 'confederacy of all peoples of the world'. To 'liberate the Negro race throughout the world' this movement was to press the following demands.

1 Complete freedom for African peoples and peoples of African descent;

2 Equality of the negro race with all other races;
3 Possession by Africans of African lands and administration;
4 Immediate abolition of forced labour and indirect taxation;
5 Abolition of all racial and class distinctions in economic and political matters;
6 Abolition of conscription;
7 Freedom of communication in the interior of Africa and along the African coasts;
8 Freedom of speech, press and assembly;
9 Recognition of the right to education in schools of every kind;
10 Recognition of the right to form trade unions.[19]

This general programme was the basic minimum to achieve the rapid modernization envisaged by the most radical Pan-Africans. All the points of this programme would be regarded in Europe as liberal and democratic demands; but put forward on a communist platform, they were bound to evoke twice as much mistrust. This was certainly the case with regard to the 'introductory measures' proposed, which were in part a résumé of the demands listed above and in part a digest of preceding resolutions.[20] Points 3 and 4 are the most important: 'Organization of a movement to liberate the Negro race; establishment of a united front with other peoples and the oppressed classes in a common fight against imperialism.'

Point 3 has a Pan-African connotation, whereas point 4 refers to a worldwide liberation movement of the proletariat. In this respect in particular the Brussels congress of 1927 may be seen as a radical sequel to the first Universal Races Congress of 1911 (which was probably unknown to most of the participants at the congress),[21] or even of the *African Times and Orient Review*, which Moore at least cannot have forgotten.[22] The Pan-African element again became evident on the margin of the Afro-Asian and Latin American proletarian liberation movement, because the two main rival groups in the United States – the Garvey movement (Moore) and the NAACP (whose delegate however did not arrive in time) – were at least brought together again on a common platform in Brussels. The historical significance of this event for the Pan-African movement should not, however, be exaggerated, if only because the extremely important anglophone element from West Africa and the West Indies was not represented. Nor did the Brussels congress bring about an understanding between the

NAACP and Garveyism. Nevertheless it did point to the theoretical possibility of a politically more radical kind of Pan-Africanism.

Nor did Brussels produce the 'movement to liberate the Negro race' anticipated in the special resolution. However it did yield the League Against Imperialism, Against Colonialism and for National Independence, which had branches in several European countries.[23] Several embryonic elements were in existence which facilitated the formation of a more wide-ranging association.[24] At a second congress, held in Frankfurt-on-Main from 20 to 31 July 1929, the Comintern tried to tighten its grip on the bourgeois nationalist elements and to depart from the old line of collaboration between the communists and bourgeois forces – but in vain. The scene was dominated by bourgeois 'reformists', including Professor William Pickens (who did in fact appear this time) of the NAACP. Africa was again represented only sparsely. Lamine Senghor, who had died in November 1927, was replaced by Kouyauté, the successor of Senghor in France[25] who delivered a speech at the congress.[26] It was at Frankfurt, too, that a figure appeared who from that time onwards was to exert a great influence upon Pan-Africanism: George Padmore.[27]

With the coming to power of Nazism in 1933, the League Against Imperialism lost its German base and had to move its centre to England, where Reginald Bridgeman, one of the most remarkable figures in the anti-colonial British left, attempted to carry on its work.[28] As early as 1934 the bottom was knocked out of any further promising activity by the Soviet Union's change of front – its entry into the League of Nations and its declining interest in supporting a colonial revolution.[29] The League Against Imperialism did remain in being for some time, but it was unable to recover from the secession of the militant element led by George Padmore.[30] The outbreak of World War II put a stop to it. Bridgeman burned its files, out of caution and concern for those who might be compromised,[31] so that a detailed description and assessment of its activity between 1933 and 1939 cannot be expected for the present.

Communist trade union activity

The communists had an even more direct and intensive influence in the countries drawn to Pan-Africanism through their activity in the trade-union field. In 1926 the Red International of Labour Unions

(RILU) formed an International Trade Union Committee of Negro Workers of the RILU; this was presided over by James W. Ford, who was the most prominent Afro-American communist at that time and in 1928 stood for the vice-presidency of the United States.[32] Ford's prominent role was in accordance with the theory current at that time in the American CP (and historically not entirely false) that the American negroes were more developed than the Africans and so should take the lead provisionally in the liberation of Africa.

> . . . from among the American Negroes must come the leadership of their race for the struggle for freedom in colonial countries. In spite of the denial of opportunity to the Negro under American capitalism his advantages are so far superior to those of the subject colonial Negroes in the educational, political and industrial fields that he is alone able to furnish the agitational and organizational ability that the situation demands.[33]

This idea was a clear parallel, in communist dress, to the vanguard thesis of Du Bois and Garvey.[34]

In December 1928 the *Negro Worker* published the working programme of the Trade Union Committee, which embraced in its geographical coverage almost all the territories to which Pan-Africanism appealed. In the northern states of the USA it planned to collaborate with the negro trade unions that already existed as well as with mixed ones, especially with the Brotherhood of Sleeping Car Porters led by Philip A. Randolph (later vice-president of AFL–CIO). In the southern states it sought to organize the Afro-American workers, centring its activities on Birmingham, Alabama.[35] A research institute was to be set up in New York as well as two trade-union schools, one in New York and the other in Chicago. In Africa the focus of its work was to be in South Africa, where the trade-union school for Africa was to be located; for the time being the South African Communist party school was to institute special trade-union courses. Furthermore, provision was made to establish contacts with West, East and Central Africa, in order to forge an organizational link with the centre in South Africa. In the West Indies it was intended, building on existing foundations, to found a separate trade-union centre and to seek contacts with the revolutionary trade-union movement in Latin America. In all the major regions a workers' conference was to be held to elaborate a detailed programme. It was decided to publish a monthly paper, the *Negro*

Worker, as well as a series of pamphlets dealing with the condition of the working class. Finally an International Conference of Negro Workers was to be called in the latter part of 1929 'in order to lay a basis for international connections of Negro workers throughout the world, and to bring them into close contact with the International Trade Union Movement'.

These resolutions guided Profintern activity which was now stepped up in the United States, in the West Indies and in Africa. The latter did not attain all its far-reaching objectives; nevertheless the last points were realized either completely or approximately. In particular, from 1928 onwards the *Negro Worker* appeared in hectographed form.[36] The international trade-union conference planned for late 1929 did not take place, but on the fringe of the second congress of the League Against Imperialism in Frankfurt a special session was held on 26 July 1929 which the African and Afro-American delegates to the congress as well as other representatives from the colonies and from European countries attended.[37] Ford provided a detailed report on the economic, social and political situation of the Black population and launched into a polemic against 'bourgeois' and 'reformist' groups such as the French socialists and the British Labour party, Du Bois's Pan-African Congress movement, the Garvey movement, the NAACP and WASU.[38] On this occasion an appeal was issued for the holding of an international conference of negro workers in London in July 1930. Ford chaired a provisional committee to prepare for this gathering. This committee had fifteen members of whom no fewer than seven came from the USA; among the latter was Pickens of the NAACP whom Ford had just strongly criticized. In addition to two South African representatives there was for the first time an East African, Jomo Kenyatta, who had recently (February 1929) arrived in England from Kenya;[39] Padmore was the West Indian delegate.[40] Apart from those organizations that were represented directly the following were given a voice in the committee's affairs: the American Negro Labor Congress, La Ligue pour la Défense de la Race Nègre, the Indian National Congress and the All-China Trade Union Federation. Since the British Labour government at short notice prohibited the congress from being held on British soil (under pressure from the South African government, as we are told with some plausibility by a contemporary anti-communist source), the conference was moved to Hamburg. Like London this was a great port; it also had the advantage of being a communist stronghold, so that the social-democratic Senate tolerated the congress.[41]

The congress met on 7 and 8 July.[42] Since most delegates from the colonies did not have passports, only seventeen people turned up, including one White man representing the African workers of South Africa. Other delegates came from the USA, Jamaica, Trinidad, Nigeria, Gambia, Sierra Leone, the Gold Coast and the Cameroons. This time British East Africa was absent, as was also the francophone element, so that only the classical anglophone region of Pan-Africanism was represented – exactly the reverse of the situation at the congress of the League Against Imperialism. In Hamburg the provisional committee turned itself into an executive committee of the International Trade Union Committee of Negro Workers. James W. Ford remained chairman with the additional responsibility of editing publications.

The United States representatives in the executive committee included: I. Hawkins (National Miners' Union), Helen McClain (National Needle Trades' Union) and George Padmore, who in the meantime had assumed a leading role in the Negro Bureau of the Profintern in Moscow. Africa was represented on the executive committee by four members: Kouyauté (LDRN; residence given as Dakar instead of Paris), Frank Macaulay (Nigerian Workers' party), Albert Nzulu (Federation of Non-European Trade Unions, Johannesburg) and E. F. Small (Gambian Labour Unions); the West Indies were represented by E. Reid (Trades and Labour Unions, Jamaica).[43]

The names of Macaulay and Small are indicative of the wedge the communists had managed to drive into the traditional West African nationalist establishment. Small, to judge by his name, was a member of one of the leading families in Gambia and may even be identical with an activist of the National Congress of British West Africa.[44] As the son of Herbert Macaulay and great-grandson of Bishop Samuel Crowther, Frank Macaulay belonged to one of the most esteemed families in southern Nigeria.[45] Frank Macaulay had apparently long remained under the influence of his father and according to communist ways of thinking was 'greatly handicapped by the petty-bourgeois nationalistic tendencies which have dominated the revolutionary movement in Nigeria up to the present time'. It was only the Hamburg congress and the fifth congress of the Profintern, held in Moscow in March 1931, that gave this representative of 'the toiling masses of Nigeria' his first opportunity to make international contacts, whereupon he became an orthodox communist. 'He immediately recognised the reformist policies which the Nigerian Democratic party had been following and took an active part in the deliberation of the Congress which he assisted in working out valuable political directions to aid the West African labour movement.'[46] His early death in 1931 was a severe blow to African communism, although it is an open question how his political views might have developed if he had lived longer. Small's appearance in Hamburg and the report he delivered there on the state of trade unionism in Gambia[47] indicate that the first trade unions in Black Africa developed under communist influence. I. T. A. Wallace-Johnson, one of the early trade-union leaders in the adjoining territory of Sierre Leone, played an important role later in the international communist movement as well as in that of Pan-Africanism.[48]

The Hamburg congress led to an intensification of communist efforts to win over African and Afro-American workers and to implement the two resolutions passed in Frankfurt. Several pamphlets were published on the situation of Black workers. Of the twenty-five titles which appeared in 1930 and 1931 no less than six were contributed by Padmore, including his first major work.[49] Padmore, who was transferred from Moscow to Hamburg as permanent representative of the Negro Bureau of Profintern, was also behind the implementation of another point in the Frankfurt programme: after the hectographed *Negro Worker* ceased publication, apparently in 1930, it re-emerged in Hamburg in January 1931. The first two issues bore the title the *International Workers' Review. Organ of the International Trade Union Committee of Negro Workers*; but from the third issue onwards this became the subtitle and the old name, the *Negro Worker*, was again used. It was published and printed in Hamburg, the editorial office and printing press being located at Rothesoodstrasse 8 in the harbour area. At first Ford was listed as the responsible editor, but from no. 10–11 (October–November 1931) he was succeeded by Padmore. Under the latter the journal had on its front cover a representation of the globe with the Atlantic countries turned so as to face the reader; looming over it was a huge figure of an African bursting his fetters with a mighty blow.[50] Like *La Race Nègre*, the journal was distributed mainly by African and Afro-American sailors from Marseilles. It was an appropriate camouflage that the house in Rothesoodstrasse was used as a seamen's hostel; some issues of the *Negro Worker* were smuggled on board ship by sympathetic Hamburg dockers. At the beginning of 1933 Padmore was arrested and spent some months in prison before being expelled – for a short time the *Negro Worker* appeared in Copenhagen. Later the editorial office was again moved, and in 1937 its address was given as Office 316, 40 rue de Colisée, Paris 8e.[51]

The *Negro Worker* is today a valuable source on the activities and views of communists about the situation in America and Africa. Two later exponents of Pan-Africanism collaborated on it: Padmore prior to 1934 and Wallace-Johnson in 1936 and 1937. The themes treated embraced the entire area to which Pan-Africanism exerted its appeal; nor were questions pertaining to Asia (China, India) neglected. For example the *Negro Worker* reprinted a sharp attack by S. Saklatvala on Gandhi in the communist journal *Labour Monthly*[52] and the same issue featured an article on the develpment of the Chinese working class.[53] The main emphasis, however, was upon the revolutionary movement in Africa,[54] and the *Negro Worker* joined in the campaign on behalf of the Scottsboro Boys.[55] Padmore marked his assumption of the office of chief editor with a 'special colonial number' under the slogan 'Workers of the World, Unite!' It was here that he eloquently defended Liberia from criticism over the scandal of forced labour in that country, referring to the resolutions of the Hamburg conference in July 1930.[56] Three further articles gave an optimistic account of revolutionary developments in Africa,[57] and another described the situation of negro workers in Cuba. A later issue featured Claude McKay's poem of 1922, 'If We Must Die'.

Haiti's ambivalent position was brought out well. One article, still published during the Padmore era, emphasized the ideological importance of Toussaint l'Ouverture,[58] whereas a later one contained an attack upon the dictatorial régime in contemporary Haiti.[59] In the mid-1930s all Pan-African groups identified themselves with the fight against fascism; consequently we find the *Negro Worker* taking a stand against the Italo-Abyssinian War and the possible return of Germany as an African colonial power.[60] The journal also paid much attention to the West African Youth League, on which reports were written by its general secretary, Wallace-Johnson, among others.[61]

The themes and content of the journal were thus Pan-African in the widest sense of the word. The very title the *Negro Worker* points in this direction, as does its cover design while Padmore was chief editor.[62] Except for Garvey's *Negro World*, which in the meantime has almost been forgotten, and his journal the *Black Man*, which appeared only sporadically,[63] the *Negro Worker* was at that time the only organ with a Pan-African coverage; it thus fulfilled a Pan-African as well as a communist function. Presumably the readers likewise had Pan-African sympathies – at least those who were no longer satisfied with a trade-unionist orientation.

Copies of the *Negro Worker* turn up in the most unexpected places. Ten copies of no. 3, year 1, of the first series seem to have been forwarded to WASU. Unless the reader's letter signed 'L. S.' published in no. 2, year 2, is a forgery, Lapido Solanke on behalf of WASU expressed thanks for the consignment, the contents of which, he said, had been 'a good eye-opener because it is full of valuable information which hitherto our Union [WASU] has not been aware of'. He promised to 'distribute the copies forwarded on to among the members' and added that 'there is nothing like co-operation between all organizations of the world, especially first among the Negro Organizations, with a view to defending their rights and liberties'.[64] It cannot as yet be ascertained whether copies of the *Negro Worker* were sent to WASU on this single occasion. Some years later Reginald Bridgeman, when inviting Solanke to an event organized by the League Against Imperialism, addressed him as 'comrade',[65] from which it may be concluded that (unless this was just a mistake or a matter of routine) the otherwise rather conservative Solanke seems to have been linked for a time with communist groups. This would also afford a better explanation why in this period anti-imperialist formulas penetrated into the journal *WASU*.[66]

One copy of the *Negro Worker* is to be found in the Du Bois papers, which should not surprise us considering the growing interest which Du Bois showed in Marxism. It was probably due to an oversight or misunderstanding that a number of copies of the *Negro Worker*, together with an optimistic letter by Padmore, found their way to the bourgeois nationalist Kobina Sekyi who was apparently more embarrassed than delighted by this consignment.[67]

Termination and historical impact

Stalinism provoked apostasy among most communist Pan-Africans (who in any case were few and far between) as soon as they realized that Comintern's interest in colonial revolution predominantly served the ends of Soviet foreign policy. After Germany left the League of Nations and Soviet Russia entered it, Stalin's policy of collective security against fascism led to close collaboration between the USSR and the Western powers; this involved discreetly dropping the revolu-

tionary nationalists in Africa and Asia. It was at this juncture that
Padmore in particular broke with Comintern, as Kouyauté in Paris
had done shortly before.[68] Owing to the USSR's change of line, in 1934
Communism lost its tenuous base in the area of interest to Pan-African-
ism. Most coloured communists or fellow-travellers left the movement
to become active as independents within the Pan-African movement.
This development may be followed particularly clearly in the cases of
Padmore and Kouyauté, as well as Kenyatta.[69] After Padmore's
breach with Comintern there was a decline in communist agitation
which affected the League Against Imperialism as well as the *Negro
Worker*. The impact which this change of course in 1934 had upon
Reginald Reynolds, the independent left-wing socialist writer, is described as follows in his memoirs:

> The Communist somersault of 1934 left radical pacifists like myself
> in a political Cave of Adullam, but not for long. The Independent
> Labour Party . . . still held in the main to a line that we could
> support. . . . Some Labour Party rebels, now well to the Left of
> the Communists, were also willing to join in forays against im-
> perialism. But most important was the effect of the new Soviet
> policy on the colonial peoples. When the Popular Front came into
> power in France, with full support of the Communist Party, any
> move against French imperialism was regarded as a betrayal of
> Russia, since France was now her ally. The League Against
> Imperialism abandoned all propaganda relating to the French
> colonies, concentrating almost the whole of its attention on Ger-
> many, Italy and Japan. Worse still, French colonials in revolt were
> denounced as 'fascists' – or at least as inspired and provoked by
> fascist agents. . . . Their betrayal . . . had a prompt reaction in the
> French colonies and even on many of the colonial intellectuals in
> Britain. Of these George Padmore . . . was an outstanding
> example.[70]

On the other hand during the mid-1930s the Popular Front growth
caused West European left-wingers who collaborated with nationalist
and Pan-African groups to become more receptive to Marxist ideas,
which indirectly trickled back again to Pan-African groups; the result
was that even the more conservative elements such as WASU and the
League of Coloured Peoples were unable completely to escape these
influences.[71] The outbreak of World War II brought about a total

change in the situation and after two decades of activity the communists found themselves practically empty-handed.

Thus the communists' foray into the history of Pan-Africanism was no more than an episode for both sides. For Pan-Africans Communism was from the first an uncertain ally. Everywhere they were a small and for the most part persecuted minority. During the early post-war years even the Soviet communists had to fight stubbornly to maintain their power; subsequently Soviet Russia remained isolated for nearly two decades. An alliance between Pan-Africanism or African national- ism and communism could only weaken, at least from a short-term view, the emancipation movement and expose it to massive oppression by the colonial powers. Moreover the atheistic views propagated by the communists disturbed members of the African élite who had been educated in Christian missionary schools, especially in British West Africa.[72] For these reasons only a few representatives of Pan-Africanism felt themselves drawn to Communism, even at the height of its influence; for them sympathy for Communism was no more than a transitional phenomenon. Even if they had wished otherwise, those who adhered to such radical principles would have deprived themselves of every chance of exerting political influence after their return to a still pre- dominantly traditional African society.

Thus the Pan-African relevance of communist endeavours through the League Against Imperialism and the Negro Bureau of the Profintern lies in the fact that, in purely formal terms, the communists filled the gap in the development of Pan-Africanism between 1927 and 1934.[73] Beyond this for some Pan-African leaders the time they spent in the communist movement was a formative political experience, especially for Padmore, Kouyauté, Kenyatta and Wallace-Johnson. For Padmore in particular his years of communist activity prepared him for his later rise to become one of the most significant brains in the Pan-African movement. His experiences left him distrustful of communist intentions, so that in due course he endeavoured to make Pan-Africanism an ideological alter- native to Communism for Africa.[74]

17 Conservative and radical Pan-Africanism in England (1934–9): Harold Moody and George Padmore

In the mid-1930s a new tendency set in towards a *rapprochement* among the various groups and movements in Britain, which culminated in the fifth Pan-African Congress in Manchester.[1] Hitherto in the literature on the subject the merit for this has been ascribed entirely or predominantly to George Padmore, the most significant representative of radical Pan-Africanism, possibly because his own autobiography was the chief source upon which these authors relied.[2] Fresh material, however, leads one to conclude that right up to 1944 the conservatives were sufficiently strong within the Pan-African movement for this view to be revised. The representative of this conservative trend was Dr Harold Moody from Jamaica, with his organization the League of Coloured Peoples. At least for a time Moody and his followers were of greater significance than Padmore and his group. There developed between them tense competition, but also a degree of co-operation hitherto unknown. Moreover the League of Coloured Peoples came into existence before the more radical movement and had greater organizational stability. It therefore seems justifiable to begin this chapter with a discussion of its affairs.

Moody and the beginnings of the League of Coloured Peoples (LCP)

The League of Coloured Peoples (LCP) was founded by Dr Harold Moody in 1931 and remained so closely bound up with his person that it lasted only a few years after his death. Moody was born in Kingston, Jamaica, on 8 October 1882, and was thus just five years older than his fellow-countryman Garvey.[3] Like Garvey he came from a family that had originally been relatively well-to-do. His father was a light-complexioned mulatto who was ruined by the great earthquake of 1907. At that time Harold Moody had already been in London for three years studying medicine at his father's expense. Although he himself was dark-skinned, Moody was entirely a product of the racially and class stratified society of the West Indies. Culturally he felt himself to be British, and he emphasized this by his lifelong work for church and mission – especially within the framework of the Christian Endeavour Union, for which he had worked while still resident in Jamaica. He was thus still completely rooted in the earlier tradition of Christian missionary activity which was of such importance in the development of modern élites in the Pan-African milieu.[4]

At first Moody deliberately kept himself at a disdainful distance from Africa and Africans; however, he received a great shock when he came to Edwardian Britain in 1904, filled as he was with idealistic concepts about England and false ideas about the actual position he would occupy in British society. Immediately on his arrival he had difficulty in finding a room, even in the relatively liberal atmosphere of London. To his consternation he suddenly discovered that the Europeans put him on the same level with the Africans whom he despised and rejected. This psychological shock was made bearable only by his Christian faith and by the aid he repeatedly received from churchmen and members of liberal and humanitarian groups. Constant racial discrimination, mitigated by examples of genuine helpfulness, became for Moody a stimulus to social and political activity. His strong allegiance to Christianity and his bourgeois origin placed him on the conservative wing of Pan-Africanism.

Moody always attached great importance to working in conjunction with Europeans for the well-being of his coloured fellow-countrymen from the West Indies and Africa. He collaborated especially with church groups like the YMCA and the Christian Endeavour Union, of whose

London branch he became chairman in 1931. He strove for understanding between the races in a personal sense also, for he married an
Englishwoman with whom he led a long and happy married life. In
Camberwell Green, London, he built up a flourishing medical practice.
His professional standing and financial independence enabled him time
and again to help his hard-pressed fellow-countrymen, at least on an
individual basis, but in the long run this gave him no satisfaction. It
seemed a logical step to found an independent organization to represent
the interests of the coloured peoples, in the first instance of those living
in Britain. In this way the League of Coloured Peoples came into
being.[5]

A glance at its immediate prehistory indicates the role played by at
least two important elements – the Pan-African and the Christian. At
the beginning of 1931 Charles Wesley, the Afro-American historian at
Howard University in Washington DC, was invited by the YMCA to
give a talk in London, to which Moody was also asked so that he might
expound his views. He used this opportunity to develop his plan for a
new organization. The response was at first not very encouraging. At a
second event attended by Wesley – this time with Moody in the chair –
the atmosphere changed. A committee was formed which met at
Moody's house. The next meeting saw the foundation of the new
organization in the London headquarters of the YMCA in Tottenham
Court Road on 13 March 1931.[6]

In July 1933 the first issue appeared of the unpretentious organ of
the League, which henceforth appeared only once a quarter. Its original
title (which was changed during World War II), the Keys, is not to be
understood literally but is an allusion to Aggrey's parable, well known
among English-speaking Africans and Afro-Americans, whereby the
racial problem was likened to a piano and its keys: one could not play
the piano by striking only the white or only the black keys, but to
obtain a harmonious melody one had to strike both. The title of the
journal thus already indicated symbolically its programme of collaboration between all races. In the same year 1933 the centenary
celebration of the death of the great abolitionist Wilberforce enabled
the new organization to present itself to the general public. Moody
spoke at the memorial service in Hull, Wilberforce's constituency, and
invoked the heritage of the great abolitionist in surmounting present-
day problems.[7]

In the leading article of the first issue of the Keys Moody placed the

work of his group in a worldwide historical and political context, which
says much for his foresight. He did not allow himself to be circumscribed
by petty local problems and professed solidarity with coloured people
throughout the British Empire and beyond:

> We know that today the world is passing through one of the most
> critical periods in its history. . . . We believe that all races, creeds
> and colours have their part to play in evolving a new order and
> system. Our task is primarily in stating the cause of our brothers
> and sisters within the British Empire. We cannot afford, however,
> to ignore the claims of the people of colour who owe allegiance
> to a flag other than our own. All along the line there is the same
> tale. The governed and their governors are at times separated by a
> wide gulf, in that the interests of the two classes seem to conflict
> very often. Never was there a greater need for unity within our
> ranks. Never was there a greater need for vision and leadership.[8]

Apart from this he did not forget the tasks to be fulfilled on his own
doorstep in Cardiff, Liverpool and London, where in this era of
depression and massive unemployment discrimination weighed particularly heavily upon coloured people. The objectives of the LCP, printed
on the inside front cover of each number, point in the same direction
and give an interpretation of the symbolic and programmatic title of
the *Keys*: 'To promote and protect the Social, Educational, Economic
and Political interests of its members. To interest members in the
welfare of Coloured Peoples in all parts of the World. To improve
relations between the Races. To co-operate and affiliate with [White]
organizations sympathetic to Coloured People.'

Although the founding of the LCP was an answer to a real organizational need, since in Britain there were (except for WASU) no organizations for Afro-West Indians or Africans, the number of its members
remained small. In 1934 there were said to be 200 of them and in 1936
262, of which as many as 99 were White.[9] Since most of the members
were hardly well-to-do its financial position, too, was always precarious.
Moody's house at first served virtually as the central office; meetings
were held in the Memorial Hall, 16 Farringdon Street, London E.C.4.
In the late 1930s this address was considered the official one of the
League.

Moody was always the predominant figure in the organization. He
liked to call himself 'founder and president' and in his 'presidential

message' he regularly addressed his members in a slightly unctuous tone (bearing the imprint of Christian devotional literature). When at the end of 1934 he expressed an intention to resign, this merely seems to have strengthened his position. However he never succeeded completely in imposing his own conservative views, and this in a double sense. Within the League tension soon developed about the definition of the concept 'coloured', behind which there lay as a rule a purely political difference of opinion. Moody was inclined to give this concept as restricted a meaning as possible and to limit membership of the League (except for quasi-honorary European members such as Margery Perham) so far as possible to Afro-Americans (and even just to West Indians, if this could be arranged) and to Africans – although he also attached importance to maintaining good relations with the NAACP in the United States. To him 'coloured' was to a large extent synonymous with 'negro'. On the other hand a considerable number of members, including some in the executive committee, wanted to extend the meaning to include Asians such as Chinese.[10] This group consisted mainly of students who were attracted to Marxism and Communism. Moody himself had an interest in Russia, especially because of the absence of racial discrimination there, but his Christian commitment did not permit him to make any significant approximation to Marxism, let alone Communism: 'We are under a democratic government and that government is acting as trustees for us until we can stand on our feet under the strenuous conditions of modern times. We must believe that they want the best for their wards, and since we know what "the best" is we must not cease to strive until we get it. Communism won't help us. We don't want to fight, we are pacifists. . . .'[11] During the annual meeting in 1934 violent discussions broke out between the conservative Moody and the younger more radical members; these found an echo in the West African press, where attacks were launched against Moody.[12]

The membership of the League's executive committee, which changed every year, reflects Moody's tendency to confine the 'coloured' group to Africans and Afro-Americans as well as his inability to assert his influence completely. From the very first the West Indian element was predominant, which is not surprising considering Moody's origin and the existence of WASU (for African students). In 1933 and 1934 the inner core of the committee consisted of four West Indians and three West Africans; the total membership (twenty in all), however, comprised twelve West Indians, two Afro-Americans from the United States, five West Africans and one Indian.[13] Two years later the centre of gravity had shifted somewhat. The inner core of the committee now included one representative from Ceylon and one from the United States, but otherwise West Indians were dominant (Moody's daughter, the treasurer, was listed as coming from England but her father still from Jamaica); but in the full committee eight more West Africans sat alongside five more West Indians.[14]

The League of Coloured Peoples was at first mostly non-political. Its immediate aim was to provide practical aid for students and also for children in their own families, for whom they arranged annually a big Christmas party; the first of these was held in January 1933 for 350 coloured children in London.[15] In addition Moody financed out of his own pocket a children's excursion to Epsom during the summer. These excursions became a traditional event. For the first one the League wrote to 275 coloured families and obtained parental consent for 195 children aged between five and fifteen to attend.[16] From 1933 onwards Moody organized a garden party for adults each year. Receptions were given by the League at Moody's house for the West India cricket team and the delegation from the Gold Coast led by Nana Ofori Atta[17] (both in 1934); and later other receptions were held for Jesse Owens and Paul Robeson. These events rounded off the social activity of the League, the importance of which should not be underestimated as a means of bringing people together and gaining access to well-to-do White society. Another of Moody's non-political ventures was an annual service held in his parish church, the Camberwell Congregationalist church, at which only coloured clergy officiated. Of a rather different character was the publicity campaign which the League ran in 1935 on behalf of about 3000 coloured people in Cardiff, mostly dockers and seamen who had been unemployed for years and who lived in semi-slum conditions, especially in the Tiger Bay area.[18]

The growing politicization of the League

In the long run even Moody could not prevent the League from launching into the troubled waters of politics. Each year from 1933 on it organized a weekend seminar. The first one was attended by more than forty people from the West Indies (Bermuda, Barbados, Jamaica, St Lucia, Trinidad), Great Britain, Australia, the USA, the Gold Coast, East Africa,[19] India and Ceylon.

The topics treated in the lectures were wholly Pan-African in their range. A graduate of Wilberforce University (Ohio) and Yale, Harry Roberts, read a paper on 'The American Negro'. Stephen Thomas, a barrister (Middle Temple) from West Africa, gave some information about the West Africans, deploring the fact 'that there was but little contact between the Africans in various parts of Africa itself, and even less contact with their brothers and sisters in other parts of the world . . .'[20] – quite an appropriate statement for a meeting called for purposes of exchanging information. C. L. R. James spoke about the West Indians, R. S. Nehra (an Indian) about the East Africans, and C. F. Strickland, apparently an Englishman, about trade unions in Africa. Harry Roberts from the USA also reported on the Scottsboro case,[21] whereupon the meeting resolved to support the campaign by taking a collection.

By backing the Scottsboro campaign the League had taken its first step along the road to political activity. The next move came in December 1933 with a resolution protesting against the revival of lynching in the United States.[22] As early as the spring of 1934 C. L. R. James, who was able to write with surprising empathy about the West India cricket team (and about cricket in general),[23] demanded self-government for the West Indies.[24] The reception for Nana Ofori Atta, held on 14 July 1934 at Moody's house, also had political overtones for Africa, although these were still rather faint.

All this, however, was just a prelude to the rapid politicization which occurred after 1935, unleashed by Italy's attack on Ethiopia and Germany's demands for the return of her colonies.[25] C. L. R. James gave a Marxist analysis of the Abyssinian war, which the gentle Moody allowed to be printed in his journal, evidently under pressure, although he himself may have been the target of the following passage: 'Africans and people of African descent, especially those who have been poisoned by British Imperialist education, needed a lesson. They have got it. Every succeeding day shows exactly the real motives which move imperialism in its contact with Africa, shows the incredible savagery and duplicity of European Imperialism in its quest for markets and raw materials. Let the lesson sink in deep. . . .'[26] More than six months earlier a particularly well-attended annual meeting, held on 4 September 1935, had passed a resolution urging 'upon the European countries which now wield authority in Africa and upon the League of Nations that the time is now ripe for them to consider a plan for the future of

Africa, which plan should be nothing less than the ultimate and complete freedom of Africa from any external domination whatsoever
. . .'[27] In the situation as it then existed the hope that such a request
might be granted by the colonial powers was quite illusory; but the
resolution does throw light upon the kind of response the conquest of
Ethiopia evoked among Africans and Afro-Americans. 'The League of
Coloured Peoples calls the attention of His Majesty's Government and
Parliament to the great movement of solidarity which the Italian
attack upon Abyssinia has brought about among the African and
African-descended peoples in reaction against European violence, conquest and domination.'[28] Even sharper was the response evoked by
Germany's colonial demands, which drove the League further to the
left, at least for the time being.[29] At an early date it had noted the
emergence of racism in the Third Reich, in the first instance in the case
of racial discrimination against four West Indian students on a German
liner, the *Caribia*. The conclusion drawn was clear: 'to warn their
coloured friends of travelling in German boats and to plead for a
boycott'.[30] For this reason the League was from the first against the
policy of appeasement, especially at Africa's expense by satisfying
German colonial claims.

> The peoples of the British Empire are bound to be affected. The
> Chamberlain government has cleverly pursued the policy of satis-
> fying the German claim for territorial expansion by directing
> Hitler's attention to Central Europe and so away from the British
> Empire. Meanwhile the British Government is conducting a cam-
> paign of the most savage repression in all colonial countries.
> Africans and other inhabitants of the British Empire can only give
> their support to a policy which secures peace, neither at the
> expense of the weaker peoples nor by the complete abolition of
> every vestige of freedom at present existing in the world.[31]

At the beginning of 1937 the League went so far as to seize upon a
protest by the (communist) International Trade Union Committee of
Negro Workers against the alleged plan to return the African colonies
to Germany, which it supported 'gladly'. In explaining this decision, it
said: 'Although some of our people are suffering under British Rule,
their fate is heavenly compared with what it was or would be under
the rule of Fascist Germany.'[32] At the 1937 annual meeting (presided
over by George Lansbury, leader of the pacifist wing of the Labour

party) Gallacher, the communist MP, made a speech. Pacifists, Jews and negroes were not sub-human, Gallacher asserted, countering Nazi propaganda; he went on to point to the absence of racial barriers in Soviet Russia.[33] A report was also given by an unnamed African about a visit to the part of Togo administered by the French, in which he said the return of Germany as a colonial power would be unpopular ('Germans not wanted'), *inter alia* because a considerable number of the French officials originated from the West Indies and from Africa and because there was no racial barrier there.[34]

The opposition to Germany's colonial claims was asserted on the level of political and ideological principles at the sixth annual weekend seminar, held from 25 to 27 March 1938, when a resolution was adopted that

> these territories should be developed primarily for the benefit of their indigenous inhabitants and with a view to their self-govern- ment. . . . The League of the Coloured Peoples believes that, on the other hand, such development and such self-government can only be hindered and retarded if these territories pass into the hands of countries with a totalitarian philosophy and dictatorial system of government which would certainly be reflected in their control of such territories, whose inhabitants have moreover ex- pressed and are expressing through their leaders their resolute opposition to control by Germany. [And then in a restrained and unmistakable language] the League calls the attention of His Majesty's Government and Parliament to the dissatisfaction which would not fail to manifest itself throughout His Majesty's Colonial territories and the possible resistance of the population of the mandated territories which the contemplation of transfer would bring about.[35]

The League as the moderate wing of Pan-Africanism

The emphasis put upon solidarity among the coloured people (whether this was understood in the narrower or wider sense) neces- sarily led to what one might call 'Pan-African domestic politics'. If one refers back to Aggrey's remark about the need to strike the black and white piano keys simultaneously, it is obvious that to attain harmony the first requirement was to see that the notes struck on the black keys were in tune. It was precisely this harmony that Moody and the

League were striving to achieve at a time when George Padmore, the hitherto best-known exponent of Pan-Africanism in Britain, was slowly beginning to gain influence.[36]

The militants around Padmore despised Moody because of the links he maintained with British groups, his conservative attitudes and his quasi-clerical style.[37] In spite of this Moody was better able to become active organizationally than Padmore with his radicalism, his communist past and his lack of contacts with the White establishment. Moody found support in men like C. L. R. James and Kenyatta, who belonged to both movements at the same time. Dr C. B. Clarke, a West Indian physician in London, was able to act as an intermediary. As chairman of the Aggrey House Committee and member of the League he was obliged to Moody in two ways. On the other hand Clarke was close to Padmore. Later he became the latter's family doctor and medical adviser until Padmore's death in 1959.[38] Finally Paul Robeson may be included in this centrist group, for politically his tendencies were towards the radical wing, but at least once he spoke about the League and gave two concerts to help improve their financial situation;[39] moreover, as patron of WASU while he was in London, he maintained good relations with this important group of African students.[40]

As an admirer of Aggrey, Moody had joined the committee of the hostel for African students, Aggrey House, which was financed by the Colonial Office; and the *Keys* claimed that the merit of founding the hostel should go to the League.[41] In the conflict with WASU over Aggrey House Moody acted as a mediator[42] and the final agreement was no doubt due to his effort to reconcile the two parties: the Colonial Office and WASU. Moreover the League and Moody tried to overcome the traditional animosity between West Indian and African students – an elementary precondition for successful collaboration between the two groups. Even if the debate once held at Aggrey House on 'the advantages of greater co-operation' between these two groups was not exactly organized by the League, at least the latter gave further publicity to it through its journal, thus recording it for the historian.

> West Indians came in for the usual trouncing for their vanity, their ignorance of the cultures of their forefathers, their desire to be imitation Europeans, and their blindness to the advantages of mutual understanding. . . . It is in our view impossible to exaggerate the necessity for West Indians to make an effort to break

through the anti-African propaganda with which their educational
system is saturated, and to try to re-establish contact with the
civilisations in which they have their roots.[43]

Above all it was a matter of checking the arrogance of the West
Indians and their pride in their higher European civilization vis-à-vis
backward Africa – a prejudice Moody knew only too well from his
own experience.[44]

To the same end were directed Moody's endeavours to unite the
various groups which had been formed in Britain during the 1930s
and to get them to formulate and propagate in public his own ideas
about the future of Africa and his West Indian homeland. Even if he
seemed too reflective and conservative to the impatient young men of
the left wing, it was precisely because of his well-known links with the
White establishment that he could act as a consolidator. Coming from
Padmore the slogan of national independence for Africa inevitably
sounded utopian, considering how matters stood, but from Moody's
lips, as spokesman of the League of Coloured Peoples, it seemed more
persuasive; it led the left-wingers to make further advances. Thus the
historian may discern a certain interplay between the two main wings
of Pan-Africanism in Britain: the tension between the two movements
strengthened both of them, although at the time, as is so often the case
in history, they did not realize that their friction was anything more
than a minor matter. Although they were led by men of different
political and personal temperaments, in the last resort they were
playing the same game and tending in the same direction. Sources
permitting, we shall therefore try to treat the two movements together
in their interrelationship with other groups and personalities.

George Padmore and radical Pan-Africanism

George Padmore, Moody's counterpart on the radical left wing of
Pan-Africanism, began the purely Pan-African phase of his career in
1934–5. At this point we must give a sketch of his life, a task facilitated
by Hooker's biography.[45]

George Padmore was born as Malcolm Ivan Meredith Nurse in
Trinidad, probably in 1902 (as Hooker reckons, although Padmore
himself always gave the date as 1903).[46] As a schoolmaster his father
belonged to the native middle class. From his grandfather, a farmer on
Barbados who lived to be over a hundred, Padmore received at an

early age a first-hand idea of the historical background to the twentieth-century world in which he was to live. At the beginning of 1945, in a letter to Du Bois, he claimed that he was 'a nephew of the late Sylvester Williams, a West Indian barrister who initiated the project with which you, Bishop Walter and others have been associated'.[47] Should such a close relationship really have existed, it would be a fascinating link within the intricate chain of Pan-African tradition. Even if Padmore's statement is exaggerated (or actually invented), it would still speak for his sense of historical continuity, in so far as he endeavoured to set Du Bois, Sylvester Williams, who in 1945 had almost fallen into oblivion, and his own self in close relationship to the Pan-African movement.

After visiting the high school at Port-of-Spain and spending an interlude as a journalist, Nurse went to the USA at the end of December 1924 to study medicine at Fisk University (the university which Du Bois attended). Before this, however, he read sociology for a while at Columbia University in New York. At Fisk he studied international relations, negro sociology, botany and zoology; he was also active as a speaker and as editor of the student newspaper, the *Fisk Herald*. In 1926 he established contact by correspondence with Azikiwe, and in the following year they made each other's acquaintance personally at Howard University, where Azikiwe had found a key position as secretary to Alain Locke. While still at Fisk Padmore began to take an interest in Liberia and in student organization. By way of New York, where he joined the Communist party, he came to Howard University to study law. Here one of his professors was Dr Ralph Bunche (Nobel peace prize-winner and later deputy secretary-general of the UN).

In 1928 at the latest Malcolm Nurse adopted the pseudonym George Padmore. Basing himself in Washington, he became active on the campus of Howard University as well as in various states on behalf of the party and its dependent organizations such as the American Negro Labor Congress led by Richard B. Moore. At the same time he wrote for the Communist party paper, the *Daily Worker*, in New York.[48] By 1929 this brilliant young man had already worked his way up to such heights within the party hierarchy that he was sent to the second congress of the League Against Imperialism in Frankfurt, where he made the acquaintance of Kouyauté.[49] In 1930 he went to Moscow where he quickly advanced to become head of the Negro Bureau of Profintern (RILU),[50] moving among the top persons in the Soviet hierarchy. He stayed for a spell in Vienna and then, after the Hamburg congress of July 1930, moved to that city in the autumn of 1931 to take over the editorship of the *Negro Worker*. At this time he devoted himself wholeheartedly to literary activity on behalf of Profintern,[51] building up an enormous network of international contacts in the colonies; according to Hooker he had about 4000 contacts in the coloured world.[52] In May 1932 he attended a conference in Hamburg-Altona at which the International of Seamen and Harbour Workers was founded. On this occasion he became close friends with Kouyauté. He undertook journeys, probably on behalf of the party, which in 1931 took him to West Africa, where in Nigeria he established contact *inter alia* with Herbert Macaulay's son, whom he won over to Communism;[53] in 1932 he went to London and Paris. In London he met his old schoolboy friend from Trinidad, C. L. R. James, whom he tried in vain to recruit for the Communist party. In Paris Padmore made the acquaintance of Miss Nancy Cunard and persuaded her to raise money in Britain for the campaign to save the Scottsboro Boys.[54] He contributed several articles to the great anthology which Nancy Cunard published in 1934,[55] mostly consisting of reprints from the *Negro Worker*. After 30 January 1933 Padmore was arrested and spent several months in Hamburg jails, and in the summer of 1933 was deported from Germany to Britain where he was not enthusiastically received since he was a well-known communist. As early as August 1933 Comintern decided to dissolve the International Trade Union Committee of Negro Workers as a sop to the Western Powers. Thereupon Padmore broke with the organization and resigned from all his posts. In February 1934 he was expelled as a 'petty-bourgeois nationalist'. Now living in Paris, Padmore thus shared the fate of his friend Kouyauté, who was likewise expelled from the communist movement at about this time.[56]

In 1935 Padmore moved to London where he joined up with several West Indians, as penniless as he was himself, in order to scrape through. He gave private lessons in the evenings, which brought him a little money, and pursued his journalistic activities: for *Crisis* in the States, and later also for other Afro-American newspapers (in World War II for the Chicago *Defender*), as well as for Gold Coast papers.[57] Politically he was closely linked to the Independent Labour party and became its colonial expert, although he never became a member and always refused to stand for election to Parliament. He contributed frequently to the *New Leader*, the central organ of the Independent Labour party, which remained fundamentally opposed to colonial imperialism, and also to other left-wing journals such as the *Tribune*, the *Socialist Leader*, *Controversy* and *Left*, usually on current colonial questions.[58] From that time dates his close collaboration with Fenner Brockway (after 1945 the Labour party's most radical colonial expert) and with an informal group of left-wing socialist and pacifist intellectuals such as Reginald Reynolds, who held weekly discussions with the Padmore group.[59]

Padmore personified several of the historical elements which played an essential role in the development of Pan-Africanism. His career extended to all the terminal points of the classical 'triangle' of Pan-Africanism – the West Indies, the USA, Europe and Africa. The memory of his direct descent from slavery was combined with a middle-class education and studies at Afro-American universities; his temporary proximity to Garveyism was combined with work for the Communist party on a national as well as an international level, in both the trade-union and the purely political arena. His great veneration for Blyden, which found expression in the name given to his daughter (whom, together with his wife, he left behind when he went to Moscow)[60] and in his homage to Blyden in his best-known book,[61] and also his respect for Du Bois[62] fitted well into the relationship he maintained (or at least claimed to have maintained) with Sylvester Williams. Through Kouyauté he established a link with the francophone wing of Pan-Africanism. In England he came into contact with the humanitarian liberal and socialist element of the British left; the latter for their part consciously placed themselves in the abolitionist tradition which led from Wilberforce and Clarkson,[63] by way of the Fabian Society (which during World War II opened the Colonial Bureau under Arthur Creech-Jones and Miss Rita Hinden) and the Union of Democratic Control (Margery Perham etc.) to the left wing of the Labour party with its colonial experts, Reginald Sorensen and Fenner Brockway.[64]

With his dynamism and his insistence on intellectual precision and political action he exerted a strong influence upon the young African and Afro-West Indian intelligentsia between 1935 and 1958 – by the strength of his personality, and by means of articles and several books,[65] lectures, contributions to discussions and a wide circle of personal contacts. From the Manchester congress onwards Padmore was the theorist, propagandist, organizer, co-ordinator and first amateur historian of Pan-Africanism; all this in one person and with financially and technically limited means – one has to take this into account to arrive at a fair assessment of his written work.[66]

In the last two years of his life Padmore was personal political adviser to Nkrumah on Pan-African questions in Ghana. It was he who was behind the first All-African Peoples' Conference, held in Accra in December 1958, which may be regarded as the sixth Pan-African Congress. There he met the youngest generation of African nationalists whose activities have so powerfully affected the world in which we live.

In his person Padmore underlines the great historical importance of the seemingly insignificant West Indies, especially in so far as Pan-Africanism is concerned; his education brings out the importance of Afro-American universities in the USA; his work for Communism over many years emphasizes the influence of modern radical ideas; his stay in London demonstrates the important role played by Britain, with its liberal and humanitarian tradition, which left its imprint on the nascent Pan-African movement; his rise to the status of a Pan-African leader around 1945 underlines the significant effect of World War II in accelerating the pace of historical change. Padmore's great share in the fifth Pan-African Congress, his contact with African nationalists and trade-union leaders – from Ralph Bunche, R. B. Moore and Azikiwe to Nkrumah and Lumumba – points to the most recent history of the Pan-African movement. He never referred to Horton, but with his wholly modern rational approach he came closest to the trend of which Horton is the lone representative in Pan-Africanism and in African nationalism.[67] Only his sentimental and uncritical love of Liberia, and during the last years of his life his similarly uncritical veneration of Nkrumah,[68] led him to deviate from his line.

In London Padmore again worked with his one-time school friend C. L. R. James. In 1935 the latter had founded a new organization, the International African Friends of Abyssinia (IAFA),[69] out of the *ad hoc* committee formed in 1934 to welcome the second delegation from the Gold Coast, the rump Aborigines Protection Society.[70] The new group managed to secure the moral support of Danquah, who as secretary had accompanied the bigger and more 'official' delegation of the Gold Coast led by his half-brother Nana Ofori Atta,[71] and also of the two ARPS delegates George E. Moore and Samuel R. Wood; in spite of this it was more an affair of West Indians than of Africans. C. L. R. James (Trinidad) was chairman; Dr Peter Milliard (British Guiana) and T. Albert Marryshaw (Grenada)[72] acted as deputy chairmen; the honorary secretary was Kenyatta and the treasurer Mrs Amy Ashwood Garvey – Garvey's first wife, whom he had divorced and who was living in London. Mohamed Said (Somaliland), Sam Manning and Padmore (both from Trinidad) made up the executive committee. With the sparse means at their disposal the members of this organization arranged a welcome for Emperor Haile Selassie when the latter arrived at Waterloo Station in London in 1936. This apparently was the limit of their practical activity. The historical importance of the group consists in the fact that it underlines once again the politicizing effect of the Abyssinian War; it also represented the first preparatory step in the establishment of the Pan-African Federation, which arranged the fifth Pan-African Congress in Manchester in 1945.

The next step along the road to Manchester was the transformation at the beginning of 1937 of what remained of the IAFA into the International African Service Bureau (IASB), which at first was no stronger than its predecessor.[73] In this organization, too, the West Indian element was predominant. The main posts were held by the same people (Padmore, C. L. R. James, Kenyatta); Padmore now took the chair. The most important new faces were the general secretary Wallace-Johnson, whom we have already met as a trade unionist from Sierra Leone,[74] and T. R. Makonnen, who was treasurer. The latter is a somewhat mysterious figure. He originated from British Guiana where he bore the name of Griffiths, but on his arrival in Britain in January 1936 he called himself T. Ras Makonnen[75] – in solidarity with Ethiopia and because he had an Ethiopian grandfather. He seems to have been an efficient organizer and something of a financial wizard. Padmore gives him the credit for having financed the fifth Pan-African Congress.[76] From the late 1930s he ran various restaurants in Manchester, which became centres for the African and Afro-American intelligentsia.[77]

The IASB arranged debates and lectures, but nothing is as yet known about their content. According to Padmore the general tone was Marxist but non-communist, with a strong orientation to Pan-African ideas which cannot be defined more closely.[78] A medium for the propagation of their ideas was the journal *International African Opinion*, which appeared in July 1938 edited by C. L. R. James.[79] Occasionally the IASB collaborated with the League of Coloured Peoples, since C. L. R. James and Kenyatta belonged to both groups.[80]

On 8 May 1938 the IASB organized a mass meeting in Trafalgar Square, a traditional rallying-point of the left, to protest against the threatening possibility that the British protectorates of Basutoland, Swaziland and Bechuanaland might be ceded to the Union of South Africa. In January 1939 it organized, together with certain socialist groups, an international conference at Friends' House in Euston Road, London, to warn the nationalists in the colonial countries against the communists' Popular Front tactics.[81]

Pre-war precursors of the fifth Pan-African Congress

Before the fifth Pan-African Congress met in 1945 several gatherings were held which, viewed historically, have the appearance of preliminary conferences prior to the congress proper, even though it seems that there was no direct link between them and the Pan-African congresses that had been held between 1919 and 1927. In these endeavours between 1934 and 1944 Moody played a surprisingly large part.

After the failure of his plans to hold a fifth Pan-African Congress in Tunis[82] during the depression years, Du Bois apparently never gave up hope of reviving the Pan-African Congress movement. He reacted positively and hopefully to every stirring of Pan-African sentiment.

The first symptom of this did not come from the traditional centres of Pan-African activity, but from Paris – which need no longer surprise us after what has been said above.[83] It was in Paris at the beginning of 1934 that Garan Kouyauté, after his expulsion from the communist movement, organized a conference to work out a programme on which Africans and Afro-Americans could unite on a worldwide scale. Padmore, who stayed in Paris after his break with Comintern, attended this conference of the francophone element, at which he gave an account of the NAACP and Du Bois. He wrote about this in a letter to Du Bois, which for the moment is our only source about this conference:

> The French Negroes recently held a conference under the leadership of . . . Kouyauté, the editor of *La Race Nègre*. The Negro problem was discussed relative to the present economic and social crisis the world over, and the fascist danger which threatens our racial extermination. . . . The Conference decided to take the initiative to convene a Negro World Unity Congress, for the pur-

pose of hammering out a common program of action around which world unity among the blacks can be achieved.[84]

This big congress was to take place in the summer of 1935 – 'providing the war-makers give us so much time'. The Paris group invited the NAACP to attend the proposed gathering and Padmore appealed to Du Bois to give vigorous support to the project.

About the fate of this initiative all that is known at present is that no congress of this kind took place either in 1935 or later. But the idea made an impact on the other side of the Atlantic, for under the impression of the welcome news from Paris Du Bois seems to have regained hope in the Pan-African movement. In that same month, February 1934, he urged 'dozens of Negro leaders . . . to help organise a militant youth movement for the world liberation of coloured peoples' (Hooker). One year earlier, at the Armenia conference held in the home of the NAACP's patron Joel Spingarn near New York, he had put forward similar ideas to the NAACP leaders, but apparently unsuccessfully.

Several months later, on 14 and 15 July 1934, another conference on Pan-African themes took place, this time in London.[84a] It coincided with the visit of the delegation from the Gold Coast. Nana Ofori Atta spoke at it as well as Moody, who held a reception in his own house on 14 July for this important tribal prince and conservative politician.[85] The general theme of the conference was 'The Negro in the World Today'. It was intended to give expression to the hopes and aspirations of the Black race and to depict its present situation in Africa, Britain, the West Indies and the United States. One of the motives given for convening the conference was the racial discrimination which faced coloured workers and students in Britain. If all the organizations which according to *Keys* promised their support in fact did take part, this must have been predominantly a meeting of the conservative and moderate element.[86] These groups were: WASU, the Student Christian Movement Joint Council,[87] the Friends' Service Council (British Quakers, whose Friends' House in Euston Road later became a centre for Pan-African meetings in London), the YWCA (possibly a misprint for YMCA?), the Negro Welfare Society (no details known; possibly a predecessor of the Negro Welfare Association?), the Gold Coast Union (again no details known), the League Against Imperialism, the Ceylon Students' Union, the Universities Mission (in which Moody likewise held a leading position), the Church Missionary Society (CMS) and the League of Coloured Peoples.[87a] A special position was occupied by the League Against Imperialism, although in a Pan-African sense it can no longer be regarded as radical after 1934.[88]

About the conference proceedings little is as yet known. It took place in the Royal Albert Hall, and according to Hooker no more than forty-three delegates were present, 'without exception reformers who deplored conditions and called for a change of heart on the part of white men'.[89] The speakers were announced as 'mainly coloured',[89a] from which it may be deduced that some Whites also spoke, or at least were expected to speak. Besides Nana Ofori Atta and Moody, whom we have already mentioned, the name of Jomo Kenyatta is worthy of note.

Unfortunately nothing is known either about the content of the addresses delivered by him or by any of the others, except for Hooker's summary description. In a complacent and typically exaggerated report on the conference, *Keys* said of Moody's addresses on 'The Negro in the Future' – long since forgotten – that it would one day be regarded as 'classical' and that it was far and away the best contribution at the conference.[90] It may be assumed that the speeches mainly served to impart information.

Apparently as a result of the subsequent trend towards political involvement and radicalization, at the beginning of 1938 the seventh annual general meeting of the League of Coloured Peoples instructed its executive committee 'to explore the possibilities of calling a World Conference for 1940. If this is to be made a reality and to accomplish any valuable result, then Africans and persons of African descent throughout the world must give us their fullest co-operation,' as Moody put it in his 'president's message'. The conference was to take place in London and was to include 'the powerful group of the coloured American citizens'.

> In view of the present state of transition of the world [the conference intended to discuss the future of the African and Afro-American groups] so that we should not be taken by surprise when the question of deciding our future and fate will be brought up. A fear was voiced that if we do not come together and state what we want, taking a hand in the formation of our own future, we might wake up one morning and find our fate fixed for us by those who are interested in our exploitation and our advancement jeopardised for generations. . . .[91]

The available documentation does not contain any mention of the key-word 'Pan-African' or any reference to earlier Pan-African endeavours. In spite of this the decision to hold such a comprehensive conference may be categorized as a manifestation of Pan-Africanism in the narrower sense of the term. It is all the more regrettable that the 1940 conference could not take place. Nevertheless the preparations for it did engender some noteworthy activities.

In the same annual general meeting at which the League adopted two separate resolutions calling attention to the politicizing effect of the Italian attack on Ethiopia and German colonial claims,[92] it put forward some proposals on colonial policy. It demanded 'universal free education for the entire colonial population' and 'the immediate enfranchisement of all literate colonial citizens, in places where this does not yet obtain'. Within ten years the League was hoping to achieve these ends 'so as to prepare a people who would be fitted to determine their own destiny through self-government'.[93]

During these months Moody's League and Padmore's IASB began to collaborate with one another, at least temporarily. They joined with the Negro Welfare Association in presenting a memorandum to the Royal Commission on Rhodesia and the West Indies.[94] This collaboration seems to have continued at the next big conference, which may be regarded as a preparation for Manchester. From 7 to 9 July 1939 a Conference on the African Peoples, Democracy and World Peace was held at the Memorial Hall, Farringdon Street, London – the traditional meeting-place, which had been the headquarters of the League of Coloured Peoples. Although Moody put in a claim for it as the largest and most important meeting of the League,[95] it does not seem to have amounted to a substitute, one year premature, for the worldwide conference planned in 1938 for 1940. Perhaps it was only intended as a preliminary to this latter conference.

The 1939 meeting was arranged by several organizations: the LCP, the Negro Welfare Association, the Coloured Film Artists' Association and the Gold Coast Association. Originally it was planned that WASU should participate, but because of some procedural error Solanke objected to it being included among the organizers.[96] It is not yet known whether Solanke later withdrew his formal objection to its presence. At any rate the meetings of the coordinating committee[97] to be discussed below took place without WASU, which would seem to suggest that it did not. Padmore and his International African Service Bureau (IASB) were apparently, according to the available evidence, not formally involved in the undertaking, but probably did take some part both in the preliminary moves and in the discussions that ensued. Moreover, Padmore was one of the speakers at the conference and took part in the debates. To arrange the gathering and to follow it up a committee was formed, which (so far as is known) held three of its four meetings in Moody's home under his chairmanship. This points to the important role that Moody played. The secretary and treasurer were Keith Alleyne and Peter Blackman respectively, both of them from Aggrey House.[98]

The theme of the Conference on the African Peoples, Democracy and World Peace points to the fact that the groups responsible, who represented different nuances of the Pan-African movement in Britain, were now more conscious than ever of the connection between their wishes and the world political situation.[99] The conference seems at times to have become rather rough, for the communists tried to win control of the proceedings and launched a violent attack on Padmore.[100] It was no doubt in line with Moody's intentions that Padmore, who spoke on behalf of the IASB and the Sierra Leone Youth League led by his friend Wallace-Johnson, rejected these attacks calmly but firmly.

The resolutions of the conference contained demands which in some details went considerably beyond the positions adopted the preceding year. They called for

1 the right of self-determination;
2 condemnation of the mandate system and any attempt to extend it;
3 freedom of speech, press and assembly;
4 repeal of repressive legislation;
5 free trade unions and other working-class organizations;
6 social legislation and universal compulsory education free of charge.[101]

Their programme provided the basis for further collaboration after the conference. The latter gave this collaboration a fresh boost. At the instigation of Dr C. B. Clarke who was close to Moody and Padmore the committee discussed, two weeks before it met on 21 June 1939,[102] 'ways and means for bringing about greater co-operation between the various bodies representing coloured opinion in England'.[103] After this session, of which so far nothing else is known, another meeting took place in Moody's house on 5 July.[104] Those present included, besides Moody as chairman, Alleyne, Philipps[105] and Roberts[106] for the LCP; Dr Wallen as non-official representative of the Coloured Film Artists' Association (CFAA)[107]; Padmore and Kenyatta for the IASB; and J. E. Worrell[108] as secretary. Moody opened the meeting by referring to the preceding meeting, which had been suggested by Dr Clarke, and to the need for greater unity. To this end he suggested forming a strong umbrella association, both for reasons of economy and in the interest of better representation. When Kenyatta put a sceptical question Moody explained that he did indeed have in mind co-operation within the framework of his League of Coloured Peoples, but that this should not prevent each of the various organizations from retaining its individual identity. Wallen and Kenyatta at once opposed this, pleading for an umbrella association outside the League. Kenyatta was in favour of bringing about integration from above by federating the executive committees of the participating organizations. Moody was concerned with creating a new organization which could win the confidence of the African and West Indian element. He therefore proposed that the already extant committee for the preparation of the 1940 conference should become a permanent body and serve as a preliminary step towards an umbrella organization incorporating all these other groups but remaining above them. On this basis agreement was reached. In reply to a question on this point, Padmore replied that he thought it unlikely that the activities of such a coordinating committee would clash with those of his own organization, the IASB, because the latter was more concerned with the mass of workers and peasants and with the question of civil rights.

This was followed by a discussion of the question whether the new committee should publish a journal of its own. The idea, mooted by Moody, met with general approval. But the realistic Padmore warned against taking premature decisions: in the first place, he said, it was necessary to agree upon the general programme which the journal would present to the world. A final decision was therefore put off once more. A programme commission was set up, consisting of Padmore, Alleyne and Worrell, who were to work out such guidelines.

Between the meeting of 5 July and the following one, held on 26 July at the same place, came the big conference of 7 to 9 July 1939. In working out its resolutions[109] a considerable role was undoubtedly played by the three persons who comprised the programme commission of the conference committee. On 26 July, as reporter of the programme committee, Padmore made the conference resolutions the basis of his proposals for a common programme.[110] This nine-point programme differed only in a few nuances of phrasing and substance from the resolutions, of which they were a summary. The only new point was a demand for an agrarian policy on co-operative lines (if 'a co-operative agrarian policy' may be interpreted in this sense). It was resolved to submit the whole document to other organizations – both those represented at the conference and those who might be interested, such as WASU, so that they might each discuss it and pass appropriate resolutions. The committee went on to discuss the name, constitution and financing of the planned umbrella organization, without coming to definite decisions. The delegates were first to ask for instructions from their respective organizations.

The next meeting of the coordinating committee was arranged for 6 September. About it nothing is yet known; perhaps it fell victim to the outbreak of the war. This event was bound to change the situation so far as the Pan-African movement was concerned. First of all, so far as the incomplete sources go, it seems to have put an end to the collaboration between Moody and Padmore, between the conservative and radical wings of Pan-Africanism in London – a collaboration which was more intensive and institutionalized, at least in embryo, than anything hitherto known. Immediately before World War II it seemed that the Pan-African movement would be united under the leadership of its conservative element. The war interrupted this process and the longer it went on the more the relationship of forces was reversed. Towards the end of the war Moody tried to realize his earlier plans, at least in part, but the politicizing effect of World War II favoured the radicals more than the conservatives. The former won such an influence over the leadership that Moody and his League of Coloured Peoples were not even represented at the fifth Pan-African Congress.[111]

18 Reawakening interest in Pan-Africanism in the USA during World War II: Du Bois and Nkrumah

General effect of World War II

The impact of World War II upon African and Asian nationalism in general and upon Pan-Africanism in particular resembles that of World War I: the outbreak of hostilities at first led to a paralysis of organizational activity, but later the war brought about an acceleration and intensification of earlier developments.[1] The paralysing effect of the outbreak of the war is obvious and needs no lengthy explanation. Oversea links became difficult or impossible to maintain. In both the British and French colonies some activists were taken into protective custody or sent to prison, as happened to Wallace-Johnson and Émile Faure. The uncertainty about how the war would end unsettled men's minds; the Hitler–Stalin pact of 23 August 1939 confused and split the left; and the defeat of France led to the dissolution of the francophone groups.

Even in Britain the first year of the war brought trouble and loosened old ties. Moody's son and daughter, of whom at least the latter was active in the League of Coloured Peoples, volunteered for the services;[2] Kenyatta had to do war work as a farm-hand in the south of England.[3]

When the office of the Independent Labour party in London was bombed out in 1941,[4] Padmore moved to new lodgings at 22 Cranleigh House, Cranleigh Street, London N.W.1. This became the new head-quarters of Pan-African activities in London until Padmore moved to Ghana late in 1957. The efforts to create a Pan-African umbrella organization and to hold a conference came to a standstill.[5]

The accelerating effect of World War II[6] was even more marked than that of World War I, because this time the war was proclaimed from the start as one for democracy. Nazi racism discredited racism as such, against which Pan-Africanism and its predecessors had always fought.[7] The entry of the USSR and the USA into the war on the side of the Western Powers brought a shift to the left and led to the restoration of old links, since Germany and her allies were now isolated in the world.

After the defeat of France, when Britain for a time had to face Germany and Italy alone, the British colonies became of greater economic and strategic importance than ever. Once the United States had joined the Allies, its massive commitment of material resources to the war effort gave a mighty stimulus to the modernization of Africa through the construction of roads, supply depots, harbours, airports, repair shops etc. The increased demand for labour furthered urbanization. The trade-union movement, particularly in West Africa which was always further ahead, received a powerful impetus.

During the 1930s a legal framework had developed for a trade-union movement in the West African colonies. The social unrest in the West Indies during 1938 demonstrated the need for trade unions as negotiating partners, so that steps were taken to fill the gap in Africa as well: trade unions were encouraged in the hope of preventing social conflicts becoming as acute as they were in the West Indies. This new conception took shape in the Colonial Development and Welfare Act, which had been drafted before the outbreak of the war but was not passed until 1940. This made grants to the colonies conditional on their respective governments permitting trade unions to operate.

The colonies' participation in the economic war effort brought social changes in its train. Thus in Nigeria the number of wage and salary earners rose from about 183,000 to about 300,000 between 1939 and 1946[8] – a development which was more dramatic than it may seem, especially in the cities of the south. The new workers and employees organized trade unions for the first time on any considerable scale,[9] and some of the peasants also formed co-operative societies. Moreover a large number of Africans serving in the British and French armies now often encountered modern forms of social life and organization which they had never seen before. From the British territories in Africa during World War II 372,000 Africans served in the British army, of whom 166,000 were stationed outside their own countries – some of them outside Africa, as for example in Burma, where West Africans fought the Japanese in units of their own up to divisional strength. From the French African territories came another 141,000 men who saw service outside their homeland.[10]

Urbanization and military service brought about a widening of horizons and a new wave of politicization. Like the infantrymen from Dahomey and Senegal after World War I,[11] many Africans who fought in the war took back home with them a new political awareness. This time it was transformed directly into dynamic action, so that returning veterans played a significant part in the African nationalist movement. In the rapidly growing cities they found new political and quasi-political organizations with a keener sense of reality and, at least in British West Africa, a local press which was more critical of the administration than ever before. Despite the war education had made progress.[12] Africa's war effort necessitated an expansion of administrative activities but led to a reduction of the European administrative apparatus, so that after four decades of retrogression and stagnation a beginning was made on its Africanization.[13]

All these factors made themselves felt against the background of great changes in world politics. Broadcasting became significant for the first time. Just as at the end of World War I, Africans claimed for themselves the great principles of democracy and national sovereignty – originally only intended for European peoples – but in a more emphatic and vigorous manner than ever before. The Atlantic Charter had a particularly electrifying effect.[14] Clement Attlee, deputy prime minister under Winston Churchill, encouraged the African nationalists by interpreting the Atlantic Charter in such a way that it gave scope to *their* aspirations as well: 'You will not find in the declaration . . . any suggestion that the freedom and social security for which we fight should be denied to any of the races of mankind. We fight this way not just for ourselves alone, but for all peoples. I look for an ever-increasing measure of self-government in Africa and for an ever-increasing standard of life for all the peoples of Africa.'[15] Churchill on the other hand immediately and unequivocally opposed any attempts to extend its meaning to the colonies: 'The Joint Declaration does not qualify in any way the various statements of policy which have been made from time to time about the development of constitutional government in India, Burma and other parts of the British Empire.' This exchange gave a foretaste of the political battle that was to take place in Britain after the end of the war.

The war had a similar effect upon Afro-Americans in the West Indies and in the USA. Here, too, the wartime economic situation stimulated political consciousness. In the West Indies additional jobs and earnings were provided by the bases which the United States set up in exchange for British destroyers. Here, too, modern trade unions and political parties first developed during the war years. In the United States the arms boom put an end to the Great Depression which had so afflicted the Afro-Americans, encouraging them to participate actively in war production; those in the armed forces developed a new political awareness.[16]

In the long run the war also gave a new stimulus to Pan-Africanism. During the latter half of the war the movement was reformed and exerted itself politically. The symptoms were to be seen on both sides of the Atlantic. From here onwards it could be said that all roads led to Manchester – i.e. to the fifth Pan-African Congress, held in October 1945.

New beginnings in the USA: the Council on African Affairs

The new phase of Pan-African activity begins, logically enough, with the man who still personified the origins of Pan-Africanism, W. E. B. Du Bois. Even during the depression years he had apparently never given up completely the hope that Pan-Africanism would revive, as is suggested by his action in 1934.[17] During World War II his vague hopes began to take concrete shape. Early in 1941, when the Carnegie Peace Endowment sent out a questionnaire about international movements and organizations, he was rather evasive in giving information about his Pan-African Congress movement. Du Bois was honest enough to admit that he himself

> was not sure whether the Pan-African [Congress] ought to be regarded as an existing institution or not. It was planned as a

conference without specific organization. . . . The ideas back of the Congress are still alive and discussed and if the world ever settles down to peace again, there will be another meeting of the Congress. At present, however, it is only an idea on paper and in the memory of a considerable number of former participants in Africa, the West Indies and America.[18]

This did not sound very dynamic, but after all Du Bois was already seventy-three years old. At any rate he indicated, although in a purely academic and speculative way, the general direction to be taken by subsequent events. He still enjoyed a high reputation in militant Afro-American circles. Towards the end of the war he again collaborated actively on the executive committee of the NAACP and took on a regular column in one of the most important Afro-American journals, the Chicago *Defender*, for which Padmore also worked as a correspondent.

The US entry into the war led to increased interest in Africa. An important organization catering to this interest was the Council on African Affairs in New York, which had been founded by Paul Robeson (on his return from Europe and West Africa), and by Max Yergan.[19] The board of management included Ralph Bunche and René Maran,[20] so that now also a certain link was forged in the USA between the francophone and anglophone elements – personified by the man who more than twenty years before had brought about the first contacts and interpenetration of ideas through his novel *Batouala*. The organization was financed, or so it appears,[21] by Frederick V. Field, a White millionaire who was a supporter of left-wing causes. At first the organization engaged in charitable activities from New York until, in the middle of World War II, it came into contact with a group of African students, mostly from West Africa. Their most vigorous spokesman was Francis N. Nkrumah or, as he called himself from about 1945, Kwame Nkrumah.

In the middle of April 1944 the Council on African Affairs in New York held a Conference on Africa which brought together a group of personalities and organizations with an active interest in that continent. Nkrumah played a considerable part in the preliminaries of the conference,[22] and it was here that he made his début on the Pan-African stage, after having already made his name as an African student leader in the United States. The 1944 conference was for Nkrumah the beginning of a career which led him by way of London and Manchester to Accra, where he became first prime minister and later president of Ghana until, in 1966, he was toppled from the pinnacle of power and became an exile in Guinea, where he died in 1972.

Nkrumah's life and education up to 1944

Nkrumah was born (probably in 1909) in Nkroful, in the Nzima area, in the extreme south-western part of the Gold Coast.[23] The Nzima are the most westerly tribe of the Fanti and the least respected. The nearest town is Axim, some miles to the south-east, and like Nkroful situated on the coast. As early as 1638 two French Capuchin friars had come to Axim as missionaries,[24] and by Nkrumah's time the Catholic church had acquired a certain strength in this area. Nkrumah's father was a goldsmith; his mother, a pious Catholic, was descended from two chiefs and on her son's departure for America she tried carefully to imprint upon his memory the fact that by family and local tradition he had a claim to these 'stools'. Thus in contrast to all the other exponents of Pan-Africanism discussed hitherto, Nkrumah came directly from the village, 'the bush'; he did not originate from an urban, intellectual milieu, rooted in a modern tradition sometimes reaching back for two or three generations – as was often the case in the Gold Coast.[25]

He was also the first figure of importance on the Gold Coast who was not brought up in a Methodist environment. From his childhood onwards he maintained strong links with traditional society. This point has generally been ignored hitherto, although it explains much about his later career. In his native village Nkrumah attended the simple Catholic village school and had himself baptized through the influence of a German missionary, Pater Georg Fischer. As a schoolboy Nkrumah frequently acted as acolyte during church services. After eight years of Catholic primary school education, at about the age of seventeen, he became a so-called 'pupil teacher' at a school in Half Assini. In 1926 he was enrolled as one of the first students in Achimota College, the newly opened teachers' training college near Accra, where during his first year Aggrey was the most influential of his teachers.[26] It was in Achimota (and not in his native village) that he became familiar with the traditional drumming and dancing of his tribe; he also founded an Aggrey Students' Society to honour the memory of his teacher and also to serve as a platform for debates.

Although Nkrumah's piety greatly diminished while he was in Achimota, after completing his studies in 1930 he became an elementary school teacher at the Catholic Junior School in Elmina. At that time he helped to found a teachers' association, a kind of trade union. In 1931 he was transferred as head teacher to a Catholic school of the same kind in Axim. Here he founded the Nzima Literature Society and through it established contact with S. R. Wood of the National Congress of British West Africa, which virtually only functioned on paper. Wood was simultaneously also secretary of the rump ARPS led by Sekyi;[27] in this capacity he was a member of the second delegation which went to London from the Gold Coast in 1934, indirectly giving the impetus to the embryonic predecessor of what became the Pan-African Federation.[28] Wood introduced Nkrumah to the history and politics of the Gold Coast and later wrote a letter recommending him for admission to Lincoln University in Pennsylvania.[29]

Around 1934 Nkrumah decided to study in England, but failed his entrance examination to the University of London. Recalling the example of his teacher Aggrey who had given him such encouragement, he decided to try his luck in the United States. He was supported in his decision by Nnamdi Azikiwe who in 1934 had returned from the USA to Africa after studying there for ten years. With Wallace-Johnson he edited the *African Morning Post*, and so contributed appreciably to the growth of Gold Coast nationalism.[30] In 1935 Nkrumah was accepted as a student at Lincoln University, and in the autumn of 1935 he travelled to the USA by way of Liverpool. During a week's stay in London he heard of Italy's attack on Ethiopia. In his *Autobiography* Nkrumah gives a somewhat dramatized account of this which, however, seems quite plausible in the light of his character and the general effect this event had upon Africans and Afro-Americans:[31] he says that in a time of depression and a confusing flood of fresh impressions this news roused him to take a firm and energetic stand in favour of nationalism and anti-colonialism.[32]

By way of Harlem Nkrumah went to Lincoln University, where he became a member of a fraternity (whose cruel inauguration ceremonies he graphically described) and a freemason. After taking his B.A. in 1939 he obtained a job at the university as assistant lecturer in philosophy, did research for his M.Sc. in philosophy and pedagogy at the University of Pennsylvania in Philadelphia, and meanwhile took a course in theology at Lincoln University. In 1942 he passed his B.A. Theol.

examination with the best marks in the course and had to give the formal speech at the final celebration. As his theme he chose the symbolic verse of the psalm: 'Ethiopia shall stretch forth her hands unto God',[33] apparently with considerable success. In 1942 he passed his M.Sc. examination in Philadelphia and became an instructor in Greek (for beginners) and in negro history at Lincoln University. In February 1943 he became an M.A. of the University of Pennsylvania and started work on his Ph.D.

During the university vacations Nkrumah earned his living by doing casual work. Among other jobs he was, prior to 1939, a steward on a passenger liner between New York and Vera Cruz (Mexico). While studying in Lincoln University's theological seminar he preached in negro churches in the eastern United States. In his spare time Nkrumah (according to his own statements) read Kant, Hegel, Descartes, Schopenhauer, Nietzsche, Freud 'and others' for his philosophical studies, and Marx, Engels, Lenin, Mazzini and Garvey out of political interest; of these thinkers it was Garvey who impressed and influenced him most.[34]

His political interests impelled him to have dealings with all sorts of political organizations in the USA in the hope of learning from them: these ranged from the Republicans and Democrats to the Trotskyites and Communists; from the Council on African Affairs through the Committee on African Students to the NAACP and the Urban League.

Nkrumah's eclecticism: the schism between traditional and modern elements

We have described Nkrumah's complex educational career in Africa and America in such detail because it contains several elements which became significant in the development of Pan-Africanism. Moreover, the abundance of academic subjects Nkrumah studied or even taught (philosophy, pedagogy, political economy, theology, ancient Greek, negro history and sociology) give an impression of the range of his interests, of the superficiality of his heterogeneous knowledge. If one adds the diverse influences left on him by freemasonry, religion and politics we have a rich blend of elements that accounts for his characteristic eclecticism. To complete the picture we have to add to this confusing wealth of modern intellectual and political notions the component of African nationalism and traditionalism. This aspect of Nkrumah's outlook, hitherto entirely neglected, may be illustrated by reference to new material. It explains his pronounced oscillation between modern and traditional ideas, which can be illustrated by the following example.

In November 1942, at the instigation of Robert K. A. Gardiner,[35] a member of WASU who had just come from London, the newly founded African Students' Association of the United States and Canada organized, in collaboration with WASU in New York and in Salisbury, North Carolina, memorial celebrations to mark the anniversary of Aggrey's death. In New York, where Aggrey died in 1927, a memorial church service was held on 22 November; four days later a ceremony in African style was held at Salisbury, where Aggrey had worked. In front of Aggrey's friends and relatives as well as African students there was a remarkable scene at Salisbury cemetery: a memorial to Aggrey was unveiled, covered with bright kent (a traditional cloth from the Gold Coast). Subsequently a representative of the African Students' Association (ASA) led the mourning. He spoke prayers in Fanti, offered libations to the gods, and then broke the turf near Aggrey's grave, removed some soil and put it into a box which was later taken to the Gold Coast to be interred in Aggrey's homeland. This ritual act was followed by further prayers, whereupon Aggrey's spirit was commanded to leave this alien continent and to return to Africa, where it might find eternal peace among the ancestral spirits.

After all this was over the master of ceremonies explained their meaning to the audience: this was a rite which was normally celebrated on the battlefield if there was no time to inter the dead. Moreover Africans believed that the spirits of their relatives could find no peace outside Africa, which was why this ceremony had been necessary.

The master of ceremonies was none other than Francis Nkrumah, at that time president of the ASA. This story is not an invention by malevolent enemies but is taken from an unsigned report which the ASA journal, the *African Interpreter*, published in its first issue of February 1943.[36] As we are told at the end of the report, several photographs were taken during the ceremony and even films which were later shown in New York cinemas. It was announced that material pertaining to the Aggrey memorial celebrations would be published, but it probably never saw the light.

That it was Nkrumah of all people who, at the grave of the pious Aggrey, should have assumed the role of a pagan fetish priest and uttered magic spells should no longer astonish us now that we are

familiar with his biography. By contrast with all other African nationalists and Pan-African leaders, Nkrumah stemmed directly from the
traditional tribal milieu. The years he spent in Achimota and as a
village schoolmaster can only have strengthened his ties to traditional
Africa and, as it were, intellectualized them. During his spell at Lincoln
University Nkrumah wrote, apparently for the theological seminar,
several term papers on aspects of Akan traditional society,[37] whose two
main groups are the Fanti and Ashanti. His projected dissertation, too,
was to have dealt with the same traditional themes.[38] It was at this
stage in his career, if not earlier, that Nkrumah may have learned or
written down the pagan spells which he recited at the grave of his
teacher Aggrey.

One can imagine the surprise of Dr Johnson, dean of the theological
seminar of Lincoln University, when he learned from the *African
Interpreter* about the activities of the young Bachelor of Theology. To a
sharp letter Nkrumah replied evasively, but with the sense of missionary
vocation peculiar to him: 'The Burden of my life is to live in such a way
that I may become a living symbol of all that is best both in Christianity
and in the laws, customs and beliefs of my people. I am a Christian
and will remain so but never a blind Christian.'[39]

The dichotomy between the modern and the traditional world
could hardly be expressed more succinctly, garbed in religious concepts.

As well as working his way through college and fulfilling his academic
duties, Nkrumah engaged in an intense quasi-political activity, partly
on the student level and partly through writing articles and attending
conferences, although still before a limited public. Some letters from
the American period of his life give an impression of his restless dynamism and his predilection for a slightly eccentric hyperbolic style, as
well as the dogmatic sharpness with which he set forth his anti-colonial
principles. In a letter of 1 July 1942 addressed to his compatriot,
K. A. B. Jones-Quartey (today professor at the university of Legon,
Ghana), he called himself simply an anti-imperialist in contrast to the
more subtle language preferred by the latter:

> You speak of a choice between the British and the Germans. For
> the true renascent African there should be no choice. Why must
> we choose between the ruthless Nazi barbarism and the cold, selfish,
> heartless exploitation and domination to which the British have
> subjected our people for so many years? No! It is our task to build,

not to make a choice, but to unite and develop so that no matter who wins this war, those who hope to exploit and maintain an empire, whether they be British, German or anything else, will find a living hell in Africa.[40]

The political programme which Nkrumah enclosed with this letter has not survived, but it may be reconstructed from other evidence. At the beginning of 1943 Nkrumah wrote to Dr Ralph Bunche, Padmore's former teacher (the simultaneous rejection of British colonialism and German national socialism was by the way identical with Padmore's position): 'The voice of the youth of Africa is crying in the wilderness of international relations and we dare not be silent. We have one object: The flag of West African Nationalism must be unfurled, now or never. . . .'[41] Thus Nkrumah's principal concern at this time was a West African nationalism rooted in an earlier tradition.[42]

In an article which appeared in the United States at the end of 1943 Nkrumah either changed his opinion on one essential point or else concealed it for tactical reasons. Now he described it as the African youth movement's aim 'to raise the voice of Africa to join that of the people throughout the world for the defeat of fascism and to help build a post-war world based upon the principles of freedom as expressed in the Atlantic Charter'.[43] He warned against any attempt to restore the colonial empires after victory since this would provoke a revolution among the colonial peoples. This was an absolutely realistic prognosis, as was proved only a few years later, but probably here the wish was father to the thought.

In the same article, originally a lecture given at a teachers' conference in Philadelphia, Nkrumah expounded in detail the dilemma facing Africa (and himself), on this occasion with reference to educational problems. After outlining earlier efforts to promote education – both of the traditional kind and that transmitted by the missions – he hit the nail on the head by declaring: 'The problem now is how to educate and then initiate the African into modern life without uprooting him from his home and tribal life. Thus the present-day educational problem in West Africa is that of educational acculturation. This calls for correlation between African culture and that of the Western world.'[44] Here Nkrumah's eclecticism is combined with an error of logic to which all romantics succumb, for the modern world and especially industrialization cannot but dissolve the old tribal society. To attempt simultaneously to modernize *and* to retain the traditional social structure must necessarily lead to desperate compromises which cannot last.

It is therefore not surprising that in the same article Nkrumah should have criticized the 'alienated . . . so-called educated Africans' who had become 'divorced from their native tradition'.

> Education in West Africa [he went on] should produce a new class of educated Africans imbued with the culture of the West but nevertheless attached to their environment. This new class of Africans should demand the powers of self-determination to determine the progress and advancement of its own culture. It must combine the best in western civilization with the best in African culture. Only on this ground can Africa create a new and distinct civilization in the process of world advancement. . . .[45]

Nkrumah and the African Students' Association (ASA)

Nkrumah played a considerable part in the African Students' Association (ASA). The history of African student politics in the United States may be told quite briefly. The first wave of students who came from South Africa around 1900 forged a link between South African Ethiopianism and the AME church in the United States; then World War I and the foundation of Fort Hare as Bantu College (1916) for the time being put an end to study by non-White South Africans in the United States.[46] Around 1900 two students from the Gold Coast came to the AMEZ college in Salisbury NC, Aggrey and Pinanko. Aggrey remained in the United States, where he was active in academic life for about a quarter of a century, whereas Pinanko returned to his homeland to set up the AMEZ church.[47] After World War I some students from the English-speaking African territories went to the USA – most of them from West Africa (Nigeria, the Gold Coast, Sierra Leone, Liberia), but also some from Uganda and South Africa. Most of these men remained in the United States, where they became professors, physicians or lawyers. They were not very numerous, probably about sixty or seventy strong.[48] Later they may have given moral and material support to the new generation of African students in the United States.[49]

Of the West African students who returned to Africa between the two World Wars the most important were Eyo Ita and Nnamdi

Azikiwe. They both went back to Africa in 1934, Ita directly to Nigeria and Azikiwe first to the Gold Coast.[50] Ita is one of Nigeria's leading educational experts, and helped to set up a national school system in that country. As first prime minister of the Eastern region he intervened occasionally in politics until he was replaced by Azikiwe. The latter was encouraged, or even persuaded, by Aggrey to go to America, and the same is true of Nkrumah.[51]

Other students from Africa besides Nkrumah went to the States before 1939. Between 1920 and 1937 twenty students in all left Nigeria; in 1938 another twelve followed. A popular choice was Lincoln University, the *alma mater* of Azikiwe and later of Nkrumah; eleven of the twelve Nigerians who arrived in 1938 studied at Lincoln.[52] In 1938 and 1939 there were so many African students there that they could form a football team which won a game against Howard University and the Hampton Institute. At one of these matches if not more, Nkrumah acted as referee.[53]

Apart from Lincoln, African students chose to go to Columbia University (New York), Harvard, Yale, the Universities of Pennsylvania (Philadelphia) and Chicago, Howard University (Washington DC), the University of Michigan and to McGill University in Montreal, Quebec. Most of them registered to read social sciences (sociology, economics, anthropology and political science); others took medicine, engineering, physics and biology. All students, except for some from Liberia, came at their own expense, or rather that of their parents and relatives – they did not receive any scholarships. Adjei took a favourable view of this, since he thought it demonstrated the Africans' urge towards modernization.[54]

These students felt a greater need than their predecessors to set up their own organizations. Some founded or collaborated in cultural and scholarly institutions, such as the African Academy of Arts and Research or the American Council on African Education (both in New York in 1944); there was also an Institute for African Studies at the University of Pennsylvania, which Nkrumah assisted by providing data on the Fanti language. Of greater importance was the establishment of the African Students' Association (ASA) to represent African students' interests in the USA and at the same time to serve as a political instrument. Nkrumah claimed most of the merit for this step: 'It was also there (Philadelphia) that I began to organise the African Students' Association of America and Canada.'[55] But new material throws some doubt on this claim. In a historical sketch which appeared in the first issue of the ASA journal, the *African Interpreter*,[56] and is thus a primary source, Nkrumah's name is not mentioned once in the sections dealing with the prehistory of the ASA. This does not necessarily mean that he played no part at all in its foundation. The fact that Lincoln University is mentioned as the most important centre of such endeavours suggests that he did take part, since he must have been an important figure among the African students at Lincoln – first as a relatively mature student and later on as a faculty member.

If one accepts the information given in the *African Interpreter* the following picture emerges. The first attempts to found a union of African students were made in 1939 and centred upon Lincoln University. But even earlier discussions had taken place elsewhere about the need to form such an organization. At the beginning of 1940 these ideas apparently assumed concrete form in conversations between A. A. N. Orizu[57] and John K. Smart. At the beginning of June 1940 these two men sent out letters inviting their African fellow-students in America to put forward their ideas on the subject; two months later they issued invitations to the first general meeting in New York. This gathering took place on 18 and 19 August at the YMCA in New York – probably in the YMCA building in Harlem on 135th Street almost opposite the Schomburg Collection. It was only on 1 January 1941 that an organization was founded at Lincoln University with the name of the African Students' Service. On 3 January a draft statute was drawn up and the first executive committee appointed. Mbonu Ojike became president, K. O. Mbadiwe secretary and Orizu 'director of information'. Later another body was constituted, a 'board of directors'. The new association even appointed its own chaplain, the Rev. Dr Don R. Falkenburg, probably to underline the members' desire to appear socially acceptable. Between 2 and 5 September 1941 the first annual meeting took place at the YMCA in New York (this time unquestionably the one in Harlem), at which officers were appointed for 1941–2; to the three just named were added Ernest Kalibala as vice-president and Udo Akpabio as treasurer. On the same occasion the name of the organization was changed to the African Students' Association.

It is not until the second annual meeting, held in New York from 7 to 10 September 1942, that we come across the name of Nkrumah, when he was elected president of ASA. This evidence undermines the credibility of Nkrumah's subsequent statement that 'at the conference I was elected president, a position I held until the day I left for England'.[58] He was not elected president at the first conference but at the second; moreover, he did not retain this office until the last day of his stay in the United States, for the fifth issue of the *African Interpreter*, published in the spring of 1944, contains a photo of Nkrumah with an accompanying caption identifying him as 'former president'. One may therefore assume that Nkrumah either resigned or was voted out, probably at the third annual meeting held in Harlem from 10 to 12 September 1943.

Also doubtful is Nkrumah's other assertion that he personally ensured the admission to the union of Africans in America who were not students. The four issues of the *African Interpreter* at present available (for the time being the most important source for the development of ASA) contain no reference to this point, which would surely have been of some interest to members if it were true; nor is there any mention of it in Adjei's article in *WASU* published at the beginning of 1945.

At its second conference in 1942 ASA gave itself an even more top-heavy executive committee than before. For a total of twenty-eight members[59] it required an executive of nine, so that almost every third member was on the committee. The distribution of offices was as follows: president, Nkrumah; vice-president, Orizu; general secretary, James L. Nsima; director of information, Adjei; treasurer, Ibanga U. Akpabio; financial secretary, Frederick S. Rowland; recorder, William F. Fitzjohn; ex-officio member, Mbadiwe; deputy secretary, J. Nnodu Okungwe. Most members of the executive also figured in three other bodies along with two ordinary members, K. A. B. Jones-Quartey[60] as member of the Bureau of Publications and member of the editorial board of the *African Interpreter* and J. E. A. Schandorf on the Publications Advisory Board.

On going through the list of ASA's twenty-eight members one is struck by the fact that only ten of them have European names, plus one (Jones-Quartey) whose name was Anglo-African. The other seventeen have unquestionably African names. Most of them came either from Nigeria (and were Ibos) or from the Gold Coast. If one proceeds from the assumption that most of the students with African names (though not all of them, on account of the tendency to revert to African names which made itself felt at the turn of the century)[61] came from a traditional, possibly rural milieu, whereas those with European names belonged to the middle class which had been in existence for about a century,[62] Nkrumah with his family background would be no exception. He would merely be the most dynamic representative of a new group of African intellectuals who deliberately tried to combine traditional and modern elements.[63] Their particular dynamism could be explained at least partly by their awareness that, hailing as they did from the common people, they thought that they represented the real, unadultered Africa.

After they returned to their homelands most ASA members became active nationalists. Three of them had already published books written from a nationalist point of view[64] while in the USA and during lecture tours they had appealed for sympathy towards African nationalism. Seven of these twenty-eight men had spectacular careers ahead of them in Africa.[65] Thus when Nkrumah was in America he was by no means the only leader among African students. His career was simply the most spectacular one until the beginning of 1966. He evidently retrojected some of his later glory into the American period of his life, perhaps to make his charisma shine still more brightly. That Nkrumah had a leadership complex even as a young man in America may be seen from the fact in issue 4 of the *African Interpreter* he addressed his fellow-students a message in the style of an imperial proclamation: 'Message from F. N. Nkrumah, President of African Students' Association, Philadelphia, Pa.; Fellow Africans – Greetings.' The content, too, was couched in the best declamatory style, as heavy as brocade and full of clichés:

> The future of our country, like the future of most countries throughout the world, lies at stake today. Only action will remove the threat to oppressor and oppressed alike. The cause of Africans everywhere is one with the cause of all peoples of African descent throughout the world. . . . Unity, Freedom, Independence, Democracy – these should be our watchwords, our ideals, and not the barbaric totalitarianism of the Fascists or perverted colonial 'democracy' of the imperialists. . . . We must rise and join hands together, for in unity alone can we find our strength and future. This is the time to remember Mother Africa and build for her a glorious and independent future.[66]

His African colleagues may not have appreciated this style, for one year later Nkrumah was no longer president of ASA, as we have seen, and the next issue of the *African Interpreter* did not contain any such message from Nkrumah's successor, Akpabio.[67]

The second annual conference of ASA in 1942, stimulated by Gardiner's presence, resolved to hold the ceremony to commemorate the anniversary of Aggrey's death alluded to above[68] and also to affiliate with WASU in London.[69] From then on ASA considered itself a collective member of WASU. It had thus established contact with what was then the most important centre of Pan-Africanism, London. After his arrival in London at the beginning of 1945 Ako Adjei wrote for the WASU journal,[70] and Nkrumah, shortly after he came to Britain in the summer of 1945, was elected vice-president of WASU. This no doubt facilitated his rise to power in Pan-African circles.

The union's plans to publish a separate journal seem to have matured about the time of the conference held in September 1942. Nkrumah had already conceived the idea of publishing a hectographed periodical from Philadelphia with the title *African Crisis* (modelled on *Crisis*). Now, apparently on Nkrumah's initiative, there came into being the Bureau of Publications which for its part published the first issue of the *African Interpreter* in February 1943.[71] The first two numbers appeared in an unassuming format and had fifteen hectographed pages. Page 16 bears only the address of the editorial office – International House, 500 Riverside Drive, New York City – and an appeal for subscriptions to US government bonds.[72] The first issue also had a front cover, the upper third of which bore the title and subtitle (The *African Interpreter*. Monthly Organ of the African Students' Association of the United States and Canada) and the motto 'For Progress and Democracy'. This was accompanied by a sketch-map of Africa (including Madagascar) with the frontiers marked, a simple graphic illustration of Africa's unity in diversity. The second number is even more modest in appearance, since the title and the map (with Africa now shown without frontiers and simply designated 'Africa') were both compressed into the upper third of the page, the rest of the page being devoted to the leading article. Inside the journal, on pages 1 or 2, there is a complete list of the executive committee, the various bodies and members (now a valuable source). The leading article in issue 1 is entitled 'We Make our Bow', which, as is candidly explained, was borrowed from the first leading article in the *African Morning Post*, published by Azikiwe in December 1934 – a clear sign of Azikiwe's influence, confirmed once more *expressis verbis* in the second paragraph.

The journal aimed to bring Africa and America closer together (to 'interpret' them to each other), so easing the task of the non-Africans who had hitherto dedicated themselves to this cause. The editors sought to explain the rapidly changing international scene to their compatriots at home and to keep them abreast of the academic progress attained by ASA members. They also sought to inform their own members about ASA's activities and to keep up the affiliation to WASU, 'our older sister organization in England', as well as with all organizations in America and Africa fighting for humanity and justice. In this way a Pan-African horizon is clearly indicated.

The political line of the editors was summed up in the following four-point programme:

1 To support the highest ideals of the Democratic Nations with special emphasis upon the principle of complete economic and political freedom for all nations;

2 To uphold the American Constitution and system of government, and to do nothing calculated to bring the United States into disrepute, hatred, danger or conflict;

3 To co-operate fully with the governments of the Democratic Nations interested in the progressive development of Africa and working for the eventual freedom of all Colonial Races, in fulfilment of ideals set forth in all the declarations of rights of such Democratic Nations, particularly those of England and America, both ancient and modern;

4 To take prompt and vigorous issue with all governments, institutions, groups or individuals, who by word or deed demonstrate antagonism to the economic, political and social aspirations, plans, and programs of renascent Africa [again reminiscent of Azikiwe].

Thus Nkrumah was evidently unable to push through the more radical line which he propagated within the organization, an unconditional and uncompromising rejection of the 'imperialist' nations.[73] Pan-African concepts break through where the same leading article ecstatically expounds an African student's emotions on hearing the word 'Africa': 'He is speaking, whether he knows it or not, of Africa as an ideological whole, as a symbol, the whole concentration, the whole dimensional range of all he best wishes, dreams, and hopes! He means the continent-home, the Fatherland, Mother Africa!'[74] The romantic exuberance and rhetorical phrasing are quite in keeping with Nkrumah's style, but might equally well originate with Azikiwe or Orizu, and are thus to some extent typical of the basic attitude of many Pan-African spokesmen.

The journal was planned as a monthly, but this ambitious scheme could not be kept up for long. When and how the third issue was prepared is uncertain; number 4 did not appear until the summer of 1943, in a larger format, more copious in content, and printed on glossy paper with photographs. After an even longer interval the fifth issue appeared in the spring of 1944. The hiatus was explained in the journal as due to a necessary reorganization.[75] No more details were offered, but the reason may have something to do with Nkrumah's withdrawal as ASA's president (which he later kept secret). The *African Interpreter* printed 'The Atlantic Charter and British West Africa. Memorandum on Post-War Reconstruction of the Colonies and Protectorates of British West Africa', Azikiwe's memorandum which had appeared one year earlier (and is rare today). This was accompanied by a leading article which expressed general agreement with the memorandum but was not wholly uncritical. Above all Azikiwe did not go far enough for the students. They rejected the dominion status he proposed: 'Such a political destiny is not that to which we look forward as befitting a proud and numerous race of men. On the contrary we look forward to the day of complete political independence for the various countries of our great continent.'[76]

However one may interpret ASA's pronouncements today in the light of Africa's turbulent recent history, a reading of this journal, together with other fragmentary knowledge about the group, conveys an impression of dynamic intellectual activity. There is no doubt that it had an impact upon interested groups in the USA during World War II. One may readily appreciate that these energetic young men, carried away by their political ideas, were in demand as experts on Africa in a continent about which even Afro-Americans knew little. For this reason it is understandable that certain ASA members – Akpabio, Nkrumah and Jones-Quartey – played a considerable part in preparing and carrying through the great Conference on Africa organized by the Council on African Affairs in New York in April 1944, the point at which we began this survey of Nkrumah's early career and the history of ASA.[77]

The New York Conference on Africa of April 1944 and Du Bois's new initiative

The historical significance of the Conference on Africa arranged by the Council on African Affairs under Robeson and Yergan lies chiefly in the fact that it tells us who in America at that time had an interest in Africa. The report submitted to the conference was compiled by a committee composed of the following: Mrs A. A. Garvey (Garvey's first widow), Mrs Edith C. Field, Elewelly Ransom, Jones-Quartey, Yergan and A. W. Hunton[78] – i.e. predominantly members of the Council on African Affairs. Also active in promoting the conference as 'co-operating sponsors' were Akpabio and Nkrumah of the USA, Mrs Mary M. Bethune, chairman of the National Council of Negro Women,[79] and Rayford Logan.[80] A. W. Hunton is presumably related to Mrs Hunton, who in her time had arranged for the fourth Pan-African Congress to be held in New York. An element of continuity was also represented by Hubert H. Delany, presumably a grandson of Martin R. Delany,[81] and by two Afro-American bishops, one of whom, David H. Sims, belonged to the AME church.

There were 112 persons at the conference, representing numerous organizations, some of them White bodies such as trade unions. The presence of certain African and Afro-American groups was of particular importance. Besides the African Students' Association and its journal the *African Interpreter* there were representatives from well-known and established Afro-American journals and organizations such as the *Afro-American* (Baltimore) and the *New Age* (New York), the NAACP and the Urban League. There were other groups about which hardly anything is known except their name. Their bizarre titles certainly suggest an interest in Pan-Africanism, but also a lack of real substance and firm roots. Besides the First Abyssinian Baptist church (the church of the pastor and congressman Adam C. Powell in Harlem) these included the following: the Ethiopian School of Research History, Ethiopian World Federation Local 26, the International African Goodwill Society, Pioneer Negroes of the World and the World Federation of African Peoples. Also represented were a West Indies National Council and the Farmers' Committee of British West Africa.[82] Particularly among the Afro-American groups there were some which, if one knew more about them, would probably have to be categorized as belonging to an irrational wing of Pan-Africanism.[83]

The results of the Conference on Africa are in themselves of little significance. Its main resolution called upon the US government to promote every effort which, in keeping with the Atlantic Charter, would lead to the independence and development of Africa.[84] Just as for Nkrumah, so also for Du Bois (who apparently did not attend), the Council on African Affairs provided a new opening: in his case for the revival of the Pan-African Congress movement. As early as the beginning of 1944 Mrs Amy Jacques Garvey (Garvey's second widow, who lived in Jamaica) and Harold Moody[85] had turned to him for help to hold a conference after the end of the war 'in order to discuss the needs and demands of the Negroes'.[86] In reply to this, Du Bois submitted a draft appeal at the beginning of April, to which he invited signatures from the leading personalities on the Council on African Affairs, Paul Robeson and Max Yergan, as well as Moody and Mrs Garvey. The persons mentioned were to declare their intention to hold the fifth Pan-African Congress in London as soon as possible after the end of the war. Du Bois had no intention of demanding African independence at the conference, as one might have expected in view of his reputation as 'father of Pan-Africanism'. As in 1919, Du Bois was concerned rather with the African mandated territories and with objectives of a more general nature such as 'economic emancipation, a voice in government, education and the introduction of peoples of Negro descent into modern life'.[87]

To prepare the congress Du Bois sought the collaboration of colonial governments, colonial peoples and the free nations of the world. He wanted to invite the heads of state of Ethiopia, Liberia and Haiti (for Pan-Africans, the three classical and symbolic independent states),[88] as well as organizations and individuals such as the National Congress of British West Africa and the Aborigines Protection Society,[89] representatives from the Senegal and other French colonies, and others from Tanganyika, the Sudan, the Belgian Congo, South and South-West Africa and Rhodesia. Furthermore he wanted to invite delegates of the Garvey movement in Jamaica (but not in the United States, where only splinter groups still existed), as well as 'select representatives of the other West Indies and from South and Central America with a strong Negro population'; and finally various Afro-American organizations from the USA were to attend.

It is not yet clear what became of the draft and whether at any time an official appeal was issued for the holding of such a conference. From the data at present available it does not appear that Du Bois's letter was discussed at the Conference on Africa, although he approached those responsible for convening it, among others. The draft's main value lies in the fact that it tells us what ideas Du Bois had at that time on the composition, character and tasks of a fifth Pan-African Congress. He simply wanted to pick up the thread again where he had dropped it in 1927–9, except that he now expected to include some of the survivors of Garvey's movement. His programme was moderately reformist, and not even anti-colonial, as one might have expected from him. He was rather naïve in expecting that he could collaborate with the colonial powers. Du Bois was certainly interested in African representation being as strong and broadly based as possible, for he wrote to Solanke in London in this sense one month later, but even this attempt to realize his Pan-African plans showed once more how little he knew about Africa. He did not render correctly the (admittedly complicated) names of the two large West African organizations and did not even know that they existed. He asked Solanke whether there were any strong organizations in British West Africa to which he might turn. At the same time he expressed reserve about giving prominence to individuals and organizations from outside Africa, i.e. to Afro-Americans.[90]

This letter from Du Bois to Solanke is at present the first piece of evidence we have that Du Bois tried to put into practice the original suggestion of Moody and Mrs A. J. Garvey. It is not clear whether this or other initiatives contributed to the further development of Pan-Africanism in Britain, as one might imagine was the case. For the centre of the movement's activities lay in Britain, and the fifth Congress turned out very differently from what Du Bois had had in mind in the spring of 1944.

The fifth Pan-African Congress in Manchester: origins and development

During the war more West Indians and Africans came to Britain as a result of the immigration of skilled workers and agricultural labourers needed to help in war production. Their intellectual and political leaders were no longer a half-tolerated, half-persecuted minority but enjoyed respect as Commonwealth citizens with more or less equal rights; some of them were even courted by politicians.[1]

In September 1939 Pan-African spokesmen did not comment on the outbreak of the war in the same enthusiastic terms as had been employed by Mohamed Ali Duse in August 1914.[2] Yet they will have appreciated the political opportunities which the war was likely to bring. Moody's group at least contemplated sending a letter to the British Foreign Secretary, Lord Halifax, in October 1939 to remind the government of the hopes and aspirations of the colonial peoples, as part of the endeavour to keep the colonial problem constantly before the public eye. This raised the question whether volunteers from the colonies could become officers (which was later agreed to after some hesitation by the government);[3] but the main point of the letter was to win from the government a clear statement about the colonies' future. However after lengthy deliberations the idea was dropped. Loyalty to the Commonwealth was stronger than the temptation to exploit the mother country's predicament for political ends. Instead it was decided to draw up a programmatic statement on the part of the coordinating committee. The draft was to be written by Peter Blackman, if possible with Padmore, who was not present at the meeting.[4] This decision implied restraint for the time being in pressing demands. Pan-Africanism had not yet become active; nevertheless this episode illustrates the existence of a political mood out of which Pan-African activity could develop anew when the time was ripe.

This hour struck as hostilities drew to an end. During the latter years of the war Moody came back to the project of a major conference on Africa.[5] As early as July 1943, acting in the name of the London Missionary Society, in which he played a leading role, Moody wrote an open letter to Africans, suggesting a kind of Pan-African body. Taking his stand upon the Atlantic Charter, Moody felt 'that a representative council of Africans should be summoned to meet a representative council of Europeans and Americans in order to discuss fully the future of Africa in every aspect'.[6] In August 1944 the *News Letter*, the organ of the League of Coloured Peoples, noted the conference held by the Council on African Affairs in New York on 14 April.[7] Already in the preceding June it had announced that the League would shortly arrange the conference which had been planned in 1938 to be held in 1940. In the same context Moody recalled 'that the masses of the people in England are now beginning to see something of the evil of race discrimination and how incongruous it is to be fighting ostensibly against the Herrenvolk idea and then to be supporting it within their own communities'.[8]

The conference of the League took place in London from 21 to 23 July 1944. About its character and composition little is yet known, and in particular we are in the dark as to whether other groups besides the League attended, as had originally been planned.[9] It may however be assumed that the Afro-American groups to which Moody had appealed in 1938 were unable to appear owing to wartime difficulties. The most important result of the conference was a 'Charter for Coloured Peoples' which in itself illustrates the radicalizing effect of World War II. This Charter demanded first of all basic equality of economic opportunity for Africa. The second (and last) part contained the really explosive demands: that the colonial powers should draw up plans for the economic, political, social and educational advance of the African territories under their control; that economic development should benefit only the inhabitants of the territories concerned; that a comprehensive educational programme be adopted; that Africans should at once be given a majority in all legislative bodies to prepare for full self-government at the earliest possible opportunity; and that the colonial powers should assume the obligation to render account to an international body about their administration in Africa and about the steps they were taking to transfer sovereignty.[10] One copy of the 'Charter for Coloured Peoples' was sent to the prime minister, Winston Churchill, who answered with a rebuff. Moody, however, dug in his heels and in his reply to Churchill took up Padmore's point that the Soviet Union's victories during the war had been won because that country had solved the racial problem within its frontiers.[11] The conference was followed by a weekend conference of the League presided over by Moody and John Fletcher of the Friends' Service Council. The principal speakers were: Arthur Creech-Jones (later Secretary of State for the Colonies in the Labour government), Miss Rita Hinden (at that time in charge of the Fabian Society's Colonial Bureau), K. A. Korsah (later a judge in the Supreme Court of Ghana but removed from this post by Nkrumah), A. Taylor-Cummings (Sierra Leone), the Rev. I. Ransome Kut, (headmaster of Abeokuta Grammar School), H. W. Springer and C. W. W. Greenidge (Barbados), M. L. Joseph Mitchell (Trinidad) and Peter Abrahams (South Africa).[12] Abrahams belonged to Padmore's group, which henceforward was constantly to grow in importance.

Preparations for the fifth Pan-African Congress

The climax of Padmore's career and the history of his group came towards the end of World War II. It was then that their Pan-African and nationalist aims harmonized with the Allies' policy declarations about the future of the world after the war. In 1944 several groups which had emerged in the meantime coalesced in a loose umbrella association, the Pan-African Federation (PAF).[13] The initiative in this apparently did not come from Padmore but from Dr Peter M. Milliard and T. R. Makonnen (both from British Guiana), who had lived in Manchester. Padmore's International African Service Bureau (IASB) formed the nucleus of the PAF but continued to exist independently. The most important other organizations which joined the PAF included: the Negro Welfare Centre, the Negro Association (Manchester) the Association of Students of African Descent (Dublin), the Kikuyu Central Association and the African Youth League (Sierra Leone Section).[14] The League of Coloured Peoples was not affiliated to the PAF, just as it was not affiliated to WASU.[15] The president of the PAF was Milliard, the treasurer J. E. Taylor[16] and the general secretary T. R. Makonnen. The most significant point about the new organization is the fact that – for the first time since the fourth Pan-African Congress in 1927 – it once again adopted the word 'Pan-African' in its title, thereby placing itself firmly in the historical tradition. The fifth Pan-African Congress of October 1945 was held under its leadership.

Outwardly Padmore at first took only a minor part in the new organization. This only changed when the preparations began for the fifth Pan-African Congress, in which he played a key role, greatly surpassing that of Du Bois. This disproves Padmore's later assertion that 'the preparation of the Fifth Pan-African Congress was assigned by Dr Du Bois, the International President, to the executive of the British section of the Pan-African Federation.'[17] Padmore seems to have allotted Du Bois a greater degree of influence than he actually deserved; possibly this was for tactical reasons, in order to use Du Bois's great prestige for the Pan-African movement of which Padmore himself was now the *de facto* leader. From the material in the Du Bois papers it is clear that the latter scarcely participated in the practical steps taken to prepare the congress; nor could he have directed it from the USA. It was from the press that he learned of the preparations that were made by Padmore's group.[18] Du Bois referred with unusual modesty to the dominant role played by groups in Britain in bringing the Congress about.[19]

At first it looked as though the leadership was again being provided from the United States, for at the beginning of 1945 Du Bois took up his initiative of the preceding year by writing a letter to Moody which was read out at the annual meeting of the League of Coloured Peoples on 16 March. In this letter Du Bois asked the League for its co-operation in convening a Pan-African congress; this was now no longer to take place in London, as Du Bois had planned in 1944,[20] but in West Africa. A similar letter was sent by Du Bois to WASU; the reply from London must have confirmed him in his views, for WASU pointed to Liberia as the most suitable country in which to hold the fifth Pan-African Congress.[21] His initiative, however, overlapped with that of the Padmore group which actually led to the fifth Pan-African Congress in Manchester.

Formally the stimulus came from an external source, but this only gave concrete shape to earlier ideas and plans.[22] At the beginning of 1945 the International Labour Office resolved at a meeting in Philadelphia to hold a first preliminary conference towards the establishment of a World Federation of Trades Unions; this met in London at the beginning of February 1945. This development in itself is testimony to the radicalizing effect of World War II, for this preliminary conference was attended both by representatives of the Soviet trade unions and for the first time also by some delegates from the colonial countries, including the British West Indies and British West Africa (Jamaica, British Guiana, Gambia, Sierra Leone, the Gold Coast and Nigeria).[23] One of the delegates, Wallace-Johnson (Sierra Leone), was discharged from an internment camp especially for this conference and put on a plane for London.

At the end of February 1945 the delegates from British West Africa and the British West Indies were invited by Makonnen and Milliard's group to come to Manchester on 4 March. Here they conferred with leaders of the IASB, the Negro Welfare Association and the Negro Welfare Centre (Manchester). On this occasion, if not earlier, Padmore launched the idea of a fifth Pan-African Congress. He had already talked about such a congress during the mid-1930s.[24] As yet we do not know whether the idea of such a Pan-African congress was mooted in 1939, during the discussions about holding a great African conference in 1940.[25] This would seem likely, but it cannot be proved. In February 1945 the presence on British soil of trade-union delegates from his West Indian homeland and from West Africa seems to have inspired Padmore to bring into play his contacts in trade-union circles from his days in Comintern and Profintern.[26] Perhaps he was even behind the invitation tendered to the colonial delegates to come to Manchester. However this may be, at the beginning of March 1945 Henry Lee Moon, the correspondent of the Chicago *Defender*, was able to give a detailed account of the meeting of the three organizations in Manchester on 4 March and of their resolution to convene a conference in Paris in September of the same year.[27] The date was fixed in such a way that the trade-union delegates from the colonies to the second Congress of the World Federation of Trades Unions could go on to the Pan-African conference afterwards. The Pan-African Federation was prominent in all these preparations, entrusting the practical details to a provisional committee composed of J. E. Taylor, Jomo Kenyatta, Milliard and

Wallace-Johnson (all of the PAF). It 'was instructed to communicate with leading African Negro organizations in America, the West Indies and Africa, seeking their co-operation in the sponsorship of a conference to formulate proposals to present to the peace conference.'

The meeting held on 4 March was followed by a public gathering of 300 persons, 'the largest Negro mass meeting in Manchester's history.' The principal speakers were Kenneth Hill (Jamaica), Wallace-Johnson (Sierra Leone), Hubert H. Crichlow (British Guiana) and other speakers included an official from the Ministry of Labour responsible for welfare matters in the colonies, as well as Kenyatta, Taylor, Milliard, Makonnen (now referred to as an Ethiopian), Chester Grey,[28] Padmore and Moon himself. The audience comprised members of the Allied forces from the colonies and the USA, Afro-American Red Cross nurses and collaborators, and workers from Africa and the West Indies who had come to Britain during the war.

A noteworthy aspect of the conception behind the congress in this early stage (so far as can be ascertained from the scanty press report) is that it was supposed to formulate proposals for a general peace conference; it may have been assumed that such a conference would meet in Paris, as it had done in 1919. It was also hoped that European and North American workers would support Negro demands at the peace settlement.[29] Just one week later Padmore reported about the preparations in the *Defender*. He expressly emphasized the inspiring effect which the visit of the colonial trade-union delegates had evoked and referred to them as partners in the decision to convene the conference. Padmore further published the draft of a manifesto compiled in Manchester, designed to serve as a working basis for a final text.[30]

WASU was apparently not yet involved in the proceedings in Manchester in March 1945, but sanctioned the manifesto subsequently. The position of the League of Coloured Peoples is somewhat unclear. In the *Defender* it was not mentioned, presumably because of the tension between Padmore and Moody. At any rate in his first letter to Du Bois after a long interval[31] Padmore criticized the League for its 'single-handed attitude'; as late as mid-April 1945 he still had doubts whether it would collaborate at all with the provisional organizational committee, although he assumed that the pressure of public opinion would force it to do so.[32] Padmore's criticism of the League at this point was not quite fair: the League had at least approved the draft of the Manchester manifesto and had published it in its *News Letter*, where

Moody was first among the signatories.[33] The same issue of the *News Letter* claimed that the manifesto was 'prepared under the aegis of the League with the assistance of representatives of the Colonial groups in the United Kingdom'.[34] Padmore even complained in the letter to Du Bois mentioned above that the League had had the draft manifesto printed on paper with its letter-heading, from which it may be deduced that the League was more strongly committed on the matter than has hitherto been assumed by writers who have followed Padmore's account.[35]

Padmore attributed to Desmond Buckle (Gold Coast)[36] the author-ship of the first draft of the manifesto. This seems to contradict statements by the League. However, if one makes a comparative analysis of the Charter for Coloured Peoples of 1944[37] and of the manifesto of 1945[38], the two statements can be reconciled, especially if one correlates the six demands of the manifesto with those in the Charter. In essence the manifesto of 1945 demanded the following:

1 Equal and rapid economic, cultural and social development of Africa and the setting up of competent authorities for this under the United Nations (corresponds in part to point 2d of the Charter of 1944)
2 Maximum participation by Africans in the administration of their countries at all levels (corresponds in part to point 2d)
3 An end to exploitation by foreign monopolies; instead, system-atic planning and development, above all in the interests of the Africans (corresponds to point 2b)
4 Hand in hand with economic development, participation by Africans in administration with an eye to full self-government within a certain period (corresponds to point 2d)
5 Measures to overcome illiteracy (corresponds to point 2c)
6 Former Italian colonies to be put on a par with the former German ones (new point).

Essentially these were the same objectives as those expressed in 1944, given a sharper and more concrete form in the 1945 document. It may thus be possible that the author of the original draft of this part of the manifesto recalled or even had before him the Charter of 1944; Buckle may even have been a member of the League. On the other hand the introduction and conclusion were new and reflected the radicalization which the Pan-African movement had undergone. The basic attitude is that of solidarity with the Allies against fascism. Setting out from the resolutions of the Yalta conference, the manifesto demanded that Africa be treated as an integral part of all attempts to promote world prosperity.

> Africa is a land of varied political forms, economic interests and social and cultural standards. This situation is complicated by the fact that among the powers with imperial possessions in Africa are Fascist Spain and Fascist Portugal. The United Nations are pledged to secure the moral and political as well as the military defeat of Fascism and must also eliminate the influence of the Spanish and Portuguese Fascist régimes.

After enumerating the concrete demands mentioned above, the manifesto listed the reasons why

> the African peoples by their contribution in manpower and material resources in the war against Fascism; by their services in Ethiopia, East Africa, the Western Desert, Italy, in the battle of Germany, by their labor in factory, field, mine and on the high seas; and by their present service in Burma in the eastern war against Japan, have earned the right to expect that they shall benefit as a result of the new concept of international co-operation which has been achieved in the course of the grim ordeal of the war of liberation against Fascism.

After the manifesto had been completed and approved by the participating organizations, the idea arose of sending it to the NAACP in New York, which was to assemble a representative delegation from America. The final decisions were to be made at a discussion with representatives from Africa, the West Indies, Brazil, Cuba, Haiti, Liberia, Abyssinia 'and other countries'. 'Fraternal delegations' from India, China, the Arab lands of the Near East and open-minded White organizations were to be invited to send to the Paris conference observers without the right to vote.

It was only now, through the press, that Du Bois heard about the preparations for a Pan-African congress in Britain. Immediately, on 22 March 1945, he wrote a letter to Padmore, with which he apparently restored the contact between them that had been interrupted for some time.[39] His letter was cool; evidently he felt that he had been bypassed and cast aside by the newer group. Briefly he reminded Padmore of his former services to the Pan-African movement and hinted about his current initiatives, especially the two letters to Moody and WASU of March 1945.[40] In four succinct passages he formulated his objections. First, it was not at all certain whether many delegates from the colonies would obtain permits to attend. Secondly, 'a Pan-African Congress ought to be held in Africa. We [sic] have held them in the past in London, Paris, Brussels and New York. We should meet this time in Africa. This seems to me of the greatest importance.'[41] Thirdly, he was against fixing a date, suggesting instead a flexible formula such as 'six months after the end of the European (or World) War'. Finally he criticized as premature the publication of the manifesto before the conference convened and before representatives of the colonial peoples had had an opportunity to define their stand. The manifesto ought to appear at the end of the congress, not before. In conclusion he informed Padmore in plain words that the NAACP – with almost 500,000 members, as he did not fail to emphasize – had stated in its programme that a Pan-African congress should be held after the end of the war and that this had induced him to carry out his project. In an authoritarian tone Du Bois concluded his letter to Padmore with the words: 'I should be very glad to hear from you at your convenience and to know what organizations are participating and just what has actually been done to this point.' Thus Du Bois wanted to restore the situation of 1919 by mobilizing the NAACP for his Pan-African congress idea, and apparently did not want power to be wrested from his hands by the groups in London.

Padmore replied on 12 April.[42] He was quick to assure the older man that the use of the term 'Pan-African' by no means implied 'an attempt to monopolise or by-pass the work of others engaged on a similar undertaking'. He placed himself deliberately in the Pan-African tradition by affirming that: 'We are well acquainted with the historical origin of the Pan-African movement, especially me [sic], as I am the nephew of the late Sylvester Williams, a West Indian barrister who initiated the project with which you, Bishop Walters and others have been associated.'[43]

As proof that he was willing to co-operate he mentioned that he had arranged for the NAACP secretary, Walter White, to give a lecture to WASU and had discussed with him the convocation of a Pan-African congress. He explained the fixing of the date by the presence of colonial trade-union delegates in Paris for the meeting of the World Federation

of Trades Unions. He and his friends had intended to utilize this opportunity to hold at least a preliminary conference prior to a congress
once travel restrictions had been eased. So far as the place of the meeting
was concerned, Padmore avoided this question elegantly. He replied
that he, too, thought it would be ideal to hold the congress in Africa if
possible, perhaps in Sierra Leone or in Nigeria, but it was doubtful
whether the colonial powers would grant permission for this. For this
reason he asked Du Bois to inquire through the NAACP and other
organizations what chances there were to hold a congress in Monrovia,
Liberia. He did not bother to go into Du Bois's criticism of the choice of
Paris as the venue.

Also on the question of pre-eminence in organizing the congress
Padmore remained diplomatically firm. Du Bois had put forward a
veiled claim to leadership based on tradition and the funds at the
disposal of the NAACP, which if it had come to pass would have made
Padmore Du Bois's auxiliary; to this Padmore counterposed the democratic principle of decentralization. Du Bois should set up a committee
in New York to get together the delegation from the USA and the West
Indies and to prepare draft resolutions etc.; in exchange he (Padmore)
would be more than willing to place at his disposal the contacts he had
established with West Indian mass organizations. Previously he had
mentioned the names and addresses of the three organizations in Britain
which had worked out the manifesto (and in so doing had again
obstinately said nothing about the League of Coloured Peoples), but
he was apparently wary of giving away his other contacts in Britain; of
African organizations Padmore did not speak at all. Instead he designated it as a task of the groups in Britain to transform the provisional
committee into a Pan-African Convening Committee in Great Britain
by bringing in other groups, and 'to contact all organizations in Africa',
which Padmore thought 'we should consider our sphere'. Only after
all the preparatory moves had been made should the two coordinating
committees in New York and London finally decide upon the place and
date of the congress.

In this way Padmore politely but determinedly staved off the claim
to leadership from New York. Finally he went a step further by building
up into a fundamental attack his muffled criticism of the League of
Coloured Peoples (which hitherto, apart from WASU, had been Du
Bois's only important contact in London). The League, he declared,
was mainly concerned with students and therefore had a continually

fluctuating membership, whereas the other organizations were much more closely identified with the masses of workers and peasants as was particularly evident in the case of the trade-union delegation from the West Indies and West Africa. This was a skilful appeal to Du Bois's proletarian mystique, a product of his increasing interest in Marxism, and was designed both to discredit the League in Du Bois's eyes and to put him in a conciliatory mood.

These differences did not lead to any conflict across the Atlantic. On the day before Padmore wrote his letter, Du Bois had sent Padmore a second letter which sounded much more relaxed and amicable.[44] In the meantime he had somehow heard directly from the Pan-African group in Manchester who had apparently succeeded in convincing him that their ideas were correct. Du Bois immediately turned to the executive committee of the NAACP, urging that the Pan-African congress be held in Paris; he also changed his opinion about the date. Finally he announced that the NAACP had decided to contribute a sizeable sum to the financing of the congress, but without stating the exact amount.

This removed the handicaps to co-operation between Du Bois and Padmore, between what was now already a past generation of Pan-African leaders and its successors. Padmore's first letter, written on 12 April, fell upon fertile soil. A noteworthy division of labour developed: Du Bois contributed the prestigious tradition of the early Pan-African Congress movement but, since difficulties arose in the NAACP, he had to come to Manchester as a private person without being able formally to commit the NAACP, let alone other Afro-American organizations.[45] Padmore contributed the organizational contacts he had forged with West Indians and Africans, especially in Britain, as well as his political and intellectual dynamism.

In Manchester an end was put to another divergence between the 'father of Pan-Africanism' and the younger generation, this time purely political in nature. In contrast to the cautious and moderate line which Du Bois had had in mind in 1944,[46] Padmore and his group were much more militant. In a letter addressed to Du Bois Padmore gave a remarkable description of the political mood of the various groups in Britain:

> Living under alien rule, their first manifestation of political consciousness naturally assumes the form of national liberation, self-determination, self-government – call it what you may. They want to be able to rule their own country, free from the fetters of

alien domination. On this all are agreed, from even the most conservative to the most radical elements. There might be differences as to the rate at which improvement is made towards the goal and regarding the political form which the objective should take. For example, Left-wing elements among Colonials emphasize self-determination to the point of secession from the British Empire, while the more conservative elements, although endorsing our claim for self-determination, clarify it in terms of Dominion status within the British Empire.[47] This does not mean that there are no individual Negroes who subscribe to political philosophies, whether they be Socialism, Communism, Anarchism, etc. But these are more in the nature of personal idiosyncrasies than practical policies. In brief, even those who call themselves Communists are nationalist. That is to say, they realise that their countries must first be nationally free before they can begin to practise their Communism.

Padmore here classified himself as standing on the extreme militant wing, although he was of course no longer a Communist. He made it clear, at least to Du Bois, that he was 'uncompromisingly opposed to all form of Imperialism'. He and his friends 'would like to break up the French Empire as much as we would like to liquidate the British Empire'. But he was objective enough to refer in the same context to the point that 'while we hold no brief for British Imperialism, the latter is a humanly run institution by comparison with [the] French', since the British colonies permitted political and trade-union organizations, whereas the neighbouring French colonies did not. After the Labour party's victory in the British election of 1945, the Pan-African groups had even greater scope. 'After all, the Negroes here voted for the Labour Party and supported them.' Frequently they joined the party (on an individual basis naturally), whereas in France the régime was a semi-dictatorial one. Padmore added: 'Unless France makes a bloodless revolution like the one which occurred here a few weeks ago, we see no prospect for French black Colonials.'

With this Padmore gave another retroactive explanation why in the past the Pan-African movement had been mainly supported by English-speaking Africans and Afro-Americans,[48] and also why the francophone element was completely absent from Manchester. In French-speaking Black Africa modern politics had begun in 1944–5 under the slogan of assimilation and integration with the motherland, so that there was no reason for nationalist let alone Pan-African tendencies.[49] At the same time, speaking here as a consistent anti-colonialist who at the beginning of the war had condemned the British Empire as 'the worst racket ever invented by man',[50] Padmore gave it the most positive evaluation. Finally he criticized Du Bois, though perhaps not purposely, because in the early 1920s at least the latter had entertained the same idealized concepts of French colonial rule against which Padmore inveighed so ardently in his letter.[51]

In the meantime the preparations for the conference had gone ahead. In June Nkrumah had arrived in London from the United States, armed with a letter of recommendation to Padmore from his old school friend C. L. R. James, whom Nkrumah had met in Harlem; according to Nkrumah, Padmore welcomed the new arrival at the station.[52] During his first days in London Nkrumah happened to run into his ASA colleague Ako Adjei on a bus; the latter introduced him to WASU, where he quickly rose to become deputy president. Within a month Nkrumah was appointed one of the two secretaries of the provisional organizing committee and participated actively in its practical work.[53]

At the same time the character of the planned conference changed. In his first letter to Du Bois of 12 April Padmore had spoken of inviting as observers as many Asiatic and Arab delegates as possible.[54] Indeed there took place on 10 June 1945 an All Colonial People's Conference, organized by the Pan-African Federation, the Federation of Indian Associations in Britain, WASU, the Ceylon Students' Association and the Burma Association. Its demands coincided to a large extent with those put forward in the Charter for Coloured Peoples of 1944[55] and need not concern us here.[56] The conference had a certain significance because from then onwards Padmore – who was the most outward-looking and internationally minded exponent of Pan-Africanism – centred his interest more and more upon Africa. Thus from the middle of 1945 Pan-Africanism again forfeited its character as a movement embracing all the colonial peoples. This limitation of the sphere of geographical interest continued in Manchester, for the fifth Pan-African Congress was the last demonstration of African and Afro-American solidarity.

At a later discussion in Manchester on 11 and 12 August further preliminary decisions seem to have been taken. Despite the accommodating attitude of the French minister for the colonies it was decided to abandon the idea of holding the meeting in Paris because of travel difficulties and the shortage of food in France immediately after the war; instead the congress was to be convened in London. Since the World Trades Union Congress in Paris ended on 9 October, the Pan-African Congress was to start on the 15th of that month, which would give sufficient time for the union delegates to cross the Channel and for the organizers in Manchester to complete their preparations.[57] Moreover, possibly under the influence of the arguments developed by Du Bois and WASU, who had originally pleaded for a congress in Africa, it was now generally realized that the forthcoming conference 'should be merely a preliminary one to a greater, more representative Congress to be held some time next year'.

The question of representation was settled in the following way. In accordance with the undertaking by most of the organizations approached in Africa and in the West Indies to send delegates to the conference, it was decided that wherever it was impossible for technical reasons to send delegates in so short a time trade-union representatives from Paris were to step in; alternatively their mandates were to be transferred to fellow-countrymen living in Britain. In this way a maximum of representation would be achieved with a minimum of personal effort and financial expenditure.

Finally it was decided to keep the present provisional committee in being until the congress opened, and then to turn it into a standing orders committee which was to undertake the task of admitting delegates and choosing speakers; further organizational matters were to be decided in full session once the congress got under way. Some time between mid-August and the opening of the congress the locale of the conference was changed once more. For some reason London was ruled out, so that the choice fell upon Manchester, the official headquarters of the Pan-African Federation.

Composition of the Congress

On 15 October 1945 matters had reached such a point that the fifth Pan-African Congress could meet in Charlton Town Hall, Manchester. Altogether it was attended by ninety delegates (including Du Bois) and eleven observers.[58] From the British press only John McNair, the representative of the ILP organ the *New Leader*, was present; the event was ignored by the major newspapers.[59] Nevertheless we are relatively well informed about developments at the congress and its results, since

for the first time its minutes were published, although only in an abbreviated form.[60] If one bears in mind the various elements contained in
Pan-Africanism and the phases in its development from the nineteenth
century onwards, the list of delegates at the 1945 meeting acquires a
new dimension. The strong block of delegates (twenty in number) from
West Africa need not surprise us in view of the traditional social and
political advantages enjoyed by those territories; nor is it surprising
that East, Central and South Africa should be underrepresented (with
only six delegates), that francophone delegates should be completely
absent, and that the West Indian element should be much in evidence
(thirty-three delegates). There were, however, no Afro-Americans
present from the USA except Du Bois, and he came only in a private
capacity and did not officially represent any Afro-American organization; he had been unable to make his influence felt in the NAACP or to
get that organization to provide the massive organizational and
financial commitment which he had promised Padmore.[61] The 'father
of Pan-Africanism', who is said to have assigned the organization of the
Congress to the British section of the Pan-African Federation,[62] does
not even appear in the official list of delegates, although he invariably
presided over the conference after his delayed arrival on its second day.
The absence of Afro-Americans may be explained by the difficulty of
obtaining permits from the USA after the end of the war, for even Du
Bois had to appeal personally to President Truman to obtain a passport
at short notice.[63] It may be that other reasons were of equal importance,
such as the aversion of younger groups in the NAACP to the idea of
squandering their energies upon Africa, so that the interest in Africa
among Afro-Americans was not so strong as might at first sight be
thought from the conference held in April 1944 by the Council on
African Affairs.[64]

   Only at second glance does one notice other absentees: none of the
three traditional symbolic states of Pan-Africanism – Haiti, Ethiopia
and Liberia – were officially represented in Manchester, although Du
Bois and Padmore had originally thought of inviting them.[65] From
Liberia there were only two delegates, but the name of their organization (Progressive Society) shows that the government was taking a
cautious line. None of the three governments took any notice of the
event by sending telegrams of greeting or similar action. The absence of
these three states from Manchester may be explained on political
grounds: to their conservative leaders the militant intellectuals and

trade-union leaders may have seemed too sinister for them to wish to identify themselves with their cause in public. Nevertheless, even without such official representation the congress was aware of the symbolism that attached to these three states, for at the start of the congress the hall was decorated with the flags of Ethiopia, Haiti and Liberia.

The countries represented were as follows (number of delegates given in brackets): Sierra Leone (three), Nigeria (six), Gold Coast (six), Gambia (two), Liberia (two); Uganda, Tanganyika, Nyasaland, Kenya (one each), Union of South Africa (two); West Indies (thirty-three) including Jamaica and Trinidad (six each). In addition to these there were various groups in Great Britain including the Negro Association (Manchester), the Negro Welfare Centre (Liverpool), the United Committee of Coloured and Colonial Peoples Association (Cardiff), the International African Service Bureau (five each), WASU (four), the Association of Students of African Descent (Dublin) and the African Students' Union of Edinburgh (one each). In classifying the delegates according to place of origin it must be borne in mind that the most important ones were once again represented by delegates of groups in Britain, some of whom, like Padmore and Peter Abrahams, had two mandates, one from a native and the other from a British organization, while others, such as Nkrumah, appeared only on behalf of a group in Britain (in his case for the International African Service Bureau). The Pan-African Federation (PAF), although it figured as one of the organizations that sent out invitations, was not represented directly but only through the presence of most groups associated with it.

The League of Coloured Peoples is completely absent, although in mid-August it had still appeared on Padmore's notepaper as one of the organizations extending invitations to attend, and in the same month it had drawn attention to the forthcoming congress in its bulletin:

> The Pan-African Federation, comprising several of the coloured organizations in Great Britain, the League of Coloured Peoples and the West African Students Union, are arranging to sponsor a conference of African peoples in England some time in September next. It is expected that representatives from the USA, British West Indies, British West Africa, East Africa, South Africa, Belgian Congo, Ethiopia, Somaliland and the Sudan will attend.[66]

Perhaps the League withdrew from the entire undertaking before the congress began. But we can only speculate about the reasons for its

absence. In view of the differences in personal and political temperament between Moody and Padmore one might think that Moody would
find it an unbearable prospect that he, the president and founder of the
League, should be unable to play a star role while Nkrumah and Padmore, who were by comparison plebeian and radical types, should
exercise such a commanding influence. It is also possible that the break
occurred after a mighty conflict, which left its traces in a determination
by both sides to hush up the incident.[67]

Among the delegates some stand out because they have already been
mentioned above or else became known later: Wallace-Johnson,[68]
Obafemi Awolowo,[69] H. O. Davies,[70] Jomo Kenyatta,[71] Dr Hastings
Banda,[72] Peter Abrahams,[73] J. E. Taylor,[74] Ako Adjei,[75] Mrs Amy A.
Garvey,[76] Ja-Ja Wachuku,[77] T. R. Makonnen[78] and finally of course
Padmore and Nkrumah. For most of these their career still lay before
them and nearly all had to spend some time in prison on account of
their political commitments. Those assembled at Manchester comprised,
to a considerable extent, the future political leadership of British territories in Africa around 1960; the West Indies were represented as
strongly as ever but did not send any of their major future political
leaders.

On going through the list of organizations represented, one is immediately struck by the great contrast with earlier Pan-African congresses: the relative prominence of delegates from trade unions, even though
these had only just come into existence in West Africa and in the West
Indies. As compared with the bourgeois notabilities, ministers and
academics who attended earlier Pan-African meetings one can now
sense a turn towards the masses, which later on was to acquire an
almost ideological force.[79] Trade-union representatives came from
Sierra Leone, Nigeria, the Gold Coast, Gambia and most of the West
Indian areas (Antigua, Barbados, Bermuda, British Guiana, Jamaica,
St Kitts, St Lucia, Trinidad and Tobago.) Among organizations of
historical significance that were represented we may note the Aborigines
Rights' Protection Society[80] and the Garvey movement of Jamaica, led
by Mrs Amy Jacques Garvey. Mrs A. J. Garvey was not present in
Manchester but the UNIA of Jamaica sent no fewer than four delegates.
Garvey's first wife, Mrs Amy Ashwood Garvey, on the other hand, was
in London as a delegate of the IASB. Finally one should mention the
presence of WASU.

The increased politicization of the movement was reflected in the fact that for the first time four political parties were represented – the National Council of Nigeria and the Cameroons (the oldest of the African political parties in Black Africa, which had been founded by Herbert Macaulay, Mohamed Ali Duse and Azikiwe in Lagos the year before), the Labour party from Grenada, and the West Indies People's National party and the Labour party, both from Jamaica. To these may be added mass organizations equivalent to political parties – the Nigerian Youth Movement, the Nyasaland African Congress and the African National Congress of South Africa. Also present for the first time was a farmers' organization, the Gold Coast Farmers' Association.

Almost all the various tendencies and groups within modern Pan-Africanism were represented in Manchester. True, the Afro-American block from the USA was absent, but it did at least have a spokesman in the person of Du Bois, who was honoured as the surviving founder of Pan-Africanism. Moreover, this element was at least present indirectly in all the Pan-African activitists who had been through Afro-American colleges and universities in the USA – in particular Padmore, Nkrumah, Adjei and Banda. Du Bois likewise represented the continuous tradition that ran from the London Conference of 1900 through the four Pan-African congresses of 1919–27 to the present gathering in Manchester. Here the old bitter conflict that had raged between Du Bois and the Garvey movement was stilled, at least in so far as the Garvey movement in Jamaica now entered into the stream of official Pan-Africanism. The presence of one of Garvey's two widows in Manchester may be understood in a similar sense – and quite definitely the active participation of Nkrumah, since the latter was later to emphasize the great influence that Garvey had exerted upon him.[81] The 'historical' organizations mentioned above – the ARPS, WASU and the South African National Congress – represented the earlier more bourgeois element, while the various student groups (including WASU) and the Padmore group represented the more modern and intellectual strain. The fact that the delegate of the People's National party from Jamaica at the same time represented the ex-British West India Regiment Association is particularly fascinating if one remembers the role which the West Indian regiments had played (indirectly, at any rate) during the mid-nineteenth century in establishing contact between the West Indies and West Africa.[82]

Among the 'historical' elements that were almost completely absent were the Christian missions or any of the African or Afro-American churches. It may be assumed that at least all the Africans present had been through mission schools – or at least through schools that had been fashioned or originally founded by the missions. But the missionary element already lay so far back that it was only feebly represented in Manchester.[83] The single minister present came – as was historically justified – from Sierra Leone, but he was the delegate of a modern organization, the teachers' union. He symbolized four historical traditions: that of the missions, of education, of Sierra Leone and of modern forms of organization. It is equally characteristic of the situation at this time that, except for this delegate, Nkrumah was the only man present who had studied theology (even if in a very rudimentary way) and had also preached. By 1945 he could hardly be regarded any longer as a practising Christian. The fact that a few years later he got his party supporters to sing the Methodist hymn 'Lead, kindly light' on Chapel Square at Cape Coast, the traditional place associated with the Methodist church and early Gold Coast nationalism,[84] was more a tactical adjustment to social realities than the expression of a religious attitude, let alone proof of a bond to the church. With Moody's withdrawal or exclusion before the beginning of the congress the Pan-African leadership had lost the last offshoot of a historical force that could be traced back to the late eighteenth century and which had contributed so much indirectly to the movement. It is not known whether a common religious service was held at the beginning or end of the congress, as had been the case in 1923 at the conference of the National Congress of British West Africa in Freetown. Such a ceremony, or a welcoming address by the bishop of Manchester.[85] would probably have struck the leaders gathered in Manchester as absurd. They kept their distance from the establishment, whether by design or because they had to. The only exception to this was a message of greetings to the congress from the Lord Mayor of Manchester.

Likewise absent from Manchester were representatives of the White abolitionist and philanthropic element, in former days so closely associated with the missions.[86] Pan-Africanism had indeed to a large extent become emancipated, both politically and socially: 'The days of dependence upon the thinking and direction of their so-called left-wing European friends who had so often betrayed them, were over. From henceforth Africans and peoples of African descent would take their destiny into their own hands and march forward under their own banner of Pan-Africanism in co-operation with their own selected allies.'[87] It no longer sought moral and political support from outsiders, as had still been the case under Du Bois.[88] A last reflex of this tradition was the presence of John McNair of the Independent Labour party and of a lady representing the politically even less significant Commonwealth party (as an observer). The Pan-Africanism of 1945 no longer asked modestly for some form of recognition or for favours from on high: it demanded political and social rights.

The strong representation of West India and West Africa brings out once again the extraordinary importance of these two areas; the under-representation of South and East Africa indicates that these areas were only of peripheral (and in the case of South Africa diminishing) significance; the location of the conference in Manchester, in the heartland of British industry, showed the key position of liberal Britain, now head of the Commonwealth (which had replaced the British Empire).

Proceedings and results of the congress

This stronger political self-awareness was matched by a more highly developed organizational framework and political content. As had been projected, the plenary session of the congress appointed a number of committees, five all told, including an entertainment committee staffed exclusively by ladies. In these bodies an unquestionable pre-dominance lay with the Padmore group, to which Du Bois also now has to be reckoned. In all of them this group provided the chairman and four other ordinary members, some of whom also served as chairman of other committees.[89] If one adds that Padmore and Nkrumah acted jointly as chief secretaries of the congress and that on the second day Du Bois was appointed its permanent president, it is quite obvious that the Padmore group, i.e. the International African Service Bureau (ISAB), exerted a decisive influence.

The commanding position of this group may be seen from the course taken by the congress and the results it produced. These matters will be dealt with only in a summary fashion here, since the sources are relatively plentiful.[90] The proceedings of the congress, published in an abbreviated form, contain a paper by Du Bois on the 'History of Pan-Africanism'. (It is not clear whether this was made available, e.g. in hectographed form, to the delegates as a working paper.) In more than one respect it is characteristic of Du Bois. After an introductory passage dealing accurately with the general background of Pan-Africanism before 1900[91] he mentioned for the first time the name of Sylvester Williams as initiator of the 1900 London conference.[92] The rest is almost exclusively concerned with himself. His survey of the Pan-African congresses up to 1927 was based mainly on newspaper quotations about the congresses, their most important resolutions, demands and proclamations, and the role he had played in them. Also the brief intervening passages strongly emphasized the first person singular. The prehistory of the fifth Pan-African Congress was covered mainly by quotations, partly from WASU's letter to him[93] and partly (but without giving the source) from Padmore's letter to him of 17 August 1945.[94] Du Bois's speech was published in 1946, in a slightly abbreviated version, in his book *Africa and the World*; later its ideas were taken over by Padmore and have ever since been responsible, directly or indirectly, for the generally accepted crude and cliché-ridden picture of the history of Pan-Africanism.[95] However, Du Bois's self-adulatory depiction of his role accords with the fact that he did indeed embody almost all the important tendencies of the past. It is therefore doubly understandable that until recently Pan-Africanism has usually been equated with those official Pan-African events since 1900 which were linked with Du Bois's name.

As at earlier Pan-African congresses, the papers delivered and the contributions to discussions served predominantly to exchange information. Each day the congress held two working sessions, each devoted to a general theme. These topics were arranged according to geographical areas and were introduced by a rapporteur. On the first day, when Mrs Amy A. Garvey was in the chair, both sessions dealt with 'The Colour Problem in Britain'. Complaints were voiced about racial discrimination, but a note of self-criticism was also sounded where speakers deplored the existence of a social gulf between students and workers. The second day began with a session on 'Imperialism in North and West Africa'; for the first time it was presided over by Du Bois, whom Padmore welcomed warmly. Nkrumah, as rapporteur, took the recent war as his starting-point and attacked imperialism as being primarily responsible. There followed supplementary statements by representatives of the four British West African colonies on the situation in their respective countries. At the beginning of the second session Dr Raphael Armattoe (Togo) spoke on the situation in francophone Africa south of the Sahara, including the Belgian Congo; he emphasized the higher level of education in the French colonies as compared with British ones, and apparently refrained from any criticism of the French colonial authorities. The second session was devoted to 'Oppression in South Africa' with Peter Abrahams and Marko Hlubi, the representatives of the African National Congress, acting as rapporteurs. Their speeches consisted wholly of complaints about apartheid – which was to become still more intense three years later, when the Boer Nationalist party under Malan won its electoral victory. All the following contributions to the discussion, so the minutes recorded, were on the theme of 'down with imperialism' and expressed sympathy and support for the Africans in South Africa.[96]

The first session on 17 October began with a minor *coup de théâtre*. Padmore announced that, contrary to the practice followed previously, according to which each session was presided over by a different chairman, the standing orders committee as a sign of its recognition and respect for Du Bois had recommended that he be appointed permanent president of the congress, and that the chairmen designated to officiate at each session should become deputy chairmen. The motion was apparently passed without any discussion or vote, and Du Bois took up his duties as president until the end of the congress. The first session held on 17 October, with Wallace-Johnson as deputy chairman, dealt with the situation in East Africa. It was introduced by Kenyatta with a survey of Uganda, Tanganyika, Kenya and Somaliland, concentrating on the Africans' social disadvantages and the low wages they received. At the end of the session Padmore contributed a few additional remarks on Rhodesia and Nyasaland.

The second session was officially devoted to 'Ethiopia and the Black Republics', but the introductory paper by Makonnen on Ethiopia was not matched by any similar ones on Liberia or Haiti. Peter Abrahams merely made an appeal to defend the interests of the only free negro states – Haiti, Liberia and Ethiopia – and countered the criticisms expressed by 'extreme socialists' who sought to deny a country like Ethiopia the attributes of sovereignty (as Makonnen had done previously). Du Bois intervened to draw attention once again to the symbolic value of these three states, which by their existence demonstrated the ability of Blacks to govern themselves. He had visited these countries himself and was impressed by their achievements.[97]

The second session on 18 October had 'The Problem in the Caribbean' as its theme. The rapporteurs were Padmore and Ken Hill (Jamaica). Padmore gave a brief survey of the history of the West Indies from Colombus to the present day, whereas Hill confined himself to Jamaica. He was followed by several other speakers who commented on the situation in their native island (as well as in British Guiana).

The first session on 19 October apparently had no general theme. Since Du Bois was listed as rapporteur, Milliard took the chair. The minutes, however, do not contain any report by Du Bois, nor is there any suggestion that he may have presented on this occasion his speech on the history of Pan-Africanism just mentioned; only at the end of the session do we find him making some remarks, which read like a concluding speech to the debate. At this session the speakers included Mrs Amy A. Garvey and a delegate from Jamaica on the special problems faced by women in the West Indies.

In his final remarks Du Bois pointed out that all those present wanted self-government for Africa, and warned that errors were inevitable; nevertheless they deserved freedom 'even if we do make mistakes'.

The congress passed resolutions on the topics treated: on various regions of Africa, on Ethiopia, Liberia and Haiti;[98] on South and South-West Africa, and on the colour bar in Britain and the West Indies. These resolutions defined more closely the demands put forward. Their substance was summarized in two brief resolutions of more general nature which expressed the real political dynamism of the congress. The first of these, 'The Challenge to the Colonial Powers', took an intermediate line between the revolutionary impatience of Padmore and Nkrumah on the one hand and Du Bois's more cautious conception of 1944 on the other.[99] 'The delegates to the Fifth Pan-African Congress believe in peace. . . . Yet if the Western world is still determined to rule mankind by force, then Africans, as a last resort, may have to appeal to force in the effort to achieve Freedom, even if force destroys them and the world.'[100] The second general statement was the 'Declaration to the Colonial Workers, Farmers and Intellectuals', drafted by Nkrumah, which expresses once again the limitless desire for independence: against imperialist exploitation the colonial peoples should concentrate upon winning political power, and for this an effective organization was essential. The tactics recommended were strikes and boycotts – non-violent methods of struggle. The intellectuals in the colonies and the educated élite generally had to play their part in organizing the masses. The declaration ended with a slogan reminiscent of the concluding passage of the Communist Manifesto: 'Colonial and Subject Peoples of the World – Unite!'[101]

The congress terminated on the afternoon of 19 October with a mass meeting at which messages of greetings were despatched to various peoples: to the Afro-Americans, 'the masses of India', Indonesia and Vietnam. These statements – to say nothing of the presence at the congress of a few observers from Asia – gave expression to the Afro-Asian element in the movement.

When the delegates parted they no doubt had the feeling that they had participated in a historic event. Indeed the congress was a landmark both in the history of Pan-Africanism and in that of decolonization. So far as Pan-Africanism was concerned, it was the first evidence of vigorous self-assertion after an interval of almost two decades; at the same time it gave an impetus to efforts to achieve the immediate goal of national independence. Thus, looking ahead, the congress served as the pace-maker of decolonization in Africa and in the British West Indies. The strategy proclaimed was to organize the masses through trade unions and political parties and to engage in a struggle for political power, first with non-violent means and only if necessary by the threat of force; this strategy was put into effect with surprising ease. The moment was, after 1945, far more favourable for the fifth Pan-African Congress than for any of its predecessors. Social progress in Africa and in the West Indies favoured efforts to win independence; so too did the general world situation at the end of World War II. An additional factor was the greater political dynamism of the younger men, who either bypassed the more cautious and conservative representatives of the older generation (Moody) or else carried them along with them (Du Bois). Thus it is quite explicable that our account of Pan-Africanism to this point may evoke the impression that all previous events in its history had been just a prelude to the Manchester meeting. For the same reason we may break off our historical description in 1945. For what followed is to a great extent the implementation of the Manchester resolutions. Moreover, these subsequent events are relatively well known,[102] so that it will be sufficient to offer a brief sketch of them here.

Part III Retrospect and conclusions

20 Development of Pan-Africanism after Manchester (1945–1966)

After a series of failures and disappointments Pan-Africanism reached its climax with the Manchester congress of October 1945. Although not much attention was paid to it at the time, it appears in retrospect as a significant event in the history of decolonization as well as of Pan-Africanism. After the congress was over the Pan-African Federation tried to keep up the impetus and to translate it into political action. At first, however, it seemed as though the fate of earlier initiatives would be repeated,[1] for in the following years the Pan-African movement gained little in internal cohesion and organizational strength. The Pan-African Federation, it is true, continued to exist but apparently did not engage in any very impressive activity. It organized some events in London and through Du Bois tried to exert an influence upon the UN; it also sought to establish contact through Nehru with the Indian national movement, but without any tangible results.[2]

The West African National Secretariat (1946–7)

To follow up the congress and to concentrate its impact more narrowly Nkrumah and Wallace-Johnson, encouraged by Padmore, founded the

West African National Secretariat in London at the beginning of 1946. In March 1946 it was able to publish the first issue of its monthly, the *New African*.[3] Nkrumah assumed the position of general secretary; Wallace-Johnson was chairman. The aims of the new Pan-African regional organization were: 'to maintain contact with, co-ordinate, educate and supply information on current matters to various political bodies, farmers' organization, co-operative societies, educational, cultural and other progressive organizations in West Africa with a view to realizing a West African Front for a United West African National Independence'. It also endeavoured 'to foster the spirit of national unity and solidarity among the various territories of West Africa for the purpose of combating the menace of artificial territorial divisions now in existence'.[4] It was intended to 'serve as a clearing-house for information on matters affecting the destiny of West Africa; and to educate the peoples, and the working class in particular, of the imperialist countries concerning the problems of West Africa'; and finally 'to work for Unity and Harmony among all Africans who stand against imperialism'. Its credo was that 'imperialism and colonial liberation are two irreconcilable opposites; a compromise between them is impossible. The death of the one is the life of the other. . . . Without political independence the talk of economic independence is mere waste of time.'

Politically the West African National Secretariat stood for

1 The complete liquidation of the colonial system;
2 Absolute independence of all West Africa;
3 The right of peoples everywhere to organise trade unions, co-operative societies, farmers' organisations without the shackles of imperialist officialdom;
4 The industrialisation of West Africa including technical and scientific knowledge.

It was opposed to 'any form of reactionary nationalism in West Africa. Any form of opportunism and reformism in matters affecting the political and economic destiny of West Africa.'

Apart from its Marxist language the West African National Secretariat does not seem to have been much more than a more radical sequel to earlier West African organizations. In fact the concept of West Africa was expanded considerably for its spokesman asserted:

By a united West Africa we mean that strip of land with all its waterways, hills, mountains and habitations stretching from 30 degrees south of the Sahara and 10 degrees west of the Congos on the south of the Atlantic Ocean. In the inland, it borders the Sudan and Kenya. It therefore follows that West Africa comprises all the territories which have been invaded and are now temporarily occupied by foreign powers. Such territories known as 'British' West Africa, 'French' West Africa', 'Portuguese' West Africa, the 'Belgian' Congo, 'Spanish' West Africa and the Republic of Liberia – all put together into one united country, is what we mean by West Africa. Upon the hills and mountains of West Africa with its hamlets and villages, its towns and cities, in the heart of the approximately seventy million people of West Africa, the rising star of West African liberty shall for ever unfurl. Our cry now is: ONE AIM! ONE PEOPLE! ONE UNITED WEST AFRICA!

It was apparently felt that the West African vanguard would lead the national Pan-African movement throughout the entire continent. 'We call upon all Africans everywhere – individuals, organizations and federated organizations in Africa, to join the West African National Secretariat and to rally the fullest support behind the Secretariat's movement for unity and freedom. The day when West Africa, as one united country, pulls itself from imperialist oppression and exploitation it will pull the rest of Africa with her.'

Not much is as yet known about the activities of the West African National Secretariat except for the statements made by Nkrumah. The inner nucleus of leaders combined to form a kind of secret society, the Circle, whose members solemnly promised to work for a Union of West African Socialist Republics. Nkrumah and his Circle were reputed to have contacts with or even to be members of the Communist party.[5] This assertion seems plausible if one takes into account the revolutionary language of Nkrumah's journal and the latter's predilection for reading the communist *Daily Worker* ostentatiously in the London tube during rush hour.[6] In mid-April 1946 Nkrumah attended a conference called by the Fabian Colonial Bureau at which, referring to the results at the Manchester congress and speaking on behalf of 'the West African delegation' (not specified more closely) he demanded in harsh and uncompromising terms 'complete and absolute independence for the peoples of West Africa as the only solution of existing problems'.[7] At that time Nkrumah wrote a pamphlet which he had privately printed and circulated in a limited edition. In this he was likewise very outspoken in calling for speedy political independence.[8]

In order to realize his West African plans Nkrumah sought contact with West African deputies in the French National Assembly, especially S. M. Apithy, L. S. Senghor, Lamine Guèye and Félix Houphouet-Boigny. Nkrumah paid a visit to Paris, but without achieving any success; equally fruitless was the presence of the West African deputies at two conferences held by the West African National Secretariat in London, one from 30 August to 1 September 1946 and the other at the beginning of April 1947.[9] The African parliamentarians adhered to the policy of assimilation, equality of rights and integration; they did not want to hear anything about Pan-Africanism, let alone a Union of West African Socialist Republics.

At the end of March 1947 there was talk about a major West African conference to take place in 1948.[10] Nkrumah went to Paris in 1947 for a second time to make preparations for it. But after he returned to Africa in November 1947 these plans came to nothing. Soon afterwards his organization folded up. Its importance lies in the fact that it provided a further platform for Nkrumah's rise to power; it was also in the tradition of earlier (British) West African nationalism although suspected by Makonnen and others of communist tendencies.

An important contribution made by the West African National Secretariat was its publication of the *New African*. This had as its motto: 'For Unity and Absolute Independence'.[11] The imprint is reminiscent of the first series of ASA's journal the *African Interpreter*:[12] in both cases the symbol chosen was a simple sketch-map of Africa bearing the single word 'Africa'. The introductory leading article, which among other things features the objectives quoted above, bears the heading 'We Bow'; this again recalls Azikiwe's first leading article in the *African Morning Post*, which the *African Interpreter* had taken over for its first issue. The conclusion of this leader suggests that the title of the journal, the *New African*, was likewise inspired by Azikiwe, for it ends with a free paraphrase, not identified as such, from Azikiwe's *Renascent African*: 'The *New African* . . . goes fearlessly to inspire the youths of Africa for definite political action, and arouse in them a burning desire for freedom, as well as bitterness against imperialism. The African of today is neither young nor old. He is just new, and his voice is the voice of the Awakened African.' It is not yet known how many numbers of the journal appeared. Presumably it ceased publication even before Nkrumah had returned to the Gold Coast, leaving behind a debt of £150 which Nkrumah later settled.[13]

The journal 'Pan-Africa' (1947–8) and activities in London

International African Opinion, the journal of the International African Service Bureau, whose dates of publication are uncertain, was replaced in 1947 for more than a year by a journal whose very title set forth the Pan-African programme: *Pan-Africa. A Journal of African Life, History and Thought.* On the front cover is a picture of a Black version of the Statue of Liberty against the background of the Atlantic and the surrounding continents; the light from the torch illuminates Africa, America and Western Europe – the classical areas to which Pan-Africanism appealed. It was edited by Makonnen and published in Manchester, except for issues 2–8 of the first year of publication which were edited by Miss Dinah Stock, a British sociologist. Miss Stock, together with some left-wing socialist friends such as Reginald Reynolds, had become interested in African nationalism even before 1945.[14] The editorial staff included Peter Abrahams (South Africa) and Frank Blaine, and among the permanent collaborators were Padmore, H. W. Springer (Barbados), Magnus C. Williams (Nigeria) and Nkrumah. All of them except Springer had been present at the Manchester congress.

This journal lived up to its Pan-African responsibilities in more senses than one: articles were devoted to topics both from the past and the present, and covered the whole geographical area of interest to the Pan-African movement; the contributors also were drawn from the same wide field.[15] It is fascinating to see that in issue 4, which was dedicated to the West Indies, Reginald Reynolds put together several excerpts from Anthony Benezet's *A Caution and Warning to Great Britain and Her Colonies* (1766).[16] Mrs Amy J. Garvey supplied some thoughts about the key issues facing the world at that time.[17] Dinah Stock contributed some information about African unions.[18] Proceeding from a speech by General De Gaulle in Bordeaux, according to which France's destiny was dependent upon events in French overseas territories, Padmore criticized the British left for not yet being anti-colonial enough: 'Unlike many British "socialists" and so-called progressives he realises that in the modern world the Western Powers cannot hold back the revolutionary upsurge of the common people in Europe, and the national liberation movements in the Colonies, unless the old colonial systems are maintained by force.'[19] A certain Frank Johnson, 'Englishman by birth, African by adoption', as he introduced himself, dreamed of a forthcoming United States of Africa.[20]

Yatu (Uganda), who had likewise attended the Manchester congress, expressed in several issues his thoughts about Africa's future.[21] In an article on African unity he gave an intelligent critique of African society which provided an alternative to the view propounded by all the Pan-African social romantics, such as Du Bois and Nkrumah. Just as Horton had sneered at the little 'village kings' on the Gold Coast,[22] so Yatu saw a radical reconstruction of African society resulting from the desire to obtain independence and modernization, since this required an end to tribalism and the narrow-mindedness of the village:

> Africa, the Dark Continent, . . . opened its door wide to western civilisation. . . . Her [colonial power's] aim is to develop these territories into future prosperous nations, strong units of people able to get along with the other nations, contributing to the social welfare of the world. . . . The African people, however, seem to be passing through what I can rightly call 'the dark ages', a period of semi-civilized and semi-primitive life. Tribal feelings and interests have kept them backward. . . . Inter-marriage is as criminal as adultery. Nepotism is prevalent in every African occupation. 10,000 people or less, because they happened to speak the same language and have the same taboo, feel, not without conceit, strong enough to stand by themselves. . . . Year in, year out, they live in this small area, enclosed not by natural boundaries but by fantastic tribal claims. They spend most of their time and money in rearing their pet chief, in discussing their primitive customs and defending what they fancy to be their inheritance. . . .
>
> For surely no one can imagine Africa made up of independent villages. It would be a dreamy Africa, parasitic in every way; for none of these tribes, numerically and economically poor, can support industrial activities. . . . Either Africa would live completely cut off from the outside world (which is impossible) or she would be obliged to make internal reforms; reforms that would admit of the world-wide recognition of her people. Such reforms are the amalgamation of these small tribes into larger units which can adequately claim their independence and position as civilized nations. . . . There can be no hope of fulfilling of national obligations to others . . . and, strictly speaking, no internal peace in a polysected Africa.[23]

With regard to East Africa Yatu expected that 'Kenya, Tanganyika, Nyasaland, Zanzibar, and all Indian Ocean Islands near the African coast, can pull together and form one country,' especially as Swahili could serve as the lingua franca of the new state. 'Their union is favoured by the absence of any marked physical boundary between one country and another. . . .'[24] Just as almost one hundred years earlier the railway was to play an important role in creating this federation: Yatu wanted to establish a direct rail link between Mombasa (Kenya) and Kampala (Uganda).

In contrast to Yatu's modern-style rationalism the Rev. T. K. Utchay (Nigeria) broke a lance in favour of the traditional African heritage. He gave a sentimental and idealized picture of pre-colonial Africa,[25] which did not however lead to a discussion between representatives of the two trends that might have cleared the air. Émile Faure, Kouyauté's counterpart in Paris during the 1930s, criticized French colonial policy in an article taken over from *Crisis*.[26] An unsigned obituary for Moody, who had died in his West Indian homeland on his first visit after over forty years' absence, found noble words of appreciation. There were, however, traces of earlier tensions: '. . . Among those who helped him to found the League of Coloured Peoples there may have been some who wished it had served other, more militant purposes than those with which he inspired it. . . . But all admired him and recognised the value of his work.'[27] One number was dedicated to the West Indies;[28] the last one dealt with the NAACP and its work in the USA,[29] so underlining for the last time the traditional Pan-African component of Pan-Negroism.

A journal that began in this spirit could not last for long. The British colonial government banned it, with the result that *Pan-Africa* ceased publication as early as the beginning of 1948.[30] Unfortunately for Pan-Africanism, this eliminated the possibility that Yatu's initiative (which Padmore took up again later in a more general and thus less effective form)[31] might have led to a fruitful exchange of ideas on the social consequences of Pan-Africanism, which in turn might have helped to provide a rational basis for Pan-Africanism.

Another important centre of Pan-African activity was WASU, especially after Solanke returned from his second recruiting foray to West Africa. Solanke's diary (in his papers – unfortunately it is only available for 1947) gives the impression that he was in close and frequent touch with all the important figures in Pan-Africanism at that time: Padmore, Nkrumah, Adjei, de Graft-Johnson, Hastings Banda, the

West African deputies in Paris, Azikiwe, the Rev. Michael Scott and Dr St Clair Drake (USA).[32] Solanke also organized a WASU parliamentary committee as an African lobby, which frequently met in the House of Commons with Solanke in the chair. Padmore exerted an influence in the same direction with his *Colonial Parliamentary Bulletin*, which provided a documentary record of debates and questions on colonial matters in the House. With his extensive contacts and journalistic activities Padmore remained the most important figure in Pan-Africanism during these years, especially once the centre of political decision-making had moved to Africa.[33]

The triumph of African nationalism (1948–58)

In 1946 Kenyatta returned to Kenya; at the end of 1947 Nkrumah likewise went back to the Gold Coast in order to take up the position of general secretary of Danquah's newly founded United Gold Coast Convention. Since *Pan-Africa* was suspended at the beginning of 1948, at which time the West African National Secretariat also ceased to exist, and since the West African conference planned for 1948 did not take place, the Pan-African movement now seemed to have dissolved completely into its diverse national constituent parts. The West Indian element dropped out almost completely as an organized force, apart from groups in Britain and those who went to the Gold Coast individually. The Afro-Americans, especially Du Bois and Paul Robeson, were virtually paralysed by the onset of McCarthyism and had to fight for their political lives. Only Padmore in London gave a certain inner consistency to the Pan-African movement, which seemed to have lost its way. In spite of the lack of a central organ he kept up an interest in political developments in Africa among left-wing socialist groups in London.[34]

While Nkrumah was still in London he had stigmatized as reactionary the nationalism of the individual colonial territories;[35] however, soon after his return to the Gold Coast he identified himself with the Gold Coast nationalism that had become so powerful during his twelve years' absence. He was now intent upon establishing a national base from which he could launch a campaign for the realization of his more far-reaching objectives. He threw all his dynamic personality into the political battle, turned what had been planned as a party of the local élite into a party of the masses, split the UGCC and after a few years of impetuous agitation had pushed his upper-class seniors to the wall. Basing himself on the so-called 'Standard VII boys', the mass of urban youths who had completed some sort of secondary education but were usually unemployed, he founded the Convention People's Party (1949) In February 1951, while still in prison, Nkrumah won the first general parliamentary elections, fought on a restricted franchise, by resorting to extreme nationalist and populist propaganda; thereupon he was released and appointed Leader of Government Business. With this step the decisive turning-point had taken place: internal self-government and full sovereignty were now but a question of time. On 6 March 1957 the Gold Coast became independent as Ghana. Nkrumah immediately proclaimed that 'the independence of Ghana is meaningless unless it is linked to the liberation of Africa'.[36]

In London Padmore had tried as well as he could to give political and propaganda support to the developments on the Gold Coast, especially in his book *The Gold Coast Revolution* which was written after his first visit to the Gold Coast, then already autonomous.[37] In his introduction Padmore gave a quite respectable survey of the early history of the country from the earliest times to the present and then went on to describe the political situation in a manner wholly favourable to Nkrumah. A few years later he followed this up with a more influential book, *Pan-Africanism or Communism?*, in which he endeavoured to set Pan-Africanism in a historical perspective.[38]

In 1958 Nkrumah underlined the Pan-African significance of Ghana's acquisition of independence by bringing Padmore to Ghana and making him his adviser on African questions. Since there was some opposition within the ruling party against a foreigner from the West Indies (Padmore was not the first Pan-African leader from the West Indies to have come to Ghana), Nkrumah could not give him a cabinet post; instead he established for him the Bureau of African Affairs.[39] It was Padmore's task to continue the pursuit of his Pan-African objectives on African soil. Already in 1953 Nkrumah had held a conference at Kumasi, the capital of Ashanti, which was intended to be the equivalent of a sixth Pan-African Congress. But apart from Azikiwe and a few other Nigerian representatives, only three observers appeared from Liberia; the National Congress of West Africa founded at Kumasi remained a fiction,[40] so that the conference may be written off as a failure.

Pan-Africanism in Africa (1958–66): success and crisis

Padmore was the first to bring a grand sweep to these Pan-African endeavours. As early as April 1958 he organized in Accra a conference of the eight African governments independent at that time (Ethiopia, Liberia, Morocco, Tunisia, Libya, Egypt, Sudan; Ghana). In the name of Africa as a whole they issued joint declarations condemning colonialism and the apartheid system in South Africa and giving the Algerian revolution their full moral support.[41] At the end of 1958 the first All-African Peoples' Conference was held, likewise in Accra. It placed itself consciously in the Pan-African tradition and may be regarded as the sixth Pan-African Congress. Here the same themes were broached as at the conference of governments; however, this time the participants were representatives of political parties and various mass organizations and for this reason the tone was considerably more bitter and further to the left. Padmore skilfully managed to thwart the communists' attempt to take over the conference, and likewise cut down radically the size of the Egyptian delegation, very much to Nasser's annoyance. The conference in Accra was the first genuinely all-African assembly, since francophone Black Africa was represented, as were the Arab lands of the north, East Africa, and the Belgian Congo (Lumumba). Pan-Africanism was now centred completely on the African continent itself, for the West Indies and the Afro-Americans were only present symbolically. It had returned, as it were, from the diaspora to the promised land.

Several historical events had made it possible for Pan-Africanism to expand and assume a continental framework: the Egyptian revolution (1952–3), the Algerian revolution (1954–62), the independence of Guinea (October 1958), and finally – carrying on a movement that had started in the pre-war years[42] – the expansion of the Négritude conception through the Présence Africaine group, manifest in the two congresses of African writers and artists held in Paris (1956) and Rome (1959). For Nasser the rediscovery of Egypt's African identity and the interest in the rest of the continent were means of consolidating his own position.[43] The Algerian revolution, like the apartheid régime in South Africa, became respectively positive and negative symbols of the Pan-African movement. The independence of Guinea followed two years later by that of Mali put an end to Ghana's isolated position in Black Africa and broke the traditional language barrier, just as the cultural barrier had been broken by the two writers' congresses of 1956 and 1959, which had been attended by writers and artists from both linguistic areas.[44] It is noteworthy that in East Africa, too, there now appeared a regional Pan-African movement which has some unspec-

tacular but relatively solid achievements to its credit.[45] Thus towards
the end of the 1950s there took place a fusion of all the different groups
in Pan-Africanism – the traditional (anglophone) ones and the new
(Arab and francophone) ones. In Ghana Pan-Africanism seemed to
have obtained a strong base in a sovereign national state. After Padmore's death in 1959 Nkrumah claimed the leadership, and in several
speeches and books endeavoured to promote the unification of Africa,
now under the slogan 'Union Government for Africa'.

An initial climax was reached in 1960, the 'year of Africa', when at
one sweep approximately half the continent became politically independent. On the other hand the inflated number of small and hardly
viable African national states meant a watering down of the Pan-
African idea. On top of this the troubles in the Congo plunged the
continent into its first major crisis. The immediate consequence was to
split Africa into two blocs of unequal strength. The beginning of 1961
saw the formation of the 'progressive' Casablanca group and the 'conservative' Monrovia–Brazzaville group. The 'progressive' Casablanca
group was, however, by no means homogeneous, not so much because
it comprised three Arab and three Black African governments
(Morocco, the FLN revolutionary government, Egypt; Ghana, Guinea,
Mali) as because Morocco itself was thoroughly conservative in its
domestic policies. The Casablanca group therefore lacked substance
and dissolved at the first opportunity with the foundation of the
Organization of African Unity (OAU) in Addis Ababa in 1963. By
contrast the Monrovia–Brazzaville group was more homogeneous and
also a compact bloc in the geographical sense. Even after its formal
dissolution in 1963 most francophone states still remained members of
the Union Africaine et Malgache.[46]

The foundation of the OAU in Addis Ababa under the leadership of
conservative but prestigious Ethiopia[47] was at that time equivalent to
a compromise, in that Nkrumah temporarily suspended his far-
reaching campaign for 'union government for Africa' so as to allow
the OAU to create a minimal basis for it. However, at later conferences
of the OAU, the last time in Accra in September 1965, he failed to make
headway against the new national states, which were in the process of
developing a considerable momentum of their own.

Besides this Nkrumah became more and more isolated in Africa,
since his Pan-African programme was all too obviously designed (in
part at least) to satisfy his personal ambition. He was suspected of

trying to promote the unification of Africa by subversive means, so that he alienated all his neighbours near and far. A ray of light seemed to be offered by the development of the Pan-African trade union movement, since the All-African Trade Union Federation, founded in Casablanca in 1961, after years of stagnation appeared to be consolidating its position firmly after 1963 and to be asserting itself against the rival western ICFTU and its dependency, the African Trade Union Federation (which had its headquarters in Dakar).[48] The second congress of the All-African Trade Union Federation especially, held in Bamako in May 1964, seemed to demonstrate and further this development.[49] But the All-African Trade Union Federation was much too dependent upon its Ghanaian base. When Nkrumah was overthrown on 24 February 1966 the All-African Trade Union Federation lost its main base, and ever since it has hung in the air. Nkrumah's fall was due mainly to domestic reasons[50] but it led to the temporary collapse of Pan-Africanism as a political movement, all the more so since only six weeks earlier Azikiwe, the president of Nigeria, had likewise been overthrown. Pan-Africanism has been obliged to fall back upon Guinea (and Mali) in West Africa and Tanzania in East Africa, where Nyerere today stands for a much more sober and pragmatic form of Pan-Africanism,[51] more defensive than dynamic. Another effect of Nkrumah's overthrow was to deprive some organizations in London and in Africa of material support. For the moment at least Pan-Africanism is so badly paralysed that a new beginning seems only conceivable after its intellectual premises and content have been re-examined.

The fact that the almost simultaneous overthrow of Nkrumah and Azikiwe could plunge Pan-Africanism into such a crisis points to a lack of inner solidarity. This should no longer surprise us after what has been said above. After the Pan-African movement had attained the goal of national independence with relative ease it found it difficult, in view of the contradictions in African society especially under the influence of modernization, to develop a common rational platform whence it could have launched a campaign for its next major objectives – national unification in one form or another and the modernization of African society.

After Padmore's death efforts to clarify matters theoretically were undertaken almost solely by Nkrumah and members of his entourage. It is doubtful whether Padmore, had he lived longer, would still have found the strength to carry through this intellectual renaissance. However that may be, Nkruman's ideological efforts were too hastily conceived, too polemical[52] or too trivial[53] for them to represent a constructive contribution to the rethinking that was so essential. 'Nkrumahism' and 'Consciencism' were too obviously designed to further the Pan-African glorification of Nkrumah. They were, so to speak, an extension of the cult of personality to the Pan-African plane, and thus failed to yield the desired effect.

Besides this, during the last months before Nkrumah's overthrow there took place in Ghana a strange self-destruction of the very substance of Pan-Africanism. It was not just that a man like Makonnen was driven into opposing Nkrumah:[54] the latter's organ of theoretical discussion and propaganda, the *Spark*, which at the same time represented the most radical and Marxist–Leninist wing of Nkrumahism and Pan-Africanism, ended by denying that there had been any Pan-Africanism prior to Nkrumah. This was a response to a critical review of the first sixteen issues of the *Spark* which first appeared in Germany and which *inter alia* pointed to the contrast between the *Spark* and Padmore in their assessment of Communism.[55] The chief editor of the paper replied with two unsigned articles in which even Du Bois, Garvey and Padmore were ruled out as champions of Pan-Africanism. Instead of utilizing the movement's historical traditions, as one might have expected, Pan-Africanism for the *Spark* began with Nkrumah, its first and only prophet.[56]

Thus the most radical representatives of Pan-Africanism were finally led to the absurdity of destroying their own historical justification. In doing this they overshot the mark and helped to reduce Pan-Africanism to little more than a mere façade, which collapsed with surprising ease and alacrity on Nkrumah's overthrow at the beginning of 1966.

21 The place of
Pan-Africanism
in history

It is no doubt too early as yet to express a definite opinion on Pan-Africanism. The entire movement is too vague, too ill-defined, too unclear in its purposes. For this very reason we have deemed it essential to describe it in as much detail as possible as a twentieth-century historical phenomenon with nineteenth-century roots and precursors. Our object has been to give some structure and form to this fluid movement, and so to make it possible to master it intellectually. Only on such a tolerably reliable basis of facts may one establish a provisional balance-sheet – remembering that Pan-Africanism may recover from its present state of crisis, and that fresh detailed studies will enlarge our knowledge and modify or correct some of our findings.

Our present knowledge does at any rate make it clear that Pan-Africanism was always the concern of tiny minorities – of the modern intellectual élites among Afro-Americans in the United States and the West Indies as well as in Africa itself (especially in West Africa). In most cases we have been dealing with small and weak groups who united to form ephemeral organizations and articulated their plans and ideas in no less ephemeral journals or pamphlets, most of which are nowadays difficult of access, if not entirely lost. It is thus only too understandable why historical scholarship has till now virtually ignored Pan-Africanism. The recent awakening of interest in it is due mainly to modern historians' greater concern with problems outside Europe and with social history. But it is also a product of history itself, especially of the decolonization of Africa. For it was this that allowed Pan-Africanism to achieve its first successes, which in turn led people to inquire into the historical roots of a movement which seemed to have appeared from nowhere.

Exuberant about this new discovery and reacting against the preceding period of colonialism European and North American commentators at first quite naturally drew conclusions about the character of Pan-Africanism on the basis of its remarkable achievements around 1960. Lacking detailed knowledge, or at the most possessing knowledge only about certain questions, their general tendency was to regard Pan-Africanism in a wholly uncritical spirit. Only a comprehensive and at the same time relatively detailed historical account enables us to appreciate the movement's inner weaknesses. The criteria of judgement which we should use become apparent on closer examination of the historical material. The existence of a few spokesmen for consistent modernization, notably Horton and Yatu,[1] make it possible for us to criticize the prevalent trend of romanticizing eclecticism, from Ahuma to Nkrumah, without running the risk of falling into neo-racism, especially as this historical analysis also makes intelligible the reasons for these inner weaknesses of the Pan-African movement.

Already our discussion of the historical and geographical background provides an explanation for the occasionally irritating ambiguity and lack of intellectual precision found among most representatives of Pan-Africanism. Slavery and colonialism inevitably led to an emotional attitude of protest, so that it required a maximum of intellectual discipline to adopt a more rational approach. Another factor was that only very few Pan-African leaders had a chance to acquire a comprehensive modern education which could have broadened their horizons beyond the parochial concerns of the society in which they lived and encouraged them to go beyond emotional protests against oppression. During the late eighteenth and throughout the nineteenth century most persons active in the movement were self-taught men. Most of them had escaped from slavery, which was such infertile soil for education, and had to depend more or less upon themselves in order to find their way in a world that was becoming ever more complex. On top of this these men had for almost two centuries to exhaust their mental energies on exposing the falseness of the absurd doctrines of European racial superiority, which denied them their dignity as human beings and any chance to attain equal rights. If one bears in mind how unfavourable their situation was at the start one must acknowledge that it is remarkable how often rational and modern arguments were used in refuting European racial theories.[2]

To this must be added the geographical factor. The classical triangle of the slave trade, which was also that of Pan-Africanism,[3] did indeed compensate to some extent for the limitations and oppressiveness of the social conditions from which the Pan-African leaders sprang; this explains why their political horizons were often so surprisingly broad. However, the social and political conditions at the terminal points of this triangle were always so diverse that they could not easily supply a common Pan-African denominator for their aspirations and interests. Vast distances were involved which made it difficult to know what conditions were really like in the various areas to which Pan-African sentiments appealed – notwithstanding the fact that many individual leaders travelled about a good deal and that their ideas circulated rapidly to and fro across the Atlantic, as well as up and down the West African coast. All these factors intensified the movement's tendency to emotionalism and lack of precision, since in order to arrive at a rational analysis of one's situation and to formulate a rational programme it is clearly necessary to have reliable information at one's disposal. The Pan-African leaders were frequently aware of this lack of knowledge and tried to remedy it so far as their modest means allowed. This is why most Pan-African meetings and journals primarily served to impart information. So preoccupied were they with instructing one another that they were usually satisfied with issuing general lists of demands or declamatory statements, and did nothing to clarify the movement's basic theoretical principles. The result was that such statements did not commit anyone to a specific course of action.

All this accounts for the fundamental weaknesses of Pan-Africanism which it has scarcely been able to overcome to this day. Although it is itself a product of the modern era, it has never been able to master the tensions between modern and traditional society in a fruitful way, or even to counter their dichotomous effect. Instead of becoming the ideology of consistent modernization, Pan-Africanism either took flight into a romanticized past, into the 'lost paradise' of Africa,[4] or else painfully attemped to combine modern and traditional elements, displaying an eclecticism which in the long run was untenable. Two striking manifestations of this inner contradiction are Du Bois's enthusiasm for Liberia in 1923-4 and Nkrumah's pagan ritual at Aggrey's grave in Salisbury NC in November 1942. Only a few leaders, either in the period of proto-Pan-Africanism or in that of Pan-Africanism proper, arrived at the sensible insight that the supposedly typical African social forms and customs which they wanted to preserve were simply the specific African version of a semi-nomadic and semi-agrarian tribal society, and that these social forms inevitably had to disappear as progress was made towards modernization and industrialization, just as they had disappeared in Europe. So far as we know, only Horton and Firmin in the nineteenth century and Padmore and Yatu (who has been completely forgotten) in the twentieth appreciated the logic of this historical process and endorsed it. But their ideas were not taken up and developed into a rational theoretical basis for the Pan-African movement.

Decolonization has sometimes led to convulsive efforts to 'Africanize' public life, to restore the African cultural heritage, to mystical cults of Négritude or the 'African personality' and an allegedly specifically African humanism; all these phenomena seem to have something in common with Ahuma's 'Backward movement' at the beginning of this century.[5] Certainly it is desirable that scholars should now make up for their past neglect of African history; however, there is a danger that African historians' recent preoccupation with their own past may lead to intellectual isolation and to increased provincialism. The present political difficulties, most distressingly symbolized in the sanguinary civil war in Nigeria, seem likely to intensify these tendencies towards neo-isolationism.

It remains to be seen whether the present difficult crisis of Pan-Africanism will give place to a renaissance. Such a new beginning could only come about on the basis of a consistent rationalist outlook which would make a clear break with the immature romanticism of the preceding period. For in default of a consistent and modern outlook the Pan-African movement will not be able to achieve the next two aims which it has set itself, at least verbally: namely, some kind of social modernization and political unification on a continental scale. The paradox in the present situation is that most African leaders pay lip service to both these ideals but in practice avoid doing anything to implement them because of the strength of the traditional conservative element in African society. As yet the power of this element appears to have been broken only by Sekou Touré in Guinea and Nyerere in Tanzania, although it remains to be seen how their policy will work out in the long run.

Despite its chronic organizational weakness and its lack of intellectual balance, Pan-Africanism has had an enormous political and historical impact, by striving for the decolonization of Africa. This may be explained by the fact that the modern (as opposed to the traditional) élites of Africa, reinforced by Afro-American and West Indian intellectuals, took up the European idea of popular sovereignty and impetuously transferred it to Africa. During World War II this took all the colonial powers (except Portugal) literally by surprise. African nationalism and Pan-Africanism profited from two factors: firstly, the guilty conscience of the colonial powers, who contrary to their official ideology of the 'White man's burden' did not follow any consistent policy of modernization in their colonies; secondly, their fear that the colonies would revolt if the African nationalists should be frustrated and turn to Communism.[6] The triumph of African nationalism, which on the whole took place with startling speed and smoothness, simultaneously deprived the Pan-African movement of the opportunity to prepare itself mentally for the far more difficult post-independence period.

One of the serious errors which the Pan-African leaders made was to overestimate the speed with which African society could develop. In principle they were quite correct in thinking that Africa would need less time to modernize than Europe, but they were mistaken about the time needed before Africa could attain a level of historical development corresponding to that reached by Europe at the time when the modern nation state came into being. Most of them admitted that Africa was very backward socially and therefore politically. Comparisons were frequently drawn (in principle quite rightly) with the development of the Greek tribes in pre-classical times or of the Teutons and Celts 2000 years ago.[7] Even Ahuma believed that African society was still at a stage akin to that of early medieval Europe.[8] But later authors wanted Africa to catch up on its lag in civilization within a very brief span, as Japan and the Soviet Union were doing. Solanke thought in terms of twenty-five years and half a generation later Danquah spoke of a single decade.[9]

Understandably reacting against racist theories which asserted on biological grounds that Africa must remain in its present backwardness for ever, and impatient to attain national independence and thus at least formal equality, they overlooked several factors. It is true that individuals, if placed as children in a modern environment and given appropriate educational opportunities, can catch up within a decade on the advantages enjoyed by others; but this applies only to individuals, each of whom is an entity to himself. The representatives of the modern African élites were too quick to judge their societies by their own personal experience, ignoring the fact that it takes far longer for societies, with all their traditions and conflicting interests, to effect a major change. Moreover, Japan and Soviet Russia, when they turned consistently and purposefully to policies of modernization and industrialization, had already achieved a level of development which will not be attainable in Africa before several decades have elapsed, if then. The discrepancy between Japan or Russia on one hand and Western Europe and North America on the other was not then so great, and in the meantime the gulf between the world's industrialized nations and Africa has widened even further.

By pushing ahead so impatiently the Pan-African leaders allowed illusions to grow up about the tempo at which African society might develop after national independence had been won. The disenchantment which inevitably followed contributed to the major 'crisis of consciousness' which Africa has been passing through during the last few years. By and large they were apparently not aware how difficult it was to try to raise traditional society as quickly as possible to the level of the modern African élites. If African society were to become rapidly modernized and amalgamated – the indispensable condition for any kind of African unity – it would require much patience and a rational outlook. Neither of these qualities has yet emerged in the Pan-African movement. It was not enough to recognize, as Du Bois did in Manchester, that mistakes would inevitably be made after independence.[10] Many African nationalists after 1945 said that they would rather govern themselves badly than go on being governed well by others; but this, too, was no more than a rhetorical flourish expressing defiance and revolt: it was not a substitute for a realistic view of the tasks before them.

To a certain extent the present crisis of Pan-Africanism helps one to assess it historically by making the main issues stand out more clearly than they do from a purely historical analysis.

An attempt to give Pan-Africanism its rightful place in modern history naturally invites comparison with other modern 'Pan' movements. Without a close study of the latter on a scale equivalent to that of the present work it would be rash to venture a detailed comparison, but one may at least formulate a provisional hypothesis.[11] All 'Pan' movements (except Pan-Americanism and Pan-Germanism) appeared in underdeveloped countries which possessed no states of their own, or whose statehood was only partial: this was the case with Pan-Slavism, Pan-Arabism and Pan-Turkism, to mention only the most important. Pan-Americanism was not much more than a diplomatic instrument in the hands of an emerging great power (USA) in the age of imperialism, and Pan-Germanism the ideology of the most extreme groups of German imperialism and proto-Fascism. The other 'Pan' movements originated among an intelligentsia exposed to contact with the modern Western world. Here the desire for national statehood was combined with the ideal of solidarity between all members of the same linguistic or cultural groups – Slavs, Arabs, Turks, Africans or Afro-Americans. This was associated with a desire to rehabilitate these 'nations without a history' and their peasant cultures; it automatically gave their ideas a dash of romanticism. Pan-Turkism and Pan-Arabism (with its religious variant, Pan-Islamism) found in history the memory of a proud imperial past which the more recent nationalisms of more limited scope were invited to match. In lieu of this Pan-Slavism developed the myth of 'mother Russia' which would bring national rebirth to the oppressed Slav nationalities of the Balkans, albeit under Russian leadership. From this point onwards Pan-Slav ideology, at least as preached in Russia, became fused with a pronounced element of Russian imperialism.

So far as historical memories were concerned Pan-Africanism, however, had not much more to offer than the claim that ancient Egypt had had an African or negroid character or origin,[12] and the vague recollection of the medieval empires of western Sudan, which in any case it owed in part to European scholarship.[13] Without much in the way of territorial statehood in the past to look back to, they were left with the continental or racial category (continental Pan-Africanism in the narrower sense, or Pan-Negroism) and the appeal to common rejection of White predominance and colonialism. It was impossible to restore the vanished empires; it was also impossible to make the surviving pre-colonial states the basis of modern national entities (although there were exceptions: Morocco, Tunisia, Egypt, Ethiopia,

Upper Volta – former Mossi empire – and to some extent Buganda). This meant that African nationalism had to take over the units of colonial administration as the framework for the emergent nations. As far as possible they were given the names of medieval African empires (e.g. Ghana and Mali). Since these nations still barely existed, and were therefore generally regarded as artificial, Pan-African leaders like Nkrumah hoped that as soon as possible after independence an all-encompassing, all-African state and consciousness might come into being which would prevent national particularism from consolidating itself and impeding the drive for African unity. Nkrumah erred in his estimate of the speed with which this Pan-African awareness could be formed, and his impatient pressure contributed to Pan-Africanism's failure in the post-independence period up to the present time.

Hitherto what one may term the classical 'Pan' movements – those in backward societies – have all failed except for Pan-Slavism. Since 1945 the Pan-Slav programme has been virtually fulfilled. The Slav peoples have their own autonomous states in close collaboration while fulfilling a radical social revolution on the Soviet Russian model. The condition for this success may lie in the fact that from the start Pan-Slavism could look for support to a strong Russian state and that the Slavs had common enemies: before 1918 the Ottoman and Austro-Hungarian empires and after 1939 Germany.[14] The other 'Pan' movements, by contrast, hung in the air in terms of power politics. French and British imperialism in the Near East put an end to the Pan-Arab unity to which the Arabs aspired at the end of World War I. After World War II the Arab nation states that had sprung up in the meantime were strong enough to prevent the champion of Pan-Arab unity, Nasser's Egyptian Republic, from achieving its ends. In addition to this the Pan-Arab movement came up against Zionism – a movement which in some respects resembles the 'Pan' movements – and its most important creation, the state of Israel. The situation became further involved with the rise of Pan-Africanism after 1958, which led to an overlapping of the two 'Pan' movements in North Africa.

Hitherto Pan-Arabism and Pan-Africanism have only obtained their objective of national independence, but not that of forming some kind of larger unit. The Arab League and the Organization for African Unity have as yet played only an embryonic role and have lacked the strength to achieve their ultimate goals. Pan-Arabism and Pan-Africanism have differed in the extent to which they have permitted social change: here the Arabs have had a considerable historical advantage over the Africans. All 'Pan' movements in underdeveloped societies face the same basic problem, the clash between the traditional world and modern influences. In trying to solve this conflict, universal to our age, the modernized élites of each country have acted in very different ways, according to their specific historical circumstances.

A critical analysis of Pan-Africanism may in some ways turn out to be disappointing, especially in view of the major crisis in which the movement currently finds itself. On the other hand a study of its history seems more fruitful. It offers an approach to the history of Africa and of the Afro-Americans. It throws light upon new aspects of European racism and colonialism, against which Pan-Africanism rose in revolt. Beyond this it opens up some of the major problems of modern history and recent historiography: the ways in which modern society has developed, especially under the influence of industrialization, the tensions between tradition and innovation, and the relationship of the individual to the society of which he forms a part.

Notes and bibliography

Notes

Introduction

1 W. E. B. Du Bois, *Dusk of Dawn: an Essay towards an Autobiography of a Race Concept* (New York, 1940) pp. 260–62, 276–8; *The World and Africa : an Enquiry into the Part which Africa has Played in World History* (New York, 1946, second edition 1965) pp. 6–12, 236–45 (identical with the paper in *History of the Pan-African Congress*, ed. G. Padmore (London, 1947, second edition 1963) pp. 13–27). For earlier sketches not taken into account in more recent works cf. R. L. Buell, *International Relations* (New York, 1925) pp. 84–6; H. Kohn, 'Pan Movements', *Encyclopaedia of the Social Sciences* (New York, 1933) volume XI, pp. 544–54, especially pp. 549f., with some factual errors but astonishingly accurate in its general assessment.

2 G. Padmore, *Pan-Africanism or Communism? The Coming Struggle for Africa* (London, 1956) pp. 117–44. I have used the edition published in Accra, which has the same subtitle but an abbreviated title: *Pan-Africanism.*

3 P. Decraene, *Le Panafricanisme* (Que sais-je?, No. 487) (Paris, 1959, third edition 1964) pp. 11–25.

4 C. Legum, *Pan-Africanism: A Short Political Guide* (London, 1962, second edition 1964) especially pp. 20–33. Also his 'The Roots of Pan-Africanism' in *Africa: a Handbook to the Continent* (London, 1961) pp. 452–62; 'Pan-Africanism and Nationalism', *Africa in the Nineteenth and Twentieth Centuries*, ed. J. C. Anene and G. Brown (London, Ibadan, 1966) pp. 528–38.

5 G. Shepperson, 'Notes on Negro American Influences on the Emergence of African Nationalism', *Journal of African History*, volume I, no. 2, pp. 299–312.

6 Especially 'Pan-Africanism and "pan-Africanism": Some Historical

Notes', *Phylon*, XXIII/4, Winter 1962, pp. 346–58.

7 G. Shepperson and T. Price, *Independent African: John Chilembwe and the . . . Nyasaland Native Rising of 1915* (Edinburgh, 1958, second edition 1963).

8 R. W. Logan, 'The Historical Aspects of Pan-Africanism, 1900–1945', *Pan-Africanism Reconsidered*, ed. American Society of African Culture (Berkeley, Los Angeles, 1962) pp. 37–52.

9 H. F. Strauch, *Panafrika: Kontinentale Weltmacht im Werden?* (Zurich, 1964) pp. 18ff.

10 Ibid., especially pp. 27, 37f.

11 E.g. I. Wallerstein, 'Pan-Africanism as Protest', *The Revolution in World Politics*, ed. M. A. Kaplan (New York, 1962) pp. 137–51. Among German works one may mention P. Coulmas, *Der Fluch der Freiheit: Wohin marschiert die farbige Welt?* (Oldenburg, Hamburg, 1963) pp. 34f.; F. Ansprenger, *Auflösung der Kolonialreiche* (dtv-Weltgeschichte des 20. Jahrhunderts, volume 13) (Munich, 1966) pp. 136–41; P. Berteaux, 'Afrika. Von der Vorgeschichte bis zu den Staaten der Gegenwart' (*Fischer Weltgeschichte*, volume 32 (Frankfurt, 1966) pp. 268–72) goes beyond the conventional limitations. Now also, V. B. Thompson, *Africa and Unity: the Evolution of Pan-Africanism* (London, 1969) pp. xxi–xxiv, 3–63.

12 Eduardo dos Santos, *Pan-Africanismo de outem e de hoje* (Lisbon, 1968).

13 Cf. the pronounced autobiographical element in many of his works, e.g. in the subtitle of *Dusk of Dawn: an Essay towards an Autobiography of a Race Concept.*

14 E.g., where he commences the prehistory of Pan-Africanism with the founding of Sierra Leone: *Pan-Africanism*, pp. 23f.

15 E.g. J. R. Hooker, *Black Revolutionary. George Padmore's Path from Communism to Pan-Africanism* (London, 1967); H. R. Lynch, *Edward Wilmot Blyden: Pan-Negro Patriot, 1832–1912* (London, 1967); E. A. Ayandele, 'Holy Johnson' (London, 1970); C. Fyfe, 'Africanus Horton, 1835–1883', *West African Scientist and Patriot* (New York, London, Toronto, 1972). Among theses unpublished when my own research was in progress one may note: J. S. Spiegler, 'Aspects of Nationalist Thought among French-Speaking West Africans, 1921–1939' (Ph.D., Oxford, 1967); P. Walshe, 'The South African National Congress' (Ph.D., Oxford, 1967); J. L. Hymans, 'L'Élaboration de la pensée de Léopold Sédar Senghor: esquisse d'un itineraire intellectuel' (Thèse pour le doctorat de recherche, Paris, 1964). I was also able to utilize dissertations in progress by Ian Duffy, Edinburgh (biography of Mohamed Ali Duse) and Samuel Rohdie, Accra (biography of Kobina Sekyi).

16 I was not permitted to consult the part of the papers in New York in the custody of H. Aptheker.

PART I

Chapter 1

1 This term was already in use in the United States during the nineteenth century, as an alternative to 'negro' and 'colored', which were thought to be discriminatory. In the present work it is used as a synonym for these terms. For a more detailed discussion of this point see I. Geiss, *Die Afro-Amerikaner* (Frankfurt, 1969) pp. 19–21; also R. B. Moore, *The Name 'Negro': its Origin and its Evil Use* (New York, 1960).

2 Cf. also H. P. Marc, 'Pan-Africanism: a Dream Come True', *Foreign Affairs*, April 1955, pp. 445ff.

3 The German term *Panafrikanisten*

was coined by Strauch on an analogy with *Panslawisten* (Pan-Slavs).

4 The best of the recent works on decolonization include H. Grimal, *La Décolonisation, 1919–1963* (Paris, 1965); R. V. Albertini, *Dekolonisation: die Diskussion über Verwaltung und Zukunft der Kolonien, 1919–1960* (Cologne, Opladen, 1966); F. Ansprenger, work cited in Introd., n.11.

5 For the origins of German conservatism, which was most strongly imbued by the idea of reverting to medieval values, cf. the first volume of the work by K. Epstein, *The Genesis of German Conservatism* (Princeton, 1966); the author's untimely death prevented him from completing the three volumes originally planned.

6 Cf. especially H. Kohn, *Die Slawen und der Westen: eine Geschichte des Panslawismus* (Vienna, 1956).

7 Cf. T. L. Hodgkin, *Nationalism in Colonial Africa* (London, 1956, fourth edition 1962) pp. 16f.

8 K. Nkrumah, *Consciencism: Philosophy and Ideology for Decolonization and Development with Particular Reference to the African Revolution* (London, 1964).

9 Cf. above, p. xii, n. 6.

10 Cf. below, Pt II, ch. 10, pp. 176–98.

11 Cf. below, pp. 30–40.

12 Cf. below, pp. 41–57, 58–65, 71ff., 169ff.

13 Cf. below, Pt II, ch. 9, pp. 161–75.

14 Cf. above, p. 5, n. 2.

15 Cf. below, pp. 37–40.

16 Cf. below, Pt II, ch. 13, pp. 263–82.

17 G. Padmore, *Pan-Africanism*, p. 87.

18 *The Interesting Narrative of the Life of Oloudah Equiano, or Gustavus Vassa, the African, written by himself* (London, 1789). This contains an instructive description of Ibo society in the late eighteenth century (pp. 3–25), recently reprinted in T. L. Hodgkin, *Nigerian Perspectives: an Historical Anthology* (London, 1960) pp. 155–66.

19 V. C. Ikeotuonye, *Zik of New Africa* (London, Geneva, 1961); K. A. B. Jones-Quartey, *A Life of Azikiwe* (London, Baltimore, 1966).

20 Cf. below, pp. 52–7.

21 For a general survey see J. H. Parry, P. Sherlock, *A Short History of the West Indies* (London, 1956, third edition 1973).

22 The literature on Haiti is likewise vast. The most modern and satisfactory monograph is J. G. Leyburn, *The Haitian People* (New Haven, 1941, second edition 1966) especially pp. 14–110.

23 Cf. below, pp. 78f.

24 J. G. Leyburn, *The Haitian People*, p. 16.

25 Cf. especially C. L. R. James, *The Black Jacobins: Toussaint L'Ouverture and the San Domingo Revolution* (London, New York, 1938, second edition 1963).

26 Cf. above, p. xii, n. 5. It would be instructive to make a similar analysis of West Indian influence on African nationalism.

27 On the West India Regiment in Sierra Leone, cf. C. Fyfe, *A History of Sierra Leone* (Oxford, 1962, second edition 1963) especially pp. 135f., 215, 348f.; also A. Nicol, 'West Indians in West Africa', *Sierra Leone Studies*, new series, no. 13, 1960, pp. 14ff.

28 Cf. below, pp. 14f.

29 Cf. below, p. 91ff.

30 Cf. J. H. Kopytoff, *A Preface to Modern Nigeria: the 'Sierra Leoneans' in Yoruba, 1830–1890* (Madison, Milwaukee, London, 1965) pp. 41–3.

31 Cf. below, Pt II, ch. 15, pp. 305–13.

32 Especially Padmore, C. L. R. James and their circle.

33 Cf. below, pp. 32–7.

34 E.g. Horton: cf. below, pp. 67f.

35 Cf. below, Pt II, ch. 15, pp. 305–13.

36 Cf. below, Pt II, ch. 15, pp. 305–13.

37 Cf. below, pp. 240ff., 254f.

38 Cf. below, Pt II, ch. 11, pp. 199–202.

39 Cf. J. S. Nye Jr, *Pan-Africanism and*

East African Integration (Cambridge – Mass., London, Nairobi, 1966) p. 31.

40 Cf. below, pp. 145, 210.
41 Cf. below, pp. 207–10.
42 Cf. below, pp. 32–5.
43 Cf. below, pp. 35–7, 42–9.
44 Cf. below, pp. 90, 166–9, 177f.
45 Cf. below, pp. 30–40.
46 Cf. below, Pt II, ch. 10, pp. 176–98.
47 Cf. below, Pt II, ch. 12, pp. 229–62.
48 Cf. below, Pt II, ch. 19, pp. 385–408.
49 Cf. below, pp. 421.
50 Cf. below, pp. 350–56.

Chapter 2

1 Cf. below, pp. 51, 91, 145f., 156f.
2 On this see the detailed treatment by E. W. Bovill, *The Golden Trade of the Moors* (London, 1958) pp. 28, 114ff., 191ff.; also B. Penrose, *Travel and Discovery in the Renaissance, 1420–1620* (Cambridge – Mass., 1952, third edition 1960).
3 The best recent account is D. P. Mannix and M. Cowley, *Black Cargoes: a History of the Atlantic Slave Trade* (New York, 1962, second edition 1965). For a critical survey of the earlier literature, cf. C. Fyfe, 'A Historiographical Survey of the Transatlantic Slave Trade from West Africa' (duplicated; Centre of African Studies, University of Edinburgh, n.d.).
4 On the trading forts see the excellent and lavishly illustrated monograph by A. W. Lawrence, *Trade Castles and Forts of West Africa* (London, 1963). On Brandenburg's part, cf. pp. 218–26; there is an earlier German account: R. Schück, *Brandenburg–Preussens Kolonialpolitik*, 2 volumes (Leipzig, 1889). On the unsuccessful attempt to establish a foothold in the West Indies, see H. Kellenbenz, 'Die Brandenburger auf St Thomas', *Jahrbuch für Geschichte von Staat, Wirtschaft und Gesellschaft Lateinamerikas* (2/1965) pp. 196–217; cf. also Georg Nørregard,

Danish Settlements in West Africa 1658–1850 (Boston–Mass., 1966).
5 The best account of Haitian history prior to independence is still Pierre de Vaissière, *Saint Domingue (1629–1789): la société et la vie créole sous l'ancien régime* (Paris, 1909).
6 The first study of one of these Gold Coast families, the Brews, is M. Priestley, 'The Emergence of an Elite: a Case Study of a West Coast Family', P. C. Lloyd (ed.), *The New Elites of Tropical Africa. Studies Presented . . . at the University of Ibadan, Nigeria, July 1964* (London, 1966) pp. 87–100. Here on p. 87 is a general indication of the significance of the mulatto element. Studies of other families would be most welcome; they would, however, probably not greatly affect the general picture.
7 Cf. below, p. 68f.
8 S. R. B. Attoh Ahuma, *Memoirs of West African Celebrities, Europe etc. (1700–1850) with Special Reference to the Gold Coast* (Liverpool, 1905) pp. 15ff.; on Quaque cf. also F. L. Bartels, *The Roots of Ghana Methodism* (London, 1965) pp. 4, 6.
9 Cf. below, pp. 60–63.
10 This thesis, inspired by Marxist thinking, is adduced by E. Williams, *Capitalism and Slavery* (Chapel Hill-NC, London, 1944, second edition 1964); also E. Mandel, *Traité d'économie marxiste*, 2 volumes (Paris, 1962) vol. 2, pp. 71–4.
11 In Haiti Napoleon's attempt to reintroduce slavery in 1802 failed as a result of the war of Independence which it unleashed.
12 Cf. below, pp. 34f.
13 Cf. above, n. 5; also J. G. Leyburn, *The Haitian People*, pp. 16ff.
14 It was a real parlour game in Haiti to try to establish the exact fraction of a person's mulatto blood, according to whether his or her mother was White, half-, quarter- or one-eighth negro etc. Each of these shades had

its particular name, producing a most complicated system that today is only of curiosity value.

15 An impressive account of these practices is given by the Haitian author E. Edouard, *Essai sur la politique intérieure d'Haiti. Propositions d'une politique nouvelle* (Paris, 1890). A modern Haitian scholar has also dared to call things by their true name (although he is a member of the Haitian emigration, opposed to the Duvalier régime): L. F. Manigat, *Haiti of the Sixties: Object of International Concern . . .* (Washington, 1964).

16 On this see L. E. Lomax, *The Negro Revolt* (New York, 1962).

17 G. Vassa, *The Interesting Narrative . . .*, I, p. 97.

18 Ibid., pp. 86f.

19 Cf. H. Aptheker, *American Negro Slave Revolts* (New York, 1943, fifth edition 1964) especially the chapters 'The Fear of Rebellion', pp. 18–52 and 'The Machinery of Control', pp. 53–78. On slavery in the USA in general cf. now especially K. Stampp, *The Peculiar Institution: Slavery in the Ante-Bellum South* (New York, 1956; London, 1964); also J. H. Franklin, *The Militant South, 1800–1861* (Cambridge – Mass., 1956).

20 Cf. below, pp. 52f.

21 For the earlier hypothesis, cf. F. Tannenbaum, *Slave and Citizen: the Negro in the Americas* (New York, 1947); his view is endorsed by H. S. Klein, *Slavery in the Americas: a Comparative Study of Virginia and Cuba* (London, 1967).

22 On this phase see now especially D. L. Dumond, *Antislavery: the Crusade for Freedom in America* (Ann Arbor, 1961); L. Lader, *The Bold Brahmins; New England's War against Slavery, 1831–1863* (New York, 1961). A critical assessment is given by J. C. Furnas, *The Road to Harpers Ferry: Facts and Follies of the War on Slavery* (New York, 1959; London, 1961).

23 Cf., e.g., below, p. 86.

24 Cf. especially R. C. Wade, *Slavery in the Cities: the South, 1820–1860* (New York, 1964).

25 One of them was A. A. Schomburg from Puerto Rico, who came to the United States around 1900 and later became the founder of the Schomburg Collection in Harlem.

26 Cf. the concise but accurate formulation by W. E. B. Du Bois, *The World and Africa*, p. 7: 'The idea of one Africa to unite the thought and ideals of all native peoples of the dark continent belongs to the twentieth century and stems naturally from the West Indies and the United States. Here various groups of Africans, quite separate in origin, became so united in experience and so exposed to the impact of new cultures that they began to think of Africa as one idea and one land.'

27 Cf. below, pp. 38–40, 98–102.

28 Fyfe, *History of Sierra Leone*, p. 13, thinks it possible that these writers were aided by Englishmen in producing these works, but does not attach much importance to the fact.

29 One group had a predominantly negative view of Africa: see below, p. 85.

30 Cf. below, pp. 258–62.

31 M. J. Herskovits, *The Myth of the Negro Past* (New York, 1941) stresses above all the strength of the African cultural heritage in the New World, whereas F. E. Frazier contests the significance of these 'survivals'. Cf. Frazier, *The Negro Family* (New York, 1939); idem, *The Negro in the United States* (New York, 1957); idem, *The Negro Church in America* (New York, 1963). Cf. also L. D. Turner, 'African Survivals in the New World with Special Emphasis on the Arts', J. A. Davis (ed.), *Africa Seen by American Negroes* (Paris,

1958) pp. 101–16. For a discussion of this controversy, see also H. R. Isaacs, *The New World of Negro Americans* (New York, 1964) pp. 107–11.

32 This hypothesis, based on the literature, needs to be elaborated in detail and if verified could put an end to the dispute about 'survivals' by providing a differentiated analysis of the conditions in various areas. An initial attempt at this is R. Bastide, *Les Amériques noires: les civilisations africaines dans le Nouveau Monde* (Paris, 1967) especially pp. 29–50.

33 Cf. especially M. J. Herskovits, *The Myth of the Negro Past*, the chapter 'Africanisms in Religious Life', pp. 207–48. On the Voodoo cult in Haiti, see the chapter 'Vodun' (as it is spelt) in J. G. Leyburn, *The Haitian People*, pp. 131–65; R. Bastide, *Les Ameriques Noires*, pp. 138–55.

34 Cf. M. M. Fisher, *Negro Slave Songs in the United States* (Ithaca – New York, 1953).

35 Ibid., p. 67 (on Haiti).

36 Cf. below, p. 371.

37 W. E. B. Du Bois, *Dusk of Dawn*, p. 114.

38 Particularly informative on this is H. R. Isaacs, *The New World*, the chapter 'Negroes and Africa', pp. 105–322.

39 Cf. below, p. 85f.

40 Cf. below, pp. 82f., 93ff.

41 Cf. below, Pt II, ch. 13, pp. 263–82.

Chapter 3

1 D. L. Dumond, *Antislavery*, pp. 8–10.

2 Ibid., p. 17.

3 Cf. W. Sypher, *Guinea's Captive Kings* (Chapel Hill, 1942); E. B. Dykes, *The Negro in English Romantic Thought* (Washington, 1942); also H. N. Fairchild, *The Noble Savage . . .* (New York, 1928). For a more recent treatment of this theme see P. D. Curtin, *The Image of Africa:*

British Ideas and Action, 1780–1950 (Wisconsin, 1964; London, 1965) pp. 49–51; more recently also D. B. Davis, *The Problem of Slavery in Western Culture* (Ithaca – New York, 1966) pp. 472–9.

4 Further details and references in Davis, *Problem of Slavery*, pp. 308f.

5 For the earlier period cf. ibid., pp. 304f.; on the conflicts in the late eighteenth and early nineteenth centuries, see especially H. Aptheker, 'The Quakers and Negro Slavery', *Journal of Negro History (JNH)*, 25/1940, no. 3, pp. 331–62. This destroys the recent suggestion doubtless put forward in good faith but nevertheless erroneous, that the Quakers were 'the only religious group who never compromised with slavery'; cf. N. Mühlen, *Die Schwarzen Amerikaner: Anatomie einer Revolution* (Stuttgart, 1964) p. 49. Mühlen's account is also inaccurate at other points, especially pp. 44, 47, 50–52, 62.

6 Dumond, *Antislavery*, p. 51.

7 A. Benezet, *Some Historical Account of Guinea . . .* (fourth edition London, 1788) with biographical details about the author; also *A Caution and Warning to Great Britain and her Colonies* (Philadelphia, 1766).

8 On his influence in England, particularly on John Wesley and Thomas Clarkson, see D. P. Mannix and M. Cowley, *Black Cargoes*, p. 172; B. Quarles, *The Negro in the American Revolution* (Chapel Hill, 1961) pp. 35f.

9 On this see especially W. E. B. Du Bois, *The Suppression of the African Slave-Trade to the USA, 1638–1870.* Harvard Historical Studies, no. 1 (Cambridge – Mass., 1896, third edition New York, 1954).

10 On the history of the AME and AMEZ churches there is as yet nothing other than accounts written by churchmen of one denomination or the other. There is a need for a

modern history of their rivalry based on these accounts. Cf. C. G. Woodson, *History of the Negro Church* (Washington, 1921); cf. also below, pp. 134–41.

11 Cf. below, pp. 98–106.

12 Cf. below, pp. 145, 182.

13 The literature on Afro-American freemasonry is likewise very sketchy. Most interest is centred on its establishment by Prince Hall. The only monograph is H. van B. Voorhis, *Negro Masonry in the United States* (New York, 1940); the other works merely provide details about the formal history of these organizations. The Schomburg Collection in Harlem has some manuscripts by H. A. Williamson dating from the period 1931–5 which deal with these problems: 'A History of Freemasonry among the American Negroes (1931); 'A Chronological History of Prince Hall Masonry, 1784–1932' (1934); 'A Brief History of Negro Masonry' (1935).

14 H. Aptheker, *A Documentary History of the Negro People in the United States*, 2 volumes (New York, 1951, second edition 1964) vol. I, p. 19.

15 For details see the monograph by Sir R. Coupland, *The British Anti-Slavery Movement* (London, 1933, second edition 1964) which still preserves its usefulness; also H. A. Wyndham, *The Atlantic and Slavery* (London, 1935). A valuable synopsis is provided by Mannix and Cowley, *Black Cargoes*, pp. 171–90.

16 Cf. below, pp. 49–57.

17 Cf. K. L. L. Little, *Negroes in Britain: a Study of Racial Relations in English Society* (London, 1947) p. 71, where the author cites a British writer of 1778.

18 On the following see especially C. Fyfe, *A History of Sierra Leone*, pp. 13–18; also P. D. Curtin, *Image of Africa*, pp. 80–106.

19 On this see C. B. Wadstrom, *An Essay on Colonization . . .* , 2 parts

(London, 1794–5) Pt II, pp. 3f. It is interesting that in Smeatham's project provision was made for the eight-hour day and Sunday holidays: 'Only eight hours of fair labour each day will be required in summer or winter; and on Saturdays only six hours. The sabbath will be set apart as day of rest, instruction, and devotion.'

20 Fyfe, *History of Sierra Leone*, pp. 52f.

21 O. Cugoano, *Thoughts and Sentiments on the Evil and Wicked Traffic of Slavery* (London, 1787).

22 Fyfe, *History of Sierra Leone*, pp. 18f.; also G. Vassa, *The Interesting Narrative*, II, p. 230f.

23 Cugoano, *Thoughts and Sentiments*, p. 139f.

24 Idem, *Réflexions sur la traite et l'esclavage des Nègres* (Paris, 1788) p. vi.

25 Cugoano, *Thoughts and Sentiments* pp. 130–34.

26 Ibid. pp. 75f.; cf. also T. Jefferson, *Notes on the State of Virginia* (London, 1787:) 'I tremble for my country when I reflect that God is just; that his Justice cannot sleep forever; that considering numbers, nature and natural means only, a revolution of the wheel of fortune, an exchange of situation is among possible events.'

27 Cf. above, p. 8.

Chapter 4

1 Cf. below, pp. 176–92.

2 Cf. below, pp. 134–48.

3 There are two recent comprehensive studies: S. Neill, *Christian Missions*. The Pelican History of the Church, vol. 6 (Harmondsworth, 1964, second edition 1966) with an ample and well-arranged bibliography, and C. P. Groves, *The Planting of Christianity in Africa*, 4 volumes (London, 1948–58). Cf. also the chapter on Christian missionary activity in Africa between the sixteenth and nineteenth centuries in R. Cornevin, *Histoire de L'Afrique*,

3 volumes, vol. 2 (*L'Afrique pré-coloniale du tournant de XVIe au tournant du XXe siècle*) (Paris, 1966) pp. 446–73, which provides a useful synopsis. Cf. also the earlier standard work by K. S. Latourette, *A History of the Expansion of Christianity*, 7 volumes (London, 1938–45).

4 For relevant bibliography, see above, ch. 3, n. 15.

5 Cf. above, pp. 38f.

6 Cf. also E. Williams, *Capitalism and Slavery*.

7 On the the following see especially C. Fyfe, *A History of Sierra Leone*, pp. 25ff.

8 C. B. Wadström, *An Essay on Colonization . . .* ; cf. above, ch. 3, n. 19.

9 *Ibid.*, pp. 341–53, gives a list of the original signatories and the amount of their shares.

10 *Letters of the Late Ignatius Sancho, an African . . .* , 2 volumes (London, 1782, first edition 1781); the then customary list of subscribers is on pp. xvii–lvii.

11 Cf. below, pp. 98–106.

12 Fyfe, *History of Sierra Leone*, p. 48; Curtin, *Image of Africa*, p. 133f.

13 Fyfe, *History of Sierra Leone*, pp. 59–61.

14 *Ibid.*, p. 105.

15 This is the general hypothesis of Eric Williams (see above, n. 6), which, although it may be faulted on some details, is in general borne out by the facts.

16 For informative details see Colonial Papers, House of Commons, *Report . . . 24th July 1807*, pp. 3–5.

17 We cannot at this point go more deeply into this question, which was of such importance in the development of international law. For the immediately relevant facts see Mannix and Cowley, *Black Cargoes*, pp. 205–23, and Du Bois, *The Suppression of the American Slave-Trade*, pp. 141–9.

18 The figure is given by C. Fyfe,

Sierra Leone Inheritance (London, Ibadan, Accra, 1964) p. 131.

19 H. A. Wyndham, *The Atlantic and Slavery*, p. 221.

20 Fyfe, *History*, pp. 75f.; also for the following information.

21 E. Stock, *The History of the Church Missionary Society*, 4 volumes (London, 1899–1916).

22 Cf. above, pp. 42ff.; on Venn, see below, p. 51.

23 T. S. Johnson, *The Story of a Mission. The Sierra Leone Church: First Daughter of the C.M.S.* (London, 1953) pp. 20, 25, 29; J. H. Kopytoff, *A Preface to Modern Nigeria*, p. 25, gives a figure of over 11,000 settlers in Sierra Leone between 1814 and 1824.

24 *Ibid.*, pp. 32f.

25 T. J. Thompson, *The Jubilee and Centenary Volume of Fourah Bay College . . .* (Freetown, 1930) contains a chapter by J. Denton, 'History of Fourah Bay College', pp. 9–26.

26 Cf. below, pp. 157f.

27 A. E. Tubuko-Metzger, *Historical Sketch of the Sierra Leone Grammar School, 1845–1935* (Freetown, 1935).

28 *Ibid.*, p. 15.

29 Instructive on this point is P. Foster, *Educational and Social Change in Ghana* (London, 1965) especially pp. 125, 130f., 155ff.

30 Cf. below, pp. 52–7.

31 From data in Tubuko-Metzger, *Historical Sketch*, pp. 18–46f.

32 Johnson, *Story of a Mission*, p. 22.

33 J. B. Hamilton, *Entrance Register of the C.M.S. Grammar School* (Freetown, 1935).

34 Cf. below, pp. 132ff.

35 Cf. below, pp. 148–53.

36 Johnson, *Story of a Mission*, p. 23; E. A. Ayandele, *The Missionary Impact on Modern Nigeria, 1842–1914: a Political and Social Analysis* (London, Ibadan, 1966) p. 178.

37 Fyfe, *History of Sierra Leone*, p. 388.

38 *Ibid.*, p. 238: 'The Colony-born

children were called "Creoles", a name used in many countries with different connotations, but in Sierra Leone for recaptives' descendants. The Creoles naturally included the descendants of the original settlers before 1800, who coalesced with the "Recaptives" to form a single social group.' Cf. the more sociologically oriented study of A. T. Porter, *Creoldom* (London, 1963). The first biography of a 'Creole' is J. D. Hargreaves, *A Life of Sir Samuel Lewis* (London, Ibadan, Accra, 1958); see also C. Fyfe, *Africanus Horton*.

39 A detailed analysis of the ambivalent position of the 'Sierra Leoneans' would be a tempting task. In the heyday of colonial imperialism the 'degenerate' and 'uprooted' Creoles were time and again contrasted with the 'pure' and 'uncorrupted' natives of the interior – a reversal of the view taken at the beginning of the nineteenth century which at first seems rather curious. On the animosity towards the 'Sierra Leoneans' in Yorubaland cf. also Ayandele, *The Missionary Impact* . . . , pp. 41, 47, 51; Kopytoff, *A Preface to Nigeria*, p. 129f. On the hostility of the natives towards the Creoles, see W. T. Thomas, 'The Position of the Sierra Leonians in Sierra Leone', *African Times and Orient Review*, April 1913, pp. 311–13.

40 Tubuko-Metzger, *Historical Sketch*, p. 15; Curtin, *Image of Africa*, p. 423.

41 Fyfe, *History of Sierra Leone*, p. 173.

42 As Johnson, *Story of a Mission*, p. 101, believes.

43 His ancestry seems to be in some doubt. Two writers refer to him as an Afro-American from the USA, and Fyfe states that he came from Charleston (*History of Sierra Leone*, p. 237; Thompson, *Jubilee and Centenary Volume*, pp. 15, 17). On the other hand J. F. A. Ajayi, *Christian Missions in Nigeria, 1841–1891: the Making of a New Elite* (London, 1965) p. 41, identifies him as a West Indian.

44 *Jubilee and Centenary Volume*, p. 17: 'The reason for this was that the interior Chiefs had demonstrated their willingness to be taught, but by members of their race.' Since the entire chronology here is somewhat vague, this statement, made ninety years after the event and without any indication of its source, should be treated with caution, especially as Fourah Bay College was not originally intended to serve the needs of neighbouring tribes.

45 Cf. above, p. 48.

46 Ayandele, *Missionary Impact*, p. 180.

47 Ibid., p. 181; Curtin, *Image of Africa*, p. 423; J. B. Webster, *The African Churches among the Yoruba, 1888–1922* (Oxford, 1964) pp. 4f.

48 Fyfe, *History of Sierra Leone*, pp. 288f.; Webster, *African Churches*, pp. 5, 16; Ajayi, *Christian Missions*, pp, 180–86, 232; Kopytoff, *Preface to Nigeria*, pp. 131f., 237, 241.

49 Webster, *African Churches*, p. 5; Ajayi, *Christian Missions*, pp. 194f., 206f., 230, 275.

50 On this event see Webster, *African Churches*.

51 Thompson, *Jubilee and Ceremony Volume*, pp. 63f.; further details on the conflict below, pp. 148–53.

52 Ayandele, *Missionary Impact*, p. 181.

53 Ibid., p. 180.

54 On the meaning of the name, cf. below, p. 54f.

55 Even today picture postcards of Bahia portray black-skinned women in what is expressly called Yoruba costume. On the contribution of the 'Brazilians' to southern Nigeria, cf. also Ajayi, *Christian Missions*, pp. 40f., 49–52, 59, 112, 155–7, 163f.; for earlier contacts between Brazil and West Africa see P. Verger,

Bahia and the West Coast Trade (1549–1851) (Ibadan, 1964).

56 On the re-emigration see especially Ajayi, *Christian Missions*, pp. 25–52, and Kopytoff, *Preface*, pp. 44–60.

57 S. Johnson, *History of the Yorubas: from the Earliest Times to the Beginning of the British Protectorate* (London, 1921, second edition 1937).

58 Kopytoff, *Preface to Nigeria*, pp. 41–3, who explains why the re-emigration took place precisely at this juncture;

59 The term 'Return of the Exiles', used by Ajayi as a chapter heading, derives from a sermon delivered by Blyden in Lagos in 1891, which was later published; cf. below, p. 157.

60 T. B. Freeman, *Journal of Various Visits to the Kingdom of Ashanti, Aku and Dahomi* (London, 1844) pp. 200, 229; Kopytoff, *Preface to Nigeria*, pp. 45, 313, n. 5.

61 Ajayi, *Christian Missions*, p. 41.

62 Ibid., p. 40.

63 Ibid.

64 G. E. Metcalfe, *Maclean of the Gold Coast: the Life and Times of George Maclean, 1801–1847* (London, 1962) p. 303; A. Birthwistle, *Thomas Birch Freeman* (London, 1950) p. 82.

65 Cf. above, pp. 17–20 and below, pp. 64–5.

66 Freeman, *Journal*, p. 224.

67 Ibid., p. 231.

68 Ibid.

69 T. Clarkson, *Review of the Rev. Thomas B. Freeman's Journals . . .* (London, 1845).

70 Cf. above, p. 38.

71 Sir T. F. Buxton, *The African Slave Trade and its Remedy*, 2 volumes (London, 1839–40). Cf. also Curtin, *Image of Africa*, pp. 299–302, and J. Gallagher, 'Fowell Buxton and the New African Policy, 1838–1842', *Cambridge Historical Journal*, 10, (1950); J. B. Webster, 'The Bible and the Plough', *JHSN*, Vol. 2, December 1962, pp. 418–34.

72 Cf. above, p. 51.

73 Ajayi, *Christian Missions*, pp. 152f., 190f.; idem, 'The Development of Secondary Grammar School Education in Nigeria', *JHSN*, vol. 3, no. 1, December 1963.

74 Cf. above, p. 48f.

75 Ajayi, *Christian Missions*, p. 152.

76 P. E. H. Hair, 'An Analysis of the Register of Fourah Bay College, 1827–1950', *Sierra Leone Studies*, no. 7, December 1956, pp. 155–60; idem, 'C.M.S. "Native Clergy" in West Africa to 1900', *Sierra Leone Bulletin of Religion*, vol. 4, no. 2, December 1962, pp. 71f.

77 Cf. above, n. 57 to this chapter.

78 Herbert Macaulay's papers in Ibadan University Library were only in part available to me when I was in Ibadan in October 1964 and January 1965. There is as yet no monograph on this important figure; on his contribution to the emergence of Nigerian nationalism, see for the present J. S. Coleman, *Nigeria: Background to Nationalism* (Berkeley, Los Angeles, 1958, third impression 1965) pp. 195–9, 266.

79 Cf. below, pp. 151–9.

80 Ajayi, *Christian Missions*, pp. 111–14, 156–62.

81 Cf. above, p. 56.

82 This fascinating process promises to be a major theme of modern African historiography. The school founded by K. Onwuka Dike in Ibadan has already contributed much, notably the studies by Ajayi and Ayandele cited extensively above. For a primarily sociologically oriented account, see P. C. Lloyd (ed.), *The New Elites of Tropical Africa* (London, 1966). Apart from the works of the Ibadan school are those by Fyfe, Kopytoff and Foster mentioned above; cf. also I. Geiss, 'Das Entstehen der modernen Eliten in Afrika seit der Mitte des 18. Jahrhunderts', *Geschichte in Wissenschaft und Unterricht*, 11/1971, pp. 648–67.

Chapter 5

1 Cf. above, pp. 48, 53.
2 Especially Padmore and Nkrumah in the twentieth century; see below pp. 358–393.
3 Cf. above, p. 46.
4 On this point and what follows, cf. F. L. Bartels, *The Roots of Ghana Methodism* (London, 1965) pp. 9ff.; instructive on the origins is the earlier work by A. E. Southon, *Gold Coast Methodism* (London, Cape Coast, 1934).
5 E. Beyreuther, *Der junge Zinzendorf* (Marburg, 1957) p. 238. On Protten see R. Cornevin, *Histoire du Togo* (Paris, 1959, second edition 1962) p. 126; H. W. Debrunner, 'Frühe westafrikanische Porträts', *Basler Nachrichten*, 10 January 1965, pp. 11f.
6 Ninety years after Quaque's death the well-known early nationalist leader Attoh Ahuma stated that the former's grandchildren were still living at Cape Coast: *Gold Coast Leader*, 7 April 1906.
7 Bartels, *Roots*, pp. 6f.
8 These were other trading forts which had a similar sociological pattern to that of Cape Coast. Anomabu, which was then very small, later produced a large number of men who played a leading part in the development of Gold Coast Methodism and nationalism.
9 Cf. also above, p. 55.
10 W. Schlatter, *Geschichte der Basler Mission* (Basle, 1910); C. C. Reindorf, *History of the Gold Coast and Asante* (Basle, 1895, second edition 1951). The Basel missionary outpost at Akropong is of special interest in that after some early setbacks it formed the nucleus of its community by bringing a number of families from the West Indies. In 1851 of thirty-one parishioners twenty-five came from the West Indies: Bartels, *Roots*, p. 30.
11 Cf. above, ch. 4, n. 57.
12 W. Tordorff, *Ashanti under the Prempehs, 1888–1935* (London, 1965) pp. 200–2.
13 Cf. above, p. 53. On Freeman, see especially A. W. Birthwistle, *Thomas Birch Freeman* (London, 1950); A. E. Southon, *Gold Coast Methodism* (London, Cape Coast, 1934). The few remarks on him in R. Cornevin, *Geschichte Afrikas von den Anfängen bis zur Gegenwart* (Stuttgart, 1966) p. 290, are misleading.
14 Bartels, *Roots*, p. 41; on all these questions cf. Curtin, *Image of Africa*, pp. 259–86.
15 Bartels, *Roots*, pp. 33, 54; D. Kimble, *A Political History of Ghana: the Rise of Gold Coast Nationalism, 1850–1928*, vol. I (Oxford, 1963, second edition 1965) p. 155.
16 More details in Bartels, *Roots*, pp. 54–9; Southon, *Gold Coast Methodism*, pp. 100f.
17 Bartels, *Roots*, p. 54.
18 Ibid., p. 25; Southon, *Gold Coast Methodism*, pp. 66–8.
19 Bartels, *Roots*, p. 63; Southon, *Gold Coast Methodism*, p. 72.
20 Bartels, *Roots*, p. 63.
21 Ibid., pp. 63–6; P. J. Foster, *Education and Social Change in Ghana* (London, 1965) pp. 78–86; Kimble, *History*, pp. 70–84.
22 Cf. F. L. Bartels, *Mfantsipim, 1876–1951*, n.p., n.d. (London, 1951); this 16-page pamphlet contains much interesting information; also idem, *Roots*, pp. 163–6.
23 Bartels, *Roots*, pp. 200f.
24 Ibid., p. 21.
25 Cf. above, p. 62.
26 The significance of the Bond was stressed to such a point by George Padmore (e.g. in his *The Gold Coast Revolution* . . . (London, 1953) pp. 29–32, 35) that when Ghana achieved sovereignty on 6 March 1957, the date chosen was the same as that on which the Bond had been signed 113 years earlier.
27 Kimble, *History*, p. 162.

28 *Gold Coast Free Press*, no. 3, 19 September 1899, supplement.

29 It would be worth exploring further this ambivalence among Europeans to what resulted from their impact. Some examples from the Gold Coast at that time are referred to by Kimble, *History*, pp. 89, 221, 228, 253.

30 Ibid., pp. 65–7.

31 Ibid., pp. 15, 186, n. 2.

32 Cf. below, pp. 166f.

33 Kimble, *History*, pp. 189, 196f., 215f.

34 Ibid., pp. 192–221.

35 On the Select Committee and its consequences cf. J. D. Hargreaves, *Prelude to the Partition of West Africa* (London, 1963) pp. 64–90; Kimble, *History*, pp. 205–9.

36 On the Eyre controversy see E. Williams, *British Historians and the West Indies* (Port-of-Spain, 1964; London, 1966) pp. 87–153; on the events in Jamaica D. Hall, *Free Jamaica, 1838–1865: an Economic History* (New Haven, 1959) pp. 243–53.

37 Kimble, *History*, p. 215.

38 Ibid., pp. 204f.

39 On this episode, which led to the complete withdrawal of the Dutch from the Gold Coast, cf. D. Coombs, *The Gold Coast, Britain and the Netherlands, 1850–1874* (London, 1963).

40 J. A. B. Horton, *West African Countries and Peoples . . .* (London, 1868; reprinted Edinburgh 1969, ed. G. Shepperson) p. 256.

41 Kimble, *History*, p. 226.

42 J. A. B. Horton, *The Medical Topography of the West Coast of Africa . . .* (London, 1859); *Physical and Medical Climate and Meteorology . . .* (London, 1867); *Letters on the Political Condition of the Gold Coast . . .* (London, 1870; reprinted 1970, ed. E. A. Ayandele).

43 Kimble, *History*, pp. 230–2. On Horton see now C. Fyfe, *Africanus Horton*; G. Grohs, *Stufen afrikanischer Emanzipation. Studien zum Selbstver-* *ständnis westafrikanischer Eliten* (Stuttgart, 1967) pp. 144–6.

44 Horton, *Letters*, p. iii: 'On this Coast the English element is unquestionably the best civilizing element.'

45 Ibid., pp. 34–9; Kimble, *History*, p. 239; on the military efforts of the merchants cf. W. W. Claridge, *History of Gold Coast and Ashanti*, 2 volumes (London, 1915, second edition 1964) vol. I, pp. 549, 613f.

46 Cf. above, p. 67.

47 Cf. above, p. 62.

48 On Ghartey cf. Bartels, *Roots*, pp. 77, 82, 86.

49 Text in G. E. Metcalfe, *Great Britain and Ghana: Documents of Ghana History, 1807–1957* (Edinburgh, 1964) pp. 336–8.

50 Ibid., p. 338; on these events Kimble, *History*, pp. 222–63.

51 Cf. above, ch. 2, n. 6; Bartels, *Roots*, p. 88.

52 Cf. above, p. 69.

53 Sarbah's chief works are: *Fanti Customary Laws* (London, 1904); *Fanti National Constitution* (London, 1906).

54 All these periodicals are in the British Museum Newspaper Library, although the collections are not complete; so, too, are the newspapers from Nigeria and Sierra Leone, which have been consulted selectively.

55 In its last issue of 29 August 1885 (vol. I, no. 22) the *Gold Coast News* complained of the lack of interest shown by the public, but hoped that the young people would remedy the situation. For a similar complaint see R. Ainslie, *The Press in Africa: Communications Past and Present* (London, 1966) p. 24. The first chapter of this work (pp. 21–54) contains a survey of the presss in British West Africa which unfortunately is neither complete nor systematic.

56 *Gold Coast Free Press*, 19 September 1899.

57 For other expressions of criticism, cf. Ainslie, *The Press in Africa*, pp. 21f.

58 Cf. below, pp. 115ff.

59 Cf. above, pp. 8–12.

60 Examples in Kimble, *History*, pp. 146–50. The Anomabu Temperance Society was founded by Ghartey in 1862.

61 Dated according to *Gold Coast Times*. 8 October 1881; Kimble, *History*, p. 149, puts it at the beginning of October.

62 *Gold Coast Times*, 22 October 1881.

63 In his opening speech the president stated that one of its aims was 'to start our country on the road to enlightenment . . . to endeavour to erect a new building out of our present unsound social fabric, to seek into the requirements of the country, to instil into us the absolute necessity for the development of the resources of our land, mineral, agricultural or otherwise; in fact, to open our eyes to what is going on around us, to teach us to give our aid towards advancing our country in the paths of civilization and enlightenment'. Ibid., 22 October 1881 (the end of this passage cited by Kimble, *History*, p. 149).

64 Ibid.

65 He then speaks of intending 'to break through this shell of exclusiveness' (*Gold Coast Times*, 8 October 1881). Evidently the gap from the rest of society was already felt to be quite wide.

66 Ibid., 24 December 1881. At the initial meeting it was stated that 'the need of a municipality; the lighting of our streets; the absence of all protection from thieves and the like at nights' were among the points that should be left for later discussion. Ibid., 22 October 1881.

67 Kimble, *History*, p. 150; on Sarbah's works, see above, n. 53.

68 Cf. the report in the *Gold Coast*

Express, vol. 4, no. 162, 23 August 1897; also Kimble, *History*, p. 518.

69 This was said in 1892. Kimble, *History*, p. 518.

70 Nkrumah mentioned him in his speech in Parliament motivating the demand for independence: K. Nkrumah, *The Autobiography of Kwame Nkrumah* (Edinburgh, 1956, fourth edition 1961) p. 164.

71 *Methodist Times*, 15 November 1897, p. 2; other examples in Kimble, *History*, p. 348.

72 *West Africa*, 1st year, no. 7, November 1900, p. 208; the others depicted were M. F. Ribeiro, C. J. Reindorf and W. G. Mensah.

73 For a sketch of his life cf. M. J. Sampson, *Gold Coast Men of Affairs* (London, 1937) pp. 77–82; cf. also Bartels, *Roots*, p. 77.

74 Bartels, *Roots*, p. 144.

75 Cf. below, pp. 148, 225, 278, 288, 369.

76 Bartels, *Roots*. Chapel Square was for decades the chief meeting-place in Cape Coast; it was here that J. H. Brew published the *Gold Coast Times* (cf. above, p. 70). Half a century after the 1897 protest meeting Nkrumah had his followers join him in singing the Methodist hymn 'Lead, kindly light' during a political demonstration at the square. Bartels, *Roots*.

77 Cf. above, p. 74. Characteristic was the conflict between the leading English Methodist missionary, the Rev. Dennis Kemp, and his parishioners around 1890, details of which are given by Bartels, *Roots*, pp. 138–40. The tension reached such a pitch that several African Methodists sent a collective letter to the mission's headquarters in London and called for Kemp's removal; cf. Methodist Missionary Society archives, London (Gold Coast, 1893–6: letters from Chiefs W. P. Arnosie and Attah Coffie and also from the Rev. M. Pondol of 23 February 1893

James H. Rigg, chairman of the Wesleyan Conference, London).

78 Cf. below, p. 222.
79 Cf. below, pp. 283–93.
80 Cf. below, p. 354.
81 Cf. below, pp. 120, 202–7.
82 Cf. below, pp. 117f., 203f., 283–93.

Chapter 6

1 Cf. below, pp. 172f.
2 Literature on the history of Afro-Americans has become so immense recently that it is hopeless to cope with it here. The *Journal of Negro History* provides an excellent *entrée* into a vast subject.
3 Cf. below, pp. 163–7.
4 T. Paine, *African Slavery in America*, 1775.
5 J. Otis, *The Rights of the British Colonies Asserted and Approved* (Boston, London, 1764) p. 43.
6 On 22 September 1774 she wrote to her husband: 'I wish most sincerely there was not a slave in the province. It always appeared a most iniquitous scheme to me to fight ourselves for what we are daily robbing and plundering from these who have as good a right to freedom as we have. You know my mind on this subject.' Cited from H. Aptheker, *American Slave Revolts* (New York, 1943, fifth edition 1964) p. 201; also in L. Bennett Jr, *Before the Mayflower: a History of the Negro in America, 1619–1964* (Chicago, 1962, third edition Baltimore, Harmondsworth, 1966) p. 49.
7 Cf. above, pp. 32f.
8 H. Aptheker, *A Documentary History of the Negro People in the United States*, 2 volumes (New York, 1951, second edition 1962) vol. I, pp. 6–14; cf. also B. Quarles, *The Negro in the American Revolution* (Chapel Hill, 1961) pp. 39–43.
9 Aptheker, *Documentary History*, I, pp. 14–16.
10 Quarles, *The Negro*, p. 45.
11 Cf. above, p. 34.

12 C. Wesley, *Richard Allen: Apostle of Freedom* (Washington, 1935) p. 36.
13 Cf. above, p. 33.
14 Aptheker, *Doccumentary History*, I, pp. 20f., 23–6. Banneker was an autodidact who published an almanac and took part in the town planning of the new capital.
15 On this and the following, cf. Quarles, *The Negro*, pp. 51–3, 58f., 75f., 94ff.
16 Ibid., pp. 111–57.
17 Ibid., pp. 163–73.
18 Cf. above, p. 44.
19 Quarles, *The Negro*, p. 82.
20 Aptheker, *Slave Revolts*, pp. 42f., 96–8, 214, 246. Denmark Vesey, leader of a major slave conspiracy discovered in 1822 in Charleston SC, corresponded with Haiti and asked for aid from that country: Aptheker, *Slave Revolts*, p. 272. Vesey is also said (ibid., p. 98, without indication of source) to have thought of getting help from Africa as well.
21 Cf. below, p. 128.
22 C. L. R. James, *Black Jacobins: Toussaint L'Ouverture and the San Domingo Revolution* (London, New York, 1938) p. 411.
23 Cf. below, pp. 86, 89, 92f.
24 T. Jefferson, *Notes on the State of Virginia* (London, 1787) p. 240.
25 P. J. Staudenraus, *The African Colonization Movement, 1816–1865* (New York, 1961) pp. 1–4, 15–30.
26 Ibid., p. 65; cf. also pp. 37, 58–65, and for the following pp. 66f.
27 O. T. Tiffany, *Africa for the Africans . . .* (Washington, 1884) p. 4, says there were 15,655 such settlers and 5722 ex-slaves freed by the US Navy, D. L. Dumond, *Antislavery: the Crusade for Freedom in America* (Ann Arbor, 1961) p. 129, puts the total of re-emigrants from the USA to Liberia at 12,000.
28 For Afro-American criticisms of Liberia, cf. below, pp. 123–6.
29 Cf. especially E. W. Blyden, *Liberia's Offering: the Call of Providence to the*

Descendants of Africa in America . . . (New York, 1862). On Blyden's propaganda on behalf of Liberia in the USA during the Civil War, see now H. R. Lynch, *Edward Wilmot Blyden: Pan-Negro Patriot, 1832–1912* (London, 1967) pp. 26ff.

30 Lynch, *Blyden*.

31 On this aspect of the question there is as yet only one unpublished thesis and two articles by H. H. Bell: 'A Survey of the Negro Convention Movement, 1830–1860' (Ph.D., Northwestern University, 1953); 'The Negro Convention Movement, 1830–60: New Perspectives', *Negro History Bulletin*, XIV, February 1951, pp. 103–5, 114; 'National Negro Conventions of the Middle 1840's: Moral Suasion vs. Political Action', *JNH*, XLII (1957) as note 43, pp. 247–60.

32 The year 1835 was another turning-point in the history of abolitionism, and thus of the Afro-Americans, and indirectly also of Pan-Africanism. To indicate these connections and to interpret them thoroughly would take us too far from our theme.

33 Cf. below, pp. 84f.

34 Cf. above, p. 28.

35 Aptheker, *Documentary History*, I, p. 8.

36 Cited from Quarles, *The Negro in the American Revolution*, pp. 39f. Evidently some slaves were first-generation arrivals from Africa, for they complained that 'some of them were stolen from the bosoms of our tender parents'.

37 Cf. above, p. 34.

38 Cited from Wesley, *Richard Allen*, pp. 66f.

39 Ibid., p. 67.

40 Cf. above, p. 81.

41 C. Fyfe, *History of Sierra Leone*, p. 112.

42 Cf. above, p. 44.

43 The Quakers gained few converts among Afro-Americans, on account of their strict piety, their tendency to exclusiveness and in part because one can detect traces of racism in their

views. Cf. T. E. Drake, *Quakers and Slavery in America*; H. Aptheker, 'The Quakers and Negro Slavery', *JNH*, XXV (1940), no. 3, pp. 331–60.

44 Cf. above, p. 78.

45 R. B. Moore, 'Africa Conscious Harlem', J. H. Clarke (ed.), *Harlem: a Community in Transition* (New York, 1964) p. 80. According to this writer one of Cuffee's descendants, Harry Dean, made another attempt with the object 'to rehabilitate Africa and found an Ethiopian Empire as the world has never seen'; ibid., p. 81. No source reference is given in either case.

46 Cf. above, p. 44.

47 The number of emigrants whom Cuffee had on board is generally given as thirty-eight; Fyfe, *History*, gives thirty-four. A discrepancy in the date (1815 or 1816 for Cuffee's second trip to Sierra Leone) is probably due to the fact that Cuffee left the USA at the end of 1815 and arrived in Sierra Leone at the beginning of the following year. On his first journey, cf. Fyfe, *History*, pp. 112f.

48 Staudenraus, *Colonization Movement*, p. 19.

49 Ibid., p. 32.

50 Aptheker, *Documentary History*, p. 70.

51 Cited from ibid., p. 71f.

52 'Let not a purpose be assisted which will stay the cause of the entire abolition of slavery.' Staudenraus, p. 33.

53 On this and the following, ibid., pp. 82–5; Wesley, *Richard Allen*, pp. 214–17.

54 Cf. below, p. 140f.

55 Cf. below, p. 92f.

56 In 1829 about 2200 Afro-Americans lived in Cincinnati, when they comprised about 10 per cent of the population. They had their own slum, called 'Little Africa'. In that year the city authorities suddenly demanded a surety of more than $500 a head for their good be-

haviour, threatening that in the case of non-payment they were to leave the city within thirty days. The Afro-Americans naturally could not and did not want to pay such sums, and in consternation asked for an extension of the term; meanwhile they sent a delegation to explore the possibilities of emigration to Canada. Before these men had returned a race riot broke out in Cincinnati – on the pattern that was so typical in American history – in which several Afro-Americans were killed and many injured. In that same year more than 1000 of them fled from the city and went to Canada; others followed in the next years. Staudenraus, *Colonization Movement*, pp. 139f.

57 J. W. Cromwell, *The Early Convention Movement* (American Negro Academy. Occasional Papers, no. 9) (Washington, 1905) p. 5.

58 On Delany's life cf. F. A. R. Whipper, *Life and Public Services of Martin R. Delany* (Boston, 1883).

59 Cf. above, p. 32.

60 W. L. Garrison, *Thoughts on African Colonization* (Boston, 1832). Garrison himself was active on behalf of the American Colonization Society until the strong opposition by the free coloureds took him aback and made him change his views.

61 Cf. below, p. 164.

62 M. R. Delany, *The Condition . . . of the Colored People . . .* (Philadelphia, 1852).

63 Idem, *Official Report of the Niger Valley Explorating Party* (New York, Leeds, 1861).

64 Whipper, *Delany*, pp. 19f., 29.

65 On Blyden cf. below, pp. 108f., 150.

66 Delany, *Report*, p. 8.

67 Cf. below, Pt. I, ch. 7, pp. 96–131.

68 Delany, *The Condition*, pp. 173–5.

69 Ibid., p. 48.

70 Ibid., p. 173.

71 Ibid., p. 172.

72 Ibid., pp. 166–71. On Delany's contribution to the criticism of

Liberia by Afro-Americans, cf. below, pp. 123f.

73 Delany, *The Condition*, pp. 173–5.

74 Some authors describe Delany as a Canadian, e.g. J. F. A. Ajayi, *Christian Missions in Nigeria, 1841–1891: the Making of a New Elite* (London, 1965) p. 48. On the other hand Whipper, whose biography was published one year before Delany's death, mentions that he was in Chatham, Ontario, but not for such a long time as to merit his becoming a Canadian citizen.

75 Delany, *The Condition*, p. 178.

76 Ibid., pp. 209ff.: 'A Project for an Expedition of Adventure to the Eastern Coast of Africa'. In this context he mentions – possibly for the first time – the idea of a rail link across Africa from the east coast to the west. Ibid., p. 213.

77 One year later Frederick Douglass estimated that one negro in four in Ohio was in favour of emigration: H. H. Bell, 'The Negro Emigration Movement, 1849–1854: a Phase of Negro Nationalism', *Phylon*, XX (1959), no. 2, p. 138. The following account is also based on Delany, *Report*; Staudenraus, *Colonization Movement*, p. 244; Whipper, *Delany*, pp. 70ff.; E. U. Essien-Udom, *Black Nationalism: a Search for an Identity in America* (Chicago–London, 1962, second edition New York, 1964) pp. 34–6; L. F. Litwack, *North of Slavery: the Negro in the Free States, 1790–1860* (Chicago, 1961, third edition 1965) pp. 258–62; Lynch, *Blyden*, pp. 17, 24f.

78 Delany, *Report*, pp. 8f.; this elasticity, evidently forced on him, led to the splitting and weakening of the emigration movement. Cf. Litwack, *North of Slavery*, p. 262.

79 Staudenraus, *Colonization Movement*, p. 244; Essien-Udom, *Black Nationalism*, p. 34.

80 Lynch, *Blyden*, p. 24.

81 Cf. below, p. 171.

82 Ajayi, *Christian Missions*, p. 191, is cautious and adds 'probably'; Kopytoff, *Preface to Nigeria*, p. 347, n. 15, gives a similar account without making such reservations.

83 Delany, *Report*, pp. 35ff.

84 Dates of their stay in Yorubaland from *Lagos Observer*, 2nd year, no. 27, 31 January 1882, pp. 2f., referring to Campbell.

85 According to Delany, *Report*, pp. 62ff.; Ajayi, *Christian Missions*, p. 48, dates the founding of the African Aid Society prior to 1859 and has Campbell and Delany acting in Abeokuta on behalf of the group in London. I prefer Delany's chronology; the difference could be cleared up by a study of the African Aid Society, if its archive can be located in Britain. One could follow up the names of Lord Alfred Churchill and its secretary, F. Fitzgerald.

86 Ajayi, *Christian Missions*, pp. 191f.

87 Thomas Hodgkin papers, Hodgkin to W. Coppinger, 30 June 1860. After their departure on 29 August 1860 he wrote to Henry H. Garnet, their contact in the USA: 'It is to be regretted that they did not . . . promptly return to America. . . . They proved rather in the way and while *I* acquit all concerned of intentional impropriety it was very evident that our friend Bourne was not helped by their presence. . . .'

88 F. Fitzgerald to T. Hodgkin, 21 August 1861.

89 Cf. below, pp. 163–8.

90 R. Campbell, *A Pilgrimage to my Motherland* (Philadelphia, 1861).

91 These data are taken from Campbell's obituary (cf. above, n. 84). This settles the query raised by Kopytoff (*Preface*, p. 347, n. 15), who wondered whether Campbell only returned to Lagos 'for at least a few years'.

92 Cf. above, p. 66.

93 Year 3, no. 29, 23 October 1865.

94 J. M. McPherson, *The Struggle for Equality . . .* (Princeton, 1964) pp. 77–97; J. H. Franklin, *The Emancipation Proclamation* (New York, 1963).

95 J. Redpath (ed.), *A Guide to Hayti* (Boston, 1861).

96 Cf. above, pp. 88f.

97 Cf. below, pp. 107f.

98 Cf. above, p. 86.

99 McPherson, *Struggle*, p. 85, also p. 79.

100 Tiffany, *Africa for the Africans* (see n. 27).

101 Ibid., pp. 12f.

102 J. W. E. Bowen (ed.), *Africa and the American Negro . . .* (Atlanta, 1896) pp. 85ff., report by Thomas G. Addison, 'The Policy of the American Colonization Society'.

103 On the following cf. W. E. Bittle and G. Geis, *The Longest Way Home: Chief Alfred C. Sam's Back-to-Africa Movement* (Detroit, 1964).

104 Ibid., p. 70.

105 Ibid., p. 190.

106 Ibid., p. 196.

107 Cf. below, pp. 258–62.

108 Bittle and Geis, ibid., pp. 217f.

109 Cf. below, pp. 279–82.

Chapter 7

1 On European racial theories, cf. now P. D. Curtin, *The Image of Africa*, pp. 28–57, 363–87. On America cf. T. F. Gossett, *Race: the History of an Idea in America* (Dallas, 1963).

2 A. Meier, 'The Emergence of Negro Nationalism: from the American Revolution to the First World War' (M. A. thesis, Columbia University, 1949), p. 53. This work may be consulted in the Schomburg Collection.

3 Cf. above, pp. 32f.

4 G. Sharp, *Just Limitation of Slavery*; idem, *The Law of Liberty*; idem, *The Law of Passive Obedience* (all London, 1776).

5 P. D. Curtin, *Image of Africa . . .*, p. 55.

6 J. Ramsay, *Essays on the Treatment and Conversion of African Slaves in the British Sugar Colonies* (London, 1784).

7 On Blumenbach see now Curtin, *Image of Africa*, pp. 38–41, 47f., 230f.; he would merit a detailed monograph.

8 Abbé H. B. Gregoire, *De la Littérature des nègres* . . . (Paris, 1808); the English edition, which made it possible for his ideas to become known in English-speaking areas, appeared under the title: *An Enquiry concerning the Intellectual and Moral Faculties, and Literature of Negroes* . . . (Brooklyn, 1810).

9 C.-F. Volney, *Les Ruines, ou Méditations sur les Révolutions des Empires* (Paris, 1794); Eng. ed.: *The Ruins; or a Survey of the Revolutions of Empires* . . . (London, 1822).

10 W. Armistead, *Tribute for the Negro* . . . (Manchester, 1848). This work is dedicated to Pennington, Douglass and Crummell.

11 A. Benezet, *Account of Guinea* (cf. above, pp. 32f., n. 7), pp. 58f.

12 Cf. below, pp. 100–9, 113–14.

13 *African Repository*, vol. I, no. 1, March 1825. The logic of the propaganda directed towards abolitionist circles in the North led the American Colonization Society (cf. above, pp. 81f.) at least formally to reject the doctrine of racial inferiority.

14 As it was, e.g. for Cugoano: cf. above, p. 38.

15 J. E. J. Capitein, *Dissertatio Politico-Theologica de Servitute, Libertati Christianae non Contraria* (Leiden, 1742); Dutch ed.: *Staatkundig-Godgeleerd Onderzoekschrift over de Slavery, . . . als niet strydig tegen de Christelyke Vryheid.*

16 I. Sancho, *Letters* (see above, ch. 4, n. 10), I, p. i. The relatively wide dissemination of racist ideas is indirectly evident from another sentence by the editor: 'He who could penetrate the interior of Africa, might not improbably discover negro arts and policy, which could bear little analogy to the ignorance and grossness of slaves in the sugar islands, expatriated in infancy, and brutalized under the whip and the task-master; and he who surveys the extent of intellect which Ignatius Sancho had attained by selfeducation will perhaps conclude, that the perfection of the reasoning faculties does not depend on a peculiar deformation of the scull or the colour of a common integument, in defiance of that wild opinion, "which", says a learned writer of these times, "restrains the operations of the mind to particular regions" and supposes that a luckless mortal "may be born in a degree of latitude too high or too low for wisdom or for wit".' (Ibid., p. xv.)

17 Ibid., I, pp. 113, 180; II, pp. 92, 98, 102.

18 Ibid., pp. 95–8.

19 Ibid., II, p. 174. In reality Sancho was not born in Africa but on a slave ship to a mother who had just been enslaved (in 1729); at the age of two he came to England (cf. ibid., I, p. v). What Sancho means here is that he was not ashamed of his African descent; for the analogous attitude of Delany, cf. above, pp. 86f.

20 O. Cugoano, *Réflexions sur la traite et l'esclavage des Nègres* (Paris, 1788) pp. 34f.; on Cugoano cf. above, pp. 38ff.

21 Among other things by Benezet's school: cf. above, p. 32.

22 G. Vassa (Equiano), *The Interesting Narrative of the Life of Oloudah Equiano* . . . (London, 1789) I, pp. 5, 48ff., 103; II, pp. 4, 217f., 226, 230–32, 243f. Equiano introduced his work with a vivid description of Ibo society as he remembered it in his youth (I, pp. 1–27); a lengthy extract from this is reprinted in the anthology by T. Hodgkin, *Nigerian*

Perspectives: an Historical Anthology (London, Ibadan, Accra, 1960) pp. 155–66. Hodgkin evidently deserves the credit for having rediscovered Equiano, and I am also grateful to him for putting me on to Cugoano.

23 G. Vassa (Equiano), *Life*, I, pp. 38ff.

24 Ibid., pp. 42f.

25 H. Easton, *A Treatise on the Intellectual Character ... of the Colored People of the United States ...* (Boston, 1837).

26 Ibid., pp. 8, 12ff.

27 As, for example, in the work of Otto von Freising in the twelfth century, who argued that the 'imperium' had been transferred from one people to another and had finally come to rest upon the 'Franks', i.e. the Germans. In a secularized form this idea re-emerged with Hegel in the early nineteenth century.

28 Easton, *Treatise*, pp. 9–11.

29 Ibid., p. 20.

30 J. W. C. Pennington, *Text Book of the Origin and History &c. &c. of the Coloured People* (Hartford, 1841) p. 7.

31 Ibid., pp. 19ff., 47f.

32 Ibid., p. 21f.

33 Ibid., p. 27.

34 Their abandonment of monotheism for polytheism, moral decline and tribal conflicts leading to wars: ibid., pp. 32–8.

35 Ibid., pp. 39f.

36 Ibid., p. 45.

37 Ibid., pp. 47–51.

38 Ibid., p. 51f.

39 Ibid., p. 54.

40 Ibid., pp. 74–85; as remedies Pennington suggested: 'Colored people must bear and forbear' (p. 87).

41 R. B. Lewis, *Light and Truth ...* (Boston, 1844) especially pp. 114–18, 123f.

42 J. E. Hayne, *The Negro in Sacred History ...* (Charleston, SC, 1887); *The Black Man ...* (Raleigh, NC, 1894): *The Ammonian or Hametic*

Origin of the Ancient Greeks ... (Brooklyn, 1905).

43 Idem, *The Negro in Sacred History ...*, p. 7.

44 J. M. Webb, *The Black Man the Father of Civilisation proven by Biblical History* (Seattle, 1910) pp. 8–11.

45 Ibid., pp. 12f.

46 J. A. Rogers, *Sex and Race: History of the Mixing of White and Black from Prehistoric Times to the Present*, 3 volumes (New York, 1940); idem, *World's Great Men of Color: 3000 B.C. to 1946*, 2 volumes (New York, 1946–7). This 2-volume work is the climax of the biographical line of argument, which goes back to Grégoire.

47 In his autobiography *A Long Way from Home* (New York, 1937) pp. 315–18, Claude McKay attacks Rogers, whom he does not mention by name: 'Besides Negro news, the journalist [i.e. Rogers] specialized in digging up obscure and Amazing Facts [cf. the following note] for the edification of the colored people. In these "Facts" Beethoven is proved to be a Negro because he was dark and gloomy; also the Jewish people are proved to have been Originally a Negro people!' McKay said he had helped 'the journalist' to find a publisher for a novel designed to appeal to the White reading public, which never appeared. 'Our Negro journalist is very yellow and looks like a métèque in France, without attracting undue attention. Yet besides his "Amazing Facts" about Negroes he has written in important magazines, stressing the practical nonexistence of color prejudice in Europe and blaming Negroes for such as exists. ... He might have thought that as he had "passed white" a little in complexion in journalism, it would be just as easy "passing white" as a creative writer. ... The last time I heard about him, he was again a Negro in

Ethiopia, interviewing Haile Selassie and reporting the white rape of Ethiopia from an African point of view for the American Negro press.'

48 Rogers, *100 Amazing Facts about the Negro with Complete Proof*, n.p., n.d. (New York, 1934, twenty-third edition 1957). These illustrated pamphlets evidently were published by the author: pp. 19f.

49 Seen in Harlem in March 1965 and November 1966.

50 G. K. Osei, *Fifty Unknown Facts about the African* . . . (London, 1966); *The Forgotten Great Africans* . . . (London, 1965). As well as these self-styled 'books' Osei has written other pamphlets about Garvey and Nkrumah's Convention People's Party.

51 Autobiographical note on the back of the second work referred to above.

52 If one may believe the reviews published as a means of self-advertisement as an appendix to his books: e.g., *100 Amazing Facts*, pp. 50–54. George Padmore also seems to have held Rogers in high esteem: cf. *Pan-Africanism*, p. 13; he cites him frequently.

53 Some samples are reproduced (in black and white) in R. Italiaander, *Schwarze Haut im Roten Griff* (Düsseldorf, Vienna, 1962). Copies of these paintings could be bought as coloured postcards in Accra up to the time of Nkrumah's fall. Some typical titles: 'Africans taught the Greeks the alphabet . . .', 'Tyro, African secretary to Cicero, originated shorthand writing in 63 B.C.', 'The science of law originated in Africa . . .', 'The science of chemistry was originated in Africa . . . , 'Aesop imparting the wisdom of Africa to the Greeks', etc. The sources were indicated: J. G. Wilkinson, *The Ancient Egyptians;* de Graft-Johnson, *African Glory;* Volney, *The Ruins;* J. A. Rogers, *World's Great Men of Color.*

54 H. H. Garnet, *The Past and Present*

Condition, and the Destiny of the Colored Race . . . (Troy–New York, 1848) p. 7.

55 Psalm 68: XXXII.

56 Garnet, *Past and Present*, p. 12.

57 B. T. Tanner, *The Negro's Origin* and *Is the Negro Cursed?* (Philadelphia, 1869); *The Descent of the Negro* . . . (Philadelphia, 1898); *The Negro in Holy Writ* (Philadelphia, 1902).

58 M. R. Delany, *Principia of Ethnology* . . . (Philadelphia, 1878, second edition 1880).

59 Cf. below, pp. 163–6.

60 Delany, *Principia*, p. 49. For Garnet (see n. 54) too, Haim was identical with Mesrain and the (legendary) Pharaoh Menes.

61 Cf. above, p. 88.

62 By Pauline E. Hopkins (Cambridge, Mass., 1905).

63 A. Crummell, *The Future of Africa* . . . (second edition New York, 1862) pp. 327ff.

64 Ibid., p. 344.

65 Ibid., pp. 283 ff.; in the title of the sermon its date is given as 21 April 1852, but later (p. 289) as 1853.

66 Ibid., p. 288.

67 Ibid., pp. 107f.

68 A. Crummell, *Africa and America: Addresses and Discourses* (Springfield–Mass., 1891).

69 W. W. Brown, *The Rising Son: or, the Antecedents and Advancement of the Colored Race* (Boston, 1874).

70 Idem, *The Black Man: his Antecedents and Achievements* (Boston, 1863) p. 32.

71 Ibid., p. 34. The reference to Caesar and/or Cicero in connection with the low commercial value of British slaves is frequent in the literature and seems to be widely known in intellectual circles in Africa today: cf. also L. J. Bennett, *Before the Mayflower* . . . (Chicago, 1962) p. 33.

72 Brown, *The Black Man*, pp. 35f.

73 Brown, *Rising Son*, pp. 43ff., 86.

74 Ibid., pp. 93, 106.

75 'The Negro in Ancient History', E. W. Blyden, *The People of Africa: Series of Papers* ... (New York, 1871). The editors of the *Methodist Quarterly Review* added a footnote: 'This is, so far as we know, the first article in any Quarterly written by a hand claiming of pure Ethiopic lineage.'

76 Ibid., pp. 17–19. What Blyden meant becomes plain from one of his earlier works, *A Vindication of the African Race* ... , introd. A. Crummell (Monrovia, 1857) p. 28: Here he defended the view that the external beauty of human beings was related to their level of development: 'Give Africans the same amount of culture from generation to generation, which Europeans have enjoyed, and their features will assume the same proportion and symmetrie.' A psychoanalyst might perhaps deduce from this passage that Blyden suffered from an inferiority complex on account of his origin, which he tried to compensate by an ostentatious emphasis on his pride in his race.

77 Ibid., pp. 23f.

78 E. W. Blyden, *A Vindication*, p. 11.

79 Ibid., p. 31. On the other hand Blyden could also use the Old Testament arguments about Ham, Nimrod etc., as for instance when he visited the Pyramids: E. W. Blyden, *From West Africa to Palestine* (Freetown, Manchester, London, 1872) pp. 105–208.

80 Cf. also below, p. 150.

81 On Blyden cf. H. R. Lynch's detailed biography, especially pp. 54–83, and now also G. Grohs, *Stufen afrikanischer Emanzipation: Studien zum Selbstverständnis westafrikanischer Eliten* (Stuttgart, 1967) pp. 139–44, although this is very inaccurate in regard to dates etc.; further E. Holden, *Blyden of Liberia: an Account of the Life and Labours of Edward Wilmot Blyden, LL. D. as recorded in Letters and in Print* (New York, 1966).

82 As by Casely Hayford, who wrote an introduction to a collection of Blyden's speeches: E. W. Blyden, *West Africa before Europe and other Addresses* ... (London, 1905) p. i: 'The work of Edward Wilmot Blyden is universal, covering the entire race and the entire race problem'; p. iii: 'The voice that was aforetime crying solitarily in the wilderness has suddenly become the voice of a nation and of a people, calling unto their kindred across the Atlantic to come back to their way of thinking ...' The first quotation also occurs in C. Hayford, *Ethiopia Unbound* (London, 1911) p. 168.

83 Cf. below, p. 150.

84 Cf. below, p. 207.

85 T. E. S. Scholes (ed.), *Industrial, Self-supporting Missionaries* ... (Colwyn Bay) n.d. [ca. 1895], p. 5.

86 Idem, *The British Empire and Alliances* ... (London, 1899); Bartholomew Smith (= Scholes), *Chamberlain and Chamberlainism* ... (London, 1903); idem, *Glimpses of the Ages* ... , 2 volumes (London, 1905–8).

87 A copy of Scholes's *Chamberlain and Chamberlainism* in the Schomburg Collection contains a personal dedication for Schomburg by the author, dated 19 August 1926, and also a letter to Schomburg from an Afro-American friend telling him of his having met Scholes in London.

88 Personal communication from T. R. Makonnen in Accra, 27 November 1964. According to Makonnen, who could not give a more precise date, Scholes was deeply moved. I am most grateful to Makonnen for putting me on to Scholes.

89 Scholes, *British Empire*, p. 272; the idea of the Empire becoming transformed into a Commonwealth is particularly apparent in *Glimpses of the Ages*, vol. II, p. 446.

90 Scholes, *British Empire*, pp. 264f., 276f.

91 Ibid., pp. 278f., 282.
92 Ibid., pp. 280, 282.
93 Scholes, *Glimpses of the Ages*, vol. I, pp. xiii, xv; vol. II, pp. 428f.
94 Ibid., vol. I, pp. xv f.
95 Ibid., p. 67.
96 Ibid., pp. 173 f., 178.
97 Ibid., pp. 283–345.
98 Ibid., p. 339.
99 Ibid., p. 384.
100 Ibid., p. 393.
101 Cf. above, n. 86.
102 Scholes, *Glimpses of the Ages*, vol. II, pp. 230–33.
103 Ibid., pp. 289–300.
104 Ibid., pp. 327–416, esp. pp. 397, 406, 416.
105 G. Padmore, *Pan-Africanism*, p. 18.
106 W. H. Ferris, *The African Abroad* . . . , 2 volumes (New York, 1913). Ferris was a graduate of Yale University: cf. R. B. Moore, 'African Conscious Harlem', J. H. Clarke (ed.), *Harlem: a Community in Transition* (New York, 1964) p. 84.
107 Cf. below, pp. 211, 214.
108 Ferris, *The African Abroad*, vol. I, pp. 182–92; also p. 276, where he calls Du Bois the 'long-awaited Messiah' of the coloured people; further pp. 371–82.
109 Cf. below, pp. 246, 270.
110 Ferris, *The African Abroad*, vol. I, pp. 429–522.
111 Ibid., vol. I, pp. 449–506.
112 Ibid., vol. II, pp. 822–52; there are even photographs of Casely Hayford and Agbebi (p. 822).
113 Ibid., pp. 927ff.; on Mohamed Duse and his journal, cf. below, pp. 221–228.
114 G. W. Ellis, *Negro Culture in West Africa* (New York, 1914).
115 Ibid., p. 24; on the influence of Egypt, pp. 22f.
116 W. E. B. Du Bois, *The Negro* (New York, 1915).
117 Idem, *Black Folk Then and Now* (New York, 1939, fourth edition 1945).
118 Ibid., pp. 15–34, 127f.
119 E.g., the two best recent accounts of Afro-American history in the USA: J. H. Franklin, *From Slavery to Freedom* (New York, 1956), pp. 3ff. (on ancient Egypt); pp. 11ff. (on Ghana, Mali, Songhai); L. Bennett Jr, *Before the Mayflower*, pp. 3–28. Cf. also C. G. Woodson, *The African Background Outlined* (Washington, 1936).
120 Franklin, *From Slavery to Freedom*, p. 3.
121 Cf. above, pp. 67, 98f.
122 J. A. B. Horton, *Letters on the Political Condition of the Gold Coast* . . . (London, 1870).
123 Cf. above, p. 106.
124 Horton, *Political Condition*, p. 13.
125 Ibid., p. 15.
126 *Sierra Leone Weekly News*, 9 February 1901.
127 Cf. above, ch. 6, n. 81.
128 *Gold Coast Free Press*, no. 4, 24 October 1899.
129 C. Hayford, *Ethiopia Unbound* (London, 1911) p. 215.
130 Ibid., especially pp. 64–75, 98f., 109, 127f., 163f., 192–5; cf. now G. Grohs, *Stufen afrikanischer Emanzipation*, pp. 146–50.
131 Hayford, *Ethiopia Unbound*, pp. 182f.
132 Ibid., pp. 196, 207.
133 Ibid., p. 167: 'In the name of African nationality the thinker [i.e. the hero of the novel, Kwamankra = C. Hayford] would, through the medium of Ethiopia Unbound, greet members of the race everywhere throughout the world. Whether in the east, south or west of the African continent, or yet among the teeming millions of Ethiopian sons in America, the cry of the African, in its last analysis, is for scope and freedom of action in the struggle for existence, and it would seem as if the care of the leaders of the race has been to discover those avenues of right and natural endeavour which would, in the end, ensure for the race due recognition of its individuality.'

134 Ibid., pp. 169f.
135 Cf. above, pp. 67f., 108f.
136 Ibid., pp. 108–10, 170. At another point Hayford synchronizes 'Japan's political awakening' with that of the Gold Coast.
137 Ibid., pp. 108ff., 115ff; cf. in general H. Gollwitzer, *Die gelbe Gefahr. Geschichte eines Schlagwortes. Studien zum imperialistischen Denken* (Göttingen, 1962).
138 Hayford, *Ethiopia Unbound*, p. 5.
139 Ibid., p. 10.
140 Ibid., p. 27.
141 A. Quaison-Sackey, *Africa Unbound: Reflections of an African Statesman* (New York, 1963) p. 16: a reference to Casely Hayford and *Ethiopia Unbound*.
142 J. M. Webb, *The Black Man* (see above, n. 44), pp. 41–9; W. H. Ferris, *The African Abroad* (see above, n. 106), vol. I, pp. 436–9; the following cited from Ferris.
143 Ibid., p. 437.
144 Ibid., pp. 438f.
145 Ibid., p. 439.
146 Cf. below, p. 209.
147 In a speech delivered at the opening of the International Africanists' Congress in Accra, 1962.
148 Cf. above, p. 73.
149 Cf. also below, pp. 202–7.
150 *Gold Coast Nation*, no. 22, 15 August 1912.
151 S. R. B. Attoh Ahuma, *Memoirs of West African Celebrities* . . . (Liverpool, 1905).
152 Cf. above, p. 97.
153 Attoh Ahuma, *Memoirs*, pp. 15–17, 19–23, 25–7, 45–7, 48–52, 61–3, 75–94.
154 On WASU, see below, pp. 297–304.
155 L. Solanke, *United West Africa at the Bars of the Family of Nations* (London, 1927) p. 57; cf. also G. Grohs, *Stufen afrikanischer Emanzipation*, p. 161.
156 J. B. Danquah, *Self-help and Expansion: a Review of the Work and Aims of the Youth Conference* . . . (Accra)

n.d. [1943] p. 16; cf. Grohs, *Stufen afrikanischer Emanzipation*, pp. 169f.
157 Ibid., p. 17.
158 Ibid., pp. 18f.
159 Danquah in his *West African Times*, 2 July 1931. In 1947 Danquah recalled to the Gold Coast Nkrumah, the man who seemed to fulfil the requirements he had laid down. Nkrumah modernized the country, raised loans abroad, and became sole leader; Danquah, however, died in 1965 in one of Nkrumah's jails.
160 N. Azikiwe, *Renascent Africa* (Accra, 1937, second edition London, 1966).
161 Ibid., p. 25.
162 Ibid., p. 67.
163 Ibid., p. 163.
164 Cf. above, pp. 102–4.
165 K. Nkrumah, *Ghana: the Autobiography of Kwame Nkrumah* (Edinburgh, Toronto, New York, 1957, fourth edition 1961) p. 18: 'My nationalism was also revived at about that time through articles written in the *African Morning Post* by Nnamdi Azikiwe.' Cf. also A. A. N. Orizu, *Without Bitterness: Western Nations in Post-War Africa* (New York, 1944) p. 294, where it is said of the book *Renascent Africa*, somewhat excessively, that it became 'the Bible of West African youth' and that 'his *West African Pilot* became the daily oracle of the Nigerian youth' (ibid., p. 295).
166 A keen analysis, made before his fall, is D. Austin, *Politics in Ghana* (London, 1964, second edition 1966).
167 K. Nkrumah, *Towards Colonial Freedom: Africa in the Struggle against World Imperialism* (London, 1947, second edition 1962) p. 37.
168 K. Nkrumah, *Africa must Unite* (London, Melbourne, Toronto, 1963) pp. 1–3.
169 H. Aptheker, *David Walker's Appeal to the Colored Citizens of the World, 1829–1830: its Setting and its Meaning* (New York, 1965) p. 70.

170 F. Douglass, *The Claim of the Negro Ethnologically Considered: an Address* (Rochester–New York, 1854) pp. 17, 25.

171 Cheikh Ante Diop; *Nations nègres et culture* (Paris, 1955, second edition 1964).

172 E.g., by G. Padmore, *Pan-Africanism*, pp. 16, 44ff.

173 Cf. above, pp. 81f.

174 M. R. Delany, *The Condition* (cf. above, ch. 6, n. 62), pp. 160, 169.

175 Ibid., pp. 169f.

176 T. McC. Stewart, *Liberia: the Americo-African Republic* . . . (New York, 1886).

177 Ibid., pp. 106f.

178 Ibid., pp. 70–80 (quoted from p. 71).

179 Ibid., p. 77.

180 S. Barret, *A Plea for Unity amongst American Negroes and the Negroes of the World* (Waterloo–Iowa, 1926, fifth edition 1943) p. 82.

181 L. Buell, *A Century of Survival, 1847–1947* (Philadelphia, 1947) p. v.

182 Ibid., p. 2.

183 Ibid., p. 13.

184 Ibid., p. 67.

185 A. Crummell, *The Relations and Duties of Free Colored Men in America to Africa* (Hartford, 1861) p. 28.

186 Idem, 'Our National Mistakes . . .', *Africa and America: Addresses and Discourses* (Springfield – Mass., 1891) pp. 169–71.

187 Ibid., pp. v f.

188 W. W. Brown, *The Rising Son* (see n. 69), pp. 129–39.

189 E. W. Blyden, *Liberia's Offering: the Call of Providence* . . . (New York, 1862) pp. 18f., 74f., 80.

190 Ibid., pp. 26f., 67; cf. now also H. R. Lynch, *E. W. Blyden* . . . (London, 1967) pp. 10–31, 32–53; further E. W. Blyden, *Christianity, Islam and the Negro Race* (London, 1887, reprinted Edinburgh, 1967) especially pp. 198–240 and other references noted in the index.

191 G. W. Ellis, 'Liberia in the Political Psychology of West Africa', *Journal of the African Society*, 1912, pp. 52–70.

192 Cf. below, pp. 258–62.

193 F. L. Broderick, *W. E. B. Du Bois: a Negro Leader in a Time of Crisis* (Stanford, 1959) pp. 134f.

194 Cf. below, pp. 270f.

195 T. Padmore, *Pan-Africanism*, pp. 44–75.

196 N. Azikiwe, *Liberia in World Politics*, 2 volumes (London, 1934); idem, 'In Defence of Liberia', *JNH*, XVII/1932 (January), no. 1, pp. 30–51; 'Liberia: Slave or Free?', N. Cunard (ed.), *Negro Anthology* (London, 1934) pp. 780–83.

197 C. L. R. James, *The Black Jacobins: Toussaint L'Ouverture and the San Domingo Revolution* (London, New York, 1938, second edition 1963).

198 Aptheker, *David Walker's Appeal* (see n. 169), pp. 83f.; also A. Crummell, *The Future of Africa* . . . (second edition New York, 1862) p. 168 (sermon in Monrovia on 30 July 1854).

199 Especially W. H. Ferris, *The African Abroad* . . . (see n. 106), vol. II, pp. 613f.

200 On Haitian history cf. J. G. Leyburn, *The Haitian People* (New Haven, 1941, second edition 1966).

201 Cf. also below, p. 317.

202 L. J. Rosemond, *Le Réveil de la conscience nationale* (Bibliothèque Haitienne) (Port-au-Prince – Haiti, 1932) p. 40.

203 On Firmin as foreign minister in Hyppolite's revolutionary government cf. A. Firmin, *Diplomates et diplomatie* . . . (Cap-Haitien, 1899) pp. 59ff.; R. W. Logan, *The Diplomatic Relations of the United States with Haiti, 1776–1891* (Chapel Hill, 1941) pp. 438–52; W. H. Ferris, *The African Abroad* . . ., II, pp. 611f.; on Firmin's unsuccessful candidacy for the presidency of Haiti at the turn of the century cf. also G. J. Benjamin, *La Diplomatie d'Anténor Firmin: ses péripéties, ses aspects* (Paris,

1960); on pp. 88–98 is an account of his negotiations with Douglass in 1891; cf. also the recent account of H.-U. Wehler, 'Stützpunkte in der Karibischen See: die Anfänge des amerikanischen Imperialismus auf Hispaniola', *Jahrbuch für Geschichte von Staat, Wirtschaft und Gesellschaft Lateinamerikas*, 2/1965, pp. 399–428, esp. pp. 401–17.

204 A. Firmin, *De l'Egalité des races humaines: Anthropologie positive* (Paris, 1885) pp. xiiif.

205 Cf. above, n. 204. Cf. Arthur de Gobineau, *Essai sur l'inégalité des races humaines*, 4 volumes (Paris, 1853–5).

206 Firmin, *L'Egalité* pp. 333–77, 582–594.

207 Ibid., pp. 644–9.

208 Ibid., pp. 644f. 'L'égalité des races humaines généralement reconnue entraine avec elle une consecration définitive et supérieure de l'égalité de toutes les classes sociales dans tous les peuples de l'univers. . . . Partout où lutte la démocratie, partout où la différence des conditions sociales est encore une cause de compétitions et de résistances, la doctrine de l'égalité des races sera une salutaire remède. Ce sera le dernier coup porté aux conceptions du moyen âge, la dernière étape accomplie dans l'abolition des privilèges.'

209 Ibid., p. 645: 'Les savants et les philosophes, qui affirment que les races ne sont pas égales, en viendraient-ils donc à désirer un régime de distinction, l'établissement de vraies castes, dans la nation même à laquelle ils appartiennent?'

210 Ibid.: 'De telles conceptions, si contraires aux aspirations modernes, ne seraient-elles pas la meilleure preuve d'une abérration d'esprit, chute dont n'est exempt aucun de ceux qui plaident contre la vérité et les lois naturelles?'

211 Gobineau, *L'Inégalité*, vol. II, p. 563.

212 Firmin, *L'Egalité*, p. 647: 'N'est-ce pas le signe d'un esprit malade?'

213 Ibid., p. 658: 'Tous les hommes sont frères. Ce sont là des paroles d'or.'

213 According to one Haitian writer Firmin was influenced by German philosophy, especially by Fichte; he learned German in order to be able to read his works in the original. Cf. G. Benjamin, *La diplomatie*, pp. 19, 21.

215 Firmin, *L'Egalité*, p. 659: 'L'égalité des races démonstrée par la science, affirmée par des faits chaque jour plus nombreux, plus éloquents et incontestables, sera donc la vraie base de la solidarité humaine. Carr on ne cimente jamais une alliance sincère par une injustice patente.'

216 Ibid., p. 660: 'Il est certain que dans l'alliance universelle des peuples et des races, il y a et il y aura toujours des groupes avancés et des groupes arrièrés. . . . Mais au lieu de diviser les hommes en races supérieures et races inférieures, on les divisera plutôt en peuples civilisés et peuples sauvages ou barbares. Parmi les civilisés même, il y aura des nations de premier ordre et des nations de dernier ordre, avec de nombreux intemédiaires. En un mot, chaque communauté nationale pourra être étudiée et reconnue inférieure ou supérieure en civilisation, quand on considère le degré de son développement sociologique comparé à l'idéal que nous faisons de l'état civilisé; mais il ne sera plus question de race.'

217 Ibid., pp. 661f.: 'Ce dernier mot [la race] implique une certaine fatalité biologique et naturelle, qui n'a aucune analogie, aucune corrélation avec le degré d'aptitude que nous offrent les différentes agglomérations humaines répandues sur la surface du globe.' Despite this Firmin used the concept of 'race' later on in his work.

218 Ibid., p. 653: 'Le monde ne reste

pas stationnaire. Les nations, les races, en se coudoyant sur le théâtre de l'histoire, passent sans cesse et reviennent sur la scène avec des rôles différents.'

219 Ibid., p. 653: 'La race noire aura-t-elle un jour à jouer un rôle supérieur dans l'histoire du monde, en reprenant le flambeau qu'elle a tenu sur les bords du Nil et dont toute l'humanité s'est éclairées dans les premiers vagissements de la civilisation? Je crois avoir prouvé que rien ne lui manque pour y parvenir. Tout indique en effet, qu'il lui est reservé d'accomplir une nouvelle transformation d'où sortira le plus beau rayonnement du génie humain.'

220 Ibid., pp. 635f., 655: 'Non, il ne sera jamais trop tard pour qu'un individu ou une race fasse sons apparition dans le monde de la lumière, dans le domaine de la science. La race noire qui doit évoluer sans cesse et franchir à pas précipités toutes les étapes qu'il faut traverser pour atteindre à la civilisation, telle qu'elle se montre dans toute l'exubérance de sa floraison européenne, n'a pas à se décourager dans cette voie ascensionelle où il lui faut monter et monter toujours!'

221 Ibid., p. 655: 'Il faut que, de jour en jour, elle renforce le sentiment, la conviction de son égalité avec toutes les autres races humaines répandues sur notre planète. Croire à l'égalité, c'est s'engager moralement et la prouver par les faits et les résultats, au prix de tous les efforts. Elle y répondra'. One might add that when an exile at the end of his life Firmin became so disillusioned that he took more from social Darwinism than one might expect from reading his principal work. Twenty-five years later he accepted, in a spirit of resignation, 'la doctrine du struggle of life', which he tried to distinguish from Nietzsche's

theories. Cf. A. Firmin, *Lettres de Sainte-Thomas: études sociologiques, historiques et littéraires* (Paris, 1910) p. 291. Ibid., p. 293: 'La race noire doit accepter le struggle for life dans son inéluctabilité. Nous devons nous armer de toutes les qualités indispensables pour combattre le bon combat . . . par la science comme par la politique, de l'égalité de droit de toutes les hommes, quelle que soit leur origine, dans l'évolution morale et mentale de l'espèce. C'est seulement par cette égalité de lutteur, . . . que nous devons établir l'édifice d'une solidarité sociale.'

Chapter 8

1 O. Cugoano, *Thoughts and Sentiments* (Paris, 1788) p. 29.
2 R. A. Young, *The Ethiopian Manifesto* . . . (New York, 1829); ample extracts in H. Aptheker, *Documentary History of the Negro People* (New York, 1943, fifth edition 1964) vol. I, pp. 90–93; citation on p. 92.
3 Cf. above, p. 101; this usage corresponds to that of Herodotus, who distinguished between light-skinned Africans ('Libyans') and dark-skinned ones ('Ethiopians').
4 Cf. above, pp. 100f.
5 H. H. Garnet, *The Past and the Present Condition, and the Destiny of the Colored Race* . . . (Troy – New York, 1848) p. 7.
6 E.g. W. E. Blyden, *The People of Africa* (New York, 1871) p. 10; W. E. B. Du Bois, *Black Folk* (New York, 1939, fourth edition 1945) p. 15.
7 R. B. Lewis, *Light and Truth* . . . (Boston, 1844) pp. 40ff.
8 W. W. Brown, *The Black Man* . . . (Boston, 1863) pp. 32f.; idem, *The Rising Son* . . . (Boston, 1874) pp. 43ff.
9 Idem, *The Rising Son* . . ., pp. 97ff., 127.
10 P. K. Seme (cf. ch. 7, n. 142).

11 W. H. Ferris, *The African Abroad . . .* (New York, 1913) vol. I, pp. 440–506; W. E. B. Du Bois, *The Negro* (New York, 1915; London, 1916) pp. 30ff.; idem, *Black Folk*, pp. 27–38.

12 C. Hayford, *Ethiopia Unbound* (London, 1911) pp. 1ff., 5, 10, 98f., 161, 167, 169, 182, 207.

13 Cf. above, p. 101.

14 Hayford, *Ethiopia Unbound*, p. 91.

15 Cf. above, p. 92.

16 E.g. E. C. Kinch, *West Africa: an Open Door* (New York, 1917) p. 48; cf. also above, p. 105, and below, p. 137.

17 E.g. A. Crummell, *The Future of Africa . . .* (New York, 1862) p. 312.

18 Cf. below, pp. 292, 370; also E. W. Blyden, 'Ethiopia stretching out her hands unto God', *Christianity, Islam and the Negro Race* (London, 1887, reprinted Edinburgh, 1967, with an introduction by C. Fyfe) pp. 113–129.

19 *Biblischer Kommentar. Altes Testament*, ed. M. Noth, vol. XV/1; H. J. Kraus, *Psalmen*, first pt (Neukirchen, 1960) p. 464.

20 J. F. H. Gunkel, *Die Psalmen: Göttinger Handkommentar*, 2nd general pt (fourth edition 1926) pp. 469, 477.

21 Ibid., p. 477; he names Zeph. 3: x, Is. 18: vii and Zach. 14: xvi ff.

22 Cf. above, p. 34, and also pp. 41–57, 58–65.

23 Cf. above, p. 34.

24 R. R. Wright Jr, *Centennial Encyclopaedia of the African Methodist Episcopal Church* (Philadelphia, 1916) p. 5.

25 C. S. Smith, *A History of the African Methodist Episcopal Church . . .* (Philadelphia, 1922) p. 19. Cf. also D. A. Payne, *History of the African Methodist Episcopal Church* (Nashville – Tenn., 1891).

26 C. S. Smith, *History of AME*, p. 348f.

27 According to the AMEZ bishop, J. J. Moore, *History of the African Methodist Episcopal Zion Church in America* (York – Pa., 1884) pp. 34ff.; or Bishop J. W. Hood, *One Hundred Years of the African Methodist Episcopal Zion Church . . .* (New York, 1885) p. 131: 'It has fallen to the lot of AMEZ Church to have the AME (Bethel) Church as its great antagonist . . .'

28 Cf. W. A. Davenport, *The Anthology of Zion Methodism* (Charlotte, NC, 1925) p. 24, where we read of a 'silly struggle between AME and AMEZ as to seniority'. On p. 27: 'It would be a benediction if the century-old struggle between Zion and Bethel would end with this discussion. These two great denominations should be one. Nothing but jealousy, conceit, envy and ambition have kept them apart all these years.'

29 C. S. Smith, *History of AME*, pp. 370, 377. In 1966 another merger was attempted.

30 L. L. Berry, *A Century of Missions of the African Methodist Episcopal Church, 1840–1940* (New York, 1942) pp. 91–3; one source (*Centennial Encyclopaedia*, p. 6) states that the Missions Department was founded in 1840. On its origins, cf. C. C. Alleyne, *Gold Coast at a Glance* (New York, 1931) p. 11.

31 Both Richard Allen and James Varick, the founders of AME and AMEZ respectively, were very light-skinned; the same is true of many bishops in both churches. There are pictures and photographs of them in several of the books, pamphlets and newspapers mentioned here; cf. also H. T. Medford, *Zion Methodism Abroad . . .* (Washington, 1937) pp. 152ff. Another useful pictorial source is J. H. Anderson, *Biographical Souvenir Volume . . .*, n.p., n.d., p. 17. This has forty photographs on a single page, illustrating Bishop James Varick and thirty-nine AMEZ churchmen who were then living; of these only twelve

had pronounced negroid features, so far as one can make these out at all from the tiny illustrations.

32 Cf. Aptheker, *Documentary History*, vol. I, pp. 145ff.

33 Ibid., p. 159.

34 E. U. Essien-Udom, *Black Nationalism* ... (Chicago, London, 1962, second edition New York, 1964, Harmondsworth, 1966) p. 33.

35 Cf. above, pp. 27ff.

36 Payne, *History of AME*, p. 477.

37 J. H. Smith, *Vital Facts concerning the AME Church* ..., n.p., n.d. (second edition 1941) p. 160.

38 Kinch, *West Africa*, p. 41.

39 Cf. above, pp. 93f.

40 G. Shepperson and T. Price, *Independent African* ..., p. 101.

41 Douglass, 'Haiti and the United States: Inside History of the Negotiations for the Mole St Nicolas', *North American Review*, September 1891, p. 34.

42 Shepperson and Price *Independent African*, p. 73.

43 Rev. G. G. Daniels, 'The Day Dawn of the Past; Resolutions for the Future', *Voice of the Missions*, vol. IX, no. 1, January 1901, p. 3.

44 'The Twentieth Century', ibid., p. 7f.

45 Rev. H. A. Attaway, 'The Part the 20th Century Negro will Play in the World's Civilization', ibid., no. 2, February 1901, pp. 4f.

46 For a biographical sketch of Coker cf. Payne, *History of AME*, pp. 88–92; also C. Fyfe, *A History of Sierra Leone* (Oxford, 1962, second edition 1963) p. 132, who erroneously refers to Coker as a Baptist.

47 Payne, *History of AME*, p. 91; Berry, *Missions of AME*, p. 41; in Fyfe, *History of Sierra Leone*, not mentioned although he is the greatest authority on the country.

48 Cf. above, p. 86.

49 Payne, *History of AME*, pp. 64ff., 477f.; Berry, *Missions of AME*, p. 43.

50 Payne, *History of AME*, pp. 477–80.

51 Cf. above, p. 140.

52 Payne, *History of AME*, pp. 477, 843.

53 Cf. above, pp. 92f, 129ff.

54 Cf. above, pp. 89f., 92ff. The Holly family played an active part in Haitian life and has been 'Haitianized' for generations.

55 Cf. below, p. 180.

56 Berry, *Missions of AME*, pp. 78–89.

57 Ibid., pp. 119, 124.

58 Cf. above, p. 141.

59 Berry, *Missions of AME*, pp. 123f.; Fyfe, *History of Sierra Leone*, p. 469; idem, 'The Countess of Huntingdon's Connexion in Nineteenth-Century Sierra Leone', *Sierre Leone Bulletin of Religion*, 4, no. 2, 1962, pp. 53–61; Payne, *History of AME*, pp. 486–91.

60 Payne, *History of AME*, p. 483f.

61 On this and what follows cf. Shepperson and Price, *Independent African*, pp. 73f.; B. G. M. Sundkler, *Bantu Prophets* (London, 1948, second edition 1964) pp. 38–43; Berry, *Missions of AME*, pp. 73–8, 158f.; L. J. Coppin, *Observation of Persons and Things in South Africa, 1900–1904*, n.p., n.d. [ca. 1905], pp. 8–14; C. P. Groves, *The Planting of Christianity in Africa* (London, 1958) vol. IV, p. 179.

62 Berry, *Missions of AME*, pp. 167f. What is said here very truly of the independent African churches and sects in South Africa is also in general true of the rest of the continent. Cf. especially T. Hodgkin, *Nationalism in Colonial Africa* (London, 1956, fourth edition 1962) pp. 93–114.

63 J. B. Webster, *The African Churches Among the Yoruba, 1888–1922* (Oxford, 1964) p. xiv.

64 By Frederick Douglass. L. F. Litwack, *North of Slavery* ... (Chicago, London, 1961) p. 213. On the other hand the AMEZ church cites in its favour Douglass's statement that it had been very valuable to him at first, especially when he was a lay preacher. W. A. Davonport,

Anthology (see n. 25), p. 10; Hood, *One Hundred Years* ... (see n. 27), p. 15. For the recurrence of this theme: 'God a Negro', *Lagos Standard*, 16 March 1898, p. 2.

65 On Kimbanginism Werner Ustorf is preparing his Hamburg doctoral thesis, to be completed in 1974.

66 On this complex of questions cf. especially Sundkler, *Bantu Prophets*; K. Schlosser, *Propheten in Afriko* (Brunswick, 1949); Hodgkin, *Nationalism*, pp. 93-114, which gives more detailed references; G. Balandier, 'Messianismes et nationalismes en Afrique Noire', *Cahiers internationaux de sociologie*, XIV/1953; Southon, *Gold Coast*, Methodism (London, Cape Coast, 1934) pp. 144-8. For a contemporary reaction to the phenomenon of the 'people's missionary' William W. Harris by a Gold Coast nationalist leader, cf. C. Hayford's rather mystical pamphlet, *William Waddy Harris: the West African Reformer* ... (London, 1915). According to Hodgkin (*Nationalism*, p. 107) Harris is said to have baptised 120,000 persons.

67 Berry, *Missions of AME*, p. 77. The romantic history of the first contacts between the AME church and Ethiopianism is related by various sources: Berry, *Missions of AME*, p. 158; Coppin, *Observations in South Africa*, pp. 11f.; M. Benson, *African Patriots* ... (London, 1963, second revised ed. *South Africa: the Struggle for a Birthright*, Harmondsworth, 1966) p. 41. According to these writers at the beginning of the 1890s a group of young African singers came from South Africa to England, where they performed before Queen Victoria and then went on to the United States. Their plan to give a series of concerts broke down and they were left without resources. A young AME minister in Ohio, the Rev. R. C. Ransom (later an AME bishop), gave them the opportunity

to study at Wilberforce. Among those who did so were Miss Charlotte Manye and Marshall Maxeke. Charlotte Manye wrote an enthusiastic letter from Wilberforce to her sister, who had remained behind in the Transvaal, and she showed this to the Rev. M. M. Mokone after his secession. Mokone read it to his parishioners, who thereupon decided to contact the AME church. Charlotte Manye passed her B.Sc. examination in 1905, married Marshall Maxeke who had been studying theology, and they went back to South Africa. There they opened a school; Mrs Maxeke published a local paper for Africans and was active in the 'Native Congress' which later became the South African National Congress.

68 Sundkler, *Bantu Prophets*, pp. 40f.

69 Cf. above, pp. 135, 138f.

70 *Voice of Missions*, vol. 12, no. 12, December 1904, p. 3.

71 Shepperson and Price, *Independent African*, p. 145.

72 R. R. Wright Jr, *Centennial Encyclopaedia*, p. 287.

73 Sundkler, *Bantu Prophets*, p. 74.

74 Ibid., appendix, with an endless list of the African sects noted since 1945.

75 The panic fear of 'Ethiopianism' had tragic consequences in what was then German South-west Africa. The German commander-in-chief, von Trotha, rejected the Hereros' offer to submit after their rising in 1904-5, for he 'saw in the entire insurrectionary movement in the German protectorate the first signs of a race war that threatened the colonial possessions of all the European peoples. In this situation any leniency on the German side would encourage the idea that Africa belonged solely to the Blacks and reinforce the so-called Ethiopian movement.' Thus the order was issued to seal off the Omaheke

Desert and to let the remainder of the Hereros die there. Cf. *Die Kämpfe der deutschen Truppen in Südwestafrika*, ed. Grosser Generalstab, Kriegsgeschichtliche Abteilung, I, vol. I: *Der Feldzug gegen die Hereros* (Berlin, 1906) p. 212. Cf. also H. Drechsler, *Südwestafrika unter deutscher Kolonialherrschaft: der Kampf der Herero und Nama gegen den deutschen Imperialismus* (Berlin, 1966) pp. 209f.

76 For this process cf. E. Roux, *Time Longer than Rope* (Madison, 1948, second edition London, 1964); M. Benson, *The African Patriots*; P. Walshe, Ph.D. thesis on the South African National Congress (Oxford, 1967).

77 Shepperson and Price, *Independent African*, also for what follows.

78 Cf. above, pp. 138f.

79 Cf. below, pp. 171, 182, 185f., 192, 196.

80 Biographical data on Small cited from Hood, *One Hundred Years*, pp. 233–6; *Gold Coast Aborigines*, 10 November 1898; Rev. Dr I. Sackey, 'A Brief History of the A.M.E. Zion Church West Gold Coast District', *Ghana Bulletin of Theology*, vol. I, 1957, no. 3, pp. 16–20, especially pp. 16f.; cf. also above, pp. 14f.

81 Cf. also below, p. 152.

82 Cf. also above, p. 14.

83 Cf. above, pp. 142f.

84 Cf. above, pp. 72–6.

85 Medford, *Zionism Abroad* (see n. 31), p. 153.

86 On this episode cf. *Gold Coast Aborigines*, 10, 26 November 1898; *Gold Coast Chronicle*, 15 November 1898; Medford, *Zionism Abroad*, pp. 35f.; D. Kimble, *History of Ghana*, vol. I (Oxford, 1963) p. 163. Strangely enough the origin in 1898 is not mentioned either by Bartels or by Sackey.

87 Cf. above, pp. 61ff.

88 Cf. above, p. 74.

89 Cf. above, n. 86.

90 Cf. above, p. 62.

91 *Gold Coast Aborigines*, 10 November 1898, p. 3; '1700' must be a misprint for '1800'.

92 Cf. above, p. 75.

93 Ibid.

94 *Gold Coast Aborigines*, 26 November 1898. For this and a similar quotation from the same paper, 25 February 1899, cf. Kimble, *History of Ghana*, p. 163.

95 *Gold Coast Aborigines*, 26 November 1898.

96 Cf. above, p. 15.

97 Medford, *Zionism Abroad*, pp. 36f.; Sackey, 'History of AMEZ district', p. 17.

98 Cf. below, pp. 348f, 371.

99 Cf. above, p. 56.

100 Cf. above, pp. 46–50.

101 Cf. above, pp. 52–7.

102 J. F. A. Ajayi, *Christian Missions in Nigeria*, p. 203; J. B. Webster, *African Churches* ..., p. 33; E. A. Ayandele, *Missionary Impact* ..., p. 178. For a later example, from 1904, cf. J. C. Anene, *Southern Nigeria in Transition, 1885–1906. Theory and Practice in a Colonial Protectorate* (London, 1966) p. 244.

103 Cf. above, pp. 48f.

104 A. E. Tubuko-Metzger, *Historical Sketch of the Sierra Leone Grammar School, 1845–1935* (Freetown) n.d., [1935] p. 23; also Ayandele, *Christian Missions*, p. 178; copy in the CMS Archive, London, CAI/022/44; personal communication from Mr C. Fyfe.

105 E. A. Ayandele, 'An Assessment of James Johnson and his Place in Nigerian History, 1874–1917', *Journal of the Historical Society of Nigeria*, 2, no. 4, December 1963; 3, no. 1, December 1964; now expanded into E. A. Ayandele, *Holy Johnson* (London, 1970).

106 H. R. Lynch, 'Native Pastorate Controversy and Cultural Ethnocentrism in Sierra Leone, 1871–1874', *JAH*, 5 (1964), no. 3, pp. 395–413.

107 Cf. above, p. 51.

108 Fyfe, *Sierre Leone*, p. 388; more details on the group in ibid., pp. 388f., 392f.; Ayandele, *Missionary Impact*, pp. 252f. Only one copy of the *Negro* has survived: Lynch, *Blyden*, p. 94, n. 34. Some quotations are available from contemporary and later publications, e.g. *Centennary Volume Fourah Bay College*, p. 54.

109 See above, p. 68.

110 *Centennary Volume*, pp. 54, 56.

111 Ibid., p. 56.

112 Cf. now Lynch, *Blyden*, esp. pp. 59f.

113 Ayandele, *Missionary Impact*, p. 253, with several examples; cf. also Blyden's letter of 1895 to a missionary conference about Africa held at Atlanta, Ga., in J. W. E. Bowen (ed.), *Africa and the American Negro* . . . (Atlanta, 1896) p. 16.

114 Ayandele, *Missionary Impact*, p. 253.

115 Cf. above, ch. 7, n. 82.

116 Cf. also above, p. 7.

117 Cf. below, pp. 258–62.

118 For more details about Johnson see the two works by Ayandele.

119 *Centennary Volume*, p. 64.

120 Ibid., pp. 63, 66.

121 On Venn cf. above, p. 51.

122 'The Negro', *Church Missionary Intelligencer: a Monthly Journal of Missionary Information*, IX, new series, 1873, pp. 225–50, especially pp. 225–7.

123 Ibid., pp. 247f.

124 Cf. above, pp. 52–7.

125 On this and what follows cf. Ayandele, *Missionary Impact*, pp. 186–92; Ajayi, *Christian Missions*, pp. 235–8.

126 Ayandele, *Missionary Impact*, p. 187.

127 On this important personality in proto-colonial Nigerian history cf. J. E. Flint, *Sir George Goldie and the Making of Nigeria* (London, Ibadan, Accra, 1966).

128 Ajayi, *Christian Missions*, pp. 238f.; Webster, *African Churches*, p. 7.

129 Ayandele, *Missionary Impact*, pp. 201f.; also Webster, *African Churches*, s.v. 'polygamy'.

130 Ayandele, *Missionary Impact*, p. 192.

131 Ibid., pp. 198–200; Webster, *African Churches*, pp. 49–56.

132 On Agbebi the most details are provided by Ayandele, *Missionary Impact*, especially pp. 254–6; on Bruce and 'Agbebi Day' cf. G. Shepperson, 'Notes on Negro American Influences . . .', *JAH*, vol. I, no. 2, pp. 309f.; also Bruce Papers in Schomburg Collection, N.Y.

133 Cf. below, p. 217f., 275.

134 The earlier literature was by and large uncritical towards the European missions; one of the last examples in S. Neill, *Christian Missions*, Pelican History of the Church, vol 6 (London, 1964, second edition Harmondsworth, 1966); see pp. 377f. for Crowther's alleged incapacity. For modern accounts based upon archive material of the secession movement in Nigeria, cf. Webster, *African Churches*, Ajayi, *Christian Missions*, pp. 250ff. and Ayandele, *Missionary Impact*, pp. 213ff.

135 Cf. above, p. 48.

136 Ajayi, *Christian Missions*, p. 253; cf. also Ayandele, *Missionary Impact*, p. 215.

137 Ibid., p. 211.

138 Ibid., pp. 216f.

139 Ibid., p. 217; Webster, *African Churches*, p. 65.

140 Ayandele, *Missionary Impact*, pp. 221f.

141 Neill, *Christian Missions*, p. 378.

142 Webster, *African Churches*, pp. 37f., 70.

143 Cf. below, pp. 185f.

144 Cf. below, p. 207.

145 Cf. below, pp. 180, 193, 197.

PART II

Chapter 9

1 Cf. above, pp. 98–101, 164f., 197f.

2 Cf. above, Pt I, ch. 15, n. 169.

3 Cf. above, p. 80.

4 Cf. above, pp. 88f.

5 M. R. Delany, *The Condition . . . of the Colored People of the United States* . . . (Philadelphia, 1852).

6 *Proceedings of the National Emigration Convention of Colored People* . . . (Pittsburgh, 1854) pp. 40f. This source was first utilized by L. F. Litwack, *North of Slavery* . . ., pp. 26of. The numerical argument is, however, older. In 1706 a White minister warned the White slave-owners: 'Whereas it is well-known, that the Whites, are the least part of Mankind. The biggest part of Mankind, perhaps, are Copper-Coloured; a sort of Tawnies.' G. Osofsky, *The Burden of Race: a Documentary History of Negro–White Relations in America* (New York, Evanston, London, 1967) p. 37.

7 According to Litwack in *North of Slavery*, although this is not to be found in the *Proceedings* . . . (see n. 6) which he gives as his source.

8 Cf. above, p. 88.

9 M. R. Delany, *Official Report . . .* (New York, Leeds, 1861).

10. Ibid., p. 52.

11 Cf. below, p. 173.

12 Cf. below, p. 190.

13 Cf. above, p. 89f; material from the Hodgkin Papers, Oxford.

14 T. Hodgkin to Thomas Hughes (Cape Coast), 22 June 1859, copy. Ibid., Letters from Dr Hodgkin, 22 June 1859–November 1866. On Hughes cf. above, pp. 65f.

15 Ibid. Hodgkin's handwriting is difficult to read; according to the sense, the penultimate sentence should include the word 'not'. This passage is of particular historical interest since it shows that Hodgkin discerned the beginnings of colonial imperialism and that he was able to see the outlines of the coming national emancipation of Africa a century before it occurred.

16 Ibid. What was needed was not banquets and speeches, but debating clubs, 'mechanics' institutes' and the spreading of the Bible in many languages.

17 Ibid.

18 Ibid., Hodgkin to Hughes, 23 September 1859.

19 Cf. below, p. 177.

20 Cf. above, p. 90.

21 Hodgkin to W. Coppinger, 8 July 1859, copy, Hodgkin Papers: 'For years the Society of Friends here and many others cherished the object which was obviously analogous to those of Granville Sharp, Paul Cuffee and others . . .' William Coppinger was a prominent Presbyterian in New York and secretary of the Pennsylvania Colonization Society, later the American Colonization Society, which in 1850 made it possible for Blyden to sail to Liberia: cf. Lynch, *Blyden*, p. 5, for further details.

22 Note by T. Hodgkin: 'Native African Association and their Friends at Dr. Hodgkin's, 7 November 1861.' Hodgkin Papers.

23 Illegible abbreviation of the Christian name. Josiah and Robert Forster took part in a meeting of the executive of the Anti-Slavery Society on 7 June 1861: cf. Anti-Slavery Papers, Oxford, Minute Book, vol. 4.

24 Business man in London; like Chinery (see below), he was a representative of Liberia.

24a Merchant with commercial interests in Liberia and Lagos.

25 On Taylor cf. S. O. Biobaku, *The Egba and their Neighbours, 1842–1872* (Oxford, 1957, second edition 1965) p. 71; J. H. Kopytoff, *A Preface to Nigeria* . . ., pp. 145f., 179, 186. At this juncture Taylor had just been appointed first vice-consul; early in 1862 he arrived in Lagos.

26 Linstant Pradine to Anti-Slavery Society, 12 April 1860, original, Anti-Slavery Papers, Oxford: 'Le Gouvernement Haitien . . . s'intéresse aux luttes qu'elle [Anti-Slavery Society] soutient en faveur

de l'émancipation de la race
Africaine . . .'

27 Cf. above, p. 89. Although Campbell is of course a common name, it would be possible that the two are identical, since Robert Campbell returned to Lagos in 1862 and the most convenient way there from the USA was via Liverpool.

28 Hodgkin Papers, ibid.; reading of phrases and words in brackets uncertain.

29 Ibid., a continuation of the almost endless sentence that comprises the bulk of this record of a session and the resolution adopted there.

30 Ibid., copy, n.d.

31 Cf. above, p. 36.

32 Cf. above, pp. 69–76, 157f.

33 Sundkler, *Bantu Prophets*, p. 43.

34 Cf. below, pp. 182f.

35 Cf. above, pp. 89f.

36 We may mention here a few of the most recent works on this period of American history: W. E. B. Du Bois, *Black Reconstruction in America* . . . (New York, 1935, third edition 1964); J. H. Franklin, *Reconstruction: after the Civil War* (Chicago, London, 1961, fourth edition 1963); K. B. Stampp, *Reconstruction* . . . (New York, London, 1964); R. W. Logan, *The Betrayal of the Negro* . . . (New York, London, 1965); A. Meier, *The Negro in American Thought, 1880–1915* (Ann Arbor, 1964).

37 P. Lewinson, *Race, Class, Party: a History of Negro Suffrage and White Politics in the South* (New York, 1932, second edition 1965); C. Vann Woodward, *The Strange Career of Jim Crow* (New York, 1955, third edition 1966). On this question and that referred to in the preceding note, see also the abundant material in Aptheker, *Documentary History*, vol. II.

38 S. Spencer, *Booker T. Washington and the Negro's Place in American Life* (Boston, 1955) pp. 128f.; the annual average after 1900 was 100 or more.

39 There is as yet no comprehensive and comparative analysis of the various race riots; there is some material in Aptheker, *Documentary History*, pp. 812–15, 866–9.

40 Cf. Spencer, *B. T. Washington*.

41 This resistance is stressed in Aptheker, *Documentary History*, II, pp. 727–43, 804–12.

42 Material on the National Afro-American Council in ibid. On Walters see his autobiography, *My Life and Work* (Chicago, Toronto, London, Edinburgh, 1917).

43 Cf. below, pp. 211, 213f.

44 On Washington's interest in Africa cf. now L. R. Harlan, 'Booker T. Washington and the White Man's Burden', *American Historical Review*, 71, no. 2, January 1966, pp. 441–67; Harlan has promised a new biography of Washington.

45 Ibid., p. 459, especially in South Africa.

46 Ibid., pp. 442–6.

47 W. E. B. Du Bois, *The Conservation of Race* (American Negro Academy. Occasional Papers, no. 2) (Washington, 1897) p. 10.

48 Ibid.

49 Ibid., p. 12.

50 Ibid.

51 Cf. above, p. 171.

52 Cf. above, pp. 141f.

53 Cf. above, pp. 153.

54 Cf. above, pp. 63, 64.

55 Fyfe, *History of Sierra Leone*, pp. 577ff.

56 Cf. above, pp. 74, 144–7.

57 Cf. above, pp. 153–8.

58 Cf. above, p. 73.

59 Cf. above, pp. 140–3.

60 Cf. above, pp. 132f. The official name for Ethiopia was then Abyssinia. See in general Fyfe, *History of Sierra Leone*, p. 578.

Chapter 10

1 A. Walters, *My Life and Work* (New York, Chicago, Toronto, London,

468 Notes to pages 176–178

Edinburgh, 1917), p. 253; cf. also *Report of the Panafrican Conference . . .* (London) n.d. [1900 or 1901], p. 1.

2 G. Padmore, *Pan-Africanism*, p. 117. Padmore does not give his source; perhaps he obtained details about Williams from members of his family, for he was Williams's nephew, as he himself states; cf. below, p. 351.

3 *Aborigines Friend*, November 1899, pp. 452f.

4 W. E. B. Du Bois, *The World and Africa . . .* (New York, 1947, second edition 1965) p. 7; previously in *History of the Pan-African Congress*, ed. G. Padmore (London, 1947, second edition 1963) p. 13. It is worth citing in full the paragraph on which our knowledge of the 1900 London conference as yet mainly rests: 'It was not, however, until 1900 that a black West Indian barrister, practising in London, called together a Pan-African Conference. This meeting attracted attention, put the word "Pan-African" in the dictionaries for the first time, and had some thirty delegates, mainly from England and the West Indies, with a few colored North Americans. The conference was welcomed by the Lord Bishop of London, and a promise was obtained from Queen Victoria, through Joseph Chamberlain, not to "overlook the interests and welfare of the native races".'

5 Padmore, *Pan-Africanism*, pp. 117f., with some flourishes.

6 H. F. Strauch, *Panafrika . . .* (Zurich, 1964) pp. 25f., virtually a paraphrase of Padmore.

7 Walters, *My Life*, pp. 253–64. This chapter of his autobiography appeared soon after the Conference as an article in *AME Zion Quarterly Review*, XI, no. 2, April–June 1901, pp. 164–72.

8 *Report*, p. 1.

9 Cf. above, p. 174f.

10 *Report*, p. 1, gives 1898, a misprint for 1897; cf. below, pp. 178.

11 *Report*, ibid.

12 *Lagos Standard*, 27 July 1898, 28 December 1898.

13 Cf. below, pp. 291f.

14 *Aborigines Friend*, November 1897, pp. 297f.

15 According to C. Fyfe, *History of Sierre Leone*, p. 453, in 1900 he was a law student in London.

16 Further details about Miss Colenso may be found in S. Marks, 'Henrietta Colenso and the Zulus, 1874–1913', *JAH*, IV, 1963, no. 3, pp. 402–11.

17 *Aborigines Friend*, March 1898, p. 349; *Report*, p. 1.

18 Cf. above, pp. 166–9.

19 *Report*, p. 1f.; identically in *Lagos Standard*, 27 July 1898.

20 *Aborigines Friend*, March 1898, pp. 348f.

21 An island off the coast of Sierra Leone. Farquhar was a missionary who came from the West Indies.

22 An older brother of the well-known Casely Hayford. Both brothers went to the Wesleyan Boys' High School in Freetown, Sierra Leone. Later E. J. Hayford was one of the first teachers at the Wesleyan High School at Cape Coast, founded in 1876, which in 1905 became the Mfantsipim (cf. above, p. 64). Details from D. Kimble, *Political History of Ghana* (Oxford, 1963) pp. 84, n. 2, 85, n. 1.

23 *Aborigines Friend*, March 1898.

24 *Lagos Standard*, V, 6, 26 October 1898, p. 2. Nothing came of this project, or so it seems; nevertheless it was a pointer to the future, for the Labour party later sometimes put up a coloured candidate (e.g. the Indian Krishnam Menon) and the Communist party in the 1920s actually got another Indian, Saklatvala, elected to Parliament as member for Battersea, one of its few MPs.

25 *Lagos Standard*, 28 December 1898, p. 2; cited from *Daily Chronicle*, 24 November 1898.
26 Ibid.
27 'The African Association', *Lagos Standard*, 27 July 1898.
28 Ibid; reprinted in *Gold Coast Chronicle*, 30 August 1898.
29 Ibid.
30 In October 1898 it was planned to hold a great protest meeting in London against the actions of the governor of Sierra Leone during the so-called Hut Tax War; ibid.
31 Ibid.
32 *Lagos Standard*, V, no. 15, 4 January 1899, p. 2.
33 Ibid.
34 *Report*, p. 2.
35 Cf. above, pp. 89, 92.
36 Cf. above, pp. 148–53, 158.
37 Cf. above, pp. 93, 143.
38 Cf. above, p. 155, and below, p. 217f.
39 Cf. above, p. 178.
40 Professor, then Vice-President (in 1908 President) of the AME's Wilberforce University; on its significance, see above, p. 134. There is a sketch of Scarborough in the *African Times and Orient Review*, August 1912, p. 70.
41 Cf. above, pp. 153, 158.
42 Cf. above, pp. 172, 211–15, 218.
43 Cf. above, pp. 93, 143.
44 Cf. above, pp. 89, 92, 139.
45 Cf. above, p. 138.
46 Walters, *My Life*, p. 260; *Report*, p. 2f.
47 Cf. above, n. 4.
48 Cf. above, p. 173.
49 On Du Bois's stay in Germany, cf. below, p. 212.
50 Walters, *My Life*, pp. 253f.
51 Fyfe, *History of Sierra Leone*, p. 545, gives his first names as Frederick William.
52 According to Walters 'Ribero'. The name indicates that he belonged to one of the relatively few families of 'Brazilians' who settled on the Gold Coast. A certain F. J. Ribeiro was Chief Clerk to Colonial Secretary Slater in Accra in 1919: Kimble, *History of Ghana*, p. 103.
53 Apparently identical with Dr John Alcindor of Trinidad: cf. below, p. 243.
54 Nothing is as yet known of these men. A certain J. E. Worrell played a part in the events of 1939: cf. below, pp. 360f.
55 *Report*, p. 4.
56 Cf. below, p. 192; on Archer, see p. 243.
57 W. H. Ferris, *The African Abroad* . . . (New York, 1913) vol. I, p. 475; a Georges Sylvain was later leader of the opposition in Haiti to the American occupation of 1915.
58 *West Africa*, I, no. 5, September 1900, p. 147.
59 Du Bois, *The World and Africa*, p. 7 (see above, n. 4); our italics.
60 Cf. above, n. 7; *The Times* (London), 24–6 July 1900, under the heading 'Pan-African Conference'.
61 Cf. above, pp. 149, 157ff.
62 *Report*, p. 3.
63 Ibid., p. 5.
64 *The Times*, 24 July 1900, p. 7.
65 The seemingly so impressive figure of 753 million dollars' worth of property in the hands of Afro-Americans in the USA turns out to be quite modest when one bears in mind that they numbered about ten million persons, so that this works out at roughly seventy-six dollars per head.
66 *The Times*, 24 July; also Walters, *My Life*, pp. 255f.
67 *The Times*, 24 July.
68 Ibid., 25 July 1900.
69 Ibid.
70 Cf. below, p. 192.
71 Cf. above, p. 188.
72 *Report*, p. 7.
73 Ibid., p. 6f.: 'That this Pan-African Conference, the first of its kind ever held in London, representing the African and his descendants in every part of the world . . .';

for the conclusion, see above, n. 72. The other resolutions in ibid., pp. 7f.

74 Ibid., p. 9.

75 Du Bois, *The World and Africa*, p. 7; cf. also Padmore, *Pan-Africanism*, p. 118; P. Decraene, *Le Panafricanisme* . . ., (Paris, 1959, third edition 1964) p. 12; C. Legum, *Pan-Africanism* . . . (London, 1962, second edition 1965) p. 25; H. F. Strauch, *Panafrika* . . . (Zurich, 1964), p. 28.

76 Du Bois used this sentence, without referring to the 1900 London Conference, three years later in the foreword to his volume of essays *The Souls of Black Folk*; cf. p. v.

77 In view of the growing differences between the modernized industrialized countries and the developing countries; on this cf. also the recent encyclical of Pope Paul VI, 'Populorum Progressio'.

78 Text from the *Report*, pp. 10–12; Walters, *My Life*, pp. 257–60; more recently also W. E. B. Du Bois, *An ABC of Color: Selections* . . . (Berlin, 1963) pp. 19–22.

79 Ibid.

80 Cf. above, Pt I, ch. 7.

81 Ibid.

82 This 'etc. etc.' is a literary hyperbole, for apart from Abyssinia, Liberia and Haiti there were at that time no other free negro states in the world.

83 Du Bois was chairman of the editorial committee, and the appeal is numbered among his works: e.g. *An ABC of Color* (cf. above, n. 78).

84 Cf. above, pp. 186–9.

85 Cf. above, pp. 172f.

86 Cf. above, p. 190.

87 Cf. above, pp. 164f.

88 A brother of Miss Henrietta Colenso.

89 Details from *Report*, p. 18; cf. Walters, *My Life*, p. 260.

90 Cf. above, pp. 178f.

91 *Report*, p. 13f.

92 Cf. above, pp. 73f.

93 Cf. above, pp. 129–31.

94 Cf. above, p. 182.

95 Cf. above, p. 177.

96 Fyfe, *History of Sierra Leone*, pp. 400f., 440, 517, 573.

97 On Sir Samuel Lewis see John D. Hargreaves, *A Life of Sir Samuel Lewis* (London, Ibadan, Accra, 1958).

98 On Payne cf. above, pp. 153, 158, 180; on Holm see p. 183.

99 'An Interesting Speech by Mr Sydney Olivier, C.M.G., on the Work of the Pan-African Association', *The Pan-African*, I, no. 1, October 1901, pp. 2f.; the article consisted mainly of a reprint of a report in the *Daily Gleaner*, Kingston, Jamaica, 30 March 1901.

100 *Report*, p. 14.

101 This conclusion is, however, not certain, for I discovered in the course of my research that the British Museum, despite the provisions of the Copyright Acts, does not have copies of all the periodicals published in Great Britain which are relevant to our theme and that some holdings are incomplete. There may therefore have been other issues of this periodical, which may be discovered in private libraries; they are not to be found in those of the Du Bois papers preserved in Accra.

102 Heading on p. 4: 'The Pan-African, Motto: "Liberty and Light". A Monthly, Issued for the express purpose of diffusing information concerning the interests of the African and his Descendants in the British Empire.' It was planned to feature in the second and later numbers photographs 'of our Leading Men and Women and Families, showing the race's progress and culture'.

103 Ibid.

104 Ibid.

105 Ibid., p. 8.

106 Cf. above, n. 104.

107 Cf. above, p. 146.

108 Cf. above, pp. 153, 158, 183;

nothing is as yet known of Love and Lazare.

109 Mr Owen C. Malhurin, Trinidad, informed me that he has completed a biography of Sylvester Williams in manuscript.

110 Walters, *My Life*, p. 260.

111 Cf. above, n. 4; in his report delivered at Manchester in 1945 Du Bois mentioned the name of Sylvester Williams, but in the version printed in *The World and Africa* (1946), which is otherwise identical, he suppressed the reference. He did not even mention his own participation in the Conference or his election to the post of vice-president of the US branch of the Pan-African Association.

112 H. R. Isaacs, *The New World of Negro Americans* . . . (New York, 1964) p. 223.

113 On Du Bois, cf. below, ch. 11, pp. 212f.

114 Cf. above, n. 75.

115 Cf. above, pp. 180, 182, 192f.

116 Cf. above, pp. 178f.

117 'The Pan-African Conference', *Lagos Standard*, 17 October 1900.

Chapter 11

1 Cf. above, p. 197.

2 African critics of British colonial rule, especially in West Africa, always compared the position of the governor with that of an absolute monarch, in order to contrast it with the democratic principles of the British constitution and to support their demand for a voice in their own affairs.

3 On the effect on Du Bois cf. his celebrated poem 'Atlanta Litany', a reaction to the race riot in Atlanta in 1906. Cf. also J. H. Franklin, 'The Transformation of the Negro Intellectual', A. M. Rose (ed.), *Assuring Freedom to the Free* (Detroit, 1964) p. 251.

4 Cf. above, p. 145, and below, p. 210.

5 W. H. Ferris, *The African Abroad* . . . (New York, 1913) vol. II, p. 840.

6 Cf. above, p. 177.

7 D. Kimble, *History of Ghana*, p. 136, n. 2.

8 Ibid., p. 144.

9 Cf. the notice in *Gold Coast Nation*, 1, no. 20, 1 August 1912; on Asaam see above, p. 146.

10 *Gold Coast Nation*, 30 October 1920, 'Opulent Natives'.

11 P. Foster, *Education and Social Change in Ghana*, p. 113.

12 Cf. above, p. 48f.

13 Cf. R. Ainslie, *The Press in Africa* . . . (London, 1966) pp. 27ff.

14 *Gold Coast Leader*, no. 209, 23 June 1906, 'Our National Crisis'.

15 Ibid., followed by the passage on the Rev. Mark Hayford cited above.

16 Ibid., no. 186, 13 January 1906.

17 Cf. above, p. 98f.

18 *Gold Coast Leader*, no. 198, 7 April 1906. Similar pleas were uttered by Mensah Sarbah in 1906 and by the *Gold Coast Nation* in 1914 against the word 'Native' and for 'African': Kimble, *History of Ghana*, vol. 1, p. 540.

19 *Gold Coast Leader*, no. 229, 10 November 1906.

20 Foster, *Education*, p. 102; Kimble, *History of Ghana*, pp. 85f.; cf. also above, p. 70. It was planned to have £7500 capital, divided into 15,000 shares. The new school was merged as early as 1905 with the Collegiate School (formerly the Wesleyan Boys' High School) to form a new institution, Mfantsipim. Thus, apart from the founding of Mfantsipim, the venture was a failure.

21 London, 1906; cf. also above, p. 73.

22 London, 1903.

23 A. Ahumah, 'The Gold Coast Nation and National Consciousness', *Gold Coast Leader*, no. 432, 19 November 1910; this is a subtitle to a

chapter in Kimble's *History of Ghana* (p. 520).

24 C. C. Reindorf, *History of the Gold Coast and Asante* ... (Basle, 1895, second edition 1951).

25 *Gold Coast Aborigines*, 1, no. 1, January 1898.

26 Cf. above, p. 98.

27 Cf. above, pp. 38f., 98f.

28 *Memoirs of West African Celebrities* ... (Liverpool, 1905).

29 M. Sampson, *Gold Coast Men of Affairs* (London, 1937).

30 Liverpool, 1911.

31 Cited from Kimble, *History of Ghana*, vol. 1, p. 524.

32 Ahuma spoke of his hope for 'an era of Backward Movement' among 'all cultural West Africans . . . Intelligent Retrogression is the only progression that will save our beloved country.' Cf. G. Grohs, *Stufen afrikanischer Emanzipation* ... (Stuttgart 1962) pp. 162f. The Gold Coast National Research Association, founded by C. Hayford in 1911, proclaimed it as its aim 'to restore "national respect and self-confidence" by observing native custom alone, without European intrusions, and by reconstructing "on paper" the native State "before the disintegrating foreign element intruded or insinuated itself into it" '. (Cited from Kimble, *History of Ghana*, vol. 1, pp. 524f.)

33 C. Hayford, *Gold Coast Native Institutions* ... (London, 1903) pp. 254f.

34 Cf. above, p. 150.

35 Kimble, *History of Ghana*, p. 524.

36 This was the title of a leading article by Ahuma in the *Gold Coast Leader*, 26 November 1910 ('The Difficult Art of Thinking Nationally').

37 Ibid., 26 November 1910.

38 Cf. above, p. 132.

39 *Gold Coast Leader*, 26 November 1910.

40 Ibid. The meaning of the word 'catholic' in this connection is not quite clear.

41 Ibid., no. 448, 11 March 1911.

42 Cf. also above, p. 65.

43 According to the terminology of the time, artisan activity is evidently what is meant here.

44 *Gold Coast Nation*, no. 5, 18 April 1912. The passage ends: 'So may He help us. God save the King-Emperor!' Only two years later did Garvey use the phrase 'One God! One Nation! One Destiny!'

45 Ibid., no. 22, 15 August 1912.

46 Kimble, *History of Ghana*, vol. 1, pp. 529–33.

47 Material on the Colwyn Bay Institute and its work in Africa is to be found in the *African Times*, 1896–1900, *Gold Coast Aborigines*, November 1898, *Sierra Leone Times*, 8, no. 51, 30 July 1898; on Scholes see above, pp. 110–12.

48 Cf. also above, pp. 158, 184.

49 E. A. Ayandele, *Missionary Impact* . . ., pp. 234–7.

50 Cf. above, Pt I, ch. 8, no. 46.

51 P. Walshe, 'The Rise of African Nationalism in South Africa: The African National Congress 1912–52' (1971), ch. I p. 49: 'The belief had been established in African minds that the Boer War was being fought to establish British non-racial justice throughout South Africa. . . . There had been good causes for non-European optimism.'

52 Cf. above, p. 177.

53 Walshe, ibid., ch. IV, pp. 9ff.; on Seme cf. also above, p. 119; on his further part in the national movement among Africans in South Africa cf. E. Roux, *Time Longer than Rope* (Madison, 1948, second edition London, 1964) pp. 108–13; M. Benson, *South Africa* (Harmondsworth, 1966) pp. 23–34, 64–6.

54 Cf. below, p. 217.

55 Walshe, ibid.

56 Cf. above, p. 197.

57 'The Constitution of the African National Congress' (hectographed copy); I am grateful to Peter Walshe for putting me on to this

document. One leader of the Congress, Solomon Plaatje, took part in the first Pan-African Congress in Paris in 1919 before he went on to the USA: cf. Benson, *South Africa*, p. 42.

58 Cf. above, p. 144.

59 J. Booth, *Africa for the Africans* (Nyasaland, 1897).

60 Cf. above, p. 152.

61 Cf. below, ch. 15, pp. 305–21.

62 Cf. above, p. 172.

63 Cf. above, p. 171.

64 Cf. above, pp. 182ff, 190f.

65 On Du Bois's life cf. especially F. L. Brodrick, *A Negro Leader in a Time of Crisis* (Stanford, 1959); E. M. Rudwick, *W. E. B. Du Bois: a Study in Minority Group Leadership* (Philadelphia, 1960); various autobiographical works by Du Bois, especially his most recent and detailed book, *Mein Weg, meine Welt* (Berlin, 1965); also some material from the Du Bois papers in Accra.

66 H. Herzfeld (ed.), *Geschichte in Gestalten*, 4 volumes (Frankfurt, 1963) vol. I, p. 329. This opinion goes back to Padmore, *Pan-Africanism*, p. 106, where we are told that 'he was born . . . into a comfortable middle-class family' and has been taken over uncritically by other writers, e.g. R. Zastrow, 'Panafrikanismus und Kommunismus', *Der Ostblock und die Entwicklungsländer . . .*, August 1963, p. 23. Information to the contrary comes from the Du Bois papers in Accra; cf. now also W. E. B. Du Bois, *Mein Weg*, pp. 22–7.

67 Georges Sylvain, after 1915 the leader of the Haitian opposition, maintained that Du Bois was the great-nephew of Elie Dubois, the most important minister of education in Haiti and the founder of modern school education in that country; cf. G. Sylvain, *Dix Années de lutte pour la liberté, 1915–1925*, 2 volumes (Port-au-Prince, n.d., [1955?]) vol. I, p. 81.

68 Manuscript of an undated interview with Du Bois, apparently after World War II; Du Bois papers, Accra.

69 Ibid.

70 There is some information about Du Bois's stay in Germany in his diary, which needs to be supplemented by the notes made by Rudwick, made available by the Schomburg Collection in Harlem; cf. now also Du Bois, *Mein Weg*, pp. 154–77.

71 Du Bois is said to have graduated in Heidelberg. This claim occurs first in Decraene, *Le panafricanisme*, p. 13, and was taken over by some German writers (Herzfeld, Strauch). In fact he only passed through Heidelberg on a summer vacation. There are no informative documents about his stay in Berlin in the University Archive of the Humboldt University.

72 W. E. B. Du Bois, *The Suppression of the African Slave-Trade to the USA, 1638–1870*. Harvard Historical Studies, no. 1 (Cambridge – Mass., 1896, third edition New York, 1954).

73 Cf. also above, p. 135.

74 *The Philadelphia Negro* (Philadelphia, 1899); on the historical significance of the Philadelphia negroes cf. above, pp. 32f, 85f.

75 The titles of these studies, in German translation, now in Du Bois, *Mein Weg*, pp. 239f.

76 Chicago, 1903, and many reimpressions. On the Washington–Du Bois controversy, cf. Brodrick, Rudwick and Spencer; also B. Mathews, *Booker T. Washington: Educator and Interracial Interpreter* (Cambridge – Mass., 1948; London, 1949) pp. 273–315.

77 One well-intentioned biographer called him a 'benevolent despot': Spencer, *Washington*, p. 162, with details of his manipulative methods.

78 Cf. above, p. 172.

79 Woodson was the founder of the *Journal of Negro History*, which is still going strong. Of his many works we may mention here only *The Negro in our History* (Washington, 1922, and frequently reprinted).

80 Text in Padmore, *Pan-Africanism*, pp. 112–15.

81 Cf. above, p. 83.

82 As an intermediate account of the NAACP: L. Hughes, *Fight for Freedom: the Story of the NAACP* (New York, 1962); cf. also E. M. Rudwick, 'The National Negro Committee Conference of 1909', *Phylon*, XVIII (1957), no. 4, pp. 413–19; C. F. Kellog, *NAACP, A History of the National Association for the Advancement of Colored Peoples*, vol. 1 (Baltimore, 1967).

83 Cf. above, pp. 173, 190; and below, ch. 12, 18, 19.

84 E.g., *Horizon*, August 1907, pp. 22–25; November 1907, pp. 15f. ('The Tuskegee Budget'); March 1908, pp. 12f.; November 1909, p. 5; September 1908, 'The Negro Vote: Talk no. 4', 'Thesis: that the Democratic Party deserves a Trial at the Hands of the Negro', February 1907, pp. 7f.; 'Negro and Socialism'.

85 No. 2, February 1907, gave news and comment about Austria (introduction of universal suffrage!) and Lagos; that for April 1907 included information about South Africa, Nigeria and the Congo.

86 The number for October 1907 (pp. 9f.) cited from Scholes, *Glimpses of the Ages* (see above, p. 111) passages in which Scholes, relying on Herodotus, spoke of the negroid origin of the ancient Egyptians. In the February 1908 issue (pp. 23–5) there appeared a reprint of a review in the *Manchester Guardian* of the book by Mensah Sarbah, *Fanti National Constitution* (London, 1907); in July 1908 there was a reprint of an article by C. Hayford, 'An African on his Race', *African Mail* (pp. 7f.). Du Bois was thus fairly well informed about current intellectual trends among the African élite.

87 A. Bontemps, *One Hundred Years of Negro Freedom* (New York, 1961) p. 216. According to G. Shepperson, 'Notes on Negro American Influences', JAH, vol. I, no. 2, p. 307, n. 24, this department was rather pompously called 'The Pan-African League Department of the Niagara Movement': from a letter in J. E. Bruce's papers in the Schomburg Collection.

88 Cf. below, ch. 12, pp. 234ff.

89 G. Spiller (ed.), *Papers on Inter-Racial Problems. Universal Races Congress* (London, 1911); on the congress see also W. E. B. Du Bois, *Darkwater* (New York, London, 1920) pp. 275f.; idem, *The World and Africa*, pp. 3–5; E. M. Rudwick, 'W. E. B. Du Bois and the Universal Races Congress of 1911', *Phylon*, XX, 1959, no. 4, pp. 372–8; 'Report of the First Universal Races Congress', *African Times and Orient Review*, I, no. 1, July 1912, pp. 27–30. There is a little material on the preparation of the congress in manuscripts British Empire, S 22, Anti-Slavery Papers, G. 441, Congress on Univercal Races, 1909–1911, Rhodes House, Oxford. These papers contain a note by 'A. Tr. B.' dated 22 December 1909 about a preparatory meeting of the congress held in the Westminster Palace Hotel, London, on 13 December 1909. Spiller is called 'Herr Spiller', which suggests that he was a German, although the surname is common in England.

90 Anti-Slavery Papers.

91 Bontemps, *One Hundred Years*, p. 217. Du Bois claimed recently (*Mein Weg*, p. 306) that he was 'among the organizers of the famous races congress'.

92 Spiller, *Papers*, pp. xxxi f.
93 Ibid., p. xxxvii.
94 On Agbebi see above, pp. 155, 180.
95 Rudwick, 'Du Bois' (see n. 89), p. 373, quoting Washington's papers.
96 Ibid., p. 375.
97 Spiller, *Papers*, pp. 348–64; it was so long that it alone had to be set in smaller type.
98 Printed in Du Bois, *Darkwater*, pp. 275f. and *The World and Africa*, p. 4. Some specimens from the beginning and the conclusions:

So sit we all as one
So, gloomed in tall and stone-swathed groves.
The Buddha walks with Christ!
And Al-Koran and Bible both be holy!
Almighty Word!
In this Thine awful sanctuary,
First and flame-haunted City of Widened World,
Assoil us, Lord of Lands and Seas!

Save us, World-Spirit, from our lesser selves!
Grant us that war and hatred cease,
Reveal our souls in every race and hue!
Help us, O Human God in this Thy Truce,
to make Humanity divine.

99 Rudwick, *Du Bois*, p. 372.
100 M. W. Ovington, *The Walls Came Tumbling Down* (New York, 1947) p. 132.
101 Cf. also B. G. M. Sundkler, *Bantu Prophets* (London 1948, second edition 1964) p. 43. The Natal Native Affairs Commission of 1906–7 discovered that at least 150 Africans had left South Africa to study in the USA. This led to the notion of founding the Bantu College of Fort Hare, which was opened in 1916 with the object of channelling the Africans' zeal for learning within the country and of so controlling it.

102 Spiller, *Papers*, pp. 336–41.
103 Cf. above, p. 150f.
104 Ibid., pp. 341–8, citation on p. 346.
105 Rudwick, *Du Bois*, p. 375; also Mohamed Ali Duse, 'Leaves from an Active Life', *Comet*, 5, no. 12, 11 October 1937, p. 7.
106 The Du Bois papers in Accra contain a letter from the secretariat of the Races Congress about the preparations for the next gathering, with the printed letter-head 'Ie Congrès des Races. Paris, 1915'.
107 Cf. above, p. 208.
108 Cf. above, pp. 172, 179.
109 Rudwick, *Du Bois*, p. 209 (no source indicated).
110 Information about this congress is provided by L. R. Harlan, 'Booker T. Washington . . .', pp. 464–7; *African Times and Orient Review*, 1, no. 1, July 1912, pp. 10–12; *Gold Coast Leader* and *Gold Coast Nation*, 1912.
111 The text of the invitation from a reprint from the *Scotsman*, 7 April 1911, in the *Gold Coast Leader*, 18 November 1911 with the heading 'Dr Booker T. Washington's Invitation'.
112 On the persons named see above, pp. 93, 143, 180, 182–92, 202.
113 Cited from 'The Negro Conference at Tuskegee Institute', *African Times and Orient Review*, 1, July 1912, pp. 10f.; now also in Harlan, 'Washington', p. 464.
114 Cf. above, pp. 116f., 147.
115 *African Times and Orient Review*, 1, July 1912, p. 11.
116 Cf. above, p. 218.
117 *African Times and Orient Review*, loc. cit.
118 *Gold Coast Nation*, 9 May 1912, p. 3; perhaps this is an allusion to Casely Hayford's letter. According to J. S. Coleman, *Nigeria: Background to Nationalism* (Berkeley, Los Angeles, 1958, second edition 1960), p. 187, Hayford took part personally in the

conference, but this cannot have been the case.

119 *Gold Coast Nation*, loc. cit.; Harlan, 'Washington', p. 466. The report in the *Gold Coast Nation*, 6 February 1913, reads: '. . . It has been a question of great concern whether or not the Gold Coast is a nation. . . . The Gold Coast is a nation, . . . can be nothing less than a nation . . . The Lord has not left the Negro without a hope to rise. Here and there, in the wilderness of the Race's struggle for greater heights are found oases refreshing and invigorating and Booker T. Washington is a Moses for his race. As a country, we cherish the hope of a continued fraternal relationship with all Negroes upon the broad field of life, especially with you on this side of the terrestrial ball.'

120 Cf. above, Pt I, ch. 6, n. 102.

121 Cf. above, pp. 143f.

122 *Gold Coast Nation*, 9 May 1912; the report in the *African Times and Orient Review* refers in brief to some other reports given by White missionaries which are not of interest here.

123 *African Times and Orient Review*, 1 July 1912, p. 12; Harlan, 'Washington', pp. 466f.

124 *African Times and Orient Review*, loc. cit.

125 Cf. below, p. 265.

126 Ian Duffield, a pupil of George Shepperson, is preparing a thesis in Edinburgh on Duse's life. The following sketch is based above all on Duse's autobiographical notes which appeared serially in the *Comet* (Lagos) in 1937–8 with the title 'Leaves from an Active Life'.

127 Duse Mohamed Ali, *In the Land of the Pharaos* . . . (London, 1911). An advertisement inside the book reads: 'An Answer for Cromer. An Answer to Roosevelt!' It also reproduces some favourable reviews from the British press.

128 J. E. Taylor is still an obscure

figure. Although he reappears later, nothing is yet known about him. The name suggests that he came from Sierra Leone, but C. Fyfe has not heard of him.

129 Cf. above, pp. 9, 168.

130 Cf. above, pp. 195f.

131 This is followed, as in the *Pan-African*, by a reference to the need for better information, since 'the truth about African and Oriental conditions is rarely stated with precision and accuracy in the columns of the European press'.

132 Cf. above, p. 75.

133 Cf. above, pp. 164, 190.

134 *Gold Coast Nation*, 23 January 1913, also for the following quotation; cf. ibid., 21 November 1913: 'We once again draw the attention of our readers to the *African Times and Orient Review* and the good work it is doing for the coloured races the wide world over. It is the duty of every patriotic African, not only to subscribe to the paper, but to take shares in the Company owning it. . . .'

135 *Gold Coast Nation*, 6 February 1913. For another member of the Betts family from Sierra Leone, presumably a relative, cf. below, p. 296.

136 *African Times and Orient Review*, September 1912, p. 101.

137 Cf. above, p. 179.

138 *African Times and Orient Review*, November 1912.

139 R. B. Moore, 'Africa Conscious Harlem', *Harlem: a Community in Transition*, ed. J. H. Clarke (New York, 1964) p. 82.

140 *African Times and Orient Review*, November 1912; the German frontier was not marked in.

141 Ibid., pp. 151f.: 'Peter the Painter, Peter of Servia and Peter the Hermit', by E. Schaap; ibid., p. 111, 'Turkey's Fallen'.

142 Dr J. Kunst, 'German Policy in Africa: Some Leading Facts', ibid., February–March 1913, pp. 238–43; Quashie, 'The Gold Coast

and German Togoland: Togoland Ground to Powder', ibid., July 1913, pp. 20f.; his is a reprint, although the fact is not stated, of an article of the same title which appeared in the *Gold Coast Leader* of 30 December 1911; 'German Atrocities in Togoland', by 'A Native of Ancho', ibid., November–December 1913, pp. 201f.

143 Ibid., June 1913, p. 58: 'Race Purity', by an 'Afro-American'; a contrary view was expressed by J. Carmichael Smith, 'Hybridisation', ibid., 9 June 1914.

144 Sundra Raja, 'China and Her Mission', ibid., November 1912, pp. 148ff.: 'European observers have been repulsed by the phantoms, as they had no patience to withstand their racial prejudices. They saw in the Chinese Revolution a mere violent movement of phantom figures that might well have escaped from a cinema film.... Great Powers in the world who have been credited with invincibility are being shattered before our eyes, and the strength of new forces is destroying old ones with vigour and rapidity. ... Europe has played its part, and the Russo-Japanese War was the first signal of a mighty change. It ushered a new force into existence, that force which has stimulated the revival of Asia. ... The awakening of China follows in the wake of the astounding revival of Japan. The contagion of progress has caught the yellow-man. ... He is not the same individual, but a renovated, regenerated and awakened man. ... The Chinese Revolution is one of the few incidents of history which shows the accomplishment of the work of ages in a day. It is a historical miracle, taking higher rank than similar ones in America and France. ... China of today is not China of yesterday, and New China stands in

triumph after having achieved one of the most hazardous tasks in history. It symbolises not only its uprising, but the uprising of all the East. The awakening of all the coloured races of the world. ... It marks out the future for Asia and stimulates all Asiatic countries to awake and arise. It is the stimulator, the inspirer, the uplifter of suffering humanity, and China is the apostle of the East. ... One can read positive signs of China's glorious future in the entire frustration of the pettifogging schemes of Western Powers. To-day these prospects are glimmering, and a few decades, perhaps the next decade, will reveal the full fire which will shine brilliantly over the East.'

145 Ng Kow Chin, 'Russia's Territorial Aggrandizement and England's Pacivity [*sic*]', ibid., April 1913, pp. 300f.: 'Russia is cowardly and aggressive. I do not mean to say that she fears China as she is. But I do mean to say that she fears China as she will be in about twenty or thirty years' time. ... She fears lest she may suffer the same humiliation as she received from the hands of the Japanese. Therefore, Russia wishes to hinder, and if possible to prevent forever, China's awakening and progress. ... Russia craves for Chinese territory, but she has not the courage to face China single-handed. ... Unless she is blotted out from the surface of the earth, it is quite possible that China will become powerful. As soon as she finds herself in a position to wreak vengeance on her enemies, she will repay Russia with compound interest the humiliations and persecutions to which she has been subjected in her weaker days. ...'

146 Ibid., November–December 1913, pp. 213f.; July 1912, pp. 10–12; 16 June 1914, p. 219.

147 Ibid., November 1912, p. 111:

'There is a lesson in all of this. If the people of Africa, and the people of Asia will but profit by Turkey's misfortunes. Lack of unity, lack of patriotism, were the basic elements of Turkey's humiliation. The house was divided against itself and it fell. Europe stretches forth her arms on every side to squeeze the darker races to her own advantage, because she knows the people of Africa and the people of Asia to be divided. It therefore behoves you, men of Asia, and you, men of Africa, to join yourselves in one common bond of lasting brotherhood. . . . Sink your petty religious differences. Curb your insane pride. The only pride you require is the pride of country and pride of brotherhood. For in that pride must you gain the respect of the nations of Europe, and in that bond of brotherhood will you give pause to the European aggressor.'

148 Ibid., 23 June 1914, p. 313f.: 'Combination White and Black' commented on a speech by Dernburg in London, in which he spoke of German–British solidarity vis-à-vis the coloured peoples, in the following Terms: 'The Anglo-Saxon and Teuton are obsessed by the question of how to deal with "all mankind of darker colour, how to retain our hold and domination over them". This is the crux of the matter and the warning is clear. Turk, Japanese, Indian, Egyptian and other Africans are *all* to go into the melting pot. They are all to be controlled and dominated by these two people.'

149 Ibid., 4 August 1914, p. 449f.: 'The day has arrived and the arms are being put to the proof, and the Teuton is doing the battle for the mastery of Europe. With that he will attain his long desired "place in the sun", in the form of tropical Colonies and India. This is why the Coloured peoples

are deeply concerned in this war Are the Germans to extend their rule over vast numbers of Black and Brown men? We who know something of what German rule means, of their treatment of Africans in Togoland, Kamerun and their other African colonies, say fervently, God forbid!'

150 Ibid., 11 August 1914, p. 468, Delta (= Duse), 'Rotten Row Conversations': 'The modern Hun of Germany is a danger to Europe and to the world at large. . . . He will devastate Belgium and practice unprintable cruelties upon its population – which by the way is the chastisement of an Allwise Creator for the abominations practised upon the defenceless population of the Congo.'

151 M. A. Baa, 'Nemesis, or the Situation in Europe', ibid., October 1913, p. 160.

152 Ibid., 16 June 1914, p. 295.

153 'The Future of Subject Peoples', October–December 1917.

154 'The British West Indies in the Mirror of Civilization. History Making by Colonial Negroes', ibid., October 1913, pp. 158–60. For the passage of interest here cf. below, ch. 5, n. 4.

155 Ibid., 19 May 1914, p. 195. Duse offered his services in answering questions and providing contacts at two shillings a time, and also said he was ready to make sales at an additional commission of 5 per cent.

156 *Africa*, I, no. 1, p. 2.

157 The first issue, Summer 1928, is in the British Museum Library.

158 Danquah's daily paper, the *West African Times*, for 30 September 1931 reported under the heading 'Duse Mohamed Refused Landing on the Gold Coast' that Duse had 'many friends' on the Gold Coast.

159 'Leaves from an Active Life', the *Comet*, 1937–8; cf. above, n. 126. The *Comet*'s publicity slogan was

'Best and only Penny Weekly News Magazine in the British Empire'.

Chapter 12

1 D. Kimble, *History of Ghana*, p. 375.
2 'War!', *African Times and Orient Review*, 4 August 1914, pp. 449f. Cf. also C. Hayford to J. E. Bruce, 7 April 1915: 'I have been anxious to know the exact attitude of America over a war which I am sure is going to alter people's point of view upon many matters. I am sure if we live long enough we shall see changes that will astound us. Out here we are going steadily to work to make good use of the opportunity, and I am quite certain that there is going to be a tremendous advance.' On the later impact of the War cf. also *African Times and Orient Review*, March 1917, pp. 45f.: 'We hope that we shall not be misunderstood when we say that a Franco-British success will mean a greater freedom of the peoples we represent than they have previously experienced. . . . Here again, we are forced to observe that the once despised black man is coming to the front in the battle for freedom, and the freedom which he helps to win for the white man, must also be meted out to him when the day of reckoning arrives. . . . In helping the British Empire and the French Republic in the hour of need you are helping yourselves to a freedom which cannot be denied to you.'
3 W. E. B. Du Bois, 'The African Roots of War', *Atlantic Monthly*, May 1915, pp. 707–14.
4 Ibid., pp. 711f.: 'In addition to these national war-engendering jealousies there is a more subtle movement arising from the attempt to unite labor and capital in a world-wide free-booting. Democracy in economic organization, while acknowledged an ideal, is to-day working itself out by admitting to a share in the spoils of capital only the aristocracy of labor – the more intelligent and shrewder and cannier workingmen. The ignorant, unskilled, and restless still form a large, threatening, and to a growing extent, revolutionary group in advanced countries.

The resultant jealousies and bitter hatreds tend continually to fester along the color line. We must fight the Chinese, the laborer argues, or the Chinese will take our bread and butter. We must keep Negroes in their places, or Negroes will take our jobs. All over the world leaps to articulate speech and ready action that singular assumption that if white men do not throttle colored men, then China, India, and Africa will do to Europe what Europe has done and seeks to do to them.'
5 Ibid., p. 713.
6 Ibid., p. 713f.
7 C. McKay, *A Long Way from Home* (New York, 1937) pp. 67f.
8 Cf. below, pp. 305f.
9 Cf. above, p. xi, n. 1.
10 Cf. above, p. 176.
11 W. E. B. Du Bois, *The World and Africa* (New York, 1947, second edition 1965) pp. 8–10.
12 Ibid., p. 10.
13 Ibid. This claim was contradicted decades later by Rayford W. Logan, despite all the respect he felt for Du Bois: 'The Historical Aspects of Pan-Africanism', *Pan-Africanism Reconsidered*, ed. American Society of African Culture (Berkeley, Los Angeles, 1962) pp. 41f. Cf. also idem, *The Senate and the Versailles Mandate System* (Washington, 1945); W. R. Louis, 'The United States and the African Peace Settlement of 1919: the Pilgrimage of George Louis Beer', *JAH*, 4, 1963, no. 3, pp. 413–33.
14 Cf. above, pp. 212–15.

15 *The Negro* (New York, 1915; London, 1916); *Black Folk Then and Now* ... (New York, 1939, fourth edition 1945).

16 *Darkwater* (New York, 1920).

17 *Black Reconstruction in America* ... (New York, 1935, third edition 1964); cf. also above, Pt II, ch. 9, n. 36.

18 *Dusk of Dawn: an Essay towards an Autobiography of a Race Concept* (New York, 1940).

19 *In Battle for Peace* (New York, 1952).

20 The militant quarterly *Freedomways*, the editorial committee of which included Du Bois's widow, issued a number in spring 1965 entirely dedicated to Du Bois and arranged a commemorative ceremony in his honour in Harlem. Roy Wilkins, the secretary of the now conservative NAACP, also rendered high praise to Du Bois in the form of a commentary on *The Souls of Black Folk* (reprinted in paperback, Greenwich, Conn., 1961).

21 Du Bois, *The World and Africa*, p. 8.

22 Broadhurst to Du Bois, 4 January 1919, Du Bois papers, Accra.

23 Harris to Du Bois, 7 February 1919, ibid.

24 The signature was omitted in error from the author's microfilm and cannot be verified now, since after Nkrumah's fall Mrs Du Bois was expelled from Ghana and the fate of the Du Bois papers is uncertain.

25 On the beginnings of Diagne's political career cf. now G. Wesley Johnson, 'The Ascendancy of Blaise Diagne and the Beginning of African Politics in Senegal', *Africa*, 36, October 1956, pp. 235–53.

26 *Crisis*, March 1919, p. 215.

27 "Memorandum to M. Diagne and others on a Pan-African Congress to be held in Paris in February 1919', Du Bois papers, Accra; this has hitherto been mentioned only in *Crisis*, March 1919, pp. 224f.

28 Ibid.

29 Ibid: 'Faire une histoire de la Race Noire. Étudier les conditions présentes de la Race. Publier des articles, brochures et un compte-rendu de ce congrès. Encourager le développement de la littérature et l'art parmi les Noirs. Arrangement d'un second Congrès Pan-Africain en 1920.' (The French version of this memorandum is cited here because the microfilm copy of the English version lacks one page.)

30 'Mémoire pour la Réunion préparatoire à l'organisation du Congrès PAN-AFRICAIN pour la protection des Indigènes d'Afrique & les Peuples d'origines Africains', ibid. Only the French version has survived. In the first sentence it is stated: 'Après plusieures réunions des personnes intéressées, il a été décidé ...'; this also gives the composition of the provisional executive committee.

31 C. Fyfe, *History of Sierra Leone*, contains no reference to Fredericks and Mr Fyfe was unable to give me any information about him when I consulted him.

32 'Ce Congrès a un double but: (1e) Nous désirons dans ce moment critique de l'Histoire du Monde, revendiquer une sérieuse considération des Droits de la Race Noire et réclamer la suppression de toutes négociations touchant les Colonies Africaines qui n'envisagent pas les droits et la volonté des Africains eux-mêmes. (2e) De prendre le premier pas vers l'union et l'entente entre des divers groupements des peuples d'origine Africaine disséminés partout, sans diminuer leur loyauté de Français, Anglais, Libériens, Haytiens ou Américains; leur inspirer que, comme Membres d'une race grande et puissante, ils ont une mission particulière sur la terre, qu'ils proposent à l'avenir de travailler en unité pour la défense de leurs droits et le développement de leur génie.' Ibid.

33 Cf. also Du Bois, *Mein Weg...* (Berlin, 1965) p. 314.

34 Idem, *The World and Africa*, p. 10.

35 Ibid.; G. Padmore, *Pan-Africanism ...*, p. 121; H. F. Strauch, *Panafrika ...* (Zurich, 1964) p. 32.

36 Du Bois, *The World and Africa*, loc. cit.

37 *Crisis*, March 1919, pp. 271–4; the following details on p. 271.

38 M. Delafosse, 'Le Congrès Panafriccain', *Afrique Française*, March–April 1919, supplément, p. 53. The representatives of the Bambara, Bobo and Baziri 'n'auraient vraisemblablement pas pris part aux délibérations, non seulement parce qu'ils n'auraient pu le faire qu'avec le concours de multiples interprètes, mais aussi et surtout parce qu'ils se seraient trouvés dans une atmosphère à laquelle rien ne les aurait préparés. Et, s'ils avaient pris part aux délibérations, il est fort possible qu'ils eussent exprimé des opinions étranges manifestant une préoccupation uniquement concentrée vers des petits intérêts locaux et nullement orientée vers l'intérêt commun de la race.'

39 Cf. above, p. 214;

40 The chief sources on the proceedings of the congress are: a report in *Crisis*, March 1919, pp. 271–4, which is said to have been compiled on the basis of reports and 'bulletins' from Du Bois, and the article by Delafosse mentioned above. There is also a document whose nature is not quite clear: it is a typed, apparently literal, version of the papers read and contributions to the discussion by the French-speaking delegates Diagne, Candace, Boisneuf and La Grosillière. This has no heading but bears a handwritten note, perhaps by Du Bois: 'Paris Session, Sept. 4, 1921'. The order of the speakers (those papers read in English by King and a certain Franklin Bouillon are only

referred to in passing) accords with the report in *Crisis*; the sharply critical tone adopted towards Germany and its colonial policy indicates that it may have been compiled shortly after the end of the war. Thus the writer of the note may have erred and this may have been a record of the first session or the first day of the 1919 congress.

41 Du Bois, *The World and Africa*, pp. 11f.; Padmore, *Pan-Africanism*, pp. 124f.; Strauch, *Panafrika*, p. 33.

42 Strauss errs in translating this 'sodass zuletzt Afrika von den Afrikanern selbst regiert wird'.

43 As Strauch, *Panafrika*, maintains.

44 Cf. above, p. 191.

45 *New York Herald*, 24 February 1919 (cited in Du Bois, *The World and Africa*, p. 12); Delafosse, 'Le Congrès Pan-Africain'.

46 *Crisis*, May 1919, p. 9, 'My Mission'.

47 I. Béton to Du Bois, 5 February 1920, Du Bois papers, Accra.

48 *Crisis*, May 1919, pp. 8f. The First Congress had cost a mere 750 dollars.

49 Cf. above, n. 27 to this chapter.

50 Cf. above, n. 30, point 4 in the text. The sentence is somewhat imprecise, so that it is better to quote it here: 'Il est proposé que des séances seront tenues à Londres et à New York en 1919 qui seront affiliées à ce congrès PAN-AFRICAIN et qu'un Secrétariat permanent résultera de ce Congrès, lequel sera chargé d'une réunion des délégués du monde entier pour 1920–1921.' This suggests that the 1919 congress was thought of as just a preliminary to other preliminary conferences in London and New York, prior to a large representative congress in 1920 or 1921.

51 Du Bois to Diagne and Candace, 28 October 1920; Diagne to Du Bois, 19 November 1920; Candace to Du Bois, 9 November 1920; all in the Du Bois papers, Accra.

52 Du Bois, *The World and Africa*, p. 236.
53 C. Hayford to Du Bois, 29 December 1920. Cf. also Hayford's dream of a Pan-African conference on the Gold Coast (above, p. 117). Earlier, at the end of March 1919 Hayford had expressed interest in this in a letter to Du Bois: cf. Hayford to Du Bois, 29 March 1919; both letters are in the Du Bois papers, Accra.
54 Du Bois, *The World and Africa*, loc. cit.
55 Du Bois papers, Accra; the list is undated; since in one report the AME Bishop Cary of Chicago is mentioned as taking part, this seems to relate to 1921.
56 Details of Logan's activities in Paris in his correspondence with Du Bois: Du Bois papers, Accra.
56a E. dos Santos, *Pan-Africanismo*, pp. 121–3, 130–4.
57 Cf. Candace's pamphlet *Le Deuxième Congrès de la Race Noire en 1921*, which appeared as an offprint from the newspaper *Colonies et Marine*, November 1921, pp. 725–41; here on p. 729 are the names of some participants in the discussion. Bellegarde was then Haitian minister in Paris.
58 Du Bois, *The World and Africa*, pp. 236f.
59 MSS. British Empire, p. 22, Anti-Slavery Papers, G. 432. Pan African Congress, Correspondence, Harris to Du Bois, 6 May 1921.
60 Harris to Du Bois, 10 June 1921, ibid.
61 Harris to Norman Leys, 12 October 1921; idem to H. W. Bevingson, Washington, 12 October 1921; idem to Rev. J. R. M. Stephens, Baptist Missionary Society, London, 23 February 1922. Cf. also Harris to Gilbert Murray, 8 October 1923, in response to his inquiry about the third Pan-African Congress: 'I am very doubtful! Du Bois is a queer fish; his anti-British and pro-French sentiment, which he expresses so strongly in public meetings, makes it very difficult for Englishmen to co-operate with him.' Ibid.
62 *Observer*, 28 August 1921; *Sunday Times*, 28 August 1921; *African World*, 3 September 1921; *West Africa*, September 1921; *Gold Coast Independent*, 1 October 1921; *Manchester Guardian*, 30 August 1921 – for the reports. On Alcindor and Archer cf. above, pp. 183, 193.
63 Cf. above, p. 222.
64 Nothing more is known of him.
65 Du Bois, *The World and Africa*, p. 238f.; Padmore, *Pan-Africanism*, pp. 130–32.
66 Cf. above, Pt I, ch. 7, pp. 96ff.
67 This demand was Point 3. Its formulation is so characteristic of Du Bois that it is worth citing in the original: 'Education in self-knowledge, in scientific truth, and in industrial technique, undivorced from the art of beauty.'
68 Cf. above, p. 239.
69 The end of the sentence is somewhat obscure. It would be characteristic of Du Bois if he meant by this a world government.
70 Du Bois, *The World and Africa*, p. 237.
71 *Northern Whig*, 6 September 1921.
72 *Challenge*, London, 2 September 1921.
73 Du Bois, *The World and Africa*, p. 236.
74 F. Challaye, 'Le Congrès Pan-Africain', *Les Cahiers*, pp. 420–24, especially p. 422; *Le Petit Parisien*, 6 September 1921; on the debate in Brussels cf. also E. dos Santos, *Pan-Africanismo*, pp. 87–9.
75 According to E. dos Santos, *Pan-Africanismo*, p. 90, who used sources in Portuguese, particularly an article in *Correio d'Africa*, Lisbon, 22 September 1921 on the Congress.
76 See n. 74.
77 'hommes de couleur'; this presumably refers only to Africans and Afro-Americans, not to Asians.

78 *Le Temps*, 6 September 1921: 'On a fait l'appel à notre solidarité pendant la guerre et elle n'a jamais fait défaut. N'avons-nous pas le droit de la demander à notre tour pendant la paix?' A full report of the first day of the conference is also given in *Le Figaro*, 5 September 1921.

79 *Le Temps*, ibid.: '. . . qui est peut-être un noir, a dit l'un d'entre eux, puisque la mort qui a frappé les défenseurs de la France ne distinguait pas entre les couleurs des combattants.'

80 *Le Temps*, ibid. These statements corresponded to the London resolution. Cf. above, p. 244.

81 F. Challaye, 'Le Congrès Pan-Africain', p. 422; *Le Temps*, ibid. Candace was, however, mistaken, for the Labour party never belonged to the Third (Communist) International; on the debate also E. dos Saulos, *Pan-Africanismo*, pp. 87–9: the author explicitly contradicts the 'traditional version' of how the Lisbon session came about by reconstructing 'the true facts'; ibid., pp. 98–101.

82 The complete text of the petition is in the Du Bois papers, an extract of which can be found in Du Bois, *The World and Africa*, p. 240; it was also published by the League of Nations: Mandates. *Second Pan-African Congress. August–September 1921.*

83 Cf. also above, p. 244.

84 Cf. above, n. 56 (p. 740 in the text cited).

85 Cf. above, p. 38; there is as yet no detailed account of the Société des Amis des Noirs. For the time being see P. Grunebaum-Ballin, *Henri Grégoire, l'ami des hommes de toutes les couleurs* (Paris, 1948). In the society as later reconstituted Victor Schoelcher, the protagonist of slave emancipation in 1848, was a member of the executive (1828): cf. V. Schoelcher, *Homme d'État et Écrivain Fran-*

çais . . ., *Correspondance inédite*, Pt 2 (Paris, 1935) p. 14.

86 E. dos Santos, *Pan-Africanismo*, p. 97.

87 Béton to Du Bois, 4 February 1922; Candace to Béton, 18 January 1922; Du Bois to Béton, 4 March 1922; all in Du Bois papers, Accra.

88 Béton to Du Bois, 5 April 1922, ibid.

89 Béton to Du Bois, 29 May 1922, ibid.

90 Du Bois to Béton, 15 June 1922, ibid.

91 Béton to Du Bois, 1 July 1922, ibid.

92 Béton to Mrs Addie W. Hunton, 2 August 1922, ibid.

93 E. dos Santos, *Pan-Africanismo*, p. 100.

94 'Third Pan-African Congress', *West Africa*, 29 September 1923, p. 1.

95 *Crisis*, vol. 26, 1923, p. 249.

96 Du Bois, *The World and Africa*, p. 241; apparently he had in mind the participants in the Lisbon meeting; this, however, seems hardly plausible in the light of new information on the session: see below, p. 254.

97 A newspaper extract, unidentified and undated, in the Du Bois papers which seems to come either from *Challenge* or from the *African World* and definitely deals with the 1923 London meeting.

98 Cf. above, p. 194.

99 On this and what follows cf. the long report in *West Africa*, 10 November 1923, pp. 1352, 1367f.

100 Lady Lugard, *A Tropical Dependency* . . . (London, 1905).

101 The most impressive study in modern times of the reality and psychology of ghetto life is K. B. Clark, *Dark Ghetto: Dilemmas of Social Power* (New York, Evanston, London, 1965).

102 *West Africa*, 29 September 1923; cf. also above, pp. 171f.

103 'The wrong way of pronouncing the name of a town, for instance, is enough to dispel the interest of those who come from that particular town.' Ibid.

104 *West Africa*, 10 November 1923, p. 1352.
105 Ibid.
106 Padmore, *Pan-Africanism*, p. 141; the same error in Strauch, *Panafrika*, p. 36; moreover, the third Pan-African Congress did not take place in summer, as Padmore states here.
107 And not in Paris, as Strauch, *Panafrika*, p. 35, maintains.
108 'Pan-Africa in Portugal', *Crisis*, February 1924, p. 170.
109 E. dos Santos, *Pan-Africanismo*, p. 99f.
110 Ibid., p. 100f.
111 For details cf. below, pp. 258–62.
112 Cf. above, p. 251.
113 Du Bois, *The World and Africa*, p. 242.
114 Du Bois to Mrs Hunton, 12 April 1926; 'Memorandum to Mrs Hunton with regard to the fourth Pan-African Congress', Du Bois papers, Accra.
115 'The Pan-African Congress: the Story of a Growing Movement'. *Crisis*, October 1972, pp. 263f.
116 Du Bois, *The World and Africa*, p. 243. An imposing list of names with the note '4th Pan-African Congress' in the Du Bois papers, Accra, mentions sixty-four Africans from the Gold Coast, Nigeria and Sierra Leone as well as from London, but they were probably only invited to the Congress in New York. If they actually appeared, Africa will not have been represented 'sparsely' (Du Bois) but on quite a respectable scale. The list nevertheless gives an idea of the personal contacts which Du Bois apparently then possessed. Some Africans (W. F. Hutchinson, Peter Thomas) had participated in previous Pan-African meetings; others had become prominent in other connections (Francis T. Dove, Freetown; C. Hayford; Sekyi; Dr O. Sapara, Lagos; Dr A. Savage, Lagos; J. P. Brown, Cape Coast);

while others again were politically prominent either then or later (Nana Ofori Atta and Prempeh, the Kumasihene).
117 Cf. below, p. 326.
118 Du Bois, *The World and Africa*, p. 243.
119 Du Bois says he first became racially conscious when he was rejected by a White girl in his neighbourhood. *The Souls of Black Folk* (Chicago, 1903) p. 16. Cf. also *Dusk of Dawn* (New York, 1940) p. 24.
120 Cf. above, pp. 20, 245.
121 'African Roots of War', *Atlantic Monthly*, May 1915, p. 713: 'We must train native races in modern civilization. This can be done. Modern methods of educating children, honestly and effectively applied, would make modern, civilized nations out of the vast majority of human beings on earth to-day. This we have seldom tried.'
122 *Horizon*, January 1908, pp. 5f.
123 *Crisis*, April 1924, pp. 248–51; Du Bois, *Dusk of Dawn*, pp. 122–5; cf. also the brilliant critical analysis by H. R. Isaacs, *The New World of Negro Americans . . .* (New York, 1964) pp. 205–20.
124 Du Bois, *Dusk of Dawn*, pp. 116f.: 'As I face Africa, I ask myself: what is it between us that constitutes a tie that I can feel better than I can explain? Africa is of course my fatherland. Yet neither my father nor my father's father ever saw Africa or knew its meaning or cared overmuch for it. My mother's folk were closer and yet their direct connection, in culture and race, became tenuous; still, my tie to Africa is strong. On this vast continent were born and lived a large portion of my direct ancestors going back a thousand years and more. The mark of their heritage is upon me in color and hair.'
125 *Crisis*, April 1924, p. 274.
126 On his visit to Liberia cf. *Crisis*,

April 1924, p. 250: 'We climbed the upright shore to a senator's home and received his kindly hospitality – curious blend of feudal lord and modern farmer – sandwiches, cake and champagne. Again we glided up the drowsy river – five, ten, twenty miles and came to our hostess. A mansion of five generations with a compound of endless native servants and cows under the palm thatches. . . . We sat at a long broad table and ate duck, chicken, beef, rice, plantain and collards, cake, tea, water and Madeira wine.'

127 Cf. above, pp. 125f.
128 Du Bois, *Dusk of Dawn*, pp. 126f.
129 Ibid.: 'And now a word about the African himself – about this primitive black man: I began to notice a truth as I entered southern France. I formulated it in Portugal: I knew it as a great truth one Sunday in Liberia. And the Great Truth was this: efficiency and happiness do not go together in modern culture. Going south from London, as the world darkens it gets happier. Portugal is deliciously dark. . . . But if this of Portugal, what of Africa? Here darkness descends and rests on lovely skins until brown seems luscious and natural. . . . And laziness, divine, eternal languor is right and good and true.' On the other hand in his official report to the State Department Du Bois maintained the opposite, defending the Liberians against the charge of being lazy: 'Your Envoy believes such persons deceived. He takes no stock in tales of incurable Liberian laziness and absolute unreliability. No people who could build and maintain this Republic for a century can be wholly lazy and unreliable. That they have lazy citizens and a conservativism and lethargy often annoying is true, but one cannot indict a whole people because of its

worst representatives.' Du Bois to Secretary of State, 24 March 1924, Department of State, Decimal File 882.00/739. On praise for laziness, cf. Du Bois's contribution to A. Locke (ed.), *The New Negro* . . . (New York, 1927) p. 409.
130 Cf. below, p. 309.
131 *Crisis*, December 1923, pp. 57f.

Chapter 13

1 Especially E. D. Cronon, *Black Moses: the Story of Marcus Garvey and the Universal Negro Improvement Association* (Madison, 1955); this may now be supplemented by Amy Jacques Garvey, *Garvey and Garveyism* (Kingston, Jamaica, 1963). These works modify the distorted pictures of Garvey as a ridiculous visionary, which has been given by Padmore and by Gunnar Myrdal, *An American Dilemma: the Negro Problem and Modern Democracy*, 2 volumes (New York, London, 1944, twentieth impression 1964). The discovery of the Garvey papers in Harlem some time ago will hopefully contribute to a more sober assessment of Garvey's position.
2 Cf. H. F. Strauch, *Panafrika* . . . (Zurich, 1964), pp. 22, 366, n. 4; P. Decraene, *Le Panafricanisme* . . . (Paris, 1959, third edition 1964) p. 15; G. Padmore, *Pan-Africanism* . . ., pp. 87ff.
3 Cf. above, p. 9; biographical details based mainly on Cronon.
4 Cf. above, Pt II, ch. 11, n. 154. The last sentence runs: 'As one who knows the people well, I make no apology for prophesying that there will soon be a turning point in the history of the West Indies; and that the people who inhabit that portion of the Western Hemisphere will be the instruments of uniting a scattered race who, before the close of many centuries, will found an Empire on which the sun shall shine as

ceaselessly as it shines on the Empire of the North to-day. This may be regarded as a dream, but I would point my critical friends to history and its lessons. Would Caesar have believed that the country he was invading in 55 B.C. would be the seat of the greatest Empire of the world? Had it been suggested to him would he not have laughed at it as a huge joke? Yet it has come true. England is the seat of the greatest Empire of the World, and its king is above the rest of monarchs in power and dominion. Laugh then as you may, at what I have been bold enough to prophesy, but as surely as there is an evolution in natural growth of man and nations, so surely will there be a change in the history of these subjected regions.'

5 M. Garvey, *Philosophy and Opinions*, ed. A. J. Garvey, 2 volumes (New York, 1923–6) vol. I, p. 37. New edition (London, 1967) ed. E. Essien-Udom.

6 Ibid., vol. II, pp. 37f.

7 Cf. also above, p. 221.

8 On this process see now G. Osofsky, *Harlem: the Making of a Negro Ghetto, New York, 1890–1930* (New York, 1966). The same author has contributed a sketch with the same title to J. H. Clarke (ed.), *Harlem: a Community in Transition* (New York, 1964) pp. 16–25.

9 Schomburg Collection, New York, J. E. Bruce Collection, 14–5. Handwritten and typed text, without title or date, probably published (perhaps in Garvey's *Negro World*?).

10 Cf. above, p. 225.

11 *African Times and Orient Review. Christmas Annual* (London, 1912) pp. 26–30.

12 Handwritten note, 30 April 1915, without address or signature; the letter-heading reads 'UNIA, Jamaica Division'.

13 Bruce Collection, ibid.

14 Cf. above, p. 218.

15 Cf. above, p. 113; Ferris also wrote for the *African Times and Orient Review*, April 1914, pp. 77f.

16 Cf. above, p. 227; Duse and Bruce were in correspondence: cf, Bruce Collection, 1731, B.L. 4a–63. Duse to Bruce, undated: 1814, Duse to Bruce, 12 September 1919.

17 Incredible as it may seem, not one major library contains copies of *Negro World*. A set exists in the Institute of Jamaica, Kingston, but this is for technical reasons unable to supply a microfilm copy. (Information from the Schomburg Collection, November 1966.)

18 Bruce Collection, 1843, Br. 372, Akinbami Agbebi Jr to Bruce, Lagos, 8 April 1920; on Agbebi Senior cf. above, pp. 154, 180, 217.

19 Cf. above, pp. 132f.

20 Myrdal, *American Dilemma*, p. 747. For a lively and ironical description of this spectacle, cf. R. Ottley, *New World a-Coming: inside Black America* (Boston, 1943) p. 76, cited in Padmore, *Pan-Africanism*, pp. 94f.

21 Padmore, ibid., p. 92. Garvey (or in Padmore's account he himself) also erred in that Queen Victoria did not succeed to the throne until three years after the first phase of the emancipation had come into effect. This lapse is, however, instructive in that it testifies to the almost legendary authority which Queen Victoria enjoyed among her coloured subjects, who attributed to her responsibility for this measure.

22 Even today simple stickers can be bought in Harlem in the colours of the UNIA.

23 Cronon, *Black Moses*, p. 65.

24 *African World*, 31 August 1921, Supplement, pp. xviii–xxi: 'The Mayor of Monrovia's Speech. Sanest Utterance at the Second International Negro Convention. Marcus Garvey attacks the Pan-African Congress.' On pp. xviii f. is the text

25 Cf. above, p. 21f.

26 Cf. also L. E. Lomax, *The Negro Revolt* (New York, 1962) pp. 43f.

27 Cf. below, pp. 271f.

28 Cf. above, pp. 122–8.

29 Perhaps identical with Manuel Garcia, who a few years earlier had written an article entitled 'The Truth about Cuba' in the *African Times and Orient Review*, September 1912, p. 105, in which he argued that the unrest in Cuba since the American occupation was due to the racial discrimination which the Americans had introduced.

30 Cronon, *Black Moses*, p. 124.

31 Cf. above, p. 238.

32 Cronon, ibid., pp. 127f.

33 Duse to Sekyi, 19 August 1922. Sekyi Papers, Cape Coast, National Archives; I am indebted to Samuel Rohdie for showing me this document.

34 Cf. above, n. 5.

35 Cronon, ibid., p. 147.

36 P. Garigue, 'The West African Students' Union: a Study in Culture Contact', *Africa*, 23 January 1953, pp. 55–69; the reference to Garvey is on p. 58 (as Dr Garvey, a title which he assumed without any justification during his second visit to London).

37 Cf. above, p. 236.

38 Cronon, ibid., p. 148.

39 Cf. above, p. 269. An impressive photograph of the event is in A. J. Garvey, *Garvey and Garveyism*.

40 Cf. above, p. 178.

41 This is clear from the only study made of a large city, Chicago: cf. H. R. Cayton and St Clair Drake, *Black Metropolis* (New York, 1945) pp. 751f.; the best example of the left wing going over to the communists is Richard Moore, and to a certain extent Padmore too. On Moore cf. above, p. 225, and below, pp. 327, 329.

42 As yet there is no account of this influence. It would be necessary to make a number of local and regional studies before tackling such a task.

43 Cf. above, p. 226.

44 Cf. above, p. 271.

45 Cf. above, n. 33 to this chapter.

46 On Agbebi cf. G. Shepperson, 'Notes on Negro American Influences . . .', *JAH*, 1, no. 2, pp. 309f.; on Hayford, cf. below, p. 276.

47 Akinbami Agbebi Jr to Bruce, Lagos, 8 April 1920. Bruce Collection, 1843, Br. 372. V. B. Thompson, *Africa and Unity*, p. 37, quoting a long article from *Lagos Weekly Record*, 27 November 1920; among the main speakers during the first public meeting of the newly founded UNIA branch were the Revs. W. B. Euba and S. M. Abiodun.

48 Cf. above, Pt II, ch. 12, n. 2. The tone of Hayford's letter is so natural and cordial that they must have been in contact earlier. Perhaps this contact was established through the medium of the *African Times and Orient Review*.

49 Bruce Collection, B.M.S. 11–22, 1873, newspaper cutting, undated (early 1920); it is striking that despite his good relations with Hayford Bruce wrongly reproduced the name of his organization, calling it the 'Native African Congress'.

50 On Du Bois's first trip to Africa cf. above, pp. 260–1.

51 Bruce Collection, B.L. 4–33, J. E. Bruce to Mrs Florence Bruce (his wife), 2 January 1924. She was asked to send the following letter to Garvey (which she presumably did):

'Dear chief,

If you think it worth while (I think it is), you may cable in my name the following to Hayford at once. "Du Bois – Crisis – on trip to Africa, bent on mischief due to failure of his Pan-African

(following the preceding note)

of the resolution, which is too long to be cited here. Cf. also A. J. Garvey, *Garvey and Garveyism*, p. 67.

Congress scheme. Financed by Joel Spingarn, a Jew, and other interests (white) inimical to African independence. Watch him. Letter follows. Make no committals."

Yours   Bruce Grit.'

The letter to his wife ran: 'Tell Mr G[arvey] to send this Cable to Hayford. I will tell Hayford what to do to break the force . . .' (the rest is illegible).

52 Cf. above, n. 49: 'The Native African Congress is a movement similar in character to that of the Universal Negro Improvement Association.'

53 Jacob Akinpelu Obisesan Diary, 1920–1960, Ibadan University Library. I was kindly permitted to consult this document by Dr James B. Webster, History Department, Ibadan University.

54 Duse visited West Africa for the first time in 1920, before he went to live for a time in the USA.

55 Obisesan Diary, ibid.

56 Ibid., entry for 23 December 1920.

57 Idib., entries for 14 February, 15 August, 2 November 1921.

58 Ibid., entry for 1 December 1921.

59 Ibid., entry for 3 March 1922.

60 Ibid., entries for 12 and 14 April 1922; cf. also Horton's view, above, p. 68.

61 Ibid., entry for 12 April 1922. One year earlier he had said (19 August 1921): 'Garveyism one is glad to note is also gaining ground everywhere in the world. No one can predict what will be the fate of the black race in the near future. Mr Marcus Garvey is trying to build a Negro Empire. The possibility or impossibility of which I am not concerned to say, but the downtrodden and oppressed Black knows that His redeemer liveth.'

62 Ibid., entry for 29 June 1922.

63 It is interesting to note that Obisesan read Booker T. Washington and Thomas Paine (entries for 3 April and 10 July 1923). On 20 December 1923 he mentions a meeting of the Blyden Brotherhood, to which however only five pilgrims turned up. On 20 September 1927 he registered Aggrey's death in New York and noted that an African paper had compared Aggrey to Aristotle.

64 V. C. Ikeotuonye, *Zik of New Africa* (London, Geneva, 1961) p. 28.

65 J. Cary, *The Case for African Freedom* (London 1941, second edition 1944) pp. 19ff.: 'Somewhere down the Niger valley, 20 years ago, a horse boy was arrested by the local Emir, and sent to my camp for talking sedition. He had been telling the local pagans, wild inlanders, that a black king was coming, with a great iron ship full of black soldiers, to drive all the whites out of Africa. The Emir suggested that he ought to be flogged and deported. My political agent, Musa, an old Hausa from the North, said that the village markets were full of this talk and asked if there were any truth in it. I told him that it was nonsense. But he looked unconvinced. . . . The notion of a ship with black officers and crew, coming across the ocean, moved him to some deep and private excitement. He was unwilling to believe that such a ship did not exist. . . . It was not for many years afterwards that I heard of the Black Star Steamship Company and its founder, Marcus Garvey, provisional President of Africa. . . . Yet Garvey's manifesto went all through Africa. I cannot be sure, of course, that the story which came to my remote district, four days' journey from a telegraph office and eight from a railway, was about Garvey and his ship. I thought it nonsense, asked for no particulars, and don't remember its date.'

66 P. Walshe, 'African National Con-

gress', ch. V, p. 22, citing *Christian Express*, May–June 1921. E. W. Smith, *Aggrey of Africa: a Study in Black and White* (London, 1929) p. 122, says the same and generalizes it to all South and West Africa.

67 Walshe, ibid.

68 K. Nkrumah, *Ghana: the Autobiography* . . . , p. 37.

69 It is therefore a mistake to assume that the Black Star over Independence Arch in Accra was a Soviet one – as was done by a German reviewer of Nkrumah's book: H. Lehmann, 'Literaturbericht. Entwicklungsländer, besonders Afrika', *Geschichte in Wissenschaft und Unterricht*, 9/1964, p. 585.

70 Cf. above, pp. 28 and Pt I, ch. 6, pp. 77ff.

71 Cf. above, pp. 96ff.

72 Cf. above, n. 63. It would be worth compiling these hyperbolic utterances by Africans and Afro-Americans about their 'great men'. This tradition may account for the cult of the individual which is so widespread in modern Africa. Cf. F. E. Frazier, *Black Bourgeoisie* (Glencoe-Illinois, 1957) pp. 173ff., especially p. 180: 'Sometimes historical figures whose features or dark complexions can be made the basis of a claim that they are of Negroid ancestry are presented as evidence of the importance of the Negro in history.' What Frazier says of the living is true also of the dead: 'petty achievements of living Negroes . . . are reported as if they were of great importance'. Cf. also p. 193, where he speaks of 'gross exaggeration of achievement of Negroes in Europe'.

73 Frazier, ibid., p. 173. For a detailed analysis of the phenomenon cf. 'The World of Make-Believe', pp. 153ff., with a study of 'Negro business men' in the early twentieth century.

74 Cf. above, pp. 114, 122f., 93.

75 A. P. Randolph, publisher of the socialist periodical *Crusader*: 'People

are now fighting for the erection of democracies, not of empires' (cited from Cronon, *Black Moses*, p. 107). For an acute and perceptive critique of this side of Garveyism cf. the pamphlet of a Basuto who was presumably then a student in the USA, M. Mokete Manoedi, *Garvey and Africa* (New York) n.d. [approx. 1924], p. 4: 'My people are not favorably impressed either with the unmitigated presumption of this man in electing himself Provisional-President of a Republic Knighting Citizens! Only Kings and Emperors confer titles upon subjects. A Republic is supposed to rest upon a citizenship-equality. But I suppose this small matter of political civics has no weight with the self-styled saviour of the African people.'

76 G. Shepperson and T. Price, *Independent African* . . . (Edinburgh, 1958, second edition 1963) p. 184.

77 E. W. Smith, *Aggrey of Africa* (London, 1929, fifth edition 1930).

78 A. J. Garvey, ibid., pp. 92ff.; according to her Garvey responded to critics in the Klu Klux Klan by explaining that his programme did not cater for a mass emigration to Africa but for 'select colonization' – which was no less problematical. In 1924 Garvey thought that with foreign aid it would be possible to bring all the volunteers to Africa within fifty years: *Philosophy and Opinions* (New York, 1926, second edition London, 1967) vol. II, p. 122.

79 Ibid., pp. 5, 8f., where it is stated that Negroes could only assert their right to equality 'when of our own initiative we strike out to build industries, governments, and ultimately empires . . .'. On p. 13: 'The world does not count races and nations that have nothing.' For other quotations which show Garvey's use of the term 'Empire', cf.

ibid., vol. I, pp. 34, 70; vol. II, pp. 5, 10, 24, 34, 106.

80 First in J. A. Rogers, *The World's Great Men of Color* . . . (New York, 1947) vol. II, p. 602; then in Padmore, *Pan-Africanism*, p. 97; and frequently quoted since.

81 *The Black Man*, I, no. 10, October 1935, p. 1.

82 Ibid., no. 8, July 1935, p. 9.

83 Thus he was wholly in favour of capitalist production (a legacy of B. T. Washington) and against communism; on the other hand he regretted the death of Lenin (Cronon, *Black Moses*, p. 197). His reputation as a 'Black man with red ideas' (cf. above, p. 246) was probably not unjustified in view of his sincere commitment to the cause of the masses of Black people.

84 Garvey, *Philosophy and Opinions*, vol. I, pp. 11, 19.

85 Ibid., vol. I, pp. 71f.

86 Cf. above, pp. 258–62.

87 Garvey, *Philosophy*, vol. I, p. 11.

88 Cf. above, p. 279.

89 Garvey, ibid., vol. I, p. 12: 'We are not a race of Haters, but Lovers of humanity's cause.' Ibid., vol. II, p. 98: 'Not Preaching Hate'.

Chapter 14

1 Cf. below, pp. 305–21.

2 Cf. below, pp. 322–39.

3 Cf. below, pp. 340–62, 385–408.

4 Cf. above, pp. 340–62. For more detailed accounts, cf. E. Roux, *Time Longer than Rope* . . . (Madison, 1948, second edition London, 1964); M. Benson, *South Africa* . . . (Harmondsworth, 1966); P. Walshe, 'South African National Congress' (Ph.D. thesis, Oxford, 1967). On the general historical background, cf. the best general history of South Africa: C. W. de Kiewiet, *A History of South Africa: Social and Economic* (London, 1941, second edition 1964).

5 There is as yet no monograph devoted to this theme. On Kadalie and the ICU cf. for the time being Roux, ibid., pp. 153–97; Benson, ibid., pp. 45–9, 54f.; Padmore, *Pan-Africanism*, pp. 348–52.

6 This has hitherto been done only rarely; cf. above, Introduction, p. xiii, n. 15.

7 The most detailed account of the National Congress hitherto is in D. Kimble, *History of Ghana* . . ., vol. I, pp. 374–403; a biography of Hayford would be welcome.

8 Cf. above, pp. 75.

9 Cf. above, pp. 73f., 117–20, 202–7.

10 Cf. above, pp. 223f.

11 Cf. above, p. 75.

12 Kimble, *History of Ghana*, vol. I, pp. 375ff.

13 Ibid., p. 379. The text of the resolution and related correspondence is in Gold Coast Legislative Council. *Sessional Papers*, no. VII, 1919–20.

14 Kimble, *History of Ghana*, p. 381 ('over 40'). The names of all the participants are in *Sessional Papers*, no. VII. Among those attending from the Gold Coast were: A. B. Quartey-Papafio, Dr C. C. Reindorf, the Rev. Mark C. Hayford, J. Henley Coussey (who in 1949 was chairman of the Coussey Committee, which took the decisive preparatory measures to achieve independence for Ghana), Tim Laing (publisher of the *Eastern Star and Akwapem Chronicle*), J. J. Arkrong (publisher of the *Gold Coast Independent*), the Rev. Osam Pinanko (cf. above, p. 148), and S. R. Wood (Secretary of the ARPS in Axim).

15 *Sessional Papers*, no. VII, which includes the speeches made at the opening session.

16 Ibid.; Kimble, *History of Ghana*, p. 382f.; Campbell was Patriarch of one of the independent Yoruba churches, the West African Episcopalian church, and in 1918 had

expressed nationalistic views; cf. J. G. Campbell, *Some Thoughts on Abeokuta during the Reign of H. H. King Gbadebo the Alake, 1898–1918* (Lagos) n.d. [1918], especially pp. 9f.

17 Text of the resolutions in *Resolutions of the Conference of Africans of British West Africa* ... (London, 1920). A brief summary of them is given in Kimble, *History of Ghana*, vol. I, pp. 383f.

18 Cf. above, p. 69.

19 This was apparently the only indirect reference to similar movements outside West Africa. But the Congress was in contact at least with Du Bois and the Garvey movement, through the intermediacy of Hayford: cf. above, pp. 240f, 275.

20 Text of the petition in *Sessional Papers*, no. VII; now reprinted in G. E. Metcalfe, *Great Britain and Ghana: Documents of Ghana History, 1807–1957*, pp. 583–5.

21 This was a mistake which Africans traditionally made, for the Select Committee could only make recommendations which the government did not have to accept; cf. also above, p. 66.

22 Extracts from Clifford's speech to the Nigerian Legislative Council are now in J. S. Coleman, *Nigeria* pp. 193f., M. Crowder, *The Story of Nigeria* (London, 1962) p. 227f. For an immediate critical response to Clifford see the *Gold Coast Independent*, 29 January 1921.

23 Legislative Council *Debates*, Session 1919–1920. Brown, 30 December 1920, pp. 367ff.; in the debate Ofori Atta and Dr Quartey-Papafio also spoke against the Congress, whereas C. Hayford was unable to defend his point of view since he was absent in London.

24 On Macaulay's origins cf. above, p. 56.

25 On developments in Nigeria there is already extensive literature. The best introduction is Crowther, *Story*, which has an excellent bibliography; also Coleman, *Nigeria*; R. L. Sklar, *Nigerian Political Parties: Power in an Emergent African Nation* (Princeton, 1963) especially ch. II, 'Nationalism and the Roots of Partisanship in Southern Nigeria', pp. 41–86. The Nigerian Civil War has provoked a flood of literature on Nigeria impossible to cover here.

26 For details cf. Kimble, *History of Ghana*, vol. I, pp. 441–8; also M. Wright, *The Gold Coast Legislative Council* (London, 1947).

27 Cf. above, p. 148.

28 J. Jones, *Education in Africa: a Study of West, South and Equatorial Africa* ... (New York, 1922).

29 Kimble, *History of Ghana*, vol. I, p. 113. For views about the need for education to be provided by Achimota, cf. the article by its first rector, the Rev. A. G. Fraser, 'Denationalisation', *Gold Coast Review*, I, no. 1, June–December 1925, pp. 71–5; for an earlier account. G. Kingsley Williams, *Achimota: the Early Years, 1924–1948* (London, Accra, Ikeja, 1962). For a more recent and detailed analysis and description of the curriculum, cf. H. N. Weiler, *Koloniale Erziehung und afrikanische Umwelt. Zur erziehungspolitischen Diskussion in der britischen Kolonialverwaltung seit 1920* (Freiburg, 1966) pp. 45–88. For the origins of the college from the vantage-point of one of the first students there, cf. K. Nkrumah, *Ghana: the Autobiography* ... (Edinburgh etc., 1957) pp. 12–16; for a modern critical analysis of the educational theories behind the venture, cf. P. J. Foster, *Education and Social Change in Ghana* (London, 1965) pp. 161–5.

30 On Achimota cf. also Kimble, *History of Ghana*, pp. 114–17; E. W. Smith, *Aggrey of Africa* ..., ch. XIV, 'The Genesis of Achimota'.

31 On this conflict see especially Kimble, *History of Ghana*, pp. 389–396.
32 Cf. below, p. 298.
33 Cf. above, pp. 235, 243.
34 C. Hayford, in a speech at the Native Club, Accra, on 15 March 1923; cf. *Gold Coast Independent*, 24 March 1923.
35 Cf. the similar views expressed by Sylvester Williams and Duse, above, pp. 178 (and n. 19), 223.
36 Ibid.
37 C. Hayford's speeches at the Congress and some other addresses have been collected and published by M. J. Sampson, *West African Leadership* (Bristol, 1951); the speech at Freetown is in ibid., pp. 67–76; it was previously published in the *Gold Coast Independent*, 24 February 1923.
38 *Gold Coast Independent*, 3 February 1923.
39 Cf. above, p. 288.
40 'The advance of science has brought about a contraction of our globe, which compels contact and interdependence among peoples, creeds and races. So strong is the impact that you cannot escape it. As a congress therefore, we cannot be indifferent to world problems which affect us more nearly than we have yet realised. The African, for one thing, is called upon for his contribution to the maintenance of the conditions of modern life. . . . There is no reason why we, as Africans, should not also harness the discoveries of science to our everyday need and make them productive of wealth and prosperity within our borders. . . .' *West Africa*, 6 March 1923, p. 225; in Sampson, *West African Leadership*, p. 78f.
41 Ibid: 'We, as Africans, want to reach the kernel and will not be satisfied with the husks. If the civilisation which we have imbibed leaves us without backbone and makes us incapable of helping our-

selves economically, politically, educationally, and religiously, we must be prepared to shed that civilisation'.
42 Cf. above, p. 287.
43 *Gold Coast Independent*, 29 January 1923; Sampson, *West African Leadership*, p. 75.
44 Ibid.: 'The African Progress Union forms a link in the heart of the Empire between the African at home and the African abroad. As such, it deserves every encouragement and support.'
45 Cf. above, pp. 240f, 275.
46 Cf. above, n. 40.
47 Sampson, *West African Leadership*, p. 87.
48 Ibid., pp. 87f.
49 Cf. above, pp. 118.
50 Sampson, *West African Leadership*, pp. 88–90.
51 *West African Times*, 11 August 1931.
52 Ibid., 31 August 1931. Among the leading personalities named were Charles A. Taylor (publisher of the periodical *The Nationalist*), E. Lloyd Henry, C. Gumbs, G. S. Franklin, W. A. Hyam, G. F. Hoyte, L. E. Simpson, Clement Payne and J. Holder. A similar group appeared in British Guiana, called the Negro Progress Convention, led by H. A. Britton and C. F. Fredericks, who sought to establish contact with the Congress. Further research in the regions concerned would be necessary to elucidate their importance.
53 Ibid.
54 Ibid., 1–2 September 1931. Already on 8 April 1931, under the title 'The National Congress: a Memento' the paper had written 'Casely Hayford is not dead one year, and already the Congress seems to have been forgotten.'
55 On Danquah cf. also above, Pt I, ch. 7, n. 159. On the beginnings of Nkrumah's political career in the Gold Coast, when he was in permanent opposition to Danquah, cf. also D. Austin, 'The Working Com-

mittee of the United Gold Coast Convention', *JAH*, 2, 1961, no. 2, pp. 273–97, and idem, *Politics in Ghana* ... (London 1964, second edition 1966) pp. 53f., 73ff.

56 On this R. L. Sklar, *Nigerian Political Parties*, pp. 48ff.

57 Cf. above, Pt II, ch. 13, n. 36.

58 Cf. above, p. 182.

59 Cf. above, pp. 119, 209.

60 Cf. L. R. Harlan, 'Booker T. Washington and the White Man's Burden', *American Historical Review*, 71, no. 2, January 1966, pp. 441–67.

61 Ibid., p. 463.

62 Founded in 1900 in memory of the young traveller to West Africa and journalist Miss Mary Kingsley.

63 Formed in 1909 by a merger of the Anti-Slavery Society and the Aborigines Protection Society.

64 Cf. above, p. 55.

65 *Journal of the African Society*, 12 July 1913, pp. 425–31; mentioned in Coleman, *Nigeria*, p. 457, n. 6.

66 Undated note by Duse on paper with the letter-heading of the *African Times and Orient Review*; it was probably written in mid-February 1913. Cf. also Anti-Slavery Papers, Rhodes House, G. 431, 'Conference with Africans in England, 1912–1916'.

67 A. B. Merriman to Harris, 28 June 1912, ibid.

68 Cf. above, p. 285, n. 14.

69 Cf. above, pp. 222ff.

70 'Conference with Africans', *Journal of the African Society*, 12 July 1913, p. 425.

71 Hutchinson was a collaborator with Duse.

72 'Conference with Africans', p. 428: 'The African arriving in London felt himself in a great desert, and, as a great many of his countrymen knew, they were often treated in a manner which went to their hearts, as coming from subjects of the same Crown to which they themselves belonged.'

73 Obisesan Diary (see Pt II, ch. 13,

n. 53), entry for 20 July 1920; also Harold Moody had had some difficulty a few years earlier in finding a room; cf. also p. 341 below.

74 Anti-Slavery Papers, G. 431, Colonial Office to Anti-Slavery and Aborigines Protection Society, 9 May 1914.

75 Unsigned duplicated letter on notepaper of the House of Commons to Harcourt, 24 July 1913; Anti-Slavery Papers, G. 431.

76 Ibid., unsigned letter to Harcourt, 14 July 1914, headed 'House of Commons', probably from Wason, the MP.

77 Harcourt to Wason, 20 July 1914, ibid.

78 P. Garigue, 'The West African Students' Union', *Africa*, vol. 23, January 1953, p. 56.

79 Coleman, *Nigeria*, pp. 203f.; the right name seems to be that used by Coleman.

80 *African Times and Orient Review*, February 1917, p. 36; August 1917, p. 36; December 1917, p. 113.

81 Cf. above, p. 294.

82 Cf. above, n. 80.

83 Cf. also above, p. 224.

84 *African Times and Orient Review*, December 1917.

85 Ibid., February 1917.

86 Ibid., December 1917.

87 E. S. Beoku Betts, 'The Negro: Prehistoric and Historic', ibid., August 1917.

88 Cf. above, pp. 96ff.

89 Cf. above, p. 233.

90 Coleman, *Nigeria*, p. 457, n. 6, citing *West Africa*, 25 October 1924.

91 C. F. H. Benjamin, president of the Union for Students of African Descent, to Du Bois, 6 November 1923, Du Bois papers, Accra: 'Its object is simply to foster a spirit of brotherhood among the sons of Africa who happen to be studying in Great Britain.'

92 Cf. above, pp. 183, 192, 193, 243.

93 Coleman, *Nigeria*, p. 202.

94 Cf. above, n. 44.
95 Cf. especially Garigue, 'The WASU'; additional material in the Solanke papers, including an unfortunately incomplete set of the periodical *WASU*; the latter is not available in the British Museum, apart from the series that began in the 1950s. Despite numerous attempts the author was unable to see the documents of the union, which still exists.
96 Garigue, 'The WASU', p. 56.
97 Solanke to Macaulay, 16 March 1925, Macaulay Papers, Ibadan University Library, 'Papers concerning WASU and Ladipo Solanke'.
98 Cf. above, p. 286.
99 Garigue, 'The WASU', p. 56; on p. 57, n. 1, he gives the names of the ten founding members; cf. also below, n. 101.
100 *WASU*, 2, no. 1, January 1933, p. 1.
101 Ibid., p. 18; this would contradict the data given by Garigue, who omits to mention Olatunde Vincent. The complete list in *WASU*, 7, no. 1, May 1940, p. 13, mentions the following in addition to those given by Garigue: H. J. L. Boston (Sierra Leone), Emil Luke, O. E. O. Asafu-Adjaye (Ashanti), C. H. H. Benjamin, Akanni Doherty.
102 *WASU*, January 1929, December 1932, January 1933, April–June 1933, the inside cover of the issues named, which give the past presidents and their deputies. Since African names appear in many variants, it is not certain whether he is identical with the president of the Union for Students of African Descent (see above, n. 91), or one of his relatives; in the former case there must have been a misprint in *WASU*.
103 *WASU*, January 1933, caption to picture facing p. 1.
104 On Robeson cf. the biography written by a (White) friend of the family, M. Seton, *Paul Robeson* (London, 1958).
105 Cf. above, p. 121.
106 *WASU*, 6, no. 1, January 1937, p. 14.
107 Ibid., and 6, no. 3, p. 52.
108 Ibid., p. 43; 7, no. 1, May 1940, pp. 3, 13.
109 *WASU Magazine*, 12, no. 2, March 1946, p. 5 (report for 1944–5).
110 *WASU*, 1, no. 8, January 1929, p. 39; 2, no. 2, April–June 1933, pp. 45f.
111 Cf. above, p. 272.
112 Cf. above, p. 48.
113 *WASU*, I, no. 9, December 1932, pp. 6–11; 2, no. 1 January 1933, which gives the names of members of the local executive; cf. also Garigue, 'The WASU', p. 58.
114 *WASU*, 2, no. 2, April–June 1933, p. 1; 4, no. 4, October 1935, p. 45: 'Those of our American and West Indian brothers who now realise that the salvation of the race lies with the African are watching with solicitation every attempt made by the African towards emancipation.'
115 One of the two speakers at the opening ceremony was another mysterious J. E. Taylor; cf. *WASU*, 2, no. 2, April–June 1933, p. 13.
116 *WASU*, 7, no. 1, May 1940, pp. 6f.
117 *WASU*, 5, no. 1, May 1936, pp. 7f.: 'A List of Important Visitors to the Union and Hostel'.
118 *WASU*, 6, no. 3, Christmas Number 1937, pp. 45f.
119 'Aggrey House and African Hostel. List of Residents . . ., 1933–6.' Solanke Papers, London. Among the West Indian visitors were J. O. Bethune and Thomas Griffith (identical with T. R. Makonnen?).
120 *WASU*, 5, no. 1, May 1936, pp. 2, 6; Christmas Number 1936, p. 53. The same carelessness was shown by several agents of the journal in Africa, who distributed it without settling accounts with the headquarters in London, which caused serious financial problems: ibid.

121 At this time there was a conflict with the Colonial Office about Aggrey House, a student hostel established for African students by the Colonial Office. This led to a split in WASU, all the students from the Gold Coast except one going over to Aggrey House.

122 This list on the basis of a set of *WASU*, unfortunately incomplete, in the author's possession.

123 He wrote about this time a pamphlet with the programmatic title *Towards Nationhood in West Africa* (London, 1928) in which he made reference to Casely Hayford among others (p. 79).

124 Coleman, *Nigeria*, p. 204.

125 A short story written under a pseudonym, 'A Student's Romance', *WASU*, 1, no. 3–4, March–June 1927, pp. 20–28; cf. ibid., p. 29, the poem by J. B. Danquah, 'Achimota'.

126 We may mention here two of Solanke's contributions: 'The Customary Constitution of the Yoruba Commonwealth', ibid., pp. 34–6; 'Yoruba (or Aku) Constitutional Law and its Historical Development', 1, no. 8, December 1932, pp. 21–5; and others too numerous to mention.

127 *WASU*, 4, no. 4, October 1935, p. 49; much more sharply after 1945, by which time WASU had moved further to the left. There was however an early sharp critique of Nkrumah's régime: cf. *West African Student*, May 1957, p. 7.

128 A. Locke, 'Afro-Americans and West Africans: a New Understanding', *WASU*, 1, no. 8, January 1929, pp. 18–24; E. J. Langford Garstin, 'Pitfalls of Civilisation', ibid., 6, no. 3, Christmas 1937, pp. 55–7. *WASU*, 10, no. 1, May 1943, is completely devoted to the WASU conference of 29–30 August 1942 on West African problems.

129 L. Solanke, *United West Africa* [or

Africa] *at the Bar of the Family of Nations* (London, 1927). This is by no means 'unpublished' as Coleman has it (*Nigeria*, p. 205), but is hardly to be found; the author came across a copy in the possession of Mrs Solanke in London. On de Graft-Johnson cf. above, n. 123.

130 *WASU*, 2, no. 1, January 1933, p. 27.

131 *West Africa Times* or *Times of West Africa*, 1932–4.

132 Cf. above, p. 121. It is therefore necessary to avoid drawing hasty conclusions from the passage in *WASU* (4, no. 1, July 1935, p. 3) cited by Garigue ('WASU', p. 61): 'The answer to oppression is not servility, but self-assertion, courage, and determination to win for one's people the same opportunities which the others enjoy, irrespective of the wishes of the overlord. This is precisely what Hitler has done, hence: Hats off to Hitler.'

133 *WASU*, January 1929. It would be worth investigating the use of the swastika by non-fascist African or Afro-American groups. *Crisis* used it in the same way, at least in 1915 and 1921. Before World War I there was a 'Swastika Club' in Kansas, USA, which called for the erection of a monument to honour the composer S. Coleridge-Taylor (prominent participant in the Pan-African Conference of 1900; cf. above, pp. 183, 192); cf. *African Times and Orient Review*, Christmas Annual 1912, p. 3.

134 *WASU*, 2, no. 2, April–June 1933, p. 5.

135 *WASU*, 1, no. 1, 1926, p. 7.

136 *WASU*, 4, no. 4, October 1935, p. 49. Already in March 1934 in the course of a protest meeting against Aggrey House it was said that its tutelage by the Colonial Office would make it impossible to use it 'for any revolutionary propaganda, not even for any ordinary criticism

of the Government measures, if such criticism should become regular, systematic and effective': cf. Macaulay Papers, 'Papers concerning WASU and L. Solanke'.

137 Cf. the text of a resolution adopted at a WASU meeting on 26 November 1938, in Macaulay Papers, at which the principal speaker was the Labour MP Creech-Jones. More than seventy students and other friends of WASU were present. Another public meeting with Labour MPs had taken place already in April 1938; cf. Garigue, 'The WASU', p. 62. The question how far the Africans' suspicions were justified can now be settled since the relevant British Government documents have become available.

138 Cf. below, pp. 384, 393, 400, 417.

Chapter 15

1 L. R. Harlan, 'Booker T. Washington and the White Man's Burden', *American Historical Review*, 71, no. 2, January 1966, p. 464.

2 Cf. above, p. 235.

3 D. A. Vaughan, *Negro Victory: the Life Story of Dr. Harold Moody* (London, 1950), p. 75.

4 Cf. J. Lacouture, *Cinq hommes et la France* (Paris, 1961) pp. 16–24; idem, *Ho Chi-Minh* (Paris, 1967). Ho Chi-Minh came to Paris in 1917 and in 1920 joined the Comité pour la IIIe Internationale; in December of that year, directly after it was founded, he became a member of the French Communist party (PCF). He gave speeches at the Club du Faubourg where in 1928 Garvey also spoke (cf. above, p. 272); so too did Tovalou-Houénou (1924) and Kouyauté (1935); on both cf. below, pp. 307–11.

5 This chapter is based mainly on two as yet unpublished theses: J. S. Spiegler, 'Aspects of Nationalist Thought among French-speaking West Africans, 1921–1939' (Ph.D., Oxford, 1967) (quoted here from the provisional text); J. L. Hymans, 'L'Élaboration de la pensée de Léopold Sédar Senghor: esquisse d'un itinéraire intellectuel' (Paris, 1964). On 'Négritude' cf. R. Bastide, *Les Amériques Noires* . . . (Paris, 1967), the chapter 'Les Chemins de la Négritude', with bibliography. There is also material (consulted by Spiegler and the author) in the Archive of the Ministère des Colonies, Archives Nationales, Section d'Outre-Mer, Rue Oudinot, SLOT-FOM, ser. 5 cart. V.

6 Spiegler, 'Aspects', ch. II.

7 R. Maran, *Batouala: Véritable roman nègre* (Paris, 1921).

8 Spiegler, 'Aspects', ch. III.

9 *Les Continents*, no. 2, cited from Spiegler, ibid., p. 13. The Africans were *sujets*, 'mais de quelle monarchie, s'il vous plaît? Nous autres Africains nous serions les humbles féaux des monarques républicains Loubet, Fallières, Poincaré, Millerand. . . . Vous avez chassé vos rois, mais leurs valets sont venus chez nous singer leurs anciens maîtres.'

10 Ibid., no. 4, cited by Spiegler, p. 23: 'Nous voulons être citoyens d'un pays quelconque. Voilà pourquoi si la France nous rejette, nous exigeons l'autonomie. Si elle nous acceuille, l'assimilation totale et intégrale.'

11 Ibid.

12 Ibid., p. 24: '. . . développer les liens de solidarité et d'universelle fraternité entre tous les membres de la race noire; les regrouper pour la reconstitution de leur terre d'origine: l'Afrique, le plus vieux de tous les continents.'

13 Ibid., p. 30.

14 Ibid., ch. V.

15 In his eagerness to claim too much for his hero Léopold S. Senghor and the Négritude movement, J. Jahn recently was guilty of an important

oversight. The personage referred to by C. McKay (*Banjo* [New York, 1927; Moscow, 1930; Paris, 1931] p. 267; and *A Long Way from Home* [New York, 1937] pp. 277–91) is of course Lamine Senghor, not L. S. Senghor. The older man is not related to the younger; he died in November 1927, the year that *Banjo* was published. The younger Senghor came to France for the first time in 1928. Cf. *A Long Way from Home*, p. 288; J. Jahn, *Geschichte der neoafrikanischen Literatur: eine Einführung* (Düsseldorf, 1966) p. 223.

16 Cf. below, p. 326.

17 Cf. above, pp. 248–50.

18 In the first no. 1 of *La Voix des Nègres*, January 1927 (a second no. 1 appeared on different paper and in another format in March 1927) Lamine Senghor formulated the programme of the CDRN in the following terms:

> À tous nos Frères! À tous les Nègres du Monde! À tous les Humanitaires du Monde! À tous ceux qui s'intéressent à la Race Nègre! . . . . 1. La tâche de combattre avec la dernière énergie la haine de race. 2. Travailler pour l'évolution sociale de la Race Nègre. 3. Refuser de renforcer l'appareil d'oppression dans les colonies dirigé contre la Race Nègre ou contre toute autre race humaine et travailler à briser plutôt cet appareil; 4. Collaboration permanente avec les organisations qui luttent véritablement pour la libération des peuples opprimés et pour la révolution mondiale. Enfin et pour tout: lutter sans merci contre le colonialisme, contre tous les imperialistes du monde, de quelque couleur soient-ils.

19 Cf. the informative long article 'Qu'est-ce que la civilisation?', *La*

Race Nègre, November–December 1927.

20 Ibid.: 'La colonisation c'est la négation du droit des Peuples à disposer d'eux-mêmes. . . .Notre mot d'ordre de combat, c'est vous-mêmes, blancs, qui nous l'avez dicté: "Droit des Peuples à disposer d'eux-mêmes".'

In the previous issue of September 1927 an article signed 'S. R.' entitled 'Le Réveil de la Conscience Nègre', using some arguments from the anglophone tradition, had maintained: 'L'Afrique a ses coutumes et ses traditions séculaires; il a aussi son histoire, sa civilisation, car, tandis que les Gaulois et les Germains n'étaient encore des barbares, resplendissait déjà sur les bords du Nil une belle civilisation qui a laissé des empreintes profondes dans le processus de transformation des sociétés européennes. Dans de pareilles conditions, il est logique, il est légitime pour les nègres de poser la question de leur liberté et de leur indépendance, d'aspirer à une vie nationale propre.' It is not difficult to see in this an example of Garvey's influence; in the same number there appeared a translation of an article devoted to Garvey's fortieth birthday in the *Negro World* of August 1927, entitled 'L'Afrique aux Africains'.

21 *La Race Nègre*, March 1929: 'Vers l'élaboration d'un programme': 'Détruire et reconstruire, élever des institutions nationales sur les ruines de celles imposées par le conquérant, c'est là un programme qui répond aux besoins impérieux de tous les peuples opprimés, notamment les colonisés. Les annamites, les nord-africains et les nègres devraient être d'accord sur ce point essentiel afin de coordiner leurs efforts.'

22 Ibid.: 'Pour réaliser ledit programme à bref délai, les nègres doivent s'entendre, adhérer en

498 Notes to pages 312–313

masses à la Ligue, s'appuyer sur les peuples opprimés qu'ils soient d'Europe, d'Asie ou d'Amérique, sur les travailleurs intellectuels et manuels de France. Le préjugé de race aura vécu le jour où un grand État nègre sera constitué sur des bases modernes; sionisme africain. Les peuples s'aimeront parce qu'ils vivront dans le cadre de la liberté nationale et de l'égalité internationale.'

23 Cited by Hymans, 'L'Élaboration', p. 111: 'Plonger jusqu'aux racines de notre race et bâtir sur notre propre fond, ce n'est pas retourner à l'état sauvage, c'est la culture même.'

24 Cf. above, Pt I, ch. 7, pp. 96ff.

25 *La Race Nègre*, July 1935: 'Nous Voulons': 'Nous voulons retrouver notre indépendance politique et ressusciter, à sa faveur, notre antique civilisation nègre. Le retour aux usages de nos ancêtres, à leurs philosophies, à leurs organisations sociales, est une nécessité vitale. . . . L'apport Nègre, dans la civilisation blanche, depuis la négresse Marie, mère de Jésus, depuis Hérode d'Alexandrie, inventeur de la turbine à vapeur, depuis Moise et les sorciers Nègres étonneraient bien des gens, si on le révélait. Il est légitime de vouloir continuer ces apports à l'humanité en restant nous-mêmes. Notre race est le champion d'un système humain dont on sentira bientôt la nécessité grande. Nous sommes la variété opposée à l'uniformité blanche, qui engendre l'ennui. Nous sommes créateurs de civilisations paysannes et artistiques et non des artisans, qui, abusant des armes qu'ils forgent, courbent au sol et anéantissent spirituellement les campagnes. Et pourquoi aurions-nous le fétichisme de la science des blancs! Ce progrès dont ils sont si fiers, il y a longtemps qu'il est arrêté. . . . Nous voulons un État Nègre unique en-

globant toute l'Afrique noire et les Antilles, et, au sein de cet État, nous ferons de la question des races ce qu'elle était avant: un élément de diversité, d'agréments et de compétition joyeuse et non un prétexte à des antipathies bilieuses. . . .'

26 *La Race Nègre*, January–February 1936, on the protest movement. It mentioned among other organizations the Union des Travailleurs Nègres, which was expressly called 'notre adversaire' and the equally hated Kouyauté, 'dont le rôle a surtout été de réaliser l'entente négro-arabe'.

27 Cf. below, p. 339.

28 For details about Algeria, cf. now W. Ohneck, *Die französische Algerienpolitik von 1919–1939* (Beiträge zur Kolonial- und Überseegeschichte, ed. T. v. Albertini and H. Gollwitzer, vol. 2) (Cologne, Opladen, 1967) pp. 156–85. A certain relaxation benefited the trade unions, but only those of French West Africa (AOF) and the Maghreb. On the AOF cf. E. Ansprenger, *Politik im Schwarzen Afrika: die modernen politischen Bewegungen im Afrika französischer Prägung* (Cologne, Opladen, 1961) pp. 219–26, 410–20. On the Maghreb cf. W. Plum, *Gewerkschaften im Maghreb. UGTT – UMT – UGTA* (Hanover, 1962) pp. 14, 16, 20f., 26.

29 On the post-war period to 1960 cf. Ansprenger, ibid.

30 This is the great merit of Spiegler's thesis.

31 An important source on the recent past and present period is *Présence Africaine*, a periodical appearing in Paris, which to a certain extent is the heir and executor of the movements and groups in the interwar period whose history has been sketched above. In Germany the Négritude movement had a zealous advocate in Janheinz Jahn, who is the author of a vast number of

works (anthologies, translations, bibliographies and articles as well as book-length studies).

32 Rayford W. Logan was an important intermediary in the political sphere, but only within the narrow sector of the Pan-African Association; cf. above, pp. 252, 256.

33 On this and what follows cf. especially J. Hymans, 'L'Élaboration', p. 73.

34 Cf. above, n. 15.

35 Cf. above, Pt II, ch. 12, p. 261

36 A. Locke (ed.), *The New Negro: an Interpretation* (New York, 1927).

37 Hymans, ibid., p. 110.

38 On the history of jazz there is already a considerable literature, but this is only tangential to our theme. On the Blues, cf. J. Jahn, *Neoafrikanische Literatur . . .*, pp. 150–61.

39 Spiegler, 'Aspects', ch. III, pp. 28f.

40 McKay, *A Long Way from Home*, p. 312f. Locke had also studied in Berlin in 1910–11, and like Du Bois had a sentimental affection for Germany. Locke's introductory essay to *The New Negro* was rejected by McKay as 'a remarkable chocolate soufflé of art and politics, with no ingredient of information inside'; ibid., p. 322.

41 For a deliciously ironical account of this literary expedition to Paris cf. McKay, ibid., p. 306.

42 Hymans, 'L'Élaboration', p. 111.

43 Cf. especially L. Frobenius, *Kulturgeschichte Afrikas: Prolegomena zu einer historischen Gestaltenlehre* (n.p., 1933, second edition Zurich, Cologne, 1954). A critical analysis of Frobenius's romantic ideology would certainly be worth undertaking, especially of the link with the Négritude movement.

44 These biographical details I owe to Dr Leslie F. Manigat, at present in Paris; cf. above, Pt I, ch. 2, n. 15.

45 The most recent account of the American occupation of Haiti is

D. G. Munro, *Intervention and Dollar Diplomacy in the Caribbean, 1900–1921* (Princeton, 1964) pp. 326–87; for the impact on Haiti cf. especially J. G. Leyburn, *The Haitian People* (New Haven, 1941, second edition 1966) pp. 99–110.

46 More details in Jahn, *Neoafrikanische Literatur*, pp. 203–5.

47 Cf. especially J. W. Johnson, *Self-determining Haiti . . .* (New York, 1920) which contains a devastating critique of the American occupation. For an evaluation of Johnson's own mission to Haiti, cf. D. Bellegarde, *Un Haitien parle* (Port-au-Prince, 1934) pp. 262–4.

48 Leyburn, *Haitian People*, pp. 131–65. An over-enthusiastic and uncritical account is J. Jahn, *Muntu: Umrisse einer neoafrikanischen Kultur* (Düsseldorf, 1958) pp. 30–64; Jahn makes some questionable assumptions about the existence of a single 'African religiosity', linked to the Voodoo cult.

49 J. Price-Mars, *Ainsi parla l'oncle . . .* (Port-au-Prince, Paris, 1928). Just ten years earlier Price-Mars had criticized the Haitian élite because it denied its African heritage: idem, *La Vocation d'élite* (Port-au-Prince, 1919).

50 Jahn, *Neoafrikanische Literatur*, p. 205.

51 Ibid., p. 203.

52 Cf. now L. F. Manigat, *Haiti of the Sixties . . .* (Washington, 1964).

53 'Au bout de ma quête, je devais trouver Alain Locke et Jean Price-Mars. Et je lus Ainsi parla l'oncle . . . d'un trait comme l'eau de la citerne, au soir, après une longue étape dans le désert.' Cited by P. Decraene, *Le Panafricanisme . . .*, p. 18.

54 According to L. F. Manigat the book is due to appear in Paris shortly.

55 'Dans les heures de graves difficultés, dans les heures de découragement et de doute, il nous suffit de penser

à l'Égypte des Pharaons pour nous convaincre que l'Afrique a joué dans l'élaboration de la civilisation un rôle primordial.' Cited by J. Hymans, 'L'Élaboration', p. 144.

56 Cf. above, pp. 96ff.

57 Cf. above, p. 123. Since Diop knows no English, this was an autonomous development of the initiative taken in the francophone area by Price-Mars.

58 Jahn, *Neoafrikanische Literatur*, p. 222; on the following also pp. 223f.

59 Hymans, ibid., p. 160.

60 Cf. above, pp. 307–13.

61 Cf. below, pp. 322–39.

62 Senghor himself said: 'À la suite des ethnologues nous redécouvrîmes la Négritude.' Cited by Hymans, ibid., p. 135.

63 Ibid., pp. 129f.

64 Cf. Casely Hayford, *Notes on the Truth about the West African Land Question* (London, 1911) pp. 118f.: 'The phenomenon of the educated native and the part he may play in the colonial administration is not confined to British waters. It invades our friends the Germans. It appears that German colonial opinion has a tendency to regard it as being to the interest of German colonial expansion not to encourage the cultivation of knowledge on the part of the Native. It is fair to point out that this tendency is not encouraged by the Kaiser's Government. . . . It is suggested that in German territories no Native has yet shown a capacity for intellectual attainments that would attract the German world. If so, it is a pity. But I should like, all the same to place in the hands of the German Emperor and German pro-Consuls the thought-moving works of the late D. E. W. Blyden. I am sure German psychologists and scientists will appreciate E. W. Blyden. They will recognize in him a kindred soul, and he may help to correct German colonial opinion.'

65 'L'émotion est Nègre, comme la raison hellène; le nègre est la créature la plus énergiquement saisie par l'émotion artistique.' Cited by Hymans, ibid., p. 133.

66 Cf. above, p. 129.

67 Cf. now H.-G. Zmarzlik, 'Der Sozialdarwinismus als geschichtliches Problem', *Vierteljahreshefte für Zeitgeschichte*, 11, no. 3, July 1963, p. 265.

68 Cf. Senghor himself, in his thoughtful contribution on Goethe to a publication of UNESCO to mark the Goethe Year 1948, reprinted in L. S. Senghor, *Négritude et humanisme* (German edition, tr. J. Jahn, Düsseldorf, Cologne, 1967) p. 81: 'In the wake of [Prometheus] we rose up against order and values, especially against reason. . . . As new Prometheuses, as Fausts with ebony faces we opposed to the platitudes of reason the tall trees of our forests, to the smiling wisdom of the "pale-faced God with pink ears" the bush-fire of our minds, and above all the unquenchable flow of blood in our veins.' Cf. also the example cited by Jahn (op. cit., p. 225); 'Ma tête bourdonnant au galop guerrier des dyoun-dyoungs, au grand galop de mon sang de pur sang.' For Senghor on his private war against civilization, cf. Hymans, ibid., p. 147.

69 Jahn, *Neoafrikanische Literatur*, pp. 222f.

70 Cf. ibid., pp. 239–46; especially E. Mphalehle, 'The Cult of Négritude', *Encounter*, 17, no. 3, March 1960, pp. 50ff.; the author here arrives at the rather sharp formula that Négritude is equivalent to an inverse racism or mysticism. A similar view is taken by A. J. Shelton, 'The Black Mystique: Reactionary Extremes in "Négritude"', *African*

Affairs, 63, no. 251, April 1963, pp. 115ff.

71 Cf. above, Pt I, ch. 7, pp. 96ff.

Chapter 16

1 Cf. below, pp. 350–5.

2 Cf. above, pp. 178, 196, 242, 251f.

3 Cf. above, p. 231.

3a On Roy, cf. G. Padmore, *Pan-Africanism*, p. 298.

4 On the background to this question see J. Degras (ed.), *The Communist International 1919–1943, Documents*, 2 volumes (London, New York, 1956–60); also W. I. Lenin, *Über die nationale und die koloniale Frage: eine Sammlung ausgewählter Aufsätze und Reden* (Berlin, 1960) pp. 615ff.; also R. Italiaander, *Schwarze Haut im Roten Griff* (Düsseldorf, Vienna, 1962) pp. 21ff.; F. Schatten, *Communism in Africa* (London, New York, 1966) pp. 53–70; F. Ansprenger, *Auflösung der Kolonialreiche* (Munich, 1966) pp. 141–6.

5 Padmore, ibid., pp. 298, 318; J. R. Hooker, *Black Revolutionary*, p. 14.

6 The following sketch is based on a contemporary communist account: L. F., 'The Influence of the Communist International among Negroes', *Negro Worker*, 2, no. 2, March–April 1929, pp. 1f.

7 Cf. above, pp. 307–12.

8 The most important source is a rare volume: *Das Flammenzeichen vom Palais Egmont. Protokoll des Kongresses gegen koloniale Unterdrückung und Imperialismus, Brüssel, 10–15. Februar 1927*, ed. League against Imperialism (Berlin, 1927). This gives on pp. 229–41 a complete list of the organizations represented at the congress and the names of the delegates and guests who appeared. The list of delegates is also in Italiaander, *Schwarze Haut*, pp. 27–31. This work is so far as I know the first to deal with the Brussels congress, but it does so in a super-ficial and sensational way and in a Cold War spirit; cf. pp. 21–52; I learnt recently that the International Institute for Social History at Amsterdam has rich material on the 'League Against Imperialism', although unfortunately I was unable to make use of the material for the present study.

9 Cf. now also B. Gross, *Willi Münzenberg: eine politische Biographie . . .* (Stuttgart, 1967) especially pp. 196–210.

10 Schatten, *Communism in Africa*, p. 65.

11 Schatten, ibid., warns against such crude and over-hasty judgments.

12 On both these men and Boncourt, cf. above, p. 307.

13 *Flammenzeichen*, pp. 128–30.

14 The reports, in German translation, in ibid., pp. 113–28.

15 Ibid., p. 115. One automatically thinks of the revolutionary chain reaction which took place in 1954 when Algerian soldiers returned from Vietnam after Dienbienphu to Algeria and began the revolution in their own country that same year.

16 *Flammenzeichen*, pp. 116f.

17 Cf. above, pp. 207f.

18 Cf. above, pp. 270, 273f.

19 *Flammenzeichen*, pp. 129f.

20 Ibid., p. 130:

'1. The economic and political organization of peoples:
  (a) organization of Negro workers;
  (b) organization of co-operatives;
2. Struggle against imperialist ideology:
  (a) propaganda against chauvinism, fascism, the Klu Klux Klan and racial prejudice;
  (b) admission of coloured workers to trade unions and workers' organizations on the basis of equality of rights;
3. Organization of a movement for emancipation of the Negro race;

4. Creation of a united front with other peoples and the oppressed classes in a common struggle against imperialism.'

21 Cf. above, pp. 215–17.

22 Cf. above, pp. 221–7, especially p. 225.

23 The composition of the general council elected in Brussels in *Flammenzeichen*, pp. 241f.; also Italiaander, *Schwarze Haut*, pp. 27–9; on p. 251 is a group photograph, in which unfortunately the individuals concerned are not identified.

24 Thus the official list of participants mentions the following organizations, among others, whose names indicate that their aims were similar to those of the League against Imperialism: All-American Anti-Imperialist League (USA); Liga Anti-Imperialista de las Americas. Comite Continental Organizador (Mexico, with associations in Cuba, Puerto Rico, Panama, Nicaragua, Venezuela, Peru), League against Colonial Oppression in the Colonies (England, with branches in France and Germany, the latter called the Liga gegen koloniale Unterdrückung). From Belgium there came a representative of a Ligue contre l'Impérialisme and from Holland one from a like-named body.

25 Cf. above, p. 311.

26 *Negro Worker*, 2, no. 4, August 1929, pp. 23–6, gives the English version of the text.

27 Hooker, *Black Revolutionary*, pp. 12f.

28 Reginald Bridgeman is a member of an old and respected English family. After visiting Harrow School (near which he still lives) and continuing his studies at Cambridge, he entered upon a diplomatic career. In July 1914 he was third secretary in the British embassy in Paris, and during the war an officer in the army. After the war he went on an officially sponsored trip to India where his experiences led him to give up his diplomatic career and to break with the traditions of his family and the milieu whence he sprang. He moved by way of the anti-imperialist left to the CPGB and the League against Imperialism. His aristocratic and conservative exterior and his cultivated background stood in marked contrast to the sectarian narrowness of his new surroundings and the shabbiness of the Daily Worker building in London. I am indebted to the library of the *Daily Worker* for information as to Mr Bridgeman's present whereabouts. Cf. also Padmore, *Pan-Africanism*, pp. 328, 365.

29 According to one writer one of its affiliated organizations in England was the Negro Welfare Association: cf. G. Choubelle, 'Les Organisations Nègres d'Angleterre', *La Race Nègre*, 9, no. 1, January–February 1936, p. 2. On the end of the League, cf. also Padmore, *Pan-Africanism*, pp. 328–30.

30 For further details cf. below, p. 351.

31 Bridgeman to the author in London in 1966.

32 On Ford cf. Hooker, *Black Revolutionary*, pp. 12f., 25, 36f.

33 J. W. Ford, 'The Negro and the Struggle against Imperialism', *U.S. Communist*, January 1930, cited by Padmore, *Pan-Africanism*, p. 319.

34 On Du Bois cf. above, pp. 172f.; Garvey did not make this explicit himself, but he put the idea into practice in his whole career. The parallels are indicated by Padmore, *Pan-Africanism*, p. 319.

35 On this and what follows cf. 'Plan of Work of the International Trade Union Committee of Negro Workers of the RILU', *Negro Worker*, 1, no. 4, December 1928, p. 2.

36 An incomplete set of the *Negro Worker* (both series) is to be found in the Morehouse Library, Howard University, Washington DC; R.

Italiaander treated this paper (*Schwarze Haut*, pp. 54-62), but again in a journalistic spirit; he consulted the complete set of the paper in Moscow, but apparently was unaware of the existence of the earlier hectographed series, for he does not refer to it. The documents of the Profintern seem to have been lost in World War II, when they were evacuated from Moscow as the Germans approached the city in the autumn of 1941: personal communication from Professor A. A. Guber, Academy of Sciences, Moscow.

37 'Call for International Trade Union Conference of Negro Workers', *Negro Worker*, 2, no. 4, August 1929, p. 2.

38 The complete report in ibid., pp. 3-22. It is too long to be reproduced here. It is mentioned in Hooker, *Black Revolutionary*, pp. 12f.

39 On the date of his arrival in England cf. G. Delf, *Jomo Kenyatta . . .* (London 1961) p. 69. Delf did not, however, mention Kenyatta's membership of the committee.

40 The provisional committee was made up as follows:

USA: William Pickens (NAACP), E. L. Doty (Plumbers' Union), Isaac Munsey (Miners' National Union), F. Premice (Furriers' Union), Otto Hall (Negro Department, Trade Union Educational League), Mary Burroughs (Teachers' Union);

South Africa: W. Thibodi (Federation of Non-European Trade Unions), Andrews (Trade Union Congress);

East Africa: Johnstone Kenyatta (Central Association of Kenya, or more correctly Kikuyu Central Association);

Haiti and West Indies: G. Padmore (Printers' Union), Henry Rosemond (Furriers' Union, USA), Dicadosse;

France: Ali (CGTU);

England: M. E. Burns (Transport & General Workers' Union).

Source: cf. above, n. 35.

41 Hooker, *Black Revolutionary* p. 17; also the extreme anti-communist French paper Ami du Peuple, 15 December 1930, an article by F. Coty, 'Le Péril rouge en pays noir', which in a strongly polemical tone reported factually the Hamburg congress of 1930.

According to Hooker, the KPD not only had a relatively good relationship with the Hamburg Senate but even had a few members in the Hamburg police. According to a communication from the Hamburg Archive, all documents which might have thrown light on the congress were destroyed during World War II.

42 The date according to *Negro Worker*, new series, I, no. 1, January 1931, p. 19; Hooker, *Black Revolutionary*, p. 17, gives 7-9 January.

43 Composition according to *Negro Worker*, ibid., p. 31; Hooker gives a different spelling of some of the names or different initials: Macauley instead of Macaulay, G. (instead of N.) Reid, G. (instead of E. F.) Small, Nzula instead of Nzulu. Kouyauté is written Kouyate, as is the general practice in English works, but I prefer the French spelling, as does Spiegler.

44 Cf. above, p. 286.

45 Cf. above, pp. 55f.

46 'Death of Comrade Macaulay' (obituary), *Negro Worker*, 1 (new series), no. 10-11, October-November 1931, pp. 42f.

47 *Negro Worker*, January 1931, pp. 22-4.

48 The first biographical sketch of Wallace-Johnson is in Hooker, *Black Revolutionary*, pp. 51f.; cf. also above, p. 292, and below, pp. 389f, 401; also I. T. A. Wallace-Johnson, *Trade Unionism in Colonial*

and Dependent Territories (London, 1946), published by the West African National Secretariat.

49 Hooker, *Black Revolutionary*, p. 22; Padmore's contributions were as follows: *What is the International Trade Union Committee of Negro Workers?; Life and Struggle of Negro Toilers* (London, 1931) (still an informative work); *Negro Workers and the Imperialist War; Forced Labour in Africa; American Imperialism Enslaves Liberia; Labour Imperialism and East Africa.*

50 An illustration which, slightly amended, later appeared on the front page of the semi-official paper *Voice of Africa* under Nkrumah, but one should not draw too many ideological conclusions from this. The historical explanation is simple: what links them is not Communism but Padmore. On Hamburg at this juncture cf. Italiaander, *Schwarze Haut*, pp. 55-7, 61; also Hooker, *Black Revolutionary*, p. 18.

51 *Negro Worker*, 7, no. 3, March 1937, p. 13.

52 S. Sklatvala, 'Who is this Gandhi?', *Labour Monthly*, reprinted in *Negro Worker*, 1, no. 3, March 1941, pp. 4-6; on Saklatvala cf. above, p. 244, and Padmore, *Pan-Africanism*, p. 328.

53 Wang (Canton), 'Development of the Chinese Workers' Movement', ibid., pp. 12-14.

54 E.g., on South Africa, ibid., January 1931, pp. 7-13, an unsigned article 'South Africa'; T. Ring, 'The Revolutionary Forces of Africa', ibid., pp. 13-16 (tr. from German); J. W. Ford, 'Negro Seamen and the Revolutionary Movement in Africa (Some lessons from Chinese Seamen)', ibid., 1, no. 4-5, April-May 1931, pp. 7-10.

55 At the beginning of the Depression eight Afro-American youths from the South who had secretly boarded a railway wagon to go to the North in search of work, were accused of having raped two girls (of dubious reputation, as it turned out, who were in any case at the other end of the train), and sentenced to death. Although the girls' statements were shown to be false, the judgment was not rescinded but merely suspended. After years of agitation and ten court proceedings the Scottsboro Boys were eventually set free shortly before the outbreak of World War II. On the agitation cf. especially *Negro Worker*, no. 7, July 1931, p. 3, with reports of protest meetings at Berlin, Hamburg, Dresden, Cologne, Paris and in South Africa, often in front of US Consulates; also 2, no. 6, June 1932, pp. 9-11, report by B. J. (Hamburg), 'The Scottsboro Campaign in Europe'.

56 Ibid., 1, no. 10-11, October-November 1931, pp. 8-11, 'Hands off Liberia'; on the significance of this country cf. above, pp. 122-8.

57 Ibid., pp. 13-16, 18f.; ibid., 2, no. 7, July 1932.

58 In the number preserved in the Du Bois papers in Accra; the microfilm copy is unfortunately spoiled so that no exact reference can be given.

59 J. Roumain, 'Haiti: a Dictatorship – Lessons and Results', ibid., 5, no. 5, May 1935, p. 14.

60 Unsigned leading article, 'End the Bloody Slaughter in Abyssinia', ibid., pp. 14f.; 'German Imperialism seeks Colonies in East Africa' (unsigned); Wallace-Johnson, ibid., 5, no. 4, pp. 3f.; cf. also above, p. 302, and below, p. 346.

61 Wallace-Johnson, 'The West African Youth League . . .', ibid., 5, no. 5, May 1935, pp. 9, 13; ibid., p. 8: E. E. Strong, 'The Negro Youth Offensive'.

62 Cf. above, p. 335.

63 Cf. above, p. 273.

64 *Negro Worker*, 2 (first series), no. 2, March-April 1929, p. 16.

65 Bridgeman to Solanke, 11 November 1933, Solanke Papers.

66 Cf. above, p. 304.
67 S. Rohdie, 'The Gold Coast Aborigines Abroad', *JAH*, 6, no. 3, 1965, pp. 392–4.
68 Cf. below, p. 352.
69 Cf. below, pp. 351–7.
70 R. Reynolds, *My Life and Crimes* (London, 1956) p. 116.
71 Cf. above, p. 304, and below, pp. 346f.
72 An important exception are the French Antilles and French Africa where colonial élites, and especially the autodidactic revolutionary elements, grew up in a much more secular atmosphere. Also in the British West Indies the religious element seems to have lost much of its early force.
73 Cf. above, p. 305.
74 Padmore, *Pan-Africanism*, p. 379, especially the concluding remarks.

Chapter 17

1 Cf. below, pp. 385ff.
2 Cf. above, p. xi.
3 D. A. Vaughan, *Negro Victory*, pp. 9ff.; Vaughan was Moody's local pastor and a close friend.
4 Cf. above, Pt I, ch. 4, 5, pp. 41–57, 58–76.
5 The first relatively detailed account of the League is in K. Little, *Negroes in Britain . . .*, pp. 85–104; but it was ignored by later writers, including Hooker, *Black Revolutionary*; on the point of most interest here cf. Little, pp. 82ff.
6 The above following Vaughan, *Negro Victory*, pp. 23–58; the founding of the League in ibid., pp. 54f.; Little, *Negroes in Britain*, pp. 82f., gives a different version which contradicts that of Vaughan only in the matter of the dates. According to Little an organization came into existence in 1931, led by Quakers, the Joint Council to Promote Understanding between White and Coloured People in Great Britain. Some months later this gave birth to the League. The Joint Council ceased to exist in 1934 because the League made it superfluous.
7 Vaughan, *Negro Victory*, p. 62; the text of his speech in *Keys*, 1, no. 2, October 1933, pp. 224, 34. C. L. R. James, historian, publicist and Trotskyist politician from Trinidad, spoke in Hull and also on the BBC: ibid., p. 16. Apart from the festivities in Hull there were celebrations in British Guiana, Trinidad, Barbados, Grenada and West Africa (not specified more closely): ibid., p. 35.
8 *Keys*, 1, no. 1, July 1933, pp. 1f.; also for the following.
9 Ibid., 2, no. 2, October–December 1934, p. 22; the figures for 1936 in ibid., 3, no. 4, April–June 1936, pp. 52f.
10 Vaughan, *Negro Victory*, p. 65; on the following pp. 64–6.
11 *Keys*, 2, no. 3, January–March 1935, p. 46.
12 Especially the *Gold Coast Spectator*; cf. also *Keys*, ibid., p. 58.
13 Ibid., no. 2, Oct. 1933, pp. 24f.
14 *Keys*, 1, No. 1, p. 16.
15 Ibid., no. 2, October 1933, pp. 24f.: 'Coloured Children's Outings to Epsom, Friday, July 14th, 1933'.
16 Ibid., 1, no. 1, p. 16.
17 On the Pan-African significance of the delegation cf. below, p. 354.
18 Cf. also Little, *Negroes in Britain*, pp. 104f.
19 *Keys*, 2, no. 2, October–December 1934, p. 21; 2, no. 3, January–March 1935, p. 52; he may be identical with Jomo Kenyatta since there were few East Africans in England at that time and he appears later in connection with the League: cf. below, p. 358.
20 Ibid., 1, no. 1, pp. 4f.
21 Cf. above, Pt II, ch. 16, n. 55.
22 Keys, I, no. 3, January 1934, p. 42.
23 Ibid., 1, no. 3, pp. 11ff.: surprising because otherwise he was a dyed-in-the-wool Trotskyist.
24 Ibid., 1, no. 4, April–June 1934, pp. 72, 84.

25 Like WASU at this time: cf. above, p. 302f.

26 *Keys*, 3, no. 3, January–March 1936, pp. 32, 39f.

27 Ibid., p. 31.

28 Ibid., 5, no. 4, April–June 1938, p. 26, resolution of the annual general meeting on 11 March 1938.

29 Ibid., 1, no. 3, January–March 1934, p. 63.

30 Ibid., 3, no. 3, January–March 1936, pp. 29f. They pointed out later that there was no racial discrimination on French boats, whereas it existed on British ones: ibid., 5, no. 4, April–June 1938, p. 83.

31 Ibid., 6, no. 2, October–December 1938, p. 3.

32 Ibid., 4, no. 3, January–March 1937, p. 31.

33 Ibid., 5, no. 1, July–September 1937, pp. 7–10; another speaker was the Labour MP, the Rev. Reginald Sorensen (today Lord Sorensen).

34 Ibid., 5, no. 4, April–June 1938, p. 83.

35 Ibid., p. 86.

36 Cf. below, pp. 351–6. Padmore's treatment of Moody is grotesque. Although Moody worked with him for a time, he is mentioned only once (*Pan-Africanism*, p. 361). On the other hand he devotes a whole sub-chapter (pp. 159–61) to a biographical sketch of Dr Peter M. Milliard, whose contribution, so far as can be seen, was much slighter than that of Moody. Hooker in his biography also failed to do justice to Moody, perhaps because he did not consult the important work by Little (*Negroes in Britain*), and made less use than he should have done of Vaughan's *Negro Victory* and the League's organ.

37 Hooker, *Black Revolutionary*, p. 41.

38 *Keys*, 2, no. 3, January–March 1935, p. 52; Hooker, *Black Revolutionary*, p. 40, note.

39 *Keys*, 2, no. 3, January–March 1935,

p. 42; no. 4, April–June 1936, p. 64.

40 Cf. above, p. 298.

41 Ibid., 4, no. 3, January–March 1937, p. 34.

42 On an early stage of the talks which later ended in success, cf. *Keys*, 2, no. 1, July–September 1934, p. 16.

43 Ibid., 4, no. 2, October–December 1936. In 1941 the same tensions reappeared at the annual general meeting of the League. One of the reasons was 'the idea dominant among West Indians that they are a cut above the Africans, because they have acquired European civilisation, and on the other hand, the African, knowing that he has a home, a heritage and a national soul (*sic*!), regards himself as miles above the West Indian'. Cf. Vaughan, *Negro Victory*, pp. 118f.

44 Cf. above, p. 341 and n. 5; for a parallel in the francophone area, cf. above, p. 307.

45 Cf. Introduction, n. 15.

46 Hooker, *Black Revolutionary*, p. 2 and n.

47 Padmore to Du Bois, 12 April 1945, Du Bois papers, Accra. In reply Du Bois wrote about this relationship in an article about the preparations for the fifth Pan-African Congress (*Defender*, 29 September 1945); Hooker, *Black Revolutionary*, 93 n., is sceptical about this information, but he was unacquainted with Padmore's letter.

48 Hooker, *Black Revolutionary*, pp. 6–10.

49 Cf. above, p. 311.

50 Cf. above, p. 331.

51 Cf. above, p. 335.

52 Hooker, *Black Revolutionary*, p. 26.

53 Ibid., pp. 26f.; the data here are, however, very vague.

54 Cf. above, Pt II, ch. 16 n. 55.

55 N. Cunard, ed., *Negro Anthology*, London, 1934.

56 Hooker, *Black Revolutionary*, p. 37, thinks it plausible that Kouyauté

embezzled money because in World War II he was shot by the Germans for the same offence. Nevertheless one should not underestimate the strength of political motives here, as also in the case of Padmore. Hooker considers that Padmore was absolutely scrupulous in money matters.

57 Especially for the *Gold Coast Spectator*.

58 A list of the fifty most important articles by Padmore is in Hooker, *Black Revolutionary*, pp. 154–6.

59 R. Reynolds, *My Life and Crimes* (London, 1956) p. 116; I am obliged to Lord Brockway for telling me that the meetings were held regularly; as his memory on these matters was a little vague when I spoke to him about them his statement may refer to the immediate post-war years as well.

60 Cf. above, p. 351; Hooker, *Black Revolutionary*, pp. 4f.

61 Padmore, *Pan-Africanism*, pp. 54f.

62 Hooker, *Black Revolutionary*, p. 87 n.

63 Cf. above, pp. 35, 47.

64 A long list of those whom Padmore considered true friends of the African in the twentieth century is in ibid., p. 365; among them is Reginald Reynolds, who thus assumes his place in the 'apostolic succession of radicals' to which he makes an ironical reference: 'This feeling of pride in belonging to an Apostolic Succession of Radicals is something I never lost' (p. 108).

65 Padmore's books (not counting pamphlets) are the following:

Life and Struggles of Negro Toilers (London, 1931);
How Britain Rules Africa (London, 1936);
Africa and World Peace, (London, 1937);
How Russia Transformed her Colonial Empire. . . (London, 1946);
Africa: Britain's Third Empire (London, 1949);

The Gold Coast Revolution: the Struggle of an African People from Slavery to Freedom (London, 1953);
Pan-Africanism or Communism? (London, 1956).

66 The sheer scope of Padmore's work cannot but inspire respect, the more so since he did not write his books in the material security and relative calm of an academic career but under the pressure of an active political engagement. Moreover Padmore was no learned historian, as is evident from the historical passages in his books, and the modern historiography of Africa did not begin until the last years of his life. One must therefore be lenient about the undoubted weaknesses in his work: the frequent repetition of favourite themes (e.g. the history of African nationalism on the Gold Coast), or the vacillation between severe condemnation of imperialism and colonialism in his early works and his almost uncritical acceptance of the abolitionist clichés in his last book. His most successful volume, *Pan-Africanism or Communism?*, is on closer inspection a somewhat abortive construct: it neither succeeded in giving a history of Pan-Africanism nor in supplying it with a theoretical framework. But it was written with his unusual verve and intellectual courage and will always retain its significance. The author gladly acknowledges his debt to it, for it was this book that led him to take up African history and the study of Pan-Africanism.

67 Padmore only once mentioned Horton, and then only in passing (ibid., p. 41).

68 Hooker, *Black Revolutionary*, pp. 6, 12, 22, 24, 33, 36, 116–20, 123, 131.

69 The only source at present is ibid., pp. 144–6.

70 For more details cf. S. Rohdie, 'The Gold Coast Aborigines Abroad', *JAH*, 6, no. 3, 1965, pp. 389–411.

71 Cf. above, p. 345.

72 Participants in the second Pan-African Congress; cf. above, pp. 343f.

73 Hooker, *Black Revolutionary*, p. 49; Padmore, *Pan-Africanism*, pp. 146–9.

74 Cf. above, pp. 292, 336.

75 Little, *Negroes in Britain*, p. 110, n. 1; cf. also Hooker, *Black Revolutionary*, p. 42.

76 Padmore, *Pan-Africanism*, pp. 146f.; also Ras Hakounen, *Pan-Africanism from within*, pp. 113–77.

77 Hooker, *Black Revolutionary*, p. 83 n.

78 Padmore, *Pan-Africanism*, p. 74.

79 This is to be found only in the documents of certain colonial governments, and not in a public library. Cf. Hooker, *Black Revolutionary*, p. 49, where unfortunately he gives no indication of the character or content of the paper.

80 Cf. above, p. 349, and below, p. 358.

81 Hooker, *Black Revolutionary*, pp. 54f.

82 Cf. above, p. 258.

83 Cf. above, Pt II, ch. 15, pp. 305ff.

84 Hooker, *Black Revolutionary*, pp. 39; also for the following, p. 40f.

84a On Atta cf. above, p. 288.

85 Cf. above, p. 288, 345.

86 Hooker, *Black Revolutionary*, p. 41.

87 See above, n. 6.

87a *Keys*, 2, no. 1, July–September 1934, p. 1.

88 Cf. above, pp. 325–31.

89 Hooker, *Black Revolutionary*, p. 41.

89a Cf. above, n. 87a.

90 *Keys*, 2, no. 2, October–December 1934, p. 21.

91 *Keys*, 5, no. 4, April–June 1938, pp. 79, 83f.

92 Cf. above, p. 346 and n. 28.

93 Ibid., p. 85.

94 In 1938 there were serious disorders in the British West Indies, which began in Trinidad. They were soon quelled by British troops. They began over the grave economic consequences of the depression. During the troubles the first steps were taken towards the creation of an indigenous trade union movement. The *Keys* and the League followed these social movements with interest, as did most members of Padmore's group. Cf. *Keys*, 6, no. 2, October–December 1938, pp. 3f.

95 Ibid., 7, no. 1, July–September 1939, p. 5.

96 Solanke to Secretary Conference Committee, 24 April 1939; Keith Alleyne to Solanke, 27 April 1939; both in Solanke papers.

97 Cf. below, pp. 360, 362.

98 Details from the letter-heading of Alleyne's communication to Solanke.

99 Cf. also P. Blackman, 'Propaganda and Knowledge', *Keys*, 7, no. 1, July–September 1939, p. 4, on the projected conference: '. . . German demands for living room in Africa may make most people vaguely aware that maybe one day their children will die in battle because of some place called Togoland. How sixpence a day in India, and the ravages of tuberculosis on the Rand, how starvation and illiteracy in Bahamas are bound up with the ever-increasing wretchedness of the Jews in central Europe, have their ties with the threat to liberty in the so-called democratic countries, remains to be seen. . . . We would recommend this conference to all who are interested in the welfare of the African peoples, and who through understanding would contribute to the furthering of their welfare.'

100 Hooker, *Black Revolutionary*, p. 55; he gives a summary account of Padmore's unconcerned reaction.

101 'Minutes of a meeting held at Dr Moody's house, 164 Queen's Road, Peckham, on July 26th 1939', Solanke papers.

102 Cf. above, p. 349.

103 Report of a meeting on 5 July 1939, ibid.

104 Cf. above, n. 101.
105 Nothing more is known of him.
106 Perhaps identical with Harry Roberts (see above, p. 346)?
107 A body founded by Paul Robeson.
108 Cf. above, p. 183.
109 Cf. above, p. 350 and n. 101.
110 Cf. below, p. 260.
111 Cf. below, pp. 400f.

Chapter 18

1 Cf. above, pp. 229ff, 305f.
2 J. R. Hooker, *Black Revolutionary*, p. 59.
3 Ibid., cf. also G. Delf, *Jomo Kenyatta* . . . , pp. 117–19.
4 Hooker, *Black Revolutionary*, pp. 48f.
5 Cf. above, p. 361.
6 Cf. also J. S. Coleman, *Nigeria*, pp. 142–56; R. v. Albertini, *Dekolonisation* . . . , pp. 34–40; R. Oliver and J. D. Fage, *A Short History of Africa* (second edition Harmondsworth, 1962) pp. 221–4.
7 Cf. above, Pt I, ch. 7, pp. 96ff.
8 Coleman, *Nigeria*, p. 255. On Africa in general cf. Lord (W. M.) Hailey, *An African Survey* (Oxford, 1938, second edition 1956) pp. 253f.
9 Cf. also I. Geiss, *Gewerkschaften in Afrika*, pp. 44f., 51.
10 Figures from Hailey, *African Survey*.
11 Cf. above, pp. 305f.
12 On Ghana see P. J. Foster, *Education in Ghana*, pp. 114f.
13 Cf. above, p. 174.
14 Cf. esp. N. Azikiwe, *The Atlantic Charter and British West Africa* (Lagos) n.d. [1943]; cf. also below, p. 383.
15 Cited from D. A. Vaughan, *Negro Victory*, p. 122.
6 For the effects on the Afro-Americans, cf. I. Geiss, *Die Afro-Amerikaner* (Frankfurt, 1969).
17 Cf. above, p. 356.
18 Du Bois papers, Accra.
19 Hooker, *Black Revolutionary*, p. 81 n., also for what follows. Yergan was an Afro-American YMCA official, who spent seventeen years in South Africa and was able to combine his work for the YMCA with an active communist commitment. He also belonged to the activists of the International African Service Bureau (IASB). On Yergan's anti-communist phase after 1945, cf. Padmore, *Pan-Africanism*, pp. 315–17.
20 On René Maran cf. also above, p. 311.
21 Hooker, *Black Revolutionary*, who uses the word 'supposedly' to indicate his doubts.
22 *Proceedings of the Conference on Africa: New Perspectives* . . . (New York, 1944); Hooker, *Black Revolutionary*, p. 81.
23 The following details from K. Nkrumah, *Autobiography*, 1957, pp. 8ff.
24 Cf. above, p. 59.
25 Cf. above, pp. 64–5, 69f.
26 Cf. also above, pp. 288f.
27 Cf. above, p. 292.
28 Cf. above, pp. 354f.
29 Nkrumah, *Autobiography*, p. 24. Cf. now J. M. Akita (ed.), *Commission on Kwame Nkrumah Papers* . . . , n.p., n.d. [Accra, 1965], p. 5: communication from Wood, 25 January 1934, in which he confirms that Nkrumah, on the occasion of his posting to Axim, was general secretary of the Nzima Literature Society.
30 Especially with his leading articles, which he published in book form: N. Azikiwe, *Renascent Africa*; cf. also above, p. 121f.
31 Cf. above, pp. 304, 346.
32 Nkrumah, *Autobiography*, pp. 22f.
33 Cf. above, pp. 132f; on his stay in the USA much information may be gleaned from B. Timothy, *Kwame Nkrumah* . . . (London, 1955, second edition 1963) pp. 25–35.
34 Nkrumah, *Autobiography*, pp. 26, 37.
35 Gardiner came from the Gold Coast

and studied in Oxford; later he taught at Fourah Bay College and became a senior official in Ghana. In protest against the Nkrumah régime he left to become an international official of the UN and is at present secretary-general of the UN Economic Commission for Africa in Addis Ababa.

36 'Aggrey Memorial Celebration', pp. 8–10. The ceremony is briefly mentioned in B. Timothy, *Nkrumah*, p. 31.

37 'The Significance of African Art'; 'The History of Religion in a Critique of West African Fetichism'; 'Primitive Education in West Africa': all term papers for Lincoln University from 1940, cited by M. M. Fisher, *Negro Slave Songs*, who was evidently able to consult these papers. The last of them was later published as an article with the same title in *Educational Outlook*, January 1941.

38 The title and subtitle of the uncompleted thesis are interesting: 'Mind and Thought in Pre-Literate Society: a Study in Ethno- Philosophy with Special Reference to the Akan People of Ghana', as cited by Akita, *Commission*, p. 6.

39 Cited by B. Timothy, *Nkrumah*, p. 32.

40 Kwame Nkrumah Papers, Ghana: National Archives, Accra. This is one of the letters which Mr J. M. Akita of Accra kindly allowed me to see and take excerpts from before the exhibition in Accra (cf. n. 29).

41 Ibid., Nkrumah to Ralph Bunche, 12 March 1943.

42 Cf. above, pp. 202ff.

43 F. N. Nkrumah, 'Education and Nationalism in Africa', *Educational Outlook*, November 1943, p. 8.

44 F. N-K. Nkrumah, 'Educational Trends and Potentialities in West Africa', University of Pennsylvania. School of Education. *Challenge to Education: War and Post-War . . .*

(Philadelphia, 1943) pp. 83–92; citation from p. 91.

45 Ibid. Previously the author stated that 'traditional Africans' often had more 'fine personalities, more culture, public spirit, spiritual and moral wealth than had been discovered among many so-called educated Africans who had been uprooted, detribalized and divorced from their native tradition . . .' Cf. in a similar spirit, a generation earlier, Attoh Ahuma: above, pp. 205f.

46 Cf. above, p. 170.

47 Cf. above, p. 148.

48 Ako Adjei, 'African Students in America', *WASU*, 12, no. 1, March 1945, pp. 14–17, states that in the previous twenty-five years 'about 100' African students had gone to the USA and stayed there. The African student association founded in 1941 had twenty-eight members, who should be deducted from this figure if Adjei included them.

49 Ibid., p. 14.

50 Cf. above, p. 121.

51 On Ita cf. Coleman, *Nigeria*, pp. 218–20; R. L. Sklar, *Nigerian Political Parties . . .* (Princeton, 1963) pp. 121–4.

52 On this and the foregoing see Coleman, *Nigeria*, p. 242.

53 According to a photograph with caption in the *African Interpreter*, 1, no. 4, Summer 1943, p. 15.

54 A. Adjei, 'African Students in America', p. 15. Also for the following.

55 Nkrumah, *Autobiography*, p. 35.

56 *African Interpreter*, 1, no. 1, February 1943, pp. 5–7.

57 Orizu, born in 1920 in the eastern region of Nigeria, came from a local princely family and for this reason referred to himself as 'Prince'. At the age of twenty-four he wrote a large book, when in the USA, which coined the term 'Zikism' and laid the ideological foundations of

the 'Zikist movement', a radical new nationalist movement in Nigeria. Cf. A. A. N. Orizu, *Without Bitterness* . . . (New York ,1944); on the Zikist movement especially Coleman, *Nigeria*, pp. 288, 296–302, and Sklar, *Nigerian Political Parties*, pp. 73–80, 89f.

58 Nkrumah, *Autobiography*, p. 35.

59 To the executive members and activists named below may be added seventeen other members: Franklin S. Anthony, Bassey A. U. Attah, Mrs Tanda Bennett, Philip K. Brown, Abdul K. Disu, S. W. George-Coker, Efion Odok, Mbonu Ojike, J. B. C. E. Okala, Thorgue Sie, John K. Smart, Thomas Udoh, Thomas Williams.

60 In all known documents from his period in America Jones-Quartey has the initial 'H.', but now he is always referred to by the initials '*K*. A. B.'

61 Cf. above, p. 73.

62 Cf. above, pp. 64–5, 70.

63 Cf. also above, pp. 370f.

64 K. O. Mbadiwe, *British and Axis Aims in Africa* (New York, 1942); Orizu, *Without Bitterness;* Mbonu Ojike, *My Africa* (New York, 1946). All three were Ibos: Coleman, *Nigeria*, p. 243.

65 In 1945 Adjei helped Nkrumah obtain valuable contacts in London and in 1947 recommended him as general secretary of the newly formed United Gold Coast Convention. After the foundation of the Convention People's Party (CPP) in 1949 he waited for a while before joining the new ruling party. Finally he became a minister, in the end for foreign affairs, in the CPP government. In 1961 he was arrested for allegedly plotting against Nkrumah and remained in jail until Nkrumah's fall in February 1966. Akpabio was in 1960 minister of education and deputy prime minister of the eastern region of

Nigeria; Fitzjohn was a professor at Fourah Bay College and a member of the executive of the Sierra Leone People's Party. Jones-Quartey became a professor at Legon University near Accra and wrote a biography of Azikiwe. Mbadiwe was in 1960 minister of trade and industry in the Nigerian federal government. Nkrumah's later career is too well known to be discussed here. Smart was in 1960 minister of labour in Sierra Leone. These data, except those relating to Adjei, from Coleman, *Nigeria*, p. 244.

66 p. 5. It is worth noting the emphasis on the 'Pan-African' element at the end of the first paragraph and the return to an uncompromising hostility towards the fascists and the 'democratic' imperialists.

67 Akpabio's presidency in April 1944 is recorded in the report on the conference on Africa held by the Council on African Affairs (cf. above, n. 22).

68 Cf. above, p. 371

69 *African Interpreter*, 1, no. 1, p. 7.

70 Cf. above, n. 48.

71 *African Interpreter*, no. 5, p. 10, 'Secretarial Report'. This paper has hitherto scarcely been mentioned in the literature: cf. Nkrumah, *Autobiography*, pp, 35f.; Timothy, *Nkrumah*, p. 33; Coleman, *Nigeria*, p. 242. Only one number was analysed by Coleman, but his data are somewhat confusing. Ostensibly he is referring to no. 4, March 1943; but this is the date of publication of no. 2; the citation he adduces from ASA's constitution would suggest no. 2. The paper is very rare. The Schomburg Collection has nos. 4 and 5; I found nos. 1 and 2 in Solanke's papers; no. 3 seems to be lost.

72 'Let us know what you think of your magazine by return mail. Meantime – Support the fight for Justice and Democracy by buying

U.S. War Bonds and Savings Stamps.'
73 Cf. above, pp. 372f.
74 Ibid., p. 4.
75 'A New Lease on Life', p. 5.
76 'Africans and the Atlantic Charter', ibid.
77 Cf. above, pp. 366f
78 A. W. Hunton was a colleague of Du Bois and his successor as director of the *Encyclopedia Africana* in Accra. Early in 1967 he was expelled by the military government that acceded to power after Nkrumah's fall. For his earlier career cf. A. W. Hunton, *Decision in Africa* (New York, 1954).
79 And therefore the representative of a group which in 1927 had saved the fourth Pan-African Congress for Du Bois by arranging for it to be held in New York: cf. above, p. 256.
80 Cf. above, pp. 241, 251, 256.
81 Cf. above, pp. 86–93, 161–5.
82 A full list is in *Proceedings of the Conference on Africa*, pp. 36f.; on p. 38 is a list of the organizations represented.
83 Cf. above, pp. 102–4.
84 *Proceedings of the Conference on Africa*, pp. 6f.; all plans for the development of Africa were to 'be directed in a systematic manner toward the achievement of self-government and the right of self-determination by these people'.
85 Cf. above, pp. 340ff.
86 Du Bois to Mrs Amy J. Garvey, Harold Moody and Max Yergan, 7 April 1944, Du Bois papers, Accra.
87 Ibid.: 'The object shall be for consultation and information so as to set before the world the needs of African Negroes and of their descendants overseas. No political changes in the relation between colonies and mother countries will necessarily be contemplated in cases where it is evident that no freedom of development is possible under present circumstances . . .'

88 Cf. above, pp. 122–8, 130ff.
89 Du Bois wrongly gave the names as 'Congress of Western Africa' and 'Aborigines Protective Society' – a symptom of the degree to which he had lost contact with political realities in Africa.
90 Du Bois to Solanke, 9 May 1944, Solanke papers.

Chapter 19

1 Cf. above, p. 366.
2 Cf. above, p. 229.
3 Cf. above, p. 365.
4 J. E. Worrell to Solanke, 30 October 1939, Solanke papers, on the meeting of the Coordinating Committee in Moody's house on 17 October: 'The Chairman, Dr Moody, in opening the meeting referred to the subjects on the agenda. The first he thought of very great importance in view of the conditions prevailing at the present time and the necessity of keeping Colonial questions constantly before the Government and Public. The subject concerned the sending of a letter to Lord Halifax, reminding the Government of the hopes and aspirations of the Colonial Peoples, especially in view of the findings of the recent Commissions, and soliciting a statement as to the Government's plans for the future of the Colonies. After a full discussion the meeting agreed that it would not be opportune to forward such a letter at the present time. Mr Blackman suggested instead the drawing up of a statement of the aims and principles of the Coordinating Committee. His suggestion was accepted.'
5 Cf. above, pp. 359f.
6 *News Letter*, 8, no. 49, October 1943, p. 4.
7 Ibid., August 1944, p. 80; cf. also above, pp. 366f.
8 Ibid., 10, no. 57, June 1944, pp. 34–6.

9 Cf. above, pp. 357f.; J. R. Hooker, *Black Revolutionary*, pp. 82f., only mentions the conference briefly in one sentence.

10 Text in *News Letter*, 10, no. 59, August 1944, p. 73.

11 Hooker, *Black Revolutionary*, p. 83.

12 Abrahams, then still a young writer, later, in the first part of his *roman à thèse A Wreath for Udomo* (London, 1956) gave a bitterly realistic and not quite fair description of the Pan-African milieu around Padmore and Nkrumah just after the war.

13 For the immediate preliminaries cf. above, p. 355.

14 The organizations are given in Padmore, *Pan-Africanism*, p. 149 n. and also in the letter-heading of the official notepaper of the PAF in 1945–6 (in Du Bois papers, Accra). As well as the IASB there were the following groups: African Progressive Association, London; Coloured Workers' Association, London; Friends of African Freedom Society, Gold Coast; Coloured People's Association, Edinburgh; United Committee of Coloured and Colonial Peoples' Association, Cardiff; African Union, Glasgow University.

15 Hooker, *Black Revolutionary*, p. 83; Padmore, *Pan-Africanism*, mentions WASU as a member, but the official letter-heading – the most reliable source – does not do so.

16 Probably Duse's original publisher (cf. above, p. 222).

17 Padmore, *Pan-Africanism*, p. 154.

18 Cf. below, p. 393.

19 *History of the Pan-African Congress*, ed. G. Padmore (London, 1947, second edition 1963) p. 24; W. E. B. Du Bois, *The World and Africa*, p. 244.

20 Cf. above, p. 383.

21 *News Letter*, 12, no. 67, April 1945, pp. 13f.; WASU's reply is printed *in extenso* in *History*, p. 25, but without giving the date.

22 Cf. above, pp. 356–61.

23 Hooker, *Black Revolutionary*, pp. 85f.

24 Ibid., p. 86.

25 Cf. above, p. 361.

26 Cf. above, pp. 351f.

27 *Defender*, 10 March 1945; also for the following quotations.

28 Of the American Red Cross.

29 *Defender*, ibid.: 'The meeting following the labor conference will permit Negro labor delegates to attend both conferences, and it is hoped that the Pan-African groups will gain the support of labor for Negro demands in the peace settlement.'

30 *Defender*, 17 March 1945; briefly mentioned by Hooker, *Black Revolutionary*, p. 86.

31 Padmore to Du Bois, 12 April 1945, Du Bois papers, Accra: 'Now that I have had the good fortune of establishing direct contacts with you . . .'; on earlier correspondence between them, cf. above, p. 356.

32 Padmore to Du Bois, *Pan-Africanism*, where Padmore mentions WASU as one of the organizations that had 'promulgated and supported' the draft manifesto.

33 *News Letter*, 12, no. 67, April 1945, p. 12. The draft was published simultaneously in the communist paper *Labour Monthly* (27, April 1945, p. 154).

34 Ibid., pp. 13f.

35 Padmore does not mention Moody or the League in this context; Hooker, *Black Revolutionary*, p. 88, merely notes that Moody signed the manifesto.

36 In a letter to Du Bois, 12 April 1945, Du Bois papers, Accra.

37 Cf. above, pp. 386f.

38 Text in *Defender*, 17 March 1945 and *News Letter*, April 1945, pp. 9–12; also for the following quotations.

39 Cf. above, p. 390 and n. 31.

40 Cf. above, p. 388.

41 Du Bois papers, Accra; also for the following quotations.

42 Du Bois papers, Accra; also for the following quotations.

43 Cf. above, Pt II, ch. 17, n. 47.

44 Du Bois to Padmore, 11 April 1945, Du Bois papers, Accra.

45 In a letter to Padmore of 12 September 1945 (ibid.), Du Bois announced that according to a resolution by the NAACP he would represent that organization, if only as an observer, since the congress had been called without the participation of the NAACP. In a subsequent letter to Padmore (12 July 1947) he mentioned serious resistance, but not a withdrawal of his mandate on behalf of the NAACP; there was no longer any talk of money.

46 Cf. above, p. 383.

47 Padmore to Du Bois, 17 August 1945, Du Bois papers; also for the following quotations.

48 Cf. above, p. 11.

49 Cf. especially F. Ansprenger, *Politik im Schwarzen Afrika* . . . (Cologne, Opladen, 1961).

50 G. Padmore, 'The British Empire is the Worst Racket Yet Invented by Man', *New Leader* (the ILP organ), 15 December 1939.

51 Cf. above, pp. 242f.

52 Cf. K. Nkrumah, *Autobiography*, p. 41.

53 Hooker, *Black Revolutionary*, p. 92.

54 Du Bois papers, Accra.

55 Cf. above, p. 386.

56 This is treated rather broadly in Hooker, *Black Revolutionary*, pp. 89f.; see also for the following.

57 Padmore to Du Bois, 17 August 1945; also for the following quotations; cf. also *History of the Pan-African Congress*, pp. 24f.; Padmore, *Pan-Africanism*, p. 155f.; Hooker, *Black Revolutionary*, p. 91.

58 The official list of delegates in *History*, pp. 71–3. Hooker, ibid., p. 94, speaks of 'about one hundred delegates' presumably counting in the observers. Nkrumah, *Autobiography*, p. 43, doubles the number to

'over 200'; he is followed by H. F. Strauch, *Panafrika* . . . , p. 39. P. Decraene, *Le Panafricanisme*, p. 23, makes a further error by stating that Du Bois organized the fifth Pan-African Congress in Manchester in March 1945; this error was taken over by F. Ansprenger in his article on Du Bois in *Geschichte in Gestalten* and in his *Auflösung der Kolonialreiche*, p. 176. C. Legum, *Pan-Africanism*, p. 31 n., calls the congress the sixth because he includes the London Conference of 1900 in his reckoning; but since Du Bois numbers them from the first Congress in Paris in 1919 there seems no reason to change the accepted enumeration.

59 P. Abrahams, in *New Leader*, 20 October 1945.

60 *History of the Pan-African Congress*; Padmore, *Pan-Africanism*, pp. 152–70; Hooker, *Black Revolutionary*, pp. 94–7; Nkrumah, *Autobiography*, pp. 43–5.

61 Cf. above, p. 395

62 Cf. above, p. 388 n. 17.

63 Du Bois to Padmore, 5 October 1945, Du Bois papers, Accra.

64 Cf. above, p. 382.

65 Cf. above, pp. 383, 392.

66 *News Letter*, 12, no. 71, August 1945, p. 107.

67 On Padmore's suppression of references to Moody, cf. above, ch. 17, n. 36. Padmore for his part was completely ignored by the League during the Manchester congress, and the gathering itself was only mentioned belatedly and briefly with a reprint of the 'Declaration to Imperialist Powers' and the 'Manifesto to the Colonial Workers': cf. *News Letter*, 13, no. 76, January 1946, pp. 77f.; Moody's friend and biographer did not mention Padmore in his life of the former.

68 Cf. above, pp. 292, 335.

69 Later the founder and leader of the Action Group, the Yoruba party;

after three years in jail for alleged high treason he was appointed Commissar for Finance in June 1967 by General Gowon, the head of the Nigerian military government. On the early period of his career cf. Awo, *The Autobiography of Chief Obafemi Awolowo* (Cambridge, 1960).

70 In Solanke's absence acting warden of the WASU hostel in London; later (until January 1966) a Nigerian federal minister.

71 Now president of Kenya after several years in exile.

72 Now president of Malawi (formerly Nyasaland).

73 Cf. above, p. 387.

74 Cf. above, n. 16.

75 Cf. above, pp. 379, 397.

76 Cf. above, p. 272.

77 Until January 1966 Nigerian minister of foreign affairs.

78 Cf. above, p 355 and ch. 17; after Ghana achieved its independence and until Padmore's death in 1959 Makonnen (whose first name is not 'Otto', as stated by Legum, *Pan-Africanism*, p. 31) was director of the African Affairs Centre in Accra, but he quarrelled with Nkrumah and in 1964 was downgraded to the post of director of hotels and tourism. After Nkrumah's fall he seems to have been expelled from Ghana as an undesirable alien and all trace of him has been lost; perhaps he went back to Manchester.

79 Nkrumah, *Autobiography*, p. 44.

80 Cf. above, pp. 74f, 354.

81 Cf. above, p. 370.

82 Cf. above, p. 11.

83 Cf. above, Pt I, ch. 4, 5, pp. 41ff, 58ff

84 F. L. Bartels, *Ghana Methodism*, p. 144.

85 Cf. above, pp. 185, 188, 290.

86 Cf. above, pp. 41f.

87 Padmore, *Pan-Africanism*, p. 152.

88 Cf. above, pp. 235, 241f.

89 Composition of the commissions in *History*, p. 74.

90 Cf. above, n. 60.

91 Cf. above, p. 174.

92 Cf. also above, p. 252.

93 Cf. above, p. 388.

94 Cf. above, pp. 395f.

95 Cf. above, p. xi.

96 See *History* also for the following.

97 In his zeal Du Bois was guilty of an exaggeration here, for so far as is known he had never visited Ethiopia.

98 *History*, p. 63. The resolution 'Ethiopia, Liberia, Haiti' is instructive enough, considering the historical background (cf. above, pp. 198–206, 209–12), to be quoted here in full: 'The Fifth Pan-African Congress sends fraternal greetings to the Governments and peoples of Ethiopia, Liberia and Haiti, and pledges its support in mobilising world public opinion among Africans and peoples of African descent in defence of their sovereign independence. We assure the Governments and peoples of these States that we shall ever be vigilant against any manifestation of Imperial encroachment which may threaten their independence. We take this opportunity to inform the Imperial powers that we look with jealous pride upon these nations and regard them as symbols of the realisation of the political hopes and aspiration of African peoples still under Imperialist domination.' Cited in part in Padmore, *Pan-Africanism*, p. 168.

99 According to Nkrumah, *Autobiography*, p. 44, Du Bois drafted the declaration.

100 *History*, p. 5; Padmore, *Pan-Africanism*, p. 170.

101 The resolution is reprinted in K. Nkrumah, *Towards Colonial Freedom* . . . , (London, Melbourne, Toronto, 1947, second edition 1962) pp. 44f.; Nkrumah ended his pamphlet of 1945 with a similar slogan: 'Peoples of the Colonies Unite: the Working Men of All Countries are behind You!'

102 Cf. especially Decraene, *Le Pan-africanisme*; Legum, *Pan-Africanism*; Strauch, *Panafrika;* Thompson, *Africa and Unity.*

PART III

Chapter 20

1 Cf. above, pp. 166–9, 196f.
2 On this there is some material in the Du Bois papers, Accra.
3 Hitherto only mentioned briefly in K. Nkrumah, *Autobiography* p. 47; H. F. Strauch, *Panafrika*, p. 42; but not in G. Padmore, *Pan-Africanism*.
4 'Aims and Objects of the West African National Secretariat', cited from *New African*, 1, no. 1, March 1946, p. 4; also for the following quotations. This paper is likewise not available in public libraries, but I have a xerox copy of no. 1 in my possession.
5 Nkrumah wrote of 'the Circle' later (*Autobiography*, p. 70); further de-dails in the Watson report of 1948: cf. D. Austin, *Politics in Ghana* p. 76.
6 Nkrumah, *Autobiography*, pp. 40f.; on p. 43 he gives an assessment of the British communist leaders Palme Dutt and Harry Pollitt.
7 *Domination or Co-operation?* (London, 1946) pp. 4f.
8 K. Nkrumah, *Towards Colonial Freedom*; on pp. ix f. is an account of the way it first appeared.
9 Unsigned note to Makonnen, 30 March 1947, on paper with the heading 'West African National Secretariat', presumably from Nkrumah, in the Solanke papers: 'The West African Deputies of the French National Assembly will be coming to London this Easter on the invitation of the Secretariat to continue the deliberations of the Conference held last year, and to implement the decisions taken, especially to make plans for calling

the All-West African Congress next year.'
10 Strauch, *Panafrika*, p. 4.
11 Makonnen, *Pan-Africanism*, pp. 262f. *Africanism*, pp. 8, 92f.
12 Cf. above, pp. 412f.
13 Nkrumah, *Autobiography*, p. 47.
14 On Dinah Stock cf. R. Reynolds, *My Life and Crimes*, pp. 85f., 118f.; cf. also *Pan-Africa*, 1, no. 8, August 1947, with an evaluation of her after her return to India; cf. also G. Delf, *Jomo Kenyatta.*
15 The following were also members of the enlarged editorial board: David S. Talbot (Ethiopia), Dr C. Piliso (England), W. E. G. (Kobina) Sekyi (Gold Coast); of these men nothing else is as yet known. Talbot was a cousin of Makonnen *Pan-Africanism*, pp. 8, 92f.
16 *Pan-Africa*, 1, no. 4, April 1947, pp. 3–7.
17 Ibid., no. 5, May 1947, pp. 3–5.
18 Ibid., no. 6, June 1947, pp. 15–18.
19 Ibid., no. 7, July 1947, pp. 12–17.
20 Ibid., no. 6, June 1947, pp. 3–7.
21 Ibid., 1, no. 4, April 1947, pp. 37–40; ibid., May 1947, pp. 21–4.
22 Cf. above, p. 68.
23 Ibid., no. 4, pp. 37–9.
24 Ibid., no. 5, p. 21.
25 Ibid., no. 8, August 1947, pp. 26–32.
26 Ibid., no. 7, July 1947, pp. 17–26; on Émile Faure cf. above, pp. 307, 311–12.
27 Ibid., p. 39.
28 Ibid., 1, no. 4, April 1947, pp. 3–7; cf. above, n. 16.
29 Ibid., 2, no. 1–2, January–February 1948.
30 Cf. Padmore, *Pan-Africanism*, p. 174; Strauch, *Panafrika*, p. 43. Padmore spoke exaggeratedly of 'several years' during which the paper had been published.
31 Padmore, ibid., p. 373.
32 St Clair Drake, an Afro-American political scientist at the University of Chicago, took part in the Manchester congress as an observer and

thereafter belonged to Nkrumah's circle (in the broader sense of the word); cf. his article 'Philosophical Consciencism: the Role of Social Philosophy and Political Theory in New Nations', *Pan-Africanist Review: a Quarterly of the African Revolution*, 1, no. 3, September 1964, pp. 5–14.

33 On the London period of Padmore's career, between Manchester and his move to Ghana, cf. now J. R. Hooker, *Black Revolutionary*, pp. 99–108.

34 Cf. below, pp. 419f.

35 Cf. above, pp. 413f.

36 A sentence frequently cited during the Nkrumah era in Ghana. On this period cf. D. Austin, *Politics in Ghana*, and D. E. Apter, *Ghana in Transition* (Princeton, 1963).

37 G. Padmore, *The Gold Coast Revolution* (London, 1953).

38 (London, 1956); for critical remarks cf. above, Pt II, ch. 17, n. 66.

39 Hooker, *Black Revolutionary*, pp. 132f.

40 P. Decraene, *Le Panafricanisme*, p. 28.

41 Further material in *Awakening Africa . . .*, n.p., n.d. [Accra, 1959] edited by the Bureau of African Affairs. On this and the following conference cf. also Hooker, *Black Revolutionary*, pp. 135f.

42 Cf. above, p. 319f.

43 Cf. especially G. A. Nasser, *The Philosophy of the Revolution*, n.p., n.d. [Cairo, 1954], pp. 62f.: his theory of the three circles in which Egyptian policy revolves: the Arab countries, Africa and the Third World.

44 Material on both congresses in *1er Congrès International des Écrivains et Artistes Noirs* (Présence Africaine, Paris, 1957); *2e Congrès . . .* (Paris, 1959).

45 Further details in J. S. Nye Jr, *Pan-Africanism and East African Integration* (Cambridge – Mass., London, Nairobi, 1966); cf. above, Pt I, ch. 1, n. 39; R. Cox, *Pan-Africanism in Practice* (London, 1964).

46 On this recent period cf. the works by Decraene, Legum and Strauch; in more detail now, Thompson, *Africa and Unity*. On the Union Africaine et Malgache cf. now the work of its former general secretary, Albert Tevoedjre, *Pan-Africanism in Action: an Account of the UAM* (Cambridge – Mass., 1965).

47 Cf. above, pp. 130ff.

48 Cf. in this context I. Geiss, *Gewerkschaften in Afrika* (Hanover, 1965), especially the chapters on the AATUF and ATUC, pp. 87–96, 97–102.

49 Cf. especially the documents in *Second Conference of the All-African Trade Union Federation . . . .* , n.p., n.d. [Accra, 1964].

50 For the reasons, as analysed before Nkrumah's fall, cf. D. Austin, *Politics in Ghana*. Also useful is the earlier work by J. Philips, *Kwame Nkrumah and the Future of Africa*, (London, 1960). Philips was an early White associate of Nkrumah from South Africa who soon became disillusioned in him, as did the Nigerian Bankole Timothy. A critical attitude is taken from the beginning by H. L. Bretton, *The Rise and Fall of Kwame Nkrumah: a Study of Personal Rule in Africa* (London, 1967); Davidson, *Black Star*, pp. 202ff.

51 Cf. now also J. K. Nyerere, *Freedom and Unity: a Selection from Writings and Speeches, 1952–1965* (London, Dar es Salaam, 1967), especially pp. 1–122 and various articles and speeches on the problem of African unity. Even so sober an observer as Nyerere makes the mistake of idealizing and romanticizing precolonial African society (pp. 9–11) although he is well aware of the necessity for radical changes in society as a result of modernization.

52 Nkrumah, *Neo-Colonialism: the Last Stage of Imperialism* (London, 1965).

53 Idem, *Consciencism: Philosophy and*

Ideology for Decolonization and Development.

54 This is the impression I gained from a four-hour conversation with Makonnen in Accra in November 1964.

55 *Der Ostblock und die Entwicklungsländer. Vierteljahresbericht der Friedrich-Ebert-Stiftung,* no. 12–13, August 1963, p. 70. The review is by the present author, apart from a few (polemical) additions by the editor of the journal.

56 *The Spark,* 16 October and 20 November 1964.

Chapter 21

1 Cf. above, pp. 115, 416.
2 Especially Pennington, Crummell, Brown, Scholes and Firmin: cf. above, pp. 167, 174–8, 179–85, 205–8.
3 Cf. above, p. 205.
4 Cf. above, pp. 258–62, 371.
5 Cf. above, pp. 258–62, 371.
6 Cf. above, this section, ch. 20, n. 1.

7 Cf. above, p. 204.
8 This is Padmore's thesis in *Pan-Africanism or Communism?*
9 Scholes (cf. above, pp. 111f).
10 Cf. above, p. 121.
11 Cf. above, p. 121.
12 Cf. above, p. 407.
13 For the first comparative surveys cf. R. L. Buell, *International Relations* (London, 1925, printed in USA 1926), pp. 72–94, the chapter 'Pan-Nationalism', where he gives a sketch of the most important 'Pan' movements, including 'Pan-Germanism', the 'Pan-Anglo-Movement', 'Pan-Latinism', 'Pan-Hispanism' and the 'Pan-Asiatic Movement'. Cf. also H. Kohn, 'Pan Movements', *Encyclopaedia of the Social Sciences,* vol. XI (New York, 1933) pp. 544–54, which is less comprehensive.
14 Cf. above, pp. 100ff.
15 Cf. above, p. 317.
16 Although the USSR itself destroyed Slav solidarity by invading Czechoslovakia on 21 August 1968.

Bibliography

I. Unpublished sources

A. ARCHIVES

Archives Nationales, Section d'Outre-Mer, Paris, Rue Oudinot:
SLOTFOM, sér. 5.
Methodist Missionary Society Archives, London.
National Archives, Washington DC: Department of State Decimal
File 882.00/739.
Rhodes House, Oxford: MSS. British Empire, S. 22, Anti-Slavery
Papers.

B. PRIVATE COLLECTIONS

John Edward Bruce Papers, Schomburg Collection, New York.
W. E. B. Du Bois Papers, Accra.
Thomas Hodgkin, Oxford.
Herbert Macaulay, Ibadan University Library, Ibadan.
Kwame Nkrumah Papers, Ghana National Archives, Accra.
Jacob A. Obisesan Diary, 1920–1960, Ibadan University Library,
Ibadan.
Ladipo Solanke, London.

II. Published sources

A. PROTOCOLS, OFFICIAL DOCUMENTS ETC.

Africa and the American Negro. Addresses and Proceedings of the Congress on Africa, December 13–15, 1895. Ed. J. W. E. Bowen (Atlanta, Ga., 1896).

Awakening Africa. Conference of Independent African States, Accra Conference (15th–22nd April 1958). n.p., n.d. [Accra, ca. 1962].

Colonial Papers, House of Commons. *Report on the Commercial State of the West Indian Colonies* (London, 1807).

The Communist International. 1919–1945. Documents. 2 volumes, ed. Jane Degras (London, 1956).

Premier Congrès International des Écrivains et Artistes Noirs (Présence Africaine, Paris, 1957).

Deuxième Congrès International des Écrivains et Artistes Noirs (Présence Africaine, Paris, 1959).

Das Flammenzeichen von Palais Egmont. Protokoll des Kongresses gegen koloniale Unterdrückung und Imperialismus, Brüssel, 10–15. February 1927. Ed. Liga gegen Imperialismus (Berlin, 1927).

Gold Coast Legislative Council. *Sessional Papers*, no. VII. 1919–1920.

HAMILTON, J. B., *Entrance Register of the C.M.S. Grammar School* (Freetown, Sierra Leone, 1935).

History of the Pan-African Congress. Ed. George Padmore (London, 1947, second edition, 1963).

League of Nations Mandates. *Second Pan-African Congress, August–September 1921.*

METCALFE, G. E., *Great Britain and Ghana: Documents of Ghana History, 1807–1957* (London, Edinburgh, 1964).

Pan-Africanism Reconsidered. Ed. American Society of African Culture (Berkeley, Los Angeles, 1962).

Papers on Inter-Racial Problems. Universal Races Congress, London, 1911. Ed. Gustav Spiller.

Proceedings of the Conference on Africa: New Perspectives. Under the auspices of the Council on African Affairs, New York City, 23 West 26th Street, New York City, April 1944 (New York, 1944).

Proceedings of the National Emigration Convention of Colored People: held at Cleveland, Ohio (Pittsburgh, 1854).

Report of the Pan-African Conference held at the 23rd, 24th and 25th July, 1900, at Westminster Town Hall, Westminster S.W., London (n.d. – ca. 1900).
Resolutions of the Conference of Africans of British West Africa held at Accra, Gold Coast, from 11th to 29th March 1920 (London, 1920).
Second Conference of the All-African Trade Union Federation: Bamako, 10th–14th June 1964. Reports and Resolutions. n.p., n.d. [Accra, ca. 1964].

B. CONTEMPORARY NEWSPAPERS AND PERIODICALS

Aborigines Friend, London.
The African Interpreter, New York.
African Mail.
The African Repository.
African Times, London.
The African Times and Orient Review, London.
African World, London.
A.M.E. Zion Quarterly Review.
Ami du Peuple, Paris.
Atlantic Monthly.
The Black Man, London.
Challenge.
The Church Missionary Intelligencer: a Monthly Journal of Missionary Information, London.
The Comet, Lagos.
Crisis: a Record of the Darker Races, New York.
The Defender, Chicago.
The Gold Coast Aborigines, Cape Coast.
The Gold Coast Chronicle, Cape Coast.
The Gold Coast Express, Cape Coast.
The Gold Coast Free Press, Cape Coast.
The Gold Coast Independent, Cape Coast.
The Gold Coast Leader, Cape Coast.
The Gold Coast Methodist Times, Cape Coast.
The Gold Coast Nation, Cape Coast.
The Gold Coast News, Cape Coast.
The Gold Coast Review, Cape Coast.
The Gold Coast Spectator, Cape Coast.

The Gold Coast Times, Cape Coast.
Horizon: a Journal of the Color Line.
Journal of the African Society, London.
The Keys (continued as: *News-Letter*), London.
Labour Monthly, London.
The Lagos Observer, Lagos.
The Lagos Standard, Lagos.
The Negro Worker, Hamburg, Copenhagen, Paris.
The New African, London.
The New Leader, London.
News Letter, London.
North American Review, London.
Pan-Africa, London.
The Pan-African, London.
The Pan-Africanist Review, Accra.
La Race Nègre, Paris.
Sierra Leone Times, Freetown.
Sierra Leone Weekly News, Freetown.
The Spark, Accra.
Le Temps, Paris.
The Times, London.
Voice of Missions.
La Voix des Nègres.
WASU (continued as: *WASU Magazine* etc.), London.
West Africa, London.
West African Times (continued as: *Times of West Africa*), Accra.

C. CONTEMPORARY PAMPHLETS AND BOOKS

ABRAHAMS, PETER, *A Wreath for Udomo* (London, 1956).
AGBEBI, MAJOLA, *Inaugural Sermon: Delivered at the Celebration of the First Anniversary of the 'African Church', Lagos, West Africa, December 21, 1902.* n.p., n.d. [Lagos, ca. 1903].
AHUMA, S. R. B. ATTOH, *Memoirs of West African Celebrities, Europe etc. (1700–1850). with Special Reference to the Gold Coast* (Liverpool, 1905).
ALLEYNE, CAMERON C., *Gold Coast at a Glance* (New York, 1931).
ANDERSON, J. HARVEY, *Bibliographical Souvenir Volume of the 23rd Quadrennial Session of the A.M.E.Z. Church, May 8–30, 1908.* n.p., n.d.

ARMISTEAD, WILSON, *Tribute for the Negro: being a Vindication of the Moral, Intellectual and Religious Capabilities of the Coloured Portion of Mankind* (Manchester, 1848).

AZIKIWE, NNAMDI, *Liberia in World Politics*. 2 volumes (London, 1934).

—— *Renascent Africa* (Accra, 1937, second edition London, 1966).

—— *The Atlantic Charter and British West Africa*. n.p., n.d. [Lagos, 1943].

BARRET, SAMUEL, *A Plea for Unity amongst American Negroes and the Negroes of the World* (Waterloo – Iowa, 1926, fifth edition 1943).

BELLEGARDE, DANTÈS, *Un Haitien parle* (Port-au-Prince, 1934).

BENEZET, ANTHONY, *Some Historical Account of Guinea, its Situation, Produce, and the General Disposition of its Inhabitants, with an Inquiry into the Rise and Progress of the Slave-Trade, its Nature and Lamentable Effects* (London, 1762, fourth edition 1788).

—— *A Caution and Warning to Great Britain and her Colonies* (Philadelphia, 1766).

BERRY, L. L., *A Century of Missions of the African Methodist Episcopal Church, 1840–1940* (New York, 1942).

BLYDEN, EDWARD W., *Christianity, Islam and the Negro Race* (second edition London, 1889, reprinted Edinburgh, 1967).

—— *From West Africa to Palestine* (Freetown, Manchester, London, 1873).

—— *Liberia's Offering: the Call of Providence to the Descendants of Africa in America*. Delivered to Colored Congregations in the Cities of New York, Philadelphia, Baltimore, Harrisburgh etc. during the Summer of 1862 (New York, 1862).

—— *The Negro in Ancient History* (Washington, 1869).

—— *The People of Africa*. Series of Papers of their Character, Condition and Future Prospects (New York, 1871).

—— *A Vindication of the African Race: being a Brief Examination of the Arguments in Favour of African Inferiority*. With an Introduction by Alexander Crummell (Monrovia, 1857).

—— *West Africa before Europe and Other Addresses Delivered in England in 1901 and 1903*. With an introduction by Casely Hayford (London, 1905).

—— *The West African University* (Freetown, Manchester, 1972).

BOOTH, JOSEPH, *Africa for the Africans* (Nyasaland, 1897).

BUXTON, THOMAS FOWELL, *The African Slave Trade and its Remedy*. 2 volumes (London, 1839–40).

CAMPBELL, J. G., *Some Thoughts on Abeokuta during the reign of His Highness King Gbadebo, the Alake, 1898–1918* (Lagos), n.d. [1918].

CAMPBELL, ROBERT, *A Pilgrimage to my Motherland: an Account of a Journey among the Egbas and Yorubas of Central Africa in 1859–60* (Philadelphia, 1861).

CAPITEIN, JACOBUS ELISA JOANNES, *Dissertatio Politico-Theologica de Servitute, Libertati Christianae non Contraria* (Leiden, 1742). Dutch edition, *Staatkundig-Godgeleerd Onderzoekschrift over de Slavery, als niet strydig tegende Christelyke Vryheid.*

CARY, JOYCE, *The Case for African Freedom* (London, 1941, second edition 1944).

CLARKSON, THOMAS, *Review of the Rev. Thomas B. Freeman's Journals of Visits to Ashanti &c.: with Remarks on the Present Situation of Africa, and its Spiritual Prospects* (London, 1845).

COPPIN, LEVIN J., *Observation of Persons and Things in South Africa, 1900–1904.* n.p., n.d. [ca. 1905].

COULMAS, PETER, *Der Fluch der Freiheit. Wohin marschiert die Farbige Welt?* (Oldenburg, Hamburg, 1963).

CRUMMELL, ALEXANDER, *Africa and America: Addresses and Discourses* (Springfield – Mass., 1891).

—— *The Future of Africa: Being Addresses, Sermons, etc. etc. Delivered in the Republic of Liberia* (second edition New York, 1862).

—— *The Relations and Duties of Free Colored Men in America to Africa* (Hartford, 1861).

CUGOANO, OTTOBAH, *Thoughts and Sentiments on the Evil and Wicked Traffic of Slavery and Commerce of the Human Species, Humbly Submitted to the Inhabitants of Great Britain by Ottobah Cugoano, a Native of Africa* (London, 1787). French translation, *Réflexions sur la traite et l'esclavage des Nègres* (Paris, 1788).

CUNARD, NANCY (ed.), *Negro Anthology 1931–1933* (London, 1934).

DANQUAH, J. B., *Self-Help and Expansion: a Review of the Work and Aims of the Youth Conference, with a Statement of its Policy for 1943, and the Action consequent upon that Policy.* (Accra) n.d. [1943].

DAVONPORT, W. A., *The Anthology of Zion Methodism* (Charlotte – North Carolina, 1925).

DE GRAFT-JOHNSON, JAMES W., *Towards Nationhood in West Africa* (London, 1928).

DE GRAFT-JOHNSON, J. C., *African Glory* (London, 1954).

DELANY, MARTIN R., *The Condition, Elevation, Emigration and Destiny of the Colored People of the United States, Politically Considered* (Philadelphia, 1852).

—— *Official Report of the Niger Valley Exploring Party* (New York, Leeds, 1861).

—— *Principia of Ethnology: the Origins of Race and Color, with an Archaeological Compendium of Ethiopian and Egyptian Civilization from Years of Careful Examination and Enquiry* (Philadelphia, 1878, second edition 1880).

Domination or Co-operation? Report on a Conference on the Relationship between the British and Colonial Peoples. Fabian Colonial Bureau Pamphlet. Controversy Series no. 1 (London, 1946).

DOUGLASS, FREDERICK, *The Claim of the Negro Ethnologically Considered: an Address* (Rochester, New York, 1854).

DU BOIS, W. E. B., *An ABC of Color. Selections from over a Half Century of the Writing of W. E. B. Du Bois* (Berlin, 1963).

—— *In Battle for Peace* (New York, 1952).

—— *Color and Democracy: Colonies and Peace* (New York, 1945).

—— *The Conservation of Race.* American Negro Academy. Occasional Papers no. 2 (Washington, 1897).

—— *Darkwater: Voices from within the Veil* (New York, London, 1920).

—— *Dusk of Dawn: an Essay toward an Autobiographv of a Race Concept* (New York, 1940).

—— *Mein Weg, meine Welt.* German translation of: *A Soliloquy on Viewing my Life* (Berlin, 1965).

—— *The Souls of Black Folk: Essays and Sketches* (Chicago, 1903, reprinted New York, 1964).

—— *The World and Africa: an Inquiry into the Part which Africa has Played in World History* (1947, second edition 1965).

EASTON, HOSEA, *A Treatise on the Intellectual Character and the Political Condition of the Colored People of the United States and the Prejudice Exercised towards Them* (Boston, 1837).

ÉDOUARD, EMMANUEL, *Essai sur la politique intérieure d'Haiti: propositions d'une politique nouvelle* (Paris, 1890).

ELLIS, GEORGE W., *Negro Culture in West Africa* (New York, 1914).

FERRIS, WILLIAM H., *Alexander Crummell: an Apostle of Negro Culture* (Washington, 1920).

FIRMIN, ANTÉNOR, *De l'égalité des races humaines (Anthropologie positive)* (Paris, 1885).

—— *Diplomates et diplomatie. Lettre ouverte à M. Solon Menos* Cap-Haitien, 1899).

FIRMIN, ANTÉNOR, *Lettres de Saint-Thomas. Études sociologiques, historiques et littéraires* (Paris, 1910).

FREEMAN, THOMAS B., *Journal of Various Visits to the Kingdom of Ashanti, Aku and Dahomi* (second edition, London, 1844).

GARNET, HENRY H., *The Past and the Present Condition, and the Destiny of the Colored Race: a Discourse Delivered at the 15th Anniversary of the Female Benevolent Society of Troy N.Y., February 14, 1848* (New York, 1848).

GARRISON, WILLIAM L., *Thoughts on African Colonization: or an Exhibition of the Principles and Purposes of the American Colonization Society* (Boston, 1832).

GARVEY, AMY JACQUES, *Garvey and Garveyism* (Kingston – Jamaica, 1963).

—— (ed.), *Philosophy and Opinions of Marcus Garvey.* 2 volumes (New York, 1923–6, second edition London, 1967, edited by E. U. Essien-Udom).

GOBINEAU, JOSEPH ARTHUR DE, *Essai sur l'inégalité de races humaines.* 4 volumes (Paris, 1853–5).

GRÉGOIRE, HENRI BAPTISTE, *De la Littérature des nègres ou recherches sur leurs facultés intellectuelles, leurs qualités morales et leur littérature: suivies de Notices sur la vie et les ouvrages des Negrès qui se sont distingués dans les Sciences, les Lettres et les Arts* (Paris, 1808). English edition, *An Enquiry concerning the Intellectual and Moral Faculties, and Literature of Negroes; Followed with an Account of the Life and Works of Fifteen Negroes and Mulattoes, Distinguished in Science, Literature and the Arts* (Brooklyn, 1810).

HAYFORD, CASELY, *Ethiopia Unbound* (London, 1911).

—— *Fanti Customary Laws* (London, 1904).

—— *Fanti National Constitution* (London, 1906).

—— *Gold Coast Native Institutions: with Thoughts upon a Healthy Imperial Policy for the Gold Coast and Ashanti* (London, 1903).

—— *Notes on the Truth about the West African Land Question* (London, 1911).

—— *William Waddy Harris, the West African Reformer: the Man and his Message* (London, 1915)

HAYNE, JOSEPH E., *The Ammonian or Hametic Origin of the Ancient Greeks, Cretes and All the Celtic Races* (Brooklyn, 1905).

—— *The Black Man: or the Natural History of the Hametic Race* (Raleigh, North Carolina, 1894).

—— *The Negro in Sacred History, or Ham and his Immediate Descendants* (Charleston, South Carolina, 1887).

HOOD, J. W., *One Hundred Years of the African Methodist Episcopal Zion Church; or the Centenial of African Methodism* (New York, 1885).

HOPKINS, PAULINE E., *Primer of Facts Pertaining to the Early Greatness of the African Race and the Possibility of Restoration by its Descendants* (Cambridge – Mass., 1905).

HORTON, JAMES AFRICANUS B., *Letters on the Political Condition of the Gold Coast since the Exchange of Territory between the English and Dutch Governments on January 1, 1868, together with a Short Account of the Ashantee War, 1862–1864, and the Awoonah War, 1866* (London, 1870, reprinted London, 1970, edited by E. A. Ayandele).

—— *Physical and Medical Climate and Meteorology of the West Coast o, Africa* (London, 1867).

—— *West African Countries and Peoples, British and Native, with the Requirements Necessary for Establishing that Self-Government Recommended by the Committee of the House of Commons; and a Vindication of the African Race* (London, 1868, reprinted Edinburgh, 1969, edited by G. Shepperson).

HUNTON, A. W., *Decision in Africa* (New York, 1954).

IKEOTUONYE, V. C., *Zik of New Africa* (London, Geneva, 1961).

JEFFERSON, THOMAS, *Notes on the State of Virginia* (London, 1787).

JOHNSON, JAMES W., *Self-Determining Haiti: Four Articles Reprinted from 'The Nation' embodying a Report of Investigation made for the NAACP* (New York, 1920).

JONES, JESSE, *Education in Africa: a Study of West, South and Equatorial Africa by the African Education Commission* (New York, 1922).

Die Kämpfe der deutschen Truppen in Südwestafrika. Ed. Grosser Generalstab, Kriegsgeschichtliche Abteilung 1. Vol. 1: *Der Feldzug gegen die Hereros* (Berlin, 1906).

KINCH, E. C., *West Africa: an Open Door* (New York, 1917).

LENIN, W. I., *Über die nationale und die koloniale Frage. Eine Sammlung ausgewählter Aufsätze und Reden* (Berlin, 1960).

LEWIS, ROBERT B., *Light and Truth: Collected from the Bible and Ancient and Modern History. Containing the Universal History of the Colored and Indian Races, from the Creation of the World to the Present Times* (Boston, 1844).

LOCKE, ALAIN (ed.), *The New Negro: an Interpretation* (New York, 1927).

MANOEDI, MOKETE M., *Garvey and Africa* (New York) n.d. [1924?].

MARAN, RENÉ, *Batouala. Véritable Roman Nègre* (Paris, 1921).

MBADIWE, KINGSLEY O., *British and Axis Aims in Africa* (New York, 1942).

MCKAY, CLAUDE, *Banjo* (New York, 1927; Moscow, 1930; Paris, 1931).

—— *A Long Way from Home* (New York, 1937).

NASSER, GAMAL ABDEL, *Egypt's Liberation* (Washington, 1955).

—— *The Philosophy of Revolution.* n.p., n.d. [Cairo, 1954].

NKRUMAH, KWAME, *Africa Must Unite* (London, Melbourne, Toronto, 1963; London, 1965).

—— *Consciencism: Philosophy and Ideology for Decolonization and Development with Particular Reference to the African Revolution* (London, 1964). German translation (Cologne, Opladen, 1966).

—— *Ghana: the Autobiography of Kwame Nkrumah* (Edinburgh, Toronto, New York, 1957, fourth edition 1961).

—— *I Speak of Freedom* (London, 1961, second impression 1962).

—— *Neo-Colonialism: the Last Stage of Imperialism* (London, 1965).

NYERERE, JULIUS K., *Freedom and Unity: a Selection from Writings and Speeches, 1952–1965* (London, Dar es Salaam, 1967).

OJIKE, MBONU, *My Africa* (New York, 1946; London, 1955).

ORIZU, A. A. NWAFOR, *Without Bitterness: Western Nations in Post-War Africa* (New York, 1944).

OSEI, GABRIEL K., *Fifty Unknown Facts about the African with Complete Proof* (London, 1966).

—— *The Forgotten Great Africans, 3000 B.C.–A.D. 1959* (London, 1965).

OTIS, JAMES, *The Rights of the British Colonies Asserted and Approved* (Boston, London, 1764).

OTTLEY, ROI, *New World A-Coming: Inside Black America* (Boston, 1943).

PADMORE, GEORGE, *Africa and World Peace* (London, 1937).

—— *Africa: Britain's Third Empire* (London, 1949).

—— *The Gold Coast Revolution: the Struggle of an African People from Slavery to Freedom* (London, 1953).

—— *How Britain Rules Africa* (London, 1936).

—— *How Russia Transformed Her Colonial Empire: a Challenge to the Imperialist Powers* (London, 1946).

—— *The Life and Struggles of the Negro Toilers* (London, 1956).

—— *Pan-Africanism or Communism? The Coming Struggle for Africa* (London, 1956).

PAINE, THOMAS, *African Slavery in America*. n.p. (1775).

PENNINGTON, JAMES W. C., *Text Book of the Origin and History &c. of the Colored People* (Hartford, 1841).

PHILIPS, JOHN, *Kwame Nkrumah and the Future of Africa* (London, 1960).

PRICE-MARS, JEAN, *Ainsi Parla l'oncle. Essais d'ethnographie* (Port-au-Prince, Paris, 1928).

—— *La Vocation d'élite* (Port-au-Prince, 1919).

QUAISON-SACKEY, ALEX, *Africa Unbound: Reflections of an African Statesman* (New York, 1963).

RAMSAY, JAMES, *An Essay on the Treatment and Conversion of African Slaves in the British Sugar Colonies* (London, 1784).

REDPATH, JAMES, *A Guide to Hayti* (Boston, 1861).

REYNOLDS, REGINALD, *My Life and Crimes* (London, 1956).

ROGERS, J. A., *One Hundred Amazing Facts about the Negro with Complete Proof*. n.p., n.d. [New York, 1934, twenty-third edition 1957].

—— *Sex and Race: History of the Mixing of White and Black from Prehistoric Times to the Present*. 3 volumes (New York, 1940).

—— *World's Great Men of Color, 3000 B.C.–A.D. 1946*. 2 volumes (New York, 1946–7).

ROSEMOND, LUDOVIC J., *Le Réveil de la conscience nationale*. Bibliothèque Haitienne (Port-au-Prince, 1932).

SAMPSON, MAGNUS J., *Gold Coast Men of Affairs, Past and Present* (London, 1937).

—— (ed.), *West African Leadership: Public Speeches* (Bristol, 1951).

SANCHO, IGNATIUS, *Letters of the Late Ignatius Sancho, an African, in Two Volumes, to which are Prefixed Memoirs of His Life*. 2 volumes (London, 1781, second edition 1782).

SARBAH, JOHN MENSAH, *Fanti Customary Laws* (London, 1897, second edition 1904).

—— *Fanti National Constitution* (London, 1906).

SCHOLES, THEOPHILIUS E. SAMUEL, *The British Empire and Alliances: or, Britain's Duty to her Colonies and Subject Races* (London, 1899).

SCHOLES, THEOPHILIUS E. SAMUEL, Bartholomew Smith,
   [i.e. T. E. S. Scholes]: *Chamberlain and Chamberlainism: his Fiscal Proposals and Colonial Policy* (London, 1903).
—— *Glimpses of the Ages: or, the 'Superior' and 'Inferior' Races, so-called, Discussed on the Light of Science and History.* 2 volumes (London, 1905, 1908).
—— (ed.), *Industrial Self-supporting Missionaries: a Practical Scheme.* Inaugurated by the Congo Training Institute, Colwyn Bay, North Wales (Colwyn Bay) n.d. [ca. 1895].
SENGHOR, LÉOPOLD S., *Négritude et humanisme.* German translation: Janheinz Jahn, *Negritude und Humanismus* (Düsseldorf, Cologne, 1967).
SHARP, J., *Just Limitation of Slavery* (London, 1776).
—— *The Law of Liberty* (London, 1776).
—— *The Law of Passive Obedience* (London, 1776).
SMITH, JAMES H., *Vital Facts Concerning the African Methodist Episcopal Church: its Origin, Doctrines, Government, Usages, Polity, Progress.* n.p., n.d. [1931].
SOLANKE, LAPIDO, *United West Africa (or Africa) at the Bar of the Family of Nations* (London, 1927).
SOUTHON, ARTHUR E., *Gold Coast Methodism* (London, Cape Coast, 1934).
STEWART, T. MCCANTS, *Liberia: the Americo-African Republic. Being Some Impressions of the Climate, Resources and People, Resulting from Personal Observation and Experience in West Africa* (New York, 1886).
SYLVAIN, GEORGES, *Dix Années de lutte pour la liberté, 1915–1925.* 2 volumes (Port-au-Prince) n.d. [1955].
TANNER, B. T., *The Descent of the Negro. Reply to Rev. Drs. J. H. Vincent, J. M. Freeman and J. L. Hurlbut* (Philadelphia, 1898).
—— *The Negro in the Holy Writ* (Philadelphia, 1902).
—— *The Negro's Origin, and Is the Negro Cursed?* (Philadelphia, 1869).
TIFFANY, OTIS T., *Africa for the Africans.* Being the Annual Discourse Delivered at the Sixty-Seventh Anniversary of the American Colonization Society (Washington, 1884).
VASSA, GUSTAVUS, *Equiano's Travels: the Interesting Narrative of the Life of O. Equiano or Gustavus Vassa, the African, written by himself* (London, 1789; abridged edition New York, London, Ibadan, 1967).
VOLNEY, C. F., *Les Ruines, ou méditations sur les révolutions des empires*

(Paris, 1794). English translation, *The Ruins, or a Survey of the Revolutions of Empires, to which is added the Law of Nature* (London, 1822).

WADSTRÖM, CARL BERND, *An Essay on Colonization. Particularly Applied to the Western Coast of Africa, with Some Free Thoughts on Cultivation and Commerce; Also Brief Descriptions of the Colonies Already Formed or Attempted, in Africa, Including those of Sierra Leone and Bulama.* 2 parts (London, 1794–5).

WALLACE-JOHNSON, ISAAC T. A., *Trade Unionism in Colonial and Dependent Territories.* West African National Secretariat Publication (London, 1946).

WALTERS, ALEXANDER, *My Life and Work* (New York, Chicago, Toronto, London, Edinburgh, 1917).

WEBB, JAMES M., *The Black Man, the Father of Civilization, Proven by Biblical History* (Seattle, 1910).

WRIGHT, RICHARD R., JR, *Centennial Encyclopaedia of the Methodist Episcopal Church* (Philadelphia, 1916).

YOUNG, ROBERT A., *The Ethiopian Manifesto, Issued in Defence of the Black Man's Rights in the Scale of Universal Freedom* (New York, 1829).

D. SCHOLARLY WORKS

Africa Seen by American Negroes. Ed. John A. Davis (Paris, 1958).

AJAYI, J. F. A., *Christian Missions in Nigeria, 1841–1891: the Making of a New Élite* (London, 1965).

AKITA, J. M., *Commission on Kwame Nkrumah Papers: Catalogue of Special Exhibition, May 1965.* n.p., n.d. [Accra, 1965].

ALBERTINI, RUDOLF VON, *Dekolonisation: die Diskussion über Verwaltung und Zukunft der Kolonien 1919–1960* (Cologne, Opladen, 1966).

ANENE, J. C., *Southern Nigeria in Transition, 1885–1906: Theory and Practice in a Colonial Protectorate* (London, 1966).

ANENE, J. C. and BROWN, G. N., *Africa in the Nineteenth and Twentieth Centuries: a Handbook for Teachers and Students* (Ibadan, London, 1966).

ANSPRENGER, FRANZ, *Politik im Schwarzen Afrika: die modernen politischen Bewegungen im Afrika französischer Prägung* (Cologne, Opladen, 1961).

ANSPRENGER, FRANZ, *Auflösung der Kolonialreiche*, dtv-Weltgeschichte des 20. Jahrunderts, Vol. 13 (Munich, 1966).

APTER, DAVID E., *Ghana in Transition* (Princeton, 1963).

APTHEKER, HERBERT, *American Negro Slave Revolts* (New York, 1943, fifth edition 1964).

—— *A Documentary History of the Negro People in the United States.* 2 volumes (New York, 1951, second edition 1964).

—— *David Walker's Appeal to the Colored Citizens of the World, 1829–1830: its Setting and its Meaning* (New York, 1965).

AUSTIN, DENNIS, *Politics in Ghana, 1946–1960* (London, 1964, second edition 1966).

AWO, *The Autobiography of Chief Obafemi Awolowo* (London, 1960).

AYANDELE, E. A., *The Missionary Impact on Modern Nigeria, 1842–1914: a Political and Social Analysis* (London, Ibadan, 1966).

—— *Holy Johnson* (London, 1970).

BARTELS, F. L., *Mfantsipim, 1876–1951.* n.p., n.d. [London, 1951].

—— *The Roots of Ghana Methodism* (London, 1965).

BASTIDE, ROGER, *Les Amériques Noires: les civilisations africaines dans le Nouveau Monde* (Paris, 1967).

BENJAMIN, GEORGES J., *La Diplomatie d'Anténor Firmin: ses péripéties – ses aspects* (Paris, 1960).

BENNETT, LERONE J., *Before the Mayflower: a History of the Negro in America, 1619–1964* (Chicago, 1962, third edition Baltimore, Harmondsworth, 1966).

BENSON, MARY, *The African Patriots: the Story of the African National Congress of South Africa* (London, 1963); second revised edition entitled *South Africa: the Struggle for a Birthright* (Harmondsworth, 1966).

BERTAUX, PIERRE, *Afrika: von der Vorgeschichte bis zu den Staaten der Gegenwart.* Fischer Weltgeschichte, Vol. 32 (Frankfurt, 1966).

BEYREUTHER, ERICH, *Der junge Zinzendorf* (Marburg, 1957).

BIOBAKU, SABURI O., *The Egba and their Neighbours, 1842–1872* (Oxford, 1957, second edition 1965).

BIRTHWISTLE, ALLEN W., *Thomas Birch Freeman* (London, 1950).

BITTLE, WILLIAM E. and GEIS, GILBERT, *The Longest Way Home: Chief Alfred D. Sam's Back-to-Africa Movement* (Detroit, 1964).

BONTEMPS, ARNA, *One Hundred Years of Negro Freedom* (New York, 1961).

Bibliography 533

BOURRET, F. M., *Ghana: the Road to Independence, 1919–1957* (London, 1960, third edition 1963).

BOVILL, E. W., *The Golden Trade of the Moors* (London, 1958).

BRETTON, HENRY L., *The Rise and Fall of Kwame Nkrumah: a Study of Personal Rule in Africa* (London, 1967).

BRODERICK, FRANCIS L., *W. E. B. Du Bois: a Negro Leader in a Time of Crisis* (Stanford, 1959).

BROWN, WILLIAM W., *The Black Man: his Antecedents and Achievements* (Savannah – Georgia, Boston, 1863).

—— *The Rising Son: or, the Antecedents and Advancement of the Colored Race* (Boston, 1874).

BUELL, R. L., *A Century of Survival, 1847–1947* (Philadelphia, 1947).

—— *International Relations* (London, 1925, printed in USA, 1926).

—— *The Native Problem in Africa.* 2 volumes (New York, 1928).

CAYTON, HORACE R. and ST CLAIR DRAKE, *Black Metropolis* (New York, 1945).

CLARIDGE, WILLIAM WALTON, *History of Gold Coast and Ashanti.* 2 volumes (London, 1915, second edition 1964).

CLARK, KENNETH B., *Dark Ghetto: Dilemmas of Social Power* (New York, Evanston, London, 1965).

CLARKE, JOHN H. (ed.), *Harlem: a Community in Transition* (New York, 1964).

COLEMAN, JAMES S., *Nigeria: Background to Nationalism* (Berkeley, Los Angeles, 1958, second edition 1960, fourth impression 1965).

COOMBS, DOUGLAS, *The Gold Coast, Britain and the Netherlands, 1850–1874* (London, 1963).

CORNEVIN, ROBERT, *Histoire de l'Afrique.* 3 volumes (Paris, 1962–6). German translation: *Geschichte Afrikas von den Anfängen bis zur Gegenwart* (Stuttgart, 1966).

—— *Histoire du Togo* (Paris, 1959, second edition 1962).

COUPLAND, SIR REGINALD, *The British Anti-Slavery Movement* (London, 1933, second edition 1964).

COX, RICHARD, *Pan-Africanism in Practice: an East African Study: PAFMESCA, 1958–1964* (London, 1964).

CROMWELL, JOHN W., *The Early Convention Movement.* American Negro Academy. Occasional Papers no. 9 (Washington, 1905).

—— *The Negro in American History: Men and Women Eminent in the Evolution of the American of African Descent* (Washington, 1914).

CRONON, EDMUND D., *Black Moses: the Story of Marcus Garvey and the Universal Negro Improvement Association* (Madison, 1955).

CROWDER, MICHAEL, *The Story of Nigeria* (London, 1962, second edition 1966).

DAVIDSON, BASIL, *Black Mother Africa: the Years of Trial* (London, 1961).

DAVIS, DAVID B., *The Problem of Slavery in Western Culture* (Ithaca—New York, 1966).

DECRAENE, PHILIPPE, *Le Panafricanisme*. Que sais-je? (Paris, 1959, third edition 1964).

DELF, GEORGE, *Jomo Kenyatta: towards Truth about the 'Light of Kenya'* (London, 1961).

DIOP, CHEIKH ANTA, *Nations Nègres et culture* (Paris, 1955, second edition 1964).

DRAKE, THOMAS E., *Quakers and Slavery in America* (New Haven, 1950).

DRECHSLER, HORST, *Südwestafrika unter deutscher Herrschaft. Der Kampf der Herero und Nama gegen den deutschen Imperialismus (1844–1915)* (Berlin, 1966).

DU BOIS, W. E. B. *Blcak Folk Then and Now: an Essay in the History and Sociology of the Negro Race* (New York, 1939, fourth edition 1945).

—— *Black Reconstruction in America: an Essay toward a History of the Part which Black Folk Played in the Attempt to Reconstruct Democracy in America, 1860–1880* (New York, 1935, third edition 1964).

—— *The Negro* (New York, 1915; London, 1916).

—— *The Philadelphia Negro: a Social Study* (Philadelphia, 1899, reprinted Greenwich, Connecticut, 1961).

—— *The Suppression of the American Slave-Trade to the United States of America, 1638–1870.* Harvard Historical Studies, no. 1 (Cambridge – Mass., 1896, third edition New York, 1954).

DUMOND, DWIGHT L., *Antislavery: the Crusade for Freedom in America* (Ann Arbor, 1961).

DUSE, MOHAMED ALI, *In the Land of the Pharaos: a Short History of Egypt: from the Fall of Ismail to the Assassination of Boutras Pasha* (London, 1911).

DYKES, E. B., *The Negro in English Romantic Thought; or, a Study of Sympathy for the Oppressed* (Washington, 1942).

EPSTEIN, KLAUS, *The Genesis of German Conservatism* (Princeton, 1966).

ESSIEN-UDOM, E. U., *Black Nationalism: a Search for an Identity in America* (Chicago, London, 1962, second edition New York, 1964); English edition: *Black Nationalism: the Rise of the Black Muslims in the USA* (Harmondsworth, 1966).

FAIRCHILD, H. N., *The Noble Savage: a Study in Romantic Naturalism* (New York, 1928).

FERRIS, WILLIAM H., *The African Abroad, or his Evolution in Western Civilization, Tracing his Development under Caucasian Milieu.* 2 volumes (New York, 1913).

FISHER, MILES M., *Negro Slave Songs in the United States* (Ithaca, New York, 1953).

FLINT, J. E., *Sir George Goldie and the Making of Nigeria* (London, Ibadan, Accra, 1960).

FOSTER, PHILIP J., *Education and Social Change in Ghana* (London, 1965).

FRANKLIN, JOHN H., *From Slavery to Freedom* (New York, 1956).

—— *The Emancipation Proclamation* (New York, 1963).

—— *Reconstruction: after the Civil War* (Chicago, London, 1961, fourth edition 1963).

FRAZIER, FRANKLIN E., *Black Bourgeoisie* (Glencoe – Illinois, 1957, second edition New York, London, 1964).

—— *The Negro Church in America* (New York, 1963; Liverpool, 1964).

—— *The Negro Family in the U.S.A.* (Chicago, 1939).

—— *The Negro in the United States* (New York, 1957).

FURNAS, JOSEPH C., *The Road to Harpers Ferry: Facts and Follies of the War on Slavery* (New York, 1959; London, 1961).

FYFE, CHRISTOPHER, *A History of Sierra Leone* (Oxford, 1962, second edition 1963).

—— *Sierra Leone Inheritance* (London, Ibadan, Accra, 1964).

—— *Africanus Horton, 1835–1883. West African Scientist and Patriot* (New York, London, Toronto, 1973).

GEISS, IMANUEL, *Gewerkschaften in Afrika* (Hanover, 1965).

—— *Die Afro-Amerikaner* (Frankfurt/Main, 1969).

GOLLWITZER, HEINZ, *Die gelbe Gefahr: Geschichte eines Schlagwortes: Studien zum imperialistischen Denken* (Göttingen, 1962).

GOSSET, THOMAS F., *Race: the History of an Idea in America* (Dallas, 1963).

GRIMAL, HENRI, *La Décolonisation, 1919–1963* (Paris, 1965).

GROHS, GERHARD, *Stufen afrikanischer Emanzipation: Studien zum Selbstverständnis westafrikanischer Eliten* (Stuttgart, 1967).

GROSS, BABETTE, *Willi Münzenberg: eine politische Biographie*. Mit einem Vorwort von Arthur Koestler (Stuttgart, 1967).

GROVES, C. P., *The Planting of Christianity in Africa*. 4 volumes (London, 1948–58. Vol. 3, 1955).

GRUNEBAUM-BALLIN, PAUL, *Henri Grégoire, l'ami des hommes de toutes couleurs* (Paris, 1948).

GUNKEL, J. E. H., *Die Psalmen*. Göttinger Handkommentar. 2. Allgemeiner Teil. (Fourth edition, 1926).

HAILEY, LORD (W. M.), *An African Survey Survey* (Oxford, 1938, second edition 1956).

HALL, DOUGLAS, *Free Jamaica, 1838–1865: an Economic History* (New Haven, 1959).

HARGREAVES, JOHN D., *A Life of Sir Samuel Lewis* (London, Ibadan, Accra, 1958).

—— *Prelude to the Partition of West Africa* (London, New York, 1963).

HERSKOVITS, MELVILLE J., *The Myth of Negro Past* (New York, London, 1941).

HODGKIN, THOMAS L., *Nationalism in Colonial Africa* (London, 1956, fourth edition 1962).

—— *Nigerian Perspectives: an Historical Anthology* (London, Ibadan, Accra, 1960).

HOLDEN, EDITH, *Blyden of Liberia: an Account of the Life and Labours of Edward Wilmot Blyden, LL.D. as Recorded in Letters and in Print* (New York, 1966).

HOOKER, JAMES R., *Black Revolutionary: George Padmore's Path from Communism to Pan-Africanism* (London, 1967).

HUGHES, LANGSTON, *Fight for Freedom: the Story of the NAACP* (New York, 1962).

HYMANS, JACK L., *L'Élaboration de la pensée de Léopold Sédar Senghor: esquisse d'un itinéraire intellectuel*. Thèse pour le doctorat de recherche (Paris, 1964).

ISAACS, HAROLD R., *The New World of Negro Americans: the Impact of World Affairs on the Race Problem in the United States and particularly on the Negro, his View of Himself, his Country, and of America* (New York, 1964).

ITALIAANDER, ROLF, *Schwarze Haut im Roten Griff* (Düsseldorf, Vienna, 1962).

JAHN, JANHEINZ, *Geschichte der neoafrikanischen Literatur: eine Einführung* (Düsseldorf, 1966).

—— *Muntu: Umrisse einer neoafrikanischen Kultur* (Düsseldorf, 1958).

JAMES, C. L. R., *The Black Jacobins: Toussaint l'Ouverture and the San Domingo Revolution* (London, New York, 1938, second edition 1963).

JOHNSON, SAMUEL, *The History of the Yorubas: from the Earliest Times to the Beginning of the British Protectorate* (London, 1921, sixth impression London, 1966).

JOHNSON, T. S., *The Story of a Mission: the Sierra Leone Church, First Daughter of C.M.S.* (London, 1953).

JONES-QUARTEY, K. A. B., *A Life of Azikiwe* (London, Baltimore, 1966).

KELLOG, C. F., *NAACP, A History of the National Association for the Advancement of Colored People*, Vol. 1 (1909–1920) (Baltimore, 1967).

KIEWIET, C. W. DE, *A History of South Africa, Social and Economic* (London, 1941, second edition 1964).

KIMBLE, DAVID, *A Political History of Ghana*. Vol. I. *The Rise of Gold Coast Nationalism, 1850–1928* (Oxford, 1963, second edition 1965).

KLEIN, HERBERT S., *Slavery in the Americas: a Comparative Study of Virginia and Cuba* (London, 1967).

KOHN, HANS, *Die Slawen und der Westen. Eine Geschichte des Panslawismus* (Vienna, 1956).

KOPYTOFF, JEAN H., *A Preface to Modern Nigeria: the 'Sierra Leoneans' in Yoruba, 1830–1890* (Madison, Milwaukee, London, 1965).

KRAUS, HANS JOACHIM, *Psalmen*, Vol. 1. Biblischer Kommentar. Altes Testament, ed. Martin Noth, Vol. XV, 1 (Neukirchen, 1960).

LACOUTURE, J., *Cinq hommes et la France* (Paris, 1961).
—— *Hô-Chi-Minh* (Paris, 1967).

LADER, LAWRENCE, *The Bold Brahmins: New England's War Against Slavery, 1831–1863* (New York, 1961).

LATOURETTE, K. S., *A History of the Expansion of Christianity.* 7 volumes (London, 1938–45).

LAWRENCE, A. W., *Trade Castles and Forts of West Africa* (London, 1963).

LEGUM, COLIN, *Pan-Africanism: a Short Political Guide* (London, 1962, second edition 1965).

LEWINSON, PAUL, *Race, Class and Party: A History of Negro Suffrage and White Politics in the South* (London, 1932, New York, 1963, third edition 1965).

LEYBURN, J. G., *The Haitian People* (New Haven, 1941, second edition 1966).

LITTLE, KENNETH, *Negroes in Britain: a Study of Racial Relations in English Society* (London, 1947).

LITWACK, LEON F., *North of Slavery: the Negro in the Free States, 1790–1860* (Chicago, London, 1961, third edition 1965).

LLOYD, P. C. (ed.), *The New Elites of Tropical Africa: Studies Presented and Discussed at the Sixth International African Seminar at the University of Ibadan, Nigeria, July 1964* (London, 1966).

LOGAN, RAYFORD W., *The Diplomatic Relations of the Unites States with Haiti, 1776–1891* (Chapel Hill, 1941).

—— *The Negro in American Life and Thought: the Nadir, 1877–1901* (New York, 1954); second edition entitled *The Betrayal of the Negro from Rutherford B. Hayes to Woodrow Wilson* (New York, London, 1965).

—— *The Senate and the Versailles Mandate System* (Washington, 1945).

LOMAX, LOUIS E., *The Negro Revolt* (New York, 1962).

LUGARD, LADY (Flora Louisa), *A Tropical Dependency: an Outline of the Ancient History of the Western Soudan* (London, 1905).

LYNCH, HOLLIS R., *Edward Wilmot Blyden: Pan-Negro Patriot, 1832–1912* (London, 1967).

MANDEL, ERNEST, *Traité d'Économie Marxiste.* 2 volumes (Paris, 1962).

MANIGAT, LESLIE F., *Haiti of the Sixties, Object of International Concern (a Tentative Global Analysis of the Potentially Explosive Situation of a Crisis Country in the Caribbean)* (Washington, 1964).

MANNIX, DANIEL P. and COWLEY, MALCOLM, *Black Cargoes: a History of the Atlantic Slave Trade* (New York, 1962, second edition 1965).

MATHEWS, BASIL, *Booker T. Washington: Educator and Inter-racial Interpreter* (Cambridge – Mass., 1948, London, 1949 [1950]).

MCPHERSON, JAMES M., *The Negro's Civil War* (New York, 1965).

—— *The Struggle for Equality: Abolitionists and the Negro in the Civil War and Reconstruction* (Princeton, 1964, second impression 1967).

MEDFORD, HAMPTON T., *Zion Methodism Abroad: Giving the Rise and Progress of the A.M.E. Zion Church on its Foreign Fields* (Washington, 1937).

MEIER, AUGUST, 'The Emergence of Negro Nationalism: from the American Revolution to the First World War', M.A. thesis (Columbia University, 1949).

—— *Negro Thought in America, 1880–1915: Racial Ideology in the Age of Booker T. Washington* (Ann Arbor, 1963).

METCALFE, G. E., *Maclean of the Gold Coast: the Life and Times of George Maclean, 1801–1847* (London, 1962).

MOORE, JOHN J., *History of the African Episcopal Zion Church in America* (York – Pa., 1884).

MOORE, RICHARD B., *The Name 'Negro': Its Origin and Its Evil Uses* (New York, 1960).

MÜHLEN, NORBERT, *Die Schwarzen Amerikaner. Anatomie einer Revolution* (Stuttgart, 1964).

MUNRO, DANA G., *Intervention and Dollar Diplomacy in the Caribbean, 1900–1921* (Princeton, 1964).

MYRDAL, GUNNAR, *An American Dilemma: the Negro Problem and Modern Democracy*. 2 volumes (New York, London, 1944, twentieth edition 1964).

NEILL, STEPHEN, *Christian Missions*. The Pelican History of the Church, Vol. 6 (Harmondsworth, 1964, second edition

NØRREGARD, GEORG, *Danish Settlements in West Africa 1658–1850* (Boston – Mass., 1966).

NYE, JOSEPH S. JR, *Pan-Africanism and East African Integration* (Cambridge – Mass., London, Nairobi, 1966).

OHNECK, WOLFGANG, *Die französische Algerienpolitik von 1919–1939*. Beiträge zur Kolonial- und Uberseegeschichte, ed. by Rudolf v. Albertini and Heinz Gollwitzer, Vol. 2 (Cologne, Opladen, 1967).

OLIVER, ROLAND and FAGE, J. D., *A Short History of Africa* second edition (Harmondsworth, 1962).

OSOFSKY, GILBERT, *The Burden of Race: a Documentary History of Negro–White Relations in America* (New York, Evanston, London, 1967).

——*Harlem: the Making of a Ghetto. Negro New York, 1890–1930* (New York, 1966).

OVINGTON, MARY WHITE, *The Walls Came Tumbling Down* (New York, 1947).

PARRY, J. H., Sherlock, P., *A Short History of the West Indies* (London, 1956; third edition 1973).

PAYNE, DANIEL A., *History of the African Methodist Episcopal Church* (Nashville – Tenn., 1891).

PENROSE, BOIES, *Travel and Discovery in the Renaissance, 1420–1620* (Cambridge – Mass., 1952, third edition 1960).

PLUM, WERNER, *Gewerkschaften im Maghreb. UGTT – UMT – UGTA* (Hanover, 1962).

PORTER, A. T., *Creoldom: a Study of the Development of Freetown Society* (London, 1963).

QUARLES, BENJAMIN, *The Negro in the American Revolution* (Chapel Hill, 1961).

—— *The Negro in the Civil War* (Boston, 1953).

REDDING, J. SAUNDERS, *They Came in Chains* (Philadelphia, New York, 1950).

—— *The Lonesome Road: the Story of the Negro in America* (New York, 1958).

REINDORF, CARL C., *The History of the Gold Coast and Asante, based on Traditions and Historical Facts from about 1500–1860* (Basle, 1895, second edition 1951).

ROSE, ARNOLD M. (ed.), *Assuring Freedom to the Free* (Detroit, 1964).

ROUX, EDWARD, *Time Longer than Rope: a History of the Black Man's Struggle for Freedom in South Africa* (Madison, 1948, second edition London, 1964).

SAUTOS, EDUARDO DOS, *Pan-Africanismo de outem e de hoje* (Lisbon, 1967).

SCHATTEN, FRITZ, *Communism in Africa* (London, New York, 1966).

SCHLATTER, W., *Geschichte der Basler Mission* (Basle, 1910).

SCHLOSSER, KATESA, *Propheten in Afrika* (Brunswick, 1949).

SCHOELCHER, VICTOR, Homme d'État et Écrivain Français, émancipateur de la race noire. *Sa correspondence inédite*, 2e partie.

SCHÜCK, R., *Brandenburg- Preussens Kolonialpolitik* (Leipzig, 1889).

SETON, MARIE, *Paul Robeson* (London, 1958).

SHEPPERSON, GEORGE and PRICE, THOMAS, *Independent African: John Chilembwe and the Origins, Setting and Significance of the Nyasaland Native Rising of 1915* (Edinburgh, 1958, second edition 1963).

SKLAR, RICHARD L., *Nigerian Political Parties: Power in an Emergent African Nation* (Princeton, 1963).

SMITH, CHARLES S., *A History of the African Methodist Episcopal*

Church, Being a Volume Supplemental to 'A History of the African Methodist Episcopal Church' by Daniel Alexander Payne, D.D., LL.D., Late One of its Bishops, Chronicling the Principal Events in the Advance of the African Methodist Episcopal Church from 1856–1922 (Philadelphia, 1922).

SMITH, EDWIN W., *Aggrey of Africa: a Study in Black and White* (London, 1929, fifth edition 1930).

SPENCER, SAMUEL JR, *Booker T. Washington and the Negro's Place in American Life* (Boston, 1955; reprinted Boston, Toronto, 1956).

SPIEGLER, JAMES S., 'Aspects of Nationalist thought among French-speaking West Africans, 1921–1939'. Ph. D. thesis (Oxford, 1967).

STAMPP, KENNETH M., *The Peculiar Institution: Slavery in the Ante-Bellum South* (New York, 1956; London, 1964).

—— *Reconstruction* (New York, 1965).

STAUDENRAUS, P. J., *The African Colonization Movement, 1816–1865* (New York, 1961).

STOCK, E., *The History of the Church Missionary Society.* 4 volumes (London, 1899–1916).

STRAUCH, HANSPETER F., *Panafrika. Kontinentale Weltmacht im Werden? Anfänge, Wachstum und Zukunft der afrikanischen Einigungsbestrebungen.* Mit Vorwort von Léopold S. Senghor (Zurich, 1964).

SUNDKLER, B. G. M., *Bantu Prophets in South Africa* (London, 1948, second edition 1964).

SYPHER, WYLIE, *Guinea's Captive Kings* (Chapel Hill, 1942).

TANNENBAUM, FRANK, *Slave and Citizen: the Negro in the Americas* (New York, 1947).

TEVOEDJRE, ALBERT, *Pan-Africanism in Action: an Account of the UAM* (Cambridge – Mass., 1965).

THOMPSON, T. J., *The Jubilee and Centenary Volume of Fourah Bay College, Freetown, Sierra Leone* (Freetown, 1930).

THOMPSON, V. B., *Africa and Unity: The Evolution of Pan-Africanism* (London, 1969).

TIMOTHY, BANKOLE, *Kwame Nkrumah: His Rise to Power* (London, 1955, second edition 1963).

TORDORFF, WILLIAM, *Ashanti under the Prempehs, 1888–1935.*

TUBUKO-METZGER, A. E., *Historical Sketch of the Sierra Leone Grammar School, 1845–1935* (Freetown) n.d. [1935].

542 Bibliography

VAISSIÈN, PIERRE DE, *Saint Domingue (1629–1789). La Société et la vie créole sous l'ancien régime* (Paris, 1909).

VAUGHAN, DAVID, *Negro Victory: the Life Story of Dr Harold Moody* (London, 1950).

VERGER, PIERRE, *Bahia and the West Coast Trade, 1549–1851* (Ibadan, 1964).

VOORHIS, HAROLD VAN BUREN, *Negro Masonry in the United States* (New York, 1940).

WADE, RICHARD C., *Slavery in the Cities: the South, 1820–1860* (New York, 1964; London, 1967).

WALSHE, PETER, 'The South African National Congress'. Ph. D. thesis (Oxford, 1967).

WEBSTER, JAMES B., *The African Churches among the Yoruba, 1888–1922* (Oxford, 1964).

WEILER, HANS N., *Koloniale Erziehung und afrikanische Umwelt. Zur erziehungspolitischen Diskussion in der britischen Kolonialverwaltung seit 1920* (Freiburg, 1966).

WELBOURN, F. B., *East African Rebels* (London, 1961).

WESLEY, CHARLES H., *Richard Allen: Apostle of Freedom* (Washington, 1935).

WHIPPER, FRANK A. R., *Life and Public Services of Martin R. Delany* (Boston, 1883).

WIGHT, MARTIN, *The Gold Coast Legislative Council* (London, 1947).

WILLIAMS, ERIC, *British Historians and the West Indies* (Port-of-Spain, 1964; London, 1966).

—— *Capitalism and Slavery* (Chapel Hill, 1944, second edition, London, 1964).

WILLIAMS, G. KINGSLEY, *Achimota: the Early Years, 1924–1948* (London, Accra, Ikeja, 1962).

WILLIAMS, GEORGE W., *History of the Negro Race* (New York, 1883).

WOODSON, CARTER G., *The African Background Outlined* (Washington, 1936).

—— *History of the Negro Church* (Washington, 1922).

—— *The Negro in Our History* (Washington, tenth edition 1959).

WOODWARD, C. VANN, *The Strange Career of Jim Crow* (New York, 1955, third revised edition 1966).

WYNDHAM, H. A., *The Atlantic and Slavery* (London, 1935).

E. ARTICLES

ABRAHAMS, WILLIAM, 'The Life and Times of Anton Wilhelm
Amo', *Transactions of the Historical Society of Ghana*, vol. 7, 1964,
pp. 60–81.

AGBEBI, MAJOLA, 'The West African Problem', Gustav Spiller
(ed.), *Papers on Inter-Racial Problems, Universal Races Congress*,
pp. 341–8.

AJAYI, J. F. A., 'The Development of Secondary Grammar School
Education in Nigeria', *Journal of the Historical Society of
Nigeria (JHSN)*, vol. 3, no. 1, December 1963.

APTHEKER, HERBERT, 'The Quakers and Negro Slavery', *Journal
of Negro History (JNH)*, 25/1940, no. 3, pp. 331–62.

AUSTIN, DENNIS, 'The Working Committee of the United Gold
Coast Convention', *Journal of African History (JAH)*, vol. 2, no. 2,
pp. 273–97.

AYANDELE, E. A., 'An Assessment of James Johnson and his
Place in Nigerian History, 1874–1917, Part I', *JHSN*, vol. 2,
no. 4, December 1963, pp. 486–516; Part II, vol. 3,
December 1964, pp. 73–101.

AZIKIWE, NNAMDI, 'In Defence of Liberia', *JNH*, 17/1932, no. 1,
pp. 30–51.

—— 'Liberia: Slave or Free?', N. Cunard (ed.), *Negro Anthology . . .*
(London, 1934) pp. 780–83.

BELL, HOWARD H., 'The Negro Convention Movement,
1830–1860: New Perspectives', *Negro History Bulletin*, 14,
February 1951.

—— 'The Negro Emigration Movement, 1849–1854: a Phase of
Negro Nationalism', *Phylon*, XX (1959), no. 2, pp. 132–42.

BLYDEN, EDWARD W., 'Mohammedanism and the Negro Race',
Methodist Quarterly Review, fourth series, vol. 29, no. 7, January
1877, pp. 100–27.

CANDACE, GRATIEN, 'Le Deuxième Congrès de la race noire en
1921', *Colonie et Marine*, November 1921, pp. 725–41.

CHALLAYE, FÉLICIEN, 'Le Congrès Pan-Africain', *Les Cahiers*,
1921, pp. 420–24.

DEBRUNNER, HANS W., 'Frühe westafrikanische Porträts',
Basler Nachrichten, 10 January 1965.

DELAFOSSE, MAURICE, 'Le Congrès Panafricain', *Afrique
Française*, March–April 1919, supplement.

DOUGLASS, FREDERICK, 'Haiti and the United States: Inside
History of the Negotiations for the Môle St Nicolas',
North American Review, September 1891, pp. 337–45; October
1891, pp. 450–59.

DRAKE, ST CLAIR, 'Philosophical Consciencism: the Role of
Social Philosophy and Political Theory in New Nations',
*The Pan-Africanist Review: a Quarterly of the African
Revolution*, vol. 1, no. 3, September 1964, pp. 5–14.

DU BOIS, W. E. B., 'The African Roots of War', *Atlantic
Monthly*, May 1915, pp. 707–14.

DUSE MOHAMED ALI, 'Leaves from an Active Life', *The Comet*, 1937–8.

ELLIS, GEORGE W., 'Liberia in the Political Psychology of
West Africa', *Journal of the African Society*, 1912, pp. 52–70.

FRASER, A. G. 'Denationalisation', *The Gold Coast Review*, vol. 1,
no. 1, June–December 1925, pp. 71–5.

FYFE, CHRISTOPHER, 'The Countess of Huntingdon's Connection
in Nineteenth-Century Sierra Leone', *The Sierra Leone
Bulletin of Religion*, vol. 4, no. 2, December 1962, pp. 53–60.

—— 'A Historiographical Survey of the Transatlantic Slave Trade
from West Africa', Centre of African Studies, University of
Edinburgh, *The Transatlantic Slave Trade from West Africa*
(Edinburgh, 1965).

GALLAGHER, JOHN, 'Fowell Buxton and the New Africa Policy,
1838–1842', *Cambridge Historical Journal*, vol. 10, 1950.

GARIGUE, PHILIP, 'The West African Students' Union', *Africa*,
vol. 23, January 1953, pp. 55–69.

GEISS, IMANUEL, 'Das Erblühen der modernen Eliten in Afrika
seit der Mitte des 18 Jahrhunderts, *Geschichte in Wissenschaft und
Unterricht*, November 1971, pp. 648–67.

HAIR, P. E. H., 'An Analysis of the Register of Fourah Bay College,
1827–1950', *Sierra Leone Studies*, no. 7, December 1956, pp. 155–60.

—— 'C.M.S. "Native Clergy" in West Africa to 1900', *The Sierra
Leone Bulletin of Religion*, vol. 4, no. 2, December 1962, pp. 71f.

HARLAN, LOUIS R., 'Booker T. Washington and the White Man's
Burden', *American Historical Review*, 71, no. 2, January 1966,
pp. 441–67.

JOHNSON, G. WESLEY, 'The Ascendancy of Blaise Diagne and the
Beginning of African Politics in Senegal', *Africa*, vol. 36,
October 1965, pp. 235–53.

JULY, ROBERT, 'Africanus Horton and the Idea of Independence in West Africa', *Sierra Leone Studies*, new series, no. 28, January 1966, pp. 2–17.

KELLENBENZ, HERMANN, 'Die Brandenburger auf St Thomas', *Jahrbuch für Geschichte von Staat, Wirtschaft und Gesellschaft Lateinamerikas*, 2/1965, pp. 196–217.

KOHN, HANS, 'Pan Movements', *Encyclopaedia of the Social Sciences*, New York, 1933, vol. XI, pp. 544–54.

LEGUM, COLIN, 'Pan-Africanism and Nationalism', *Africa in the Nineteenth and Twentieth Centuries*, ed. J. C. Anene and G. Brown (London, Ibadan, 1966) pp. 528–38.

—— 'The Roots of Pan-Africanism', *Africa: a Handbook to the Continent* (London, 1961) pp. 452–62.

LOGAN, RAYFORD W., 'The Historical Aspect of Pan-Africanism, 1900–1945', *Pan-Africanism Reconsidered*, ed. American Society of African Culture (Berkeley, Los Angeles, 1962) pp. 37–53.

LOUIS, WM ROGER, 'The United States and the African Peace Settlement of 1919: the Pilgrimage of George Louis Beer', *JAH*, vol. 4, 1963, no. 3, pp. 413–33.

LYNCH, HOLLIS R., 'Native Pastorate Controversy and Cultural Ethnocentrism in Sierra Leone, 1871–1874', *JAH*, vol. 5, 1964, no. 3, pp. 395–413.

MARC, HENRY PAUL, 'Pan-Africanism: a Dream Come True', *Foreign Affairs*, April 1955, pp. 445ff.

MARKS, S., 'Henrietta Colenso and the Zulus, 1874–1913', *JAH*, vol. 4, 1963, no. 3, pp. 402–11.

MOORE, RICHARD B., 'Africa Conscious Harlem', J. H. Clarke (ed.), *Harlem: a Community in Transition* (New York, 1964) pp. 77–96.

MPHALEEHLE, E., 'The Cult of Negritude', *Encounter*, vol. 17, no. 3, March 1960, pp. 50ff.

NICOL, ABIOSEH, 'West Indians in West Africa', *Sierra Leone Studies*, new series, no. 13, 1960, pp. 14ff.

OSOFSKY, GILBERT, 'The Making of a Ghetto', J. H. Clarke (ed.), *Harlem: a Community in Transition* (New York, 1964) pp. 18–25.

PRIESTLEY, MARGARET, 'The Emergence of an Élite: a Case Study of a West Coast Family', P. C. Lloyd (ed.), *The New Elites of Tropical Africa* (London, 1966) pp. 87–100.

R., T., 'Observations on the Early History of the Negro Race', *African Repository*, vol. 1, no. 1, March 1825, pp. 7ff.

ROHDIE, SAMUEL, 'The Gold Coast Aborigines Abroad', *JAH*, vol. 6, no. 3, 1965, pp. 392ff.

RUDWICK, ELLIOT M., 'The National Negro Committee Conference of 1909', *Phylon*, XVIII, 1957, no. 4, pp. 413–19.

—— 'W. E. B. Du Bois and the Universal Races Congress of 1911', *Phylon*, XX, 1959, no. 4, pp. 372–8.

SACKEY, REV. DR ISAAC, A Brief History of the A.M.E. Zion Church West Gold Coast District', *The Ghana Bulletin of Theology*, vol. 1, 1958, no. 3, pp. 16–20.

SHELTON, AUSTIN J., 'The Black Mystique: Reactionary Extremes in "Negritude"', *African Affairs*, vol. 63, no. 251, April 1963.

SHEPPERSON, GEORGE, 'Ethiopianism and African Nationalism', *Phylon*, XIV, no. 1, 1953, pp. 9–18.

—— 'Notes on Negro American Influences on the Emergence of African Nationalism', *JAH*, vol. 1, no. 2, pp. 299–312.

—— ' "Pan-Africanism" and "pan-Africanism": Some Historical Notes', *Phylon*, XXIII/4, Winter 1962, pp. 346–58.

TURNER, LORENZO D., 'African Survivals in the New World with Special Emphasis on the Arts', J. A. Davis (ed.), *Africa Seen by American Negroes* (Paris, 1958) pp. 101–16.

WALLERSTEIN, IMMANUEL, 'The Evolution of Pan-Africanism as a Protest Movement', Morton Kaplan (ed.), *Revolution in World Politics* (New York, London, 1962) pp. 137–51.

WEBSTER, JAMES B., 'The Bible and the Plough', *JHSN*, vol. 2, December 1962, pp. 418–34.

WEHLER, HANS-ULRICH, 'Stützpunkte in der Karibischen See: die Anfänge des amerikanischen Imperialismus auf Hispaniola', *Jahrbuch für Geschichte von Staat, Wirtschaft und Gesellschaft Lateinamerikas*, 2/1965, pp. 399–428.

ZASTROW, ROSWITHA, 'Panafrikanismus und Kommunismus', *Der Ostblock und die Entwicklungsländer. Vierteljahresbericht der Friedrich-Ebert-Stiftung*, no. 12–13, August 1963, pp. 21–34.

ZMARZLIK, HANS-GÜNTHER, 'Der Sozialdarwinismus in Deutschland als geschichtliches Problem', *Vierteljahrshefte für Zeitgeschichte*, 11/3, July 1963, pp. 246–73.

Subject
Index

Index of
Persons